UNIVERSITY LIBRARY
UW-STEVENS POINT

**Understanding
exceptional children
and youth**

Contributors

Henry R. Angelino
Joan H. Faubion
Wanda Fuhrmann
Cathy Groves
John S. Howland
Harry J. Parker
Marshall D. Schechter
William J. Ward
Mary Ann Weiss

Understanding exceptional children and youth

An introduction to special education

B. Marian Swanson
College of Behavioral Sciences
Northeastern Oklahoma State University

Diane J. Willis
Child Study Center
University of Oklahoma Health Sciences Center

Rand McNally College Publishing Company • Chicago

Rand McNally Education Series
B. Othanel Smith, advisory editor

Sponsoring editor: Louise Waller
Project editor: Charlotte Iglarsh
Cover illustrator: John Sandford
Designer: June Lambla

Instructor's Manual available

79 80 81   10 9 8 7 6 5 4 3 2 1
Copyright © 1979 by Rand McNally College Publishing Company
All rights reserved
Printed in USA
Library of Congress catalog card number: 77-77701

To Louis, Greg, Jane, Eric and Alyce

To Bill and Zelma Willis and Herb and Orpha Bynum

Foreword

Understanding moves from the situational and specific to the inclusive and the general. This is just as true of pedagogical inquiry as it is of other scientific endeavors. Ever since the federal government began to emphasize research on exceptionality more than two decades ago, we have become increasingly aware of its variety and complexity and how our knowledge of it illumines the total range of human behavior. The understanding of exceptionality is doubtless a condition for understanding all children, and the knowledge, procedures, and techniques presented in this book are the basis for a pedagogy that underscores their strengths and works toward maximum fulfillment of their potential. There is good reason to suppose that this approach is applicable to the whole field of education, a thesis that gains more and more support as research on exceptionality advances.

    It is becoming increasingly clear that exceptionality can be understood only in terms of relevant knowledge from a broad spectrum of disciplines. Psychology, sociology, ophthalmology, neurology, audiology, and medicine have each contributed significantly to our comprehension of the various forms of exceptionality. Thus, the complexity of exceptionality makes a team approach to the modes of coping with the problems of exceptional children an operational necessity. This approach is one of the unique features of this book. It puts pedagogical problems in a context that renders it ever more likely that educational policies and decisions will be more effective and responsive.

    Educational provisions for all the various types of exceptionality are explored in depth, and the wide range of special services are not neglected. These resources are treated in ways that sensitize school personnel, parents, and clinicians to their best use. The shift from the isolation of exceptional children, especially those who can profit from normal school environments, to mainstreaming is dealt with in ways helpful to clinicians, teachers, administrators and indeed all school personnel. The problems that arise from mainstreaming are discussed also in practical terms.

    The authors write from a rich background of firsthand experience with exceptional children in schools, hospitals, clinics and service agencies. This background, plus their wide-ranging academic and scientific credentials, has enabled them to present an important work on the facts, principles, and educational approaches applicable to exceptionality. The book has an instructive organization and a readable style, which serves to make it an excellent text for the introductory course on exceptional children and youth.

B. Othanel Smith

Preface

The impetus for *Understanding Exceptional Children and Youth* was provided by the on-site experience of teaching college and university students in a variety of courses that deal with exceptionality. In working with exceptional children and their families and guiding school personnel and professionals in community agencies, the present authors found a tremendous need for a text that would emphasize the team approach to educating this population. We experienced the validity of this approach at first hand.

An ongoing concern of helping professionals has been the need for establishing more communication and greater sharing of information among team members. Medical personnel, physical and speech therapists, school administrators, teachers, psychologists, and social service personnel, can put their shared information and ideas at the service of the exceptional child, the child's family, the community, and each other. For example, a teacher needs to know what medical problems bear on a child's behavior and ability to learn. Without this knowledge, the teacher cannot do an effective job. Yet rarely is such information provided.

Each unit in the book provides pertinent information that the future teacher or interested professional will need to know. This information includes definition of each exceptionality, its causes, theoretical and practical approaches to diagnosis and teaching strategies, and practical applications of such knowledge to the home, school and community setting of which the exceptional child and youth is a part. As already stated, the multidisciplinary approach—wherein all persons who are needed to provide appropriate services are mobilized to the task—is absolutely essential if we are to have optimum educational opportunity for these children and youth.

Understanding Exceptional Children and Youth contains five major parts: The introductory unit focuses on a number of critical topics. The monumental impact and the implications of the newest legislation concerning exceptional children and youth are surveyed; the multidisciplinary team concept is defined and explored; and parental reactions to exceptionality in their own child are treated. This latter topic is integral to better understanding of how special education can help this population of children and youth. The last unit serves as a summation and also briefly explores possible future concerns in the realms of research, advocacy and manpower needs. Each unit provides a set of valuable aids to the student: An advance organizer outlining the topics covered, a set of general and specific learning objectives, and a comprehensive reference and resource list.

Part One considers *intellectual exceptionality*. Included are Units 2 and 3, which deal with the mentally retarded, and Unit 4, which treats of the gifted and talented. Part Two presents the area of *educational exceptionality*. Within it, Unit 5 discusses the population of children and youth who experience difficulties in and out of school due to societal neglect. There are hundreds of thousands of these children in our society. Specific learning disabilities, the newest area of exceptionality, is the subject of Unit 6.

Part Three covers *emotional and social exceptionality*. Unit 7 initially presents a consideration of emotionally handicapped children and youth, and then examines forms of behavior that are viewed as "delinquent."

Part Four presents exceptionality in terms of various *sensorimotor disabilities*. Unit 8 deals with children and youth who have speech and language disabilities; Unit 9 discusses hearing disabilities; Unit 10 covers visual disabilities; and Unit 11 considers physical and health impairments.

Between the planning stage for this text and the selection of contributing authors with expertise in various areas of special education, federal legislation was enacted that "guaranteed the rights of all handicapped children and youth to free and appropriate educational and supportive services." The new mandated legislation "turned our book around," but in an even more positive direction. We became more determined than ever to provide a relevant text that includes the most current information and ideas about educating exceptional children and youth.

A continuing concern in the area of special education is the classification of exceptional children and youth into categories such as "mentally retarded," "specific learning disabled," etc. The dangers inherent in this practice are presented as a critical issue in the discussion of the labeling process in Unit 1. However, it *is* necessary to employ the terminology used in the newest legislation and/or supported by findings in current research in the professional literature for diagnostic, assessment and program planning purposes.

B. Marian Swanson
Diane J. Willis

Acknowledgments

First and foremost, we are indebted to students, teachers and other school personnel, helping professionals, exceptional children and youth themselves, and parents who provided the necessary feedback for evaluating the relevancy of material to be included in our text. These people kept us alert to newer materials, methods, concepts, and programs. Their help has proved invaluable.

Further acknowledgment is due to a number of colleagues and friends: Sam C. Ashcroft, Ph.D., Director of the National Center on Educational Media and Material for the Handicapped at Ohio State University whose valuable suggestions were incorporated in the unit on visual disabilities; Jack Foreman, head of the Department for Deaf Education at the University of Tulsa, and Michael Dennis, Ph.D., head of the Division of Audiology and Speech Pathology and Polly Patrick, M.S., audiologist and instructor, both of the Department of Otorhinolaryngology, University of Oklahoma Health Sciences Center in Oklahoma City, who contributed to the unit on hearing disabilities; and Dorothy Wright, who critically read the unit on physical and health disabilities. A special note of gratitude is extended to several members of the staff at the Child Study Center in Oklahoma City. Gertrude Forde, supervising teacher, Maxine Lavender, coordinator of the learning disabilities section and Ellidee D. Thomas, M.D., pediatric neurologist and director of the Child Study Center, all offered helpful suggestions and critiqued various units. We are also extremely grateful to Stevie Farrand, Ora Lee Parker, Betty Rose and Andrew Siegel for their help in preparing the manuscript for publication. Special thanks are due, too, to Professors John T. Braggio, Henry Leland, Patrick O'Donnell and David Sabatino for their insightful reviews of the text.

Finally we deeply appreciate the work of the staff at Rand McNally College Publishing Company: James R. Schmitt, for his recognition of the need for our proposed text and his support throughout; Charles H. Heinle, Jr., for his active personal involvement in the project; Jennifer Kurz, for invaluable assistance throughout the project; and Louise Waller and Charlotte Iglarsh for shepherding the manuscript through the editorial and production phases to completion.

Contents

Foreword   vii
Preface   ix
Acknowledgments   xi

1 Introduction to exceptionality   *B. Marian Swanson • Diane J. Willis*   1
What is exceptionality?
Exceptionality is no respector of status or race
Historical perspectives
    Early attitudes about the handicapped • Emergence of residential schools • Beginning of public day school facilities
The impact of recent legislation
    Emphasis on rights of children
Public Laws 93-380 and 94-142
The multidisciplinary team
    The composition and work of the team
The need for early diagnosis
Issues of special concern
    The efficacy of standardized tests • The labeling process
Educational placement provisions
    Residential schools today • Hospital and homebound services • Public day school provisions
Approaches to understanding human behavior
    Biophysical factors • Psychodynamic factors • Psychosocial factors • The behavioristic approach
Parental reactions to children exhibiting a disability
    Grief reactions • Family psychodynamics and its effects • Intervention techniques
Summary

Part one Intellectual exceptionality

2 Mentally retarded children and youth: assessment and causes   William J. Ward   47

What is mental retardation?
Perspectives on mental retardation
    The past · Current perspectives
Level of intellectual functioning
    The concept of mental age · The standard deviation IQ
Adaptive behavior assessment
Prevalence of mental retardation
Classification of mental retardation by causative factors
    Infection and intoxication · Trauma · Metabolic and nutritional disorders · Postnatal gross brain disease · Unknown prenatal influences · Chromosomal abnormality · Gestational disorders · Retardation following psychiatric disorder · Environmental influences · Other conditions
Summary

3 Mentally retarded children and youth: educational, home, and community considerations   William J. Ward   73

Profound and severe retardation
    The profoundly retarded · The severely retarded · Educational provisions
The moderately retarded
    Physical and motor development · Speech and language development · Academic and vocational expectations · Social and personality aspects · Educational provisions · Approaches to working with the moderately retarded population
The mildly retarded
    Physical and motor development · Speech and language development · Academic and vocational expectations · Social and personality aspects · Educational provisions
General considerations
    Mainstreaming · Home and family · Community attitudes toward the mentally retarded
Summary

4 Gifted and talented children and youth   Henry R. Angelino   99

Historical perspectives
Present considerations
What is giftedness?
Frequency of giftedness
Characteristics of the gifted population
    Physical growth and development · Emotional aspects · Social aspects

Variables in giftedness
    Male-female variance · Ethnic and socioeconomic factors
Techniques for identifying the gifted
    Use of individualized IQ tests · Group assessment · Teacher observation as an assessment technique · Identification of creativity · Current concerns
Educational provisions
    Program planning and operation · Administrative procedures
Motivation in the gifted
    The gifted underachiever
School, community, and parents as catalysts
    Community resources and school responsibility · Teachers of the gifted · Parental participation and cooperation
Summary

Part two   Educational exceptionality

5   Societally neglected children and youth   B. Marian Swanson   131

Who are the societally neglected?
Populations facing societal neglect
    Specific racial and ethnic minorities · Migrant laborers · Isolated rural poor · Inner-city ghetto dwellers
The presence of poverty
    Hierarchy of human needs as related to poverty · Poverty and malnutrition · Poverty and inadequate housing conditions · Poverty and the family unit · Assessment of feelings of self-esteem
Language of the societally neglected
    Elaborated and restricted language · Bilingualism and dialect · Reading difficulties
Intervention strategies
    Compensatory educational provisions · Language provisions · Health and nutritional provisions · Other developmental and instructional provisions
Summary

6   Children and youth with specific learning disabilities
    B. Marian Swanson · Diane J. Willis   163

Definition of specific learning disabilities
Prevalence
Identification criteria
    Discrepancy · Exclusion criteria · Maturation difficulty · Neurological correlates
Organic aspects
    Hard neurological signs · Soft neurological signs
Perceptual-motor theory of specific learning disabilities

Perception defined • Coordination, or motor functioning, difficulties • Cognitive abilities and concept formation
Specific academic area difficulties
    Reading difficulties • Spelling and writing difficulties • Arithmetic difficulties • Speech and language difficulties
Educational strategies
    Process, or modality, training • Task analysis procedure • Combination of process training and task analysis
Aspects of social and emotional behavior
    Hyperkinesis and hyperactivity • Impulsiveness, or disinhibition • Distractibility • Perseveration • Emotional lability
Correlation between juvenile delinquency and SLD
Problems of self-esteem and approaches to adaptive management
    Medical management or therapy • Operant conditioning, or reinforcement therapy • Other adaptive behavior techniques
Need for continuing research
Summary

Part three   Emotional and social exceptionality

7 Emotionally handicapped children and youth   *Marshall D. Schechter • John S. Howland • B. Marian Swanson • Diane J. Willis*   203

What is good mental health?
    Stages of healthy emotional growth • Attempts to define emotional disability
Significant influences on emotional development
    Constitutional factors • Family dynamics • School-related sociocultural influences • Ego or self development
Classification and labeling problems
Special symptoms
    Bladder and bowel control problems • Pica • Tics • Anorexia nervosa
Transient situational disorders
Aggressive and destructive behaviors
Neuroses in children and youth
    Depressive neurosis • Hysterical neurosis, conversion type • Phobic neurosis
Psychoses in children and youth
    Early infantile autism • Early childhood schizophrenia • Schizophrenia in youth • Manic-depressive psychoses
Special concerns
    Child abuse • Drug abuse • Suicide
Intervention strategies
    Individual psychotherapy • Group psychotherapy • Family therapy • Behavior modification, or reinforcement therapy • Other therapeutic techniques • The classroom teacher as facilitator

Juvenile delinquency
> What is juvenile delinquency? • Overall incidence • Causes of juvenile delinquency • Intervention techniques • Prognosis

Summary

Part four Sensorimotor exceptionality

8 Speech and language disabled children and youth
Mary Ann Weiss   253

What is a communication disorder?
> Language and speech • Examples of communication disorders

Incidence of speech and language disorders
Normal speech development
Types and characteristics of speech disorders
> Articulation disorders • Voice disorders • Fluency disorders

Normal language development
Types and characteristics of language disorders
> Causal factors • Auditory receptive and expressive language disorders • Diagnosing language disorders • Remedial techniques

Speech and language disorders related to other physical disabilities
Summary

9 Hearing disabled children and youth   Diane J. Willis • Joan H. Faubion   291

The role of hearing
Effects of hearing loss upon the developing child
Facts and fallacies
> Facts • Fallacies

Attitudes toward the "deaf-mute"
Symptoms of possible hearing disabilities
> Auditory specialists

Who are the hearing disabled?
> Incidence

Causes of hearing disabilities
> Genetically linked hearing disabilities • Hearing disabilities of nongenetic origin

The auditory system
> The external ear • The middle ear • The inner ear • The cochlea and sensory pathways

Types of hearing loss
> Conductive hearing loss • Sensorineural hearing loss • Mixed hearing loss • Central auditory disorder

Assessment of auditory disabilities
    Audiometric procedures • Hearing aids
Social and psychological impact of hearing disabilities
    Social development • Intelligence • Cognitive development • Personality development
Education of the hearing disabled
    Oral communication • Manual communication • Fingerspelling • Total communication • Parental participation in educational programs • General educational achievement • Academic curriculum • Directions in educational programs
General trends and needs in today's society
Summary

10 Visually disabled children and youth   Diane J. Willis • Cathy Groves • Wanda Fuhrmann   333

Facts and fallacies about visually disabled children
Who are the visually disabled?
    Prevalence and incidence • Causal factors • Symptoms of possible visual disorders • Eye specialists
Anatomy and function of the eye
    Protective structures • Refractive structures • Muscular structures • Receptive structures
How visual disabilities are assessed
    Snellen chart • Barraga visual efficiency scale
Personal-social development of visually disabled children
    Mother-child interaction • Stimulation techniques
Motor milestones
    Sitting • Crawling
Language development
Cognitive development
Psychological overview of the visually disabled
    Self-concept • Body image • Concept formation • Mannerisms • Adjustment problems • Psychological testing • Fostering social and emotional growth in the school environment
Academic curriculum and training programs
    Mobility training and orientation • Decisions about primary mode of learning • Braille • Reading print • The Optacon for reading
Combined visual and hearing disorders
    Causes • Diagnosis and evaluation • Prevention
Trends in educational programs
Summary

11   Children and youth with physical and health disabilities   xix
    Harry J. Parker   377
Introduction
Disorders of the nervous system—cerebral dysfunction
        Cerebral palsy • Epileptic seizures
Disorders of the musculoskeletal system
        Juvenile rheumatoid arthritis • Muscular dystrophy
Disorder of the endocrine system
        Diabetes
Disorders of the respiratory system
        Allergies and bronchial asthma
Life-threatening disorders
        Leukemia • Cystic fibrosis
Other disorders and their educational implications
Multihandicapped children
Summary

Summing up   411

Contributors' biographies   417
Credits   421
Name index   423
Subject index   431

Understanding exceptional children and youth

1 Introduction to exceptionality

B. Marian Swanson
Diane J. Willis

What is exceptionality?
Exceptionality is no respector of status or race
Historical perspectives · *Early attitudes about the handicapped* · *Emergence of residential schools.* · *Beginning of public day school facilities*
The impact of recent legislation · *Emphasis on rights of children*
Public Laws 93-380 and 94-142
The multidisciplinary team · *The composition and work of the team*
The need for early diagnosis
Issues of special concern · *The efficacy of standardized tests* · *The labeling process*
Educational placement provisions · *Residential schools today* · *Hospital and homebound services* · *Public day school provisions*
Approaches to understanding human behavior · *Biophysical factors* · *Psychodynamic factors* · *Psychosocial factors* · *The behavioristic approach*
Parental reactions to children exhibiting a disability · *Grief reactions* · *Family psychodynamics and its effects* · *Intervention techniques*
Summary

2
Introduction to exceptionality

Student learning objectives

The student will:
1. learn about the historical perspective of exceptionality, and how society currently is trying to improve services for exceptional children and youth
2. be able to define exceptionality
3. master the major provisions of Public Law 94-142
4. be able to explain the multidisciplinary approach and recognize its benefits and advantages in providing special services
5. learn about the various types of placement alternatives for the children and youth concerned
6. recognize the importance of early diagnosis
7. be able to explain *mainstreaming,* and learn about its ramifications
8. learn about the important issues of children's rights, IQ testing, and labeling
9. learn about a number of relevant approaches to understanding human behavior
10. learn about parental reactions to exceptionality, and some of the strategies used to assist families of exceptional children and youth

Through your study of exceptionality you will learn about various special segments of our school-age population. Our goal is to awaken your interest and enhance your understanding of these children and youth. Since none of us lives in isolation, we all encounter at some time in our lives those who are considered exceptional. Such children comprise at least 12 percent of the school population. To be precise, approximately eight million children and youth of school age fall into this category. This number is equal to the entire populations of Oklahoma, Nevada, New Mexico, North Dakota, and Tennessee combined! Since we are talking about a great many people, it is imperative that future teachers, educators, administrators, health officials, and psychologists have a clear understanding of this group's special needs and capabilities.

The exceptional person has been triply handicapped: first, by the nature of his or her disorder; second, by societal attitudes and prejudices; and third, by the lack of appropriate educational services in widespread areas. Recently enacted federal legislation covering the rights of the so-called handicapped has at long last forced us to reckon with these injustices. This new legislation necessitates vast changes in identification procedures. It also changes the way decisions are reached concerning the type and extent of special services provided to these young people. In this text the importance of teamwork in planning appropriate programs will be emphasized, as accomplished through the multidisciplinary team approach to diagnosis, treatment, and remediation. As you gain a greater understanding of exceptionality, we hope that you will be challenged to take an active role in improving the educational, social, economic, and humanistic opportunities for this large segment of our population.

What is exceptionality?

Often the term *exceptional* is misunderstood to refer only to gifted or talented individuals. We can clarify this term through the following definition: The study of exceptionality involves all children and youth who possess conditions that constitute significant departures from the societally defined average, or norm, in (1) *intellectual,* (2) *educational,* (3) *emotional,* (4) *social,* (5) *sensory,* or (6) *physical or health capacities.* As a consequence, special knowledge and services are required to aid them in realizing their maximum potential.

Clarifying the term

Included in this definition are: (1) the intellectually different (whether mentally retarded or gifted), (2) the societally neglected, (3) the learning disabled, (4) the emotionally disturbed, (5) those adjudged to be delinquent, (6) those with speech and language problems, (7) the hearing disabled (whether deaf or hard of hearing), (8) the visually disabled (whether blind or partially sighted), and (9) the physically or health disabled. Many children will be represented in more than one of these categories because their conditions cause multiple handicaps.

Children represented

The definition of *handicapped children* is clearly set forth in Public Law 94-142, the newest federal legislation, as follows:

> ... the term "handicapped children" means those children ... evaluated as being mentally retarded, hard of hearing, deaf, speech impaired, visually handicapped, seriously emotionally disturbed, orthopedically impaired, other health impaired, deaf-blind, multihandicapped, or as having specific learning disabilities, who because of those impairments need special education and related services (Federal Register, 1977, p. 42478).

Definition of "handicapped children"

Special education, or *exceptional learner education,* is defined in the same law as "specially designed instruction at no cost to the parent to meet the unique needs of a handicapped child" (Federal Register, 1977, p. 42480). Special education encompasses instruction in the classroom, home, hospital, or institution, including provisions for physical and vocational education if the latter is indicated to meet the aforementioned needs of the handicapped child. Its purpose is to maximize each child's potential. The related services called for in the definition of handicapped children include transportation, school health and social work services, speech, physical and occupational therapy, psychological services and counseling services. Medical services that are required in order to determine the need for special education are also included. These would be provided by a physician for diagnostic and evaluation purposes.

What is special education?

Introduction to exceptionality

Exceptionality is no respector of status or race

Exceptionality is not associated with any particular socioeconomic status or race. In many cases in the past, the family of a child with a disabling condition tried to keep the affliction secret or placed the child in a residential institution. Today, however, such a child is likely to remain within the family unit. While there is less stigma associated with having an exceptional child, some parents still have difficulty accepting a handicapping condition. During John F. Kennedy's presidency in the early 1960s, for example, mental retardation received a great deal of attention because the president's sister Rosemary was thus handicapped. More than ever it was recognized that mental retardation could occur in any family, and through President Kennedy's efforts, many programs to aid the retarded were initiated.

Disabilities may strike any child or family

Positive examples set by prominent persons have increased the public's understanding and acceptance of exceptional people. Perhaps the most famous of all those who conquered a multihandicapping condition is Helen Keller. Before she reached two years of age, she lost her sight and hearing as the result of a high fever. Despite this, she became an internationally famous writer and traveler. Her life has served as an inspiration to parents of exceptional children for many years. Anne Sullivan, her teacher, also became famous, because of her dedication and ingenuity in reaching and teaching Keller through the sense of touch.

As a child, Albert Einstein showed signs of specific learning disabilities, including late language development and difficulties in certain subject areas. President Franklin D. Roosevelt, physically disabled by polio, demonstrated that being confined to a wheelchair was not necessarily a deterrent to achievement. Vincent Van Gogh, the famous painter, suffered emotional problems. Many other examples can be cited of people who overcame their disabilities and proved that the majority of exceptional individuals can go on to lead normal and productive lives.

Historical perspectives

Early attitudes

In some ancient (and even current) cultures, people afflicted with certain exceptionalities were thought to be accursed by the gods or simply insane (Willis & Thomas, 1978). The handicapped were viewed as the dregs of society or as bad omens (Melcher, 1976). Social attitudes of society toward the exceptional in general and the retarded in particular have been slow in changing. The retarded were often characterized as delinquents and degenerates who were immoral and prone to vagrancy. They were thought to be the "root of social evils" and a burden to civilization (Davis, 1962, p. 3). Dunn (1964, p. 14) writes:

Attitude change comes very slowly

> Prior to the year 1800, society's record [toward exceptionality] was one of the most pathetic chapters in the history of man. In ancient times, Spartan

parents exposed their handicapped offspring to the elements to perish. In the Middle Ages, the retarded were exploited as fools or jesters for the pleasure of the lords and their ladies. During the Protestant Reformation most people thought handicapped persons were possessed by the Devil, and therefore the common treatment was to beat the Devil out of them.

Beginning in the thirteenth century, the Church provided asylums—the only sanctuaries available to the handicapped. Such asylums did not provide treatment or education, but they did at least furnish their residents with protection and food.

Church-sponsored asylums

While treatment and services for handicapped individuals would appear to have been very slow to emerge, we must admit that in recent years a great deal has been accomplished. After all, professional services have only been available for approximately 160 years in Western civilization and for only a century or so in the United States (Dunn, 1964).

Emergence of residential schools

Society gradually developed more charitable attitudes toward the handicapped and by the 1800s, attempts were made to provide for their special needs. Such aid was largely inadequate, however, and in some states, as many as sixty percent of the deaf, blind, insane or mentally retarded persons were inmates of poorhouses (U.S. Office of Education, 1976).

In 1817 the first full-fledged residential institutions or schools for the handicapped began to appear. During that year schools for the deaf were established in Connecticut and New York, with other states soon following. In 1829 the first private residential school for the blind was founded in New England, and Ohio and Virginia established state-supported facilities for this special group in the 1830s. The first residential school for the mentally retarded, the Massachusetts School for Idiotic and Feebleminded Youth, was started in 1859 in Boston. Other states soon followed in establishing such facilities.

These earlier efforts, however, placed greater emphasis on custodial care than they did on the true education of handicapped children and youth (U.S. Office of Education, 1976, p. 9). Not until the early 1900s did these facilities at last begin to be viewed and officially designated as educational, rather than charitable, institutions.

Beginning of public day school facilities

Even with the establishment of residential schools for the handicapped, the number of children and youth in need of specialized services exceeded the available facilities. Hence the concept of public-school day classes for children with various types of handicaps emerged. Table 1-1 lists the founding dates, locations, and types of handicaps served in the public schools during the late 1800s and early 1900s. The percentage of cities reporting special classes for the handicapped is reflected in Table 1-2. As indicated, the largest percentage of special classes were for the mentally

Introduction to exceptionality

exceptional. The second largest percentage were for the environmentally exceptional, or non-English speaking, children and youth.

Since the times reflected in Table 1-1 a great deal has transpired in the field of exceptional education. During the last seventy years we have made rapid progress in providing special services for the exceptional (see Table 1-3). The question remains, however: how can we best help the handicapped person to achieve his or her potential?

Seventy years of progress

The impact of recent legislation

During the 1960s and 1970s more laws affecting exceptional children and youth were passed by Congress than ever before. We will focus our attention on several of these laws that are designed to protect the individual's right to achieve his or her potential for living as full and as independent a life as possible.

Title I

In 1965 the highly significant Elementary and Secondary Education Act (ESEA) was passed. Called Title I, it dealt with public education for the handicapped from lower socioeconomic levels.

Table 1.1
Commonly reported dates when day classes for the handicapped were first held

Deaf	Boston, Mass.	1869
Retarded	Providence, R. I.	1896
Crippled	Chicago, Ill.	1899
Blind	Chicago, Ill.	1900
Lowered vitality	Providence, R. I.	1908
Partially seeing	Roxbury, Mass.	1913

Source: U.S. Office of Education, 1976, p.11

Table 1.2
Percentage of U.S. cities in 1911 reporting special classes for exceptional children

Type of special class	*Percentage of cities*
Mentally exceptional	42
Defective 11	
Backward 25	
Gifted 6	
Physically exceptional	10
Environmentally exceptional (non-English speaking)	39
Morally exceptional (delinquent, incorrigible)	17

Source: See Table 1.1

Two bills amending ESEA followed and emphasized provisions for special education. The second bill, Public Law 89-750, was signed into law by President Lyndon B. Johnson in 1966 and established the first version of the Education of the Handicapped Act. This became known as Title VI of the ESEA and provided grants to states to "initiate, expand, and improve" programs for all exceptional children (Martin, 1976, p. 133). Additionally, the Bureau of Education for the Handicapped and the National Advisory Committee on the Handicapped were established.

Title VI

Emphasis on the rights of children

Areas in which children's rights were violated began to receive emphasis only in recent years. Several investigators studied the policy of placing children in residential

Table 1.3
Numbers of pupils enrolled in special education services provided by local public school systems in the U.S. 1922–1972

Areas of exceptionality	1971–72	1968	1958	1948	1940	1932	1922
Total exceptional	—	—	889,560	377,615	313,722	163,950	—
1. Superior cognitive abilities (gifted)	(no data)	(no data)	52,269	20,712	3,255	1,834	(no data)
Total handicapped	2,857,551	2,251,500	837,291	356,903	310,467	162,116	26,161
2. General learning disabilities (mentally retarded)	872,113	703,800	223,447	86,980	98,416	75,099	23,252
(moderate/trainable)	no breakdown	(55,000)	(16,793)	(4,509)	(nil)	(nil)	(nil)
(mild/educable)	no breakdown	(648,800)	(206,654)	(82,471)	(98,416)	(75,099)	(23,252)
3. Behavioral disabilities (emotionally disturbed)	156,486	99,400	28,622	15,340	10,477	14,354	(no data)
4. Oral communication disabilities (speech impaired)	1,360,203	1,122,200	494,137	182,344	126,146	22,735	(no data)
5. Hearing disabilities (deaf and partially hearing)	79,539	65,200	21,616	13,977	13,478	4,434	2,911
6. Visual disabilities (blind and partially seeing)	30,630	22,700	11,600	8,216	8,875	5,308	(no data)
7. Neuromotor and other crippling and health disabilities	182,636	109,000	57,230	47,227	53,075	40,186	(no data)
8. Specific learning disabilities	166,534	120,000	(nil)	(nil)	(nil)	(nil)	(nil)
9. Multiple handicapped	9,310	9,200	—	—	—	—	—
10. Other	—	—	579	2,819	—	—	—
Total K-12 school age population (in thousands)	52,000 (est.)	50,500	39,500	28,600	28,250	28,400	25,000

Source: Dunn, 1973, pp. 18–19. Data compiled from Mackie, 1969; Martens et al., 1950; Martin, 1970; Simon & Grant, 1970; U.S. Office of Education, 1971

centers for treatment in terms of possible violations of the children's rights (Ginsberg, 1974; Hobbs, 1975; Joint Commission on Mental Health of Children, 1969; Murdock, 1974). The findings of ten federal agencies that sponsored the Classification of Exceptional Children Project were that treatment center programs across the U.S. provided almost identical services to their residents—regardless of the population served (Hobbs, 1975). These findings were appalling, when one considers that each exceptionality, and, of course, each individual, requires a unique and highly specialized program. Clearly there existed a discrepancy between that which was *known* about children, exceptionality and mental health, and that which was *implemented*.

Child advocacy programs

The development of child advocacy programs was needed to protect the civil rights of various types of exceptional and multihandicapped children (Gallagher, 1976; Koocher, 1976). Murdock (1974) reported that the mentally retarded were denied due process in cases of guardianship and decisions to institutionalize.

Despite the greater availability of special education classes in the public schools, some parents continued to have difficulty in obtaining necessary services for their exceptional children. Certain exclusionary policies still restricted such children's public school attendance. Hence, individual parents, guardians, parent organizations, and supporters of children's rights joined in challenging the courts and their state legislatures to guarantee every child—regardless of handicapping condition—the right to equal education opportunities.

Landmark court decisions

The Fourteenth Amendment of the Constitution (which guarantees equal protection) was interpreted by these vocal advocacy groups as establishing the right of every child to a free public education. In 1971, a landmark court decision set precedent by supporting this stand. The Pennsylvania Association for Retarded Children and thirteen mentally retarded children as plaintiffs won a court decision stating that retarded children had access to a free public education (Weintraub & Abeson, 1974). Later that same year in the District of Columbia, seven parents and guardians of children with various handicapping conditions (epilepsy, retardation, neurological impairment) received court stipulation that no child was to be excluded from receiving "a publicly supported education consistent with his needs and ability to benefit therefrom" (Weintraub & Abeson, 1974, p. 548).

Despite such court decisions, parents of exceptional children often found that special education classes were filled or certain types of classes or services were still not available. Particularly those living in small towns or rural areas were offered few options. The child whose exceptionality created problems in school was sent home and expected to remain there until he or she could adjust to the traditional classroom. An actual case example illustrates such a situation:

Eric Mrs. Anderson brought her six-year-old son Eric to a health sciences center for evaluation following his exclusion from school for disrupting the class. The family had been informed that Eric could not return to school until he could conform to classroom expectations. The Anderson family lived in a rural area two hours away from the center and Mrs. Anderson urgently wanted to help her son.

Eric's speech was difficult to understand, he exhibited behavior problems in the classroom, and he appeared unable to profit from regular classroom instruction. At the center he received a complete medical-neurological examination, speech and language assessment, visual and hearing checks, and psychological and educational evaluations. Results of these examinations showed Eric to be of average intelligence with normal visual and hearing acuity. He revealed a moderate to severe speech articulation problem and mild muscle coordination difficulties. He also demonstrated problems in distinguishing alphabet letters of similar appearance, in directional and spatial orientation (for instance, telling right from left), and in following a sequence of several commands or instructions.

Victoria's parents have just been informed that special education will be required for her. The placement team is discussing Victoria's specific needs.

Eric's emotional status was considered fragile. This was attributed to his school problems and the stress of not being understood when he spoke. When teased by his peers, Eric would strike out in anger and frustration.

Since his rural school had no special education services, it was recommended that Eric be reinstated in his regular class. It was also recommended that regular consultation between Eric's classroom teacher and personnel from the Evaluation Center be established to devise a program for meeting and handling his needs in the regular class setting. The principal and teacher were reluctant to reinstate Eric because (1) they lacked specific knowledge of how to remedy his difficulties and (2) they had insufficient time to give him special help. However, the classroom teacher and principal did cooperate in implementing educational suggestions for remediation and thus afforded Eric his right to an education.

Public Laws 93-380 and 94-142

Parents, educators, and interested legislators—aware that inequities in the treatment of handicapped children and youth still exist—vigorously lobbied for an additional and vitally important piece of legislation, which was passed in 1974. The Education Amendments of 1974 (Public Law 93-380) authorized increased levels of aid to states for the implementation of special education services and set forth *due process requirements* to protect the rights of handicapped youngsters and their families.

Due process requirements

This was followed in 1975 by enactment of the most comprehensive provisions ever legislated relating to handicapped individuals. Entitled *The Education for All Handicapped Children Act,* Public Law 94-142 set forth "as national policy the proposition that education must be extended to handicapped persons as their fundamental right" (Brenton, 1974, p. 6) and guarantees free appropriate public education. In this law first priority is accorded children not currently receiving special services needed and second priority is given to children who are inadequately served (see Table 1-4).

Other specific stipulations of Public Law 94-142 include assurances that:

Fair testing

1. Testing and assessment methods will be comprehensive and fair (that is, the testing must be nondiscriminatory and not based on a single criterion or index such as an IQ score).
2. The rights (due process) of handicapped children and their parents or surrogate parents will be protected. Under this provision parents or guardians have access, for example, to information regarding evaluations and may protest educational decisions made by school officials. Confidentiality of personally identifiable information is to be ensured.
3. Special services will be provided in the least restrictive environment (meaning that exceptional children may be placed in special or separate classes only for

Access to information

the portions of time deemed necessary for providing appropriate services).
4. Individualized programs to educate handicapped children will be implemented, maintained, and evaluated. Individual educational plans (IEPs) must be provided which include both short- and long-term educational goals and services with periodic review and revision of instructional goals and methods set forth.

IEPs

Enacted as a lifetime, or permanent, authorization with no expiration date, this newest legislation directed "that state and local school systems establish policies of providing free public education for all of America's handicapped children" (Martin, 1976, p. 133). Included are ages three through eighteen by the year 1978, extended to age twenty-one in 1980 (unless inconsistent with state law or court order regarding public education). Annual data is to be compiled leading to full educational opportunity for all handicapped children from birth through twenty-one years (Federal Register, 1977, p. 42481).

The multidisciplinary team

To comply with each of the four provisions cited above, as well as with others included in Public Law 94-142, school officials and other professionals must cooperate to a greater degree than ever before. The authors of this text are strongly committed

Table 1.4
Estimated number of handicapped children served and unserved by type of handicap

	1975–76 served (projected)	1975–76 unserved	Total hand. child. served & unserved	Percentage served	Percentage unserved
Total age 0–19	4,310,000	3,577,000	7,887,000	55%	45%
Total age 6–19	3,860,000	2,840,000	6,700,000	58%	42%
Total age 0–5	450,000	737,000	1,187,000	38%	62%
Speech impaired	2,020,000	273,000	2,293,000	88%	12%
Mentally retarded	1,350,000	157,000	1,507,000	90%	10%
Learning disabilities	260,000	1,706,000	1,966,000	13%	87%
Emotionally disturbed	255,000	1,055,000	1,310,000	19%	81%
Crippled & other health impaired	255,000	73,000	328,000	78%	22%
Deaf	45,000	4,000	49,000	92%	8%
Hard of hearing	66,000	262,000	328,000	20%	80%
Visually handicapped	43,000	23,000	66,000	65%	35%
Deaf-blind & other multihandicapped	16,000	24,000	40,000	40%	60%

Source: U.S. Office of Education, 1976, p. 2

to the concept of a multidisciplinary team approach and will emphasize such an approach in terms of each exceptionality. Good diagnosis, treatment, and remediation of exceptional children and youth requires a multidisciplinary team effort. Piecemeal information offered to parents and educators does not and cannot integrate all of the existing medical, social, psychological, educational, or speech results into a meaningful whole. Nor can a teacher, psychologist, health official, or others concerned take isolated reports about the child and easily integrate and translate the meaning of such results into a comprehensive educational program. It takes a coordinated effort to provide the best educational programs for exceptional children and youth.

Sharing of responsibility

To illustrate the extreme importance of a multidisciplinary team approach in diagnosing and planning of remediation or treatment, let us presume that you are the teacher, special services coordinator or school administrator charged with planning individual educational programs for two handicapped children. You have referred two children for evaluation and have received the following information (excerpted from actual reports):

Child A
(Caucasian male, 7 years of age, 2nd grade)

Teacher's report
1. writing usually very poor and almost illegible; occasionally good
2. difficult to understand when speaking
3. cannot read or spell at a second-grade level
4. good in most sports

Social history report
5. intact family constellation, history of marital problems that are now resolved; stable home

Speech and hearing report
6. normal hearing
7. moderate to severe articulation problems
8. mild dysfluencies

Psychology report
9. average intelligence on verbal tests
10. above-average intelligence on performance tests
11. poor self-esteem, rebelliousness, emotional adjustment problems
12. academic achievement at beginning first grade in reading, kindergarten level in spelling, and second grade in math

Neurology report
13. mild choreoathetosis made worse by fatigue
14. normal early developmental milestones
15. abnormal electroencephalogram
16. normal visual acuity

Child B
(Caucasian female, 6½ years of age, 1st grade)

Teacher's report	1. cannot function well in class, not reading at grade level
2. talks to herself, seems to be in a world of her own
3. sometimes hits other children
Social history report	4. good, stable family
Psychology report	5. average to above-average intelligence on verbal tests
6. reading and spelling at grade level; math achievement slightly below grade level
7. severe visual-motor-perceptual problems
8. marginal emotional adjustment
Medical report	9. walked at 17 months, talked at 1½-2 years of age
10. retrolental fibroplasia
11. normal neurological examination
Ophthalmology report	12. alternating extropia, myopia—9.00 + 100 × 180 in each eye
13. 20/800 distance bilaterally, uncorrected

Having five such separate reports on each child makes it difficult to plan appropriate individualized educational programs and to determine whether either or both of these children needs special class placement, special tutoring, special equipment, and/or psychotherapy. To interpret ophthalmological and neurological reports is nearly impossible without calling each specialist and asking for an interpretation. Even then, interpretations alone would still not tell us how the problem might affect learning or if special educational provisions would be necessary. Yet these professionals offer medical information that is critical to the understanding of these two children and to their educational and class placement. Sometimes, too, psychological and educational reports are written in such technical jargon that the information is of little benefit to the teacher who must educate the child.

The composition and work of the team
By definition a multidisciplinary team approach means that various professionals evaluate, collaborate, and cooperate with each other in planning the provision of appropriate services for an exceptional child. The team may include any combination of the following—or other needed—professionals: educators (special, regular, administrative), medical personnel, psychologists and/or psychometrists, social workers, speech pathologists, audiologists, physical therapists, vocational rehabilitation specialists. Parents are also very important and necessary contributors to the team.

A team evaluation includes social, educational, psychological or psychometric —and, as needed—medical, speech and language, physical therapy, or audiological

14
Introduction to exceptionality

assessment. These assessments are designed to identify the child's strengths and weaknesses so that educational and other services can be planned that will lead to his or her personal achievement. Figure 1-1 illustrates the four phases involved in the multidisciplinary approach: These include (1) comprehensive assessment, (2) resulting impressions, (3) initial program planning, and (4) follow-up through periodic reassessment and program modification as necessary.

Team members may vary

As a multidimensional view of the child emerges, and solutions are sought to further the child's educational and general welfare, team members may vary. Figure 1-2 illustrates a sampling of various exceptionalities and the professionals who can provide vital and relevant information for the establishment of programs for the children and youth involved. Note that no one discipline is given sole expert authority in the decision-making process. What is important is the recognition that various professionals offer valuable information that affects the plans for the child's learning the way he or she is viewed and understood.

Following the comprehensive assessment and evaluation, the team goes on to clarify its plans based on the data obtained. Figure 1-3 illustrates four major considerations that lead to the implementation of a developmental or educational program for an exceptional child. These include determination of the extent to which (1) special teaching techniques are required, (2) later vocational goals or choices may be influenced, (3) later independent living choices are involved, and (4) social and recreational choices are affected.

Public Law 94-142 clearly outlines procedures for implementing appropriate services at the local school level. These procedures include (1) the formation of a placement committee or team which will have responsibility for making specific decisions concerning a specific child and (2) the placement comittee's development of an individual education program (IEP) which is based on an evaluation of that child's needs and which contains particular kinds of information. (See the Resource Manual published by the National Association of State Directors of Special Education [NASDSE, 1976, pp. 4–5] for an in-depth presentation of these procedures.)

Placement team formation Table 1-5 indicates possible committee composition to enable local education agencies to carry out the intent of Public Law 94-142 concerning a multidisciplinary approach. Members of the committee, as previously pointed out, may vary according to the unique needs of the child whose program of services is being planned. Their first task, of course, is to determine the child's eligibility for receiving special education services according to state criteria.

Development of an individual education program Following determination of eligibility based upon information gained from the results of comprehensive assessment procedures, the placement committee then proceeds to develop an individual education program that will offer practical plans for meeting the student's specific needs. The provisions of Public Law 94-142 specify that an IEP developed at the local level should include—at the minimum—the following components:

IEP components

Figure 1.1
Multidisciplinary team approach

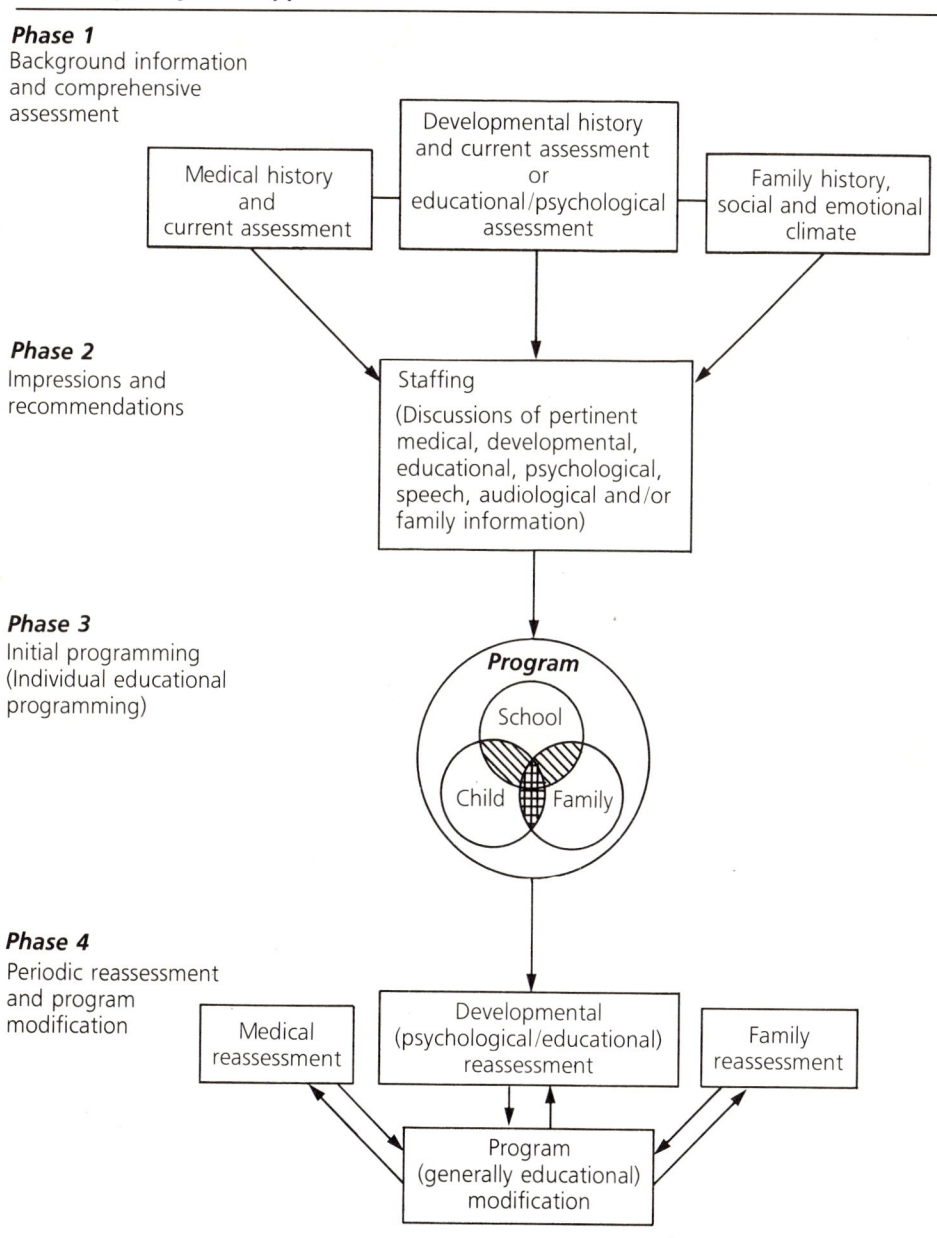

Phase 1
Background information and comprehensive assessment

- Medical history and current assessment
- Developmental history and current assessment or educational/psychological assessment
- Family history, social and emotional climate

Phase 2
Impressions and recommendations

Staffing
(Discussions of pertinent medical, developmental, educational, psychological, speech, audiological and/or family information)

Phase 3
Initial programming
(Individual educational programming)

Program
School
Child
Family

Phase 4
Periodic reassessment and program modification

- Medical reassessment
- Developmental (psychological/educational) reassessment
- Family reassessment

Program (generally educational) modification

Source: Adapted from Thomas & Marshall, 1977, p. 18

1. present level of educational performance
2. annual goals and short-term objectives
3. specific educational services to be provided
4. extent to which the child will participate in the regular classroom
5. projected date for initiation and duration of services
6. objective criteria and evaluation procedures
7. schedule and procedures for review (which must be done at least annually)

Figure 1.2
Background information and assessment of the exceptional child

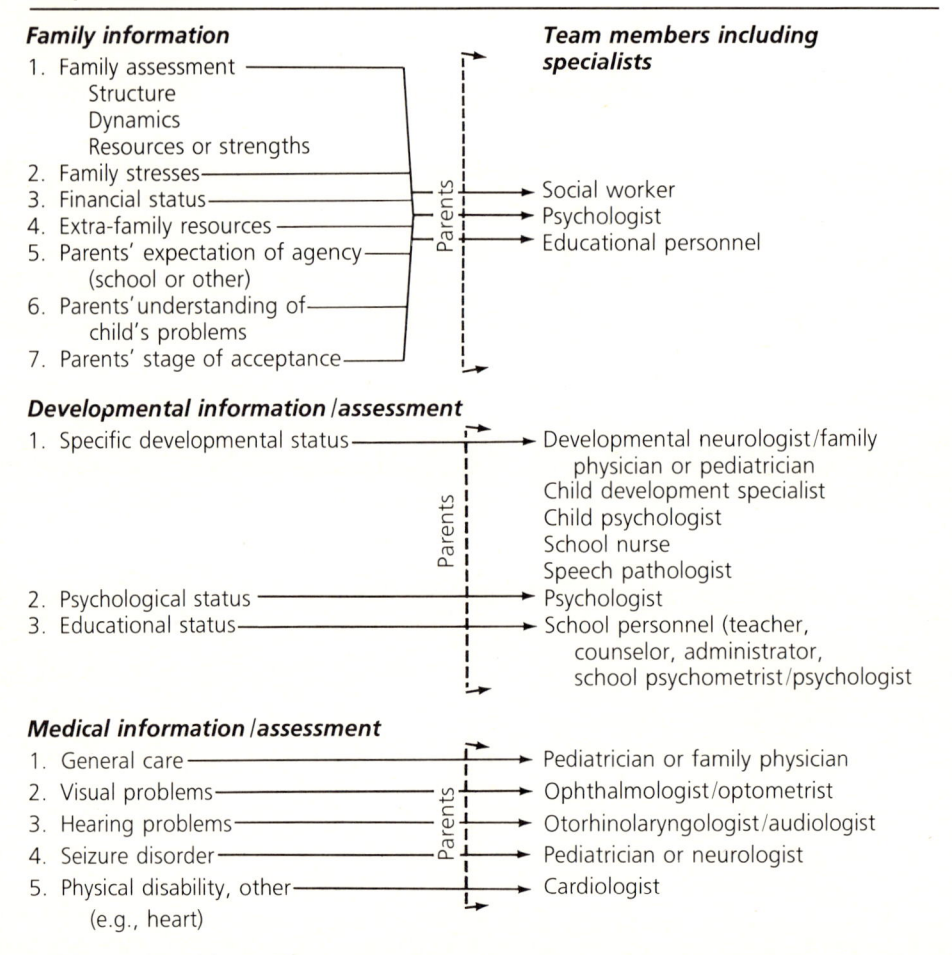

Family information
1. Family assessment
   Structure
   Dynamics
   Resources or strengths
2. Family stresses
3. Financial status
4. Extra-family resources
5. Parents' expectation of agency (school or other)
6. Parents' understanding of child's problems
7. Parents' stage of acceptance

Team members including specialists
→ Social worker
→ Psychologist
→ Educational personnel

(Parents)

Developmental information/assessment
1. Specific developmental status → Developmental neurologist/family physician or pediatrician
   Child development specialist
   Child psychologist
   School nurse
   Speech pathologist
2. Psychological status → Psychologist
3. Educational status → School personnel (teacher, counselor, administrator, school psychometrist/psychologist)

(Parents)

Medical information/assessment
1. General care → Pediatrician or family physician
2. Visual problems → Ophthalmologist/optometrist
3. Hearing problems → Otorhinolaryngologist/audiologist
4. Seizure disorder → Pediatrician or neurologist
5. Physical disability, other (e.g., heart) → Cardiologist

(Parents)

Source: Adapted from Thomas & Marshall, 1977, p. 20

Figure 1-4 illustrates a sample form which, when completed, contains these components, Figure 1-5 is an activities checklist that enables educators to document the options for a child's placement, and Figure 1-6 is a sample of the form used to review the placement on an annual basis.

One can sum up the whole purpose of the multidisciplinary team as an effort to ensure each exceptional child or youth educational services which lead to optimal development. The effectiveness of the multidisciplinary model stems from its flexibility and consideration of individual differences. No one program is suitable, for example, for all retarded children, or all deaf or visually disabled children. Each child or youth is thus now viewed as unique, and the need for careful educational programming is seen as paramount to realization of potential.

Each child is unique

Figure 1.3
Considerations in planning developmental or educational programming for sample disabilities

Sample disability	Professionals for specific care	Special teaching techniques required?	Likely to affect vocational choice?	Likely to affect independent living choice?	Likely to affect social and recreational choices?
Visual disability/ blindness	Ophthalmologist Optometrist Optician Educator	Yes	Yes	Possibly	Yes
Hearing disability/ deafness	Otorhinolaryngologist Audiologist Educator	Yes	Yes	Possibly	Yes
Seizure disorder	Primary care M.D./ developmental neurologist Educator	Possibly	Possibly	Possibly	Possibly
Mental retardation	Psychologist Psychometrist Educator	Yes	Yes	Possibly	Probably
Cerebral palsy	Primary care M.D. Developmental neurologist Physical therapist Educator	Yes	Possibly	Possibly	Probably

Source: Courtesy of Ellidee D. Thomas, M.D., Child Study Center, Oklahoma City *(adapted)*

The need for early diagnosis

The importance of early diagnosis will be emphasized throughout this text. You will learn of various techniques devised to detect medical, hearing, visual and other problems at birth. These diagnostic techniques have been developed because it has been demonstrated beyond a doubt that early diagnosis and treatment aids a child's developmental progress. The child is able to adapt more quickly to his or her environment when problems are detected early and a program for cognitive-developmental stimulation is initiated. Research by numerous investigators has demonstrated that there are critical, or sensitive, periods of development in humans as well as in other forms of life (Harlow & Harlow, 1966; Hess, 1959; Moltz, 1963; Scott, 1958). The periods are termed critical because of the events or circumstances that occurred during the exceptional child's early life, because of the physical and emotional status of the child at that stage of development, and "because of the sequence in which the developmental events occur" (Caldwell, 1962, p. 237).

Critical periods for learning

Table 1.5
Possible placement committee composition

Person	Permanent members	Recommended on core committees	Consulting members
School administrator	x		
Special education administrator	x		
Referring/receiving teacher		x	
Parent		x	
Psychologist			x
Educational diagnostician			x
Speech pathologist			x
Physical therapist			x
Occupational therapist			x
Audiologist			x
School nurse			x
Social worker			x
Guidance counselor			x
Curriculum specialist			x
Methods & materials specialist			x
Physician			x
Ophthalmologist/optometrist			x
Vocational rehabilitation counselor			x
Other consultants			x

Source: National Association of State Directors of Special Education, 1976, p. 16

Figure 1.4
Synopsis of an individual education program (IEP):
Total service plan

Child's name _____

School _____

Date of program entry _____

Prioritized long-term goals:

_____

_____

Summary of present levels of performance:

_____

_____

_____

Short-term objectives	Specific educational and/or support services	Person(s) responsible	Percent of time	Beginning and ending date
				Review date

Percent of time in regular classroom

Placement recommendation

Committee members present

Dates of meeting

Committee recommendations for specific procedures/techniques, materials, etc. (include information about learning style)

Objective evaluation criteria for each annual goal statement

Source: National Association of State Directors of Special Education, 1976, p. 29

We would hypothesize that a child's *educational readiness* corresponds to a critical, or sensitive, period. The critical-periods hypothesis appears to be used in two ways (Caldwell, 1962, p. 237):

(1) a critical period *beyond* which a given phenomenon will not appear (i.e., a point in time which marks the onset of total indifference, or resistance, to certain patterns of stimulation);
(2) a critical period *during* which the . . . individual . . . is especially sensitive to various developmental modifiers, which, if introduced at a different time in the life cycle, would have little or no effect (i.e., a period of maximum susceptibility).

Adapting the critical-periods hypothesis to the early growth and development of exceptional children is logical and demonstrates why early diagnosis and treatment are crucial to the optimal functioning of the child. Caldwell suggests that we allow the *behavior* of the child to inform us of his or her readiness period rather than let a particular time period determine what we might expect. For example, the normal

Child's behavior is a guide to readiness

Figure 1.5
Developing the IEP: Activities checklist

Activities
Check off the following activities as they are completed by the committee or individual members

_____	Parents contacted
_____	Evaluation information assembled
_____	Evaluation information compared to eligibility criteria
_____	Eligibility decision made
_____	Method for developing plan specified
_____	IEP examined for most appropriate/least restrictive placements
_____	Options for placement discussed
_____	Placement recommendation made
_____	Parent permission for placement obtained
_____	IEP signed by all members

Conference must be held within thirty days of determination of eligibility or attendance. A mutually agreed upon time and place is determined. Alternative procedures should be stated if parents are unable to attend. Documentation of attempts to arrange conference should be kept. Participation of interpreters should be arranged if a communication barrier is involved.

Source: National Association of State Directors of Special Education, 1976, p. 47 (adapted)

period of time for a child to walk varies from ten to sixteen months of age. To say that the critical period for walking is twelve months of age, a time when most children do begin walking, would not be accurate and would not take into account either individual differences or the normal *range* of development of from ten to sixteen months.

We can illustrate how early development is influenced by events that occur at certain critical, or sensitive, periods. Pregnant mothers who contract German measles during the first trimester of pregnancy are likely to have infants who have severe hearing and vision impairments, have heart problems and/or other congenital problems. Thus the first three months of intra-uterine development are critical in terms of normal infant development. If the pregnant mother were to contract measles during the latter half of her pregnancy her offspring would be free of the handicapping conditions. (See Unit 11 for a further discussion of rubella children.)

The special education teacher is working with Victoria. Her parents are interested observers of the learning activity being demonstrated.

Figure 1.6
Annual review of placement

Date of review _____

Child's name _____ Date of birth _____ C.A. _____

Address _____ Phone _____ Parent _____

1. Present placement/program:
   _____
   _____

2. Progress to date (number of objectives met):
   _____
   _____
   _____

3. Recommendations:
       Continue in the same program next year _____
       Transfer to next level of program _____
       Return to full-time regular classroom _____
       Explore other alternatives:
           Specifically, _____
       _____
       _____

4. Additional comments:
   _____
   _____
   _____
   _____
   _____

Placement team members
_____, Chair
_____
_____
_____

Source: National Association of State Directors of Special Education, 1976, p. 87 (adapted)

Animal studies using chimpanzees demonstrate that the first year of life is critical for normal visual development. In chimps who were raised in darkness for the first year of their lives, certain cells in the retina did not develop and vision was permanently impaired (Reisen, 1950). There also appear to be critical periods during which certain skills emerge. If these skills fail to evolve, the child is likely to experience a permanent delay in development. For example, a deaf child whose hearing loss goes undetected or for whom no formal speech and language stimulation program is initiated until after four or five years of age will demonstrate a serious lag in communication skills throughout life. A youngster who has serious visual impairment that goes undetected, or a blind child who does not receive early motor and cognitive stimulation until four to six years of age will be delayed throughout his or her school years. A child who does not receive appropriate maternal attention or is placed in one foster home after another during the first year or two of life will have greater difficulty forming durable, stable and close relationships. The first one or two years of life are a critical period for learning to form an attachment to a significant adult. It has also been suggested that events which occur during the first three of four years of life are critical for those who develop schizophrenia in later life (Mussen, Conger & Kagan, 1969). Thus, early diagnosis and early stimulation are crucial for the adequate emotional, physical and cognitive development of children.

Research supports critical-period hypothesis

Early intervention essential

As mentioned earlier, a child's behavior will indicate when he or she is ready to proceed to a new developmental level. For example, most children walk between the ages of ten and sixteen months. If a youngster with cerebral palsy or one who is blind is not walking by that time, can we assume that retardation is complicating development, or can we more fairly assume that the exceptionality itself may be causing the delay in walking? To understand specific exceptionalities is to understand that development may vary to an even greater degree. For example, lack of sight can delay the ability to walk until eighteen to twenty-two months of age or longer, while the child who is physically and sensorially normal but does not walk until twenty-two months of age may be retarded. A blind child whose disability is diagnosed early may walk on schedule if he or she receives appropriate stimulation. On the other hand, early diagnosis may have no effect on when a retarded child learns to walk, but it may affect the development of other cognitive abilities.

Greater developmental variation in exceptional children

Several units in this text discuss the importance of early diagnosis for specific exceptionalities. The results of early, as well as late, intervention are also discussed.

Issues of special concern

The preceding sections have dealt with early diagnosis and recent legislative provisions and procedures to ensure future educational opportunities for exceptional children and youth. A child's optimal adaptation to his or her environment occurs when individual needs are assessed by various disciplines and a program is tailored to the child's special needs. Two specific issues are intricately related to all children

IQ testing controversy

and youth but are of particular concern to the future of those who are exceptional. They are (1) the efficacy of standardized tests—particularly intelligence, or IQ tests—as traditionally used in the measurement and evaluation of student ability, and (2) the practice of applying labels to children on the basis of test performance or behavioral characteristics even though these labels serve no useful purpose in identifying a child's individual strengths or specific needs.

The efficacy of standardized tests

IQ assessment must not penalize the child

Psychological assessment is valuable and even necessary for the diagnosis and proper placement of exceptional children, but this process must not violate their rights. With unskilled examiners, unsuitable tests, or examiners unfamiliar with cultural or specific exceptionalities, such has often been the case. Appropriate assessment should be requested to answer specific questions that might be helpful in establishing a program for a child, and not simply for the sake of determining intelligence quotient. An IQ score alone does not provide sufficient information for understanding the needs of individual children.

IQ test shortcomings

The IQ test: what does it test?   What is an IQ, or intelligence quotient? Generally, it is a score based on a person's responses to a series of verbal and nonverbal tests. What does an IQ score mean? The answer is not simple. The common, but misleading, assumption is that an IQ score tells us how bright a person might be. Such an oversimplification has created problems for years. In fact, a child may be functionally bright but obtain a low score on a standardized test of intelligence. For example, a Navajo youth who has lived all of his or her life in the heart of the Navajo reservation in Arizona would be likely to score low on the Wechsler or the Stanford-Binet intelligence scales, two common test instruments used by psychologists and psychometrists across the nation. If, however, we were to place a white middle-class child from a large urban center on the reservation to live through a winter we would find that the Navajo youth would appear to be functionally brighter.

Cultural bias

In professional literature, as well as in mass-market publications, the validity of using traditional standardized tests of intelligence as a basis for placing children and youth into special school programs continues to be questioned. In 1972 intelligence testing of black children was halted temporarily in California following a court decision that the IQ tests administered there were culturally biased. The state Department of Education was ordered to cease placement of black students in classrooms for the educable mentally retarded "... on the basis of criteria which place primary reliance on the results of IQ tests" (APA Monitor, 1972, p. 7). In 1974 the U.S. Commission on Civil Rights contended that Mexican-American students are twice as likely as Anglo students to be assigned to classes for the mentally retarded.

In recent years the belief that criticism of IQ tests is well founded has resulted in either a moratorium on or abandonment of the use of group, as well as individual, testing instruments by various school systems. As a result of court suits protesting the use of such test results for school placement or assignment of students (Weintraub & Abeson, 1974) and/or genuine concern by educational and other personnel concerning the tests' shortcomings, future evaluation procedures under the latest enacted legislation (Public Law 94-142) must be in accordance with the following provisions:

> (1) Testing and evaluation materials and procedures used for the purposes of evaluation and placement of handicapped children must be selected and administered so as not to be racially or culturally discriminatory. . . . (2) Tests and other evaluation materials: are provided and administered in the child's native language; (3) have been validated for the specific purpose for which they are used; and (4) are administered by trained personnel. . . . (5) Tests and other evaluation materials include those tailored to assess specific areas of educational need and not merely those which are designed to provide a single general intelligence quotient. . . . (6) No single procedure is used as the sole criterion for determining an appropriate placement for a child. . . . (7) The evaluation is made by a multidisciplinary team or group of persons. . . . (8) The child is assessed in all areas related to the suspected disability, including, where appropriate, health, vision, hearing, social and emotional status, general intelligence, academic performance, communicative status, and motor abilities (Federal Register, 1977, p. 42496).

Safeguards to ensure proper assessment

Perhaps controversy will abate as a result of the procedural safeguards required by Public Law 94-142. If trained examiners utilize test instruments according to the newest legislation and evaluate test performance in terms of *all* factors which may affect the child (see Table 1-6), the need for moratoriums or exclusion of IQ tests may become unnecessary.

Children's rights   Assessment procedures can violate children's rights in at least five ways, according to Mercer (1974, pp. 132–36). Her opinion is that children have

1. the right to be evaluated within a culturally appropriate normative framework
2. the right to be assessed as multidimensional human beings
3. the right to be fully educated
4. the right to be free of stigmatizing labels
5. the right to ethnic identity and respect

Public Law 94-142 has addressed such needs by calling for *comprehensive evaluation*—rather than basing placement on a single index, such as an IQ test. It has further provided specific due process rights to the exceptional child and his or her family.

Rights of due process   Each of the following provisions of Public Law 94-142 deal with the *due process rights* of parents and reinforce their rights to make decisions concerning their child's exceptionality.

1. The local education agency (LEA) must secure voluntary written consent for assessment or evaluation procedures that are undertaken to determine if special services are needed and to identify educational needs. The parents retain the right to revoke such consent at any time.
2. Parents have the right to give—or withhold—permission for planned school placement into a specific program.

Right to examine pertinent school records

3. Parents have the right to examine all school records related to identification, evaluation, and placement and to question the accuracy and appropriateness of such information and decisions.
4. Parents who do not agree with the assessment results or placement plans for their child may request an independent evaluation. Information obtained is to be used in LEA's decision-making process.

Right to impartial due process hearing

5. Parents have the right (as does the public educational agency) to request an impartial hearing. When a hearing is initiated, the LEA's representative or team members generally explain the identification tests employed, the procedures used in determining educational needs, and the resulting placement recommendations. The parents, and any representative attending the meeting at the request of the parents (child advocate, private psychologist), have the right to ask questions, present any new data about the child, etc.

Right to appeal

6. In the event that such efforts do not lead to agreement among all parties concerned, the parents have the right to appeal the results of the due process

Table 1.6
Possible areas for child evaluation

Educational functioning
  Achievement in subject area
  Learning style
  Strengths and weaknesses
  Thinking processes
  (knowledge, comprehension, application, analysis, synthesis, evaluation)

Social-emotional functioning
  Social/psychological development
  (attending/receiving, responding, valuing, organizing, characterizing)
  Self-help skills

Language functioning
  Receptive
  Expressive
  Nonverbal
  Speech

Physical functioning
  Visual
  Hearing
  Speech
  Motor/psychomotor
  (gross motor, fine motor)
  Medical health

Family
  Dominant language
  Parent-child interactions
  Social service needs

Environment
  Home
  School
  Interpersonal
  Material

Cognitive functioning
  Intelligence
  Adaptive behavior

Source: National Association of State Directors of Special Education, 1976, p. 20

hearing to their state Department of Education. If the situation is not resolved at this level, the parents have the right to appeal to the civil court system. Thus both schools and the family will be responsible for seeing that the exceptional child's rights are protected.

The most recent legislation relating to due process rights of the handicapped is Public Law 94-103. Section 113 of the law mandates that every state provide a protection and advocacy agency to protect the rights of those with intellectual, emotional, and sensorimotor disabilities.

The labeling process

As we noted earlier, classification of exceptional children is made on the basis of significant departures from the so-called norm, or societal average. Such categories are societally defined as a particular culture attempts to set such norms, but changes or modifications in definitions have been seen through the years. Terms such as *exceptional, handicapped, disabled* and *disordered* have all been used interchangeably to refer to individuals in need of special services. The attempt to distinguish between the meaning of a disability as an "impairment of structure or function" and a *handicap* as a term implying "a detrimental effect on the individual's functioning level" (Telford & Sawrey, 1967) has received support. Scriven (1976, p. 61), for example, notes that we too often view handicaps as "permanent, instead of treating some of them as highly situational." Professionals, laypeople, and associations representing various conditions point to studies that demonstrate the productiveness of individuals designated as handicapped. The examples of the many people of renown who have succeeded in making outstanding contributions despite varying disabilities lend further credence to this point of view. The practice of designating people as handicapped will continue, however, due to society's sympathetic response to this term when funding is needed for various programs. Also, the term *handicapped* is included in local, state and the most recent federal legislation.

Difficulties in classifying exceptionality

The student seeking a true understanding of exceptionality must avoid the pitfall of using certain terminology as labels. A label locks individuals into a preconceived or sterotyped pattern of expectations. Gallagher (1976) notes that the nomenclature used in classifying the exceptional population needs to be used in these positive ways:

Necessity for avoiding stereotypes

1. as a basis for studying causative factors associated with different classifications;
2. as a foundation for greater understanding of the appropriate delivery of services (for example, differentiation in treatment and rehabilitative efforts); and
3. as a vehicle for obtaining needed resources (financial support, reimbursement on insurance claims and training of personnel in specialized areas)

The use of a classification system for purposes other than these will lead to continuing controversy about the stigmas attached to labeling.

Educational placement provisions

Special services

The kinds of special services for children and youth must now be carefully considered. The means through which special services for exceptional children are furnished can vary, however, along a continuum of varying degrees of segregation, *depending upon individual needs.* Again, in accordance with Public Law 94-142, special services must be provided in the *least restrictive* environment. The following alternatives for educating exceptional children are possible: residential schools, hospital and homebound services, self-contained special education classes, itinerant services, and mainstreaming in standard classrooms.

Residential schools today

Certain children still need residential schools

Because of the trend toward deinstitutionalization, certain conditions must exist to warrant placing children in residential facilities. Children who have *extensive medical or health problems and/or severe behavioral or management problems* may be candidates for placement in a residential setting. Some residential schools for the blind, deaf, or the mentally retarded cannot be ruled out when the good of the child is under consideration. Many institutions offer exemplary educational programs which cannot at present be duplicated in the public schools. Increased cooperation in integrating residential school students into any public school setting from which they can benefit will be a part of future efforts to comply with Public Law 94-142 requirements for placing the handicapped in the least restrictive educational setting possible.

Hospital and homebound services

Some children are confined to hospitals or to their homes because of the nature of their temporary or permanent disabilities. Students who must remain in full body casts or under close medical supervision must receive special educational considerations. In addition to providing a visiting homebound and/or hospital special education teacher, school personnel attempt to reduce the isolation of these children from their peers. Electronic advancements have made it possible for the child to have access to a more integrated educational experience. For example, in many larger cities, talkback television or telephone services are available, which permit the student to view and communicate with classmates. Such means are illustrated in the following case:

> **Brent** This normal, healthy child was thrown from a horse at the age of eight, sustaining severe head injuries. He began having seizures following the accident, but they were initially controllable by medication. When Brent reached adolescence, however, his seizures became pronounced and medication was no longer effective. After consultations among the attending neurologist, classroom teacher, school counselor, and psychologist, homebound instruction was recommended. It was decided that this would be the

best course of action until Brent's physical difficulties could again be brought under effective control. Through talkback television services Brent was able to remain in contact with his peers, and visitations from a teacher assigned to homebound students helped him to continue making academic progress.

Public day school provisions
Although special services provided within the public school setting represent greater integration opportunities, a number of different alternatives must be considered in determining the most appropriate placement for individual students. Sometimes a

Placement alternatives

In response to the parents' desire to help, Victoria's teacher brings them into the teaching process of basic arithmetic.

self-contained classroom setting is preferable. In this case, children who fall into a single diagnostic category, such as mentally retarded, emotionally disturbed or learning disabled, are grouped together and guided by special educators who assume responsibility for full-time educational programming. Minimum class size for self-contained classrooms varies according to type of exceptionality and may differ from state to state. In this type of program, however, the exceptional child has only limited opportunities for interaction with students from regular classrooms.

Splitting students' time

Less restrictive programming alternatives include splitting the student's time between special classes and regular classes, and placing the student in regular classes while providing him or her with special instructional personnel and facilities during portions of the school day. The latter includes periods of time, for example, for individualized instruction by the school reading specialist in a laboratory or resource room with various specialists (remedial reading or learning disabilities teacher, speech and language therapist, etc.). Such resource personnel may be full- or part-time staff members of various schools within the community. In some cases, part-time traveling specialists visit various schools on designated days and tutor children either individually or in groups.

Support for the least restrictive environment

Underlying the current emphasis on careful consideration of placement procedures is the contention that segregation into special classes fails to provide youngsters with the best possible educational experiences. Proponents of this view feel that a less restrictive placement is more likely to lead to realization of the individual's potential for effective functioning in society (Dunn, 1968; Johnson, 1962) and that too many youngsters are inappropriately assigned to special classes (Johnson, 1971; Wakefield, 1965). They also contend that more special services can be provided when regular classroom assignment is accompanied by close cooperation between classroom teachers and appropriate community or school-based resource personnel. Each of these and other considerations have resulted in local and state educational agencies being accountable under Public Law 94-142 *for providing services in the least restrictive manner deemed feasible.*

Mainstreaming considerations While the practice of least restrictive placement is currently labeled as *mainstreaming* of exceptional children and youth, the word is not used in the law. In fact, contrary to the impression of many people, PL 94-142 neither mandates that all handicapped children will be educated in a regular classroom, nor does it abolish any particular educational environment, such as a residential setting (Ballard & Zetter, 1977, p. 183). We will, however, refer to mainstreaming since this is the most popular way of conceptualizing the "least restrictive environment" clause of Public Law 94-142.

Mainstreaming may be misunderstood

Mainstreaming provisions will vary according to the kind and amount of integrative experiences that will benefit individual exceptional children and youth (Johnson, 1962; Jones, 1976). In such a program, handicapped children are integrated in regular classes with "normals" to the maximum extent appropriate. The new least restrictive educational environment will use the IEP as a guide or framework for meeting the needs of each child. When an exceptional child must be retained either full- or part-time in a self-contained special education class, his or her IEP document must clearly indicate why this is the most appropriate placement (Ballard & Zetter, 1977, p. 183). Concerns about the feasibility of mainstreaming have been voiced and a number of strategies have been offered to ensure successful placement of handicapped children in the least restrictive environment (see Table 1-7). *Mainstreaming depends on each child's needs*

It is now widely accepted that needless segregation of exceptional children is undesirable, and the reasons for integrating such youngsters into the regular classroom are more than purely academic. When ordinary children meet and begin to learn about the aids, appliances and apparatus required by some exceptional children, they can begin to look beyond the appliances and treat the disabled child as they would any other. In fact, teachers can greatly help a class by taking one or two hours to discuss the special equipment that disabled children use (Bookbinder, 1977). In a manual edited by Aiello (1975), many practical ideas for dealing with this type of situation have been suggested, and future educators may find it to be a useful resource. By learning about handicaps and sitting side by side, both handicapped and normal children cannot help but increase their own, and subsequently others', understanding. Another positive effect of mainstreaming, as demonstrated in one recent study (Peterson, Peterson & Scriven, 1977), is that exceptional children tend to imitate the behavior of "normal" children. *Imitation or modeling*

Approaches to understanding human behavior

Understanding human behavior has been approached from a number of different perspectives: biophysical or medical, psychodynamic, or psychodevelopmental; psychosocial; and behavioristic. Underlying all the assessment procedures, diagnostic classifications, and remediation or rehabilitation efforts for exceptional children, is the attempt to understand the conditions that affect human behavior.

Biophysical factors
The biophysical, or medical, approach stresses physical or biological factors that affect human behavior. From this approach vast amounts of knowledge are available concerning, for example, the functioning of the central nervous system (brain and spinal cord), the peripheral nervous system (sensorimotor functions), the endocrine and glandular systems, and other physiological influences. *Organic components*

Part of the biophysical approach is the study of genetic, or hereditary, influences. Research in this area dates back many years and continues to aid in the assessment, diagnosis, and therapeutic strategies for various conditions. Controversy still surrounds the effects of heredity and environment on behavior, but there is now

Table 1.7
Mainstreaming concerns and strategies

Concerns	Strategies
Our present and past teacher training programs provide little opportunity for regular teachers to become competent in meeting the needs of varied handicapped students.	Regular teacher training programs must undergo change to provide the increased understanding and competency needed in working with the handicapped.
Teacher training programs frequently place greater emphasis on methodology than on interpersonal needs of children in the classroom. Handicapped youngsters frequently have greater adjustment problems.	Greater emphasis on the social and emotional needs of *all* youngsters in the classroom is required.
Many youngsters are currently mainstreamed in regular classes but do not receive adequate services. Failure, frustration and social isolation are a consequence.	Careful, periodic evaluations need to be made of the benefits each child derives from the mainstreamed setting. Individual performance criteria must be examined.
Many prejudices and misconceptions exist concerning handicapped youngsters.	Personal values and present knowledge will need re-examination so as not to interfere with total commitment to all students as required in the teaching profession.
Mainstreaming will "dump" many handicapped children into the regular classroom as reluctance to make special class assignments grows.	Careful pre-assessment of a child's needs and capacity for success in the regular setting must be determined before foregoing special class placement.
Assessment procedures are controversial with regard to their effectiveness in determining needs of students.	Appropriate assessment procedures must be further identified and used by only those skilled in adequate interpretation.
Children are often inappropriately labeled as handicapped or overlooked as in need of special services because of differences in professional opinions.	A team approach must be utilized in determining if a child is in need of special services, what services are to be provided and how best to provide such services. The classroom teacher serves as a member of the professional team, working with other appropriately designated professionals.
Given current class sizes, individual differences among students are already great and preclude the teacher's adaptation to the even greater differences that would be present if handicapped children were included.	Class size needs to be restricted to a realistic number (perhaps eighteen to twenty-two students) in the elementary setting so that individual needs can be met.

Source: Data compiled from Brenton, 1974; Martin, 1976a; U.S. Office of Education, 1975

a consensus that an individual's total makeup is influenced by the interaction of both factors. The necessity of including various appropriate medical personnel in a multidisciplinary team has already been emphasized.

Psychodynamic factors

Study of human behavior from the psychodynamic, or psychodevelopmental, approach concentrates on examining the psychological aspects of an individual's makeup. Sigmund Freud, the most famous proponent of this approach to understanding human behaviors, conceptualized the view that the psyche (soul or spirit as distinguished from the body) possessed certain energizing forces that direct one's behaviors. Problems that develop in later life were viewed by Freud and his followers as often stemming from experiences during earlier developmental periods. Psychodynamic theorists may vary in their approach, but all concentrate on understanding the individual in terms of how past psychological influences affect present behaviors. This approach will be more thoroughly illustrated in Unit 7.

Psychological components

Psychosocial factors

In the psychosocial approach, the impact of ecological or environmental influences on the individual receive greater consideration. Acknowledging social influences as powerful forces, psychosocial theorists view aspects of society as determinants of behavior (Calhoun, Acocella & Goodstein, 1974). They are particularly interested in the labeling process. Needless stereotyping, as well as the promulgation of certain behaviors after a person has been labeled, are among their primary concerns. Additional emphasis is placed on the existence of societal inequities that contribute to problems experienced by many individuals and groups. The psychosocial perspective will come up throughout the text, most particularly in Unit 5.

Social components

The behavioristic approach

B. F. Skinner (1965), the most widely known behavioral psychologist at present, continues to view aspects of human behavior as primarily learned. Skinner is supported in his thinking and research by the work of earlier renowned psychologists (Pavlov, Watson, Thorndike) who also adhered to the behavioristic viewpoint. The behavioral psychologist views the *principle of reinforcement* as determining the responses individuals make to presenting conditions or situations with which they are presented. Each life is viewed as being filled with reinforcements (positive or negative consequences), which have influenced and continue to influence our behavior or actions. We are seen as operating on our environment and then doing or not doing certain things because of resulting "learned" consequences.

Learned behavior and reinforcement

The use of reinforcement principles for changing or modifying behavior is controversial (Stewart, Goodman & Hammond, 1976) and is sometimes viewed as being too manipulative or controlling. Others contend that practically every technique we use to change behavior is a form of the behavioristic, or behavior modification, approach (Brown, 1976; Madsen, 1971). "Everyone who has the responsibility for socializing, training, and educating children is involved in the process of enhancing or changing behaviors" (Blackham & Silberman, 1974, p. 1). These behavior modification advocates go on to say that we are really attempting to accomplish two basic goals: (1) to teach the child desirable behavior that may not be a part of his or her behavioral repertoire and (2) to eliminate or change unacceptable, self-defeating or undesirable behavior that the child might present. The purpose of these goals is to promote positive behavior that will aid the child as he or she relates to peers, family and neighborhood. Application of the behavioristic approach as used in this way and as applied to exceptional children will be examined in subsequent units.

Parental reactions to children exhibiting a disability

Most prospective parents look forward to their baby's arrival and fantasize a healthy child for whom they have high expectations of future success. When a handicapped child is born, it is as if the parents must bury their fantasies and reorient their thinking.

Disabilities may not be evident at birth

The fact that a child is born disabled may not always be evident at birth. Unless the child has an obvious physical deformity such as cleft palate, limb abnormalities, deviant physical characteristics (for example, Down's Syndrome), the newborn baby's condition may go undiagnosed. Sometimes a mother can sense immediately that something is wrong because the physician and nurses may delay in bringing the baby to her. She may sense something in the nurses' reactions to her, but not until the physician breaks the news are the mother's worst fears realized. In hundreds of interviews with mothers of cleft-lip/palate children, the same theme was reiterated: the delay in seeing the baby, the mother's growing apprehension that something was wrong, the physician's explanations which initially were only half-heard or half-understood, the shock to both parents when they saw their "different" baby, and, many times, the guilty feeling, as if they were somehow responsible for this unforeseen accident of nature. It is at this very early stage that parental counseling is so important for the sake of the relationships of all involved.

Grief reactions

Shock or disbelief

Parents react differently to stress depending upon their own psychological defenses, personality structures, and the support systems available to them. Almost all parents, however, begin to go through a grief reaction (see Table 1-8) once a serious handicap is diagnosed (Drotar et al., 1975; Kubler-Ross, 1969). At first they are *shocked* and *cannot believe* the news of the disability. Generally, unless the handicap is obvious, parents will seek a second, and perhaps even a third, opinion regarding the status of their child, particularly if retardation is the initial diagnosis. Parents need to be given this opportunity without adding to their guilt feelings. After a serious disability has been confirmed by one or more professionals, many parents accept and follow through on the suggestions for specialized services. Some parents continue to "shop" for better news and continue to *deny* that their child is handicapped. The longer the parents refuse to accept their child's difficulty, the longer it will be before he or she can begin to receive needed services. **Denial**

In diagnosing a baby's or young child's condition, it is crucial that the physician or other professional be gentle in discussing the findings (Noland, 1971). Time must be allotted to answer all questions the parents might ask. Indeed, the professional might even anticipate and respond to questions the parents are afraid to ask. For example, the parents of a deaf child frequently want to ask "If our baby is deaf, does that mean she (or he) will be retarded?" Much can be done to alleviate the concerns of parents by anticipating questions, spending adequate time on answers and providing reading material for more understanding.

Among other reactions experienced by parents of disabled children are feelings of *anger, guilt* and *frustration.* In anger, parents may blame each other for their child's disability or lash out at the physician or professional who diagnosed the condition. Out of guilt feelings, they may secretly berate themselves, believing they are somehow responsible for their child's disabilities. Frustration may ensue as they attempt to find suitable community resources to meet the child's needs. Sometimes parents are not informed of services, or they may be told to wait a period of time before seeking them. In the case of many disorders (for instance, deafness or blindness) a one- or two-year delay can be critical. Then the child may always be delayed and never catch up with peers or with those for whom services were provided at the earliest possible time. It is the professional's responsibility to help parents become associated with appropriate agencies or centers that offer the services they require. When such services are not available locally, as in smaller communities, the parents must be aided in obtaining services in the surrounding area. **Anger, guilt and frustration**

Not only do parents feel a sense of shock, denial, anger, guilt or frustration upon learning that their child has a serious handicap, but they can become unrealistic in their expectations for the child and look for magic cures. They might *bargain* with God or with themselves, believing that if they do certain things or act certain ways, perhaps the child's problem will disappear. Some parents may place great **Bargaining**

Table 1.8
Grief reactions experienced by parents of exceptional children

1. Shock and disbelief
2. Denial
3. Anger, guilt and frustration
4. Bargaining
5. Depression
6. Reorganization and adaptation

Depression

hope in various passing fads which purport to eradicate or alleviate certain disorders. Parents' hopes for overcoming their child's disabilities cannot be disparaged or discouraged by professionals. Rather, it is necessary to remain nonjudgmental, to continue to work in realistic ways and listen with greater sensitivity to the parents. In all of the usual grief reactions, parents feel *saddened* and *depressed* that they do not have a normal infant or child. This is a very real and normal grief reaction.

Reorganization and adaptation

Most parents will eventually *reorganize* their lives and household around their child and *adapt* to his or her limitations and potentialities (Drotar et al., 1975). When this occurs, it implies a form of acceptance of the child's exceptionality. But before the parents reach the stages of adaptation, they will have experienced a multitude of feelings. The greatest distress often is felt between the time of initial diagnosis and the first contact with an agency or center that can provide proper services to their child. During this interim stage, parents feel helpless and anxious about their child's condition; they do not know what to do, where to go, or what caused the problem. Professionals must therefore take whatever time is necessary to listen to, inform, counsel, and aid parents in every possible way.

Family psychodynamics and its effects

The psychodynamics of the family play a major role in the personality development of a handicapped child. Aside from their grief reactions, the parents soon begin to display other responses toward their child. Unless parent counseling begins early, the child and family may experience even greater stress and adjustment problems. Table 1-9 illustrates various types of negative relationships that can develop, the subsequent parental reactions, and their possible effects upon the child.

Intervention techniques

Parents will vary in their anxieties about their child's exceptionality and/or in their views concerning his or her needs. Various members of the multidisciplinary team may see the need for parental counseling and can choose any of several methods for helping the parents to interpret the results of the child's assessment and/or accept needed intervention strategies. No matter what technique is used, the goal is to increase parental understanding and thereby foster the family's continued cooperation in efforts to aid the child.

Extended feedback sessions   Extended feedback meetings are useful when the assessment data is complex and when the parents are having personal difficulties in understanding or accepting the information. Such sessions also allow the parents enough time to come to terms with the information and give the professional an opportunity to counsel them informally by focusing on the feelings and questions that arise.

Encouragement of participation in parent groups   Participation in a parent group can be invaluable to parents who feel isolated from others because of their child's exceptionality. Such groups are often extremely effective because of the mutual assistance and support the participants can provide each other as they face similar circumstances. Meeting in groups may be less threatening to some parents who might prefer to avoid individual counseling. The parent-group experience can assist parents through the grief process, help to focus on ways of alleviating the stress that may accompany rearing a child with a disability, or aid in extending knowledge of healthy parent-child relationships and child-rearing practices.

Many parents who are members of organizations that represent various handicapped children and youth (as well as other individuals) serve in the capacity of child advocates, devoting time and energy to seeing that children's rights are protected. Such individuals can help to assure parents that appropriate provisions are being made for their child and/or help them to secure needed services, thus reducing parental doubts or anxieties.

Child advocates

Parents and teacher are sharing their information about Victoria's progress and discussing her future individualized instruction program.

Table 1.9
Family relationships and psychodynamics

Type of relationship	Parental reactions	Effects on child
Confused	Concerned but unsure of how to cope with child's difficulty. Usually has tried unsuccessfully to work with child; frustrated. Sense of failure, guilt. Ambivalence may interfere with seeking professional intervention.	Child appears anxious; always testing limits. Child's self-concept reflects parents's confusion, frustration.
Inconsistent	Parent uses varying means to control child, no pattern. Parents transmit two opposite messages at same time.	Child confused. Child may withdraw. Child may become anxious and rebel.
Denial	Minimizes or does not admit to child's difficulty. Parents' goals, expectancies, dreams for child have been thwarted. Parent usually first reacts by feeling child will outgrow problem.	Child confused and frustrated because of dichotomy between reality and parents' denial. This confusion may bring withdrawal or acting out. Feeling of insecurity may occur. Self-confidence is shaky.
Vicarious	Parent lives through the child. Child is to realize aspirations parents could not achieve. Child's handicap destroys the parents' dreams for the child.	Child may be pressured to achieve despite handicap. Child may be pushed to overcome handicap. Child may have poor self-concept.
Symbiotic	Abnormally close tie between one parent and child. Parent begins to devote his/her life to this child. May reflect deep-seated emotional problems in the parent.	Child does not develop an independent personality. Lack of independence, infantile reactions, fear of separation.
Overprotective	Parents try to shield child from ordinary hazards of life, exaggerated with a child with a handicap. Parents' concerns are limitless. Parents may reflect guilt feelings.	Child may become fearful; self-confidence and esteem are low. Handicap becomes exaggerated and out of proportion to reality.
Overpermissive	Parents permit a wider range of behavior than normal. Parents cannot set limits. Parents may be ineffectual. Parents may be responding to guilt feelings.	Child with handicap may be given free rein because of misconceptions, pity, etc. Child may not conform socially. Child may become overly dependent.

Table 1.9 (Continued)

Type of relationship	Parental reactions	Effects on child
Rigid	Parents set very high standards. Parents may be perfectionists. Parents are organizers, compulsive at times. Applies these standards and rules for child; expectations higher than child's capability.	May be disappointment to parents because of handicap. Child may also strive for perfection. Child may rebel actively or passively. Child may withdraw and regress.
Disinterested	Often seen in multiproblem or disorganized households Child's problems secondary to more pressing problems/conflicts family faces each day.	Child usually withdrawn or passive; loner. Later, child is likely to act out; run away, delinquent. More likely not to conform socially.
Neglectful	Parent exhibits lack of responsibility for child. Child's handicap may create negative feelings in parent. Parent has ambivalent feelings toward child.	Range of neglect, including physical and emotional needs of child. Child feels unwanted and unloved. Child may focus on handicap as cause.
Fragmented	Parental discord of pathological degree. Parental separation usual result.	Child may see handicap as cause of parental problems. Feelings of insecurity and rejection.
Rejecting	Parents may actually reject child; may be precipitated by handicap. Something about child may cause negative feeling.	Child feels unwanted or unloved. May blame handicap for feeling of rejection. Causes poor self-concept; apprehensive about all peers and adults.

Source: From Elizabeth J. Webster, ed., Professional Approaches with Parents of Handicapped Children, *1976, pp. 197–99. Courtesy of Charles C Thomas, Publisher, Springfield, Ill.*

Helpful literature   Many parents want to read all they can about their child's exceptionality and will seek out literature that focuses on that particular disability. Some parents who do not care to attend parent groups may still be motivated to read and solve their problems personally (McWilliams, 1976). A list or collection of appropriate nontechnical pamphlets, books, and articles made available to the parents can contribute to their understanding of their specific situation.

Parent involvement in child's education   We have found that parents—especially mothers—who are encouraged to participate in specific action programs for their child (such as early stimulation or other activities and exercises) tend to feel an enhanced confidence because they are contributing to their youngster's development. Such involvement necessarily must be monitored so that the child feels *no pressure,* but when appropriately carried out, it can prove beneficial to both child and parent.

The ultimate goal of parent counseling is to enable the parents to resolve any personal anxieties and conflicts about their exceptional child so that they can provide a healthy emotional and educational environment. Parents who assume an active role in providing support for their child often join organizations that promote the interests of exceptional children. For example, it is the activist parents who have been instrumental in getting legislation passed for funding, research, and other productive endeavors beneficial to the handicapped. Out of such mobilization, parents' groups that represent various exceptional children, such as the Association for Children with Learning Disabilities and the National Association for Retarded Children, are now recognized on both state and national levels.

Summary

In this introductory unit to understanding exceptional children and youth, we have touched on a number of important topics that will serve as a foundation for subsequent discussions of specific areas of exceptionality. The definition of exceptionality was presented first, along with an overview of the historical developments that led to our current perspectives.

Because of the vast changes encountered in complying with the Education for All Handicapped Children (Public Law 94-142), we have acquainted you with some of the major aspects of this law as they apply to the provision of educational opportunities and the rights of the child and the family in the school and the community. The individual education program (IEP) is an important component of the overall procedure.

Additionally, unresolved and controversial issues in the field of exceptionality were considered, including the debate surrounding the use of standardized tests as a means of assessment and the practice of stereotyping, or labeling, individuals on the basis of societally defined norms.

Educational alternatives were explored and related to Public Law 94-142, which requires the least restrictive placement for all handicapped children. The role of the multidisciplinary team in facilitating identification and subsequent delivery of appropriate services was explained and emphasized.

We concluded with an overview of the underlying factors involved in understanding individual behavior; a discussion of certain common reactions of parents as they cope with feelings and attitudes about their child's disability; and intervention strategies used to counsel parents.

Active parental involvement benefits the child

References and resources

Aiello, B., ed. *Making It Work: Practical Ideas for Integrating Exceptional Children into Regular Classes.* Reston, Va.: Council for Exceptional Children, 1975.

American Psychological Association. "Intelligence Testing of Black Children Ordered Ceased by California Court." *APA Monitor,* nos. 9 and 10 (1972).

Ballard, J., and Zetter, J. "Public Law 94-142 and Section 504: What They Say about Rights and Protections." *Exceptional Children* 44 (1977): 177–84.

Blackham, G. J., and Silberman, A. *Modification of Child Behavior.* Belmont, Calif.: Wadsworth, 1974.

Bookbinder, S. "What Every Child Needs to Know." *Exceptional Parent,* no. 4 (1977), pp. 31–34.

Brenton, M. "Mainstreaming the Handicapped." *Today's Education,* no. 2 (1974), pp. 20–25.

Brown, B. S. "Behavior Modification: What It Is and Isn't." *Today's Education,* no. 1 (1976).

Caldwell, B. M. "The Usefulness of the Critical Period Hypothesis in the Study of Filiative Behavior." *Merrill-Palmer Quarterly* 8 (1962): 229–42.

Calhoun, J. F.; Acocella J. R.; and Goodstein, L. D. *Abnormal Psychology, Current Perspectives.* 2nd ed. New York: Random House, 1974.

Davis, S. P. *The Mentally Retarded in Society.* New York: Columbia University Press, 1962.

Drotar, D. et al., "The Adaptation of Parents to the Birth of an Infant with a Congenital Malformation: A Hypothetical Model." *Pediatrics* 56 (1975): 710–17.

Dunn, L. M. "A Historical Review of the Treatment of the Retarded." In *Mental Retardation: Readings and Resources,* edited by J. H. Rothstein, pp. 13–17. New York: Holt, Rinehart and Winston, 1964.

Dunn, L. M. "Special Education for the Mildly Retarded—Is Much of It Justifiable?" *Exceptional Children* 35 (1968): 5–22.

Dunn, L. M. *Exceptional Children in the Schools.* 2nd ed. New York: Holt, Rinehart & Winston, 1973, pp. 18–19.

Gallagher, J. J. "The Sacred and Profane Uses of Labeling." *Mental Retardation,* no. 6 (1976), pp. 3–6.

Ginsberg, L. H. "An Examination of the Civil Rights of Mentally Ill Children." In *Annual Progress in Child Psychiatry and Child Development,* edited by S. Chess and A. Thomas, pp. 577–89. New York: Brunner/Mazel, 1974.

Harlow, H., and Harlow, M. H. "Learning to Love." *American Scientist* 54 (1966): 244–72.

Hess, E. H. "Imprinting." *Science* 130 (1959): 133–41

Hobbs, N. *The Futures of Children.* San Francisco: Jossey-Bass, 1975.

Irvin, T. "Implementation of Public Law 94-142." *Exceptional Children* 43 (1976): 135–37.

Johnson, G. O. "Special Education for the Mentally Retarded—A Paradox." *Exceptional Children* 39 (1962): 1–123.

Johnson, J. L. "Special Education and the Inner City: A Challenge for the Future or Another Means for Cooling the Mark Out?" In *Problems and Issues in the Education of Exceptional Children,* edited by R. L. Jones, pp. 370–82. Boston: Houghton Mifflin, 1971.

Joint Commission on Mental Health of Children Report. *Crisis in Child Mental Health. Challenge for the 1970s.* New York: Harper and Row, 1969.

Jones, P. R. "Up Front with the President." *Exceptional Children* 42 (1976): 365.

Koocher, G. *Children's Rights and the Mental Health Profession.* New York: Wiley, 1976.

Kubler-Ross, E. *On Death and Dying.* New York: Macmillan, 1969.

Mackie, R. P. *Special Education in the United States: Statistics, 1948–66.* New York: Teachers College Press, Columbia University, 1969.

McWilliams, B. J. "Various Aspects of Parent Counseling." In *Professional Approaches with Parents of Handicapped Children,* edited by E. J. Webster, pp. 27–64. Springfield, Ill.: Charles C Thomas, 1976.

Madsen, C. L. "You Are Already Using Behavior Modification." *Instructor,* no. 2 (1971), pp. 47–56.

Martens, E. H.; Harris, C.; and Story, R. C. *Statistics of Special Schools and Classes for Exceptional Children, 1947–48: Biennial Survey of Education in the United States, 1946–48,* Chapter 5. Washington, D.C.: U.S. Office of Education, 1950.

Martin, E. W. *Programs of the Bureau of Education for the Handicapped.* HEW Secretary's Committee on Mental Retardation. Washington, D.C.: 1970.

Martin, E. W. "A National Commitment to the Rights of the Individual—1776–1976." *Exceptional Children* 43 (1976): 132–35.

Martin, E. W. "Integration of the Handicapped Child into Regular Schools." In *Mainstreaming: Origins and Implications. Minnesota Education,* no. 2 (1976a), pp. 5–7.

Melcher, J. W. "Law, Litigation and Handicapped Children." *Exceptional Children* 43 (1976): 126–30.

Mercer, J. R. "A Policy Statement on Assessment Procedures and the Rights of Children." *Harvard Educational Review* 44 (1974): 328–44.

Moltz, H. "Imprinting: An Epigenetic Approach." *Psychological Review* 70 (1963): 123–38.

Murdock, C. W. "Civil Rights of the Mentally Retarded—Some Critical Issues." In *Annual Progress in Child Psychiatry and Child Development,* edited by S. Chess and A. Thomas, pp. 590–625. New York: Brunner Mazel, 1974.

Mussen, P. H.; Conger, J.; and Kagan, J. *Child Development and Personality.* 3rd ed. New York: Harper and Row, 1969.

National Association of State Directors of Special Education. *Functions of the Placement Committee in Special Education: A Resource Manual.* Washington D.C.: 1976.

Noland, R. L., ed. *Counseling Parents of the Ill and the Handicapped.* Springfield, Ill.: Charles C Thomas, 1971.

Peterson, C.; Peterson, J.; and Scriven, G. "Peer Imitation by Nonhandicapped and Handicapped Preschoolers." *Exceptional Children* 44 (1977): 223–24.

Riesen, A. H. "Arrested Vision." *Scientific American* 183 (1950): 16–19.

Scott, J. P. "Critical Periods in the Development of Social Behavior in Puppies." *Psychosomatic Medicine* 20 (1958): 42–54.

Scriven, M. "Some Issues in the Logic and Ethics of Mainstreaming." In *Mainstreaming: Origins and Implications. Minnesota Education* no. 2 (1976), pp. 61–67.

Simon, K. A., and Grant, W. V. *Digest of Educational Statistics: 1970 Edition.* Washington, D.C.: U.S. Office of Education, 1970.

Skinner, B. F. *Science and Human Behavior.* New York: Free Press, 1965.

Stewart, W. A.; Goodman, G.; and Hammond, B. "Behavior Modification: Teacher Training and Attitudes." *Exceptional Children* 42 (1976): 402–3.

Telford, C. W., and Sawrey, J. M. *The Exceptional Individual.* 2nd ed. Englewood Cliffs, N.J.: Prentice-Hall, 1967.

Thomas, E. D., and Marshall, M. J. "Clinical Evaluation and Coordination of Services: An Ecological Model" *Exceptional Children* 44 (1977): 16–22.

Todd, M., and Gottlieb, M. I. "Interdisciplinary Counseling in a Medical Setting." In *Professional Approaches with Parents of Handicapped Children,* edited by E. J. Webster, pp. 191–216. Springfield, Ill, Charles C Thomas, 1976.

U.S. Office of Education. *Estimated Number of Handicapped Children in the United States, 1971–72.* Washington, D.C.: U.S. Government Printing Office, 1971.

U.S. Office of Education (HEW), Bureau of Education for the Handicapped. *Closer Look.* Winter 1975.

U.S. Office of Education. *The Unfinished Revolution: Education for the Handicapped.* 1976 Annual Report of the National Advisory Committee on the Handicapped. Washington, D.C.: U.S. Government Printing Office, 1976.

U.S. Office of Education. "Education of Handicapped Children: Implementation of Part B of the Education of the Handicapped Act." *Federal Register* 42 (1977): 42471–518.

Wakefield, R. A. "An Investigation of the Family Backgrounds of Educable Mentally Retarded Children in Special Classes." *Exceptional Children* 3 (1965): 143–46.

Weintraub, F. J., and Abeson, A. "New Education Policies for the Handicapped: The Quiet Revolution." *Phi Delta Kappa* 55 (1974): 526–28, 569.

Willis, D. J., and Thomas, E. D. "Seizure Disorders." *Psychological Management of Pediatric Problems,* vol. 2, edited by P. Magrab. Baltimore: University Park Press, 1978.

American Academy of Pediatrics
1801 Hinman Avenue
Evanston, Illinois 60204

American Medical Association
535 N. Dearborn Street
Chicago, Illinois 60610

American Occupational Therapy Association
6000 Executive Boulevard
Rockville, Maryland 20852

Child Study Association of America
9 E. 89th Street
New York, New York 10010

Council for Exceptional Children
1920 Association Drive
Reston, Virginia 22091
(useful for each unit)

Family Service Association of America
44 E. 23rd Street
New York, New York 10010

Foundation for Child Development
345 E. 46th Street
New York, New York 10017

National Association of Social Workers
2 Park Avenue
New York, New York 10016

National Center on Educational Media and Materials for the Handicapped (NCEMMH)
Ohio State University
Columbus, Ohio 43210

National Center for Law and the Handicapped
1235 N. Eddy Street
South Bend, Indiana 46617

National Committee for Multihandicapped Children
239 14th Street
Niagara Falls, New York 14303

National Education Association
1201 16th Street, NW
Washington, D.C. 20036
(useful for each unit)

National Information Center for the Handicapped
Box #1492
Washington, D.C. 20013

1
Intellectual exceptionality

A child's intellectual exceptionality can range from the level of genius to profound retardation in ability to learn. Society continues to seek answers to the question of what makes one child extremely bright and another child severely handicapped in mental ability. A multitude of causative factors have been identified as contributing to mental retardation (Unit 2). But, whatever the degree of limitation in learning ability, there is a need for increased individualized educational programming (Unit 3). It is now generally recognized that the mentally retarded are capable of doing much more than was believed in past years. Their potential capabilities can only be realized, however, by increasing and broadening the services and programs available to them.

Gifted children and youth in the school population (Unit 4) are not specifically provided for under the Education for All Handicapped Children Act, since giftedness is not commonly viewed as a handicapping condition. However, gifted and/or talented children and youth do meet the criterion of being "exceptional"—that is, varying from the so-called norm or average to the extent of needing special services. If our gifted population is not provided appropriate educational programs and services commensurate with their capacities they, too, can be considered "handicapped." They need to be presented with challenges that will motivate them to realize their potential.

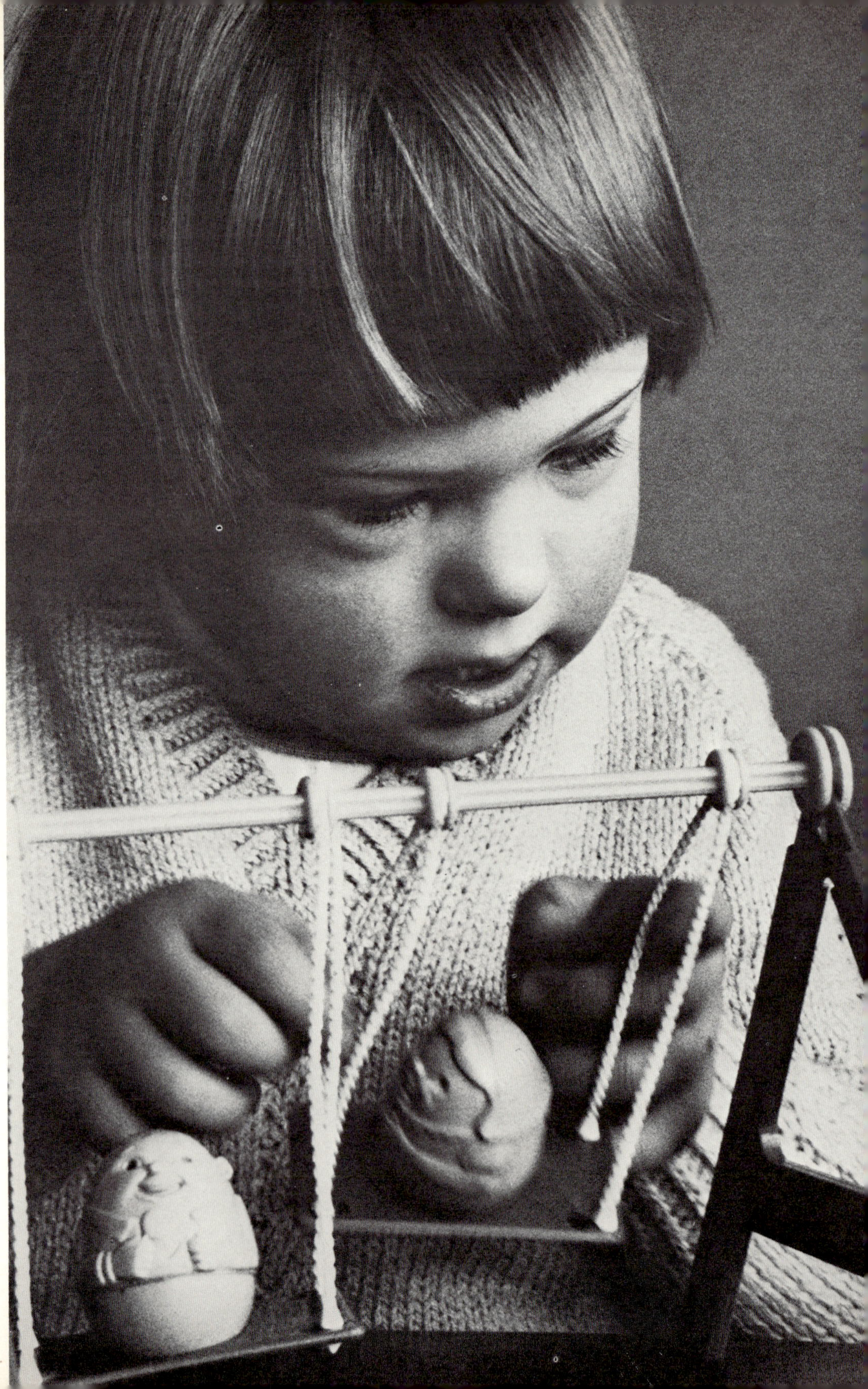

2 Mentally retarded children and youth: assessment and causes   William J. Ward

What is mental retardation?
Perspectives on mental retardation • The past • Current perspectives
Level of intellectual functioning • The concept of mental age • The standard deviation IQ
Adaptive behavior assessment
Prevalence of mental retardation
Classification of mental retardation by causative factors • Infection and intoxication • Trauma • Metabolic and nutritional disorders • Postnatal gross brain disease • Unknown prenatal influences • Chromosomal abnormality • Gestational disorders • Retardation following psychiatric disorder • Environmental influences • Other conditions
Summary

Student learning objectives
The student will:
 1. learn to see mental retardation in its historical perspective
 2. be able to define mental retardation according to AAMD criteria
 3. learn about the origins and causes of mental retardation
 4. be able to describe the concept of mental age and its uses
 5. be able to explain the adaptive behavior scale
 6. be able to list factors influencing prevalence figures of retardation
 7. be able to point out and discuss at least one type of retardation under each of the AAMD classifications

Extermination, institutionalization, and exclusion from public school—these were among the means of dealing with mentally retarded children in the past. Prevention, identification, and educational and vocational programming—these are the new methods that have evolved during the last twenty years, which have been the most significant period in history for the mentally retarded. This long-awaited transition, accomplished through the efforts of parents, educators, psychologists, and physicians, has led to legislation guaranteeing equal opportunity for the mentally retarded.

In this unit we will touch on some of the leaders and historical events that have influenced current planning and programming for this group of children. Our primary concentration, however, will be on the prevalence, terminology, and causal aspects of mental retardation.

What is mental retardation?

To define mental retardation in a way that includes information for accurate identification and methods of treatment is indeed difficult. One of the early definitions in the English Mental Deficiency Act of 1913 included the classification of levels of mental deficiency using such terms as idiot, imbecile, feebleminded person, and moral defective. This act defined mental deficiency as "a condition of arrest or incomplete development of the mind, existing before the age of eighteen years, whether existing from inherent causes or induced by disease or injury" (Kolstoe, 1970, p. 79).

Early definitions

During the 1930s, some authorities attempted to outline specific areas of deficiency in terms of social, mental, and causal aspects (Sarason, 1959); later, others sought to define mental retardation from legal and medical points of view (Porteus & Corbett, 1953; Jervis, 1952). Professional groups and parents of retarded children continued efforts to define mental retardation in a way that would promote greater understanding and acceptance. Through the leadership of the American Association on Mental Deficiency (AAMD), a more adequate definition of mental retardation was set forth in 1973. It states: *"mental retardation refers to significantly subaverage general intellectual functioning existing concurrently with deficits in adaptive behavior, and manifested during the developmental period"* (Grossman, 1973, p. 5). The developmental period referred to is from birth to eighteen years of age.

Current definition

Grossman points out that this statement applies to current behavioral performance; it does not relate to causal factors nor does it imply prognosis. While it is the basic definition to be used in this text, we will expand on it when necessary to better understand children and youth designated as mentally retarded.

Perspectives on mental retardation

Historically, social attitudes towards individuals whose intellectual abilities were substantially lower than the norm have exhibited some positive concern and much negativism. Many terms were used to describe this population: simpleminded, foolish, silly, backward, among others. The Twelve Tablets of Rome (449 B.C.) indicated concern thusly: "If a person is a fool, let his person and goods be under the protection of his family or his parental relatives" (Kolstoe, p. 77).

The past

Fortunately, through the years leaders have emerged who contributed greatly to the understanding of mental retardation. Their efforts resulted in more thorough evaluation procedures, appropriate educational efforts, and better treatment of the mentally retarded by society. One of the pioneers in this area was an eighteenth-century French physician, Jean Marc Itard. Itard undertook the education and socialization of an eleven-year-old boy named Victor, who had been abandoned in the forest and was later found by hunters (Lambert et al., 1975). Through Victor's progress, Itard demonstrated that substantial learning could result from intensive educational stimulation. His efforts served as an inspiration to others, including one of his former students, Edouard Séguin. Séguin subsequently focused on appropriate placement and educational provisions for those with substantially lowered intelligence, who at the time were frequently housed with convicts or the insane. He left France in 1848 to become superintendent of the school then known as the Pennsylvania Training School for Idiots. His accomplishments in this position served as a catalyst for increased interest in the retarded and attracted the attention of such notables as Montessori (Kirk & Johnson, 1951). In 1896, the first public school class for mentally retarded children in the United States was established in Providence, Rhode Island.

Pioneer efforts toward better understanding

Current perspectives

More recently we have seen progress made through the passage of legislation and the organization of special interest groups concerned with the welfare of retarded and other exceptional children. The National Association for Retarded Children and the International Council for Exceptional Children have emerged as powerful forces in the expansion of research, education, and public understanding of retardation. Spurred on by President John F. Kennedy's interest (see Unit 1) the President's Panel on Mental Retardation was established. President Lyndon B. Johnson continued to focus national attention on the problem of retardation with his appointment of the President's Committee on Mental Retardation. Gearheart (1975) provides a comprehensive outline and discussion of federal legislation on some of the areas that benefit the mentally retarded.

Recent efforts toward better understanding

During the 1970s new terminology and objectives emerged. *Normalization,* the opportunity for the mentally retarded to function in their culture to the best of their ability, has become a standard goal. With the passage of Public Law 94-142 (see Unit 1), the trend has turned away from institutionalization and segregation and in favor of greater integration into the regular classroom. This movement has come to be known as mainstreaming.

Normalization as the goal

Mentally retarded children and youth: assessment and causes

Level of intellectual functioning

Despite the controversy surrounding the use of an intelligence quotient derived from a standardized intelligence test as a measure of an individual's potential (see Unit 1), the AAMD definition still refers to "significantly subaverage general intellectual functioning" as a criterion for identification of retardation. One of the most widely used instruments for measuring intelligence is the Stanford-Binet Intelligence Scale (Terman & Merrill, 1973). In the early 1900s French psychologists Alfred Binet and Theodore Simon published the first scale of intelligence measurement, which was followed by the work of Louis Terman of Stanford University. Terman published 1916 and 1937 revisions of the Binet-Simon Scale (Anastasi, 1959). A third revision by Terman and Merrill appeared in 1960 and was followed in 1972 by the norms for the current Stanford-Binet Intelligence Scale.

Stanford-Binet Intelligence Scale

The concept of mental age

The Stanford-Binet Scale introduced the concept of *mental age* into the measurement of intellectual functioning. The items in a standardized intelligence test deemed appropriate to a typical chronological age (CA) are used to specify a corresponding mental age (MA). A standard intelligence quotient (IQ) index is based on the following formula: IQ = MA/CA × 100. Thus, an average twelve-year-old's IQ would be 100, and a child whose mental age lags behind his or her chronological age will have an IQ of less than 100. To compute the mental age of a twelve-year-old with an IQ of 75 the following formula is used:

Computing mental age

$$\frac{IQ \times CA}{100} = \text{Estimated mental age}$$

$$\frac{75 \text{ (IQ)} \times 12 \text{ (CA)}}{100} = \frac{900}{100} \text{ or 9 years mental age}$$

In some cases, mental age may be used to determine approximate grade-level placement or academic expectations. Mental age minus five years determines the grade level. For example, 9 yr.(MA) − 5 = 4th grade.

Like the IQ score as a basic measure of intelligence, the concept of mental age is often criticized in current literature. The utility of the MA is particularly challenged and considered inappropriate when it is applied to the expected level of functioning of adolescents and adults. Nevertheless, numerous standardized individual and group tests retain this type of score and it continues to be used by many individuals in planning educational programs or expectations for students.

The standard deviation IQ

The *Test Service Bulletin,* a journal dealing with the techniques and principles of mental measurement states that

An individual's test score acquires meaning when it can be compared with the scores of well-identified groups of people. . . . Sooner or later, every textbook discussion of test scores introduces the bell-shaped normal curve. The student . . . soon learns that many of the methods of deriving meaningful scores are anchored to the dimensions and characteristics of this curve (Seashore, 1955).

Interpreting the bell-shaped curve

The normal curve is traditionally presented in the manner illustrated in Figure 2-1. The curve is marked off into subareas by vertical lines at the zero, or exact center, point and at 1, 2, 3, and 4 standard deviation units (a measure of variance or difference) right and left from the center point. Each particular test, according to standardization and norming procedures, has its own score at the center of the curve, which is equated to the *mean,* or *average,* score. Each also has its own number of points equivalent to a standard deviation unit.

The figures printed within the various subareas indicate in percentages how many of the total number of people in a normal distribution would obtain a given score on a specific test. In Figure 2-1, for example, 34.13 percent of all people have scores falling between zero and −1 standard deviation. Similarly, 34.13 percent

Figure 2.1
Method of expressing test scores using the normal curve and Wechsler and Stanford-Binet deviation IQs

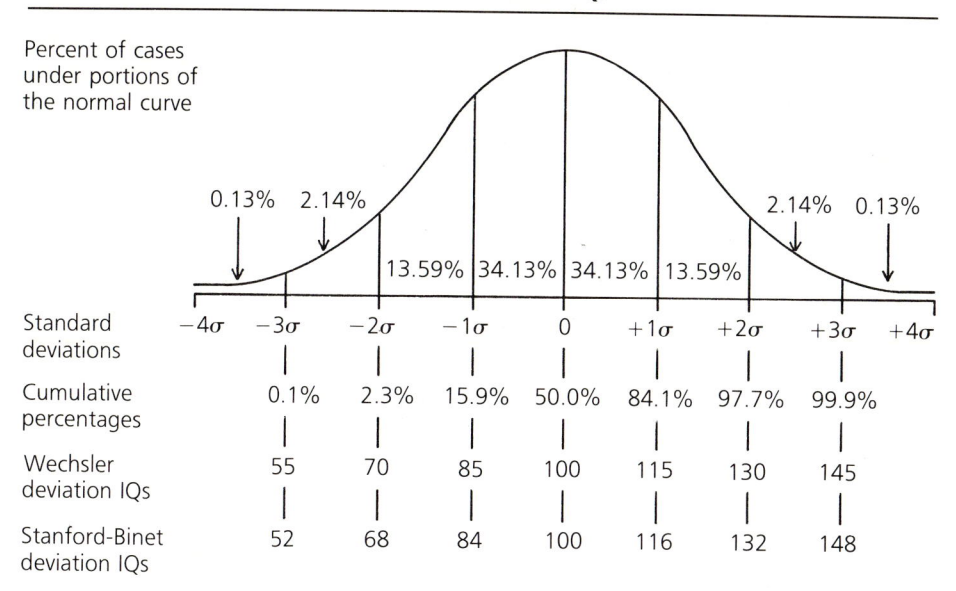

Percent of cases under portions of the normal curve

	-4σ	-3σ	-2σ	-1σ	0	$+1\sigma$	$+2\sigma$	$+3\sigma$	$+4\sigma$
Standard deviations									
Cumulative percentages		0.1%	2.3%	15.9%	50.0%	84.1%	97.7%	99.9%	
Wechsler deviation IQs		55	70	85	100	115	130	145	
Stanford-Binet deviation IQs		52	68	84	100	116	132	148	

Percentages within curve: 0.13%, 2.14%, 13.59%, 34.13%, 34.13%, 13.59%, 2.14%, 0.13%

Source: Test Service Bulletin *of the Psychological Corporation,* January 1955, p. 7.

have scores falling between zero and +1 standard deviation. Thus a total of 68.26 percent, or approximately two-thirds of all cases, lie between + or −1 standard deviation of the average.

Below the row of figures indicating standard deviation units on the curve are further percentage figures which show *cumulatively* the percentage of people included *to the left* of each standard deviation point. For example (starting from the left of the curve), we see that at −2 standard deviations, only 2.3 percent of the population has been cumulatively included. As we reach the center and other points moving further to the right on the curve, increasing percentages of the population are covered. (For example, at +3 standard deviations, 99.9 percent of the population has been included.)

Both The Stanford-Binet and the Wechsler Intelligence Scale (1974) offer comparison of an individual's relative placement on the normal curve by standard deviation IQs. Each has a mean, or average, IQ score of 100, with a standard deviation of 16 points on the Binet and 15 points on the Wechsler.

In terms of the latest AAMD definition of mental retardation, significant subaverage general intelligence as measured by IQ scores would be "greater than two standard deviations from the mean" (Grossman, 1977, p. 11). The resulting classification is illustrated in Table 2-1. (Note that it reflects the same information that was graphically depicted in Figure 2-1.)

An IQ of 69 or below on the Wechsler Scale and an IQ of 67 or below on the Stanford-Binet would indicate possible inclusion within the mentally retarded population, when combined with existing deficits in adaptive behavior. Because the latter condition is an important aspect of the 1973 AAMD definition of mental retardation, we will examine it in greater detail later in this unit.

Another popular method of classifying the mentally retarded for instructional or educational purposes is by designation as *educable, trainable,* and *custodial.* The educable usually are defined as those with IQs between 50 and 75 to 79, the train-

Table 2.1
AAMD classification by ranges of standard deviation value and IQ (Wechsler and Stanford-Binet)

Level of mental retardation	Range in standard deviation value	Corresponding IQ range for test with standard deviation	
		Wechsler 15	Stanford-Binet 16
Mild	−2.01 to −3.00	55–69	52–67
Moderate	−3.01 to −4.00	40–54	36–51
Severe	−4.01 to −5.00	25–39	20–35
Profound	below −5.00	under 25	under 20

Source: Grossman, 1977, p. 19 (adapted)

able as those have IQs between 30 and 50 to 55, and the custodial as those with IQs below 30.

    Despite all these elaborate attempts at IQ definitions, we observed in Unit 1 that controversy persists over the many abuses and misuses of standardized test scores. Classification by IQ scores is justifiable only in the hands of those skilled in test administration methods and interpretation of test results as correlated with other aspects of behavior (for example, formal measure of adaptive behavior and/or interdisciplinary examination of the child within the classroom). The danger of incorporating IQ test scores in any definition of mental retardation is that by attending to these scores, we may overlook the total child.

Introducing Chris—a five-year-old Down's Syndrome child. He is absorbed in the story and stimulated by the pictures that his Dad is sharing with him.

Adaptive behavior assessment

Earlier and continued recognition of the need for comprehensive evaluation procedures in the assessment of a child's strengths and weaknesses has resulted in wider use of various instruments that measure different aspects of a person's total level of development. The Bayley Scale of Infant Development (Bayley, 1969), the Denver Developmental Test (Frankenberg & Dodds, 1969), and the Gesell Development Schedule (1974) concentrate primarily on developmental progress made during the earlier years. The Cain-Levine Social Competency Scale (Cain et al., 1963) includes a measure of an individual's competency in such areas as self-help, social development, initiative, and communication skills. The Vineland Social Maturity Scale (Doll, 1965) focuses on measuring behavior skills as viewed from the areas of self-help, locomotive, occupational, social, communicative, and self-directional competencies for the period from birth to maturity. The new SOMPA scale (System of Multicultural Pluralistic Assessment) is especially useful for black and Hispanic children (Mercer & Lewis, 1978).

Out of concern that youngsters may be misclassified as retarded solely on the basis of IQ scores, the AAMD has included in its definition of retardation "deficits in adaptive behavior." *Adaptive behavior* relates to the individual's ability to function independently in relation to his culture and age group and thus reflects "the effectiveness with which an individual copes with the natural and social demands of his environment" (Lambert et al., 1975, p. xi).

During the early childhood years, assessment is based on maturational and developmental skills in the areas of communication, motor ability, and self-help. During later childhood and adolescence, learning and social skills receive greater emphasis because they are required for successful participation in an academic setting. During adult life, the individual's ability to carry out social and vocational responsibilities is emphasized. As noted, the developmental period from birth to eighteen years of age is used in distinguishing mental retardation from other disorders.

The AAMD Adaptive Behavior Scale (ABS) was thus devised to provide a standardized procedure for evaluating the social functioning of children along two major dimensions: developmental lines and personality aspects (see Table 2-2). The ABS provides a profile sheet on which the data are recorded and from which a profile of strengths and weaknesses can be ascertained (see Figure 2-2). The authors of the Public School Version of the AAMD Scale point out that they

> ... view assessment as the first step in the diagnostic-prescriptive process in planning education programs for all exceptional children. It is the phase during which all educationally relevant data are gathered and made available for subsequent analysis with the eventual development of an individual educational plan. For this purpose, adequate assessment requires an extensive, comprehensive approach. Interdisciplinary staffing is a necessary diagnostic procedure, and the assessment of a child's adaptive behavior is an integral part of this comprehensive effort (Lambert et al., 1975, p. xiii).

Figure 2.2
Sample profile summary sheet for a 16-year-old female

Identification __12345__
Age __16__
Sex __F__
Date of administration __July 9, 1975__

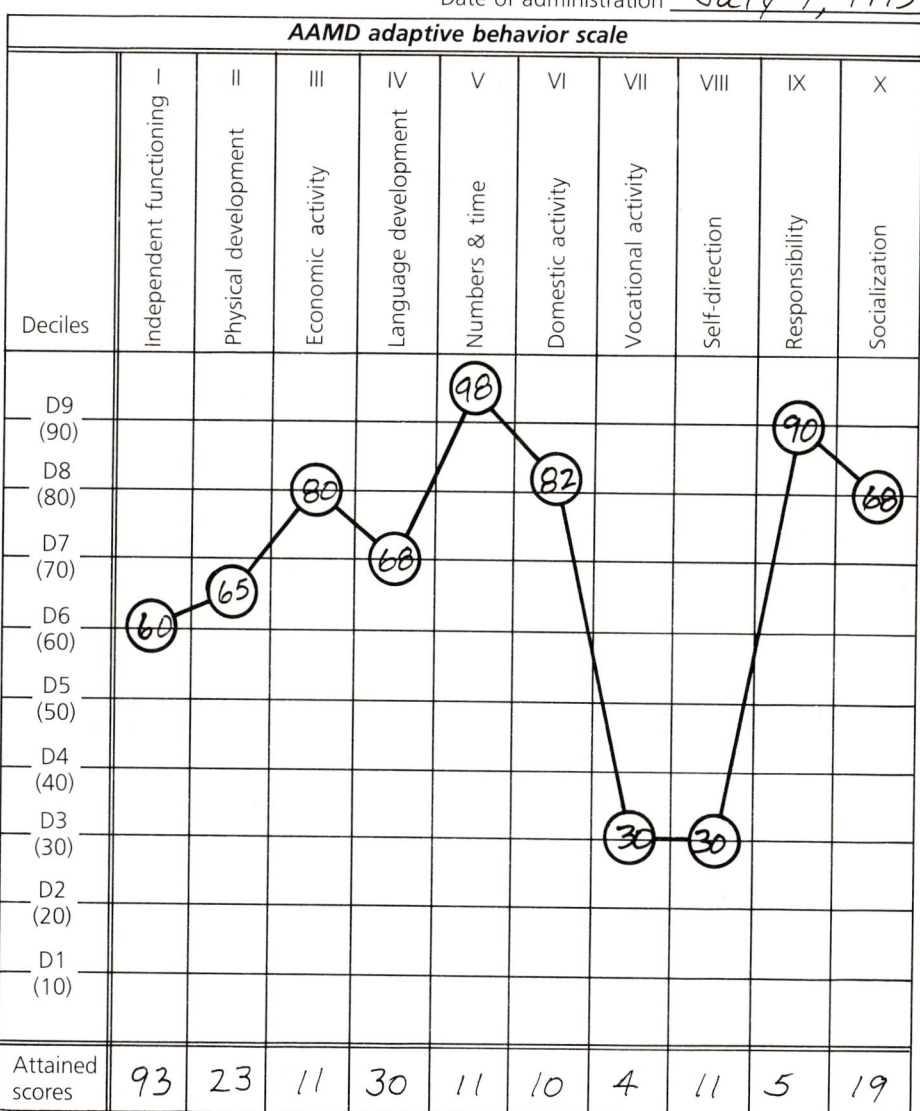

Deciles	I Independent functioning	II Physical development	III Economic activity	IV Language development	V Numbers & time	VI Domestic activity	VII Vocational activity	VIII Self-direction	IX Responsibility	X Socialization
D9 (90)					98				90	
D8 (80)			80			82				68
D7 (70)				68						
D6 (60)	60	65								
D5 (50)										
D4 (40)										
D3 (30)							30	30		
D2 (20)										
D1 (10)										
Attained scores	93	23	11	30	11	10	4	11	5	19

Source: Nihira et al., 1975, p. 14

Table 2.2
AAMD adaptive behavior scale

Part one
Developmental domains

1. Independent functioning
   (eating, toilet use, cleanliness, appearance, care of clothing, dressing and undressing, travel, general independent functioning)
2. Physical development
   (sensory development, motor development)
3. Economic activity
   (money handling and budgeting, shopping skills)
4. Language development
   (expression, comprehension, social language development)
5. Numbers and time
6. Domestic activity
   (cleaning, kitchen duties, other domestic activities)
7. Vocational activity
8. Self direction
   (initiative, perseverance, leisure time)
9. Responsibility
10. Socialization

Part two
Personality domains

1. Violent and destructive behavior
2. Antisocial behavior
3. Rebellious behavior
4. Untrustworthy behavior
5. Withdrawal
6. Stereotyped behavior and odd mannerisms
7. Inappropriate interpersonal manners
8. Unacceptable vocal habits
9. Unacceptable or eccentric habits
10. Self-abusive behavior
11. Hyperactive tendencies
12. Sexually aberrant behavior
13. Psychological disturbances
14. Use of medications

Source: Lambert et al., 1975, p. 1

As in the case of IQ scores, the measurement of adaptive behavior may not be as precise and accurate as desired because it is impractical—if not impossible—to observe an individual in all possible environmental interactions. However, information provided by informants or learned from direct observation can add to an examiner's understanding of the individual and lead to more definitive diagnosis, appropriate placement, and needed instructional emphasis.

Prevalence of mental retardation

The methods used in defining mental retardation necessarily become a factor in establishing prevalence figures. Statistics from the U.S. Office of Education for 1975 indicate that 1,350,000 children and youth received some type of special services for the mentally retarded (see Table 1-4 in Unit 1). This number will increase with full implementation of Public Law 94-142. Terman and Merrill's classification based on intelligence scores obtained on the Stanford-Binet (1973) places 2.6 percent of the population in the mentally defective range, while Wechsler's (1974) intelligence classification yields a 2.2 percent figure.

A year later, Chris is in school. Here he is mastering a specific task of identification while working with a learning box.

The number of children reported as retarded also varies from country to country and depends on differing criteria. The Dutch cite 2.6 percent; the French, depending on age levels included, record from 1.5 to 8.6 percent; and the British report educational provisions for 1 percent in special schools with 8 or 9 percent requiring special education within ordinary schools (World Health Organization, 1954). In the United States the President's Panel on Mental Retardation (1962) and most current sources estimate 3 percent of the total population as mentally retarded. In investigating the mentally retarded population, the AAMD classified 89 percent as mildly retarded, 6 percent as moderately retarded, 3.5 percent as severely retarded, and 1.5 percent as profoundly retarded.

Factors affecting prevalence figures

Penrose (1966) notes that prevalence figures, in addition to being influenced by definitions used for identification, will vary according to the ages and representation of the sample employed. Concerning identification by age, most surveys indicate that the number of children identified as retarded increases rapidly during the early school years and drops in the teen and adult years (Heber, 1970). This increase seems to reflect the emphasis placed on academics and the identification of learning difficulties during the early years following school entrance. The lowered incidence of identification of mental retardation in the "teen-plus" population may indicate that such individuals do not remain in school and are thus less likely to be detected. This is particularly true in the case of the 89 percent classified as mildly retarded, whose adaptive behavior skills in social and vocational areas may negate the presence of mental retardation. As a result of federal legislation calling for earlier identification and remediation services for high-risk children, or those showing signs of possible difficulties, an increase in the preschool population diagnosed as mentally retarded can be anticipated. However, because of earlier intervention strategies, the percentage of school-age children in this category may decrease.

In noting that the influence of socioeconomic status on measured intelligence must be considered, Heber (1970) states that

Socioeconomic level is a variable

> There is a clear difference in the mean IQs for various socioeconomic groups. These in turn give rise to substantial differences in the prevalence of IQs falling within the mentally retarded range. These socioeconomic distinctions remain regardless of whether the groups are defined in terms of family income, quality of housing, parental education, or paternal occupation (p.7).

Thus it can be seen that a clear-cut picture of the incidence or prevalence of mental retardation is difficult to obtain. Reference must always be made to various factors included within the figures cited, including definition employed, age group included, and representativeness of the sample.

Classification of mental retardation by causative factors

Beyond the wide concern for adequate definition, assessment procedures, and prevalence figures, the causative factors leading to retardation should not be neglected.

The etiological approach, though not as influential on educational programming as other perspectives, does provide pertinent information concerning the characteristics and physical limitations of the mentally retarded. Such information can be particularly useful in genetic counseling, an important service when there already is one retarded child in a family and the parents are fearful of having another. Such counseling would, of course, involve a multidisciplinary team that includes a physician with expertise in genetics and knowledge of the causative factors of mental retardation. Such knowledge could then serve as the basis for individual family counseling. Classification by cause is not always clear; there is still much that remains unknown about genetic influences and the complications before birth, during birth, and following birth (prenatal, perinatal, postnatal) that can produce or contribute to mental retardation.

Genetic counseling

The American Association of Mental Deficiency, however, has organized a classification system based on the etiological knowledge that does exist. Such classification is sometimes termed nonfunctional (Grossman, 1977), since even when etiology is known, it may not yield constructive benefits for the child. Certainly, further research in this area can help to increase understanding of the present functioning and future needs of retarded children and to plan services for them. Because of the significant role that causative factors can play in the understanding and treatment of mental retardation, the remainder of this unit will be devoted to a brief overview of the AAMD classification system.

AAMD classification system

Infection and intoxication

During the prenatal period the developing fetus is susceptible to damage from infection and intoxication. Within the first three months, or trimester, of pregnancy, the mother's contraction of rubella, or German measles, can lead to serious complications. Although a relatively mild infection for the mother, it can cause congenital heart disorders, blindness, deafness, seizures, and mental retardation in the unborn child. From 10 to 85 percent of rubella babies are reported as exhibiting some type of abnormality (Carter, 1970; Covert, 1965; Fishbein, 1963).

Rubella

In the past, syphilis was a prime cause of mental retardation. Presently, as a result of marital blood tests and new treatment techniques, syphilis is controllable and a mother under treatment may produce an uninfected child. An infected child, however, may have any number of symptoms, including inflammation of the mucous membranes of the nose and moist lesions around the mouth, anus, and genitalia. At various stages the central nervous system may be involved, causing seizures and mental retardation. The severity of retardation can range from dull normal to profound, depending upon the stage of syphilis and its treatment. With the current increase of venereal diseases, mental retardation due to congenital syphilis may again become more prevalent (Carter, 1970; Gellis & Feingold, 1968; Patterson, 1971).

Syphilis

Postnatal infections caused by viruses, bacteria, parasites, protozoa, and fungi may also lead to mental retardation. For example, meningococci meningitis, a bacterial infection usually surrounding the brain, may cause varying degrees of damage. Many infections can be treated with drugs, but the degree of success depends on the stage at which treatment is begun (Grossman, 1977).

Toxic agents such as carbon monoxide and lead can cause damage to the fetus. Similarly, a woman who uses drugs during pregnancy may give birth to a baby who is addicted or whose cerebral deterioration is sufficient to cause mental retardation (Carter, 1970).

Blood incompatibility

Mother-fetal blood group incompatibility, resulting from differences in Rh factors, can lead to the death and spontaneous abortion of the fetus. If the child lives, brain damage can occur. This blood factor, like many others, is inherited. In such cases, the mother produces antibodies which, if absorbed through the placenta, cause the destruction of the child's oxygen-carrying red blood cells (Carter, 1970; Fishbein, 1963).

Kernicterus, also due to blood incompatibility, results from the breakdown of red blood cells and the release of large amounts of bilirubin (yellowish-red bile) into the blood. Deposits of this chemical are found in the skin and brain of the child and produce jaundice (yellow skin), drowsiness, rigidity, spasms, and mental retardation. Blood transfusions given when bilirubin reaches a certain level can reduce mental retardation (Carter, 1970; Gellis & Feingold, 1968).

Trauma

Prenatal and perinatal trauma

The general category of trauma, or physical agents, includes prenatal, perinatal, and postnatal injury. Prenatal injury can result from radiation. Although it generally takes massive amounts of radiation to produce retardation, the feeling prevails that pregnant women should not be exposed to it at all (Carter, 1970).

Mechanical injury at birth can occur in a number of circumstances. Malposition or malpresentation, such as breech birth, and problems caused by postmaturity, where the fetus is disproportionately large because of an extended pregnancy, can lead to damage. Better prenatal care and hospitalization during childbirth have lessened or alleviated the risks involved in such cases (Grossman, 1977).

Perinatal anoxia, in which there is an insufficient supply of oxygen to the fetus due to premature separation of the placenta or a heart condition or anemia in the mother, can result in retardation or other abnormalities. *Postnatal anoxia* can result from shock, respiratory difficulties, or poisoning. The National Association of Retarded Citizens (NARC) has been concerned with the threat of poisoning that the ingestion of paint containing lead presents to infants and young children. Manufacturers and paint producers have cooperated in the reduction of lead poisoning by controlling the lead content in paint (Carter, 1970).

Postnatal injury

To cause mental retardation, postnatal injury must usually be severe. A skull fracture, dehydration, or any other disorder serious enough to produce prolonged unconsciousness can result in permanent damage. The extent of the injury will dictate the degree of possible retardation (Carter, 1970).

Metabolic and nutritional disorders

Neuronal lipid (fat) storage disease   The onset of *Tay-Sachs disease* usually occurs when a child is from four to six months old and leads to death within a few years. Although the child may appear normal at birth, it soon becomes noticeable that he is unable to carry out such normal tasks as holding up his head and that he suffers from visual difficulties, hearing problems, and mental retardation. This disease is hereditary and is most frequently found in the Jewish population. Prenatal detection of a carrier is possible by studying fluid obtained from the sac enclosing the fetus (amniocentesis). Although there is currently no known treatment for the disease, genetic counseling can be helpful to parents (Carter, 1970; National Institute of Child Health and Human Development, 1973).

Tay-Sachs

Carbohydrate disorder   *Galactosemia* is also transmitted genetically. In such cases, the infant fails to metabolize the galactose in milk. If the child is not placed on a low lactose (milk sugar) diet, failure to thrive and jaundice, vomiting, liver damage, cataracts, seizures, and mental retardation can result (Carter, 1970).

Amino acid disorder   In *Phenylketonuria* (*PKU*), an additional hereditary metabolic disorder, the body fails to change one of the amino acids (phenylalanine) into another (tyrosine). PKU can be detected either by urinalysis or blood analysis. Seizures, hyperactivity, and mental retardation can result if the child is not placed on a low phenylalanine diet that excludes such foods as meat, milk, and proteins in general. There have been reported cases of normal intelligence in children whose phenylalanine level was constantly monitored. The frequency rate of PKU is estimated at one in twenty thousand births, and many of the children affected are blond-haired and blue-eyed. All states currently have laws requiring that newborn babies be checked for PKU, which has resulted in a lowered incidence of retardation from this disorder (Carter, 1970; Covert, 1965; Gellis & Feingold, 1968).

PKU

Nucleotide disorders   *Lesch-Nyhan's disease* is an example of a nucleotide disorder due to the deficiency of an enzyme in nucleic acid (purine) metabolism. An increase of uric acid in the urine and blood (hyperuricemia), gout, loss of motor ability affecting speech, mental retardation, and self-mutilation are characteristic of Lesch-Nyhan's syndrome. This disorder primarily affects boys, occurs at an early age, and is genetically transmitted. Although it is possible to control hyperuricemia and other aspects of the syndrome, mental retardation and self-mutilation are not amenable to treatment (Carter, 1970; Gellis & Feingold, 1968).

Endocrine disorders   Hypothyroidism, or *cretinism,* is a common endocrine disorder that may be either congenital or acquired. The congenital form is due to a partial or complete absence of the thyroid gland at birth. While this is not an inherited disorder, iodine deficiency in the mother is a factor. In the acquired form

Cretinism

(goitrous cretinism), the thyroid gland is present but the release and formation of the thyroid hormone is affected. In cases of overstimulation of the thyroid, a visible enlargement of the gland, or goiter, develops. The symptoms of hypothyroidism are broad bridge of the nose, large thick tongue, short thick neck, hoarse cry, cold dry skin, short extremities, broad hands, and mental and motor retardation. Treatment with thyroid hormone is effective in early infancy but is not as productive at later stages of development (Carter, 1970; Gellis & Feingold, 1968; Grossman, 1977).

Nutritional disorders Nutritional disorders stemming from inadequacies or imbalances in the mother's diet can cause malnourishment of the fetus and lead to mental retardation. The importance of adequate prenatal and early childhood nutrition will be covered more thoroughly in the discussion in Unit 5 on societal neglect.

Postnatal gross brain disease

This category includes a large group of disorders whose causes are unknown. Hereditary factors involving lesions, tumors, and progressive deterioration of the central nervous system are listed in this category (Kirk & Johnson, 1951). Neurofibromatosis (Von Recklinghausen's disease) and tuberous sclerosis are two examples of gross brain disease.

Neurofibromatosis is a hereditary condition characterized by brownish spots on the skin (particularly on the back) and tumors of the peripheral and central nervous systems. The skin lesions vary in size and their development cannot be controlled. If the tumors are large and located in the central nervous system, mental retardation may occur. Tumors may also occur in such organs as the kidney and heart and there may be excessive limb growth and other bone abnormalities. Whenever possible, the skeletal defects should be corrected and the tumors removed. This disorder occurs in one in three thousand people (Carter, 1970).

Tuberous sclerosis is characterized by reddish-orange nodules in a butterfly pattern in the area of the face, particularly on the cheeks. Tumors can be found in the kidneys, heart, lungs, and central nervous system. Seizures, abnormal brainwave patterns, and intracranial calcification are present. This too is a hereditary disorder, and its treatment involves the removal of tumors whenever possible and practical and the use of anticonvulsants to control seizures (Carter, 1970).

Unknown prenatal influences

The conditions in this category, which includes microcephaly and hydrocephaly, are of unknown origin and exist prior to birth. Such disorders involve cranial and congenital defects.

Microcephaly There are two types of microcephaly—primary (inherited) and secondary (acquired). The causes of the secondary type vary; they could result from radiation exposure or could be in conjunction with other disorders. Inherited microcephaly is characterized by an extremely small, conically shaped head, a flattened bridge of the nose, and ears that appear large because the forehead slopes. The brain tissue is underdeveloped but in proportion to the size of the cranium. Retardation will range from mild to severe (Carter, 1970; Gellis & Feingold, 1968).

Chris is completing an art assignment with great enthusiasm. Part of his school time is spent with nonexceptional children.

Hydrocephaly Overproduction or underabsorption of cerebrospinal fluid is termed hydrocephaly. It may, but does not always, imply an increase in the size of the head, which depends on the age of onset and whether the sutures of the cranial cavity have closed. If the sutures have closed, pressure in the cranial cavity will become intense. In the event that they have not closed, the cranium will expand to accommodate the additional cerebrospinal fluid. In such cases the head is globe-shaped, the bridge of the nose is flat, and the eyes are pushed downward and out and become more widely spaced. Hydrocephaly is not a genetic abnormality, although some links to inheritance have been reported. Maternal age does seem to be related to its occurrence. Recent treatment consists of the surgical placement of a tube with a pump, or shunt, in the side cavity of the brain so that excess fluid can be removed. The degree of retardation will vary, depending on the treatment and associated factors. In some cases the individual's system will compensate and the production and absorption balance will stop or arrest the expansion of the cranium (Carter, 1970; Gellis & Feingold, 1968).

Varying degrees of retardation

Chromosomal abnormality

Human beings normally have twenty-three pairs of chromosomes, or a total of forty-six. Twenty-two of these pairs determine basic characteristics; the twenty-third pair determines the sex of the offspring (XX = female, XY = male). The chromosomes are grouped in pairs numbered from one for the largest to twenty-two for the smallest (see Figure 2-3). Chromosomal aberrations are known to occur as a result of gene mutation, aged gametes (sperms or eggs), and other factors. Down's Syndrome (involving non-sex-determining chromosomes) and Turner's and Klinefelter's syndromes (involving the twenty-third pair of chromosomes or gametes) are representative of such disorders.

Down's Syndrome One of the more visible conditions that society has commonly associated with mental retardation is *Down's Syndrome*. Dr. John Langdon Down first described this disorder in 1866, and because of a faint resemblance to some of the physical features of the Mongoloid race, the term *mongolism* was long used to label the syndrome. Its causative factors are associated with the age of the mother. The likelihood of Down's Syndrome approximately doubles after age thirty for each successive five-year period of the mother's age (Smith & Wilson, 1973). About one in sixty-five women over the age of forty-five who bears a child will produce a Down's Syndrome infant (Gearheart, 1975).

Nondysjunction A common type of chromosome aberration associated with older mothers, leading to Down's Syndrome, is nondysjunction. In such cases, one pair of genes fails to separate at conception, resulting in an extra, or forty-seventh, chromosome above the normal forty-six. The extra chromosome is placed in the twenty-first pair, which causes that unit to contain three chromosomes instead of two, or trisomy 21 (see Figure 2-4). This occurs by chance and is predictable only in reference to the age of the mother (Sarason, 1959).

Translocation is less common and occurs because of faulty cell division that results in the attachment of one chromosome to another. The familial reoccurrence of Down's Syndrome where translocation is present is greater than in families where nondysjunction has occurred (Carter, 1970).

Mosaicism is observed as an error in the division of an early embryonic cell. The cell receives an extra twenty-first chromosome and passes it along during cell division. In such cases, the individual will have a different number of chromosomes in different types of cells—perhaps forty-seven in blood cells and forty-six in skin cells. Generally, there are fewer abnormalities in this type of Down's Syndrome (Carter, 1970).

General physical characteristics of Down's Syndrome are small ears, protruding tongue with deep fissures, slanted eyes, broad hands with short fingers, singular palm crease, short stature, and underdeveloped genitalia. Congenital heart disorders and respiratory complications are common. Aging appears to occur much more rapidly than normal and affects the life span of the child. The degree of retardation can vary from mild to profound, although the largest percentage of Down's Syndrome individuals fall within the moderate (trainable) to severe range. Treatment would generally involve special educational programming and the control of seizures or other medical factors through medication (Carter, 1970; Covert, 1965; Grossman, 1977).

Down's Syndrome characteristics

Figure 2.3
Physical features of human chromosomes

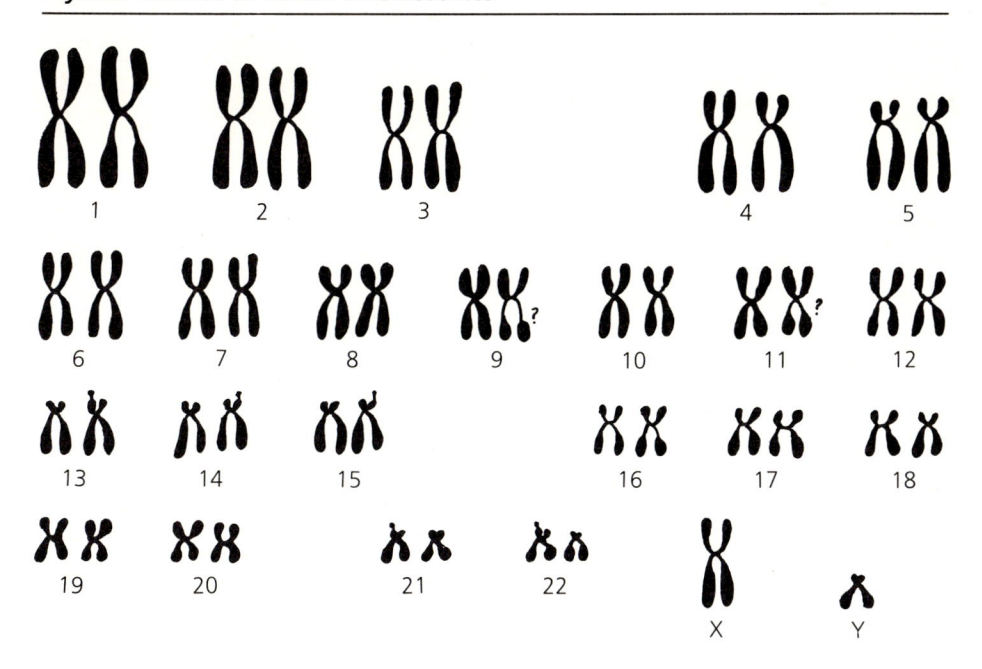

Turner's Syndrome This syndrome results from the absence of an X chromosome in the female (XO). Mental retardation is not always present; however, learning problems usually occur, probably because of the hearing loss that may accompany this syndrome. The physical characteristics of Turner's Syndrome are short stature, webbing of the neck, low-set ears, broad-bridged nose, broad chest, lack of ovary development, and female sterility. Treatment entails the use of female hormones to help develop female sex characteristics (Carter, 1970; Gellis & Feingold, 1968).

Klinefelter's Syndrome Klinefelter's Syndrome occurs in males and, in its most common form, results in an extra X chromosome (XXY), and a chromosome count of 47. The primary distinguishing features of this disorder involve decreased sexual characteristics, such as underdeveloped genitalia and testes and sterility. At puberty, the male may develop such female secondary sex characteristics as enlarged breasts. In an attempt to increase masculine appearance, hormones are usually prescribed,

Figure 2.4
Chromosomes of a Down's Syndrome male child showing trisomy—21

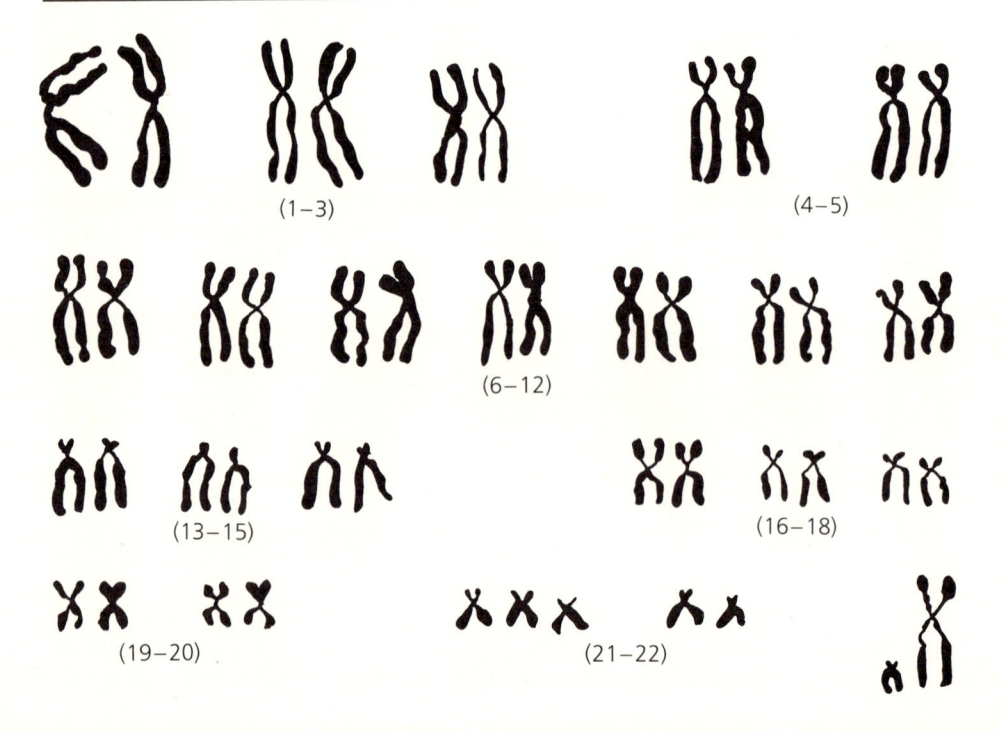

and treatment for personality problems and behavioral disorders may be necessary. Mental retardation will vary from mild to profound but is generally in the moderate range (Carter, 1970; Covert, 1965; Gellis & Feingold, 1968).

Gestational disorders
Prematurity, light birth weight, and postmaturity are gestational disorders that can result in mental retardation and other complications. Babies delivered before the thirty-seventh week from the first day of the mother's last menstrual period are classified as premature. Those born weighing less than five-and-a-half pounds may also require special care. Postmaturity may be a complicating factor if a pregnancy runs seven or more days longer than normal. Many normal births, however, take place later than anticipated and do not involve postmaturity (Grossman, 1977).

Retardation following psychiatric disorder
Grossman (1977) describes this category as "retardation following psychosis or other psychiatric disorder when there is no evidence of cerebral pathology." The exact nature of psychogenic mental retardation is difficult to delineate, although it is known that severe emotional disorders can impair intellectual functioning. Hingtgen and Bryson state that "even though many psychotic children have severely subnormal intellectual level, most investigators clearly distinguish between psychosis and mental retardation and many consider the two diagnoses mutually exclusive" (1972).

Psychogenic retardation

Environmental influences
Adverse environmental conditions may lead to retardation in a child with no known organic disease or pathology. For a child to be placed in this category, there must be evidence that one of its parents and one or more of its siblings function at subnormal intellectual levels. The child also must exhibit subaverage intellectual functioning and impairments in adaptive behavior (Grossman, 1977). Retardation of this type—most often in the mild, or educable, category—is usually found under conditions of severe environmental deprivation where inadequate pre- and postnatal medical care are likely to be factors. This topic will be discussed in more detail in Unit 5.

Other conditions
The AAMD's final general category relating to the causes of mental retardation includes the *multiple biological and social conditions* that contribute to mental retardation. Special sensory handicaps, such as deafness and blindness, fit in this category when they are the only contributing factors to retarded development. Also covered are cases of unknown etiology and previously unheard of or ill-defined conditions (Grossman, 1977).

Special sensory handicaps

A study of the effects of social conditions on mental development (Rendon et al., 1960) compared eighteen malnourished hospitalized children with a control group. All subjects had been born in normal deliveries and had no organic disease or cerebral pathology. All of the malnourished children came from extremely low socioeconomic backgrounds and broken homes, and many of their parents were of below-average intelligence. The researchers found that these youngsters were deficient in all areas of mental development and that their difficulties persisted even after nutritional inadequacies had been overcome. Other studies of the effects of severe deprivation are discussed in Unit 5.

Multihandicaps related to retardation

Disorders of perception and expression Included in the final general category are such disorders as total lack of speech, motor disabilities affecting speech, perception (sensory cortical) disabilities, and others that affect mental development (Grossman, 1977). Many of the causes of retardation discussed earlier involve these disabilities. For example, the rubella child may suffer a hearing loss as a result of the disease. This in turn will reflect on language acquisition (Fishbein, 1963), and the developmental process will lag as a result of the many factors involved. Bender (1965) points out that "mental defectiveness is not an entity; neither is it an isolated deficiency in intelligence. It is a symptom which may be associated with many different conditions."

Convulsive disorders Various kinds of seizure disorders are discussed in detail in the unit on physical and health disabilities (Unit 11). With reference to the relationship between epilepsy and mental retardation, Schmidt and Wilder (1968) state: "Although epilepsy is not characterized by definite abnormalities in intelligence or personality, cognitive and personality disorders are found more often among epileptic subjects than among those without neurological disease." The individual working with the mentally retarded needs to be aware of epilepsy, its treatment, and procedures that might be helpful to the child. Eyman et al. (1970) indicate that the mentally retarded are particularly likely to suffer from brain dysfunction and show hyperactivity and arm-hand and speech problems.

Motor dysfunction Here we refer to cerebral palsy, which is primarily associated with motor disabilities but can cause language, speech, and other disorders. Stephen (1968) studied sixty-six trainable mentally retarded children and reported 33 percent as having cerebral palsy. Robinson and Robinson (1976) indicate that 40 to 50 percent of the cerebral palsied population have IQs below 70. Based on the neurological impairment that often accompanies mental retardation and the role of brain injury in cerebral palsy, it is easy to see the relationship between the two. While mental retardation may be present in cerebral palsy, we see strong dangers in automatically classifying the cerebral palsied child as retarded. Further information regarding cerebral palsy is included in Unit 11.

Summary

In Unit 2 we have seen how difficult it is to define mental retardation comprehensively. Vestiges of the past and concerns of the present have been put in perspective. Methods of measuring levels of intellectual functioning were presented, shedding some light on the concept of mental age and the standard deviation intelligence quotient. The recent emphasis on including a measure of adaptive behavior as part of comprehensive assessment procedures underscores the fact that no single crite-

The class is keenly interested in the learning experience. Chris' teacher certainly evoked a positive response from Chris!

rion should be used for placement purposes. Causative factors of various conditions based on the AAMD classification system were introduced because of their importance in better understanding and treating mentally retarded children and youth. This information will serve as a background for Unit 3, in which mental retardation will be discussed in terms of educational, home, and community considerations.

References

Anastasi, A. *Psychological Testing.* New York: Macmillan, 1959.
Bayley, N. *Bayley Scales of Infant Development.* New York: The Psychological Corporation, 1969.
Bender, M. A. *A Visual Motor Gestalt Test and Its Clinical Use.* New York: Orthopsychiatric Association, 1965.
Cain, L. F.; Levine, S.; and Elzey, F. F. *Cain-Levine Social Competency Scale.* Palo Alto, Calif.: Consulting Psychological Press, 1963.
Carter, H. *Handbook of Mental Retardation Syndromes.* 2nd ed. Springfield, Ill.: Charles C Thomas, 1970.
Covert, C. *Mental Retardation: A Handbook for the Primary Physician.* Chicago: American Medical Association, 1965.
Doll, E. A. *Vineland Social Maturity Scale.* Minneapolis: American Guidance Service, 1965.
Eyman, R. K.; Moore, B. C.; Capes, L.; and Zachofsky, T. "Maladaptive Behavior of Institutionalized Retardates with Seizures." *American Journal of Mental Deficiency* 74 (1970): 651–59.
Fishbein, M., ed. *Birth Defects.* Philadelphia: J. B. Lippincott, 1963.
Frankenburg, W., and Dodds, J. B. *Denver Developmental Test.* Denver: Ladoca Project and Publishing Foundation, 1969.
Gearheart, R., and Litton, W. *The Trainable Retarded: A Foundations Approach.* St. Louis: S. V. Mosby Co., 1975.
Gellis, S. S., and Feingold, M. *Atlas of Mental Retardation Syndromes.* Washington, D.C.: U.S. Government Printing Office, 1968.
Gesell, A., et al. *Gesell Developmental Schedules.* 3rd ed. New York: P. B. Hoeber, 1974.
Grossman, J., ed. *Manual on Terminology and Classification in Mental Retardation.* Rev. ed. Washington, D.C.: The American Association on Mental Deficiency, 1977.
Heber, R. *Epidemiology of Mental Retardation.* Springfield, Ill.: Charles C Thomas, 1970.
Hingtgen, J. N., and Bryson, C. Q. "Recent Developments in the Study of Early Childhood Psychoses: Infantile Autism, Childhood Schizophrenia, and Related Disorders." *Schizophrenia Bulletin,* Spring 1972, p. 8.
Jervis, G. A. "Vocational Rehabilitation of Mental Retardation. Medical Aspects of Mental Deficiencies." *American Journal of Mental Deficiency,* October 1952, p. 175.
Jones, R. L., ed. *Problems and Issues in the Education of Exceptional Children.* Boston: Houghton Mifflin, 1971.
Kirk, S. A., and Johnson, G. O. *Educating the Retarded Child.* Boston: Houghton Mifflin, 1951.
Kolstoe, O. P. "Defining Mental Retardation." *Ninth Annual Distinguished Lecture Series in Special Education and Rehabilitation,* Summer 1970, pp. 77, 79.

Lambert, N.; Windmiller, M.; Cole, L.; and Figueroa, R. *AAMD Adaptive Behavior Scale.* Public School Version, 1974. Washington, D.C.: American Association on Mental Deficiency, 1975.
Mercer, J. R., and Lewis, J. F. SOMPA. New York: The Psychological Corporation, 1978.
Mesibov, G. "A Retrospective Look at Children: Bicentennial Issue 1776–1976." *Journal of Clinical Child Psychology,* Winter 1976.
National Institute of Child Health and Human Development. *Antenatal Diagnosis and Down's Syndrome.* Washington, D.C.: U.S. Government Printing Office, 1973.
Nihira, K.; Foster, R.; Shellhaas, M.; and Leland, H. *AAMD Adaptive Behavior Scale: 1975 Revision.* Washington, D.C.: American Association on Mental Deficiency, 1975.
Patterson, E. G. "VD Reaches Epidemic Proportions." *Mental Retardation News,* February 1971, p. 3.
Penrose, L. S. *The Biology of Mental Defect.* 2nd rev. ed. New York: Grune and Stratton, 1966.
Porteus, S. D., and Corbett, G. R. "Statutory Definitions of Feebleminded in the U.S.A." *Journal of Psychology* 35 (1953): 103–4.
President's Panel on Mental Retardation. *A Proposed Program for National Action to Combat Mental Retardation.* Washington, D.C.: U.S. Government Printing Office, 1962.
Rendon, R.; Hurtado, J. J.; and Arathoon, M. C. "The Effect of Malnutrition on the Physical and Mental Development of Children." In *Congenital Mental Retardation,* edited by G. Farrell, pp. 262–88. Austin, Texas: University of Texas Press, 1969.
Robinson, H. B., and Robinson, N. M. *The Mentally Retarded Child: A Psychological Approach.* 2nd ed. New York: McGraw-Hill, 1976.
Sarason, S. B. *Psychological Problems in Mental Deficiency.* 3rd ed. New York: Harper and Brothers, 1959.
Schmidt, R. P., and Wilder, B. J. *Epilepsy.* Philadelphia: F. A. Davis, 1968.
Seashore, H. G., ed. "Methods of Expressing Test Scores." *Test Service Bulletin,* January 1955, pp. 7–8.
Smith, D. W., and Wilson, A. A. *The Child with Down's Syndrome* (*Mongolism*): *Causes, Characteristics and Acceptance.* Philadelphia: W. B. Saunders, 1973.
Stephen, E. "Psychological Assessment of Severely Subnormal Children in Hospital with Associated Physical Handicap." In *Proceedings of the First Congress of the International Association for the Scientific Study of Mental Deficiency,* edited by B. W. Richards, pp. 760–62. Surrey, England: Michael Jackson Publishing, 1968.
Terman, L. M., and Merrill, M. A. *Stanford-Binet Intelligence Scale.* Boston: Houghton Mifflin, 1960.
Terman, L. M., and Merrill, M. A. *Stanford-Binet Intelligence Scale.* 1972 norms ed. Boston: Houghton Mifflin, 1973.
Wechsler, D. *Manual for the Wechsler Intelligence Scale for Children—Revised.* New York: Psychological Corporation, 1974.
World Health Organization. *The Mentally Subnormal Child.* World Health Organization Technical Report Series, no. 75, 1954.

(See Unit 3 reference list for resource agencies relating to mental retardation)

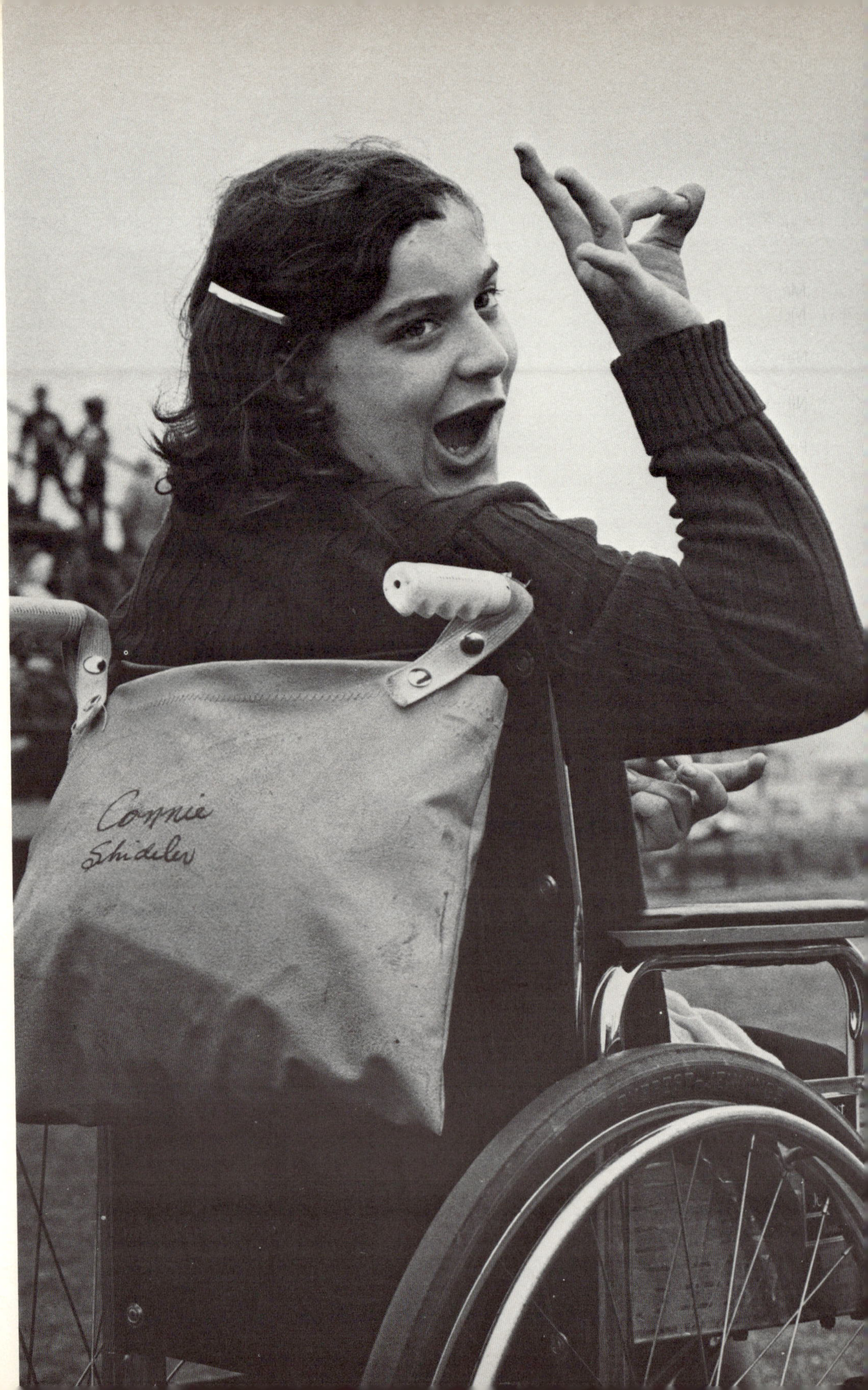
Connie
Shideler

3 Mentally retarded children and youth: educational, home, and community considerations
William J. Ward

Profound and severe retardation · *The profoundly retarded* · *The severely retarded* · *Educational provisions*
The moderately retarded · *Physical and motor development* · *Speech and language development* · *Academic and vocational expectations* · *Social and personality aspects* · *Educational provisions* · *Approaches to working with the moderately retarded population*
The mildly retarded · *Physical and motor development* · *Speech and language development* · *Academic and vocational expectations* · *Social and personality aspects* · *Educational provisions*
General considerations · *Mainstreaming* · *Home and family*
Community attitudes toward the mentally retarded
Summary

Mentally retarded children and youth: educational, home, and community considerations

Student learning objectives

The student will:
1. understand how Public Law 94-142 relates to the retarded school-age child
2. be able to describe the components of an individual learning plan
3. be able to discuss the physical, communicational, vocational and educational characteristics of the severely, profoundly, moderately and mildly retarded child
4. have knowledge of some of the educational materials used with the mentally retarded
5. be able to describe a sample classroom setting for the moderately retarded child
6. be able to describe a sample daily schedule for the moderately retarded child
7. learn about the problems involved in the home setting of the retarded child
8. recognize some of the misconceptions in the community regarding mental retardation

Public Law 94-142, which mandates educational opportunity for all handicapped children between the ages of three and twenty-one by 1980, may well provide the needed impetus to realize quality programming for the mentally retarded in all categories. As was pointed out in Unit 1, this legislation provides for (1) a comprehensive system of identification, (2) full educational opportunity, (3) a comprehensive personnel development system, (4) a system of priorities, (5) parental involvement, (6) participation in the mainstream of regular education, (7) procedural safeguards, (8) protection in evaluation procedures, (9) confidentiality, and (10) individualized educational programs.

Concrete sequential program planning

Implementing an *appropriate* individual education program (IEP) for a mentally retarded child—despite expectations for slower academic progress—requires a concrete sequence of program plans from which parents and teachers may work to meet the individual needs of the youngster. As discussed in Unit 1 an IEP consists of the following: (1) an outline of present level of performance, (2) recommendations for educational services, (3) stated goals for the year, (4) stated short-term goals, (5) planned objectives within the regular educational program, (6) support services needed, (7) designation of persons responsible for services, (8) dates for beginning and ending services, (9) review dates of IEP in terms of student progress, and (10) parental involvement in planning and approval of programming. The IEP approach may become a significant aid in reducing unneeded segregation practices as each of the above considerations are reviewed by parents and the educational team.

Reducing segregation practices

Profound and severe retardation
The profoundly retarded
The profoundly mentally retarded exhibit substantial deficiencies in the areas of physical development, communication, self-care, and overall intellectual functioning. Their measured intelligence quotients are under 25 (Grossman, 1977). Many of these children are placed in institutional settings because of major medical problems. Nevertheless, educational programs should be provided for them based on their individual needs and capabilities. The population is difficult to assess and medical evaluations play a major role in the programming procedure.

Custodial care usually required

The severely retarded
Severe mental retardation includes individuals with an IQ range of 20 to 39 (Grossman, 1977). The IQ level does not dictate the services that are offered; rather it gives the teacher some directions in planning the services. This population sometimes is included in the trainable group.

The evaluation of this population is again a difficult task and involves a full-team approach, including medical, educational, and psychological specialists. In many instances data are obtained not only from measurement tools but through observation by trained personnel.

Educational provisions for profound and severe retardation
The educational program for the profoundly retarded may be centered around self-help or simple communication skills. A frequently used teaching technique is sensory stimulation accompanied by appropriate reinforcement of the desired response. Physical and music therapists may play an important part in programming for these youngsters.

Self-help and simple communication

The educational program for the severely retarded may be centered around gross motor, communication, self-help, and social skills. In the area of gross motor skills, activities must be based on the child's developmental level rather than on his or her chronological age. Assessment of current physical abilities and desired goals must be considered. In working with the child, the teacher must first obtain a response. Then, even if the response is negative, it can be channeled constructively by using behavior modification or other special techniques.

In behavior modification, the desired or undesired behavior must first be isolated, which requires adequate study and observation of present conduct. The following experiment carried on in a community school for the severely retarded is an example:

Training through reinforcement

Toileting skills The objective was to improve toileting skills. Over a period of time the children learned to respond to their own individual color cues. A record of the number of accidents that each child had over a period of time was kept in order to obtain an indication of the time sequence during which the accidents occurred. Once this was established, a bell would ring in the classroom at the approximate time that a given student had been having the greatest number of accidents. The bell was used to call the child's attention to the colored card being held by the teacher's aide. The child responding to his or her color would then be taken to the bathroom. Upon successful completion of the toileting task, the child would be reinforced; if the child were unsuccessful, reinforcement would be withheld. At the end of six months, toileting accidents had been cut by 98 percent and 33 percent of the children were responding independently.

The teacher or home trainer should remember that intellectual assessment will play only a small role in programming for the profoundly and severely mentally retarded. By using other appropriate information, such as present skills, a baseline of behaviors from which to program can be developed. Once this baseline is established, plans can be carefully laid out to help the child overcome any deficiencies. For example, in developing self-help skills such as dressing, the teacher or home trainer must make sure that the clothes used are items that he or she can manipulate. A model to pattern oneself after and some step-by-step direction may be needed. One of the most important aspects involved in such work is the allowance of enough time to complete the task. The child should always receive praise for successful completion of a task and be given encouragement for any attempts. Once having mastered a dressing task, such as buttoning a shirt, the child should be allowed to perform the activity independently from then on.

Task analysis by teacher

Many times during the process, the teacher will need to utilize task analysis. This involves breaking a whole activity down into distinct steps which the child can handle. Each step is reinforced until the whole task is completed.

Programming for the profoundly and severely retarded must be done on an individual basis. Factors that will have an influence on programming include the availability of support personnel (physical therapists, medical specialists, etc.) and necessary physical facilities. The law provides for support services to be purchased when they are not available in the community or school setting. These could include residential care, homebound instruction, transportation to available services, or other required special arrangements. The prognosis for the profoundly and severely mentally retarded is generally impossible to predict. Early intervention programs staffed by competent personnel may allow the profoundly and severely retarded to attain goals never thought possible.

The moderately retarded

Appropriate placement procedures

In addition to assessing both IQ differences (three to four standard deviations below average and IQs of 40 to 54 [Wechsler] or 36 to 51 [Binet] as seen in Table 2-1, Unit 2) and deficient adaptive behavior, further considerations must be taken into account to ensure appropriate educational, home, and community participation for the moderately retarded. Physical, motor, and language development, learning and occupational expectations, and social and personality aspects—these are all specific areas that relate to planning appropriate placement procedures and services to be provided.

Physical and motor development

Multiple handicaps, including hearing and vision impairment, are more frequently seen within the moderately retarded population. Generally, such children tire easily and are more susceptible to health problems. Particularly in cases of Down's Syndrome, respiratory infections and heart complications are present (Gellis & Feingold,

Multihandicaps among the moderately retarded

Introducing Connie—Despite her developmental and physical handicaps, she is setting out to win a Special Olympics race, spurred on by a cheering section.

1968). Musculature may be unevenly developed (although this condition is present in other populations without resulting complications) and acquisition of motor skills is likely to lag. The moderately retarded are significantly slower in accomplishing such developmental tasks as crawling, standing, and walking. Coordination problems frequently are pronounced and result in difficulty with small muscle activities (finger and hand movements) or large muscle activities (awkwardness of gait in walking and running) (Grossman, 1977).

Speech and language development

Speech and language delay

Language development is substantially delayed in both the understanding of spoken language used by others (receptive language) and spoken language used by the child (expressive language). Speech defects, including articulation and other disorders, often need remediation after language is acquired.

Academic and vocational expectations

The moderately retarded population is usually expected to reach limited academic and vocational plateaus. Their anticipated level of achievement is generally considered to be approximately one-third to one-half the mental development of normal children, and their mental ages are expected to range from six to eight years. Academic achievement may vary from the first to the third- or fourth-grade levels. This reduced level of academic expectancy usually precludes their entry into independent vocational pursuits. Vocational potential, however, can be realized under the sheltered workshop approach (discussed below).

Social and personality aspects

Conduct needs to be monitored

Moderately retarded individuals remain more personally dependent on others during their lifetimes and are unlikely to acquire the social skills necessary for successful personal interaction within general society. Their conduct and judgment usually need to be monitored by others because they lack the ability to foresee consequences and make adequate social adjustments.

Educational provisions

Administrative organization   Certain states and educational systems may have to reorganize their administrative levels and provisions for the moderately retarded in order to meet new legal and public demands. Some individuals within the upper range of the severely retarded population may be included in the new programs. An effective reorganization of classes for the moderately retarded within the public schools would require a departure from the former common practice of providing only one classroom in which all moderately retarded children were treated alike.

Mainstreaming the moderately retarded

Under the old system there were difficulties in providing for individual needs in terms of materials, developmental and socialization processes, and prevocational and vocational training.

An effective reorganization of public school classes would include the following improvements:

Preschool level, ages three to five: The preschool child's program would involve half-day classes in which emphasis is placed on developing self-help, beginning speech and language, and motor and socialization skills.

Primary level, ages six to nine: The primary level would extend the school day to approximately five hours and involve further training in preschool-level skills and emphasis on the acquisition of visual and auditory skills necessary for participation in later learning situations.

Intermediate level, ages nine to twelve: The intermediate level would provide full-day classes. Activities would include continued work on the readiness skills indicated above, as well as beginning and ongoing functional academic training aimed at reading for protection, increasing reading ability, and acquiring additional arithmetic skills, etc. Skills useful for leisure-time activities would be emphasized, including physical education, art and music; skill building for family group and societal participation would continue.

Secondary level, ages thirteen and over: At this stage, prevocational and vocational skills would be given greater attention while work continued in all other previously introduced areas. Students may be taught to prepare simple food combinations, such as sandwiches, salads, and desserts, and do other household tasks to aid in their own personal and familial effectiveness. Training in personal grooming and hygiene become most important as a continued part of the socialization process.

Placement in a *sheltered workshop* where actual vocational productiveness is possible is an ultimate goal for the moderately retarded. The National Association for Retarded Citizens (NARC) defines a sheltered workshop thus: A work-oriented rehabilitation facility with a controlled working environment and individualized vocational goals, which utilizes work experiences and related services to assist the handicapped person's progress toward normal living and productive vocational status (Fraenkel, 1962, p. 2).

Sheltered workshop is the ultimate goal

In relation to rehabilitation workshops, Brolin (1976) states that "their work may often be too simple, routine, and unchallenging to many potential clients" (p. 51). Sheltered workshops for the moderately retarded, however, are successfully operated in many communities. In such a setting, close supervision is provided as retarded individuals perform certain tasks leading to the final production of an article or the eventual marketing of a product. Typical work might entail making and packaging ribbon bows in plastic bags, affixing labels on clothing or other items, or sorting out parts and pieces for the final product. The ingenuity of the workshop director is vital in determining what type of work can be accomplished successfully and in securing contracts for such projects. Unfortunately, too few communities have established such centers and therefore too few opportunities exist for the mentally retarded to enjoy their benefits. There are very positive effects of the workshop experience. These include increased feelings of self-worth among the workers as

Positive effects of workshops

they view themselves and are viewed by others as more productive human beings; wage-earning, which relieves them of totally dependent economic status; and exposure to comparatively greater socialization processes. Also, in terms of socialization, the individual can feel more sense of belonging as he or she participates in the working world; at the same time family responsibility for providing necessary supervision is reduced. Both of these conditions may contribute to more effective familial and societal interactions.

The following case may be cited as a typical example of the expectations for a moderately retarded child.

Stan He is an eight-year-old, diagnosed as exhibiting Down's Syndrome of mental retardation (see Unit 2). His family has a lower socioeconomic background and his siblings, three older and one younger, are all of normal intelligence. Stan's measured intelligence quotient at this time is 43, and among his adaptive behavior difficulties are language problems and sensory and motor difficulties. His social behavior has improved since he began participating in a special educational program at his local public school. Academic skills are still beyond his capabilities.

In the future, Stan might be expected to attain academic skills up to the first or second-grade level. Even with help in speech and language development, he will remain deficient in the communicative skills required by society, but he will be proficient enough to meet smaller group or familial demands. Further progress in educational, social, and vocational skills will be dependent upon the type of provisions made for him in the classroom. Later successful participation in a sheltered-workshop environment is feasible. Stan's capabilities for total independent employment are negated, however, by our present knowledge of means to overcome his intellectual and adaptive behavior deficits.

Socialization and self-help skills

Educational programs While the curriculum for the moderately retarded does include emphasis on learning to read, spell, and do simple arithmetic, greater emphasis is placed on other areas of learning. Self-help skills receive early consideration in the curriculum; they continue to be emphasized in later learning experiences designed to aid the individual to become a more effective participant within the family unit or in a sheltered workshop environment. Socialization skills are an ongoing part of the curriculum. Particularly important is the child's orientation to the community. Local field trips serve as an integral part of the learning experience and provide a concrete basis for discussion of social behavior in public, the use of public transportation, making simple purchases, etc.

Incorporation of such activities as swimming, bowling, skating, camping, and arts and crafts provide experiences that lead to more effective use of leisure time. Although the students' ages and the extent of their exceptionality may present some problems in extending activities beyond the classroom setting, many communities report excellent success when various individuals or groups within the community volunteer their services.

Classroom setting and organization   The classroom for the moderately retarded should be as large or larger than a regular classroom. Ideally, it should contain a kitchen area with sinks, stove, and refrigerator because basic food preparation

The classroom as a miniature home

Connie's determination and drive are evident. In the wheelchair race individual effort and competitive spirit are rewarded.

and household activities are a part of the curriculum. A bed, a washing machine, and even a small living area would allow the teaching of bed making and cleaning and could allow some prevocational training as well as practice in independent living skills. Toilet facilities should be in the classroom or easily accessible if the teacher is going to be successful in that aspect of the program, and there should also be access to the playground.

The size of the class should be based on (1) age—the younger the children, the smaller the class; (2) handicaps—the more handicapping conditions, the smaller the class; (3) school experiences—the less experience, the smaller the class. The area should have adequate storage space so that materials not being used can be placed out of sight. This reduces the number of distractions for the children. The classroom should contain materials in the following categories:

1. self-care: toothbrush, comb
2. writing: paper, pencils
3. social acceptance: dishes, glasses, silverware
4. protective reading: signs, films
5. physical development: balls, pegboard, blocks
6. music and art: record player, clay
7. economic usefulness: brooms, washing machine
8. language development: common objects, books, tape recorder

Figure 3-1 is a suggested distribution of time that may be helpful to classroom teachers.

Approaches to working with the moderately retarded population

The child should be observed carefully for readiness and maturational level before any training program is introduced. Allowances must be made for the fact that growth in all areas is not consistent. The following guidelines should be considered by the teacher:

1. Examine the needs of the child.
2. Set realistic goals so the child can be successful in his or her learning experience.
3. Understand and view the child's behavior in reference to development.
4. Provide support during the learning experience.
5. Allow adequate time for the child to complete the task.
6. Select the proper stimuli to elicit the desired response from the child.
7. Provide consistency in discipline and in supportive roles.

Well-planned activities that are presented in an organized manner in the proper environment enhance the child's learning and eliminate the need for external controls.

Figure 3.1
A plan for school time distribution for moderately retarded children

	Preschool 3 to 5 Yrs.	*Primary* 6 to 9 Yrs.	*Intermediate* 9 to 12 Yrs.	*Secondary Level I* 13 to 16 Yrs.	*Secondary Level II* 17 to 19 Yrs.	*Secondary Level III* 20 to 21 Yrs.
9:00	Arrival Opening exercises	Arrival Opening exercises	Arrival Opening exercises	Arrival Opening exercises	Arrival Opening exercises	Arrival Opening exercises
9:30	Self-help skills	Self-help skills	*Academics* Reading for safety Phone no. Address, etc.	*Functional* Numbers Writing Reading	*Functional* Numbers Writing Reading	On-campus work or workshop
10:00	Bread & milk Speech Language	Speech & language				
10:30	P.E. Music Art	Break	Organized games Play	Break	Break	Break
11:00	Social & group activities	Auditory skills	Speech & language	Social skills	Social skills	Work activity
11:30	Rest Prepare to go home	Music Prepare for lunch	Health Hand washing Prepare for lunch	Health	Health P.E. Music Art	
12:00		Lunch	Lunch	Lunch	Lunch	Lunch
12:30		Free time	Rest	Rest or quiet time	Prepare for work	Work activity
1:00		Rest	Unit experience	Work habits	In-school or on-campus work	
1:30		Group activities	P.E. Art Music	Job skills		
2:00		P.E.				
2:30		Dismiss	Dismiss	P.E.		Classroom reviewing Work counseling
3:00				Dismiss		Dismiss

Mentally retarded children and youth: educational, home, and community considerations

The mildly retarded

Expectations for the mildly retarded differ substantially from those for the moderately retarded population. This group is defined as exhibiting IQ differences of from two to three standard deviations below average and IQs of 55 to 69 (Wechsler) or 52 to 67 (Binet) (see Table 2-1, Unit 2) plus deficits in adaptive behavior. This child population can be characterized as the "six-hour retarded," a term used by the President's Panel on Mental Retardation (1970) to refer to those whose deficits lie primarily in the academic areas.

Physical and motor development

Mildly retarded child looks like other children

In general, mentally retarded children are apt to be smaller and lighter than normal children of the same chronological age. Such differences are minimized, however, within the mildly retarded population. These youngsters have fewer physical deformities than moderately retarded children, and many are physically indistinguishable from their normal peers.

Motor coordination may be normal

In the area of motor development, they may be slow to master standing and walking. However, the delay is not usually significant enough for many parents to see as an early concern. Motor coordination problems are not as apparent as they are in the moderately retarded population, and many mildly retarded youngsters exhibit normal agility in both fine motor and gross motor tasks. The greater the degree of retardation within the mildly retarded group, the more overlap there may be with characteristics of the moderately retarded.

Speech and language development

Functional language usually adequate

In general, language development is slower than normal, with the rate of progress in speech and language activities determined by other factors (for example, language stimulation activities), rather than simply by reduced mental potential. Speech difficulties are usually amenable to correction through speech therapy. Communicative deficiencies may involve lowered use and understanding of abstract words and ideas, generalizations, and descriptive language. However, capacity for functional language use is indicated in most cases.

Academic and vocational capabilities

Educable

Differences between the moderately retarded and the mildly retarded populations in terms of learning and occupational capabilities are *extremely pronounced.* Many of the mildly retarded (frequently termed *educable*) are expected to progress at about one-half to three-quarters the rate of normal mental development and to attain mental ages ranging from approximately eight to twelve years. Academic achievement is expected to range from the third- to the fifth- or sixth-grade levels in the basic subject areas of reading, spelling, and arithmetic.

This group's occupational potential again differs substantially from the moderately retarded population. With proper work-skill training and preparation, many can be expected to function independently in the unskilled or semiskilled labor market. The fact that 75 to 80 percent of those in the upper levels of the retarded population succeed in holding jobs attests to their capability in this area.

Upon leaving the school situation many of these mildly retarded individuals are no longer identifiable in terms of deficient adaptive behavior. In this respect it has been contended that many of the youngsters labeled as educable or mildly retarded are designated as such only on the basis of school performance or intelligence tests. Both of these assessments are influenced by sociocultural factors that tend to lower and distort measurement of potential (Jones, 1971).

This group can live and work independently as adults

Social and personality aspects

Mildly retarded youth have much potential for success in social and interpersonal interaction. Their placement in special classes that are perceived as "dumb" (Jones, 1971, p. 112), may negatively affect self-concept or motivation (Jones, 1972). A study based on the responses of 129 junior high school teachers revealed that 82 percent of their students were ashamed of being in special classes. Ninety percent of the respondents indicated that the children were aware of the derogatory labels assigned to their classes. The fact remains, however, that retarded children in regular classes may still be viewed in a derogatory manner by more academically competent classmates (Jones, 1974).

Special class placement may have negative effect

Educational provisions

Administrative organization   The need to change approaches to programming for the mentally retarded was revealed by efficacy studies which pointed out that educational objectives were not being met, and that the academic achievement levels of the mildly retarded in special classes were not as high as those of their retarded counterparts in regular classes (Kirk, 1964; Smith & Kennedy, 1967). The long-standing four educational objectives for normal children formulated first in 1938 by the Educational Policies Commission also apply to the optimum level of development of the mildly retarded. These goals cover the areas of (1) self-realization, (2) human relationships, (3) economic efficiency, and (4) civic responsibility. Another objective, education for the use of leisure time, was later added (Hutt & Gibby, 1976).

General educational goals are applicable

Effective program reorganization for the mildly retarded would include much greater integration into various aspects of the regular school program at the earliest possible level. It would include the following features:

Preschool level, ages three to six: The preschool program for the mildly retarded would include development of communication, perceptual-motor, self-help, and socialization skills, along with enrichment through new experiences.

Primary level, ages six to nine: The primary program would feature some self-contained instruction under the direction of a specially trained teacher and part-time placement and participation in a regular classroom situation for any activities from

Integration into regular classes is a right!

which the child can benefit. Curriculum emphasis would be placed on the readiness activities necessary for academic study and there would be continued work on the development of the basic skills begun at the preschool level.

Intermediate level, ages nine to twelve: Intermediate programs would begin to emphasize more formal academic training in reading, written and oral communication, and simple arithmetic. Motor and perceptual areas of development would also receive attention as a necessary adjunct to learning proficiency. The opportunity for placement with regular students would be extended.

Middle or junior high school level, ages thirteen to fourteen: Emphasis on basic academic subject areas would continue, for many students would at this point be reaching an optimum level of development for formal learning. Placement in regular classes for physical education, industrial arts, home economics, art, and music is feasible. With cooperation from the school, prevocational work experiences (such as school lunchroom responsibilities and other school-related duties) could be provided to develop the appropriate work habits and social skills related to success in later vocational training situations. The services of a rehabilitation counselor should also be provided.

Prevocational training is a "must"

Senior high school level, ages fifteen and over: Many states require certain units of study (history, science, etc.) for which the mildly retarded may need special classes. Social living skills, including money management and job-finding techniques, become increasingly important subject areas before formal education is terminated. The regular class participation begun earlier should continue, and formalized work-study program provided for all whose skills permit such involvement. Vocational rehabilitation counselors and guidance services should be available to aid the individual with school work-study programs and to provide assistance in post-school adjustment. Chaffin et al. (1971) demonstrate that this joint effort with the mentally retarded is effective, and the Rehabilitation Act of 1973 emphasizes the delivery of services to those most in need (HEW, 1976).

Work-study programs

A sheltered-workshop situation, which can also be helpful to this group, is viewed as a needed community resource by the National Association for Retarded Citizens. Some mildly retarded individuals may be permanently placed in the workshop, while others only may participate as part of a work-adjustment program. A cooperative program aimed at providing appropriate school and vocational training services is shown in Figure 3-2.

A typical example of a mildly retarded youth is discussed below.

Rosanne The parents of twelve-year-old Rosanne are in the upper-middle income bracket, and she has one younger sister of average intelligence. Her mother can recall no complications during her pregnancy and Rosanne was delivered as a normal-term baby.

Her parents did feel some concern about her slowness in motor development and language acquisition. At the age of two Rosanne experienced her first seizure, causing her parents to seek medical advice. Rosanne was placed on medication for seizure control and experienced no further difficulty in this area.

When she started school, it became evident that she lagged behind her peers in academic abilities and motor and communication skills. She was subsequently evaluated and her IQ was found to be 62, within the mildly retarded range. She was placed part-time in a special education class and was given speech and language therapy.

At the present time Rosanne is functioning at the fourth- to fifth-

Figure 3.2
Proposed distribution of services between school and community for mentally retarded persons

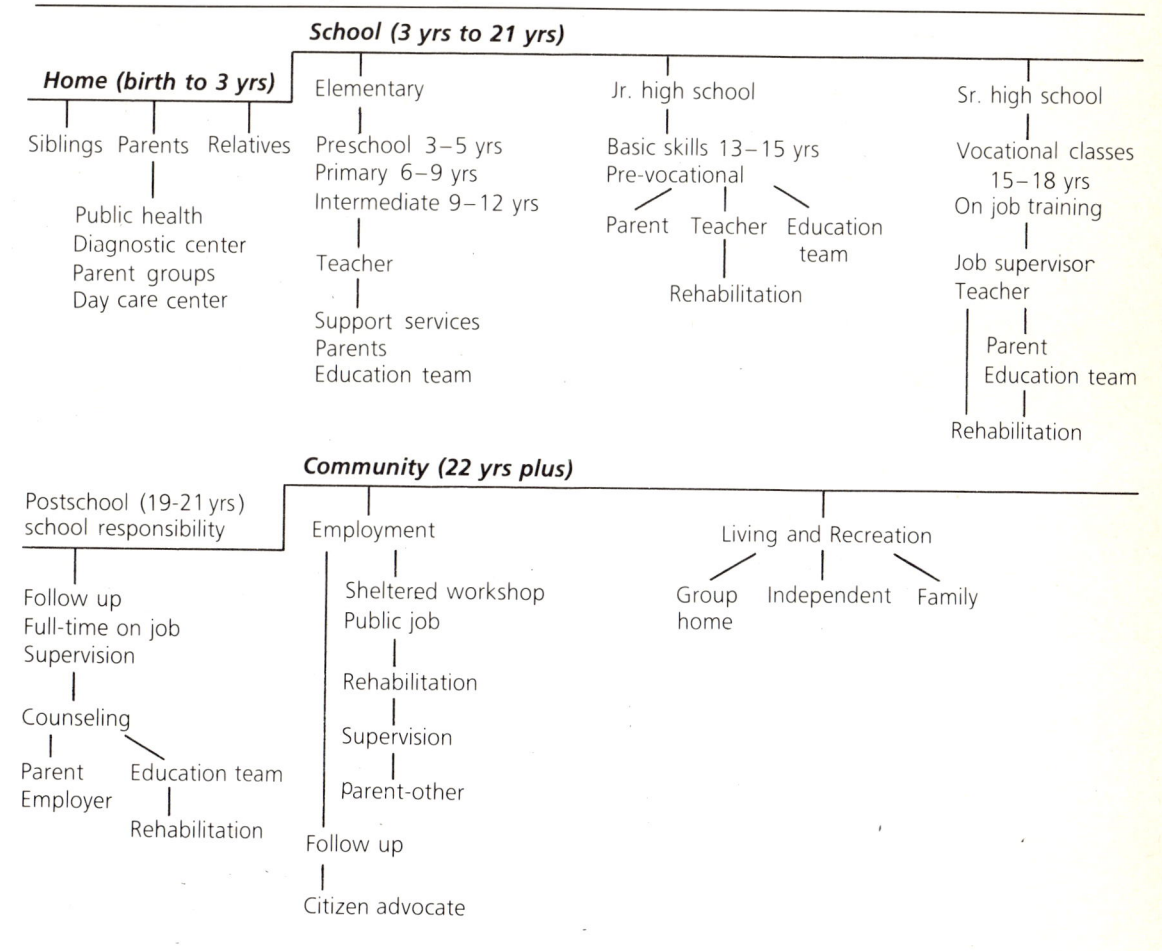

```
                        School (3 yrs to 21 yrs)
                        
Home (birth to 3 yrs)   Elementary          Jr. high school         Sr. high school
                        
Siblings Parents Relatives  Preschool 3–5 yrs   Basic skills 13–15 yrs   Vocational classes
                        Primary 6–9 yrs     Pre-vocational              15–18 yrs
    Public health       Intermediate 9–12 yrs                            On job training
    Diagnostic center                       Parent  Teacher  Education
    Parent groups       Teacher                              team        Job supervisor
    Day care center                                                      Teacher
                        Support services    Rehabilitation
                        Parents                                          Parent
                        Education team                                   Education team
                        
                                                                         Rehabilitation

                        Community (22 yrs plus)

Postschool (19-21 yrs)  Employment                          Living and Recreation
school responsibility
                        Sheltered workshop                  Group    Independent   Family
Follow up               Public job                          home
Full-time on job
Supervision             Rehabilitation

Counseling              Supervision

Parent   Education team Parent-other
Employer
         Rehabilitation Follow up

                        Citizen advocate
```

grade level in basic academic subjects. She needs continued help with some problems in social adjustment and preparation for later vocational proficiency. If such services are provided during her future school years, it is anticipated that Rosanne may eventually be able to support herself and hold an unskilled or semiskilled job under minor supervision. She may marry and have children of her own.

When children like Rosanne are integrated into regular classes, grading practices are sometimes seen as a problem. Professionals, cognizant of intra-individual differences, have long advocated grading based on individual effort and accomplishment in relation to potential. The mildly retarded child—or for that matter, any child—should not be given a failing grade if maximum effort is put forth in relation to potential, even though a desired norm may not be reached.

Grading practices

Educational programs   Referring to the manner in which learning tasks for the mildly retarded (educable) should be presented, Kolstoe (1976) makes the following recommendations:

How to present tasks

1. The tasks should be uncomplicated. The new tasks should contain the fewest possible elements, and most of the elements should be familiar, so he [or she] has very few unknowns to learn.
2. The task should be brief. This assures that [the learner] will attend to the most important aspect of the task and not get lost in a sequence of interrelated events.
3. The task should be sequentially presented so the learner proceeds in a sequence of small steps, each one built upon previously learned tasks.
4. Each learning task should be the kind in which success is possible. One of the major problems to be overcome is that of failure proneness. This major deterrent to learning can be effectively reduced through success experiences.
5. Overlearning must be built into lessons. Drills in game form seem to lessen the disinterest inherent in unimaginative drill.
6. Learning tasks should be applied to objects, problems, and situations in the learner's life environment. Unless the tasks are relevant, the learner has great difficulty in seeing their possible importance (p. 27).

Classroom setting and organization   Because of the diversity of activities, the classroom for the mildly retarded should be larger than a regular classroom. Areas of study will range from prevocational skills through academic subjects. One of the major educational goals for this group is self-management in society. Therefore space must be available in which social skill-building activities may be practiced. It is important to create a pleasant atmosphere because the students may spend several years in this environment.

Spacious and pleasant atmosphere important

The location of the classroom should be such that the children will not be excluded from the regular school environment. In compliance with Public Law 94-142, children should be placed in the least restrictive environment to provide optimum educational experience.

The furniture may be organized in units and, in many cases, tables are better than desks because they allow more student interaction. The desks, tables, chairs, and work areas should be designed to fit the children comfortably.

The classroom should contain high-interest, low-vocabulary reading material along with games of therapeutic value. The games should involve such areas as counting, muscular development, rhythmical activities, and likenesses and differences. Arts and crafts can be used to enhance self-expression and coordination. The teacher can structure these activities to include and develop work habits that will carry over into prevocational and vocational areas. Record players, tape recorders, telephones, and films are essential equipment for all levels.

At the finish line Connie's classmate Margaret is awarded the second-place ribbon. Connie is clearly delighted with her friend's success.

General considerations

Mainstreaming

Public Law 94-142 ensures the mentally retarded the right to an appropriate education in the least restrictive environment. Whenever possible, retarded children should be included in the regular school activities from which they can benefit.

The educational team, child, and parents will be involved in deciding the necessary approach to providing the best possible developmental opportunities. The educational services could be provided in any one or a combination of the following settings: special institution, home, private school, self-contained classroom, resource room with resource teacher (tutor), or part-time special education classroom and part-time regular classroom.

Those suffering from severe and profound mental retardation will be the most difficult to integrate into the public schools. Facilities must be altered; for example, ramps and toilet accommodations for wheelchairs must be provided. The greatest challenge involves staffing—getting the support personnel who are trained and skilled in educational programming to serve this population.

Table 3.1
Suggested areas of program emphasis for profoundly retarded persons

Preschool age	School age	Adults
Sensorimotor stimulation a. stimulating sight, hearing, touch, smell, and muscular response b. enriching environment and encouraging exploration of interesting and attractive surroundings	Sensorimotor development a. identifying shapes, colors, sizes, locations, and distances b. identifying sound patterns, locations, tonal qualities, rhythms c. identifying textures, weights, shapes, sizes, temperatures d. identifying familiar, aversive, and pleasant odors	Sensorimotor integration a. sorting, transferring, inserting, pulling, folding b. responding to music activities, signals, warnings c. making personal choices and selections d. discriminating sizes, weights, colors, distances, locations, odors, temperatures, etc.
Physical development a. body positioning b. passive exercising c. rolling, creeping, and crawling d. balancing head and trunk e. using hands purposefully f. standing practice g. training for mobility	Physical mobility and coordination a. practicing ambulation b. overcoming obstacles; walking on ramps and stairs, running, skipping, jumping, balancing, climbing c. using playground equipment d. participating in track and field events	Physical dexterity and recreation a. riding vehicles; participating in gymnastic-like activities and track and field events b. marking with pencil; cutting with scissors; stringing beads; pasting; and assembling c. swimming and water play d. using community parks, playgrounds, and other recreational resources

Suggestions for areas of performance to be emphasized in the profoundly retarded population are seen in Table 3-1 (Luckey & Addison, 1974, p. 124). These authors have noted that "the inclusion of profoundly retarded students in the public schools will necessitate a revision in traditional definitions of education" (p. 123).

The moderately retarded will not present the same difficulties to the schools and will be involved on a limited basis in regular school activities. Art, music, and physical education classes and school assemblies may best be utilized in the normalization process for this population.

Art, music, physical education, least difficult

The mildly retarded will benefit greatly from regular school activities. The child with interests and abilities in areas such as art, music, physical education, industrial arts, vocational education, and drama may have such programs adapted to fit his or her strengths and limitations.

Table 3.1 (continued)

Preschool age	School age	Adults

Pre-self-care
  a. taking nourishment from bottle and spoon; drinking from cup and finger feeding
  b. passive dressing; accommodating body to dressing; partially removing clothing
  c. passive bathing; handling soap and washcloth; participating in drying
  d. passive placement on toilet; toilet regulating
	Self-care development
	  a. self-feeding with spoon and cup; eating varied diet; behaving appropriately while dining
	  b. removing garments; dressing and undressing with supervision: buttoning, zipping, and snapping
	  c. drying hands and face; partially bathing
	  d. toilet scheduling; indicating need to eliminate; using toilet with supervision
		Self-care
		  a. eating varied diet in family dining situation; using eating utensils; selecting foods
		  b. dressing with partial assistance or supervision
		  c. bathing with partial assistance or supervision
		  d. using toilet independently with occasional supervision

Language stimulation
  a. increasing attention to sounds
  b. encouraging vocalization
  c. responding to verbal and non-verbal requests
  d. identifying objects
	Language development
	  a. recognizing name, names of familiar objects, and body parts
	  b. responding to simple commands
	  c. imitating speech and gestures
	  d. using gestures, words, or phrases
		Language and speech development
		  a. listening to speaker
		  b. using gestures, words, or phrases
		  c. following uncomplicated directions

Interpersonal response
  a. recognizing familiar persons
  b. requesting attention from others
  c. occupying self for brief periods
	Social behavior
	  a. requesting personal attention
	  b. playing individually alongside other residents
	  c. using basic self-protective skills
		Self-direction and work
		  a. using protective skills
		  b. sharing, taking turns, waiting for instructions
		  c. traveling with supervision

Source: Luckey & Addison, 1974, p. 124

Home and family

Family life education   Family life education should be included in any curriculum for the retarded, particularly for those in the mildly retarded, or educable, range, because they are likely to marry and bear children. Some societal concern regarding reproduction by persons designated as mentally retarded has been expressed. Twenty-four states have laws permitting the sterilization of the mentally retarded and four states do not permit the mentally retarded to marry (Krishef, 1972).

As a general rule, individuals who are moderately, severely, and profoundly retarded do not marry and reproduce. The more constant supervision required by their dependency may interfere with their possibilities for reproduction, and many individuals in these populations—by virtue of their more severe disabilities—are not capable of reproducing (as in cases of Down's and Klinefelter's Syndromes).

Within the mildly retarded population, however, sex drive and capability for reproduction approximate those of the normal population. Education in human sexuality, including its physical and psychological aspects, is felt to be an important responsibility of the family or other persons concerned with the individual's appropriate development and behavior (De La Cruz & LaVeck, 1973). This aspect of family life education has only recently gained attention, as opposition to sterilization procedures has increased, and concern over society's commercial exploitation of human sexuality has risen.

Parental attitudes   The professionals who work with retarded children and their families often hear parents express the feeling that "having a retarded child isn't easy." Most parents are genuinely interested in maintaining normal, healthy relationships among all family members, including the retarded child, but they are faced with many difficult decisions.

One of the most difficult decisions some parents face is whether or not to institutionalize their child. The fact that some retarded children require almost constant supervision allows their parents little, if any, time for rest, relaxation, and recreation. Many times parents find themselves physically unable to cope with the problems of keeping these children at home, especially if there are also normal children in the home. A study of seventy-seven institutionalized Down's Syndrome children and their families, however, indicated that if adequate counseling had been given, the majority of the patients could have been cared for at home (Kugel et al., 1964). Other researchers have found that home-reared groups were significantly superior to institutionally reared groups in the areas of intellectual and social development (Shotwell & Shipe, 1964).

It is apparent that each family must evaluate their own resources when deciding whether to keep their child at home or place him/her in an institution. If conditions exist that indicate a need for institutional services, the parents should not be made to suffer guilt feelings concerning such placement. Many families find that after the initial adjustment to institutional placement, the child will be most anxious to return there after brief home visits so as not to miss out on programs and activities of which he or she has become a part. In some cases of retardation where constant medical treatment and supervision are required, home placement is generally not feasible.

The parents of mildly retarded children also can suffer stressful situations. In one study (Wadsworth & Wadsworth, 1971) questionnaires were sent to parents concerning their feelings about the placement of their children in special classes. Responses showed intense feelings were aroused by the special class placement and labeling of their children.

Other researchers have found that parents generally react to their child's mental retardation in one of three ways: (1) they accept the child for what he or she is and try to provide appropriate services leading to achievement; (2) they have mixed feelings of both acceptance and rejection, but decide in favor of institutionalization. (3) they partially or totally reject the child (Ehlers et al., 1973). When working with parents of retarded children, say Ehlers et al. (1973), those who are counseling the family should be directed toward the following goals:

Goals of counselors

1. Help them to be more objective about their child.
2. Help them to learn about behavior their child will outgrow and behavior that can be expected to continue.
3. Help them to assimilate ideas about handling various problem situations common to families of a retarded child.
4. Advise them about the helpful books and pamphlets available and make these materials available for their study and use.
5. Assist them in learning how to handle their retarded child with greater acceptance, understanding and knowledge.
6. Aid them in providing the child with leisure-time pursuits and other constructive activities which may result in a happier child and, therefore, a happier family.
7. Advise them regarding the community resources which are available (such as clinics, evaluation centers, parents' groups, sheltered workshops, and educational institutions for the retarded) (p. 185).

Community attitudes toward the mentally retarded

As mentioned earlier, the mentally retarded in the regular school setting can suffer many pressures from their normal peers as a result of the way their disabilities are labeled. The community sometimes makes it difficult for the retarded to function because the two terms *mental illness* and *mental retardation* are mistakenly thought to be synonymous. Additionally, the way the term *mental retardation* is generalized —so that the characteristics seen in the more profoundly retarded are associated

Dispelling myths is difficult

with all retarded children and youth—leads to overreactions of sympathy or rejection rather than reality-based viewpoints.

The contributions of the mentally retarded to the community can be viewed from various perspectives, and factors within the community structure will have a significant effect. From the economic viewpoint, for example, if unemployment is high in a particular area, the hiring of the mentally retarded may be perceived as taking jobs away from other members of the community. Many times employers, consciously or otherwise, anticipate failure by their retarded workers; hence, they become more attentive to situations that reinforce this viewpoint. The following case will help illustrate this latter point.

Sam A nineteen-year-old student participating in a work-study program during the last half of his senior year of high school was employed as a general helper in a retail tire store. His responsibilities included washing windows, sweeping floors, cleaning restrooms, and assisting to mount tires in the shop. Sam had been employed for six months and all evaluations had been superior. One day Sam came to see his work-study supervisor, however, and announced that he had just been fired. He reported that he had completed all of his assigned jobs and had helped change the tires on five cars that morning. He said that the other employees had gone across the street on a break, so when he finished putting on the last tire, he lay down on a bench and was smoking a cigarette when the boss walked in and fired him for loafing.

The supervisor consulted with the employer and Sam got his job back, but his reemployment did not last long. The first firing incident produced feelings between Sam and his employer that were not conducive to a productive relationship. Although Sam had done his job, the fact that he was labeled as retarded no doubt contributed to his difficulties with his employer.

If the public were made more aware of the capabilities of a large majority of the retarded population and if appropriate educational experiences were provided for all retarded children and youth, we would see greater assimilation and acceptance of this special group into the community. A number of already existing programs are helping to meet this goal. The Special Olympics, sponsored by the Joseph P. Kennedy Foundation, is a nationwide endeavor that has generated great enthusiasm and a high degree of participation by local communities. It offers softball, basketball, track and field, volleyball, bowling, and similar activities geared to the varying ages and degrees of retardation of its participants. The Teenagers for the Retarded (TARS) have also assisted in a wide variety of programs. Scouting and camping are among the many pursuits which help to expand the horizons of children and youth at all levels of retardation. These are steps in the right direction, and it is hoped that eventually they and many similar projects will become even more widespread.

Nationwide programs

Summary

In this unit we have specifically discussed expectations for the various groups of children and youth presently designated as mentally retarded. The profoundly and severely retarded were viewed in terms of programming, appropriate placement and learning provisions based on present knowledge of their capabilities, but with further research indicated.

The moderately retarded and the mildly retarded were studied in relation to (1) physical and motor development, (2) speech and language development, (3) academic and vocational expectations, and (4) social and personality traits. Specific educational provisions for these populations were discussed, and general consideration was given to educational planning and methods, classroom setting and mainstreaming possibilities.

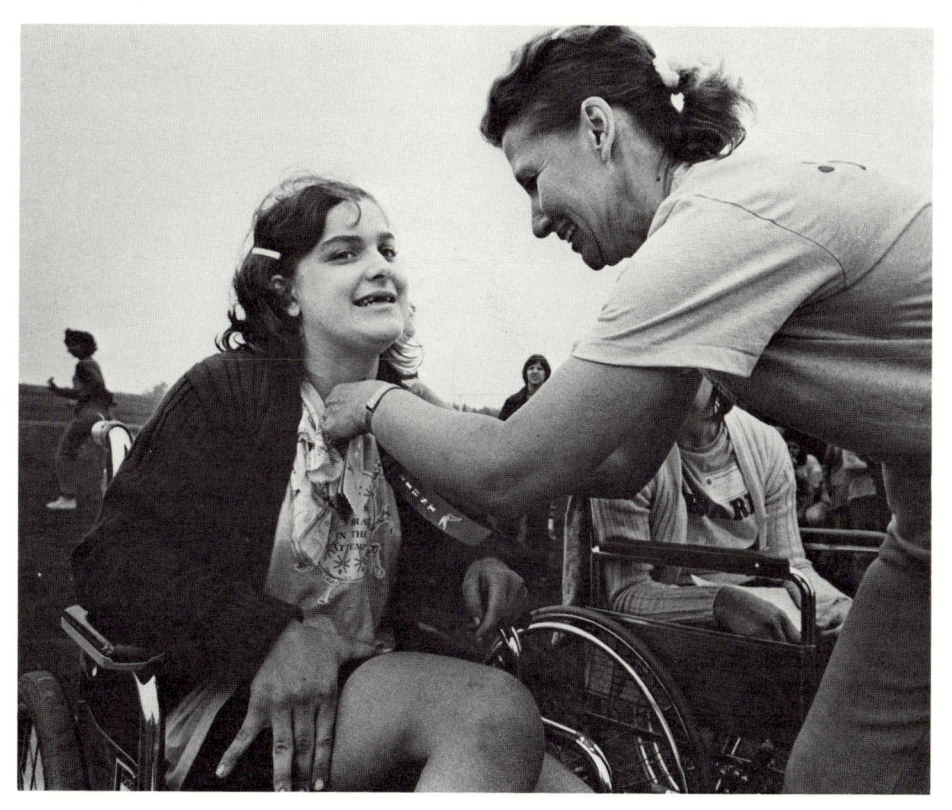

The big moment for Connie arrives. She is presented with the Gold Medal for her winning performance. Her coach, an occupational therapy aide, makes the presentation.

The need for family life education was stressed, and home and family attitudes in the presence of mental retardation were discussed. Community attitudes toward the mentally retarded were viewed, and the need for greater understanding of the potential of a large number of these youngsters was emphasized.

References and resources

Brolin, D. E. *Vocational Preparation of Retarded Citizens.* Columbus, Ohio: Charles E. Merrill, 1976.

Chaffin, J. D.; Spellman, C. R.; Regan, E. C.; and Davison, R. "Two Follow-up Studies of Former Educable Mentally Retarded Students from the Kansas Work-Study Project." *Exceptional Children,* Summer 1971, pp. 733–38.

De La Cruz, F. F.; and LaVeck, G. D., eds. *Human Sexuality and the Mentally Retarded.* New York: Brunner Mazel, 1973.

Educational Policies Commission. *The Purposes of Education in American Democracy.* Washington, D.C.: National Education Association, 1938.

Ehlers, W. H.; Krishef, C. H.; and Prothero, J. C. *An Introduction to Mental Retardation: A Programmed Text.* Columbus, Ohio: Charles E. Merrill, 1973.

Fraenkel, W. A. *Fundamentals in Organizing a Sheltered Workshop for the Mentally Retarded.* New York: National Association for Retarded Children, 1962.

Gellis, S. S., and Feingold, M. *Atlas of Mental Retardation Syndromes.* Washington, D.C.: U.S. Government Printing Office, 1968.

Grossman, J., ed. *Manual on Terminology and Classification in Mental Retardation.* Rev. ed. Washington, D.C.: American Association on Mental Deficiency, 1977.

Hutt, L., and Gibby, G. *The Mentally Retarded Child: Development, Education and Treatment.* 3rd ed. Boston: Allyn and Bacon, 1976.

Jones, R. L., ed. *Problems and Issues in the Education of Exceptional Children.* Boston: Houghton Mifflin, 1971.

Jones, R. L., ed. "Labels and Stigma in Special Education." *Exceptional Children,* March 1972, pp. 553–64.

Jones, R. L. "Student Views of Special Placement and Their Own Special Classes: A Clarification." *Exceptional Children,* September 1974, pp. 22–29.

Kirk, S. A. "Research in Education." In *Mental Retardation,* edited by H. A. Stevens and R. Heber. Chicago: U. of Chicago Press, 1964.

Kolstoe, O. P. *Teaching Educable Mentally Retarded Children.* 2d ed. New York: Holt, Rinehart and Winston, 1976.

Krishef, C. H. "State Laws on Marriage and Sterilization of the Mentally Retarded." *Mental Retardation,* June 1972, pp. 36–38.

Kugel, R. B.; Fedge, A.; Trembath, J.; and Hein, H. "An Analysis of Reasons for Institutionalizing Children with Mongolism." *Journal of Pediatrics* (1964): 64, 68–74.

Luckey, R. E., and Addison, M. R. "The Profoundly Retarded: A New Challenge for Public Education." *Education and Training of the Mentally Retarded.* Reston, Va: Council for Exceptional Children, 1974, pp. 123–30.

President's Panel on Mental Retardation. *The Six-Hour Retarded Child.* Washington, D.C.: U.S. Government Printing Office, 1970.

Shotwell, A. M., and Shipe, D. "Effect of Out-of-Home Care on the Intellectual and Social Development of Mongoloid Children." *American Journal of Deficiency* 68 (1964) pp. 693–99.

Smith, H. W., and Kennedy, W. A. "Effects of Three Educational Programs on Mentally Retarded Children." *Perceptual and Motor Skills,* 24 (1967), 174.

Wadsworth, H. G., and Wadsworth, J. B. "A Problem of Involvement with Parents of Mildly Retarded Children." *Family Coordinator* 20 (1971) 141–47.

U.S. Department of Health, Education and Welfare. *Information Memorandum.* Washington, D.C., August 26, 1976.

American Association for Education of the Severely and Profoundly Handicapped
1600 W. Armory Way
Garden View Suite
Seattle, Washington 98119

American Association on Mental Deficiency (AAMD)
5101 Wisconsin Avenue, NW
Washington, D.C. 20016

Association for the Help of Retarded Children
200 Park Avenue South
New York, New York 10003

Institute for the Study of Mental Retardation and Related Disabilities
University of Michigan
130 S. First Street
Ann Arbor, Michigan 48108

International Association for the Scientific Study of Mental Deficiency
5201 Connecticut Avenue
Washington, D.C. 20015

National Association for Retarded Citizens (NARC)
2709 Avenue E, East
P.O. Box #6109
Arlington, Texas 76011

National Association of Sheltered Workshops and Homebound Programs
1522 K Street, NW
Washington, D.C. 20005

President's Committee on Mental Retardation
Regional Office Building #3
7th and D Streets, SW
Washington, D.C. 20201

Social and Rehabilitation Services of the U.S. Department of Health, Education and Welfare
Administration Division of Developmental Disabilities
Washington, D.C. 20201

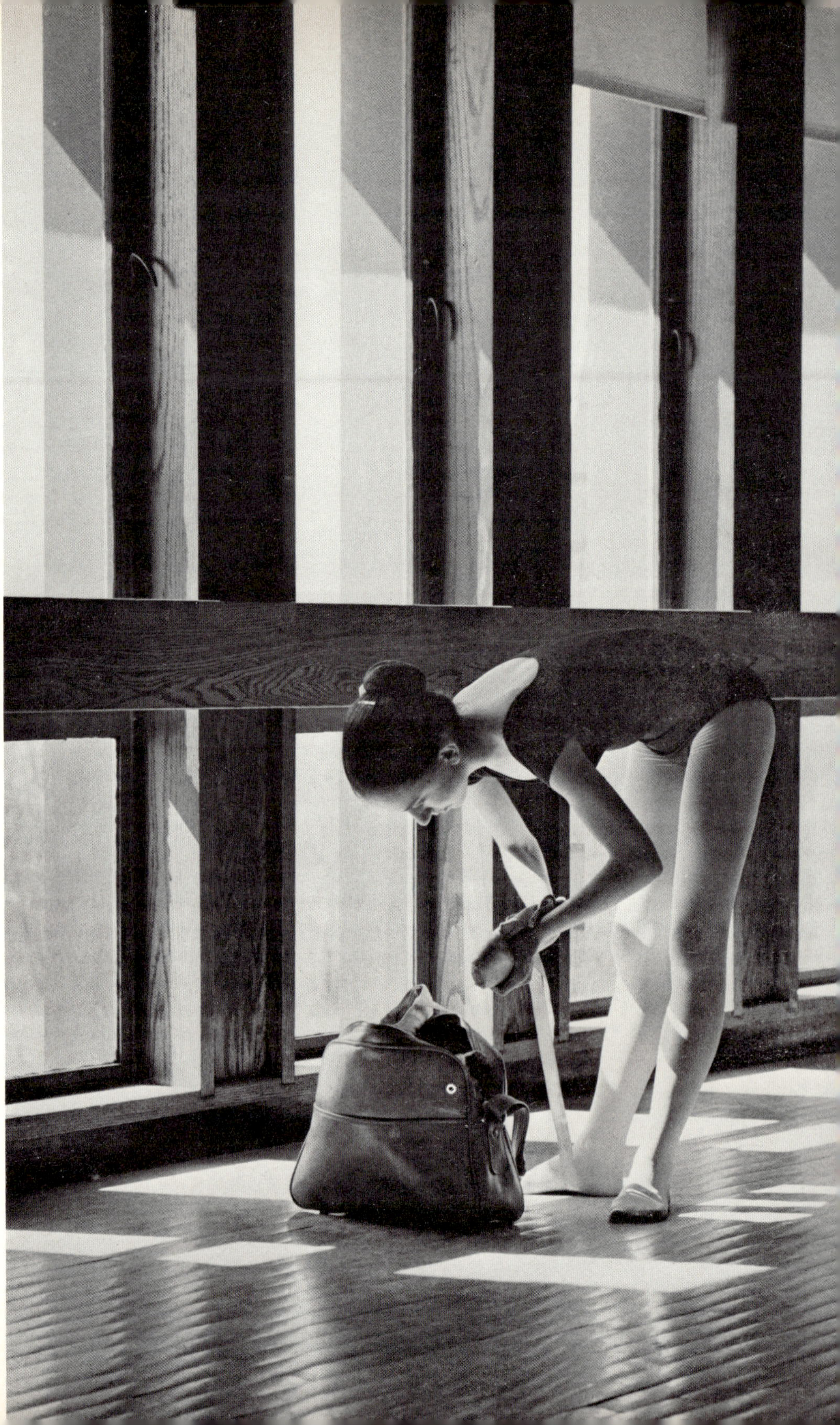

4 Gifted and talented children and youth   Henry R. Angelino

Historical perspectives
Present considerations
What is giftedness?
Frequency of giftedness
Characteristics of the gifted population · *Physical growth and development* · *Emotional aspects* · *Social aspects*
Variables in giftedness · *Male-female variance* · *Ethnic and socioeconomic factors*
Techniques for identifying the gifted · *Use of individualized IQ tests* · *Group assessment* · *Teacher observation as a technique* · *Identification of creativity* · *Current concerns*
Educational provisions · *Program planning and operation* · *Administrative procedures*
Motivation in the gifted · *The gifted underachiever*
School, community, and parents as catalysts · *Community resources and school responsibility* · *Teachers of the gifted* · *Parental participation and cooperation*
Summary

Student learning objectives

The student will:
1. become acquainted with the criteria for inclusion of youngsters into the "gifted and talented population"
2. have a broader knowledge and understanding of the characteristics found in the gifted population
3. be able to critically evaluate Terman's longitudinal study of the gifted
4. become familiar with the different procedures used to identify the gifted with respect to learning, motivation, creativity, and leadership
5. become acquainted with the societal and cultural attitudes towards the gifted (e.g., male/female, ethnic, socioeconomic considerations)
6. analyze a number of myths and misconceptions about the gifted
7. be able to identify the factors in planning an educational program for the gifted in a given community
8. learn the pros and cons of various administrative school procedures for serving gifted children and youth within the educational setting
9. become cognizant of the reasons for underachievement by the gifted and its implications for educators and parents
10. become informed about the responsibilities of various groups (parents, school, community) in nurturing the potential of the gifted and acting as facilitators of expanded services for them

One of the primary concerns of American education is to provide equal opportunity for all children to develop their maximum potential. Various learning atmospheres are required for the variety of exceptionalities found in children. To achieve this goal the field of special education was developed. The gifted, too, have been included in these programs over the years, although they have not always been accorded the kind of educational treatment necessary to fulfill their full potential.

Historically, the gifted and talented have made many significant and original contributions, including a number of techniques and types of equipment now being used in other areas of exceptionality. Our continuing need for inventors, scientists, artists, writers, performers, and political leaders requires that everyone be involved in encouraging the gifted to achieve to their maximum potential.

Whatever stance is taken on the best way to educate this group, educators are more and more concerned that the traditional curriculum and methods of instruction do not provide maximum growth and development for the gifted. This unit will focus on the various procedures that might be utilized to achieve this goal, and will point up an oft-forgotten fact: that those blessed with high ability are likely to be high in other dimensions, although there are exceptions. The main emphasis here will be on the methods of identification, the utilization of a variety of assessment instruments, and the development of programs tuned especially to fast learners and those with high creativity or special talents.

Historical perspectives

Concern for the education of gifted individuals dates far back in time. While planning his ideal social state in the fourth century B.C., Plato stressed the importance of discovering and educating the most able youths to become the future leaders of the state, speculating on ways of identifying these potentially able youth. Later the Romans, too, integrated some of Plato's ideas in their search for gifted individuals, although they were more concerned with developing leaders in politics and war.

Ancient Greek and Roman attitudes

But little systematic education for the gifted occurred until the latter part of the nineteenth century, when attention focused on them as a result of the publication of Galton's *Hereditary Genius* (1869). In 1891, Lombroso published his work on *The Man of Genius,* which purported to show (as Lombroso himself believed) that genius or intellectual brilliance is pathological. He assumed that certain physical characteristics such as short stature, emaciation, stammering, delayed development, and even left-handedness were all associated with the concept of genius. To him these were degenerate tendencies out of our primitive past. Because of Lombroso, genius and insanity came to be associated in a general way. Most nineteenth-century thought, however, centered on the philosophy that all human beings were created equal, and that any existing differences were present only because of training and other such environmental advantages.

Genius and insanity were thought to be associated

The advent of the Binet IQ tests in 1905 ushered in a long but fluctuating era of interest in intelligence. Binet's purpose was to devise an instrument that would separate the slow learners in French schools from the remainder of the group. A few years later this test was brought to the United States, where it was translated and modified somewhat to meet American interest in recording the wide variations found in a more heterogeneous society.

Then in the 1920s Terman and his associates began to investigate the concept of genius by going to the schools in California and identifying highly gifted children whose intelligence quotients (IQs) measured 140 and above. Thus began the most famous longitudinal study of highly gifted individuals ever attempted. Five volumes entitled *The Genetic Study of Genius* have already been published, with future publications to be released in the year 2015 (Burks, Jensen & Terman, 1930; Cox, 1926; Oden, 1968; Terman, 1925; Terman & Oden, 1947).

Famous longitudinal study

The current emphasis on the gifted, which followed the relative indifference of the 1930s and 1940s, may be traced to the advent of the cold war. With Sputnik in 1958, the Soviet Union suddenly forged ahead of America in the space race. Some interest was shown before Sputnik, but definitive action came only after the Russian launch. Thus it took a crisis to stimulate renewed interest in our gifted and talented

Interest in the gifted in the late 1950s

youngsters. Since then, some federal funds have been allocated to the states to promote programs for the brighter and more creative children in our schools.

In the past, gifted children in general, but those in the elementary schools in particular, have been sorely neglected. Specialized provisions and funds have been so limited that most of these children (with some notable exceptions, to be sure) have been denied any adequately organized and directed activities and learning situations. The usual result is that they are left mainly to themselves, with the occasional help of some parents, to develop their individual potential in their own way. Obviously, much wasted effort and frustration are involved in such activities.

Present considerations

Presently our main goals for these gifted individuals must involve:

Priority of concerns and goals

1. adequate and early identification
2. proper use of a variety of assessment procedures
3. challenging programs both in the schools and in the community at large
4. cooperative efforts between school personnel (administrators and teachers), parents, the gifted themselves, and an involved community
5. development of positive and humanisitic attitudes toward these able individuals by working toward dispelling the myths and fallacies that arose in the past and continue to be passed on to successive generations

In addition, professionals and lay public alike need to reassess their attitudes and values toward equal educational opportunities for all. Provision must be made for the whole range of variances in the population to achieve the betterment of everyone.

What is giftedness?

Expanded concept of giftedness

Many different definitions have been put forth in the attempt to identify this group of individuals. If we look at the broad conception of giftedness, we must include not only the academically gifted but the gifted in such other social endeavors as music, the arts, sports, mechanical skills, political and social leadership, and creativity. We can begin to identify and seek out children from all walks of life and all backgrounds to assure ourselves of having left no stone unturned in finding this small but potentially powerful social minority. Such a broad conception of giftedness, however, creates problems in our attempts to develop a common set of criteria for this exceptionality.

Definitions

Who are the gifted and talented? What is meant by these terms? The current definitions include those whose cognitive abilities place them in the upper 3 to 5 percent of the population (Marland, 1972). Broader definitions of the gifted, as noted above, include characteristics such as creativity, superior ability in the performing arts, and other socially desirable achievements (Martinson, 1973).

For the purposes of this unit, we propose to define the academically gifted as being in the upper 3 percent in measured general intelligence (IQ of 130 or above) as assessed by the popular individual assessment instruments. Included also must be those who are high in creative abilities and superior in special areas deemed desirable by the society.

Introducing Joanne—a high school student who is highly talented in the dance. This is her ballet class.

Gifted and talented children and youth

We have mentioned three major conceptions of giftedness:

1. superior cognitive ability
2. creativeness in thinking and production
3. superior talent in special areas

All of these conceptualizations of our most able and talented individuals do not receive equal amounts of recognition within our culture. It is a truism that each society rewards most lavishly the abilities or talents it prizes the most. High-ability individuals tend to enter those areas wherein the rewards—money, recognition, power—are the greatest. Currently, athletics and the performing arts are among the most rewarding areas.

Sidney Pressey (1955) has proposed several major factors as producing "precocious marked superiority" in certain fields of endeavor at certain periods of time. As examples, he compared precocious musicians of the eighteenth and nineteenth centuries with twentieth-century athletes. Pressey remarks that these individuals had certain experiences in common. Most of them had an early and favorable home environment with much parental encouragement, excellent instruction, many opportunities to practice their particular skills, stimulating interactions with famous people, and many successful experiences (Ammons & Ammons, 1962; MacKinnon, 1962).

Experiences that enhance giftedness

Frequency of giftedness

Depending on the cut-off score one is using, there will of course be considerable differences in the frequency of this trait. Also, any cut-off score *whatever* is of great significance, because if it is set either too high or too low, it could be quite self-defeating. The suggested cut-off of the upper 3 percent mentioned in our definition contains those whose IQ scores are above 130. This would exclude a number of persons who do not perform well on tests. If we were to use the top 15 to 20 percent (IQ about 115–120) as a cut-off point, we would be including a large proportion of those who could not compete in schools maintaining high academic standards. Thus we see that in itself the IQ score is an insufficient criterion, because the score does not measure motivation, creativity, athletic prowess, musical ability, and so forth.

IQ alone not sufficient

Conservative estimates place the number of gifted at somewhere between 1½ and 2 million children out of about 49 million recorded in the estimated total Autumn 1975 school enrollment (see Table 4-1) or approximately 3 to 5 percent of the school-age population (Burt, 1975; Marland, 1972; Martinson, 1973).

It should be remembered that the actual number of gifted school-age children identified within any community or area will depend upon the intellectual, educational, and cultural level of the given locale. The most neglected groups accordingly are the potentially gifted from the various minority and less advantaged groups who could provide a greater proportion of excellence of all kinds if sought out by means other than the conventional assessment instruments. Gifted children of every race,

Neglected or overlooked gifted youngsters

Table 4.1
Estimated school enrollment—Autumn 1975

Level of instruction	Total	Estimated number of gifted
Kindergarten–8th grade	33,800,000	1,014,000
9th–12th grade	15,500,000	465,000
	49,300,000	1,479,000

Source: Grant & Lind, 1976

ethnic group, and socioeconomic class could then be added to the existing pool of exceptional persons.

Continuous opportunity for realizing the potential of the gifted is dependent upon the combined efforts of the family, school, and community to encourage these individuals by providing adequate opportunities to expand their interests, curiosity, and motivation toward more and more knowledge. A genuine respect for and encouragement of excellence in intellectual spheres is just as necessary as it is in other spheres, such as athletics and the fine and practical arts. Here all three groups (family, school, and community) must assume this responsibility for the continued growth and development of these individuals with superior cognitive abilities.

Characteristics of the gifted population

Physical growth and development

In general, there is considerable agreement that in their physical characteristics the gifted show a considerably more favorable picture than the average for their age group. The longitudinal study by Terman and his associates demonstrates conclusively that his population had above-average physical development (Oden, 1968; Terman, 1925; Terman & Oden, 1959). In fact, at every age measured, they were as a group ahead of the developmental norms for the average within the same age group.

Above average in physical development

Gifted children mature earlier, a factor which may well be associated with differences in socioeconomic backgrounds rather than with giftedness itself. Frierson (1965) demonstrated that when socioeconomic status is controlled, the general health of the lower-status gifted child does not quite match that of the child from a more affluent family. However, the general population norms for height and weight increased from 1923 to 1954, which may account for some of the variations reported by Frierson (p. 85). When comparing gifted with nongifted children, it is of great importance to control for socioeconomic status. Most of Terman's population came from higher socioeconomic level families.

Baldwin conducted anthropometric (body) measurements on 594 children of Terman's gifted group with IQs ranging from 130 to 189 (Terman, 1925). Thirty-seven anthropometric measurements were taken of these children, all of whom were found to be superior in thirty-four of the thirty-seven measurements, including standing height, weight, and general physical development. Baldwin concludes that his investigation shows the gifted group, as a whole, to be physically superior to the comparison group. A follow-up study provides further evidence on the validity of the conclusions presented in the first volume of the series, while also providing other data not collected earlier (Burks, Jensen & Terman, 1930).

Excellent health through adulthood

Terman's follow-up study of his group indicates a continuance of good health into adult life. The respondents reported better-than-average health, with over 90 percent of the men and around 80 percent of the women so indicating. Oden's report (1968) on the forty-year follow-up of this group of gifted men and women mainly supports the earlier findings of a significantly lower mortality rate, excellent general physical health, satisfactory mental health, and a continuing wide range of political, social, and other leisure-time activities.

Health histories taken by Terman (1925) revealed some advanced general developments of the gifted:

1. greater weight at birth
2. earlier walking and talking
3. earlier pubescence
4. precocious dentition
5. better-than-average nutrition
6. greater height, weight, shoulder and hip width, and strength of grip
7. superior motor ability
8. less defective hearing and mouth breathing
9. less stuttering and other nervous symptoms

Emotional aspects

Myth of emotional instability dispelled

If and when the gifted suffer from emotional problems, they are not primarily due to some "built-in" emotional instability. Terman's data showed that his gifted sample as a group were no more emotionally unstable than the control group. In the follow-up studies, Terman and Oden present convincing evidence regarding the satisfactory mental health and adjustment of the gifted group (1947, 1959).

In a more recent report on the gifted group, Oden (1968) presents the results of a forty-year follow-up (see Table 4-2). Again the results indicate that the gifted are relatively free of serious maladjustment problems. Alcohol was considered a problem by a few subjects; only a total of twenty-two (fourteen men and eight women) were suicide cases. The incidence of crime and delinquency remained very low for the group. This information does help dispel the ill-founded belief that high intelligence is somehow tied in with some form of mental instability or peculiarity. It simply is not so—nature does not counterbalance in this way. However, some of the extremely gifted (those whose IQs run above 170) may have adjustment difficulties.

A recent study (Milgram & Milgram, 1976) looked at some personality characteristics of gifted Israeli children with respect to the above-mentioned myth that genius and psychological maladjustment are highly correlated. Two groups, a gifted

Table 4.2
Long-term emotional adjustment of gifted adults

	Percent Men	Percent Women
Satisfactory	69	64
Some difficulty	23	26
Serious difficulty	9	10
Serious difficulty with hospitalization, including deceased subjects who had been hospitalized for mental illness	3.2	4.3

Source: Adapted from Oden, 1968, pp. 8–9

(IQs from 140) and a nongifted group of boys and girls, were compared on a number of indices of personality adjustment. The results confirmed the researchers' predictions: the gifted group showed more positive self-concept, better self-motivation and a lower level of both general anxiety and test anxiety for both sexes.

Social aspects

In the sphere of social behavior, members of the gifted group are as successful as they are in their other activities. They have been reported to be readily accepted by others throughout their school years and later into adult life. In general, they are well-liked; they participate in a wide range of school activities, such as clubs, special-interest groups, various cultural events, and sports. On the other hand, whenever possible, they seem to prefer companions more like themselves in intellectual maturity and those slightly older than their own age group. Their interests tend toward more mature levels in reading and games, and toward the more individualized forms of recreation such as chess, tennis, swimming, and puzzlesolving.

Peer acceptance of the gifted

Terman's studies indicated that the group held twice as many leadership positions in both public schools and in college than the general school population. The follow-up studies of social adjustment as adults indicated a continuance of this favorable position. Oden (1968) reports that as adults the group continued to be involved in a wide range of interests and activities unrelated to their vocations. Besides pursuing a variety of hobbies and other leisure-time interests, they participated actively in the social, civic, cultural, and educational affairs of their communities. The highly gifted are *not* reclusive, introverted, or disinterested in their communities and society as a whole.

Diversity of interests throughout life

Variables in giftedness

Male-female variance

As far as it is possible to assess, no difference exists in the incidence of giftedness between the male and female population. In scholastic achievement, however, gifted boys as a group fail to achieve up to their maximum ability as well as girls do

Equal intellectual potential in both sexes

in the elementary and secondary school settings. But the boys who do less well in these grades do much better in college and in achievement in the outside or career world. However, these differences in career achievement in favor of males may even today be the result of cultural influences (that is, certain occupational fields were traditionally considered to be male pursuits—medicine, law, science).

Societal attitudes affect achievement

While there are admittedly some differences between the sexes in personality variables and in the differential socialization of the sexes, the fact is that females of very high achievement have not emerged in the numbers that might be expected. There is no reason, however, to assume that they lack the ability to achieve in all fields of endeavor. It is lack of encouragement and opportunity, rather than lack of ability, that has prevented women in the past from reaching high levels of professional attainment. The pressures on girls to conform to specific sex roles, and the resulting "fear of success" tend to prevent the majority of able females from realizing their potential. The usual stereotype of females that is still part of the belief systems of most male and female adults prevents many girls from developing their abilities to the maximum.

Crippling female stereotypes

Ethnic and socioeconomic factors

It is now well known that Terman's sample came from nearly all racial and ethnic groups represented in the cities he used (Terman & Oden, 1947). There was a wide disparity, however, in the proportional representation of these different groups.

Various minority racial and ethnic groups and/or lower socioeconomic groups have generally scored less well on traditional assessment tests. Because scientists have not been able to isolate or identify the interactive effects of heredity and environment, it becomes very difficult to assess the relative value of either one in determining the reasons for lowered performance on these tests by less acculturated children and youth. The youth population that is termed "societally neglected"—most often members of racial minorities or lower socioeconomic classes—will be discussed in depth in Unit 5.

Group and individual test performance

Group averages based on race, ethnicity or socioeconomic status can provide no basis for judging the intellectual capacity of any given individual. But it is clear that many potentially gifted youngsters in these groups do go unidentified as gifted. Unfavorable circumstances and experiences can account for differences in test-taking performance or other variables included in the definition of gifted potential.

Techniques for identifying the gifted

Early identification important

There is general agreement that the sooner a gifted youngster is identified, the earlier educators can prepare and provide appropriate educational experiences for his or her fullest development. Early identification then becomes the key in seeking out the wide range of potential available in our nation. However, identification is no simple matter for a large number of these gifted. Some are more easily identified because of their advanced performances in reading and vocabulary and their high degree of academic interest and curiosity. Others are not so easily identifiable through observation by either parents or teachers and, therefore, must be identified by more objective methods. We must always keep in mind that there is no single method that will identify the aspects of giftedness as previously defined. Identification is always best achieved by a combination of methods using the team approach.

Use of individualized IQ tests
The insufficiency of IQ scores for measuring other criteria in the definition of giftedness has been previously mentioned in this unit, yet measured intelligence still constitutes a part of the definition or classification of the gifted population. Included as one segment of a comprehensive assessment approach, the individual intelligence test can facilitate identification of superior cognitive ability. This identification should then in turn lead to implementation of appropriate school placement and needed educational procedures. *IQ as part of comprehensive assessment*

It is important to remember, however, that care must be taken to avoid excluding—on the basis of IQ test results (or current tests of ability and achievement)—those able youngsters whose ethnic and socioeconomic backgrounds have prevented them from developing their possible potential. In discussing the task of locating the "pool of talent" in Western Europe, Husen (1974) remarks that researchers' experiences in this effort have led them to realize that the groups tested are not to be thought of as strictly limited or fixed. Rather, the measurable assets of individuals are potentials that can be affected by changes in the environment in which the individuals develop. Continued schooling and better social conditions will most likely account for increased IQ scores.

Because of practical concerns for costs, in terms of both money and time, individual intelligence testing cannot be used extensively in the majority of school systems. A number of alternatives are used which can precede referral for individualized intelligence testing of students. *Drawbacks to individual testing*

Group assessment
Most school systems do employ periodic assessment of student potential and academic achievement as measured through group testing procedures. Such evaluations yield a mental maturity level (IQ) and grade-level performance respectively. However, results of group testing—by its necessary lack of individual interaction between the examiner and the large number of students simultaneously being tested—often prove less reliable in yielding true intellectual or achievement potential of individual students.

Group testing instruments can serve a useful purpose, however, when they are employed as *screening* devices. Students who receive IQ scores in the range of 115 to 120 on *group* mental ability tests should be referred for individual intelligence testing. Research indicates many of these youngsters will score within the gifted *Group assessment useful for screening*

range (130+) when tested individually on the Stanford-Binet or the Wechsler Scales. Similarly, students whose achievement test results indicate advanced grade levels in several academic subject areas of *two* or more years beyond present grade placement should be included in referral for further individualized assessment procedures.

Teacher observation as an assessment technique

If the identification of the gifted were left to the classroom teacher, it would be found that many of the truly gifted would go unrecognized and few would actually be selected. In the oft-quoted study by Pegnato and Birch (1959), it was shown that their sample of teachers missed more than half of the gifted pupils whom the researchers subsequently identified on the Binet intelligence test. Greater instructional emphasis within regular and special teacher-education training programs is still needed to prepare teachers to identify the gifted.

Teachers need training to identify gifted

To aid in more accurate identification, Renzulli and associates (1971, pp. 244–47) devised a rating scale. Four major areas are included for teacher (and/or parent) rating or appraisal. Higher scores obtained in these areas suggest that giftedness components are present when objectively evaluated in relation to comparatively lower ratings for more average students (see examples below):

1. Learning characteristics
   a. advanced vocabulary for age and grade level
   b. independent reading habits; prefers advanced level books
   c. quick mastery and recall of factual information
   d. grasp of underlying principles; ability to make valid generalizations
2. Motivational characteristics
   a. self-starting
   b. persistence in task completion
   c. striving for perfection
   d. bored with routine tasks
3. Creativity characteristics
   a. great curiosity about many things
   b. greater originality in problem solution and responses to ideas
   c. less concern with conformism
4. Leadership characteristics
   a. self-confidence and success with peers
   b. ready shouldering of responsibility
   c. easy adaptation to new situations and changes in routine

Identifying creativity

Difficulties in defining creativity

Past attempts at identifying creative behavior have produced considerable confusion among the creativity advocates. Among the reasons for this confusion are (1) that there is no generally accepted definition of creativity and (2) there is no standardized measure that would compete with the tests for assessing intelligence despite their shortcomings. The most widely accepted current definition, which sums up several already existing ones, was put forth by Torrance (1962, p. 218). He assumes creativity is a process that includes four basic elements: (1) sensing gaps and other deficiencies; (2) formulating ideas or hypotheses about them; (3) testing these hypotheses; and (4) communicating the results with the possibility of modifying and retesting the hypotheses.

Process or product? Yamamoto (1965) originally criticized creativity research because of the basic lack of agreement among researchers as to what the concept is

Opportunity for enrichment in this area of the performing arts is afforded by the school Joanne attends. Developing her potential involves serious study, and Joanne meets the challenge with hard work and rigorous practice.

that they are attempting to measure. Much of the disagreement has stemmed from attempts to define creativity in terms of either "process" or "product" (Golann, 1963; Arasteh & Arasteh, 1968). Overemphasis on either one or the other, however, tends to neglect the total concept. Emphasis on *process* includes fantasy, imagination, originality, curiosity, introspection. Emphasis on *product* involves a judgment concerning the amount of creativity demonstrated by the production of a work that expresses high talent and quality. But who will judge the production as creative? Despite the efforts of social scientists it is impossible to construct a totally reliable set of criteria to judge the merit of various creative products. While the product is more difficult to identify clearly (except perhaps in scientific productions), the real question here is the social criterion; that is, does the product constitute a significant contribution to society? Such a judgement necessarily is influenced by changes in societal concerns and values.

Who judges the product?

Generally, studies concerned with creativity in children have dealt primarily with the process, due to the difficulties in determining the extent of creativity expressed by the child in a production. In addition, researchers were much more concerned with identifying the potentially creative child for further enrichment of his or her potential. Whenever children's creative products have been assessed, they have been in terms either of age trends or as additional aspects of observations on children's behaviors (Arasteh & Arasteh, 1968).

Studies of creativity in children

Measures of creativity   A number of psychologists, including Getzels and Jackson (1962), Wallach and Kogan (1965), Torrance (1962), and Guilford (1965) have designed tests that purport to measure creativity. One of the leaders in developing tests is J. P. Guilford, who earlier (1959) had proposed the concept of *convergent* versus *divergent* thinking. The first type, which usually leads to one right or best answer, is more often included in current intelligence tests; the second type is represented in the mental processes that search in many directions to produce wide-ranging responses, and is more often involved in creative productions.

Convergent vs. divergent thinking

Torrance (1962), the originator of the Minnesota Tests of Creative Thinking, has included over twenty-five different kinds of tasks in his battery. A number of them are usable with young children. Torrance's have been the most commonly used tests for assessing creativity, since all of his tasks require the production of divergent solutions. (A revised manual for administering and scoring the tests was published in 1974.)

Tests of creative thinking

In their research with a gifted group, Getzels and Jackson (1962) utilized some of Guilford's ideas to develop their own measures of creativity. They devised five special tests: completing fables, making up problems, finding hidden shapes, word association, and listing uses of things. For example, in the test on uses of things, the subject is asked to give as many uses as he or she can imagine for some well-known object, such as a brick. The answers are then scored for both originality and the number of uses given.

Marsh (1964), in his re-analysis of the Getzels and Jackson data, believes that the conventional IQ is still the best single criterion for identifying creative persons. Burt (1975), too, takes issues with Getzels' and Jackson's assumptions that a test of creativity requires the answers to diverge and should measure the person's ability to deal inventively with either verbal or numerical symbols or with object-space relations. Burt suggests his concepts of *useful creativity* which he maintains "must involve the ability to deal, not only inventively but also rationally, with the material involved" (p. 296). (The recent criticism of the late Cyril Burt's findings on the nature of intelligence do not bear on his research cited here.)

Most researchers in this area take the view that *some* relationship between creativity and intelligence certainly does exist but that these factors are not mutually inclusive. Most researchers are also likely to believe that some minimum intelligence seems essential for most creative productions, but beyond that the relationship between the two constructs appears to be low. Guilford, however, who first proposed the hypothesis that the relationship between IQ and many types of creativity is low or moderate (1950), has since modified his earlier view and now believes that there is a place for creative thinking abilities and functions within the broad realm of intelligence, suggesting a closer relationship between the two concepts (1975).

Creativity-intelligence correlation

Despite controversy surrounding how best to define (process or product), and how best to test and measure, the concept of creativity is part of the current understanding of giftedness. As a term, it is probably the best synonym we can apply to describe those human behaviors we consider original, outstanding, and desirable. It is currently believed that we can enhance creative thinking by proper educational treatment (Guilford, 1975), and that we need not all be creative in similar ways.

Some additional light on how the creative process in children may be enhanced is provided by MacKinnon (1962) in his now-famous study of creative architects. He found that the home environments of these architects provided many opportunities and encouragements for them to develop their talents. Also, the mothers of these men played a very important role in providing continuous opportunities for their intellectual growth. Finally, the families themselves did not adhere strictly to the narrowly defined sex-role standards of the males as breadwinners and the females as homemakers. In fact, most of these mothers had interests and careers of their own.

Role of environment

No one can seriously doubt the importance of creative persons in any society, since this feature shows itself in so many different ways—in scientific discoveries, in musical, artistic, and literary products, in technological advancements and inventions, in athletics, and in social and political innovations. Creativity in any form must come from within the person, but then it is up to society to provide the climate in which all types of creative behavior may flourish. Fostering and nurturing any kind of intellectual and creative performance is the responsibility of everyone—parents, teachers, educators, psychologists, and all others who may come in contact with growing individuals.

Society's responsibility

Gifted and talented children and youth

Current concerns

The more subjective methods of selection, such as teacher nomination, school grades, and group test scores continue to be used by school personnel in locating gifted students. For various reasons these methods have remained popular despite their inaccuracy (Kirk, 1966) and their lack of objectivity (Marland, 1972). Marland contrasts in rank order the differences between the six most popular identification procedures being used in the United States with those recommended by a selected group of specialists in the area of the gifted.

Current and recommended selection procedure

Rank order now being used
(1) teacher observation
(2) group achievement tests
(3) group intelligence tests
(4) previously demonstrated accomplishments
(5) individual intelligence tests
(6) scores on tests of creativity

Rank order recommended by specialists
(1) individual intelligence tests
(2) previously demonstrated accomplishments
(3) teacher observation
(4) group achievement tests
(5) scores on creativity tests
(6) group intelligence tests

Additional indicators

Caution must be exercised in employing any single index or criterion as *the* most important determinant of the presence of giftedness. With more recent emphasis on the presence of creativity as an important variable in identification of the gifted, the rank order of the creativity dimension may increase in importance. Stanley (1973) has proposed also that high scores on aptitude and achievement tests designed for much older students can prove invaluable for completing identification of highly able but younger students.

Thus we can see that the process of ensuring proper procedures for identifying our gifted children and youth are incomplete. Current trends indicate more accuracy in identification procedures, however, through continued research and the efforts of classroom teachers to understand more fully the various components that comprise giftedness.

Educational provisions

Program planning and operation

Planning appropriate programs for the gifted requires a great deal of hard work and honest cooperation among the school personnel, the parents, the community, and also the student themselves. The gifted, individually and as a group, differ from other students in their ability to learn much faster and remember more. They also can use what they have learned to think more deeply.

Since gifted children and youth will represent a smaller proportion of the school population in the majority of American communities, certain aspects must be considered in any curriculum planning. The size and type of community, including its values, attitudes, general educational level, and kind of leadership (educational and/or community-based), all have an influence on how much effort it can or will make to provide programs for its gifted and talented individuals.

Community variables in curriculum planning

When planning an educational program for the gifted, the following factors should be included:

1. The administrative staff of the school should select an advisory committee of lay persons to join in the planning phases of the program.
2. The planned program must be interpreted to the local community.
3. A roster should be compiled of the various organizations, personnel agencies, and activities in the community that would aid the objectives of the program.
4. Plans should be made to utilize all existing community resources.
5. After the program is in operation, there should be both periodic evaluation and periodic reports to the community on the progress of the program.

Larger urban school systems, which sometimes contain a higher percentage of gifted and talented children, may be able to include in their programs certain experiences not feasible in rural or small town areas. In the latter locales it is even more important that all possible area resources be utilized. Qualified people can serve as an important resource and older gifted students who can contribute to the planning for their own educations should be encouraged to do so.

Rural and small town resources

Without careful planning of programs for the gifted—based on their needs and interests as well as their abilities and performances (Rice, 1970)—the gifted may remain unchallenged by educational and other experiences commensurate with their potential (Ogilvie, 1973). Typically, many gifted students do quite well in school even without much attention. Some educators and laypeople have the attitude that the gifted can take care of themselves; hence, special programs for developing their fullest potential are often overlooked.

Laissez-faire attitude toward the gifted

Due to their broad interests and thirst for knowledge, gifted children, as a whole, do involve themselves in many different types of activities. This could pose a problem for program planning unless those involved are aware of the wide range of interests that gifted and talented students possess.

Administrative procedures

Basically there are three major administrative procedures for educating the gifted: (1) acceleration, or "grade skipping"; (2) enrichment within the regular classroom setting; and (3) special, or ability, grouping. No single one of these procedures can be rated superior to the others without qualifications; individual differences among students within the gifted population are as great as those among any other group of humans, and the total person must be considered before applying any of these techniques.

Acceleration Educational acceleration refers to school services that allow a student to progress more rapidly than is usual for regular students. The youngster may complete his or her education in less time or at an earlier chronological age. There are several ways to accelerate the regular program (Khatena, 1976).

An increasing number of educators are advocating early admission to provide gifted and talented children with formal school experiences as early as possible. This form has been used primarily to permit able children to enter public schools at an earlier chronological age than the usual legal entering age. A child may be admitted to kindergarten or first grade after having been tested by a competent assessment specialist who can testify that he or she has the requisite mental age and social characteristics to assure success in the formal school program. Usually a mental age of six to eight months over the legal entrance age is sufficient.

Mental maturity and early entrance

The primary consideration in such cases is that the child has mentally matured more rapidly than the average child and will thus be able to meet the requirements for academic learning even though he or she does not meet the legal entrance age, which has been set at approximately five for kindergarten and six for the first grade. The research on early school entrance has shown favorable results for the great majority of these early entrants in terms of achievement in physical, social, and emotional growth and adjustment (Klausmeier & Ripple, 1962; Klausmeier, Goodwin & Ronda, 1968).

Other practices currently used in the public schools to achieve acceleration are the following:

1. unit plan: ungraded or multigraded classes
2. longer school year: summer programs in school and college
3. correspondence courses
4. skipping, or double promotion
5. extra subjects in high school and college
6. credit by examination in high school and college
7. college-level courses for high-school students
8. early entrance into college
9. independent study in high school and college
10. advanced placement
11. honors programs in college

Individual considerations

Significant considerations always arise when plans for acceleration are advanced. Individual student differences may show up in the special interests, motivation, needs, drive and goals of the gifted as well as in their academic competence. Acceleration must be viewed as an individual matter, with each student being assessed on his or her own merit. The amount of acceleration also depends upon individual considerations. Terman believed that a high degree of acceleration could be applied to the gifted (1925). Others caution against too much acceleration (Hildreth, 1966). A minimum of two years of acceleration up through high school for the most gifted has been applied with good success.

Enrichment As an educational procedure, *enrichment* refers to the introduction of extra provisions and experiences designed to make learning more meaningful and interesting. Enrichment is generally accomplished within the regular classroom and seems to be the least controversial of the three administrative procedures for educating the gifted. It is also the least costly and requires the least administrative atten-

The class is getting a lesson in art history. Joanne's schooling is in the educational mainstream, augmented by special instruction.

tion. The regular classroom teacher is the major source for enrichment activity, although in recent years he or she may have assistance from specialists with extra training in working with exceptional children (Burt, 1975; Love, 1972).

Enrichment experiences may be effected by providing a variety of additional activities, including independent study in the student's interests and hobbies. Time is allowed for greater *in-depth* (or *horizontal*) enrichment or more challenging above-grade-level (or *vertical*) enrichment. Extra time for creative expression and development of special abilities is also allotted. The classroom teacher—in cooperation with other school and community resource personnel—bears the responsibility of carrying out enrichment techniques, drawing the line between enrichment and just plain busy work. A great deal of knowledge, understanding, and ingenuity is required to ensure the success of this technique. Curriculum differentiation involves the use of a variety of materials and in-depth and advanced-level experiences. Enrichment, which provides for the adjustment of instructional methods and materials to fit the needs and abilities of each student, can be and has been used successfully by competent teachers to educate their gifted pupils.

Special grouping In special grouping, individuals of similar, or homogeneous, ability and special interests are brought together for greater academic progress and development of special talents. There are many who believe that homogeneous grouping is the best way to adapt to the academic needs of the gifted and develop their talents. Many questions remain as to the efficacy of this procedure, which has generated much heated controversy. Some maintain that merely narrowing the ability range in the elementary classroom on the basis of some general ability measure without a well-planned program in both content and method will produce little positive change in the academic achievement of the pupils (Goldberg et al., 1966). In a number of British studies on the topic of ability grouping, the results also have been controversial and unclear (Bridges, 1975; Daniels, 1961).

Tracking, or multiple tracking, in which students of the same grade level are placed in a number (usually three) of different tracks is another ability-grouping technique. Rapid learners, regular or average learners, and slow learners are respectively grouped in classes or programs with different expectations and demands. Tracking techniques involve many factors and potential problems, including the following: (1) teaching procedures must allow for maximum learning to take place for *every* student, regardless of the track placement; (2) student track assignments must not remain intact once the selection is made; rather, constant evaluation of student progress is needed; and (3) student feelings and emotions stemming from being labeled according to the track into which he/she is placed must be considered. The "self-fulfilling prophecy" is a danger in the track system. Attitudes of both students and faculty as to "who is who" in each track can be very destructive, both academically and psychologically.

Further research is clearly indicated concerning ability grouping, both from the standpoint of its overall desirability and its effects upon academic achievement. To date there is no educational grouping procedure which unequivocally proves its superiority in providing maximum educational opportunities for *all,* including the nurturing and developing of gifted children and youth.

Motivation in the gifted

Motivation is that which prompts people to action. Many educators and psychologists believe that motivation serves as one of the most important variables determining the learning process. Two types of motivation are delineated in psychological literature, *intrinsic* and *extrinsic.* Intrinsic motivation is directed from within the individual. It is viewed by Maslow (1970) as a personality aspect of people who live creative, effective lives, aware of their own abilities and making good use of them. He characterizes these individuals as self-actualizing. Performance and actions accomplished because of the various external rewards involved (praise by others, advantages to be gained in the form of money, other rewards) are seen as reflecting extrinsic motivation. Both types of motivation are part of the lives of all individuals and each varies in the degree to which it affects behavior. Here we will consider motivational aspects as they are particularly pertinent to the gifted population.

Intrinsic vs. extrinsic motivation

It is well known that deliberate reinforcement of any behavior strengthens that behavior. The gifted achiever, like all others, will react favorably to such extrinsic reinforcers as peer and adult recognition, good grades, getting on the honor roll and in honor societies, and successful competition for scholarships. Prizes of books and equipment are important, as is special recognition at school assemblies and banquets and in newspaper reports.

The gifted underachiever

What of the gifted underachiever? Many of the gifted tend to perform well below their singular capacities, resulting in frustrations and failures in self-fulfillment (Angelino, 1960). Terman (1925) early expressed concern with the lack of real challenge for the gifted, which results in lowered motivation. This in turn is reflected in poor study habits, superficial work, and carelessness that can affect later scholastic achievement. Deliberate attempts at some type of external reinforcer can be helpful to stimulate the gifted underachiever, who will react to some of the same types of reinforcement as will the gifted achiever.

Challenging the gifted underachiever

Failure to identify gifted underachievers also can result in their becoming bored with routine classroom work, contributing to a high dropout rate in high school (Ming, 1973). Gifted underachievers and school leavers are examples of talent wastage that, with proper identification and adequate programming, could be reduced greatly or eliminated.

Talent wastage and gifted dropouts

Hirsch and Keniston (1970) report that of the entire group of freshmen entering four-year colleges in America, fewer than half finally graduated from the school they entered. Some did eventually graduate from other colleges, but the dropout rate was still extremely high. A number of other studies (Ming, 1973; Terman & Oden, 1959; Trent & Medsku, 1968) report similar bleak studies of gifted and talented individuals who fail to complete high school or college, with one study reporting that 55 percent of the gifted were working below their mental abilities and 18 percent of high-school dropouts were gifted students.

Some of the social-psychological factors involved in the college dropout rate among talented students (Hirsch & Keniston, 1970) could also be applied to the high-school dropout rate. Of forty college undergraduates studied who were on the verge of dropping out, thirty-one did leave their schools. All were in good academic standing and none left for financial reasons. The main reasons cited were family relationships and the students' own conflicts and a transfer of negative feelings to college, which they viewed as having many of the bad features of their families.

While personality factors are significant in failure to achieve, economic, familial, and social factors also play significant roles in failure to continue with educational endeavors. Socioeconomic status of the family, with its attendant value system, is very influential. Parental encouragement is a major factor in facilitating learning efforts and achievement (Gold, 1965; Terman & Oden, 1947; Trent & Medsku, 1968). The following case illustrates this point:

Susan S. Sue is a twenty-eight-year-old professor of English at a midwestern university. Her parents separated when she was four months old and her mother assumed sole responsibility for her child's upbringing. Her mother instilled a love for learning in Sue, so that when Sue entered formal schooling she was already reading and writing simple sentences.

In the fourth grade Sue came under the tutelage of a dedicated and interested teacher who became a significant factor in her education. Sue's measured IQ was found to be over 170 and she was eligible for double promotion. Her mother decided against her advancement, however, preferring that Sue remain with her peers. Assessing Sue's potential, her teacher encouraged Sue's academic development by permitting her much freedom and independence in pursuing her schoolwork, while requiring the high academic standards of which Sue was capable. She additionally was allowed the opportunity to work with the sixth-grade teachers in two of her favorite subjects, English and science. Her mother provided many other incentives that gave Sue an increasing love for learning, and Sue came to see school and education as a challenging and enjoyable pursuit. She also was very popular with her peers and was readily chosen as a teammate or partner for most activities. Sue's early love for learning has never diminished, and in her current profession she pursues a teaching and research career and conducts numerous workshops in helping teachers become more proficient in their careers.

In contrast to Sue's motivating experiences and influence, many gifted children and youth are not detected very early. In addition to careful procedures for identifying the gifted and the provision of adequate and broadened curricula to meet their needs, increased use of competent school guidance and counseling services is recommended in conjunction with supportive services from other school personnel, parents, and the community. When these services are lacking, the risks of disinterest, unfulfilled potential and dropping out are much higher.

A total program for the gifted

School, community, and parents as catalysts

The multidisciplinary approach to identification and determination of needs has been emphasized in previous units of this book. In order to carry out the responsibility of making it possible for all children—including the gifted—to develop into productive adults, many individuals have to follow up and serve as catalysts. They must provide the right atmosphere for maximum learning and achievement to take place.

Community resources and school responsibility

Community resources must include all those individuals who can contribute to the school's gifted programs, as well as the various agencies and civic organizations that can provide input and resources for the education and training of the gifted. The key in effective school-community relations is the school superintendent, who must capitalize on his or her knowledge of the community and administrative skills to draw together and organize appropriate programs, projects, and interests to benefit the gifted. The local school principal—whose function it is to see that daily school operations are carried out effectively—greatly influences procedures for teaching and educating the gifted. Without leadership at this level of administration, teachers find it difficult to effect the kinds of programs needed for gifted students in the individual schools (Bridges, 1975).

School superintendent and principal are the key people

Guidance and counseling services   As further supportive and resource personnel within the school and/or community, guidance and counseling services are of particular significance to the gifted. Help and advice on academic potential or personal problems can lead to greater self-understanding. Educational needs may involve the development of efficient study habits and learning techniques, as well as general efficiency in all academic or talent endeavors. Personal guidance can take the form of assistance in dealing with any perceived problems about pressure to achieve or peer acceptance. Gowan and Demos (1964) divide the counselor's role into three areas of interaction: (1) with the gifted individual, (2) with teachers of the gifted, and (3) with parents of the gifted. The counselor's responsibility includes participation in the identification process, assistance in ensuring that needed educational experiences are provided, assistance with vocational guidance, and help with any personal problems (parent, teacher, student) that require resolution in order to maximize the potential of the gifted student.

Teachers of the gifted

At the classroom level it is the teacher who must set a tone that will encourage learning and favorably affect student attitudes, self-confidence, creativity, and realization of talent. Unfortunately, there is very little objectively derived and current information regarding the preparation of teachers for the gifted. With some notable exceptions, teacher education for the gifted is extremely limited compared to the training of persons to teach other exceptional children. Very recently, the availability of some federal monies has impelled a number of institutions and state departments of education to participate in programs for the gifted, including additional courses (especially at the graduate level) to train teachers in this special field. Clearly, many training opportunities need to be provided for those interested in teaching gifted and talented youngsters.

A comparison of American programs with Soviet teacher preparation for educating mathematically talented students will illustrate some of the responsibilities our educators face in this area. Vogeli, in describing the Soviet training program for secondary school teachers of computer programming for the mathematically talented, says "the program . . . is both intensive and of high mathematical quality. Its duration is five years, in contrast to four years for programs without dual specialization" (1968, p. 40). Soviet teachers receive a total of 4,388 hours of classroom and laboratory instruction as contrasted to graduates of our four-year colleges, who receive only about 2,000 hours of classroom and laboratory work. The differences are obvious.

Gold (1965) proposed these guidelines for teachers who plan to work with the gifted:

1. proper screening and selection of candidates
2. good general preparation for teaching
3. both depth and breadth in scholastic training
4. graduate study with professional specialization
5. in-service training on the job
6. maturity

What are effective teachers of the gifted like? Bishop (1968) studied selected characteristics of successful high school teachers as identified by gifted, high-achieving students and compared them with teachers who were not so identified. He reported no differences between his two groups on such variables as sex, marital status, type of educational experience, highest degree held, or participation in professional organizations. The significant differences that appeared between the two groups indicated strongly that those teachers whom the students identified as successful were those whom they identified as intellectually superior, more motivated to high achievement, more favorable toward students, liked to teach gifted students best, more stimulating and imaginative in the classroom and definitely inclined toward personal intellectual pursuits.

In an earlier study, Brandwein (1953) asked gifted science students which teacher characteristics they thought were significant in stimulating students to enter science. He reported that of the eighty-two teachers chosen as the most stimulating teachers: more than 90 percent had a master's degree in science, more than half had taught in college at some time, more than 90 percent had published at least one article in science or in education, all but one had been an officer in a local or

Teacher as role model

Joanne's academic program must not suffer because of her special talent. Here she confers with one of her teachers about a project.

national teacher organization, and all had participated in extracurricular activities in music, athletics or publications, as well as intracurricular pursuits in their own fields. In addition, these same teachers held up firm standards of scholarship to their students, thus being the type of model (exemplars) that would stimulate and gain the respect of these young people.

While we do not yet know what specific features of teacher behavior and psychological make-up are essential for being a successful teacher of the gifted, Newland (1976) suggests they ought to be in the top 10 percent of the ability distribution. In addition, they must be able to relate effectively to their students emotionally and socially. Particularly, they must be free from feeling threatened by these rapid learners. Despite lack of research concerning selection and training, there is general agreement that adequate and viable programs for training competent teachers for the gifted are needed at all levels (Gallagher, 1975).

Can only a gifted teacher do well with a gifted child?

Parental participation and cooperation

As previously noted from research, parents serve as the most influential factor in the process of motivating and educating the gifted (Terman, 1925; Terman & Oden, 1947, 1959). Many may find themselves trying to cope with a child who seems extremely active and curious, and who often frustrates them (Grost, 1970). They are no less apt to vary than their children and often they need consideration and counseling to help them rear their gifted youngster (Bridges, 1975; Rolands, 1974). Caution must be exercised, particularly to avoid applying any pressure that would be counterproductive to the intrinsic motivation that should be nurtured. A gifted child should not be expected to excel in all endeavors, although maximum potential should be encouraged. Parents are equally important in helping their gifted youngsters maintain a balanced life in terms of time devoted to academic study, recreational activities, and varied interests.

Parental encouragement, not pressure

Teachers and other interested professionals can advise parents of certain indices or signs that can be used to identify giftedness in their children. These include characteristics we noted earlier in this unit (Renzulli, 1971): the gifted child demonstrates inordinate curiosity, shows intellectual interest in a great variety of things; learns more rapidly and easily, has a greater range of interests and hobbies, has a creative imagination, likes puzzles and other complicated games, and in general, shows advanced progress, including special talents in relation to his or her average peers or siblings. Such potential will be less likely to flourish, however, without nurturance and interest from the parents.

The many aspects of parenting a gifted child go beyond the scope of this unit, but it is necessary that parents receive assurance, encouragement, and help from professionals who know and understand gifted children. Through such cooperation parents can more successfully provide appropriate motivational support, extra freedom for the child in developing potentials without pressure, and the amount of attention needed for the total development of the gifted individual.

Summary

We have seen that this population of children and youth certainly is not "handicapped," in terms of possessing the various disabilities referred to in the introductory unit, or to be discussed in subsequent units (such as hearing, visual, or physical disabilities). However, the gifted *do* fall under the definition of exceptionality because they exhibit substantial variance from the average in intelligence, creativity, or talent. Thus they are in need of special services to realize their unique potentials.

The discussion of the nature of giftedness and the characteristics of the gifted was couched in terms of physical growth and development, emotional aspects, and social characteristics. Additionally, techniques for identification of the gifted were explained and information concerning assessment of the various dimensions of giftedness was provided.

Considerable emphasis was placed on educational planning and provisions for this special group. The psychological components involved in educating gifted children (e.g., motivational aspects) were stressed, as were the roles of the school, community, teachers, and parents in fulfilling the needs of our gifted population.

References and resources

Ammons, R. B., and Ammons, C. H. "How to Foster Genius: McCurdy Extended." *Proceedings of the Montana Academy of Sciences* 21 (1962): 138–44.

Angelino, H. R. "Characteristics of Superior and Talented Youth." In *Working with Superior Students: Theories and Practices,* edited by B. Shertzer, pp. 90–104. Chicago: Science Research Associates, 1960.

Arasteh, A. R., and Arasteh, J. D. *An Interpretative Account of Creativity in Childhood, Adolescence, and Adulthood. Creativity in the Life Cycle.* Vol. 2. Leiden, Netherlands: E. J. Brill, 1968.

Bishop, W. "Successful Teachers of the Gifted." *Exceptional Children* 34 (1968): 317–25.

Brandwein, P. F. *The Gifted Student as a Future Scientist.* New York: Harcourt, Brace, 1955.

Bridges, S. A. *Gifted Children and the Millfield Experiment.* London: Pitman Publishing, 1975.

Burks, B. S., Jensen, D. W., and Terman, L. M. *The Promise of Youth: Follow-up Studies of a Thousand Gifted Children. Genetic Studies of Genius.* Vol. 3. Stanford, Calif.: Stanford University Press, 1930.

Burt, C. "Critical Notice: Creativity and Intelligence by J. W. Getzels and P. W. Jackson." *British Journal of Educational Psychology 32* (1962): 292–98.

Burt, C. *The Gifted Child.* New York: Wiley, 1975.

Cattell, R. B., and Butcher, J. J. *The Prediction of Achievement and Creativity.* Indianapolis: Bobbs Merrill, 1968.

Cox, C. M. *The Early Mental Traits of Three Hundred Geniuses. Genetic Studies of Genius.* Vol. 2. Stanford, Calif.: Stanford University Press, 1926.

Cronbach, L. J. "Intelligence? Creativity? A Parsimonious Reinterpretation of the Wallach-Kogan Data." *American Educational Research Journal* 5 (1968): 491–511.

Daniels, J. C. "The Effects of Streaming in the Primary School: I. What Teachers Believe." *British Journal of Educational Psychology* 31 (1961): 69–78.

Frierson, E. C. "Upper and Lower Status Gifted Children: A Study of Differences." *Exceptional Children* 32 (1965): 83–90.
Gallagher, J. J. *Teaching the Gifted Child.* 2nd ed. Boston: Allyn and Bacon, 1975.
Galton, F. *Hereditary Genius.* London: Macmillan, 1869.
Getzels, J. W., and Jackson, P. W. *Creativity and Intelligence: Exploration with Gifted Students.* New York: Wiley, 1962.
Golann, E. "Psychological Study of Creativity." *Psychological Bulletin* 60 (1963): 548–65.
Gold, M. J. *Education of the Intellectually Gifted.* Columbus, Ohio: Merrill, 1965.
Goldberg, M., Passow, A., and Justman, J. *The Effects of Ability Grouping.* New York: Teachers College Press, Columbia University, 1966.
Gowan, J. C., and Demos, G. D. *The Education and Guidance of the Ablest.* Springfield, Ill.: Charles C Thomas, 1964.
Grant, W. V., and Lind, C. G., eds. *Digest of Educational Statistics,* 1975 ed. National Center for Educational Statistics. Washington, D.C.: HEW, 1976.
Grost, A. *Genius in Residence.* Englewood Cliffs, N.J.: Prentice-Hall, 1970.
Guilford, J. P. "Creativity." *American Psychologist* 5 (1950): 444–54.
Guilford, J. P. "Three Faces of Intellect." *American Psychologist* (September, 1959): 470–73.
Guilford, J. P. "Varieties of Creative Giftedness, Their Measurement and Development." *Gifted Child Quarterly* 19 (1975): 107–20.
Hildreth, G. H. *Introduction to the Gifted.* New York: McGraw-Hill, 1966.
Hirsch, S. J., and Keniston, K. "Psychosocial Issues in Talented College Dropouts." *Psychiatry* 33 (1970): 1–20.
Husen, T. *Talent, Equality and Meritocracy: Availability and Utilization of Talent.* The Hague: Martinus Nijhoff, 1974.
Khatena, J. "Educating the Gifted Child: Challenge and Response in the U.S.A." *Gifted Child Quarterly* 20 (1976): 76–90.
Kirk, W. D. "A Tentative Screening Procedure for Selecting Bright and Slow Children in Kindergarten." *Exceptional Children* 33 (1966): 235–41.
Klausmeier, H. J., and Ripple, R. E. "Effects of Accelerating Bright Older Pupils from Second to Fourth Grade." *Journal of Educational Psychology* 53 (1962): 93–100.
Klausmeier, H. J.; Goodwin, M. L.; and Ronda, T. "Effects of Accelerating Bright, Older Elementary Pupils: A Second Follow-up." *Journal of Educational Psychology* 59 (1968): 53–9.
Lombroso, C. *The Man of Genius.* London: Walter Scott, 1891.
Love, D. *Educating Exceptional Children in Regular Classrooms.* Springfield, Ill.: Charles C Thomas, 1972.
MacKinnon, D. "The Nature and Nurture of Creative Talent." *American Psychologist* 17 (1962): 484–95.
Marland, S. P. *Education of the Gifted and Talented.* Washington, D.C.: U.S. Office of Education, 1972.
Marsh, R. W. "A Statistical Re-analysis of Getzels' and Jackson's Data." *British Journal of Educational Psychology* 34 (1964): 91–3.
Martinson, R. A. "Children with Superior Cognitive Abilities." In *Exceptional Children in the Schools,* edited by L. Dunn, pp. 191–244. 2nd ed. New York: Holt, Rinehart and Winston, 1973.
Maslow, A. H. *Motivation and Personality.* 2nd ed. New York: Harper and Row, 1970.

Milgram, R. M., and Milgram, N. A. "Personality Characteristics of Gifted Israeli Children." *Journal of Genetic Psychology* 129 (1976): 185–94.
Ming, R. W., and Gould, E. N. "Meeting the Needs of the Gifted." *Education Digest* 38 (1973): 34–5.
Newland, T. E. *The Gifted in Socioeducational Perspective.* Englewood Cliffs, N.J.: Prentice-Hall, 1976.
Oden, M. H. "The Fulfillment of Promise: Forty-Year Follow-Up of the Terman Gifted Group." *Genetic Psychology Monographs* 77 (1968): 3–93.
Ogilvie, E. *Gifted Children in Primary Schools.* London: Macmillan, 1973.
Pegnata, C. W., and Birch, J. W. "Locating Gifted Children in Junior High Schools: A Comparison of Methods." *Exceptional Children* 25 (1959): 200–304.
Pressey, S. L. "Concerning the Nature and Nurture of Genius." *Scientific Monthly* 8 (1955): 123–9.
Renzulli, J. S.; Hartman, R. K.; and Callahan, C. M. "Teacher Identification of Superior Students." *Exceptional Children* 38 (1971): 211–14, 243–48.
Rice, J. *The Gifted: Developing Total Talent.* Springfield, Ill.: Charles C Thomas, 1970.
Rolands, P. *Gifted Children and Their Problems.* London: J. M. Dent and Sons, 1974.
Stanley, J. C. "Accelerating the Educational Progress of the Intellectually Gifted Youth." *Educational Psychologist* 10 (1973): 113–46.
Terman, L. M. *Mental and Physical Traits of a Thousand Gifted Children. Genetic Studies of Genius.* Vol. 1. Stanford, Calif.: Stanford University Press, 1925.
Terman, L. M., and Oden, M. H. *The Gifted Child Grows Up: Twenty-Five Years' Follow-up of a Superior Group. Genetic Studies of Genius.* Vol. 4. Stanford, Calif.: Stanford University Press, 1947.
Terman, L. M., and Oden, M. H. *The Gifted Group at Midlife: Thirty-Five Years' Follow-up of the Superior Child. Genetic Studies of Genius.* Vol. 5. Stanford, Calif.: Stanford University Press, 1959.
Torrance, E. P. *Guiding Creative Talent.* Englewood Cliffs, N.J.: Prentice-Hall, 1962.
Torrance, E. P. *Torrance Tests of Creative Thinking: Norms and Manual.* Lexington, Mass.: 1974.
Trent, J. W., and Medsku, L. L. *Beyond High School: A Psychosociological Study of 10,000 High School Graduates.* San Francisco, Calif.: Jossey-Bass, 1968.
Vogeli, B. R. *Soviet Secondary Schools for the Mathematically Talented.* Washington, D.C.: National Council of Teachers of Mathematics, 1968.
Wallach, M. A., and Kogan, N. *Modes of Thinking in Young Children.* New York: Holt, Rinehart, and Winston, 1965.
Wallach, M. A., and Wing, C. W. J. *The Talented Student: A Validation of the Creative-Intelligence Distinction.* New York: Holt, Rinehart and Winston, 1969.
Yamamoto, K. "Creativity—A Blind Man's Report on the Elephant." *Journal of Counseling Psychology* 12 (1965): 428–34.

American Association for Gifted Children
15 Gramercy Park
New York, New York 10003

National Association for Gifted Children
8080 Spring Valley Drive
Cincinnati, Ohio 45236

2
Educational exceptionality

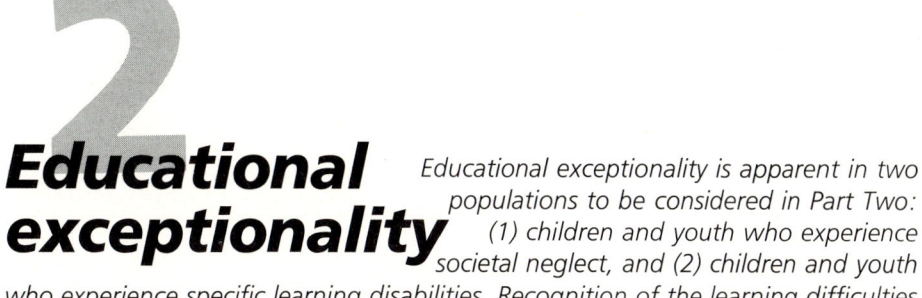

Educational exceptionality is apparent in two populations to be considered in Part Two: (1) children and youth who experience societal neglect, and (2) children and youth who experience specific learning disabilities. Recognition of the learning difficulties encountered by these two populations is among the most recent concerns of dedicated educators and other professionals.

Many of these boys and girls are known to be misclassified in terms of learning potential. Thus they experience frustration when the demands of educational procedures are not in accordance with their specific needs. Their limitations have too often been emphasized without consideration of the reasons for their particular learning problems. And too often this lack of understanding has been matched by a lack of remediation procedures for their respective educational difficulties. Our purposes in this section of the text are to provide a more thorough background for examining these two exceptional populations, to point up their educational problems, and to explore the intervention strategies that can be used to help them.

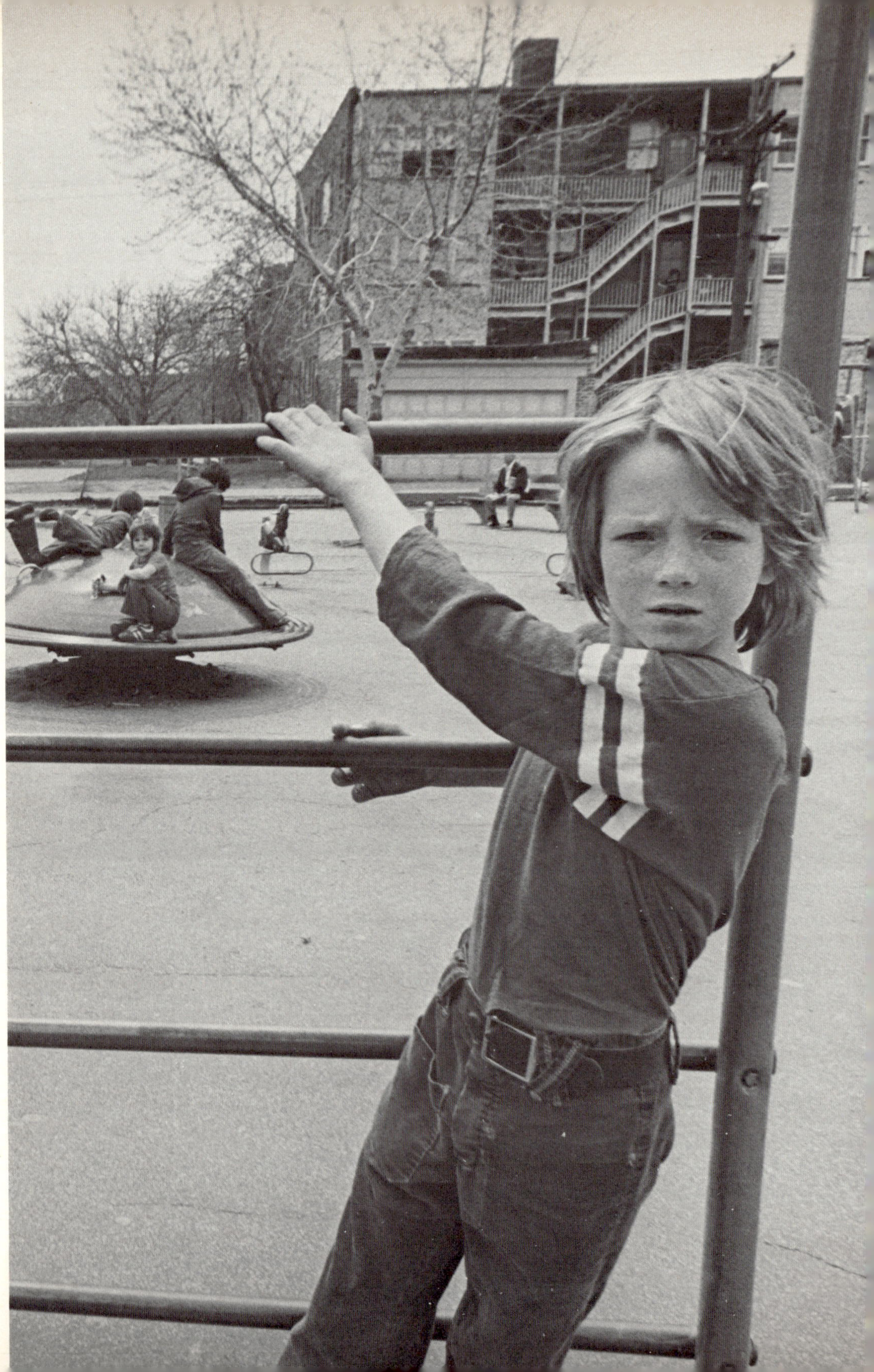

5 Societally neglected children and youth   B. Marian Swanson

Who are the societally neglected?
Populations facing societal neglect · Specific racial and ethnic minorities · Migrant laborers · Isolated rural poor · Inner-city ghetto dwellers
The presence of poverty · Hierarchy of human needs as related to poverty · Poverty and malnutrition · Poverty and inadequate housing conditions · Poverty and the family unit · Assessment of feelings of self-esteem
Language of the societally neglected · Elaborated and restricted language · Bilingualism and dialect · Reading difficulties
Intervention strategies · Compensatory educational provisions · Language provisions · Health and nutritional provisions · Other developmental and instructional provisions
Summary

Student learning objectives
The student will:
1. become acquainted with a child and youth population who experience societal conditions that constitute a handicap to realizing their potential
2. be able to define "societally neglected"
3. be able to describe the specific societal conditions that contribute to lower attainment in education, career, and social life
4. learn the concept of a hierarchy of human needs
5. recognize that there is a relationship between such conditions and the personality and psychological makeup of an individual

Societally neglected children and youth

Student learning objectives

The student will:
6. examine and analyze the impact of poverty on nutritional status, housing conditions, the family unit, and language factors
7. learn about the effects of poverty on self-motivation in this population, including the concept of locus of control
8. become aware of the components of elaborated and restricted language patterns and their differences
9. become acquainted with some of the intervention strategies that have been employed to fulfill more adequately the needs of societally neglected children and youth and to contribute to their capabilities for a constructive life

This unit deals with varied societal aspects faced by certain children and youth which prevent or make more difficult their attempt to realize their potential in our current educational, vocational, and social systems. Among our primary concerns will be those youngsters who are most frequently represented in the statistics regarding school dropouts. We will examine the circumstances that surround such failure to achieve. We will also examine the various conditions that can diminish or extinguish their potential for being constructive and contributing members of society. We will then view some of the strategies proposed to circumvent such loss of human potential.

The United States frequently is referred to as the wealthiest and most affluent of all nations. Yet there exists an exceptional group of children and youth who suffer from societal indifference and/or negligence. This is reflected educationally in the fact that only 50 percent of these children and youth will graduate from high school. During school attendance years they are plagued with reading difficulties, which place them a year or more behind in expected reading abilities and subsequent performance based on reading skills. Approximately one-third are estimated to become dependent on welfare for their subsistence in adult years.

Learning problems, we know, can be due to environmental, cultural, or economic deprivation. Although not included under the various legal definitions of the handicapped, and thus not covered by the legislation discussed in Unit 1, the children and youth we will study in this unit should be recognized as needing inclusion in the population of exceptional children—those in need of special services to realize their capabilities.

This population requires special services

These youngsters (and their families) are referred to by a number of different terms, including *educationally disadvantaged, culturally disadvantaged, socially disadvantaged, culturally deprived,* and *culturally different.* We prefer to use the term *societally neglected* because we see their problems and adjudged inadequacies as related to factors that can be eradicated through greater societal concern and social action.

Who are the societally neglected?

Our definition of the societally neglected includes *those children and youth whose experienced environmental, cultural, and/or economic societal conditions consistently prevent them from realizing their potential within the dominant educational, vocational, and social structures of present society.* Societal neglect can be defined as society's inattention to certain of its members—being remiss in attending to, caring about, or doing for them. The portrait of this exceptional population must be more clearly delineated and the conditions that represent societal neglect more clearly explored. Only in this way can we find solutions for the major problems that are presented.

Definition

Populations facing societal neglect

Despite the smaller environmental segments of society within which all of us find or place ourselves (family, neighborhood, chosen circle of friends), it is necessary to interact with the broader range of society. Each of us, for example, is expected to interact with others within the larger school environment. To be later considered productive in society, we are expected to participate with others in various job and vocational settings that have certain expectations for "successful" participants.

The individual whose earlier and/or continuing conditions have differed substantially—environmentally, culturally, or economically—from the majority of the population may find himself or herself ill-prepared for such at-large, or general, societal expectations (Bradley, 1970; Gottlieb & Ramsey, 1967). Previous opportunities for the acquisition of knowledge, skills, or even attitudes in relation to societal expectations may be lacking. As a result the individual encounters difficulty with his or her involvement in the overarching culture of the majority. In turn, receiving society's sanction and appreciation is made much more difficult. It is in these societal contacts that certain individuals find themselves entangled in unsuccessful experiences.

Unsuccessful societal encounters

Specific racial and ethnic minorities

Within the populations most often encountering societal neglect of their needs, we find a greater proportion of children and youth from certain racial and ethnic minorities as contrasted to members of the white Anglo-American majority population. The term *ethnic minority* is most often used today to refer to native American Indians, black Americans, and Spanish-speaking Americans. Being a member of such a minority is not of course equivalent to being societally neglected, since many minor-

Societal circumstances among ethnic minority children

ity group members effectively realize their potentials and contribute or perform highly. But a substantial number of members of the above three groups are included within the populations unable to fulfill potential due to encountered societal circumstances.

Also within the concept of racial and ethnic minorities are children and youth from families representing recent immigrant groups (southern Europeans, Asians, Puerto Ricans, Cubans), whether actually foreign or native born. They, too, share problems similar to the American Indian, black, and Hispanic American.

Migrant laborers

A second population includes children and youth from families of migrant laborers. Educational problems in particular can appear in children of migrant laborers as their families move across the country to follow sporadic job opportunities. Despite the existence of child labor laws and compulsory school attendance requirements, children *are* working in the fields and school attendance is spotty (Riggs, 1973).

For children of migrant workers, school time also may be lost during the numerous relocation moves and the process of resettlement in a new community. Because of a lack of continuity in the educational process, these children may encounter academic difficulty. They may be expected to progress according to the current curriculum content offered in the new classroom of which they become a part; however, their previous foundation for such adaptation may be lacking.

Isolated rural poor

A third population of potentially societally neglected children and youth come from families in isolated and/or poor rural areas. In the more remote parts of the Appalachian mountain region of America, for example, rural families remain in the areas in which they were born, even though their living conditions may reflect underemployment and undereducation. Lack of sustained school attendance in such areas has been acknowledged. Inadequate education and opportunity to progress in acquiring newer needed skills has been perpetuated through generations. The neglect and exploitation of the Appalachian region led to an inheritance of illiteracy, preventing many from rising above prevailing living conditions. The resulting deprivation has been well documented in literature (Crow et al., 1966; Parker, 1972a).

Inner-city dwellers

The fourth and last group we will identify is not as clearly definable in terms of being ethnically or racially disadvantaged or by a specific occupational category (Brickman, 1972, p. 9). It is composed of families representing all racial, national, and cultural origins. It includes the unskilled and those with occupational skills now obsolete for employment opportunities. It includes the immigrants and migrants who have attempted to flee from former undesirable conditions, as well as those already locked into a setting from which there appears no opportunity for flight. These are the families who are found settling or remaining together in the central blighted areas of our larger cities or in segregated areas of smaller cities and towns. They may be seen intermingling or remaining withdrawn and separated one from another, although living side by side.

Ghetto children

"Pockets of stability" It must be remembered that not all those who are identified as members of these four groups will qualify for inclusion within our definition of the societally neglected; some evidence no consequent deprivation or disadvantage. Many migrant working families fare well in their pursuits and their children are able to adapt easily to new locations and even benefit from their varied geographical and school experiences. Some of the families in isolated rural areas cope well in meeting their own needs and society's expectations. Even within the inner city or ghetto, many families are able to compensate for the effects of their surroundings. A Baltimore Human Renewal Study noted the variation among slum-dwellers; some families were living in "peace and dignity . . . and . . . there are occasional pockets of unusual stability with a considerable neighborhood pride" (Crow et al., 1966, p. 3).

Many in these groups cope well

Within some families included in these four groups, a richness of cultural heritage may exist. As Goodman (1971) notes, "When one approaches a group of children without preconceived notions, it is possible to discover strengths as well as weaknesses, a different cultural pattern rather than a deprived one, different language patterns rather than no language" (pp. 377–8). Despite such acknowledgement, however, we realize that members of these four groups qualify in greater number for inclusion within our definition of the societally neglected—those who experience conditions that limit their potential. Although heterogenous as far as nationality or race, skills or training, former or present location, they paradoxically represent a homogeneous group.

Their homogeneity lies in the fact they are most often all linked together by a shared or common factor, which can determine such things as where they can live and with whom they can associate, or—in other varying ways—interferes with their satisfying their own basic needs or society's expectations. This common factor is the continued presence of poverty and what has come to be known as "a culture of poverty" (Lewis, 1966).

Poverty is the common factor

The presence of poverty

"If you are poor, you suffer and may slide or be pushed down to 'skid row'. To be poor helps to flatten one on the floor of the stratified social milieu" (Crow et al., 1966, p. 38). Although the United States is frequently portrayed as a wealthy nation, the American poor approximate 24½ million people. Using federal guidelines that are defined and adjusted periodically, an income of $6,200 or less for a family of four or more currently (1978) qualifies as poverty level. (The farm family figure is

24½ million poor people in the U.S.

135

Societally neglected children and youth

$5,270.) More members of the four aforementioned groups consistently fall into this category. About 9 percent of the white population is included, along with 31 percent of the black population, 21 percent of the Spanish-speaking population and 38 percent of all Indians.

Despite attempts by the United States government to subsidize families through programs entitled "welfare spending" or "income security," we see that the pulverizing presence of poverty still has not been eradicated for millions of Americans.

Hierarchy of human needs as related to poverty

According to Maslow (1968), all individuals have needs or "deficiencies which must be optimally fulfilled by the environment in order to avoid sickness and subjective ill-being." Such needs are conceived as "related to each other in a hierarchal and developmental way, in an order of strength and of priority" (p. 153). This hierarchy of needs has been represented in pyramidal, or ascending, order as illustrated in Figure 5-1. The most basic *physiological,* or life-perpetuating, needs, such as satisfaction of hunger, thirst, rest and sleep, are represented at the lowest level of the figure. At the next lowest level are the *safety needs,* representing the search for security and safety and feelings of being free from danger. Third in the hierarchy, *love and belonging needs* emerge. These include the motivation to possess and give feelings of acceptance, affection, and love and to share identification with others for successful social interaction. The next highest level represents the *self-esteem* motives, including both the desire for self-respect and self-confidence and the need for recognition and respect from other people. Finally, at the fifth and highest level, is the need for *self-actualization.* Here self-fulfillment is sought in the form of full use of one's potential, talents, and capabilities. (Only a small percentage of persons from *any* population consistently achieve at this highest level.)

Concerning the hierarchic sequence, needs that are lower in the hierarchy are seen as more "urgent determiners of behavior when their satisfaction is lacking"

Ascending order of need

Lower-level needs must be satisfied first

Figure 5.1
A motivational hierarchy

| Self-actualization |
| Self-esteem |
| Love and belonging |
| Safety needs |
| Physiological needs |

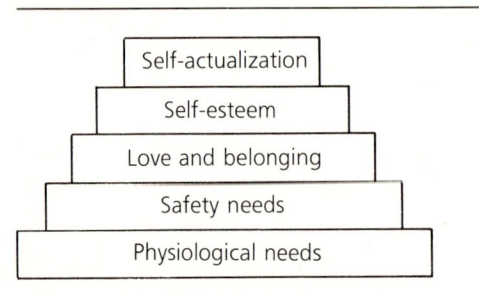

Source: Adapted from Maslow, 1970

(Hilgard & Atkinson, 1967, p. 139). Individuals, for example, who are experiencing hunger have their attention and concern focused on this hunger need. The lowest deficient level for an individual generally is seen as requiring relatively adequate satisfaction before one's behaviors can be focused on achieving satisfaction of higher-level motivational needs and concerns.

As we consider various aspects of the lives of the population of the societally neglected, we will relate certain conditions and influences to this model of human needs in order to better understand these children and youth.

Poverty and malnutrition

Proper nutrition includes the sufficient intake, in both amount and kind, of food substances that contain the essential nutrients known to be required for the proper

Introducing Ricky—whose living conditions are such that he needs special help to develop enough self-esteem to achieve successfully. Henry, a volunteer Big Brother, suggests an interesting project.

growth and functioning of the organism. Malnutrition is present when an individual is lacking or deficient in adequate consumption or absorption of one or more needed nutrients to the extent that specific symptoms and conditions appear.

The problem of malnutrition in the United States is enormous, with more than ten million Americans estimated to suffer from some form of inadequate or improper food intake (Organ, 1970a). The problem is widespread—poor eating habits or inadequate diet are found in individuals from all walks of life and not confined to any one ethnic or economic segment of the population. However, the presence of consistent nutritional deprivation, resulting from inadequate or improper food intake, is greatest among those individuals existing in poverty conditions. Children are most often the victims.

Relation to infant and child mortality Shocking data discovered during a study conducted by the Joint Commission on Mental Health of children revealed that in 1968 the United States had the thirteenth highest overall infant death rate among nations. Within the reported U.S. infant mortality rate, black and American Indian children were included three times more often than whites.

Investigators of the causes of infant and child mortality have contended that malnutrition is a major underlying factor in deaths reported to be due to infections. Further well-controlled studies are needed to fully support this contention. However, based on the clinical experiences of physicians, a relationship has been proposed between nutritional status and subsequent infections that can result in death. Organ (1970b) reports that "throughout the world, the largest part of preventable mortality is due to the combined effect of malnutrition and infection in the first years of life" (p. 1). In children with documented severe malnourishment, it is believed that increased mortality rates can result from contraction of such common childhood diseases as measles and chicken pox (Dayton, 1969).

Besides the relationship that may exist between malnutrition and infant and child mortality rates, there are other effects of nutritional deprivation that are found to be more prevalent among the poor.

Effects on physical health and development Symptoms or conditions arising as a result of malnutrition can include retardation in the physical growth and development of the child, as well as the presence of such conditions as anemia, rickets, vitamin or protein or calorie deficiencies, goiter, and other health disorders. Two types of diseases—marasmus and kwashiorkor—are the results of severe malnutrition and may culminate in death if they remain untreated.

Marasmus is the result of severe restriction in caloric intake from birth or shortly thereafter. It is manifested in the wasting of body tissues, emaciation, and severe retardation in physical growth. Kwashiorkor is a result of various nutritional deficiencies, but particularly of inadequate protein nourishment. The presence of kwashiorkor may produce extreme stunting of growth, as well as skin sores, water retention, and hair discoloration.

Studies of nutritional deprivation among the poor have focused on various differences from expected standards for the population as a whole. Such differences include variations from expected growth patterns. A most common point of reference for the measurement of growth patterns is the recording of a child's height and weight, followed by continued assessment over a period of time. Comparison of the child's progress is made with physical growth standards expected in children receiving adequate nourishment. While reasons for significant variations from expected patterns require individual consideration as to the exact cause, the presence of inadequate nutritional intake has been found to be a source of retardation in physical development. *Retardation in physical growth*

The National Nutrition Survey conducted by HEW in 1968 (Organ, 1970a; Schaefer & Johnson, 1969) was the first comprehensive study of its kind in our country. It included an analysis of physical growth patterns and other symptoms which can be associated with malnutrition. The study involved a sample population of approximately seventy thousand persons from ten states. The majority of the sample population had annual incomes of less than $3,000. *National Nutritional Survey*

Results of the study indicated that from 35 to 55 percent of the persons included suffered from various kinds of nutritional inadequacies. Among the children included in the study the results were startling, as evidenced in the following:

> Children suffer most from malnutrition. About 15 percent of all children studied showed evidence of growth retardation. Some children were retarded by two years at the age of six. All of these children run the risk of never catching up in physical development. In addition, it was observed that many of these children may not develop mentally to capacity. . . . (Organ, 1970a, p. 1).

Other findings indicated that one-third of the children suffered from anemia and one-third suffered from vitamin A deficiency. Additionally found in smaller percentages of cases were other kinds of conditions associated with nutritional deprivation, including rickets and "potbelly," which is considered to be a symptom of protein-calorie deficiency. Within the total sample, seven cases were found showing the severe general malnutrition of marasmus and kwashiorkor.

In this ten-state survey primarily involving families from low-income groups, there was a high frequency of the inadequate health conditions commonly associated with malnutrition as an underlying or contributing cause. Studies conducted with samples of poor children from various populations in America (the Apache, Navajo, and other American Indian children), as well as studies conducted in other countries such as Guatemala, have indicated significantly higher proportions of various nutritional deficiencies and related physical complications among children of the poor (Dayton, 1969). *Low income vis-a-vis nutritional deficiencies*

Effects of maternal malnutrition on offspring   Closely associated with malnutrition in children and resulting consequences for physical growth and development is the relationship between a nutritionally deficient pregnant mother and her developing fetus. This condition also has received increased attention and concern. Maternal malnutrition has been recognized as a factor that is not only associated with health problems during pregnancy, but also involves other complications. Higher incidences of actual or threatened miscarriages, premature deliveries, and even stillbirths are known to be associated with maternal malnutrition.

Reduced birth weight and size

Beyond these possible consequences, the effects of maternal malnutrition have been noted in other ways. Infants born to malnourished women have shown evidence of reduced birth weight and length beyond the expected variation existing in any population or family in regard to normal birth weight and height. Poorer health histories in postnatal and later developmental periods also have been recorded for children born to malnourished mothers.

Effects on mental development   The possible detrimental effects of malnutrition on mental development also have become a concern. The consequences of poverty as related to the learning process within the actual school situation will receive later consideration. Within the scope of our present discussion, however, the relationship of malnutrition to the development of the brain and resulting mental functioning should be examined.

Rapid growth of brain in prenatal period and early years

The human brain, as a part of the central nervous system, develops most rapidly during the latter part of the fetal period and the first six months after birth. Rapid growth continues during the first three years of life. Brain maturation is dependent, therefore, upon adequate nutrients being supplied not only to a developing fetus during the months of gestation but to the young child during the early postnatal period. Any deficit in the supply of necessary nutrients as experienced through maternal malnutrition or through dietary deficiencies in the first few years of life can result in retarded brain growth or development.

Studies have been conducted that indicate the effects of malnourishment upon the learning capacities of children. Referring to a study involving children from a South American city's slum section (Monckeberg, 1969), the following findings are reported:

1. Intellectual performance of malnourished children is significantly inferior to that of children who were adequately nourished.
2. Mental retardation was correlated with retarded growth and with degree of malnourishment.
3. Growth retardation included a deficit in cranial growth that was significantly correlated to intelligence quotient.
4. An apparent decrease of brain volume (disproportion of brain size to the skull size) was evident in those children with a history of severe marasmus.

5. Follow-up studies on apparently healthy children who suffered from severe malnutrition in infancy suggest that damage to intellectual capacity is irreversible (Organ, 1970a, p. 3).

In the United States, various relationships between prenatal maternal health and learning patterns in infants were examined (Organ, 1970a). Preliminary findings revealed that four times as many black as white pregnant women in the sample study had protein-deficient diets. Such maternal protein deficiency was suggested as being related to later poor learning responses on the part of their offspring.

As the many negative effects of malnutrition show up, it becomes apparent that a major effort is needed to eradicate this condition. Some of the intervention procedures designed to ensure proper nutrition will be discussed in a later portion of this unit. The importance of such efforts cannot be minimized, especially as the detrimental impact of malnutrition is more fully recognized.

Poverty and inadequate housing conditions

The inadequacy of housing conditions is another area of deprivation that characterizes the plight of the poor. Wooden shanties are occupied not only by the rural poor in the hills or countrysides, but on the "wrong side of the tracks" in almost any American city or town. Countless families are forced to occupy dwellings that undermine the sustenance of good physical and/or mental health. The poor live in vast expanses of single- or multifamily tenement dwellings that are overcrowded and have inadequate heating, poor ventilation, and unsanitary plumbing.

Inadequate housing facilities undermine good health

The ghetto or racially segregated sections of the inner cities are distinguished from other housing areas by squalor and wretched living facilities. Run-down conditions are reflected in the peeling paint, cracked plaster or paper-thin walls, clogged plumbing or sewage drains, and overflowing garbage. These oppressive signs may be more permanent than temporary in the dwellings of the poor.

Peeling paint and overflowing garbage

While urban-renewal projects costing millions of dollars have ameliorated some of these depressing conditions, such efforts have not been entirely free from criticism. Their effectiveness in meeting stated goals of adequate housing for all of America's citizens has been questioned. Erskine Caldwell suggests that many urban housing projects "stack people one on top of another . . . and exemplify only a new setting for dwellers in poverty. . . . It might look all right on the outside of those places, . . . but something happens inside." Referring to his best-selling novel recounting the desperation of poverty for the southern sharecropper, Caldwell further stated, "It doesn't change everything just because they've paved over part of Tobacco Road" (UPI, 1975).

The need for feeling physically comfortable

We have already viewed some of the problems resulting from malnutrition. Inadequate housing conditions, also more frequently found among the poor, deny them the needed privacy, rest, and sleeping accommodations for replenishment of energy. One is frequently too hot,

Myth of the physical toughness of the poor

too cold, or too crowded for physical comfort. The false image of physical toughness as a characteristic among the poor has been portrayed through accounts of urban gang fights or other aggressive encounters in the school or neighborhood setting. The actual effects of lowered housing standards, combined with poor or lowered nutritional conditions, do not substantiate this myth.

Fatigue and susceptibility to infection

Fatigue among the poor may be evidenced in its more common form of listlessness or in overactivity or restlessness. These latter behaviors, however, are often unrecognized as fatigue symptoms, and are frequently misinterpreted as "nonconforming."

More susceptibility to infections may be evidenced among the poor because of the substandard sanitary facilities or inadequate heating or ventilation systems often found within tenement complexes or flimsy single-family dwellings. Lowered physical stamina for adequate muscular development or pursuit of mental or educational development can result.

Attempts to escape from the sordidness of living conditions—particularly within the inner city—have resulted in a high incidence of young drug abusers; drugs may offer a transitory comfort. Increased sexual promiscuity may also result, with the possibility of added complications from venereal disease infections or unwanted pregnancy. Although these effects are not confined to the lower socioeconomic population, such involvement contributes further and more substantially to possible physiological or mental health breakdown when combined with other existing problems specifically confronting the poor.

Order and stability

The need for feeling safe and secure   As a further consequence of congested and inadequate housing, the poor also may have greater difficulty in experiencing feelings of safety, security, order, and stability in their lives. In urban disadvantaged areas, living in what is generally considered to be an unsafe neighborhood can be a continual threat to feelings of safety (Colfax, 1972).

Socially destructive behaviors

Acts of vandalism and theft occur frequently within areas inhabited by the very low-income population. Particularly within the inner core of a city—where the poor are forced to congregate because housing is cheap or segregation still exists—the incidence of hostile or destructive actions is relatively high. In discussing the problems encountered by youths of the inner city, Levine (1970) writes of "urban disorder . . . being fueled by discontent among young people who, rather than acquiring the attitudes and skills needed to succeed in our society, are demonstrating an increasing tendency to behave in a self-destructive and socially destructive manner" (p. 84). The following account of an experience recorded by the teacher of a student enrolled in a program for disadvantaged young people is illustrative of such problems:

> One morning Selma . . . seemed especially depressed. . . . After class I asked if she were ill.
> "I can't talk, Mrs. Dawson," she sobbed. "Last night while we were out,

someone came in and stole my husband's suits and sliced the furniture covers and curtains."

"Do you live in the project?"

"Yes, and I face the street. I don't know what to do. We have no money to replace these things now . . ." (Dawson, 1968, p. 35).

Poverty and the family unit

Poverty and its consequences can affect family life in various ways. The family unit has long been recognized as the means through which appropriate behaviors are modeled and adequate socialization skills learned. The importance of an intact, or nuclear, family unit—in which both parents are present—has received considerable attention in literature. Broken homes have been recognized as relating to emotional problems in children and contributing to delinquency. More recently the emotional climate of the home has been considered equal to or more important than the mere physical presence of both parents.

Emotional climate of home

Referring to families characterized by the absence of one of the parents, Haskell and Yablonsky (1978) write that

> a one-parent family, whether as a result of divorce, desertion or death, usually consists of a mother and children living together. The mother often finds it difficult to provide sustenance and guidance, and the absence of a father leaves the male children without an adult male model. Children born out of wedlock and brought up by their mothers are in much the same position . . . (p. 86).

Matriarchal family structure

Within this matriarchal pattern, the mother finds it necessary to take advantage of any available employment hours. Such absences from the home can sometimes result in periods of time during which adequate care and supervision are not provided for child members of the family.

In relation to the structural makeup of the black family unit, Parker (1972b) cites the following figures: "one-fourth of Negro families are headed by a woman. Of all married Negro women, 20.4 percent have absent husbands, as against 4.4 percent of all white married women. Over one-third of all Negro children live in broken homes or with a relative" (p. 69).

The need for feeling that one belongs   The need for feeling physically safe has been discussed, but it is also important to recognize safety in terms of its psychological component (Briggs, 1970; Maslow, 1968). Within the matriarchal, or father-absent home, the mother may find it more difficult to assume the dual role of financial provider and provider of the emotional needs of her children in relation to feelings of belongingness, love, and acceptance. It should be recognized, however, that a mother's employment, in itself, is not the determining single factor in assessing adequate or inadequate mother-child relationships.

In Rieber's study of low-income families (1968), the receptive vocabulary of children of employed mothers was compared with that of children whose mothers were not employed. From results obtained it was speculated there was increased verbal interaction by working mothers with their own children as a result of the mother's contact with other people during outside employment. Nevertheless, with further regard to poverty conditions and parenting, Wilson (1974) states:

Poverty affects parenting

Middle-class child-centered behavior, as defined . . . is not operable in the milieu of poverty. Research recently completed . . . shows that material shortages in the home and poor environmental conditions severely affect parental child-rearing methods. . . . The debate concerned with preparation for parenthood or education of parents should acknowledge the realities of life in the slums, which forces parents to adopt methods of child-rearing of which they do not approve (p. 241).

Aside from father-absent homes, there is the likely possibility of prolonged unemployment of the male provider. This factor can increase family tension and stress. Despite the male physical presence, his financial unproductiveness can cause feelings of resentment, disapproval, and lowered status. Such feelings may be coming from him and/or may be reflected by other family members. The consequence, however, can be a diminished capacity to serve as an individual to whom one can turn for identification, belonging, and acceptance needs.

Breakdown of patriarchal family pattern

The breakdown of the patriarchal pattern among various minority ethnic groups, such as blacks, American Indians, Hispanic Americans, as well as among low socioeconomic nonminority families, such as the Appalachians, may result in a change or reversal of traditional family life (Crow, et al., 1966; Fantini & Weinstein, 1968; Gould, 1967; Parker, 1972a). As the mother assumes responsibility as the wage earner, the father, unable to adequately provide for the family, may express his feelings of inadequacy in passivity or indifference or even belligerency. He may turn to excessive use of alcohol or may permanently or sporadically desert his family (Dawson, 1968; Gould, 1967).

Inadequate knowledge of child-rearing practices

Child-parent and peer relationships Beyond circumstances which may be present in the father-absent or father-unemployed home, lack of parental knowledge concerning adequate child-rearing practices can jeopardize children's chances for feeling loved and accepted. Child-rearing methods used by parents frequently reflect their own childhood experiences. It is far more difficult to be a loving, nurturant parent—sharing time, interests, and concerns with one's own children—if such experiences were not a consistent part of one's own childhood.

When children of poverty become adults, they may find themselves living in the same kind of oppressive conditions that drained their parents of the time and energy, and also the receptivity to knowledge, for appropriate child-nurturing experiences. With this inheritance of a culture of poverty, lack of knowledge and training for correcting inadequacies may continue, and parenting deficiencies may be perpetuated. This writer is reminded of a statement made by a young mother concerned about the harsh treatment she was using in disciplining her child. She noted, "I find myself repeating certain practices of my own mother which I felt as a child—and still feel—were wrong."

Because poverty-stricken parents may lack either the time, energy, or knowledge to sustain parent-child interactions that lead to the satisfaction of belonging needs, their children's increased dependence is often displaced onto peer relationships (Maslow, 1968). We have seen that the presence of poverty usually causes the existing family unit to reside in certain depressed areas. We have also noted that

Increased dependence on peers

Ricky is encouraged to begin a kite construction and flight project. After expressing some doubts about his ability to succeed and some reservations about his desire to do it, Ricky does finally pitch in.

conditions within such areas often generate threats to feelings of safety and security by virtue of higher incidences of acts of vandalism or other hostile occurrences. While group or gang affiliations may be of a positive sustaining nature and not in conflict with values and norms deemed desirable by overall society, some children and youth—as they seek feelings of acceptance—associate more easily with peer or gang groups that do not foster adequate socialization processes for success outside the particular subcultural setting.

"A delinquent subculture"

Juvenile delinquency increases as numbers of youths drop out of school and are unable to find employment (Crow et al., 1966; Sanchez-Hidalgo, 1969). Membership in some gangs which adhere to a "delinquent subculture" (Haskell & Yablonsky, 1978, p. 86) can include various negative aspects. Fulton (1972) views the situation of many black children coming from father-absent homes as resulting in their having "few, if any, close male models of behavior" (p. 82). Biller (1971) discusses several studies relating to possible negative consequences of father-absent homes. Masculinity needs on the part of the young male can be perceived as often leading to increased aggressive acts, including deliberate violations of "that other society's" norms as a basis for acceptance into some gangs. Young females—in their search for feelings of love and belongingness—may experience sexual exploitation. The higher incidence of female involvement in more aggressive behavior also is seen in figures reporting the nature and occurrence of delinquent acts. (See Unit 7 for a more detailed exploration of juvenile delinquency.)

Various approaches have been undertaken to increase the effectiveness of parent-child interactions in lower socioeconomic families as well as in other families where children's needs are not being met. But economic and social mobility are seen by some psychologists and educators as a necessary forerunner to increased parenting effectiveness. Wilson (1974), states that "A more appropriate population for education in parenthood would be a socially upward one. Parents and children in the slums need vast fiscal resources to improve their conditions before an attempt is made to change their attitudes" (p. 241).

Assessment of feelings of self-esteem

How one feels about oneself

Self-respect—including feelings of confidence, competence, and appreciation of self—is viewed as essential for psychological health. There has been a great deal of interest displayed in measuring an individual's self-concept—defined as the feelings one has about oneself—as such feelings are reflected in various behaviors.

The dependency of a person upon the environment or "various external criteria" (Colfax, 1972, p. 110) for satisfaction of the need for self-respect has been recognized. One psychologist puts it this way:

> Each child's view of himself is built from the stream of reflections that flow together from many sources: his treatment by those around him, his physical mastery of himself and his environment, and his degree of achievement and recognition in areas important to him. These reflections are like snap-

shots of himself that he pastes in an imaginary photo album. They form the basis of his identity. They become his *self-image* or *self-concept*—his personal answers to "Who am I?" (Briggs, 1970, pp. 17–18).

The numerous investigations that have been made of the influence of differing conditions—including racial and socioeconomic differences—indicate that self-esteem is not related to any one single factor or element. Rather, it is determined, as is all human behavior, by a complexity of interacting circumstances and experiences.

Circumstances and experience determine self-esteem

In racial minorities   Colfax states that "relatively little support is provided for the idea that the Negro sense-of-self is self-stigmatizing and self-derogating" (1972, p. 110). In his assessment of the self-concept of twenty-five hundred preadolescents within the setting of segregated black and white school environments, the presence of lowered self-esteem or self-derogation was less within the black school population than the white. Colfax speculates, however, that self-derogation may find greater expression beyond the years of preadolescence and in the context of wider experiences.

In a study of the self-concept of Mexican-American students, the idea that these youth necessarily hold a negative self-image is refuted (Carter, 1972). Comparing the self-concept of Mexican-American youth with "Anglo" youth, lowered self-esteem was not found to be present more often in the Mexican-American child. Carter suggests that "the supposed negative self-image of the Mexican-American is, in reality, our own stereotype projected onto him. 'Anglos' tend to think of Mexican-Americans in negative ways, and conclude they [Mexican-Americans] see themselves in the same light" (1972, p. 138).

In lower socioeconomic levels   There is awareness, however, that the task of developing and maintaining positive self-esteem is made increasingly difficult for large numbers of children in the lower socioeconomic class. Although Scott (1967) notes that many children among the societally neglected population have parents who provide the kinds of opportunities that enable their children to develop a sense of worth and adequacy, she cites the greater frequency of environmental disorganization. We have already observed that the lower socioeconomic-class youngster often comes from either a fragmented or broken home or a home in which parents may find it more difficult to provide and foster positive feelings and experiences for their children. Insecurity and feelings of personal inadequacy experienced by adults within the family also can directly affect their children's self-esteem. Scott (1967) writes that "the children are likely to be uncertain about their own worth. For the more insecure and unfulfilled a person is, the more attentive he is to satisfying his own needs, and the less supporting he can be of others" (p. 160).

Familial influences important in building self-worth

There are other patterns of familial interaction that may inhibit feelings of self-worth in children. These patterns may be found in families from *any* social or economic strata. However, lower socioeconomic-class children are more often the recipients of attention that is given in the presence of misbehavior (Fantini & Weinstein, 1968). Attention and parent-child interaction under such circumstances is usually negative in nature. When this is the case, without parent or adult focus on positive attention and praise for desirable behaviors, a lowered self-image can be developed by the child. If the child continues to experience lack of positive acknowledgement and encouragement by significant others, including teachers or peers within the school setting, self-depreciation will continue to grow.

Lack of positive attention

The effects of poverty and low self-concept on motivation

The combined undesirable effects of poverty and lowered self-esteem can be reflected in increased occurrences of nonadaptive behavior. One of the aspects of behavior considered nonadaptive on the part of individuals from lower socioeconomic environments is their seemingly lowered motivation. It goes without saying that many members experiencing societal neglect are able to extricate themselves from many negative circumstances and achieve successfully. However, many adults, as well as children and youth, have been accused of being "unwilling" to take advantage of opportunities to improve their current or future life circumstances.

Success and/or failure as variables in motivation

Those whose daily lives are surrounded by constant reminders of failure can easily suffer from reduced motivation. A perceived lack of motivation among the societally neglected population can be related to existing doubt that significant improvement can result from one's own efforts. Maslow (1968) points out that "the person who hasn't conquered, withstood, and overcome continues to feel doubtful that he could" (p. 4). The possibility of change can seem remote in terms of more pressing demands or needs. A "weak sense of the future" (Gottlieb & Ramsey, 1967, p. 30) may result in behaviors that are misinterpreted as indicating apathy and indifference.

Internal locus of control

A social learning theory involving the personality aspect of "locus of control" is particularly relevant to understanding the motivational characteristics of this population (Rotter, 1954). In terms of Rotter's theory, locus of control constitutes the degree of control one feels one possesses in determining one's own destiny or fate. An *internal* locus of control is present if one feels personally and highly instrumental in determining what happens to oneself as a result of one's own personal actions. If, however, one views factors outside oneself, or in the environment, as the major determinant of life's occurrences, and excludes personal actions as being instrumental, then an *external* locus of control is considered present.

External locus of control

Societally neglected children and youth have been recognized as more often having an external locus of control, believing their life situations are determined by outside factors such as chance, fate, or luck (Rotter, 1954). They are not convinced that they possess the personal effectiveness to significantly change their present or future environments. Motivation and self-concept are critical factors to be considered in the problems of disadvantaged youngsters in the school situation (C.

Deutsch, 1967). Vocational counselors are becoming increasingly aware of these factors as they attempt rehabilitation measures with older youth and adults. When one realizes the combination of the many negative factors producing what may appear as lowered motivational characteristics, such behavior can perhaps be better understood and dealt with more effectively.

We have considered the consequences of differences existing in nutritional status, housing conditions, family structure and interaction, and motivational aspects among poor families; now we turn our attention to another area of differences—language characteristics of the poor and/or societally neglected.

Language of the societally neglected

Speech and language disorders among children and youth will be covered comprehensively in Unit 8. Our concern here is with the academic failures and attendant problems of societally neglected children that can be related to deficiencies in language (Lively-Weiss & Koller, 1973, p. 293). Language development is viewed in this context as a necessary foundation for later success in various aspects of the learning and socialization processes.

When compared to middle-class children, economically disadvantaged children enter school with deprivation in previous language experiences (M. Deutsch, 1967). Verbal interaction—as a means of exchanging information—has been observed to be less frequent within lower socioeconomic-class families. Increased use of gestural communication, lack of reading matter in the home, and the parents' possible lack of verbal communication skills are felt to be factors contributing to deficits in the child's language experiences.

Economic status and language development

Elaborated and restricted language

Basil Bernstein's study (1962) gave early support to the contention that lower-class language patterns differ from middle-class language patterns. Bernstein reported that greater use of formal language containing instructional or informative content was found more often in middle-class verbal interaction. He termed this usage *elaborated language.* Greater frequency of informal language—or language used to satisfy more current and concrete needs or demands—was found more prevalent among lowerclass families and termed *restricted language.* We noted earlier that families in the societally neglected segment of the population were necessarily preoccupied with meeting present rather than future needs. These findings can be related to this differing emphasis.

Various samples of elaborated versus restricted language interaction can be observed in parent-child verbal exchanges in numerous kinds of daily settings. One must keep in mind that such differences are not always based on a single index, such as socioeconomic level. In a post-office where a young mother, accompanied by her approximately four-year-old child, was waiting her turn in the food stamp line, an *elaborated* form of communication was overheard. The young child—obviously bored by the process of waiting—emitted several short but piercing screams. This particular mother's reaction was to inform her young child quietly in the following manner:

> Child: (Loud screams)
> Mother: Donnie, those are kinds of noises to make outside. Those are outside noises. They are too loud inside here and can bother other people.

Elaborated parent-child verbal exchanges

The success of this mother's communication with her child was evidenced by the child's acceptance of her message, which also conveyed important information for cognitive development (Cowles, 1967; C. Deutsch, 1967). The mother had made reference to "outside noises," "too loud," "inside here" (labeling of the environment) and had clarified the quality of behavior expected among "other people." A wealth of learning information could be observed in this brief parent-child interchange, which transferred without threat to the child's sense of personal worth.

Contrasted with this situation, restricted verbal interchange lacks content for more precise definitions or distinctions and does not include the labeling process or the sharing of thought patterns for greater understanding. The following verbal encounter between another mother and her young child in a grocery store illustrates the nature of the restricted language approach:

> Child: (Loud cries)
> Mother: Michael, shut up!
> Michael: But you hit me!
> Mother: I did not, you're acting bad.
> Michael: I am not.
> Mother: Shut up, Michael, or I'll smack you!

Restricted parent-child verbal exchanges

Although this is also a verbal exchange, it is marked by the presence of short, commanding statements. There is no elaboration by explanation, and unanswered questions remain concerning the child's perception of being "hit" or "acting bad." Such observed behavior may not have been an accurate sampling of mother and child verbal interaction within the family and other extended situations. But if it did constitute an accurate sampling of behavior to be repeated, Michael's chances for gaining perceptual awareness and comprehension through a verbal interchange with his mother are greatly reduced in comparison with Donnie's opportunities for acquiring such knowledge.

Receptive and expressive language ability

Concerning language experiences, the child must first achieve success in understanding the spoken word (receptive language ability) before he can achieve success in expressing himself orally (expressive language ability). Following certain levels of achievement in these earlier language stages, the child becomes ready to comprehend and understand the reading process. Such achievement—necessary for successful transfer to the school situation—can be curtailed by restricted language patterns used in the home.

Bilingualism and dialect
Bilingualism per se does not always constitute a source of disadvantage, as many children who grow up in a natural bilingual environment have more than adequate learning and educational patterns. Justin (1970), however, reports that nearly one million Spanish-speaking children in the Southwest never will go beyond the eighth grade, with language differences considered a major factor contributing to their termination of education. Cordasco (1972) reports lack of continued education also among Puerto Rican youth on the eastern seaboard, again with language differences considered a factor. Dialect differences, too, have been reported as some-

Relation to school dropout rates

Engaged in the intricacies of keeping a kite in flight, Ricky can better appreciate what Henry meant when he spoke of "the fun of flying."

times interfering with the reading process, as some words may need to be translated into one's own dialect for comprehension (Foerster, 1974).

Reading difficulties

While many factors need to be examined concerning causes of reading difficulties, reading progress is dependent upon certain earlier stages of language experience and skills. Retardation in reading ability has been reported more prevalent among children from lower socioeconomic groups (C. Deutsch, 1967) and is believed to be related to their high dropout rate in school.

The lack of auditory discrimination ability has been found to be among the specific causes of reading failure. Many children are unable to discriminate between similar-sounding letters or words and fail to perceive their own differences in pronunciation that lead to lack of word comprehension (for example, saying "sumpin" for "something").

Lower auditory discrimination skills

Among the societally neglected population, certain environmental factors, which were discussed earlier, are seen as contributing to a lack of development in finer auditory discrimination skills. Higher noise levels are frequently found within the home and environmental setting that interfere with the use of discriminatory skills for detecting finer differences. Additionally, the lower presence of informative verbal exchange (elaborated language) among family members deters the development of general listening or attentive habits. Such differences in auditory discrimination or listening skill development can produce obstacles to successful learning, not only in the reading process but in other aspects of the total communication process (e.g. spelling, written language activities).

Intervention strategies

Various intervention strategies are employed to circumvent or alleviate the problems we have discussed. Legislation has been enacted to try to ensure adequate income for all families in the United States. Special provisions also foster maintenance of food supplies (food stamps), adequate housing facilities (project housing, rent subsidies), and free or reduced-cost health-care services. Further legislation is intended to eliminate discriminatory practices in educational provisions or employment opportunities. While no completely satisfactory solutions to any of these problems are present in today's society, various strategies have been formulated to facilitate needed programs. These strategies, however, have been controversial in terms of desired effectiveness.

Controversial intervention strategies

Compensatory educational provisions   In discussing compensatory education programs, Bronfenbrenner (1969) writes that "any program seeking to meet the educational needs of disadvantaged children must address itself not only to the development of cognitive competence but also of patterns of motivation and behavior appropriate to a productive, cooperative society" (p. 2).

The necessity for planning the curriculum carefully to provide such development involves the cooperation of many individuals. Teaching personnel must be aware of child developmental processes and must demonstrate competency in effecting needed changes (including familiarity with motivational and socialization aspects) to ensure beginning and future learning success.

The most widely known system for providing the compensatory, or equalizing, experiences necessary for successful participation in the regular public school system is the Head Start program for preschool youngsters. Although compensatory preschool education indicates some failure to produce expected outcomes (Emanuel & Sagan, 1974), it is generally supported as one of the most potent means of preventing these exceptional children from falling further behind in basic academic readiness and other skills. Continued research on Head Start has resulted in redefining and refining the specific goals to be achieved. Bronfenbrenner stresses that improvement in the child's development is also based largely on securing needed cooperation from those closest to the child (parents, siblings, other relatives) and others with whom the child associates (peers, older children, neighborhood adults). Hence, programs aimed at improving socioeconomic conditions in the community and motivational factors in the home can contribute to the success of compensatory preschool education. *Head Start*

School, family, community must cooperate

The necessity for continued later adaptation or follow-through on special needs is recognized in order to maintain the beginning equalization at school entry that preschool programs may provide (Borden et al., 1975). Upward Bound programs, for example, can assist low-income students to complete their high school educations and enter post-secondary programs. When adaptations are not made within the regular school setting, alternative schools are available in many communities to further the educational process. Alternative schools focus on remediation of any deficits in academic skills along with preparation for job entry or entry into higher education when applicable. *Follow-through programs*

Within the higher, or post-secondary, educational setting, community colleges are seen as effective in providing not only further general educational opportunities but also technical or career programs (Committee for Economic Development, 1971, p. 45). Various types of programs also are funded within many of the traditional university settings and offer assistance through tutoring services, personal and academic counseling, career information services, and work-study grants for financial assistance. Special compensatory programs also may be centered on regular university campuses, where classes are held for preparing educationally disadvantaged individuals to pass General Educational Development (GED) examinations under the High School Equivalency Program.

The necessity is also recognized for identifying talent, creativity, and intellectual giftedness within the populations we have been discussing and for following *Gifted minority children* through by offering beneficial and enriching experiences. (See Figure 5-2 for an example of such a program.)

More recent emphasis has been placed on extending prevention or intervention strategies downward to the earliest age groups possible. Under such provisions children from birth to five years of age are now being provided diagnostic services relating to developmental progress; subsequently they are provided with programs designed to alleviate, circumvent, or eliminate problems that threaten adequate future development.

Language provisions

Other programs are specifically concerned with the school's responsibility for providing appropriate language-learning experiences to every student regardless of differences in mother tongue and former opportunities. Recognizing the need for preserving individual heritage and not stripping children of their ethnic and cultural differences, the NEA Task Force on Bilingual/Multicultural Education (1976) defined bilingual education as "a process which uses a pupil's primary language as the principal medium of instruction while teaching the language of the predominant culture in a well-organized program, encompassing a multicultural curriculum" (p. 13). Such an approach is designed to ensure students' rights to appropriate education even when their primary language is not English. The U.S. Department of Health, Education and Welfare (HEW) too has issued guidelines to prevent language discrimination.

Health and nutritional provisions

Within the early childhood programs, provisions are included for monitoring health and nutritional needs. Section 3, Public Law 94-105 authorizes a school breakfast program, stating that "as a national nutrition and health policy, it is the purpose and intent of the Congress that the School Breakfast Program be made available in all schools where it is needed to provide adequate nutrition to children in attendance."

Positive results are reported from providing students with adequate nutrition prior to beginning the school day; restlessness in some children was reduced and improvement in school work was observed. Under an earlier enacted school lunch program, free and/or reduced prices for meals are available according to formulas developed for such participation.

Other developmental and instructional provisions

The range of programs or instructional strategies that can benefit this special student population is more often limited by lack of imagination, interest, and involvement on the part of those who can help rather than it is by lack of funds. Conway (1976) reports on an innovative program involving twenty-five junior-high black students in a California school. The students were considered high-risk candidates for dropping out of school, exhibited low self-confidence, and were disenchanted with the educational process. Through a "Flight Project" program, these students were provided with special study units (mechanics, radio operation, navigation, meteorology, mathematics, etc.) to prepare them for the final unit of the program: actual instructional time in a single-engine airplane. Flying time was provided by a grant from a private foundation in San Francisco. Significant gains were made by the students who participated in the flight project in terms of increased self-esteem and greater feelings of internal locus of control. For example, "I have a lot of confidence in my ability" and "If I want to become something, I will" were statements made by participants. Other programs based on the "big brother" or "big sister" approach can be successful in building self-esteem and feelings of self-mastery. Interaction is provided with role models, including those within the child's own cultural setting, who exhibit desired behavior patterns and whom the child or youth is encouraged to emulate (Bronfenbrenner, 1969, p. 3).

Using certain intervention strategies, progress *is* being made with these populations, but much remains to be accomplished. That there exists untapped potential and normal human desires for higher life goals can be aptly illustrated in the following "success story" about a migrant worker who overcame substantial economic, language, and educational deficits.

Rafael Ortiz   The success of Rafael Ortiz in his growth from migrant life to classroom teacher is one of inspiration to all who know firsthand the

Figure 5.2
Operation Eagle I

Oklahoma State Department of Education
Indian Education Section

Northeastern Oklahoma State University
College of Behavioral Sciences

A program for gifted and talented Indian students

From June 7 through June 18 a special program for talented and gifted Indian students attending junior and senior high schools will be conducted on the campus at Northeastern Oklahoma State University, Tahlequah, Oklahoma. This program, sponsored by the Oklahoma State Department of Education, Indian Education Section, and the Bureau of Indian Affairs, Muskogee Area Office, has been designed to benefit Indian students with unique academic or artistic abilities . . .

problems, obstacles, disappointments, and frustrations characteristic of the migrant stream.

Rafael was born in Mexico City. His father's people were from Mexico, and his mother's family just over the border in Texas. His parents moved to Pharr, Texas when he was seventeen years old, and the family migrated each summer to Idaho, along with Rafael's grandparents who had migrated to Idaho for eighteen years until the grandmother passed away. The family still migrates to Idaho in the summer.

Schooling was a problem, and until he was of high school age, he got his education as most migrant children do—just as they can, wherever they are at the time. Later, he was enrolled in the Adult Migrant Education Project in Edinburgh, Texas, for almost two years. Here he had bilingual teachers who understood the problems of the migrant young person. They encouraged him. They were excellent teachers, and he learned a great deal from them.

In 1971, Rafael stopped migrating. Carol Stockton, who was the director of the Head Start Program in Nampa, Idaho, told him about the COPE (Cooperative Program for Educational Opportunity) program. "She told me about it several times, but I was hesitant. Finally, I applied and got an opportunity to study and work part-time in the Nampa School District," Rafael said. He stayed a year, and during that time, a new world opened up to him. He learned through Mrs. Stockton about financial aid given by the University of Idaho, so he made application and was given assistance. He worked at the Title I Teenage Migrant Summer School in Nampa, and he was able to continue his studies at the University of Idaho, earning his bachelor's degree in education. He is now a bilingual teacher in the Lakeview Elementary School, working with fourth graders.

"More than anything else, I want to help children—all children who need help," he said. There was an intensity in his voice that underscored his dedication.

"I know the fears, frustrations, the obstacles and failures that a migrant child experiences," he said. "And I want to tell them that they *can* succeed. They can learn English. They can do anything they want, if they will preserve their culture, and remember where they came from and where they are going" (Baker, 1977, pp. 34–36).

We cannot present any panacea, or cure-all, to culminate the discussion in this unit. The complexity of the social problem under scrutiny remains enormous. One can only look to the future for more effective methods of giving "solid substance to the American dream" (Committee for Economic Development, 1971, p. 82). As in the cases of the other exceptionalities treated in this text, attitudinal changes on the part of society—stemming from greater understanding—must take place in order to make further progress.

Summary

This unit has discussed the various problems experienced frequently by children and youth from backgrounds that include racial and ethnic minorities, migrant workers, isolated rural poor families, and inner-city ghetto dwellers. Their condition has been considered as it thwarts fulfillment of human needs. Aspects of poverty as specifically related to nutrition, housing, family functioning and structure, language, and educational problems have received consideration, along with some prevention and intervention strategies to alleviate problems.

Society must concentrate further on providing better solutions to existing problems and capitalize on the many existing strengths and potentials that can be

A success! The visible interest among Ricky's peers in his accomplishment can be a motivating factor for future learning.

found within this diverse group of youngsters and their families. Attitudinal changes are a necessary part of the solution-finding process, as unwarranted prejudices and stereotypes must be eliminated to ensure needed progress. The goals for which we strive in meeting the needs of the societally neglected were put very cogently by a great Scottish essayist.

"The great law of culture is:
Let each become all that he was created capable of being;
expand, if possible, to his full growth;
and show himself at length in his own shape and stature,
be these what they may." (Thomas Carlyle)

References and resources

Baker, B. M. "Success Stories." *Delta Gamma Bulletin,* vol. 43, no. 2 (1977), pp. 31–39.

Bernstein, B. "Social Class and Linguistic Development: A Theory of Social Learning." In *Education, Economy and Society,* edited by A. H. Halsey, J. Floud, and C. A. Anderson. New York: Free Press, 1961.

Biller, H. B. *Father, Child, and Sex Role.* Lexington, Mass.: D. C. Heath, 1971.

Borden, J. P.; Wollenberg, J.; and Handley, H. M. "Extended Positive Effects of a Comprehensive Head Start Follow-Through Program Sequence on Academic Performance of Rural Disadvantaged Students." *Journal of Negro Education* 44 (1975): 149–60.

Bradley, R. C. *The Education of Exceptional Children.* Wolfe City, Tex.: University Press, 1970.

Brickman, W. W. "Varieties of the Educationally Disadvantaged: An Introduction." In *Education and the Many Faces of the Disadvantaged: Cultural and Historical Perspectives,* edited by W. W. Brickman and S. Lehrer, pp. 1–15. New York: Wiley, 1972.

Briggs, D. *Your Child's Self-Esteem: The Key to His Life.* New York: Doubleday, 1970.

Bronfenbrenner, U. "Motivation and Social Components in Compensatory Education Programs. Suggested Principles, Practices, and Research Designs." *Critical Issues in Research Related to Disadvantaged Children,* edited by E. Grotberg, pp. 1–34. Princeton, N.J.: Educational Testing Service, 1969.

Carter, T. O. "The Negative Self-Concept of Mexican-American Students." In *Education and the Many Faces of the Disadvantaged: Cultural and Historical Perspectives,* edited by W. W. Brickman and S. Lehrer, pp. 137–40. New York: Wiley, 1972.

Colfax, J. "The Cognitive Self-Concept and School Segregation: Some Preliminary Findings." In *Education and the Many Faces of the Disadvantaged: Cultural and Historical Perspectives,* edited by W. W. Brickman and S. Lehrer, pp. 105–10. New York: Wiley, 1972.

Committee for Economic Development. *Education for the Urban Disadvantaged from Preschool to Employment.* Statement by the Research and Policy Committee. New York: Committee for Economic Development, 1971.

Conway, L. "Classroom in the Sky: A Power Trip for Disadvantaged Youth." *Phi Delta Kappan* 57 (1976): 570–74.

Cordasco, F. "Puerto Rican Pupils and American Education." In *Education and the Many Faces of the Disadvantaged: Cultural and Historical Perspectives,* edited by W. W. Brickman and S. Lehrer, pp. 126–31. New York: Wiley, 1972.

Cowles, M., ed. *Perspectives in the Education of Disadvantaged Children.* Cleveland: World Publishing, 1967.

Crow, L. D.; Murray, W. I.; and Smythe, H. H. *Educating the Culturally Disadvantaged Child: Principles and Programs.* New York: David McKay, 1966.

Dawson, H. S. *On the Outskirts of Hope.* New York: McGraw-Hill, 1968.

Dayton, D. H. "Early Malnutrition and Human Development." *Children* 16 (1969): 210–17.

Deutsch, C. "Some Effects of Poverty on Children" In *Perspectives in the Education of Disadvantaged Children,* edited by M. Cowles, pp. 83–95. Cleveland: World Publishing, 1967.

Deutsch, M. "The Disadvantaged Child and the Learning Process." In *The Disadvantaged Child,* by Deutsch and Associates, pp. 39–57. New York: Basic Books, 1967.

Emanuel, J. M., and Sagan, E. L. "The Intelligence, Reading Achievement and Arithmetic Scores of Head Start Attendees Compared to Head Start Non-attendees in the First, Second and Third Grades." *American Institute for Mental Studies Training School Bulletin* (1974) 119–31.

Fantini, D., and Weinstein, G. *The Disadvantaged: Challenge to Education.* New York: Harper and Row, 1968.

Foerster, L. M. "Language Experiences for Dialectally Different Black Learners. *Elementary English* 51 (1974) 193–97.

Fulton, R. "The Negro Child and Public Education." In *Education and the Many Faces of the Disadvantaged: Cultural and Historical Perspectives,* edited by W. W. Brickman and S. Lehrer, pp. 79–85. New York: Wiley, 1972.

Goodman, Y. M. "The Culture of the Culturally Deprived." *Elementary School Journal* 71 (1971): 376–83.

Gottlieb, D., and Ramsey, C. E. *Understanding Children of Poverty.* Chicago: Science Research Associates, 1967.

Gould, N. "Cultural Perspectives on the Education of the Poor." In *Perspectives in the Education of Disadvantaged Children,* edited by M. Cowles, pp. 33–52. Cleveland: World Publishing, 1967.

Haskell, M., and Yablonsky, L. *Juvenile Delinquency.* 2nd ed. Chicago: Rand McNally College Publishing Co., 1978.

Hilgard, E. R., and Atkinson, R. C. *Introduction to Psychology.* 4th ed. New York: Harcourt, Brace and World, 1967.

Justin, N. "Culture Conflict and Mexican-American Achievement." *School and Society* 98 (1970): 27–28.

Levine, D. U. "Stratification, Segregation, and Children in the Inner-City School." *School and Society* 98 (1970): 84–89.

Lewis, O. *La Vida.* New York: Random House, 1966.

Lively-Weiss, M. A., and Koller, D. E. "Selected Language Characteristics of Middle-Class and Inner-City Children." *Journal of Communication Disorders* 6 (1973): 293–302.

Maslow, A. H. *Toward a Psychology of Being.* 2nd ed. New York: Van Nostrand, 1968.

Maslow, A. H. "A Theory of Human Motivation." In *Motivation and Personality,* edited by A. H. Maslow. 2nd ed. 1970.

Monckeberg. F. "Severe Malnutrition and Irreversible Mental Retardation." *Journal of American Dietary Association* 54 (1969): 51.

National Education Association. "America's Other Children. Bilingual Multicultural Education: Hope for the Culturally Alienated." *NEA Reporter* vol. 15, no. 4 (1976), pp. 1, 13–15.

Organ, J. J. "Malnutrition: Crisis in Early Human Development." *Public Health Currents* vol. 10, no. 1 (1970a), pp. 1–4.

Organ, J. J. "The Fight Against Hunger and Malnutrition in the U.S." *Public Health Currents* vol. 10, no. 2 (1970b), pp. 1–4.

Parker, F. "Appalachia: Education in a Depressed Area." In *Education and the Many Faces of the Disadvantaged: Cultural and Historical Perspectives,* edited by W. W. Brickman and S. Lehrer, pp. 211–25. New York: Wiley, 1972a.

Parker, F. "Historical Perspective on Negro Deprivation, Protest, and Segregated Education." In *Education and the Many Faces of the Disadvantaged: Cultural and Historical Perspectives,* edited by W. W. Brickman and S. Lehrer, pp. 67–75. New York: Wiley, 1972b.

Rieber, M., and Womack, M. "Intelligence of Preschool Children as Related to Ethnic and Demographic Variables. *Exceptional Children* 34 (1968): 609–14.

Riggs, Ronald. "Sweatshops in the Sun." *Time,* 30 July 1973, p. 56–58.

Rotter, J. B. "Social Learning and Clinical Psychology." New York: Prentice-Hall, 1954.

Sanchez-Hidalgo, E. "Juvenile Delinquency and Cultural Deprivation." *Psychological Abstracts,* 1969, vol. 43, no. 02830.

Schaefer, A. E., and Johnson, O. C. "Are We Well Fed? . . . The Search for the Answer." *Nutrition Today* 4 (1969): 2.

Scott, W. S. "Meeting the Affective Needs of Disadvantaged Children. In *Perspectives in the Education of Disadvantaged Children,* edited by M. Cowles, pp. 159–82. Cleveland, Ohio: World Publishing, 1967.

United Press International release, October, 1975.

Wilson, H. "Parenting in Poverty." *Psychological Abstracts,* 1975, vol. 53, no. 09454.

ACTION
Vista Program
806 Connecticut Avenue, NW,
Washington, D.C. 20525

American Civil Liberties Union
Juvenile Rights Project
22 East 40th Street
New York, New York 10016

Committee for Economic Development
477 Madison Avenue
New York, New York 10022

Community Services Administration
Project Head Start
1200 Nineteenth Street, NW
Washington, D.C. 20506

National Advisory Council on the
 Education of Disadvantaged Children
425 Thirteenth Street, NW
Suite 1012
Washington, D.C. 20004

National Education Association
Project URBAN
1201 16th Street, NW
Washington, D.C. 20036

Office of Child Development
Research and Evaluation Division
P.O. Box 1182
Washington, D.C. 20201

U.S. Department of Health, Education and
 Welfare
Office of Education
Educational Research Information Center
Washington, D.C. 20208

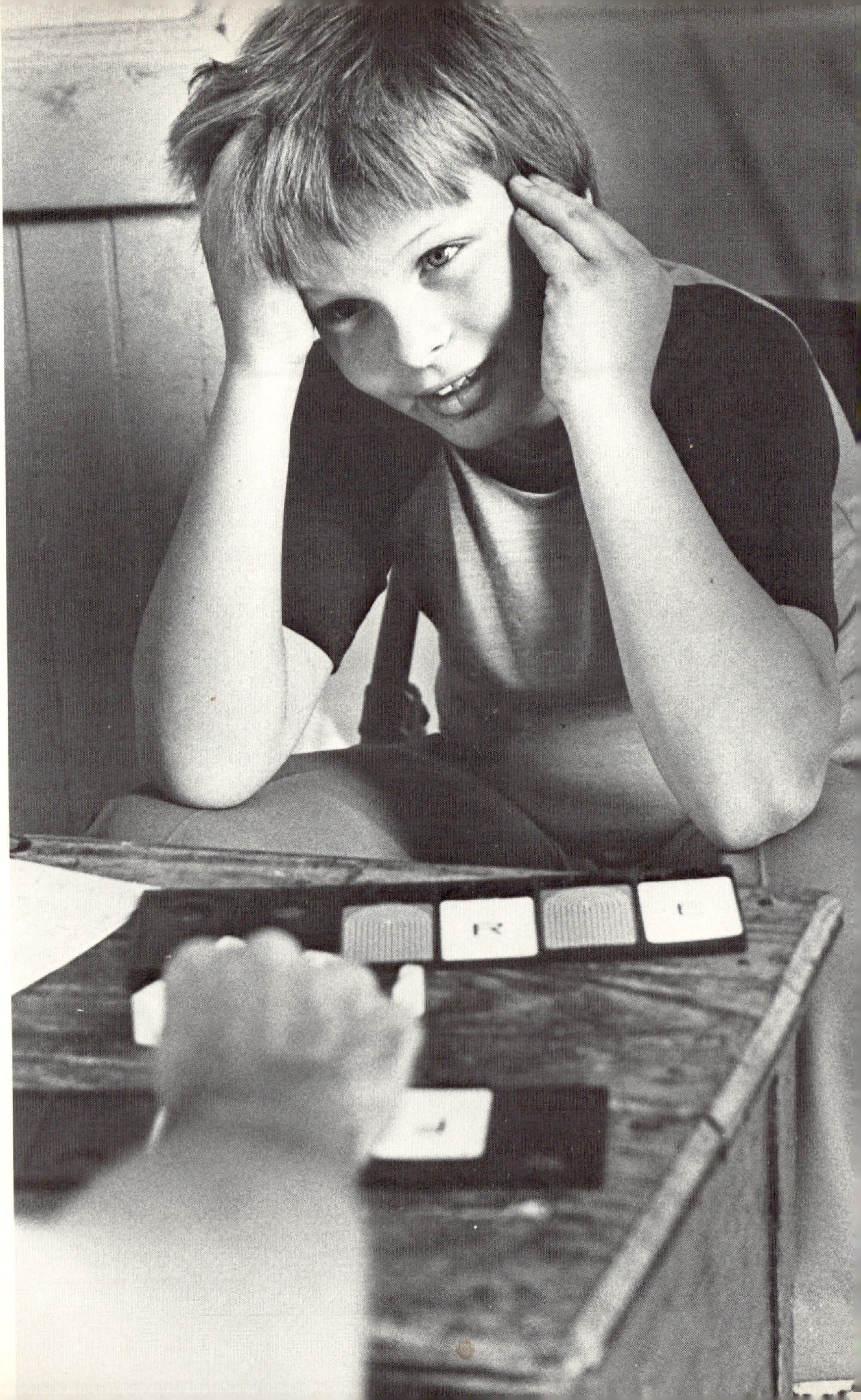

6 Children and youth with specific learning disabilities

B. Marian Swanson
Diane J. Willis

Definition of specific learning disabilities
Prevalence
Identification criteria • *Discrepancy* • *Exclusion criteria* • *Maturation difficulty* • *Neurological correlates*
Organic aspects • *Hard neurological signs* • *Soft neurological signs*
Perceptual-motor theory of specific learning disabilities • *Perception defined* • *Coordination, or motor functioning, difficulties* • *Cognitive abilities and concept formation*
Specific academic area difficulties • *Reading difficulties* • *Spelling and writing difficulties* • *Arithmetic difficulties* • *Speech and language difficulties*
Educational strategies • *Process, or modality, training* • *Task analysis procedure* • *Combination of process training and task analysis*
Aspects of social and emotional behavior • *Hyperkinesis and hyperactivity* • *Impulsiveness, or disinhibition* • *Distractibility* • *Perseveration* • *Emotional lability*
Correlation between juvenile delinquency and SLD
Problems of self-esteem and approaches to adaptive management • *Medical management or therapy* • *Operant conditioning, or reinforcement therapy* • *Other adaptive behavior techniques*
Need for continuing research
Summary

163

Children and youth with specific learning disabilities

Student learning objectives

The student will:
1. recognize the importance of understanding specific learning disabilities (SLD) as a separate entity from other known disabling conditions
2. become acquainted with the various approaches used to define such children and to explain the cause(s) of specific learning disabilities
3. recognize that there exists a diversity of professional theories concerning the cause of specific learning disabilities
4. become acquainted with the characteristics we associate with children experiencing difficulties in learning (e.g., behavior, motor coordination, perception, specific academic area difficulty)
5. be able to define various terms used in SLD literature (for example, hyperactivity, impulsivity, distractibility, perseveration, emotional lability, gross motor problems, fine motor problems, receptive language, apraxia)
6. be able to explain some of the types of problems in the visual perception process and how these may relate to the learning process
7. be able to explain some of the types of problems in the auditory perception process and how these may relate to the learning process
8. become acquainted with the various approaches to adaptive management of problems exhibited by SLD children and youth
9. be able to define dyslexia and discuss academic areas of deficiences experienced by learning disabled children
10. be aware of the current, more common approaches to identifying and teaching children with specific learning problems

The area of specific learning disabilities has generated more parental involvement, legislation, and professional interest than almost any of the other areas of exceptionality. This has led to the formal recognition that children with learning disabilities fall within the definition of the exceptional. Previous units have dealt with the reasons for certain children's failure to achieve in academic areas (mental retardation, societal neglect), and later units will deal with other conditions contributing to difficulties in learning (emotional problems, sensorimotor impairment, or health difficulties).

Bright youngsters who have difficulty in learning

The particular children with whom we are now concerned present a distinctive challenge to educators and parents because reasons for their learning problems are not as easily discernible as those of other children with handicapping conditions. In fact, much controversy still surrounds the means of identification, the underlying causes, and the strategies for remediation of learning disabilities. Despite the lack of total agreement on these and other issues, it is acknowledged that children with specific learning disabilities have greater difficulty in learning than do most other children despite the fact that they have average, above-average, or even superior intellectual potential. Hence, a bright child may be unable to achieve academically. This is a tremendous waste of potential and a devastating blow to the child's self-concept.

The field of learning disabilities is still so new that approaches to identifying and teaching this group of children are continuing to evolve. There is no "best" approach, and the teacher skilled in this field must be flexible and adapt and integrate procedures based upon the needs of the individual child. Until recent years, children with specific learning disabilities have been misdiagnosed as being hearing-impaired, emotionally handicapped, of lowered intellectual potential, or characterized in general terms as unwilling or unable to learn. There *is* one area of general agreement now, however; children diagnosed as learning disabled possess the potential for greater achievement and success than formerly recognized and acknowledged.

Definition

Samuel A. Kirk proposed the term *learning disabilities* in 1963 to describe a heterogeneous group whose learning problems were described by a variety of terms, including brain-injured, dyslexic, aphasic, and perceptually handicapped (1977). These terms are still used today although they are not inclusive of all children who are diagnosed as learning disabled. The current definition of specific learning disability is cited in Public Law 94-142:

SLD as defined by P.L. 94-142

> "Specific learning disability" means a disorder in one or more of the basic psychological processes involved in understanding or in using language, spoken or written, which may manifest itself in an imperfect ability to listen, think, speak, read, write, spell, or to do mathematical calculations. The term includes such conditions as perceptual handicaps, brain injury, minimal brain dysfunction, dyslexia, and developmental aphasia. The term does not include children who have learning problems which are primarily the result of visual, hearing, or motor handicaps, of mental retardation, of emotional disturbance, or of environmental, cultural, or economic disadvantage (US Office of Education, 1976, p. 42478; 1977, p. 52404).

In this unit the abbreviation *SLD* will refer to the nominal form *specific learning disabilities,* and to its adjectival form, *specific learning disabled,* as well.

Prevalence

Prevalence figures on the number of SLD children and youth have varied substantially, primarily because of the criteria used to determine whether or not a child is learning disabled (Lerner, 1976). The 1976 Annual Report of the National Advisory Committee on the Handicapped (HEW, 1976) estimates the number of children and youth at approximately two million (see Unit 1, Table 1-4). The prevalence of learning disabilities according to severity and the suggested types of placement program are

Two million children estimated as SLD

diagrammed in Figure 6-1. Special class programs are recommended for only a small number (1 to 2 percent) of the children diagnosed as learning disabled.

Identification criteria

The law requires that further information be set forth to clarify conditions that must exist before it is determined that a child has a specific learning disability. A multidisciplinary team approach must be used to evaluate the child. Included among the team members must be: (1) a child's regular assigned teacher or, if the child is non-assigned, a teacher qualified to teach a child of his or her age; (2) at least one individual who is qualified to conduct individual diagnostic examination of children. As a further aid to the team in determining if a specific learning disability exists, the law states that "the child's academic performance in the regular classroom setting . . . must be observed by a team member or members . . . other than the child's regular teacher" (U.S. Office of Education, 1977, p. 65083).

Multidisciplinary team approach required

Discrepancy

Using the team approach, a specific learning disability is designated if

1. the child does not achieve commensurate with his or her age and ability levels in one or more of the areas listed below when provided with learning experiences appropriate for the child's age and ability levels
2. the team finds that a child has a severe *discrepancy between achievement and intellectual ability* in one or more of the following areas:
    a. oral expression
    b. listening comprehension
    c. written expression
    d. basic reading skill
    e. reading comprehension
    f. mathematic calculation
    g. mathematics reasoning (USOE, 1977, p. 65083).

The reason for the discrepancy between achievement and intellectual ability is not clearly understood, except to say that the SLD child has a circumscribed deficit that prevents learning to read, write, or comprehend in a routine way. In presenting the SLD child with various other tasks that are not achievement-test related, however, it is evident that the child performs well.

Circumscribed deficit

Exclusion criteria

Also included in the current definition of learning disabilities are *exclusion criteria*, used as guidelines for identifying learning disabled children (Kirk, 1977). Under these criteria, children who have learning problems due primarily to other disabilities (visual, hearing, or motor; retardation; emotional; and/or environmental, cultural, economic) are excluded from the specific learning disability category. By excluding children and youth with other handicaps it by no means suggests that none of them have learning disabilities. It simply means that these children require educational services that address their specific handicaps.   *No other handicap*

The federal guidelines recognize and emphasize the identification of SLD by: (1) discrepancy between achievement and intelligence, and (2) exclusion criteria. In addition to these means of understanding children labeled learning disabled, an understanding of the maturational processes within the child can give us further insights into possible identification approaches.

Figure 6.1
Prevalence of learning disabilities by degrees of severity and types of programs they require

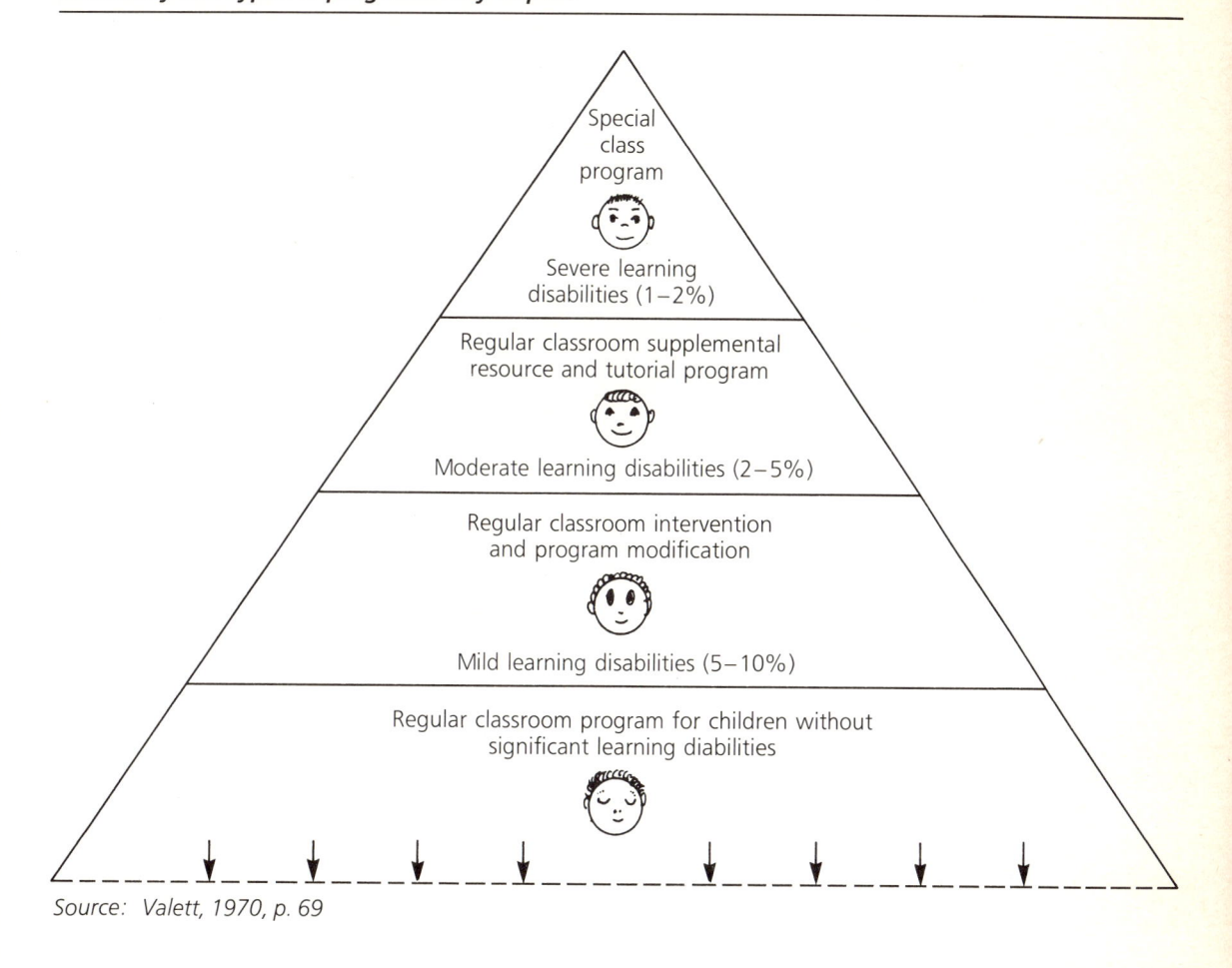

Special class program
Severe learning disabilities (1–2%)

Regular classroom supplemental resource and tutorial program
Moderate learning disabilities (2–5%)

Regular classroom intervention and program modification
Mild learning disabilities (5–10%)

Regular classroom program for children without significant learning diabilities

Source: Valett, 1970, p. 69

Maturation difficulty

The *maturational,* or *developmental,* process of children can vary. Researchers have focused on the presence of maturational unevenness, irregularity, or lag as a possible cause of learning problems (Bender, 1957; Slingerland, 1971). For example, boys mature more slowly than girls, and by age six, many boys as well as some girls may not be ready perceptually or in motor areas to learn to recognize letters of the alphabet or to print legibly. Testing instruments used to assess children five and six years of age may demonstrate visual-motor-perceptual problems that are related to a maturational lag and not to a true dysfunction within the child. Developmental disorders of language and learning may be attributed to something inherently wrong within the child, when actually these disorders may be a function of maturation (Myers & Hammill, 1976). Numerous children are diagnosed as learning disabled who are indeed merely lagging in development. Intervention may be necessary, however, in the form of developmental programming to correct imbalances that can interfere with learning processes.

Maturational lag

Neurological correlates

A fourth identification approach has focused on *organic* or *neurological dysfunction* in children with specific learning disabilities. The reference within the current definition of SLD to medical conditions such as brain injury, minimal brain dysfunction, or perceptual handicap attests to the voluminous amounts of research extending through the years that relate specific learning deficits to neurological correlates. Many professionals in the field of learning disabilities currently contend that such emphasis is outmoded. They see such research as a cause-oriented approach (Faas, 1976) that serves little purpose to educators and others in determining and implementing remediation efforts. Others contend that knowledge of neurological implications can be helpful in understanding a child's overall educational strengths and weaknesses (Gaddis, 1975). Accordingly, the medical, or organic, aspects are worthy of further consideration. This is not to imply, however, that most SLD children are neurologically impaired.

Controversy over usefulness of this approach

Organic aspects

The physician can be a crucial member of the team of professionals charged with diagnosing and remediating SLD (Bateman & Frankel, 1972; Bennett, 1966; Richardson, n.d.). When something is wrong with a child, even including learning problems in school, many parents will seek out a physician for advice. A thorough physical examination of the child frequently includes a review of the child's past history, a complete series of blood tests, and a review of the sensory system (vision, taste, hearing, speaking, etc.). In the past (and to some extent even now within the medical profession) the child with SLD was thought to have an organic or neurological problem. The next step then was to see if the child had what are termed hard neurological signs.

Physician as member of team

Hard neurological signs

Past research indicates that problems in learning (as well as behavior) could result from lesions or impairment of the central nervous system (CNS). The CNS is comprised of the brain and the spinal cord (see Figure 6-2). Difficulty, however, was encountered in corroborating the presence of hard neurological signs—that is, a *known lesion* of the central nervous system—in many children who presented learn-

Lesion of the central nervous system

Introducing Ned—a bright youngster who needs special help for his specific learning disability. Here we see him receiving individualized vocabulary instruction in the resource room from his SLD teacher.

ing and behavioral difficulties not attributable to other handicapping conditions (Wender, 1973). To date, in fact, SLD is not attributable to hard neurological factors except in those children who have had head injuries, brain surgery, or tumors. Hence, while brain damage may be one reason for learning and behavioral problems, a number of other factors can produce the same problems.

Soft neurological signs

Some children who are diagnosed as SLD do have a history of soft neurological signs of the types described by Strauss and Lehtenin in their early studies of brain-injured

Figure 6.2
Illustration of the cerebral cortex, cerebellum, spinal cord, and brain lobe areas associated with specific functions

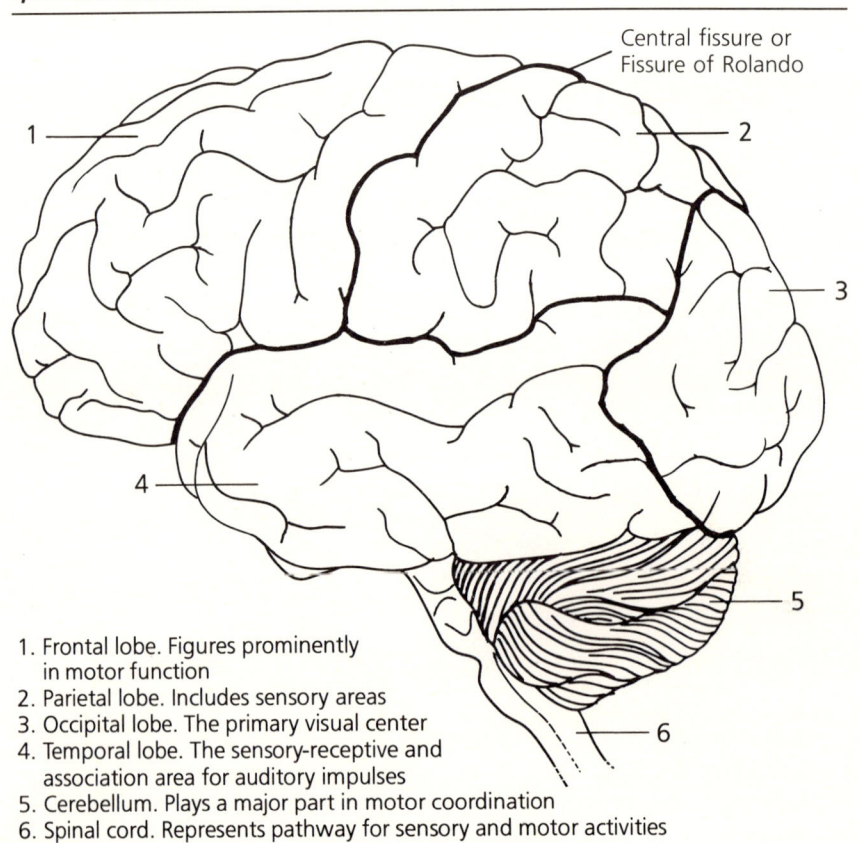

1. Frontal lobe. Figures prominently in motor function
2. Parietal lobe. Includes sensory areas
3. Occipital lobe. The primary visual center
4. Temporal lobe. The sensory-receptive and association area for auditory impulses
5. Cerebellum. Plays a major part in motor coordination
6. Spinal cord. Represents pathway for sensory and motor activities

Source: A programmed approach to anatomy and physiology: the nervous system. *Transparency No. 7, Courtesy of the Robert J. Brady Co., Washington D.C., 1974. (adapted)*

children (1947). Later termed the "Strauss syndrome" (Stevens & Birch, 1957), learning and thinking problems appeared related to (1) perceptual disorders (visual, auditory, and space perception); (2) inappropriate behaviors (distractibility, hyperactivity); (3) motor functioning difficulty (awkwardness).

The term *minimal brain dysfunction* was suggested by Clements to refer to children exhibiting soft neurological signs concomitant with learning difficulties (1966). Before discussing the characteristics most often associated with the minimal cerebral dysfunction syndrome, the student should be aware that this syndrome is *not* necessarily associated with a learning problem. Lerner (1976) points out that

May or may not be problems associated with SLD

1. A wide range of soft signs of minimal neurological dysfunction occurs among children who *are* learning.
2. Because the child's neurological system is not yet mature and is continually changing, it is often very difficult to differentiate between a lag in maturation and a dysfunction of the central nervous system.
3. Many of the tests for soft signs are psychological or behavioral rather than neurological tests (p. 51).

Despite this complexity, many interested physicians and researchers continue their efforts to detect existing conditions in children that might suggest later specific learning problems. A good medical examination of cranial nerves coupled with a good medical history is helpful in taking into account or ruling out any neurological problems. The use of an electroencephalograph, or brain wave recording (EEG), as a diagnostic tool by most physicians or pediatric neurologists is indicated only if there is a question of seizures or other brain abnormality. The efficiency of the EEG in detecting minimal cerebral dysfunction has been found to be questionable.

Perceptual-motor theory of specific learning disabilities

The use of the term *perceptual handicap* as included within the current definition of SLD children is an outgrowth of a medical orientation—relating specific learning disabilities to neurological dysfunction. So-called perceptual problems in the SLD child are not limited to his or her sensory awareness (visual and hearing acuity). While any child experiencing learning problems should first receive complete visual and hearing examinations as a part of the evaluation process, perceptual difficulties may be evidenced in the absence of sensory deficits. However, there *are* indications that children with diagnosed seizure problems are "high risk" for demonstrating perceptual-motor problems (Willis & Thomas, 1978).

Perceptual difficulties in absence of sensory deficits

Numerous theories have been postulated about perceptual-motor development and its relationship to learning. One theory deals with visuomotor development as it relates to learning (Getman, 1965). Another, which we will discuss here, deals with the stability of perceptual-motor development, stressing that a child's view of the world as a reliable place depends upon normal motor development of

Stable perceptual-motor development

the sensory modalities (Kephart, 1967). Kephart's approach, as Lerner (1976) explains it, examines the normal sequential development of motor patterns and motor generalizations and compares the motor development of children with learning problems to that of normal children.

> Normal children are able to develop a rather stable perceptual-motor world by the time they encounter academic work at the age of six. For many children with learning disabilities, however, their perceptual-motor world is unstable and unreliable. These children encounter problems when confronted with symbolic materials because they have an inadequate orientation to what Kephart calls the basic realities of the universe that surrounds them (p. 142).

> As children gain information through motor generalizations, they also begin to note perceptual information. Since they cannot investigate all objects in motor fashion, they begin to learn to investigate them perceptually. Perceptual data only becomes meaningful when it is correlated with previously learned motor information; thus, perceptual information must be matched or aligned with the built-up body of motor information. Kephart terms the process of comparing and collating the two kinds of input data *perceptual-motor match* (Lerner, 1976, p. 145).

Perception defined

Although it is difficult to explain perception, it is clear from various definitions taken from the literature that more than just sensory awareness and adequate reception of stimuli is involved. [Italics are added to emphasize the various operational components included in the perceptual process as defined below and discussed in this unit.]

> The process through which we become *aware of* our environment by *organizing* and *interpreting* the evidence of our senses (Kagan & Haveman, 1972, p. 594).

> The *interpretation* of sensory information. The mechanism by which the intellect *recognizes* and *makes sense out* of sensory stimulation. The accurate *mental association* of present stimuli with *memories* of past experience (Forgus, 1966, p. 493).

> The process of information *extraction* in man's adaptive behavior which . . . we must relate . . . to the general problem of *cognitive development* if we are to understand fully the nature of the *reception, acquisition, assimilation,* and *utilization of knowledge.* Looked at in this way, perception becomes the core process in the acquisition of *cognition* or *knowledge* . . . the *superset;* with *learning* and *thinking* as *subsets* subsumed under the perceptual process (Forgus, 1966, pp. 1–2).

Integration, interpretation, organization, memory, and other activities are indicated in the perceptual process if meaningful learning and appropriate responding behaviors are to occur. The concise operational nature of the process of perception as a function of the central nervous system is still not clearly resolved, but the importance of an intact brain and spinal cord (CNS) for effective functioning is emphasized.

Visual aspects of perception Following through on the premise that perceptual skills comprise the foundation for the development and acquisition of adequate academic skills, aspects of visual perception continue to be studied. There are variances in describing these skills, so for the purposes of this unit a composite will be presented. *Perceptual skills underlie academic skills*

1. *Visual form perception* relates to the ability to perceive the shape, size, and positional aspects of an object. If a child is unable to recognize those properties that distinguish a square from a circle or a rectangle, it may be indicative of problems in form perception. The child may also have difficulty distinguishing [dog] and [DOG] or recognizing that [1 + 1 = □] requires the same response as $\begin{array}{r}1\\+1\\\hline\Box\end{array}$.

2. *Visual figure-ground differentiation* refers to the ability of a child or youth to focus upon some selected figure or object and screen out any irrelevant stimuli in the background (see Figure 6-3). Because his attention may switch from one distracting stimuli to another, a child with figure-ground problems may show an inability to concentrate. This type of differentiation is viewed as necessary to the reading process, since letters and words must be perceived without confusion from surrounding letters and words and must also be perceived in proper sequence (Frostig, 1972; Gaddis, 1975). Skills such as keeping one's place in reading, locating a particular word in the dictionary or in a sentence, scanning for specific information, and locating places on a map are examples of activities believed to involve figure-ground differentiation. *Reading skill dependent on figure-ground discrimination*

Figure 6.3
Example of figure-ground relationship

3. *Visual discrimination* involves the ability to note likenesses and differences in shapes or forms, letters, and words. This ability has been related to success in recognizing letter forms and words involved in the reading process.

4. *Visual-motor integration* refers to an ability to integrate vision and the movement of body parts. A motor integration problem can show up in activities like cutting, pasting, buttoning, and lacing, etc. A child with motor integration difficulties may have trouble with chalkboard writing or copying designs or words. The child's printing or writing may be almost illegible. The following case example illustrates a visual-motor integration problem that was negatively affecting school performance.

Bobby This six-and-a-half-year-old boy was referred to an evaluation center because of inattentiveness and poor concentration. He was evaluated during the summer before his entrance into the first grade. Bobby had above-average intelligence on verbal tests and low-average intelligence on performance tests. He could read at a second-grade level, perform math equivalent to a first-grade level, and spell (if the examiner wrote the words for him) near a second-grade level. Bobby's printing was illegible and he had serious visual-motor integration problems. Perceptually he could discriminate letters, words, and numbers but he was unable to transduce visual (perceptual) information to the motor system; that is, he could not print or write letters or numbers. Bobby's attempt to reproduce symbols used in an achievement test is shown in Figure 6-4. Educational planning included modality training (discussed later in this unit). Results of the training over a brief period of time can be seen in Figure 6-5.

5. *Spatial integration* refers to perceiving positional aspects of objects in space. Forgus (1966) states that

it would be difficult to conceive of man's adjusting adaptively to his world if he did not respond to its spatial aspects in a relatively accurate way. We must examine the way the individual locates objects not only with respect to one another but also with respect to his own bodily orientation (pp. 182–83).

Mirror writing or reading (writing or reading words upside down and backwards), reversals or rotations of words, letters, or figures (*saw* for *was*, *m* for *w*, 6 for 9), or problems in accurate sequencing of letters or words in a sentence have been cited among the difficulties related to space perception (Frostig et al., 1963; Frostig, 1972).

6. *Visual closure* relates to the ability of an individual to perceive the entirety of an object when only fragments are presented—in other words, the ability to fill in missing aspects of a word or object. Symptoms associated with visual closure problems in the SLD child are: slowness or difficulty with close visual work, as words and pictures have to be carefully scrutinized; difficulty with similar-looking written let-

ters (*n* and *m*) or with closure of symbols required in the arithmetical process; and confusion of letters or numbers (*B* seen as *13*). Visual closure has been recognized as related to the reading process, since the eye fixates and perceives only parts of letters in a word or phrase (Kirk et al., 1968a, 1968b; Kirk & Kirk, 1972).

7. *Visual memory* is the ability to activate or recall visual images. In visual *recognition,* one indicates familiarity with the stimulus presented. In visual *recall,* memory is required without recognition cues being available. The individual must be able to activate a visual image when needed for various kinds of learning tasks. Children who exhibit deficits in the ability to visually recall letters, words, or numerals can be considered to have visual memory problems. Thus spelling from dictation, writing a sequence of numbers from memory, and other written language tasks that are to be

Visual memory as related to classroom expectation

Figure 6.4
Bobby's attempt to reproduce symbols on a part of the Wide Range Achievement Test

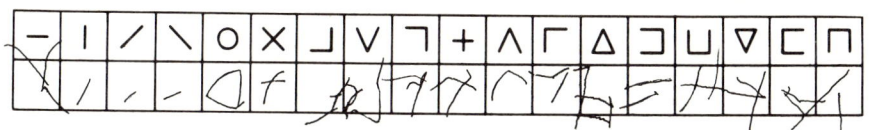

Source: Jastek et al., 1976, p. 1.

Figure 6.5
Results of modality training

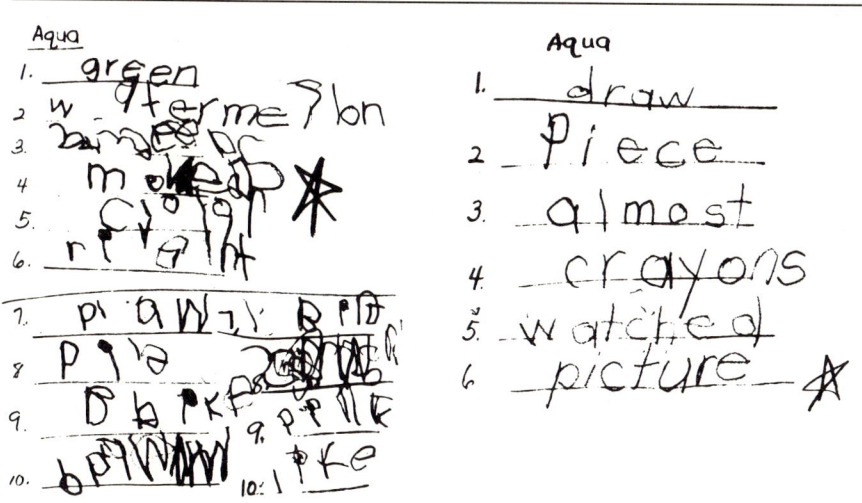

Bobby's printing before training

Bobby's printing after three months of modality training

spontaneously produced can constitute a specific area of learning difficulty. Visual memory problems also extend to difficulty in recalling aspects relating to people or objects, so that performance on drawing-from-memory tasks can be affected (Johnson & Myklebust, 1967).

The preceding discussion relating visual form, figure-ground discrimination, motor integration, closure, space, and memory is not totally inclusive of the visual perception process, but these aspects of visual perception are required in both early and later stages of the learning process.

Auditory aspects of perception The very young child progresses from an early understanding of a limited number of words to understanding more complex speech and language. As in visual perception, there are numerous components involved in auditory perception. Although there is not total agreement concerning the relationship of certain auditory perceptual abilities to general or specific abilities in the reading process (Hammill & Larsen, 1974; Martinus & Hoovey, 1972; Stubblefield & Young, 1975), various researchers cite evidence that the learning process is dependent to some degree on intact auditory perceptual skills (Bannatyne, 1971; Carpenter & Willis, 1972; Johnson & Myklebust, 1967; Kirk et al., 1968a, Kirk et al., 1968b; Kirk & Kirk, 1972; Minskoff et al., 1972). The most frequently discussed auditory skills are reviewed below:

Auditory discrimination includes the ability to recognize specific sounds in speech and to differentiate between similar-sounding letters such as *b, p,* and *d,* as well as similar-sounding whole words such as *pan* and *man*. Locating the positional arrangements of sounds in words (initial, medial, or final) is dependent upon initial discriminatory skills. A child's lack of ability in phonetics or understanding of speech sounds can complicate the process of making sense out of what he or she is hearing.

Beyond basic discriminatory skills, *auditory receptive skill*—the process of attaching meaning to incoming verbal stimuli—is essential for continued learning. Auditory receptive difficulties may result in inconsistent or inappropriate responses to the spoken word or to verbal communication.

As the visual memory process can serve as part of the foundation for further learning, *auditory memory*—or the stable retention of information presented verbally—can serve as another foundation for efficient functioning and absorption of knowledge. In the home and school, auditory memory demands are ever present; learning is extensively based upon recalling or remembering information and knowledge presented verbally. Short-term (primary) memory problems may be indicated if the child is observed as having difficulty in implementing a series of auditory directions. Long-term (secondary) memory problems may be present if difficulty is evidenced in satisfactory recall of previously learned material presented auditorally (and meaningfully, of course). A case example follows:

Jan A nine-and-a-half-year-old fourth-grader was referred for evaluation by her teacher because of an inability to spell. She was above average in intelligence and was achieving at grade level in math and reading but was two grades below grade placement in spelling. A consistent auditory sequential problem was found on a number of tests. Auditory discrimination deficits were ruled out and no other problems were apparent. Jan was asked to print a story on any topic she chose. She printed her story (shown in the top section of Figure 6-6) and then she was asked to read it aloud. (What she read is shown at the bottom of the figure.)

Gaps in comprehension

Auditory closure as a part of the organizational process leading to understanding involves integrating separate parts into meaningful wholes to extract meaning from general auditory input. Not every auditory stimulus or sound element can or should be attended to for processing overall auditory comprehension. Inadequate closure skills can produce distortions or gaps that interfere with initial comprehension of material to be learned and/or its later appropriate use. Auditory closure difficulty can show up as problems in understanding someone who speaks very rapidly or in understanding words in a song (Minskoff et al., 1972). Lack of closure in the endings of words (causing incorrect number or tense changes) can produce grammatical usage errors in later written or spoken application—for example, "the boy all voted" or "he sit over there."

The preceding discussion has acknowledged the relationship of perception to the total learning process as reflected in past and present research. Our attention now will focus on motoric or coordination skills as a part of the total learning and adjustment process and as a requirement for successful school performance.

Figure 6.6
Example of auditory sequential memory problem

This is what Jan printed:

Are dog r,ame is Jan. He is 1,yese
old. He was bane Oct. 7,1969. He ean
jume up to my hed inea much. He is
a lat dag. He is bake lake ves
iset on his neck he has a white
dot ther. He a good pet I like him.
His mom is red laki ves.

This is what Jan read:

Our dogs name is John. He is 1 year old. He was born October 7, 1969. He can jump almost up to my head. He is a little dog. He is black all over except on his neck he has a white dot there. He is a good pet I like him. His mom is red all over.

Coordination, or motor functioning, difficulties

Motor or expressive responses viewed as "a complex, coordinated series of movements which accomplish a purpose" (Kephart, 1964, p. 22) can present difficulties for a certain number of SLD children who are observed as frequently erratic or irregular in body control or are described as awkward, clumsy, or careless. While not paralyzed in any way, the body fails to react in a normal, smooth manner in the performance of certain types of motor skills. Various types of motor functioning difficulties have been cited as characteristic of learning disabled children (Boder, 1966; Koppitz, 1975). Loss of ability to perform certain purposeful movements or skilled motor acts in the absence of paralysis is defined as *apraxia* (Frierson & Barbe, 1967; Johnson & Myklebust, 1967; Kephart, 1964), with apractic-type tasks often included in pediatric neurological examinations (Boder, 1970; Thomas et al., 1973; Wender, 1973).

Erratic body control

Motor integrity often is assumed erroneously to reflect increased maturity associated with intellectual ability. The alert classroom teacher is in a position to observe coordination problems which may be present in any child, particularly the learning disabled. Difficulties with the coordination of movements of larger muscles are referred to as *gross motor problems*. Activities such as running, skipping, hopping, throwing, and catching involve the use of larger muscles, and deficiencies are noted when gross motor skills are not consistent with expected developmental levels. Lack of large muscle control or coordination can be observed in a child on the school playground. Children who are awkward and clumsy may develop a feeling of inferiority when their motor competency is compared with that of other children of their age.

Activities associated with gross motor skills

Fine motor problems involve difficulty with coordination or movement of smaller muscles. Fine motor skills are an early prerequisite to the successful completion of such school tasks as drawing, cutting, pasting, printing, or writing. These skills involve the use of the smaller muscles of the fingers and hand. When first exposed to using pencil, crayons, or scissors in preschool or kindergarten, the child is expected to make many mistakes. With experience, practice, and maturational growth, fine motor skills are expected to reach increasing refinement. These skills are reflected in writing and other more exacting motor coordination tasks required with advanced grade placement.

Classroom success depends on fine motor skills

Coordination difficulties of the apractic type have been extended to problems in producing the motor movements necessary in speech. *Expressive speech* problems are viewed as apractic in nature when the child knows what he or she wishes to say but fails in initiating or coordinating appropriate motor movements of the tongue and other oral structures needed for understandable speech. The presence of severe articulation disorders in which the child's speech is mostly unintelligible is sometimes referred to as *verbal apraxia* (Johnson & Myklebust, 1967) and is included as one of the various types of expressive communication disorders. (See Unit 8 for further discussion.)

Motoric difficulties lead to speech problems

Cognitive abilities and concept formation

Cognitive abilities or skills "refer to a collection of mental abilities that enable one to know and to be aware. Cognition refers to the manner in which humans acquire, interpret, organize, store, retrieve, and employ knowledge" (Lerner, 1976, p. 278). Adequate cognition depends upon all the processes discussed in the section on perception. If a child is evidently bright and not emotionally disturbed, yet has difficulty reasoning or making sense out of the environment or out of tasks that the teacher explains over and over, he or she is likely manifesting a specific learning disability. Children with known head injuries, for instance, may demonstrate such disturbances in their thinking processes. A child may be able to make sense out of isolated events but never be able to put everything together into a meaningful whole.

Understanding that a whole is the sum of its parts

It is like thinking of the game of baseball as throwing a ball, or as hitting a ball, or as running, without grasping the relationship among all three in terms of what these efforts are meant to achieve. In order to play the game successfully, one must

Progressing at his own pace, Ned is absorbed in the learning task his SLD teacher has assigned. She has selected an activity that will meet his needs.

grasp the whole concept BASEBALL. We learn to adapt to our environment according to the way we *perceive* and *understand* the total situation. Hence, concept-learning is extremely important. For example, some simple concepts are *cat, bed,* and *mother;* higher concepts relative to these are: *cat* is an *animal; bed* is *furniture; mother* is a *woman* or *person*. Children with language deficits may also be deficient in conceptual abilities, because through language a child can generalize rapidly to other concepts. For example, a child who understands the concept *run* after watching a teacher demonstrate the word by running, may not generalize the meaning to include *water running* or a *car running*.

Language deficits can lead to conceptual deficits

In summation, visual perceptual, auditory perceptual, motor coordination, and/or conceptual problems may and often do contribute to a child's inability to learn to read, write, or comprehend at a level commensurate with age, grade placement, or intellectual potential. It requires a thorough medical, psychological and educational evaluation to assess and delineate a child's specific strengths and weaknesses. The results of the evaluation generally demonstrate why a child is performing below grade level. According to Lerner (1976) the following steps are essential in making a diagnosis of why a child is not achieving (pp. 74–75).

Why the child is not achieving

1. Determine whether the child has a learning disability, i.e., is the child bright but achieving below expectations and does the child present developmental imbalances suggestive of SLD.
2. Measure the child's present achievement to determine where the child is failing and where the problem appears to be. For example, can the child not read because the child does not know the alphabet or has no knowledge of phonics or has serious perceptual problems?
3. Analyze how the child learns.
4. Explore why the child is not learning. Could it be due to poor auditory memory or to perceptual or conceptual problems?
5. Collate and interpret the data and formulate a diagnostic hypothesis.
6. Develop a plan for teaching in terms of the hypothesis that you have formulated. This includes delineating a child's strengths and weaknesses.

Specific academic area difficulties

Detailed explanation of specific remedial measures for varying types of academic disabilities are studied in courses on methods of teaching. Here, however, we need to consider ways in which learning problems based on perceptual, motoric, and/or conceptual problems are manifested in specific academic or skill areas as these are related to the SLD population.

Reading difficulties

Reading problems constitute one of the most frequently experienced difficulties of the SLD child or youth. Since so much learning is dependent on reading ability, problems in this area can be devastating.

Dyslexia

The term *dyslexia*, often used in discussion of reading disabilities, indicates "... the primary presenting symptom of difficulty in learning to read" (Vogel, 1974, p. 104). Specific definitions will vary according to the biases or interests of the professional groups (medical, psychological, educational) concerned with reading problems (Blom & Jones, 1970), but the term *dyslexic* should not be indiscriminately applied to children with reading difficulties. Generally excluded are those children whose reading problems stem from lowered intellectual potential, sensory acuity disabilities (speech, hearing, vision), emotional disorders (Johnson & Myklebust, 1967) or are the result of societal neglect (Kirk et al., 1968). Neurological dysfunction may or may not be present (Vogel, 1974). Frierson (1967) defines dyslexia as a "partial inability to read or to understand what one reads silently or aloud." He goes on to say that "some authors refer to genetic, affective, experiential and congenital dyslexia" (p. 491).

We have noted that definitions of dyslexia vary; it must be recognized, too, that interpretation of the term has to be considered in relation to the context in which it is discussed. In cases where the child has a specific learning disability in the area of reading, we would want to know if such reading difficulties are due to inadequate visual or auditory perceptual skills, conceptual difficulties, or perhaps even a combination of various perceptual deficits. For example, Carpenter and Willis (1972) emphasize the necessity of focusing attention on auditory perception and not just on visual perception, since children can be dyslexic because of auditory problems.

Different kinds of perceptual deficits in reading

Patterns of dyslexia   Boder (1970) suggests three patterns that reflect

> ... atypical patterns of reading and spelling among dyslexic children.... The three dyslexic reading-spelling patterns appear ... to be diagnostic in themselves ... and suggest a useful diagnostic approach. These three patterns—since they reflect the dyslexic child's functional assets as well as deficits in the visual and auditory processes prerequisite to reading—appear to have prognostic and therapeutic implications, differing for each of the three subtypes (p. 239).

Boder's three groups include a dysphonetic group (group 1), in which there is "a primary deficit in letter-sound integration and in the ability to develop phonetic skills" (p. 289). Due to this deficit and consequent lack of phonetic skill, children in this group are unable to read words that are not in their whole word or sight vocabulary. Their spelling ability also suffers, since they are unable to apply phonetic skills to correct spelling of words.

Lack of phonetic skills

A second group described by Boder is termed the dyseidetic group (group 2), which reflects a primary deficit in the ability to perceive whole words. "They read phonetically, sounding out words, familiar and unfamiliar, as if they were being encountered for the first time" (p. 289). Spelling words are written phonetically so that errors include such misspellings as "lisn" for *listen* and "laf" for *laugh* (p. 290).

Inability to perceive whole words

Boder's third group includes children who are both dysphonetic and dyseidetic

Nonreaders

(group 3). Their lack of phonetic skill causes these children to experience difficulty in "perceiving whole words as gestalts. . . . Without remedial reading therapy they tend to remain alexic, or nonreaders" (1970, p. 290). Similarly, in the same sense as they may be said to be nonreaders, they are nonspellers (Boder, 1973, p. 671).

Identification and remediation   In providing appropriate remediation for dyslexia, the discerning teacher will wish to refer the child to an examiner qualified to assess the type of specific deficits present. The classroom teacher can aid in the assessment in an informal way. With close observation the teacher can determine if the child has difficulty in hearing differences in sounds (group 1), fails to recognize words previously encountered in reading and has to sound them out all over again to incorporate them into a meaningful whole (group 2), or is more severely disabled and lacks both phonetic and whole-word recognition skills (group 3).

Following determination of these and other possible types of deficits interfering with the reading process, the classroom teacher must then adapt reading material to the student's specific needs. This necessarily implies that books from more than one basal reader series may need to be present in the classroom, since different series may have different emphases on skills required of the child in the learning-to-read process. Assisted by resource personnel (e.g., reading specialists), the teacher needs to determine what early demands each particular basal book makes on the child. For example, does it primarily use an auditory approach in which learning to read is based on sounding, or auditory skills, or does it emphasize more of a visual approach, in which visual perceptual skills are emphasized for success in beginning reading? These and other methods (such as emphasis on linguistic patterns for beginning readers), which are used as different approaches in different reading series, need to be matched to each individual child's needs.

Boder (1970, 1973) also recognizes the possible presence of "the classic dyslexic errors . . . reversals and letter-order errors" (1970, p. 290) in any of her designated three groups. Such reversals, or sequencing problems, necessarily add to difficulties in the reading or spelling process. Remediation for these types of deficits would include exercises in which emphasis is placed on developing right-left, or directional, abilities in the child, as well as exercises aiding development of auditory or visual sequencing skills.

It can be seen that the common practice of having three ability-based reading groups in the classroom may still not provide enough individualized instruction for dyslexic children. If textbooks from only one basal series are used without regard to a specific dyslexic child's assets or deficits in reading skills, placement in the usual "slow" group may still not provide the remediation steps necessary to correct the child's deficiencies or capitalize on her abilities. Certainly if a child has consistently failed in the reading process for some time, the teacher may make use of referral sources (remedial reading centers and teachers, etc.) to aid in further diagnosis and selection of appropriate remedial procedures. Seeking such help should not be considered as a weakness in the teacher's ability to teach, but should be considered as reflecting genuine concern about realizing a child's potential for a more successful school experience.

McClurg (1970) offers the classroom teacher a comprehensive list of symptoms that may be associated with dyslexia. Several of these symptoms have been discussed earlier in this section and in the section on perceptual-motor difficulties. Two of the symptoms (10 and 11) more clearly fall under the category of secondary reactions to school learning problems. Excerpts from the list follow (pp. 373–74):

Symptoms associated with dyslexia

1. The child has average or above-average measured intelligence, but is a low achiever. His [or her] learning disabilities may appear as perceptual, conceptual, or coordination dysfunction.
2. The child may show deficiencies in conceptualization, sequencing, or spatial abilities.
3. Impaired visual perception may be reflected in poor eye-hand coordination and in the perception of figure-ground, organization, or spatial relationships.
4. Impaired auditory perception is indicated when the child has trouble in blending sounds and in sequencing small words. [He or she] . . . usually gains very little phonics and other word-attack skills in the first grade. The child's functional vocabulary consists of only a few short words he or she has memorized.
5. Directional confusions and reversing letters are common.
6. Information is fed into the brain and properly decoded (input), but there is erraticism or malfunctioning in the encoding (output) processes.
7. Limitations in motor coordination are common.
8. Speech disorders are of varying degrees.
9. Attention and perseveration disorders may be found.
10. Unpredictable and disorganized behavior can be expected when the child tries to function in frustrating situations.
11. The child's primary learning disabilities may contribute to secondary psychological problems. It is a safe prediction that such problems will intensify until he [or she] gets corrective or remedial help.

Spelling and writing difficulties

In addition to problems in reading, the SLD child may encounter difficulty in spelling and writing tasks required in the academic setting. *Dysorthography* is a term used to refer to a specific disability in spelling. *Dysgraphia*, or *graphomotor problems*, refers to difficulty in executing movements made in writing. (Recall the case studies of Bobby and Jan in previous sections of this unit.) Like the reading process, both spelling and writing ability are dependent upon many subskills, so that the classroom

Spelling and writing ability depend on many subskills

teacher needs to carefully discern the specific nature of the spelling or writing difficulty underlying a particular child's problem. Despite the de-emphasis by some authorities of perceptual difficulties as the cause of specific learning disabilities, most educators acknowledge that the presence of visual or auditory discrimination, visual or auditory memory, sequencing ability, and eye-hand coordination are among the necessary prerequisites for success in spelling and writing tasks. *For successful remediation, the kinds of errors being made need to be analyzed and educational strategies must be employed to overcome specific deficits.*

Remediation techniques

It may be necessary to allow the child who has problems in remembering how letters are formed to respond orally to the spelling lesson while continuing to work on remediating this underlying disability. The child with apractic, or motor, difficulties in correctly forming letters or words also may need to utilize the oral response method to meet spelling or writing demands until motor difficulties are corrected. Such temporary adaptations can allow the student to chalk up some success, rather than experiencing constant failure because of existing deficiencies. Several researchers (Mullins et al., 1972) advocate use of a cursive script adapted for the SLD child; the technique is designed to reduce differences between writing demands and what the child experiences in book print.

Arithmetic difficulties

Disabilities specifically related to understanding calculation, relationships, and concepts in numbers or mathematics are often referred to as *dyscalculia*. As in the reading, writing, and spelling processes, symbols are used in arithmetic. Correct symbol identification and understanding of attached meaning are required. The SLD child may experience difficulty in discriminating between similar symbolic forms (*9* vs. *6*) or may exhibit motor deficiencies by writing incorrect figures (*3* instead of *5*).

Correct symbol and concept identification

Abilities in ordering and sequencing are required early—as in rote counting—and continue as a part of mathematical calculation and comprehension. Further difficulties for some SLD children can be experienced when more abstract terminology is used, such as *more than, less than,* and *equal to.* Reading difficulties also can contribute to arithmetic disabilities as computation of written or stated problems is introduced. The emphasis on conceptual understanding in the "modern math" approach can place an additional burden on some SLD children.

Using concrete objects or abacus

Using concrete objects or an abacus for counting can be beneficial in increasing the arithmetical understanding of some children who experience problems in grasping the abstractions included within numerals. There are a number of arithmetic teaching strategies available that can be related to specific disabilities and individualized educational plans.

Speech and language difficulties

Interwoven into our current discussion are a number of factors that can contribute to difficulties in the communication process—a process wherein individuals exchange information through oral or written means. We have already examined the factors involved in success or lack of success in spelling and writing.

To understand the development or acquisition of the communication process so that specific disabilities therein can be properly diagnosed and remediated re-

Ned's regular classroom teacher provides support and individual assistance. Here she helps on an arithmetic assignment.

quires more extensive analyses of speech and language disorders in children and youth. In terms of *oral* speech and language, this exceptionality will be covered separately in Unit 8. However, a specific *written language* problem can exist, beyond spelling and handwriting, wherein a child has difficulty in (1) understanding and using correct grammar or syntax and/or (2) formulating or conveying thoughts and ideas into written form (Johnson & Myklebust, 1967; Wallace & Kauffman, 1973). A case example can illustrate this specific learning disability.

> *Mark*   This bright eleven-year-old had good verbal expression and no problems in reading. However, he had great difficulty in translating or conveying his thoughts and ideas into the written language process. When describing the picture of an Indian, which he had drawn, Mark wrote the following:
>
>> 1690—The Indian play fight with the knife. Play Indian dance circle by the fire. In the morning the Indian wake up and ride float and catch the red fish for breakfast. And go far away to Squanto!
>> 1691—And then stop and make Indian house and go sleep for 1 day for sleep. The one Indian said, wow this is Squanto. The one Indian called everbuy wake up and looked all around that is Squanto.
>> 1694—The one Indian saw lot of cowboys 1,000! The one Indian ride horse and hurry and called the 900 Indians. The one Indian said Go the horse will be run and stop Get off the horse and walked up, up, up, up, all away up and stop and see the cattle. Indian said ready set go shoot with bow arrows, guns, spears, axs. Cowboys said Go Boom! Big gun power.
>> 1695—all cowboys and Indians was dead Is a skeleton 50 Indians not dead 30 Cowboy not dead
>
> When asked to read or tell his story, Mark expressed himself well, using good grammar and syntax. He used a good vocabulary and ordered the words together correctly to form phrases and sentences that transmitted his meaning.

Written language disorders may thus exist singly (as in Mark's case) or in combination with other specific areas of disability, such as the oral communication problems covered in Unit 8.

Educational strategies

Adjust the program instead of the child

Although in the past there has been a great deal of emphasis placed upon training the SLD child in specific perceptual processing skills, there is currently a swing away from such specified remedial efforts. The trend seems to be moving toward adjusting the programs used in the educational setting to meet the needs of the individual child rather than trying to adjust (train) the child to fit the program. This does not, however, mean that all efforts at improving perceptual skills in the child are dropped. Definite individual differences in a child's specific abilities may well be evident; results of research studies do not invalidate that idea. And these abilities may be assessed and deficits remediated with a comparable improvement in the child's learning. So while controversy over the educational strategies used to remediate SLD still goes on, the good classroom teacher will be adapting his or her teaching approach to the progress the child is making. Process, or modality, training, task analysis procedure, and a combination of the process and task analysis procedure are among the strategies most frequently used in the classroom.

Process, or modality, training

In this approach, the teaching plan is designed to remediate those processing functions that are deficient (Smead, 1977). For example, if a child has a reading problem due to poor auditory discrimination skills, he or she will be given exercises in differentiating one sound from another; the hope here is that this skill will continue to develop and thus facilitate progress in overall listening and reading skills at a later time. As was stated earlier, research has not substantiated the claims by some that this approach will, in fact, increase academic learning (Hammill & Larsen, 1974). But the notion is that we can overcome the deficit and eliminate the disability. And with many children this system works, as is illustrated in Figure 6-5.

Implicit in the process training approach is the recognition that training in a process has its own value without relation to academic success at some future date. In other words, certain perceptual skills are necessary for their own sake. If a child does not recognize or discriminate those things in his or her environment that can cause pain, for instance, the child will need to be taught that flame can burn or knife can cut. If a child cannot print or draw, it becomes necessary to train that child by providing exercises in drawing or printing. The preschool and kindergarten programs almost universally deal directly in this type of process training. Hence, skills in the perceptual areas mentioned in the previous section may be taught to a child in anticipation that reading or other academic skills might be improved.

Process training as an end in itself

Task analysis procedure

The task analysis procedure in remediation necessitates a thorough understanding of all the steps required in the learning of any specific task (Bush & Waugh, 1976). The procedure allows the teacher or diagnostician to determine exactly at which step the child's instruction should begin. This information is obtained through carefully designed assessment and observation, usually by the teacher. If a child fails in performing a task, the teacher analyzes that failure in an effort to determine whether the failure was in the teacher's manner of presentation or in the child's mode of response. For example, the teacher may ask students to circle a picture in their workbooks that rhymes with a word the teacher presents orally. The steps required in such a task include prior knowledge or experience with the pictures, auditory memory skills, ability to compare words, understanding of the word rhyme, and the motor skill necessary in order to make a circle. The above steps can be broken

Teacher must analyze every step in a process

down even further, but from the example it is clear that children are constantly asked to perform complicated tasks in order to succeed in the academic arena. It is also clear at this point that readiness for a particular task is vital to every student's success and that the teacher must be cognizant of the many steps involved in a specified task in order to guide each child toward successful performance.

Combination of process training and task analysis

Best remediation is through a combined approach

The majority of children will benefit from a strategy that combines the best aspects of the two preceding approaches. The resultant procedure will incorporate process and task training in the remedial program; that is, the child will be taught to utilize a specified process to accomplish the desired task. Let us say a child exhibits difficulty discriminating geometric shapes, and as a result of this perceptual problem, he or she also has difficulty discriminating letter shapes. In this instance the remedial efforts would be geared toward learning to recognize letter shapes rather than geometric shapes per se, since letter recognition is the ultimate goal (Kephart, 1971).

Aspects of social and emotional behavior

Behavior that interferes with learning

Certain kinds of social and/or emotional behavior have been (and still are to an extent) prominent in the discussion of SLD children. Such behavior is of concern because it can often interfere with or complicate the child's learning process and is seen as representing a departure from the norm.

It should be pointed out that while the types of behavior to be discussed are often associated with children with learning problems, in and of themselves they are not symptomatic of a learning disability. But despite problems in diagnosis and etiology, these symptoms need to be considered (Keogh, 1971). Parents may need counseling concerning their children's problems and special needs, educational adaptations may have to be made, and appropriate supportive or intervention strategies need to be utilized to help these children reach their academic and behavioral potential.

Classroom teachers are often the first to report these modes of behavior. Such symptoms are sometimes considered soft neurological signs when viewed from an approach that focuses on organic or neurological dysfunction in SLD children. (See the previous discussion in this unit on organic aspects of SLD.)

Hyperkinesis, or hyperactivity

The terms *hyperkinesis* (excessive and seemingly purposeless muscular movement) and *hyperactivity* are sometimes used synonymously. Walker (1975) describes them thus:

> Hyperactivity, also known as hyperkinesis, . . . is not a disease; it is merely a label for a constellation of signs and symptoms that can occur for various reasons. The hyperactive child's behavior is driven, uncontrolled. He

may have a short attention span, throw temper tantrums, and have difficulty sleeping, learning, sitting still, and responding to discipline. These symptoms may be present in whole or in part, to greater or lesser degrees. They may be present through the day, in the morning or at nighttime only, or after meals. They can occur in children of both sexes, though they are observed more frequently in boys (p. 354).

Children whose hyperactivity is believed to be of organic origin as determined by a physician may be treated by the use of individually prescribed medication. The trend, however, is away from medicating children, except for a few who may definitely require such help. Behavior modification techniques are used to moderate a child's activity level and biofeedback may be used. (See pp. 191–92 for a review of the latter two approaches to adaptive management.)

Alternatives to medication

Impulsiveness, or disinhibition
Children exhibiting this type of behavior seem to act on impulse or with sudden or unexpected thought or determination. They do not consider the consequences of their actions; they seem to act first and think later.

Distractibility
Distractible behavior is exhibited by the child whose attention is easily called away to various other stimuli. It is closely related to *short attention span,* where the child is able to focus his or her attention or concentration for only a short period of time.

Perseveration
In contrast to distractibility, *perseveration* represents a different type of attentional difficulty: the child manifests reponse behavior which is continued long after the response has value or appropriateness. Perseverating behavior can be seen either in motor activities or in verbal, ideational, or thought processes from which the child is unable to terminate appropriately. An example of perseveration is a child's repetitive drawing of dots, a line, or some other figure.

Emotional lability
Frequent changes of mood or instability of emotions in a child are referred to as *emotional lability.* From the medical point of view, such behavior is thought to represent fragility in central nervous system functioning. Emotional lability has also been related to frustration in meeting environmental demands. (A distinction must be made between emotional lability as characterized here and the manic-depressive symptoms discussed in Unit 7 relating to emotionally handicapped children and youth).

It has been noted by physicians, parents, and others that the behavioral symptoms described above tend to disappear in the preadolescent or adolescent stage. But feelings of inadequacy, a lack of confidence, lowered self-concept, anger, and

Need for early treatment program

frustration may remain with the child as a consequence of these former behavioral aspects. An early treatment program is advocated to include careful diagnosis, assistance, and cooperation from the school, counseling of the child's parents and/or the child, and consideration of possible medical or other management techniques. Through an understanding of the reasons for a child's specific behavior, the process of labeling a youngster as thoughtless, disobedient, or inattentive can be avoided.

Correlation between juvenile delinquency and SLD

The impaired delinquent is a recently delineated population (Siegal, 1976). Such youngsters show many features that have raised the possibility that learning disabilities are a causative factor in juvenile delinquency. Berman and Seigal (1976) found that of a sample of fifty incarcerated juvenile delinquents, nearly three-fifths showed evidence of at least one, and usually more than one, specific learning disability. How the factor of delinquency interrelates with various specific learning disabilities is, of course, conjectural.

Misbehavior as a signal of SLD

In the learning disabilities syndrome, the classroom teacher must be aware of causes and consequences from various directions. The youngster who is presenting behavioral difficulties can well be expressing signs of frustration, being unable to keep up with the rest of the class because of underlying learning disabilities. Often it is easy to dismiss disruptive behavior as an expression of anger, attention-getting, or showing off. While these certainly can play a part, they should not obscure the fact that frequently there may be an underlying, undiagnosed learning disability.

Self-programming for failure

The classroom teacher can be sensitive to the fact that youngsters with learning disabilities are often prone to program themselves as failures. Many of these "self-programmed" youth develop delinquent behavior in the early teenage years if not aided according to specific needs. The empathic and understanding classroom teacher—in noting the co-existence and possible relationship of these behaviors—can do a great deal to lower frustration, increase understanding, and set appropriate limits.

Problems of self-esteem and approaches to adaptive management

Self-acceptance and acceptance by others

Parents, teachers, and others who observe the many frustrations encountered by the child with specific learning disabilities in fulfilling academic or behavioral expectations are concerned with the child's capabilities for satisfying his or her need for self-esteem. As previously noted, the need for acceptance by others is paramount to one's own acceptance of self. Swanson and Parker (1971) cite the need for further research investigating the feelings that learning-disabled children have about themselves, as well as feelings they experience *from* and *toward* others.

In addition to adapting materials and techniques to reduce difficulty in specific academic areas, the treatment program may involve various managerial approaches to reduce behavioral differences that indicate difficulties in acceptance *of self or others* or acceptance *by others*. Below are some of these approaches as reflected in the current literature.

Medical management or therapy

Medical therapy is one of a number of means through which more adaptive behavior for learning and social acceptance purposes is sought. Many parents of SLD children seek out the advice of their family physician when certain behaviors seen as disruptive or disturbing are presented, either within the family or as reported by school personnel. Because one of our nation's present concerns is the abuse of drugs by a substantial percentage of the population, control through medication therapy has become a very controversial topic. Numerous studies, however, report positive gains in behavioral aspects of SLD children through the use of the prescribed medication (Knight & Hinton, 1969; Oettinger, 1970; Page et al., 1974). Many physicians do affirm that there are benefits to be derived through medication for a *very small number* of children within the learning-disordered population. But because of each child's varying response to different medications and prescribed dosages, all persons involved must carefully weigh the advantages or disadvantages of such an approach.

Pros and cons of medication therapy

The question for the physician, members of the child's family, and persons in the school setting becomes: Can medication therapy help to facilitate behaviors that lead to a greater capacity for learning and increased self- and social acceptance? If medication is employed, it cannot be effective when isolated from other remediation techniques, including educational strategies and parent and/or child counseling. It must be kept in mind, however, that medication is necessary *in only a very few cases* and that drugs are not a cure-all for learning problems.

Operant conditioning, or reinforcement therapy

The technique for increasing learning and adaptive behavior potential through methods based on learning theory or operant conditioning was discussed and illustrated in the introductory unit. It will be examined further in Unit 7, which deals with emotional handicaps. This approach has been incorporated recently as a successful strategy with SLD children in the educational setting, and with parents of SLD children who are trying to help their child reduce the frequency of maladaptive behaviors (Ryback & Staats, 1970; Simpson & Nelson, 1974). As noted earlier in the text, this technique is not free of controversy either, but it has been justified on the basis that it eliminates behaviors impeding healthy adaptation and development. Discussing the use of a reward system of positive reinforcement for the management of hyperactivity in the classroom, Fairchild (1975) notes that

Reward system for managing hyperactivity

> Classroom token *economies* can be a very effective means of improving learning and behavior. In a classroom token economy the teacher identifies some specific target behaviors that need improvement and dispenses tokens

(chips, computer cards, etc.) when appropriate behaviors occur. For example, Herbie might receive one token for beginning his work, one for remaining seated, one for task completion, and another for neatness. A reward system may be in the form of a menu which combines a variety of activity and tangible reward. The tokens could be exchanged daily or weekly. When giving tokens always pair the token with social reinforcement (p. 74).

In illustrating a reinforcement therapy approach wherein check marks received for fulfilling behavioral change objectives can be exchanged for tangible reinforcers, Blackham and Silberman (1977) emphasize the importance again of using "secondary reinforcement (praise) to further enhance the child's satisfaction in controlling himself" (p. 114). They also indicate that they have found that children who will control the behavior by themselves no longer need the check marks.

Other adaptive behavior techniques

Biofeedback

Biofeedback training, in which an individual is taught to consciously monitor electrical activity within his or her brain waves, has received recent attention as applicable to improving the classroom behavior of hyperkinetic children (Martinus & Hoovey, 1972). Dietary precautions also are cited as helping to reduce behavioral deficits. Feingold (1976) suggests that chemical additives to food, such as artificial flavors and colors, can be linked to behavioral and school problems. And Havard (1973) believes that allergies and subsequent health complications may be the basis for hyperactivity and other behavioral problems that are labeled as SLD. Hence it is apparent that many things can contribute to a child's behavioral and subsequent academic problems that are not related to a learning disability per se.

The professional classroom teacher plays a vital role in contributing to the child's sense of his or her own personal worth, thus facilitating overall adjustment. This is accomplished through positive acceptance of learning-disabled children, along with adapting materials and techniques as needed to help the child overcome specific deficits.

Need for continuing research

As we noted earlier, the field of learning disabilities represents the newest area of exceptionality included within the current definition of the handicapped. The need for further research is unquestioned. Issues relating to identification of and methods for reducing the unproductive behavior sometimes present in SLD children need clarification. Particularly in the areas of remediation, continued research is indicated. Responding to such need, the Bureau of Education for the Handicapped (BEH) in 1977 funded twenty-three additional educational agencies to establish Child Service Demonstration Centers (CSDCs) for children with specific learning disabilities (U.S.

Child Service Demonstration Centers

Office Education, 1977, p. 1), making a total of fifty-three, located in thirty-three states and Puerto Rico. The focus of efforts will include study and/or use of individualized program planning, methods of instruction, multidisciplinary assessment, the

A scrambled word exercise is one of the activities from which Ned can benefit. He and his classmates are playing a spelling game.

relationship between juvenile delinquency and learning disabilities, least restrictive placement, instructional and managerial techniques for parents and teachers, and other necessary concerns. These and other efforts remain paramount for further understanding and developing services and resources that will enable learning-disabled children and youth to maximize their potential.

Summary

Attempts to more thoroughly understand the school population referred to as children or youth with specific learning disabilities have been presented. And the ongoing controversy surrounding causes and remediation techniques was explored. Current definitions and criteria for inclusion of youngsters within this population have been examined, along with various approaches aimed at greater understanding of such children.

Some of the more specific aspects included in research and educational literature have been surveyed, such as social and emotional behavioral characteristics, perceptual-motor functioning problems, specific academic-area difficulties, and the approaches to remediation, including process training and task analysis. Some consideration was also given to the problem of self-esteem. Approaches to facilitating the SLD child's potential for learning by modifying certain modes of behavior were presented.

The chances for children with specific learning disabilities to achieve successfully will increase proportionally through early diagnosis and individualized remediation programs that address the strengths and weaknesses of the individual child. Parental, educational, and other professional efforts can then be specifically directed to aid in preventive measures and implement the kinds of services needed by this population of children and youth.

References and resources

Bannatyne, A. Language, Reading and Learning Disabilities. *Psychology, Neuropsychology, Diagnosis and Remediation.* Springfield, Ill.: Charles C Thomas, 1971.

Bateman, B., and Frankel, H. "Special Education and the Pediatrician." *Journal of Learning Disabilities* 5 (1972): 178–86.

Bender, L. "Specific Reading Disability as a Maturational Lag." *Bulletin of the Orton Society* 7 (1957).

Bennett, E. M. "The Pediatrician's Role in Evaluating the Child with a Learning Disability." *Academic Therapy Quarterly* 1 (1966).

Berman, A., and Siegal, A. W. "A Neuropsychological Approach to the Etiology, Prevention, and Treatment of Juvenile Delinquency." In *Current Perspectives in Child Personality and Psychopathology,* vol. 3, edited by A. Davids. New York: Wiley, 1976.

Blackham, G. J., and Silberman, A. *Modification of Child Behavior.* Belmont, Calif.: Wadsworth, 1977.

Blom, G. E., and Jones, A. W. "Bases of Classification of Reading Disorders, Commissioned by the National Advisory Committee on Dyslexia and Related Reading Disorders. *Journal of Learning Disabilities* 3 (1970): 605–17.

Boder, E. "A Neuropediatric Approach to the Diagnosis and Management of School Behavioral and Learning Disorders." Reprint from *Learning Disorder* 2 (1966): 15–44.

Boder, E. "Developmental Dyslexia: A New Diagnostic Approach Based on the Identification of Three Subtypes." *The Journal of School Health,* June 1970, pp. 289–90.

Boder, E. "Developmental Dyslexia: A Diagnostic Approach Based on Three Atypical Reading-Spelling Patterns." *Developmental Medicine and Child Neurology* 15 (1973): 663–87.

Bush, W. J., and Waugh, K. W. *Diagnostic Learning Disabilities.* 2nd. ed. Columbus, Ohio: Merrill, 1976.

Carpenter, R. L., and Willis, D. J. "Case Study of an Auditory Dyslexic." *Journal of Learning Disabilities* 5 (1972): 121–29.

Clements, S. D. "Minimal Brain Dysfunction in Children. Terminology and Identification. Phase One of a Three-Phase Project." *U.S. Department of Health, Education and Welfare, Public Health Service Publication No. 1415,* pp. 1–18. Washington, D.C.: U.S. Government Printing Office, 1966.

Faas, L. A. *Learning Disabilities: A Competency Based Approach.* Boston: Houghton Mifflin, 1976.

Fairchild, T. N. *Managing the Hyperactive Child in the Classroom.* Austin, Tex.: Learning Concepts, 1975.

Feingold, B. F. "Hyperkinesis and Learning Disabilities Linked to the Ingestion of Artificial Food Colors and Flavors." *Journal of Learning Disabilities* 9 (1976): 551–59.

Forgus, R. H. *Perception: The Basic Process in Cognitive Development.* New York: McGraw-Hill, 1966.

Frierson, E. C., and Barbe, W. B., eds. *Educating Children With Learning Disabilities; Selected Readings.* New York: Appleton-Century-Crofts, Meredith, 1967, pp. 85–90.

Frostig, M., in collaboration with Lefever, W., and Whittlesey, J. R. B. *Developmental Test of Visual Perception.* Palo Alto, Calif.: Consulting Press, 1963.

Frostig, M. "Visual Perception, Integrative Functions and Academic Learning. *Journal of Learning Disabilities* 5 (1972): 5–15.

Gaddis, W. H. "Neurological Implications for Learning." In *Perceptual and Learning Disabilities in Children,* edited by W. M. Cruikshank and D. P. Hallahan. *Psychoeducational Practices,* vol. 1. Syracuse: Syracuse University Press, 1975.

Getman, G. N. "The Visuomotor Complex in the Acquisition of Learning Skills." *Learning Disorders* 1 (1965): 49–76.

Hammill, D. D., and Larsen, S. C. "The Effectiveness of Psycholinguistic Training." *Exceptional Children,* Sept. 1974, pp. 5–14.

Havard, J. "School Problems and Allergies." *Journal of Learning Disabilities,* vol. 6, no. 8 (1973), pp. 492–94.

Jastek, J. F.; Bijou, S. W.; and Jastek, S. R. *Wide Range Achievement Test.* Wilmington, Del.: Jastek Associates, Inc., 1976.

Johnson, D. J., and Myklebust, H. R. *Learning Disabilities: Educational Principles and Practices.* New York: Grune and Stratten, 1967.

Kagan, J., and Havemann, E. *Psychology: An Introduction,* 2nd ed. New York: Harcourt Brace Jovanovich, 1972.

Keogh, B. K. "Hyperactivity and Learning Disorders: Review and Speculation." *Exceptional Children* 38 (1971): 101–9.

Kephart, N. C. *Aids to Motoric and Perceptual Training.* Madison, Wis.: Bureau for Handicapped Children, 1964.

Kephart, N. C. Perceptual-Motor Aspects of Learning Disabilities. *Educating Children with Learning Disabilities,* edited by E. C. Frierson and W. B. Burke, pp. 405–13. New York: Appleton-Century-Crofts, 1967.

Kephart, N. C. *The Slow Learner in the Classroom.* 2nd ed. Columbus, Ohio: Merrill, 1971.

Kirk, S. A. "Specific Learning Disabilities." *Journal of Clinical Child Psychology,* vol. 6, no. 3 (1977): pp. 23–26.

Kirk, S. A., and Kirk, W. D. *Psycholinguistic Learning Disabilities: Diagnosis and Remediation.* Urbana, Ill.: University of Illinois Press, 1972.

Kirk, S. A.; McCarthey, J.; and Kirk, W. D. *Illinois Test of Psycholinguistic Abilities.* Urbana, Ill.: University of Illinois Press, 1968a.

Kirk, S. A.; McCarthey, J.; and Kirk, W. D. *Examiner's Manual: Illinois Test of Psycholinguistic Abilities.* rev. ed. Urbana, Ill.: University of Illinois Press, 1968b.

Knight, R. A., and Hinton, C. C. "The Effects of Methylphenidate (Ritalin) on the Motor Skills and Behavior of Children with Learning Problems." *Journal of Nervous & Mental Disease* 148 (1969): 643–53.

Koppitz, E. M. *The Bender Gestalt for Young Children. Research and Application, 1963–1973,* vol. 2, New York: Grune and Stratten, 1975.

Larsen, S. C., and Hammill, D. D. "The Relationship of Selected Visual Perceptual Abilities to School Learning." *Journal of Special Education* 9 (1975): 281–91.

Lerner, J. W. *Children with Learning Disabilities.* 2nd. ed. Boston: Houghton Mifflin, 1976.

McClurg, W. H. "Dyslexia: Early Identification and Treatment in the Schools." *Journal of Learning Disabilities* 3 (1970): 372–77.

Martinus, J. W., and Hoovey, Z. B. "Bilateral Synchrony of Occipital Alpha Waves, Oculomotor Activity and Attention in Children." *Electroencephalography and Clinical Neurophysiology* 32 (1972): 349–56.

Minskoff, E. H.; Wiseman, D. E.: and Minskoff, J. G. *Inventory of Language Abilities Record Booklet, The MWA Program for Developing Language Abilities.* Ridgefield, N.J.: Educational Performance Associates, 1972.

Mullins, J.; Joseph, F.; Turner, C.; Zavadski, R.; and Saltzman, L. "A Handwriting Model for Children with Learning Disabilities." *Journal of Learning Disabilities* 5 (1972): 306–11.

Myers, P. L., and Hammill, D. *Methods for Learning Disorders,* 2nd. ed. New York: Wiley, 1976.

Oettinger, L. "Learning Disorder, Hyperkinesis, and the Use of Drugs in Children." *Rehabilitation Literature* 32 (1971): 162–67.

Page, J. G.; Janicki, R. S.; Bernstein, J. E.; Curran, C. F.; and Michelli, F. A. "Pemoline (Cylert) in the Treatment of Childhood Hyperkinesis." *Journal of Learning Disabilities* 7 (1974): 498–503.

Richardson, S. A. "Learning Disabilities: An Introduction." *ACLD Reprint.* Pittsburgh: Association for Children with Learning Disabilities.

Ryback, D., and Staats, A. W. "Parents as Behavior-Therapy Technicians in Treating Reading Deficits (dyslexia)." *Journal of Behavior Therapy and Experimental Psychiatry* 1 (1970): 109–19.

Siegal, A. W. "Toward Comprehensive Etiological Models of Delinquent Behavior in Adolescents: The Contributions of Recent Neuropsychological Studies." Unpublished manuscript, 1976.
Simpson, D. D., and Nelson, A. P. "Attention Training Through Breathing Control to Modify Hyperactivity." *Journal of Learning Disabilities* 7 (1974): 274–83.
Slingerland, B. H. *A Multi-Sensory Approach to Language Arts for Specific Language Disability Children: A Guide for Primary Teachers.* Cambridge: Educators Publishing Service, 1971.
Smead, V. S. "Ability Training and Task Analysis in Diagnostic/Prescriptive Teaching." *Journal of Specific Education* 11 (1977): 113–25.
Stevens, G. D., and Birch, J. W. "A Proposal for Clarification of the Terminology Used to Describe Brain-Injured Children." *Exceptional Children,* vol. 23, no. 8 (1957), pp. 346–49.
Strauss, A. and Lehtinen, L. *Psychopathology and Education of the Brain-Injured Child,* vol. 1. New York: Grune and Stratten, 1947, pp. 128–145.
Stubblefield, J. H., and Young, C. E. "Central Auditory Dysfunction in Learning Disabled Children." *Journal of Learning Disabilities* 8 (1975): 90–94.
Swanson, B., and Parker, H. "Parent-Child Relations: A Child's Acceptance by Others, of Others, and of Self." *Child Psychiatry and Human Development* 1 (1971): 243–54.
Thomas, E. D.; Letchworth, C. J.; Rogers, G. A.; Jones, M.; Akin, M.; and Levy, J. "The Diagnosis of Learning Disabilities: A Neurologic Screening Test to Identify Children at High Risk." *Southern Medical Journal* 66 (1973): 1286–93.
U.S. Department of Health, Education, and Welfare. *The Unfinished Revolution: Education for the Handicapped.* 1976 Annual Report of the National Advisory Committee on the Handicapped. Washington, D.C.: Government Printing Office, 1976.
U.S. Office of Education. *Federal Register, Assistance to States for Education of Handicapped Children,* vol. 41, no. 230, Washington, D.C.: 1976.
U.S. Office of Education. *Federal Register, Part 2, Implementation of Part B of the Education of the Handicapped Act,* vol. 42, no. 163, Washington, D.C.: 1977.
U.S. Office of Education, Bureau of Education for the Handicapped. *Centerfold.* National Learning Disabilities Assistance Project, Sept./Oct., 1977.
U.S. Office of Education. *Assistance to State for Education of Handicapped Children* vol. 42, no. 250, December 29, 1977.
Valett, R. E. *Effective Teaching: A Guide to Diagnostic-Prescriptive Task Analysis.* Belmont, Calif.: Fearon Publishers, 1970.
Vogel, S. A. "Syntactic Abilities in Normal and Dyslexic Children." *Journal of Learning Disabilities,* vol. 7, no. 2 (1974), pp. 103–09.
Walker, S. "Drugging the American Child: We're Too Cavalier About Hyperactivity." *Journal of Learning Disabilities* 8 (1975): 354–58.
Wallace, G., and Kauffman, J. M. *Teaching Children with Learning Problems.* Columbus, Ohio: Charles E. Merrill Publishing Co., 1973.
Wender, P. "Diagnosis and Management of Minimal Brain Dysfunction in Children." *Ross Timesaver,* vol. 15, no. 4, (1973), pp. 1–6.
Willis, D. J., and Thomas, E. D. "Seizure Disorders." In *Psychological Management of Pediatric Problems,* vol. 2, edited by P. Magrab, pp. 49–88. Baltimore: University Park Press, 1978.

References and resources

American Foundation on Learning Disabilities
P.O. Box #196
Convent Station, New Jersey 07961

Association for Children with Learning Disabilities (ACLD)
5225 Grace Street
Pittsburgh, Pennsylvania 15236
(affiliate organizations in forty-eight states)

Closer Look Newsletter
P.O. Box #1492
Washington, D.C. 20013

Directory of Educational Facilities for the Learning Disabled
Academic Therapy Publications
1539 Fourth Street
San Rafael, California 94901

National Council of Organizations for Children and Youth (NCOCY)
1910 K Street, NW
Washington, D.C. 20006

National Learning Disabilities Assistance Project (NALDAP)
The NETWORK
Merrimac, Massachusetts 01860

Orton Society, Inc.
8415 Bellona Lane
Towson, Maryland 21204

Publication List
Oklahoma Association for Children with Learning Disabilities
3701 N W 62nd Street
Oklahoma City, Oklahoma, 73112

Special Learning Corporation
42 Boston Post Road
Guilford, Connecticut 06437

U.S. Department of Health, Education and Welfare
National Institutes of Health
Publications #ADM 77-337 (1977)
Superintendent of Public Documents
U.S. Government Printing Office
Washington, D.C. 20402

3
Emotional and social exceptionality

It is increasingly clear that unfavorable prenatal, perinatal, and postnatal events affect the growing organism, creating a background for subsequent complication. Familial and social influences also are observable as playing a part in these various difficulties. In Unit 7 various perspectives will be utilized to gain more insight into emotional and social exceptionality.

No single entity has been identified as the causative factor in problems considered to be emotional or reflecting variations from social norms. The transient and tenuous nature of interpersonal relationships in our society, however, makes it more difficult to provide emotional and social support systems for children and youth.

Treatment strategies for the child and youth population with emotional problems or those classified as delinquent have varied considerably over the years as environmental influences, learning concepts, and biological mechanisms have become better understood. Of particular importance is the realization that educators play a major role in supporting treatment and are of inordinate value in facilitating major changes leading to a troubled youngster's more adequate adjustment. School personnel, along with parents, actually are the primary caretakers for most children manifesting emotional or social exceptionality. Supportive systems for such young people do come from the medical profession (psychiatrists, pediatricians, family practitioners) and personnel in psychology, social work, and the public health areas. Nonetheless, the classroom setting is where a major portion of the child's or youth's waking hours are spent, so that greater understanding by school personnel of emotional disorders and variations from social norms is essential to being a part of the mental health team.

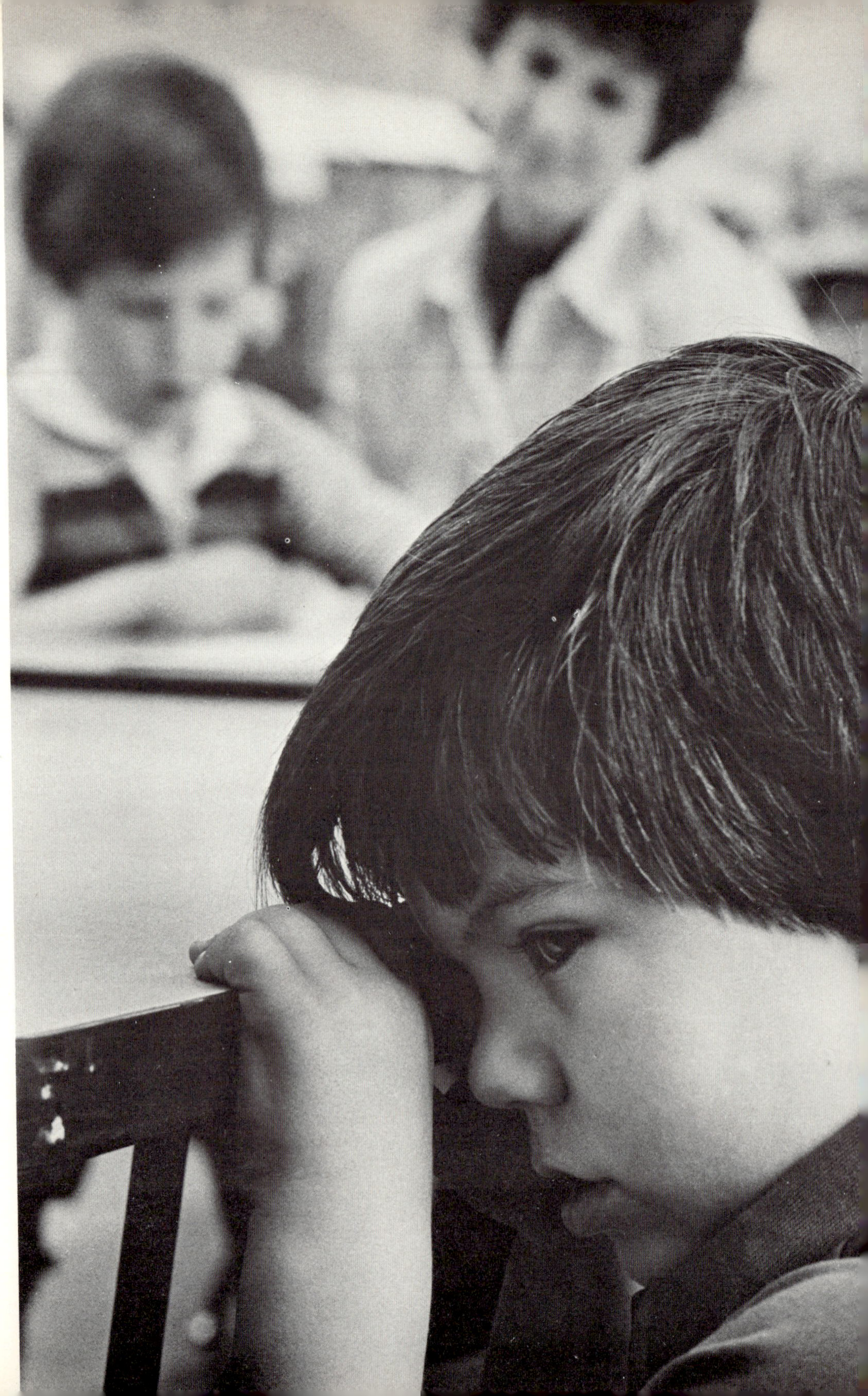

7 Emotionally handicapped children and youth

Marshall Schechter · John Howland ·
B. Marian Swanson · Diane J. Willis

What is good mental health? · Stages of healthy emotional growth ·
    Attempts to define emotional disability
Significant influences on emotional development · Constitutional
    factors · Family dynamics · School-related sociocultural influences · Ego or
    self development
Classification and labeling problems
Special symptoms · Bladder and bowel control problems · Tics · Pica ·
    Anorexia nervosa
Transient situational disorders
Aggressive and destructive behaviors
Neuroses in children and youth · Depressive neurosis · Hysterical neurosis,
    conversion type · Phobic neurosis
Psychoses in children and youth · Early infantile autism · Early childhood
    schizophrenia · Schizophrenia in youth · Manic-depressive psychoses
Special concerns · Child abuse · Drug abuse · Suicide
Intervention strategies · Individual psychotherapy · Group
    psychotherapy · Family therapy · Behavior modification, or reinforcement
    therapy · Other therapeutic techniques · The classroom teacher as
    facilitator
Juvenile delinquency · What is juvenile delinquency? · Overall incidence ·
    Causes of juvenile delinquency · Intervention techniques · Prognosis
Summary

Emotionally handicapped children and youth

Student learning objectives

The student will:
1. be able to identify long-term mental health goals and stages of healthy emotional growth
2. be able to identify criteria for defining emotional handicaps and will be aware of the difficulties inherent in such definitions
3. understand the impact on emotional development of a number of constitutional, familial, and school-related sociocultural factors
4. be able to identify specific syndromes of behavior that indicate various neurotic and psychotic conditions in children and youth, including "school phobia"
5. recognize some of the underlying factors contributing to aggressive and destructive behavior in children and youth
6. understand the distinction between the neuroses and functional psychoses
7. recognize symptomatic behavior in these areas of special societal concern: (a) child abuse (b) drug abuse (c) suicide
8. demonstrate an understanding of the various strategies employed in the therapeutic treatment of emotional disorders
9. demonstrate various ways in which the classroom teacher serves as a facilitator in the diagnosis and treatment of emotionally handicapped children and youth
10. become familiar with various theories relating to causes of juvenile delinquency, and recognize the complexity and multiplicity of causes
11. become familiar with the legal, social, and psychological approaches to dealing with delinquent behavior and the educational strategies that may be employed

Throughout this text we examine a multiplicity of factors that account for difficulties beginning with or during formal school attendance. In Unit 7 we will concentrate on emotional problems as a primary factor leading to behavioral disorders. The diagnostic entities considered will include all stages of growth and development during the regular school years. While preschool programs can help substantially in detecting and treating early symptoms of mental health difficulties, emotional problems exhibited by school-age youngsters remain a primary concern.

In the past, educators may not have played such a vital role in therapeutic intervention strategies for emotionally troubled children and youth, particularly those with disorders considered more severe. But the future outlook is for increased integration of all exceptional children into the regular classroom (as stressed in earlier units). Hence professionals in the mental health field must make greater use of outpatient treatment resources rather than inpatient hospitalization or institutionalization for emotional problems. This new orientation means that educators will need to serve effectively as members of multidisciplinary teams (psychiatrist, psychologist, social worker, teacher, parents) in dealing not only with milder forms of emotion exceptionality, but with severely troubled youngsters as well.

What is good mental health?

The firm and clear awareness of the realities of the world and how best to handle such realities is a major way of defining adult emotional health. Emotional maturity in the adult thus can include the following: (1) a capacity to be adaptable or flexible, (2) an ability to handle aggressive impulses in a socially acceptable manner, (3) a capacity to harmonize basic needs, drives, and urges with internal, or self, controls, (4) a capacity to be productive in work and play, (5) a capacity to give of oneself and to respect the needs of others, and (6) a capacity to be independent but with acceptance of dependency when needs dictate. These are reasonable long-term goals that demonstrate emotional maturity. On a very practical level we would state that good mental health means that a person is basically comfortable (physically and emotionally), appropriate in behavior, and maintains a level of efficiency in fulfilling responsibilities of his or her role, whether it be keeping house or achieving passing grades in school. This practical definition of mental health can be reversed into three criteria of abnormal behavior: (1) discomfort, comprising physical discomfort, such as fatigue or aches and pain, and psychological discomfort, such as anxiety, depression, or unhappiness; (2) bizarreness that includes striking departures from socially acceptable standards of behavior, such as phobias, hallucinations, delusions, tics, delinquency, drug addiction, and alcoholism; and (3) extreme inefficiency, or an inability to assume even a minimal level of responsibility or to perform anywhere near one's potential (Buss, 1966).

Goals of mental health

Stages of healthy emotional growth

Often, healthy human emotional development from infancy to adulthood is characterized by stages of progress from dependency to independency. Such stages are distinguished by: (1) progress in adjusting one's locus of control (see Unit 5) from external to internal, with subsequent feelings of self-determination and autonomy, (2) progress from self-centered gratification lacking concern for others to healthy need-satisfaction cognizant of the welfare of others, and (3) progress from testing out in fantasy to actually being productive according to one's capabilities.

From dependence to independence

The school-age period of development should be a time of consolidation of many basic forces leading progressively to feelings of self-worth and self-esteem. The development of positive feelings concerning one's physical self, the capacity to consider future objectives and vocations and how best to reach them, and the establishment of a core of mutually satisfying friendships, all represent stages of healthy emotional growth. The basic struggle to separate psychologically from the

Struggle to separate

family should be well under way by the later adolescent school years, and even though complete independence may not be attained, there should be a feeling that this will occur within the foreseeable future. Fantasies about future relationships, vocations, and values should be congruent with one's own abilities, talents, and interests and acted upon in a way that is of mutual benefit to oneself and others in society.

Attempts to define emotional disability

There is no clear-cut, universally accepted method of defining what an emotional handicap is. Yet parents and teachers are constantly put into a position of explaining and/or handling behavior that is considered to be at variance from a norm. The definition of what constitutes an emotional disorder is always relative to the context in which a behavior is presented. Each individual has his or her own personally derived concept of normality for all ages of people, and it is against this internalized yardstick that others' reactions are measured.

Internalized yardstick of "normalcy"

Despite the possible lack of agreement among individual observers of behavior, there exists considerable congruency within any society concerning recognition of "normal" behavior in children and youth. For example, within our society certain expectations regarding role-appropriate behavior for boys and girls are still widely held. Developmental principles and related expectations are instilled in any society through continuous life observations. These become the basis for definitions concerning emotional or behavioral norms. Individual behavior is checked against these behavioral norms of the social system in which the individual is reared. Each community and each subset within the community, however, may determine its own acceptable modes, and these can represent a complex series of learned behaviors.

Based on this myriad of constructs, the classroom teacher, among others, makes responses or decisions concerning the normality or pathology of a particular child's behavior. Such decisions may not only be determined by the formally learned and internalized constructs but may also be affected by external or more observable factors. That is to say, when the teacher can overtly see, and thus more easily understand, a particular response, there is a greater likelihood that the behavior will be considered within the realm of the norm or average. Take the case of the child walking down the aisle between rows of desks:

Example 1: external stimulus as behavior determinant

Gwen As she walks down the aisle, Gwen is deliberately tripped by another child. The teacher sees the child at the desk stick out her foot to trip the walker. The child who is tripped picks herself up and then strikes the offending classmate. The teacher may chastise both youngsters but can more clearly understand the reaction of one to the other since *external* precipitating and responsive aggressive acts were observed.

In contrast, the reasons for some behaviors are not as clearly observable, as evidenced in the following case.

Sandy   The teacher observes Sandy sitting quietly at a table, seemingly occupied with a craft. Although unprovoked by anyone, Sandy might suddenly pick up papers, pens, and crayons and violently throw them about the room, not directing the missiles at any particular individual. At this point the teacher intervenes but has no notion of what stimulated such behavior. Under these circumstances the teacher is more likely to label this action abnormal, since he or she is unable to identify or understand the *internal* stimulus that led to the child's outburst.

Example 2: internal stimulus as behavior determinant

Defining and evaluating behaviors as "normal" (or conforming) or "abnormal" (or non-conforming) is thus quite complex and involves consideration of societal expectations and individual and environmental influences.

Incidence   Desired progression in emotional maturity may go awry during various stages of a child's or youth's development. The incidence of consequent emotional handicaps in the school-age population is high, with estimates ranging from 5 to 15 percent. Of all the children who need special classes for the emotionally handicapped, such placement has been provided for only about 2 percent (U.S. Office of Education, 1971). The critical dearth of adequate psychological or psychiatric services for this group is characterized by mental health professionals as a national disaster.

A national disaster

Significant influences on emotional development

As we noted in earlier units, the controversy about the relative importance of nature and nurture—hereditary versus environmental influences—is still prominent in literature and research. Increasingly accepted, however, is the recognition that the evolution of personality development is the result of the vector forces from both one's nature and the way this nature is nurtured.

Nature vs. nurture

To further illustrate the intimate interplay between nature and nurture, we will examine a few of the factors and dynamics in this construct.

Constitutional factors

Attention has again focused on the physical, or organic, influences (prenatal, perinatal, and postnatal) that can result in various kinds of disabilities or complications. Since the days of ancient Greece, the belief has persisted that "the physical state of the organism plays an important part in personality disorganization" and that "constitution may be regarded as the total biological makeup of an 'individual'" (Kisker, 1964, pp. 74, 84). We stressed at the beginning of Part Three and in Units 2 and 5 that the physical status of the expectant mother affects the developing fetus. It has been suggested that feelings of anxiety and/or depression in a mother who is pregnant produce their own special kinds of chemicals which, in turn, can pass through

Linkage of physical and emotional disability

the placenta and have a direct effect on the growing organism (Everett & Schechter, 1972). A number of studies have identified personality characteristics with which children *seem* to be born and which remain relatively constant through development. A complete discussion of the organic basis of personality disorganization is beyond the scope of this unit, but the student needs to be aware that much research is available investigating the linkage of organic makeup to varying degrees and types of emotional disability (Quay & Werry, 1972; Ross, 1974).

Correlation of emotional disabilities with stages of physical development

We have previously noted the dilemma involved in defining "normal" versus "abnormal" behavior. A study by Schechter et al. (1972) indicated a wide variation in physical development in later childhood and middle-school period, leading in turn to a wide variation in emotional or psychological responses in the adolescent. These researchers discovered that estrogens in females began increasing around seven years of age and that the male hormone, testosterone, was beginning to rise around age eight. This suggested that the beginning of puberty in the female did not date from the onset of the menstrual function nor in the male with the beginning of nocturnal emissions. Rather, these were the end points of approximately four years of hormonal influences serving as the motor force for the psychological stage we typically call adolescence. Along with this, the actual appearance of secondary sex characteristics occurred at a younger age so that we could form a grouping of children in the middle school age (eleven to fourteen) who were no longer children in body and personality.

Physical development within all ages of the school population is unequal both within the individual and between individuals, as height and weight along with the appearance of secondary sex characteristics generally follow a familial pattern. Within the teen-age population, for example, some have already reached their adult height at fourteen, while others might take until their late teens or early twenties to do the same. This points up the difficulty in clearly differentiating and correlating certain emotional disorders with stages of physical development.

Family dynamics

The importance of family interactions in explaining emotional problems in children also has been widely researched, as reflected in medical, psychological, and sociological literature (Kiev, 1974; Quay & Werry, 1972; Ross, 1974). Children's problems have been presented as often precipitated and/or complicated by parental pathological states. Mothers diagnosed as distorting reality for themselves (schizophrenic) have been viewed as distorting reality for their children. Parents who are depressed, especially during the child's first eighteen months of life, have been found to emphasize this depression position to the point of creating possible future difficulties in their offspring. Parents who are unusually fearful have been thought to heighten anxiety states, creating a fear-based reality for the child rather than helping him or her to recognize the fantasy base for many anxieties.

Although there can indeed be quite severe familial pathology which produces emotional disturbances, it should be noted that there are no absolutely defined parental traits or characteristics that either *always* influence the child in some departure from the norms or are *specific* to certain disorders. Some children are especially sensitive to environmental events, while others seem unusually immune to extraordinary stresses.

In an interesting study conducted by a group of pediatricians (Powell, Brasel & Blizzard, 1967; Powell et al., 1967), the close and necessary association of psychological development with physical development was demonstrated as follows:

> *Tender loving care* It was noted that a group of infants were not growing or putting on weight normally. In careful examination of these children, the pediatricians discovered that there was a lack of pituitary growth hormone in the blood. Since this hormone was so scarce, it was necessary to keep the children in the hospital for a considerable time without any specific treatment except to see that they were adequately nourished and attended. After a short period of this concentrated attention —*but without the injectible growth hormone*—the children began to put on weight and grow. When the blood pituitary growth hormone was examined, the pediatricians were amazed to find almost normal levels of this substance.
>
> The children were returned to their parents and constantly reexamined in their home setting. Following a short period back home, it was discovered that the children were again without pituitary growth hormone. Reentry to the hospital followed; this time there was no thought of injective hormone but merely of giving adequate attention and affection to the children. The same results as on the previous hospitalization were again noted as near-normal levels of the hormone in the bloodstream were found.

Growth hormone deficiency and maternal deprivation

The importance of this particular study was that it unequivocally demonstrated that if they are to develop, even normal structures (such as the pituitary gland in these children) need to have their function triggered by tender, affectionate, and stimulating adults. The resultant diagnosis of failure to thrive due to parental deprivation now has become standard in the understanding of growth failures in many children even after infancy. (This deprivational syndrome is considered in more detail as a part of the child-abuse constellation discussed later in this unit.)

Deprivational syndrome

School-related sociocultural influences

The state of development signaled by the child's entry into the regular school grades represents the beginning of certain expectations different from those present in earlier childhood settings. Children with previous daycare or preschool experiences may adapt more readily to the new school environment where increasing demands are made. A number of new skills for academic learning are called for that involve intellect, sensorimotor apparatus, communication skills, and psychological maturity. This is the time when the child, in a more formal way, is pushed into establishing an identity distinct from others (the ego, or self). He or she is asked to a greater degree to shift from primarily intrafamilial ties to peer relationships and to transfer greater authority to teachers for adequate school adjustment.

Growing importance of peer relationships

As children continue in school, they become more acutely aware of sociocultural differences; also, hierarchies of class systems develop differently from the way they did earlier. Peer relationships become increasingly important as youngsters—moving through their school years—are expected to further separate from dependency on parents and to form liaisons and attachments with others of their own age. Special regard frequently is given by peers to the "right" clothes, easy availability of money, and certain other signs of social status and acceptability, such as athletic ability, physical (including sexual) development, and a quality of attractiveness that at times is dictated by fad. In any event, the student soon learns where he or she stands within the "pecking order" of the class.

Ego or self development

Teacher can affect child's feeling of self-worth

Each of the significant influences discussed above affect the child's or youth's ideas concerning *self*, or *ego*. As we saw earlier in Unit 5, positive feelings of self-worth are considered to be a major contributor to good mental health and emotional stability. A negative self-concept has the potential for precipitating unhealthy emotions (for example, feelings of emptiness, loneliness, the consuming fires of expressed or unexpressed rage). If individuals view themselves as inadequate in meeting their own or others' expectations, this low self-esteem can contribute to emotional instability. The classroom teacher plays a prominent role in the development of the feelings the child accumulates regarding himself or herself as either a worthwhile or non-worthwhile individual.

Classification and labeling problems

Short-term and chronic problems

Beginning with early childhood and continuing throughout an individual's life, any behavioral variation can range on a continuum from mild to severe to profound. Additionally, symptoms believed representative of emotional problems can exist singly or in conjunction with a number of signs pointing to the presence of disturbed behavior. Emotional problems also can be both transient (short-term) in nature or symptomatic of later or more permanent (chronic) maladaptive adjustment.

Using a common frame of reference

The fallacies inherent in and derived from the labeling process were discussed in Unit 1. Certain definitive, or classifying, terms, however, are attached to various behaviors viewed as substantial departures from the prevailing accepted norm. Terminology may undergo revision from time to time but the practice of classification is in accordance with the premise that a common frame of reference aids in communication and fosters research relating to causes and treatment of emotional disorders as well. In justification of such practice, one psychiatrist has emphasized:

If epidemiology, treatment, and etiology are to be studied on a national or international scale, a common language must be developed. If we are to make sense to our colleagues, and even if we differ violently in our underlying concepts and assumptions, we must be able to use the same terms to refer to the same patients (Fish, 1972, p. 95).

The incompleteness of the growth and development process in children and youth has been acknowledged as complicating the clear differentiation of symptoms of disorders (Ross, 1974). Also there exists uncertainty concerning "the extent of overlap between childhood and adult disturbance" (Clarizio & McCoy, 1970, p. 10). Within this complicated sphere and despite recognized limitations, it has become possible to delineate certain behaviors as representative of presently existing

Introducing Mike—Experiencing depression, he closes himself off from others. His teacher offers support and tries to build a relationship of mutual trust.

or possibly future emotional deviations. We will examine certain areas of emotional disorder that are of particular interest to educators and other related personnel concerned with the ultimate development of positive mental health in children and youth. When working with youngsters, professional help is indicated if one sees certain symptoms persist, so that appropriate treatment strategies may be initiated.

Special symptoms

Bladder and bowel control problems

To determine the causes and appropriate treatment strategies for bladder and bowel control difficulties, the possibility of organic, developmental, and environmental factors must be examined before emotional or psychogenic causes are considered. In the case of *enuresis*, or lack of appropriate control of urine elimination (Ross, 1974), the condition also may accompany the reaction to a transient stress situation in which there are no indications of personality disorder. (See pp. 216–217 for a discussion of transient situational stress.)

Enuresis   Children under three years of age frequently have not attained neuromuscular control of the bladder so that voluntary regularity is not yet present. Variations in the development of the child's voluntary muscles do occur so that some children are able to control bladder (and bowel) functions at an earlier age than others. A substantial number of bladder problems are likely the result of poor training habits, training started too early, and/or the lack of conditioning (making a connection) between the sensation of a full bladder and the arousal mechanisms in the brain.

Diurnal enuresis refers to wetting during waking hours and *nocturnal enuresis* refers to bedwetting at night. If daytime or nighttime enuresis persists (despite adequate parental training) beyond the years where voluntary control is usually obtained (four to five years), a complete medical examination is indicated to rule out physical reasons for the problem. Nocturnal enuresis can be related to any of the following: constriction of the urinary canal opening, a small urinary bladder, maturational delays in the development of the central nervous system, mental retardation in which developmental milestones (such as successful toilet training) are delayed, or simply the result of a child's being such a deep sleeper that the sensation of a full bladder does not trigger an arousal warning to the brain. If the child is a deep sleeper, the physician may place the child on medication that lessens the depth of sleep.

To leave bladder problems untreated can lead to secondary emotional strains for the child. He or she often feels ashamed about wetting, and parental or teacher irritation may develop as a result of the problem. In the case of nocturnal enuresis in the older child or youth, there is worry about overnight stays with friends for fear of being ridiculed once the problem is discovered. A case study of one treatment method follows:

Johnny The mother of a third-grade, eight-year-old boy sought assistance because her son was still wetting the bed at night. Johnny's parents were loving, warm, and supportive and had tried to help their son overcome his problem by calmly talking with him, getting him up several times during the night, limiting his liquid intake before bedtime, etc. The family physician could find no physical basis to explain Johnny's problem other than that Johnny was reported to be a very deep sleeper.

Johnny also was seen by a psychologist and, aside from the humiliation Johnny admitted feeling about his problem, no other emotional, personality, or family conflicts could be found. He was eager to overcome his problem and the family agreed to comply with the strict rules that accompanied a conditioned response treatment method. This method utilizes an alarm system (bell or buzzer) which awakens the sleeper for proper urine elimination.

Treatment by an alarm system

The procedure was explained and demonstrated to Johnny and his mother. A special pad will be placed in bed at the level of Johnny's hips and covered by the bedsheet. When urine (or water or other liquid) contacts the pad, a current will set off the alarm which is loud enough to awaken Johnny and his parents, if they are in the same part of the house. Johnny and one parent must go through a set routine for the purpose of conditioning the appropriate response. When the bell or buzzer goes off, Johnny will awaken, turn off the alarm, climb out of bed, and go to the bathroom to complete toileting *even though he may feel no further need for urination.* While Johnny goes to the bathroom, one of his parents will change the sheet, place a dry pad on the bed, and reset the alarm. Johnny will return to the bedroom, change from wet clothing, and go back to bed. In essence, a patterning procedure will be established so that soon Johnny will associate the alarm system with the sensation of a full bladder and awaken just prior to bedwetting. The conditioning device will be left in place for at least ten days to two weeks after the bedwetting has ceased, since occasional accidents may still occur.

Along with strict adherence to the routine established, and with no other emotional conflicts present, the alarm conditioning device generally is successful in reducing nocturnal enuresis within a relatively short period of time (Finley & Wansley, 1976). In Johnny's case, his nighttime bedwetting was eliminated in three weeks, and he could then safely spend the night with friends without fear of embarrassment. Other methods of eliminating enuresis in the child also are available (Walker, 1978).

Encopresis This term refers to inadequate bowel control and is evidenced as repeated soiling behavior where the child either retains the feces but leakage occurs or in behavior wherein a fully formed stool is evacuated inappropriately (Warson et al., 1954). Encopresis exhibited by school-age children is considered a more indicative sign of emotional difficulty. This problem, too, must first be checked by a physician to rule out medical causes associated with the colon. Left untreated, retention of the feces can lead to impaction of the colon, causing loss of its muscle tone and shape and making bowel elimination a much more serious medical problem.

Reinforcement therapy

A procedure using reinforcement therapy is reported as having high success in treating encopresis (Wright, 1973, 1975; Wright & Walker, 1976). If serious emotional disturbances are demonstrated by the child, these must be treated *first,* with the encopresis problem handled after the child's condition is stabilized. When a child exhibits bowel control difficulties within the school setting, referral of the child for professional help certainly is indicated. Peer relationships may suffer as a result of the inappropriate behavior, with consequent lowering of the child's feelings of self-adequacy.

Pica

Ingestion of poisonous substances

As the very young child manipulates and explores the environment, the mouth is frequently used as a means of sensory input. Childhood illnesses or death resulting from ingestion of poisonous or otherwise damaging substances point to the need for close supervision to protect the young child. With continued parental supervision and teaching, the normal child usually learns during the second year to discriminate between edible and inedible substances. *Pica* refers to the continued eating of nonnutritive or even harmful substances. The presence of pica may reflect inadequate learning (as evidenced in its occurrence among the more severely retarded), or it may serve as a symptom of emotional disturbance. It has also been suggested that in some "neglected and undernourished children pica may indicate lack of supervision and attention. These children are starved for both attention and food" (Shaw & Lucas, 1970, p. 347). The possibility of lead poisoning from eating paint is of particular concern as are gastrointestinal complications resulting from ingestion of various other substances normally considered inedible. Referral is indicated when pica is observed, particularly if it persists past the age of two to three years.

Tics

Tics are stereotyped, involuntary movements of certain muscle groups. The movements serve no useful purpose and appear as nervous habits resulting from feelings of anxiety. They may include such facial tics as unusual mouth movements, rapid eye-blinking, sniffing of the nose, or facial grimacing. Other common tic symptoms are jerking of the neck, shoulders, or body and nervous coughs or clearing of the throat.

Certain personality features

Tics have their onset in children from six or seven to twelve years of age and are thought symptomatic of emotional stress or tension often caused by parental or school demands. Children exhibiting tics appear to present common personality features in that they are restless, self-conscious, sensitive, overambitious, and overconscientious. Some of the children are cited as shy, seclusive, and easily embarrassed (Kanner, 1957).

When the source of stress or tension is removed, the milder (more singly and simply expressed) varieties of tics usually disappear. The more severe (hysterical-convulsive type) tics are more difficult to treat and may persist into adult years. In fact, many tics are highly resistant to general types of treatment. In one approach, called habit-reversal, the child practices movements that are the reverse of the tic. The child or youth learns to be aware of his/her own body movements (tic or habit), practices a reverse action, and is rewarded by social approval for eliminating the tic (Azrin & Nunn, 1973).

Habit-reversal treatment

Youngsters exhibiting the tic syndrome need to be referred to a counselor or psychologist so that the source of anxiety or tension can be pinpointed and the areas of conflict alleviated, if possible. Particular efforts by the classroom teacher and others are required to avoid criticizing the child, calling attention to the tic, or expecting more productiveness than the child is able to handle. Educationally these children usually function as well as others so long as stress or pressures do not become too great and the classroom teacher plays a supportive role.

Supportive role of teacher

Anorexia nervosa

Anorexia nervosa represents a serious and sometimes life-endangering condition resulting from voluntary, self-imposed starvation. Extreme weight loss and disturbance of body physiology (malnutrition, menstrual disturbance in females) is evidenced but a drive for persistent or continued activity may remain (Calhoun et al., 1977; Freedman & Kaplan, 1972; Ross, 1974; Shaw & Lucas, 1970). Along with refusal to eat, voluntary regurgitation sometimes takes place.

Anorexia nervosa is more commonly found in females, aged twelve to twenty-one, but can occur in both sexes at any age. The ratio cited is nine females to one male. Since dieting is common among young females, the actual presence of anorexia nervosa may not be recognized until accompanying complications have progressed. Fortunately the disorder is relatively uncommon but, because of its possible culmination in death if left untreated or treatment is substantially delayed, anorexia nervosa should be recognized as one of the more serious types of psychological disturbances.

Much more common in females

Underlying causal factors from clinical case histories of anorexics include overemphasis on the significance of food, including a history of previous overeating and obesity, with severe dieting measures subsequently employed. Family conflict (parent-parent, parent-child) is also cited as a causal factor. In addition, anorexia nervosa can serve as a mechanism for avoiding the adult sexual role. A common triad in depressive disorders includes anorexia, weight loss, and insomnia (Kiev, 1974). An actual case example of an anorexia nervosa patient follows:

A triad in depressive disorders

Sally   Sixteen-year-old Sally was five feet five inches tall and weighed eighty-four pounds when referred to the hospital. She had always been a very active person involved in social clubs in school and many extracurricular activities. She was an average student who appeared well-liked by classmates. About eight months before hospitalization, Sally weighed 135 pounds and, although she carried this amount of weight well at her height, she told her parents that she was going on a diet. Sally first refused foods that had any appreciable caloric value and then rejected food entirely, stating that she was not hungry. A big power struggle ensued at home as her parents tried to force her to eat something nutritious. Despite a fifty-pound weight loss, Sally was still energetic and able to maintain almost all of her activities.

On examination in the hospital she looked rather emaciated but still was in a surprisingly healthy condition. Sally denied any feelings of hunger, denied she looked too thin, denied she really needed hospitalization, and denied there was any danger to herself because of her restricted food intake. Although there were a few other possibilities, the most likely diagnosis was that of anorexia nervosa.

Sally was told that she could eat as much or as little as she liked, but that if she did not gain from one-fourth to one-half a pound per day an intravenous feeding would be administered. She also was told that if she did not gain the prescribed amount, she would have to remain on the ward without a pass. For the first few days, Sally stubbornly refused to eat at all. She was quite shocked that the nurses kindly but firmly persisted in giving her the intravenous feeding. For the next few days, Sally took her tray of food but then hid some of the food on the ward and flushed the rest down the toilet. The staff was quite aware of the tricks of similar patients and caught her at all her evasions. When Sally was convinced of the set position of the staff, she cooperated grudgingly. Besides, she found remaining on the ward confining and boring. This treatment, most effective in the beginning, was a crucial form of behavior modification because of the life-threatening nature of the illness. Sally's therapist helped her gain some psychological understanding of her desire for extreme skinniness, which in her case appeared related to a fear of taking on the full responsibilities of a mature adult female.

While the family physician is in the best position to notice symptoms of anorexia nervosa, the classroom teacher also may be able to detect excessive preoccupation with dieting and weight loss. The longer the condition exists, the more difficult it is to treat.

Transient situational disorders

Temporary stress

All of us at some stage of our lives experience stressful situations that present a variety of symptoms. Whether it is a disruptive home environment caused by divorce, the loss of a favorite relative through death, a personal illness, a forced separation from loved ones, or some other particularly stressful circumstance, we all react differently. The symptoms a child or adolescent might present in these instances are not the result of an *underlying* personality disturbance but are the means the individual uses in attempting to cope with stressful situations.

Educationally, the child might fall behind in classwork, act depressed and unhappy, or even become aggressive or agitated. A change in the child's functioning will alert the observant teacher to the fact that something is responsible for the child's presenting behavior. An understanding teacher can be a tremendous support to the child during a particular time of stress. With such understanding support available, the child may not require further outside assistance and time alone may well resolve the situation. An example of a transient situational disorder will illustrate some of the symptoms a child might present.

Changes that alert the child's teacher

Susie   Five-year-old Susie had always been a cheerful, happy, bright-eyed child. She related well to the other children, was curious, and learned rapidly. One day Susie came to school quite sullen, began clinging to the teacher, and wanted to be held. The teacher inquired about Susie's present home situation and learned that Susie had been sent to live with an aunt while her mother entered the hospital for a serious operation. Susie had not seen her mother in over a week and she knew something was happening because everyone at her aunt's home became so serious when they spoke of her mother. Susie was frightened and unprepared for the move; hospitalization of her mother had been abrupt, changes had been made rapidly, and she missed her mother. Once the classroom teacher understood Susie's present situation, she was more patient and tolerant of the child's clinging behavior. When Susie was able to be with her mother again, her behavior stabilized, and she once again became a cheerful, happy, eager-to-learn child.

Aggressive and destructive behaviors

All parents can document outbursts of their child's rage, even during the infancy stage. Most frequently these outbursts are associated with frustration when the child is blocked from attaining some specific goal. Temper tantrums of the "terrible twos" are well-known; these occur normally during the child's attempts to initially separate from parents and establish some independence.

Aggressive or destructive behavior that continues into later childhood and adolescence, however, is of greatest concern within the present-day school setting. The learning environment of a single classroom, or even an entire school, may suffer as the result of unsocialized, aggressive reactions that infringe upon the rights of others. The definition of aggression and destructive behavior is determined relative to societal expectations and, within that society, by familial and subgroup expectations. We will confine our discussion, however, to behavior "characterized by overt

Learning atmosphere negatively affected

or covert hostile disobedience, quarrelsomeness, physical and verbal aggressiveness, vengefulness, and destructiveness" (Freedman & Kaplan, 1972).

For continued societal advancement, it is generally agreed that a society must be able to control unsocialized aggressive tendencies in its members, both as individuals and as members of a collective group. The necessity for such control has sparked research along four lines: (1) the medical approach investigating destructive behaviors from the standpoint of biological theory (genetic or organic factors); (2) the psychodynamic approach; (3) the sociological or psychosocial approach (emphasizing cultural and environmental influences); and/or (4) the behavioristic approach (discussed in Unit 1, pp. 33–34). Each theoretical approach has given further insight into the multiplicity of causes that can be responsible for unsocialized aggressive reactions.

The concern of the classroom teacher—in addition to learning possible causes for aggressive behavior so that changes, whenever possible, can be initiated—is with maintaining a classroom environment that is conducive to the learning process for both the disruptive youngster and classmates. Corporal punishment was traditionally employed as a means of control, although extensive debate surrounds the efficacy of this approach. For example, paddling is itself an aggressive act being used to punish aggression and some state laws prohibit the use of this approach. In cases where harsh and punitive treatment of the child is employed in the home, further corporal punishment is viewed as ineffective for ultimate resolution of the child's behavioral problems. Expulsion or suspension from school is another traditional means for dealing with aggressively disruptive students. Again, proponents of mental health procedures question the efficacy of this approach when the student and family involved do not receive constructive assistance in resolving conditions leading to undesired behaviors.

Certain family patterns are among the circumstances leading to aggressive and destructive behavior by children and youth. One or more of the following are often cited: parent dissatisfaction with the child, emotional inadequacies of the parents themselves, family permissiveness towards aggression, lack of adequate parental supervision, general family discord, and the use of painful, physical punishment as the major means for control of the child.

Neuroses in children and youth

Neurotic reactions have as their major characteristics "extreme anxiety associated with ineffectiveness in meeting life demands" (Clarizio & McCoy, 1970, p. 105). It has been suggested that the clear identification and incidence of neuroses in youngsters are hampered, in part, by the reluctance of the child guidance movement to label children—who are still undergoing years of development and change—with adult classifications (Anthony & Benedek, 1970, p. 105). Additionally, responses to overwhelming anxiety felt by children and youth can take many diverse forms.

Despite problems in identification, data indicating the presence of neurotic reactions as defined above suggest that such a disability is one of the most frequent emotional handicaps in children. Estimates of incidence range as high as 1 per 100 pupils (Clarizio & McCoy, 1970, p. 107). We will examine a few of the types of neuroses that can interfere with the normal functioning of children and youth.

"One in a hundred pupils"

Depressive neurosis

One of the most common neurotic reactions is that of excessive depression. A study of depression in children found a high frequency of the following symptoms: (1) self-criticism, (2) overt sadness, (3) open aggressiveness, (4) psychosomatic bodily disturbances, such as abdominal pains, eating problems, headaches, sleep disturbances, and (5) withdrawal indicated by lack of interest and participation in activities or loss of energies, or (6) increased activity in the form of restlessness or agitation (Weinberg & Malmquist, 1971). Depression in adolescents sometimes reflected similar symptoms but could also reflect wider swings of mood and more varied symptoms. Depression is thus sometimes difficult to diagnose and many of the symptoms also can be found in varying degrees in normal children and youth. However, when excesssive depression is found to interfere with normal functioning, depressive neurosis is indicated.

Symptoms

Hysterical neurosis, conversion type

A dramatic type of neurotic reaction is seen in the conversion type of hysterical neurosis, where anxiety is converted into physical symptoms (blindness, paralysis, deafness, tics) whose dysfunction cannot be attributed to organic causes. The case of Phyllis presents this type of disorder.

> *Phyllis* One of the casualties brought into the emergency room of the community hospital following an explosion of a gasoline truck in the center of the city was thirteen-year-old Phyllis. Phyllis ostensibly was totally blind. In the accident there were a number of people killed and many severely burned; Phyllis had witnessed people who were actually aflame.
> It was found that her visual disturbance did not stem from any organic cause. Rather, it was a conversion reaction to retrospectively blot out the horrible scenes that she had witnessed and to protect her against possible future sights which might arouse feelings of fear, revulsion, and disgust.

Blotting out horrible sights

Phobic neurosis

Another type of reaction—*phobic neurosis*—is rapidly demanding more attention and concern from educators. Phobias are defined as excessive and persistent fears of some object or situation that should be consciously recognized by the individual (child or adult) as presenting no real or actual danger. Many different kinds of phobias exist, ranging from fear of animals to fear of heights. We will concern ourselves here with the most common phobia of school-age children: *school phobia*, in which anxiety is displaced onto the school situation.

School phobia   School phobia is evidenced when the child has an unwarranted fear of going to school, has poor school attendance, experiences anxiety about leaving home, may use physical complaints to avoid school, and generally manages to stay at home. In these instances the child is not playing truant by skipping school, but indeed has unrealistic fears about leaving home to attend school or to continue the school day's attendance requirements (Kennedy, 1965).

Based on reviews of case studies, the cause of school phobia is largely attributed to an overdependency between mother and child. Approximately seventeen per thousand school-age children exhibit school phobia, so it is not a rare problem.

Many school-phobic youngsters are seen repeatedly by the family physician due to complaints of recurrent abdominal pain (RAP) or headaches. The astute physician will take a very careful history and perform a thorough physical examination. The onset of symptoms can generally be related to the evening before Monday morning school attendance (or other mornings of required school participation). If there is no organic complication causing the RAP or headache (or other presenting symptoms), the physician will aid the child's family to understand that stress or anxiety can and does affect the gastrointestinal tract, as well as other bodily organs. The following example is an actual case history of a youngster exhibiting school phobia.

Randy   This six-year-old male had stomachaches every Monday morning, and while he occasionally was taken on to school, the school nurse invariably ended up calling his mother and requesting that she take him home. Once he was home, however, Randy would begin feeling better. After a few weeks of constant complaints of stomachaches, Randy was scheduled to see his pediatrician.

A thorough medical examination failed to reveal any physical causes and the physician requested a psychological consult. Consultation (with cooperation from the family, Randy, and the physician) revealed a well-adjusted family situation but one whose close-knit nature fostered overdependency in Randy. The parents, assured that nothing physical was wrong with their son, understood and accepted the idea that he was fearful of separating from them and used his stomachaches as a way to stay home.

In order to help Randy adjust to school, the following plans were agreed upon. The next morning the father would take Randy to school regardless of his physical complaints. No sympathy or attention was to be focused on Randy when he complained of a stomachache. The psychologist had a conference with Randy's classroom teacher and the school nurse, informing them that nothing physical was wrong with Randy. They agreed to follow suggestions that they positively reinforce Randy's presence in school and ignore any physical complaints. Randy's mother was not to be called to take him home.

The next morning Randy was taken to school by his father. When Randy later complained of being "ill," his teacher reassured him that he would feel better and allowed him to lay his head on the desk but not to leave the classroom. At the end of the day Randy's mother picked him up and praised him for remaining in school. No questions were asked regarding how his stomach felt or if he were sick. Within a period of two weeks Randy no longer complained of stomachaches and his school attendance became regular. It was clear that cooperation of all persons involved facilitated his school adjustment.

Considerable support must be given to the parents of a phobic child since they are crucial to the success of the treatment strategy. Unless the mother-child relationship is quite disturbed, a treatment procedure similar to Randy's is usually successful in adapting the child to continued school attendance. Treatment for school phobia necessarily involves the following steps: (1) medical examination of the youngster to rule out the presence of actual physical illnesses warranting absence from school; (2) return of the child to the school situation without undue delay; (3) cooperation among the parents, school personnel,and other professionals during the treatment procedure to reinforce the child's efforts and successes in remaining in the school setting; and (4) provision of activities that the child can successfully perform during school hours (Cooledge et al., 1957). *Steps in treatment*

The ultimate goal in the treatment of school phobia is to return the child to successful school participation. With the necessary cooperation of those involved in treatment strategies, the prognosis for recovery from unwarranted fear of school attendance is considered to be favorable.

Psychoses in children and youth

A psychosis is a severe form of emotional disorder. All forms of adaptation (interpersonal, intrapersonal, intellectual) are adversely affected and the disruption of the entire personality is extensive. The psychotic individual's capacity to recognize or judge reality is distorted. False perceptions (hallucinations) and false beliefs (delusions) contribute to impairment in meeting life's demands. *Psychotic conditions defined*

A genetic, or constitutional, basis for these severe disorders has been researched widely, and there have been many studies devoted to identifying external factors (familial and interpersonal processes) as causative. The diagnostic classifications for these profound disorders in early childhood are modeled after the conditions found in adults. The disorders actually may not be the same in origin but their symptoms do resemble those of adult psychoses. It is difficult to identify external causal factors in younger psychotic children, and many workers in this area suggest that the earlier in life children exhibit these pathological states, the more likely it is that there is an organic or genetic base for them. *Causal factors difficult to identify*

We will consider psychotic conditions as they are manifested in the early childhood years as well as in the maturing adolescent. Our consideration will include symptoms to be recognized by early-childhood teachers and by teachers and other professionals involved in the later school years. There seems to be a consistency and continuity of adaptation in psychotic conditions, however, so that difficulties earlier in life can become more severe when new stresses occur later.

Early infantile autism

Kanner (1957) was the first to use the term *early infantile autism* for a group of children with a similar cluster of symptoms. These children, often from birth onward, were amazingly withdrawn, forcibly resisted any contact with adults, developed little speech unless it was to echo what was said to them, made little eye contact with people, rhythmically and repetitiously repeated certain movements, and preferred all physical objects to be in precisely the same place and condition all of the time or they became visibly upset. The cause of autism is uncertain, but theories pertaining to organic problems as opposed to family stress seem to prevail at this time (Rimland, 1964). These children are described as being "different" at birth; they are not easy to hold or cuddle, they exhibit irritability and seem to prefer to be left alone, as illustrated in the following case.

Rhythmic repetitious movements

> **Steve**   This three-year-old was referred to an evaluation center from the speech and hearing clinic because he was not speaking. He had spoken a few words at twelve months of age but then communicative verbal language seemed to disappear. He had always been a child who pulled away from any physical contact, so that even when his parents attempted to cuddle him, he would arch his back and scream until they put him back down.
>
> Repeated physical examinations reported Steve's health as normal, and he appeared to be growing and gaining weight appropriately. About the same time that Steve's speech disappeared, his parents and relatives noted that he was doing a great deal of rocking in his crib. When he began to walk, the rocking continued, either while he stood in one spot or was seated on a chair. During these times and others, people remarked that Steve seemed to be "almost in a different world." He played insistently with twirling objects such as tops, and he never played with his parents and siblings. His eye contact with others was virtually nonexistent, and the feeling people had when he did look at them was that he was actually looking *through* them. Any time his mother cleaned his room and moved an object from where it originally was, Steve would go into a violent screaming tantrum until the object was restored to its original position.

Organic theories about autism are in the ascendency

Recently, Ritvo (1978) has hypothesized that autism is a physical disease of the brain. Developmental rate and integration or modulation of sensory input within the brain are affected, leading to language and personality disabilities. If appropriate remediation or rehabilitation techniques are applied, Ritvo views the future for children with autism as more favorable than do earlier researchers. These techniques include the use of operant-conditioning programs, employment of special education remedial strategies, and use of psychotherapy as deemed appropriate for application to specific cases.

In other recent developments, Rimland and others who investigated the effects of megavitamin therapy, using Vitamin B6 with sixteen autistic youngsters, report positive results in terms of behavioral changes (*Science News,* 1978). As is the case regarding the causes of autism, acceptance of various remediation therapies still remains controversial, with more research indicated.

Beginning to respond to his teacher's efforts, Mike engages in a type of "play therapy" with a percussion musical instrument.

Early childhood schizophrenia

Children who are called *schizophrenic* also seem to have their symptoms begin in early life. However, there are some distinct differences between the onset of this disorder and infantile autism. The onset of schizophrenia takes place more often *after* a normally developing first year of life, with many parents describing the first year as especially calm.

While the autistic child is noted as being unusually healthy, the schizophrenic child suffers from a great number of physical disturbances during his or her second and subsequent years. The brain wave tracings (EEGs) of schizophrenic children are frequently abnormal, whereas the EEGs of autistic children are more often read as normal (Rimland, 1964).

The schizophrenic child does not insist on the preservation of sameness in his environment and also is often found to hallucinate (have false perceptions), which the autistic child may not. Autistic children generally have excellent motor ability, while schizophrenics are more often characterized as having poor coordination. The schizophrenic child has been described as *disoriented* in relationship to his environment, whereas the autistic child appears *unoriented* or *detached* from events. Familial histories in schizophrenic children also indicate more emotional disorders present, while there appears to be a lower than normal incidence of psychoses in the families of autistic children (Rimland, 1964).

Schizophrenia in youth

Schizophrenia in later developmental years can appear with varying symptoms, but is characterized by disturbances of thinking, mood, and behavior (Freedman & Kaplan, 1972, p. 62). The pressures of biological drives coupled with the relative immaturity of the adolescent's personality and experience—as one psychologically shuttles back and forth from feelings of dependence to independence, from feelings of being a child to feelings of being an adult—can precipitate profound disturbance in the form of schizophrenia in some youth. In the later school setting, however, it is sometimes difficult to differentiate between normal adolescent turmoil and the more malignant emotional disorders exhibited by a student. Contrast the following illustrations:

> **Bill** Upset by the financial problems within his family, Bill became increasingly morose and withdrawn. He secluded himself and complained about his classmates talking about him. His parents were concerned and consulted a mental health specialist. She advised the parents and Bill to talk over the pressures all were experiencing and how they could work together to solve the problems. On the initial contact, the presumptive diagnosis could have been that of a schizophrenic reaction. But after a few family therapy sessions, Bill reorganized with a complete return to adequate functioning. The final diagnosis was that of an adolescent turmoil of transient

situational nature, confirmed as Bill maintained his gains through high school and later college attendance.

When irrational thoughts persist and when behaviors are seen by the outside world as bizarre, the possibility of a break with reality conditions is suggested, as in the following case:

> *Eileen*   This girl's family sustained severe financial reverses, too. She also withdrew and felt that her classmates were against her, but, in contrast to Bill, she reported hearing voices saying bad things about her. Her parents were just as concerned as Bill's but Eileen refused any help.
>
>   Her symptoms became more intense and disruptive in the school and family situation She eventually refused to go to school, refused to eat, bathe, or change her clothes, and was unable to sleep. In desperation, her parents had her admitted to the community mental health center. Despite an improvement in her symptoms as a result of treatment which included the use of medication, upon returning home Eileen gave evidence of skip-backs each time she forgot or refused to take prescribed medication. Her diagnosis was of a schizophrenic process requiring repeated hospitalizations for years afterward.

Example 2: schizophrenic process

Manic-depressive psychoses

Although some cases of manic-depressive psychosis are reported to start earlier in life, most of the cases cited in literature occur during or after adolescence. In this disorder, there are swings in mood from unrealistically elated, excited, expansive (manic) to miserably sad, inactive, and withdrawn (depressed) moods. During either of these distinct phases, the person is unable to judge realistically his or her life situation and therefore acts inappropriately.

   The adolescent judged to be psychotic may face a relatively short-lived disability or the symptoms may persist, requiring intensive therapeutic work. It is necessary to rule out possible drug effects or the results of some physical disorders in order to ascertain that a condition is one of the psychoses. The process of ego (self) development whereby the normal child or youth stabilizes as an integrated, functioning person is seriously disrupted in the psychoses. Such disorders require early appropriate referral by parents and teachers when signs of personality disorganization are evidenced.

Disruption of ego development

Special concerns

Although differential diagnosis and delineation of contributing factors in emotional disorders can be complicated, three problem areas are of particular concern in present-day society. These include the high incidence of (1) abuse of children, (2) abuse of drugs, and (3) depressive illness leading to suicide and attempted suicide.

Child abuse

One of the most serious problems in today's society is that of child abuse. For a nation as progressive as the United States it seems incredible that it took almost two hundred years to pass a federal law stating that it was illegal to abuse children. The first Society for the Prevention of Cruelty to Children was formed in 1885 in New York, approximately a year after a child by the name of Mary Ellen was found chained to a bedpost, severely malnourished from subsisting on bread and water, with multiple bruises and marks on her body from frequent beatings.

The case of Mary Ellen

When the child's situation was brought to the attention of the police, no one would take legal action because the child was the "property" of the parent and parents could do as they pleased with regard to their own children. The nurse who found Mary Ellen finally went to the Society for the Prevention of Cruelty to Animals and pleaded the case on the grounds that the child was a member of the animal kingdom. On this basis, Mary Ellen was finally removed from her home (Fontana, 1973).

The term "battered-child syndrome" was coined in 1961, and during the next year a nationwide survey was conducted to find out how many cases of physical abuse were reported during the year (Helfer & Kempe, 1964; Kempe et al., 1962). Coming from seventy-one hospitals, a total of 302 cases of battered-child syndrome were recorded. Almost one-third of the reported children had either died or sustained permanent brain damage.

In 1974 the Federal Child Abuse Prevention and Treatment Act was signed into law. The law reads:

Legal definition

"Child Abuse and Neglect" means the physical or mental injury, sexual abuse, negligent treatment, or maltreatment of a child under the age of eighteen by a person who is responsible for the child's welfare under circumstances which indicate that the child's health or welfare is harmed or threatened thereby (Public Law 93-247).

Reporting child abuse "in good faith"

It is now mandatory to report suspected child abuse and neglect to the local protective service unit of the Department of Public Welfare or the juvenile court (Paulsen, 1974). In most states, by reporting "in good faith," one is protected if a lawsuit is filed against the complainant. In the past, physicians, teachers, neighbors, and others were reluctant to get involved in family matters even if a child's life were in danger. The fear of a lawsuit and possible financial loss prevented people from reporting. Now, however, in many states, if there is knowledge of child abuse or suspected child abuse and neglect, one can be held legally liable if such knowledge is not reported.

Although children of any age may be subject to abuse, most of the victims are three years of age or younger. In fact, abuse is fast becoming the number one killer of children under age three (Williams, 1976).

Who would abuse children? While we all experience anger toward children at some time or other, most of us do not physically harm them. A number of general characteristics of parents who abuse their children are set forth, such as demanding, dependent, immature, and impulse ridden, but these characteristics describe non-child abusers as well (Steele & Pollock, 1974). Among more definitive characteristics we can include unrealistic expectations; that is, the parents demand and expect more from their infant or child than the child is capable of understanding or doing. This tendency is illustrated in the following:

Characteristics of abusive parents

> *Unrealistic expectations* Twin children, eighteen months of age, were admitted to the hospital for the second time for failure to thrive, and discussions with their mother uncovered her expectations for the infants. When the mother was charged with neglect, she stated irately that there was plenty of food in her home and that it was put on the table for everyone to eat. When asked to expand on this statement it was learned that the eighteen-month-old twins were expected to climb in their chairs, fill their own plates with food, and feed themselves.

A second characteristic of parents who abuse their children is a tendency to look to their children to supply them with love and support. This role reversal means that the children are to provide their parents with nurturance and protection, and the parents are dependent on the children (Morris & Gould, 1963). The parents primarily disregard the children's needs for healthy development and growth and concentrate instead on satisfying their own needs.

Role reversal

Third, it is not unusual for abusive parents to have had poor parental models themselves, so that they frequently repeat inadequate modes of discipline and child rearing that they learned from their own parents. A lack of mothering is felt to be a basic factor in the roots of parental abuse (Steele & Pollock, 1974). Also, abusive parents frequently are noted to have themselves been the child victims of excessively harsh punitive methods.

Parents' own parental models

All this is not to say that the causes of child abuse can be easily explained. It is important to understand that there is no one set of causal factors. Rather, the problem is multidimensional, with many social factors influencing the situation. If unemployment and social class are important variables that contribute to abuse, or if unwanted pregnancies and prematurity of birth are found to be contributory factors, then these social/psychological problems must be analyzed and alleviated (Willis, 1976).

No easy explanations

Symptoms of child abuse When may a classroom teacher or other concerned individual suspect child abuse and neglect? Some symptoms are seen when children present an overall appearance of poor care, seem malnourished and dehydrated, are unusually fearful, and are apathetic and devoid of facial expression. Further, these children may be unresponsive to toys, to other children, or to the teachers's attempts at interacting with them, and are viewed by their parents as *bad* or *different* (Muir, 1976). Certainly when one discovers burn marks, bruises that are not easily explainable, repeated injuries or lacerations, etc., child abuse may be suspected. It is at this point that a teacher will want to call the protective services division of the local Department of Welfare, after consultation with the school principal.

Team approach is a must

Teamwork is needed to aid the child victims and their families. A teacher cannot be expected to handle the problem alone; rather, child-abuse problems require close interdisciplinary work with law enforcement agencies, social workers, psychologists, protective service workers, physicians, community agencies, and volunteer groups.

Drug abuse

Drug dependence is present when there is "evidence of habitual use or a clear sense of need for the drug" aside from prescribed intake which has been medically indicated (Freedman & Kaplan, 1972, p. 72). School personnel are becoming increasingly aware that the problem of drug abuse extends downward even to the elementary or middle-school-age child. Statistics regarding actual abuse are difficult to derive because of the lack of uniformity in reporting and the variation among states in statutes relating to use of certain substances, such as marijuana.

Drugs as a means of escape

Why, many workers question, do children and youth, as well as adults, show dependency or addiction to drugs? No one reason seems applicable to all or even most drug-dependent users. Generally, however, there seems to be a disillusionment with one's current life situation from which drugs offer a temporary means of escape. Some drug-dependent minors indicate that only at the time of the use of drugs do their lives seem to have "real meaning." Other factors leading to use and potential abuse of drugs appear to include the need to satisfy one's curiosity, the desire to experiment, and pressure from peers to conform for continued association or inclusion as a member of a particular group.

Symptoms of drug abuse

In an effort to combat the enormity of the drug-dependence problem, most school systems now include in their curricula programs that explain the effects of various drugs and alert youngsters to the potential dangers inherent in their use. Teachers are thus becoming more aware of symptoms that signal the possible abuse of drugs; these symptoms can vary from a student exhibiting a false sense of well-being, or euphoria, to significant changes in attitude, irresponsible actions, and episodes of wide swings in moods (e.g., from "highs" to "lows").

Wide swings in mood

Initially, it may be difficult to differentiate behavior that is associated with chemical reactions to the abuse of drugs from those symptoms related to certain disorders previously discussed in this unit (for example, unsocialized aggressive reactions, manic-depressive psychosis). Following referral, however, ultimate accurate diagnosis separating the personality disorder of drug dependence from other disorders can be made by appropriately trained professionals.

Suicide

Suicide is classified as the second leading cause of death in youth from fifteen to twenty-one years of age, exceeded only by deaths attributed to accidents. The actual frequency of suicide may be much higher than has been estimated (Mishara et al., 1976), if, as suspected, some one-car accidents—among the most common causes of fatalities—are actually suicide attempts. When individuals who knew such auto accident victims have been interviewed, underlying dynamics seen in suicide attempts often were reported as having been present. Additionally there now seems to be a greater number of real suicidal attempts occurring earlier in life. Part of the problem in appraising this possibility is the reluctance of those responsible for reporting vital statistics. Many states do not include death by suicide below age ten; these deaths are placed in the accident column instead, as if it is unthinkable to adults that young children might wish to kill themselves.

Suicide frequency may be higher than reported

According to reported suicide statistics, three times as many females as males *attempt* suicide, but it is the males who are three times more successful in killing themselves. This unusual reversal of attempts versus successes is related to differences in the suicide method utilized. Females most frequently use medication, while males use guns or hanging. There is an obvious time lag between the life-threatening act and actual death by these different methods; death is postponed longer with the oral ingestion of medication, giving rescuers much more opportunity to act.

Male and female suicide rates

The causes of suicidal actions are not always clear, although those occurring with the psychotic panic of the schizophrenic or those in which suicidal threats are voiced to try to influence another's actions (parent, opposite sex, peer) are more easily comprehended. Theories that are advanced concerning suicide include the belief that the act of suicide represents (1) overwhelming anger toward someone which is then turned against the self, and/or (2) feelings of failure to live up to one's own expectations or the expectations of significant others (Schechter, 1957; Schechter & Sternlof, 1972). Deep depression—in which the individual sees life's problems as insolvable and suicide as the only recourse to end such suffering—may culminate in self-destructive action. When depressive illness is present, the individual may voice feelings of hopelessness about the future. Direct or indirect expressions concerning the futility of life can represent an admission that usual coping methods have failed. Symptoms of depressive neurosis and manic-depressive psychoses were discussed earlier in this unit; left untreated, either of these conditions could contribute to the incidence of suicidal acts.

When coping methods have failed

Intervention strategies

In many cases the classroom teacher or other school personnel are the first to recognize that a child or youth is in need of special help for emotional difficulties. The beginning point of intervention is usually a conference with parents outlining the difficulties as viewed by the school and exploring the parents' viewpoints and reac-

Cooperation is the key factor

tions. In some cases, if there is cooperation among the school counselor, classroom teacher, and other supportive persons in the school system and if the family is willing and able to make needed changes, additional referral of the emotionally troubled child or youth may not be necessary. In many other cases referral is indicated for a thorough diagnostic evaluation leading to determination of necessary intervention strategies. Treatment approaches can take many forms, some of which we will consider.

Individual psychotherapy

One-to-one relationship

In some cases a child or youth is so emotionally handicapped that individual therapy or a one-to-one therapist-client relationship is needed. Even in cases where this approach seems most correct, it is still necessary to engage as therapeutic allies the parents, as well as school personnel. For example, the therapist must continue to know how the child or youth handles himself or herself outside the individual therapy session. What emotional difficulties continue to exist for the client in the classroom, on the playground or athletic field, in study hall, etc? What is the status of behavior at home? Only with close feedback of relevant information concerning the child or youth can the therapist judge accurately the progress being made through individual therapy measures.

Group psychotherapy

Group situation is a testing ground

In aiding some youngsters to work out their problems, group psychotherapy is found more beneficial than individual therapy. Particularly with adolescents who may be highly resistive to individual therapy, knowing that others have problems and are seeking assistance can allay fears or reluctance about their need for help. With problems of peer relationships evidenced by many children and youth, the group situation can become a testing ground for behavioral changes to be made in interpersonal relations and can help measure the degree of success being attained.

Psychodrama

Various techniques may be employed by different group leaders to facilitate changes in individual group members. Such techniques can range from the leader's taking turns to work with each person on his or her problem to techniques utilizing more informal, consistent interchange and interaction among group members. The use of psychodrama within the group situation is widely employed. Psychodrama allows group members to actively dramatize concerns or situations for greater understanding and therapeutic release of feelings.

Family therapy

Since the family is recognized as a major influence on behavior, the use of family therapy is seen as an effective method for diagnosing, or getting at the core of a particular child or youth's problems, and also as a means of facilitating needed changes for solution of difficulties. Here again family therapists may vary in actual techniques used. Some use the total family-group session approach wherein all members of the family actively interact with one another. Other therapists may see the parents as a couple, allowing interchange between them and listening to and talking with each in the presence of the other. Family therapists concentrate, however, on observing family interactions as clues to solving child-family difficulties.

Behavior modification, or reinforcement therapy

As an intervention strategy, behavior modification has been discussed in a number of contexts earlier in this book. It calls for active participation by family members, classroom teachers, and others in reinforcing desired behavioral responses. The rewards system to be used must be individually determined; what constitutes a *reward* to one individual may be meaningless to another. Punishment in its traditional corporal form (spanking, paddling) is not used, although withdrawal of certain privileges seen as rewarding (television viewing, use of the family auto by a teenager) may be incorporated into the plan for increasing desired behavior. When administered with careful consistency and careful monitoring of results, reinforcement therapy has been found successful in extinguishing undesirable behavior and culminating in the learning of new and acceptable modes of responses (Homme & Tosti, 1971; Ross, 1974; Skinner, 1953).

Consistency and careful monitoring required

Other therapeutic techniques

With younger children, play therapy (whether conducted between a single child and a therapist or a small group of children and a therapist) can be an effective therapeutic technique. Problems in interaction with others can be voiced or observed, fears expressed or noted, and tensions and difficulties analyzed for possible resolution. Materials and activities range from arts and crafts of all kinds, to puppetry, to active participation in various games.

Play and vocational therapy

With older youths and adolescents, arts and crafts and building materials are used extensively as a form of vocational therapy. Music and dance forms, too, have been employed successfully as therapeutic devices with both young children and adolescent groups.

More recently there has been a growth in camp counseling for the emotionally handicapped older child or youth. Camping sessions offer an extended period of time for therapists or counselors and group members to interact, in both informal and more structured ways, to clarify and alleviate existing difficulties. Again, as in other therapeutic endeavors, it is necessary to employ follow-up assistance from the family of the handicapped youth whenever possible.

When emotional problems reflect greater disorientation of the child or youth and/or when conditions potentially dangerous to the individual are present, intensive *inpatient treatment* in a hospital or other institution is indicated. The psychotic conditions, anorexia nervosa, and suicide attempts can require an inpatient setting where medical and psychiatric/psychological services are readily available. Chemotherapy—in which medication is prescribed to modify or alleviate an emotional disorder—is always administered under the direct supervision of medical personnel (al-

Inpatient therapy

though its use is sometimes begun or continued on an outpatient basis). Many of the forms of therapy discussed previously are also used with the patient while in the hospital or institutional setting.

Despite the fact that inpatient treatment may be clearly indicated in certain cases, the ultimate goal of such treatment is to return the child or youth as soon as feasible to adequate functioning within the whole of society. In order to facilitate gains made through inpatient treatment, the patient's family is helped to make changes that will allow for healthful reintegration of the child or youth back into the family. In some cases where this is not possible, foster placement may be indicated. Successful re-entry into the school situation requires the dedicated efforts of school personnel, who need to be informed of any necessary changes in academic demands and/or procedures to be followed.

Ultimate goal is reintegration

The classroom teacher as facilitator

With the continued de-emphasis on institutional placement for any but the most severely disturbed, the role of school personnel as vital members of the mental health team becomes more and more important. We have previously noted the cooperation that must be maintained between the school, family, and other professional workers in the efforts to work with emotionally handicapped youngsters. As a part of the diagnostic workup and therapeutic intervention planning, many psychologists and psychiatrists rely on observations concerning behavioral and emotional difficulties as noted by classroom teachers.

Teacher observation used in diagnostic workup

Checklists have been provided for teachers to help them more clearly delineate the types of behavior that interfere with the student's success in the classroom. Hammer (1970) lists various patterns of behavior that suggest possible emotional handicaps and groups them into nine major categories: (1) disturbed classroom behavior, (2) disturbances in attitudes toward the self, (3) disturbed behavior with the teacher, (4) disturbed relationships with peers, (5) inappropriately infantile behavior, (6) disturbances in physical functioning or appearance, (7) disturbance of speech, (8) sexual disturbances, and (9) difficulties in learning (pp. 518–519). A sample of the *Behavior Problem Checklist* developed by Quay and Peterson (1967) with directions for scaling are shown in Table 7-1. Checklists can have their drawbacks, however. For example, the rater may be a rejecting parent who places emphasis only on negative aspects of the child's behavior, or the parent may not be aware that certain behavioral characteristics are a part of certain stages of development (e.g., temper tantrums in the very young child). Nevertheless, a competent classroom teacher who remains objective but is vitally interested in his students' welfare can provide valuable behavioral information that will be useful for evaluation purposes and subsequent intervention strategies.

Checklists provide valuable information

Juvenile delinquency

The rise of violence, vandalism, and other disturbing behavior in the school setting is becoming an area of increasing concern to educators and the general public. Class-

Table 7.1
Eighteen items from a behavior-problem checklist

Please complete each question carefully.
1. Name (or number) of child_____
2. Age (in years) _____
3. Sex_____(M 1, F 2)
4. Father's occupation _____
5. Name of person completing this checklist
   _____
6. What is your relationship to this child? (circle one)
   a. Mother   b. Father   c. Teacher   d. Other_____
                                                 (Specify)

Please indicate which of the following constitute problems, as far as this child is concerned. If an item does *not* constitute a problem, encircle the zero; if an item constitutes a *mild* problem, encircle the one; if an item constitutes a *severe* problem, encircle the two. Please complete every item.

0	1	2	1. Oddness, bizarre behavior
0	1	2	2. Restlessness, inability to sit still
0	1	2	3. Attention-seeking, "show-off" behavior
0	1	2	4. Stays out late at night
0	1	2	12. Crying over minor annoyances and hurts
0	1	2	13. Preoccupation; "in a world of his own"
0	1	2	14. Shyness, bashfulness
0	1	2	15. Social withdrawal, preference for solitary activities
0	1	2	16. Dislike for school
0	1	2	36. Has bad companions
0	1	2	37. Tension, inability to relax
0	1	2	38. Disobedience, difficulty in disciplinary control
0	1	2	39. Depression, chronic sadness
0	1	2	51. Profane language, swearing, cursing
0	1	2	52. Nervousness, jitteriness, jumpiness; easily startled
0	1	2	53. Irritability; hot-tempered, easily aroused to anger
0	1	2	54. Enuresis, bed-wetting
0	1	2	55. Often has physical complaints, e.g., headaches, stomachache

Source: Quay & Peterson, 1967. ©1967 by Donald R. Peterson and Herbert C. Quay

room teachers and other school personnel need to be cognizant of some of the causes and intervention techniques relating to this critical problem.

    The following is an all-too-common classroom situation: A teacher comes into the classroom and is met by several youngsters having a fist fight. He breaks it up and learns that one of the combatants accused the other of stealing. Next he is told that a fourteen-year-old girl who has been a very good student has run away over

Delinquent behavior in classroom

the weekend. He has seen numerous articles in the newspapers about school systems where teachers are attacked, knives are carried routinely by gang youths, and police are used as hall monitors. How can he understand and cope with such behavior?

The number of professions—sociology, law, criminology, psychology, and psychiatry, to name a few—that purport to speak to the problem of delinquency point up the fact that no one area of professional knowledge has been especially successful in understanding delinquency. There are many theories of causes and many treatments offered, with varying success.

"Impaired delinquent"

Recent literature has suggested that more juvenile delinquents show minimal neurological impairment then had been previously noted (Siegal, 1976). This has given rise to the term *impaired delinquent*. Traditionally, however, causative theories have focused on measures of social disruption, family problems, and peer pressures. These theories usually find that delinquency is exaggerated by the psychological stresses of adolescence. Our discussion here will examine these theories and will pay particular attention to points where delinquency overlaps certain kinds of exceptionality.

What is juvenile delinquency?

A juvenile delinquent is identified on the basis of his or her behavior. This behavior is illegal in specific ways: for example, a delinquent act in most jurisdictions is an act performed by a youth which, if performed by an adult, would be a criminal act. But juvenile delinquency is not so easy to define; it is both a popular and a legal term. Webster defines it as "a status in a juvenile characterized by antisocial behavior that is beyond parental control and, therefore, subject to legal acting." While this is a generally accepted popular definition, the legal definition differs from state to state. In part, it is age-dependent: in some places the juvenile or family court has jurisdiction over young people until they are sixteen; in others, the jurisdiction extends until they are eighteen or even twenty-one. The legal requirements that determine which particular youngsters are called juvenile delinquents vary in other ways. The ultimate definition is circular: a juvenile delinquent is a youngster who has been so adjudicated by the court. One can analogize from the baseball umpire who asserted, "It ain't a ball or a strike until I call it one."

Legal definitions vary

A delinquent . . . is a delinquent . . . is a delinquent

As noted above, the law generally provides that if a youngster of appropriate age breaks a law designed to control serious transgressions of adult behavior, such a youngster could be adjudicated a juvenile delinquent. In states in which this term is used strictly, it can be legally conferred only on those youngsters who commit serious crimes, such as homicide, manslaughter, robbery, rape, assault and burglary.

Offenses applicable only to juveniles

Status offenses But in other states, laws are more flexibly interpreted and youngsters who are considered "incorrigible" or "habitually disobedient" may be termed delinquent (Haskell & Yablonsky, 1978). Status offenses are offenses that are applicable to juveniles only. This means that if an adult were to commit any of these offenses he or she would *not* be subject to any legal sanctions. These include running away, truancy, curfew violations, and the status of being "ungovernable," "stubborn," or "wayward." Such imprecise definitions refer to behavior which is clearly *not* labeled juvenile delinquency in other jurisdictions; in fact, the use of that term is studiously avoided. Different states have different terminology for such behavior. In New York State, such youngsters are found to be "persons in need of supervision (PINS)." The laws of California use the term "ward of the court" to apply to such youngsters. To put it another way, society has established general rules for the behavior of its youth, and status offenses are clearly in violation of usual societal standards.

Mike has made progress. He has emerged sufficiently from his withdrawn state to engage in parallel, or side-by-side, play alongside classmate Tommy.

In this discussion, we will use the popular definition of juvenile delinquency, cognizant of its legal ambiguity and the problems of labeling. Thus, we are talking about a range of socially unapproved behavior that can come to the attention of the law for status and criminal reasons.

Overall incidence

The actual incidence of juvenile delinquency is difficult to ascertain. This is in part because of the variations in definition from state to state and in part because similar offenses may be handled in different ways in the same locality. The following case study illustrates how one incident may become statistically recorded while another will not be recorded in any way:

Roger and Tom Roger, a sixteen-year-old Eagle Scout on a scout troop camping trip, stopped at a supermarket for supplies. He picked up a magazine, put it under his coat, and walked out. The store manager observed this action and notified the scoutmaster. The scoutmaster called Roger's parents, they drove some thirty miles to the place where Roger had taken the magazine, paid for it, apologized to the store owner, and took Roger home.

Tom, a fifteen-year-old boy of limited intellectual capabilities, worked after school carrying bags of groceries from a supermarket to patrons' cars. He was from a poor family and living with his chronically ill grandmother. One day, after he had been working at the store for over two months, Tom took a large pack of chewing gum and put it in his pocket. This was noted by the store manager, who called the police. Tom was arrested and placed overnight in the local jail.

Of those cases that are recorded, about one-half are dealt with at the police station without referral to court or any other agency.

The U.S. population between ten and seventeen years of age is approaching thirty-five million. We know that juvenile delinquency is presently increasing. Some measurement of the numbers involved can be made through police records. Such records show that about four million youths had contact with police in 1970, and two million of these contacts resulted in arrests. About half of the youths arrested were referred to juvenile courts and if trends continued, it has been estimated that one and one-half million cases would be handled by the courts in 1977 (Haskell & Yablonsky, 1978, pp. 16–22).

Female delinquency There is abundant evidence that delinquency is increasing more rapidly among females than among males. The period 1968 to 1973 showed arrests for females under eighteen rising 35 percent, while comparable figures for males increased 10 percent. A 1972 report from HEW attributes this increase to the changing attitudes of girls towards society and society's changing attitude towards them. Instead of accepting the passivity assigned to girls in the past and society's protective role towards them, today's young females are becoming more aggressive and more independent in their day-to-day activities (United Press International, 1972).

While today's young females are engaging in types of delinquent behavior heretofore more common in males (vandalism, running away), a difference still exists when it comes to labeling sexual behavior as delinquent. Sexually promiscuous behavior by girls may be adjudged as constituting delinquency, while society tends to pay little attention to sexually active boys except for rape offenses (Herskovitz, 1969).

Still a double standard

Causes of juvenile delinquency

We have defined what is popularly and officially meant by juvenile delinquency. Yet these perspectives, definitions, and statistics serve only generally to describe a number of *socially unapproved* and/or criminal kinds of behavior. What makes youngsters act in these ways? There may be as many reasons as there are youngsters who perform such acts. Delinquency is a complicated phenomenon and it is all too often oversimplified. Theorists generally separate delinquency into behavior whose roots are felt to be intrapsychic (of psychodynamic origin) and behavior in which sociocultural (psychosocial) factors appear to be significant causes. A good deal of overlap, however, must be conceded.

Psychodynamic theories   Psychodynamically delinquent behavior is seen as "acting out." This means that the delinquent behavior keeps the individual from experiencing a symptom either by taking the place of the symptom or by providing enough outlet for the discharge of emotional energy to avoid development of the symptom. Instead of experiencing an inner conflict about what he or she might want to do that is forbidden, the delinquent avoids this situation by externalizing it, moving it from "inside" to "outside." It is theorized that in some individuals guilt from the underlying conflict is alleviated when they are caught and punished for their delinquent acts.

"Acting out"

Character disorders. The neuroses and psychoses described earlier in this unit account for but a small portion of delinquency. Psychodynamic theories point to persons with *character disorders* (also called *personality disorders*) as responsible for the bulk of delinquent behavior. Character disorders are lifelong patterns of behavior, often acceptable to the individual involved but producing conflict with others.

The subtype of character disorder most often seen in delinquency is termed *antisocial* in diagnostic manuals. These individuals get into repeated conflicts with society, have poor ability to postpone immediate gratification of impulses, find it difficult to maintain close relationships, and feel little or no guilt or anxiety over delinquent or antisocial acts.

No motivation to change lifelong patterns

Masked depression. While it has been noted for some time, this concept has only recently been given particular attention in literature. As Lesse (1974) put it:

> [Recent]reports have highlighted the fact that depressions may also be disguised by various types of "acting out" or behavioral disturbances. These behavioral masks may take the form of antisocial acts, impulsive sexual behavior, compulsive gambling, temper outbursts, destructiveness, sadistic or masochistic acts, compulsive work or behavior patterns, accident proneness, histrionic dramatizations, and more. It may manifest itself in the form of narcotics addiction, barbiturate habituation, the use of stimulant drugs, and the use of psychedelic agents such as lysergic acid or mescal derivatives (p. 4).

Is depression always recognizable?

The concept of masked depression is important in understanding some delinquents. Depression similar to that typically experienced by adults becomes increasingly common after midadolescence. This experience of depression is characterized by low spirits, loss of appetite for food and sex, disturbances in sleeping patterns, lowered motivation, and, occasionally, feelings of worthlessness and even thoughts of suicide. Some youngsters beginning to experience these symptoms of depression turn to acting-out behaviors to keep depressive feelings from being felt and experienced. An adolescent girl may involve herself in a pattern of sexually promiscuous behavior that provides a false feeling of involvement and closeness (Herskovitz, 1969). Or as Ludwig (1974) has pointed out regarding the use of psychedelic drugs:

Sexual promiscuity and chronic drug use

> There is a sub-species of depression, characterized by ennui, feelings of isolation, lack of purpose, and loneliness which tends to predispose many young people to the chronic use of psychedelic drugs. In a sense, the clinical effects of psychedelic drugs are almost specific, but temporary, antidotes for this underlying disphoric emotional state, since they provide the drug user with a sense of novelty, meaningfulness, and interpersonal rapport (p. 248).

Another researcher has estimated on the basis of matched groups that "four out of five delinquents . . . were somewhat depressed, in contrast to (a matched group of) nondelinquents, of whom only two out of five . . . evidenced the same degree of depression" (Chwast, 1974, p. 230).

Family theories   Here we examine the context in which the youngster grows up and try to understand some other important influences relevant to delinquency. Our review will look at various aspects of family structure as well as family interaction.

Broken homes. Clinical experience and a number of controlled studies (Haskell & Yablonsky, 1978, pp. 110–118) demonstrate that given a matched group of delinquents and nondelinquents, the delinquents will be significantly more likely to have come from broken homes. But this is not a single cause-and-effect relationship: one cannot assume that a broken home automatically causes delinquency. The

Stability as important as structure of family

actual number of delinquents from broken homes is not overwhelming when compared to those from intact family units, and there are clearly many other family factors to be taken into account. Delinquents also are likely to come from two-parent, but unstable, home situations. Whether or not the home is a happy one is equally as important as its structural makeup.

In the one-parent family that has experienced separation, desertion, or divorce, there is also likely to be a good deal of conflict even though the absent parent may be from time to time available to the children. For example, many people who decide to divorce have experienced a good deal of anger, frustration, and hostility preceding the event. This can seriously jeopardize efforts at consistent discipline and consistent display of reasonable affection between parents and children.

Discipline. Webster's definition of discipline emphasizes self-control, character training, orderliness and efficiency. Ideally, parental behavior that clearly communicates these expectations will help a child grow from a position of *external* controls with punishments, or sanctions by adults, to one of *internalized,* or self, control. From clinical observations and systematic studies of discipline patterns among the parents of youngsters who become delinquent, one can isolate a number of factors that give rise to maladaptive and often delinquent behavior (Haskell & Yablonsky, 1978, pp. 119–129). One such factor is the lack of consistency in discipline. When a youngster grows up in an atmosphere in which certain actions predictably have certain consequences, the world can seem safe, secure, and manageable. But if the discipline is capricious, if a certain form of misbehavior is at times ignored and at other times likely to result in vigorous physical punishment, the youngster will feel confused, frightened, and unsure. These feelings can give rise to delinquent acting out.

Consistent discipline vital to feeling of security

Professionals dealing with delinquent teenage children note that when consistent external controls and limits are set up in a predictable way, the adolescents often feel much more comfortable and relieved, even if the standards are stricter than those under which they grew up. This would imply that consistency itself can be rewarding (McCord & McCord, 1959).

Unconscious inconsistency. When confronted with the observation that they handled similar kinds of misbehavior in different ways, most parents and teachers will generally be able to recognize that fact. With help, they can be taught how to be more consistent. A more insidious form of inconsistency is shown when the parent makes one message known verbally, but provides another message, usually nonverbal, through other forms of communication. The latter message is unconscious and contradicts the first. This is found in situations first described by Johnson (1949), in which she shows how parents of delinquent youngsters may *consciously* condemn their youngsters' delinquency, yet *unconsciously* promote it.

Contradictory messages

> *Mary*   This fifteen-year-old girl was a poor student and truant to the point of suspension from school. She took drugs, was sexually promiscuous, and ran away for one or two days at a time. On her return her mother, a

tight-lipped, anxious, repressed and shy lady, would encourage Mary to tell all about her adventures during her runaway time. The mother seemed particularly fascinated by Mary's promiscuity and drug-taking. After the recital of all the misdeeds in which Mary had indulged, her mother would declare she was going to restrict Mary's activities for a month. After about two or three days, Mary was generally able to manipulate her mother into fully restoring all privileges.

It is clear that even though Mary's mother disapproved of her behavior, she was fascinated with it in contrast to her own somewhat limited life. By her careful solicitation of the exciting events Mary had experienced, and by not following through with her disciplinary plans, the mother subtly encouraged Mary to run away and then return and share her experiences.

Attention and affection. We have seen that negative attention can provide *some* of the "stroking" that is usually given through affection. The ability to demonstrate consistent love and affection in physical, verbal, and other ways between parents and children is one of the most important factors promoting healthy growth and psychological development. In cases of extreme deprivation, massive family size, and/or during particular conflicts, the necessary amount of affection for a child may simply not be available. Parents who are preoccupied with their own personal miseries can have little energy to share affection and be concerned with their children's needs.

The triangle. Theorists of complex family interactions know that frequently a youngster experiences conflicting messages as a result of parent marital disharmony. At times, he or she may be utilized as a vehicle for communication between them, a phenomenon sometimes referred to as a *triangling* (Bowen, 1971). In such situations some youngsters are pushed into delinquent behavior to express one parent's anger and frustration with the other.

David Mrs. Potter married Mr. Potter after her first marriage ended in divorce. When David, her son from her first marriage, was first seen in consultation he was fifteen. Mrs. Potter was angry with her husband because he was passive, unresponsive, and a poor provider. At the same time she was weary of his anger toward her and sought to divert it in a number of ways.

David asked his parents for money to buy a calculator that would help him in his complex studies. He was an excellent student in both physics and mathematics in high school. His mother demurred, saying that his stepfather simply did not make enough money to afford it, and she made no secret of her contempt for Mr. Potter. When David appeared at the house with a calculator some weeks later, no questions were asked. The fact that he had stolen it was not revealed until some months later, when he was caught on another shoplifting charge.

David was "triangled in," leading to his delinquent behavior.

Behavioral learning viewpoint   Earlier units in this text discussed learned behavior in a number of contexts. Skinner (1938, 1953) and others pointed out that behavior responses are sent forth in relation to certain "consequent environmental factors."

To apply these concepts to the learning of delinquent behavior, we would note that behavior results from the sum of positive and negative conditioning factors. If, for example, parents ignore or overlook behavior considered unacceptable by general society, the parent is giving *positive reinforcement* by condoning it. On the other hand, children reared in a family in which the supply of affection available is less than might be needed, may find that the only way to obtain parental attention is to misbehave. The misbehavior is then reinforced by the parents' attending to it even though their attention consists of reprimands and punishments. A history of such repeated attention for misbehavior is frequently seen in youngsters who become delinquent in adolescence.

Rewards for misbehavior

Behavioral learning principles are relevant not just for the insights gained into the causes of antisocial and delinquent behavior, but also for a better understanding of the origins and maintenance of appropriate behavior. They also have value in altering socially inappropriate behavior. It has been noted, for example, that positive reinforcement techniques work more effectively in terms of behavior modification than negative reinforcement techniques (Brady, 1975, pp. 1827–1829). Thus, praising a child's restraint, good judgment, self-control, and postponement of gratification may be more effective than punishment after trouble has occurred.

Praise more effective than punishment

Sociological perspectives   Earlier we saw how sociological factors influence motivation (Unit 5). By most statistical measures of class and delinquency there is found a significant correlation between lower socioeconomic-class youth and delinquency. Numerous theories have been advanced to try to explain this correlation.

One set of theories explains delinquency on the basis of lack of effective social controls; the other understands delinquent motivation in cultural terms. Kalogerakis (1976) has reviewed these theories recently. He notes that some environments can lack controls and be provocative, stimulating violence and other delinquent acts, making weapons available and also allowing easy access to facilitating agents such as alcohol. On the other hand, he points out, it is important to recognize that some subcultures make delinquency "culture-syntonic" (p. 113). This means that delinquent and violent behavior is culturally acceptable and indeed expected in a variety of situations.

Delinquency motivation theories

Intervention techniques

In general, the aims of any form of intervention are twofold: (1) to prevent occurence of illegal behavior and (2) to find and understand the root causes. Indeed, these were the aims when juvenile courts were first established in 1899. Quay et al. (1970) suggest *differential treatment* as a means of intervention in delinquent careers. They encourage use of their method for classifying delinquents into four dif-

Differential intervention

ferent behavioral categories: inadequate-immature, neurotic-conflicted, unsocialized aggressive or psychopathic, and socialized or subcultural (pp. v–vi). Different treatment strategies for each behavioral category are called for in rehabilitation and treatment.

Of course, primary prevention of delinquency connected to societal ills, poor child-rearing practices, divorce, and poverty requires massive intervention in these spheres. The importance of such primary *societal* prevention cannot be overemphasized. But when we discuss intervention here, we refer to *individual* intervention for a particular delinquent. Below we will consider the kinds of immediate intervention relating to individual youngsters or small groups of youngsters, which take place outside the legal system.

Family and school intervention   Intervention outside the legal system takes place before an individual's behavior comes to the attention of law enforcement officials. Most commonly such intervention will be made by social institutions, such as schools, or by the family itself. Parents may recognize delinquent behavior in their youngster or have it brought to their attention by others; they may seek outside aid or may handle the matter themselves. The aid generally sought is counseling from such individuals as the family doctor or minister, the school counselor, or a counselor from a community guidance or mental health center.

The intensity with which the school or family pursues help for a given problem of delinquency will often depend on how disruptive the behavior appears to the school or family. Some families may condone stealing as part of the cultural norm, whereas other families with the same problem might be more concerned. Similarly, a school will have to deal more vigorously with the truancy problem of a thirteen-year-old, than with the similar problem of a child who is nearly sixteen and approaching the age at which the school policy states that attendance is no longer mandatory.

Other delinquency problems impinge more directly upon the school, its staff, and other students. Some experts have estimated the cost of vandalism, arson, and theft in the nation's public schools at $500 million annually (Brenton, 1975). To deal with such problems various alternatives have been proposed, ranging from increased security measures to special training for teachers. One special training approach tries to equip teachers with (1) diagnostic and remedial teaching competence, (2) crisis intervention skills, and (3) a thorough knowledge of the community (Bell, 1975).

Another approach emphasizes special programs. High school equivalency programs have been shown to be helpful in dealing with dropouts and in reducing this group's proneness to delinquency (Rulo, 1974). Another group of youngsters prone to dropping out are those who have already been placed in an institutional setting. Briscoe (1974) describes a program designed to help youngsters readjust to regular high school after discharge from a juvenile detention center.

It is the feeling of the present authors that the therapeutic approach can be utilized by teachers, guidance counselors and others, not just by mental health professionals. Such therapeutic interactions may be carried out in either an individual or a group setting. Warmth and understanding will help to inhibit the youngster's tendency to act out unconscious impulses if the adult sets consistent, firm limits. If a trusting and supportive relationship can be established, the youngster may develop enough insight to examine and work through his or her feelings of depression and low self-esteem.

Therapeutic approach

Specific family therapy approaches that have been developed in the past decade have proven to be increasingly applicable to the field of delinquency. Family members can gain insights into the need for setting limits. Ways of avoiding the unconscious promotion of unwanted behavior can also be clarified. When the delinquent behavior is the result of pathology that can be identified in the family itself, family therapy must be considered the treatment of choice.

Family therapy

Classroom strategies   There can, of course, be no simple prescription for dealing with a juvenile delinquent in the classroom, but we can offer some suggestions for an appropriate approach. In order to deal with the delinquent, one needs to have a working understanding of *why* the behavior is taking place. Without such an understanding, one is at the mercy of one's immediate reactions, such as anger at rebellious student behavior. Feelings of anger or the desire to retaliate need to be carefully considered before acting in a classroom situation. As we have stressed in this unit, there may be a variety of reasons underlying delinquent behavior. The classroom teacher can be assisted in the search for understanding by a number of available resources. These include school professionals in guidance, social work and psychology. With the cooperation of school administrative officials, and given time and patience, valuable information can often be obtained directly from the family at a parents' conference. Family conferences that include parents, the problem youngster, and siblings can prove to be very useful in helping to explain behavior difficulties.

Teacher's own feelings

Having an understanding of the cause of the behavior can lead the classroom teacher to consider interventions that will be useful in terms of the class. This does not, of course, preclude the use of other treatment agencies when indicated. Presuming the delinquent youngster does remain in the class, firm, clear, consistent limits must be set and clear expectations must be communicated. The consistency must come not only from the individual teacher in the classroom, but also from other teachers with whom the youngster has contact throughout the teaching day and the administrative and other professional staff. In addition, once the consistent limits and expectations with appropriate sanctions have been decided upon, this plan should be adhered to for an extended period of time—at least four to six weeks. Teaching professionals might say, "We have tried everything." This may indeed be true, but often it means that the "everything" has been tried on successive

Sticking to a plan

days, so that as soon as a youngster begins to seriously test a particular limit, it is given up and another alternative is substituted.

To help set limits, it is possible to enlist the aid of the other students in the class. This can be facilitated extremely well by experienced teachers, assisted by other school personnel and professionals in social work, psychology, and guidance. In such a model, students discuss particular types of behavior that have occurred in the classroom. Suggestions are solicited from class members concerning how they themselves might handle problem behavior and how they might help structure appropriate behavior.

Using classmates to help

These general guidelines aside, individual differences that characterize every youngster need to be taken into account and considered in any appropriate program. Some youngsters need to be strongly challenged or confronted; others may need a great deal of "tender loving care." Working with youngsters judged delinquent can be difficult and highly frustrating work. The classroom teacher needs to have a great deal of patience with self and also with those over whom he or she has charge. Most important, when current efforts appear not to have been especially useful, the teacher must not think of himself or herself as a failure. It may be that the teacher's genuine efforts to assist will lead to later desired adjustment by the student.

Don't despair

Prognosis

As we have said repeatedly in this discussion, there is no one single picture of delinquency. It is a complicated syndrome, coming out of many interrelated causes. Any remedial effort must be based on a careful evaluation of all relevant causes, including familial, social, individual, and medical factors. When all the data are gathered and reasonable hypotheses about the specific factors underlying an individual's delinquency can be made, one can plan for appropriate intervention. Prospects are best if the delinquency is of sudden onset, related to a particular situation, and if the family and youngster are willing to cooperate. If there is no cooperation, if the delinquency has been long-standing, and if it seems to be very much a part of the social or familial system in which the individual has developed, then the chances for successful intervention diminish. The amount of difficulty experienced by so many professional workers serves to re-emphasize the fact that our knowledge and understanding of these kinds of complex behavior with multiple and disparate causes are still very rudimentary.

Summary

We began to explore the topic of emotionally handicapped children and youth by examining desirable long-term mental health goals and stages of healthy emotional growth. Our review pointed out some of the problems involved in defining and establishing criteria for emotional disabilities.

We considered organic, familial, and school-related sociocultural factors as these play a part in the child's or youth's concept of self and consequent emotional development. A number of syndromes exhibited in various emotional disturbances were described in terms of symptoms, behavior and possible causative factors. Additionally, some special areas of concern in today's society were discussed, including the high incidence of child abuse, drug abuse, and suicidal acts as these relate to emotionally handicapped children and youth.

General approaches as well as specific treatment strategies for various disorders were presented, and we looked at some patterns of behavior that are popularly and legally termed as juvenile delinquency. Delinquent behavior, as we noted, is a

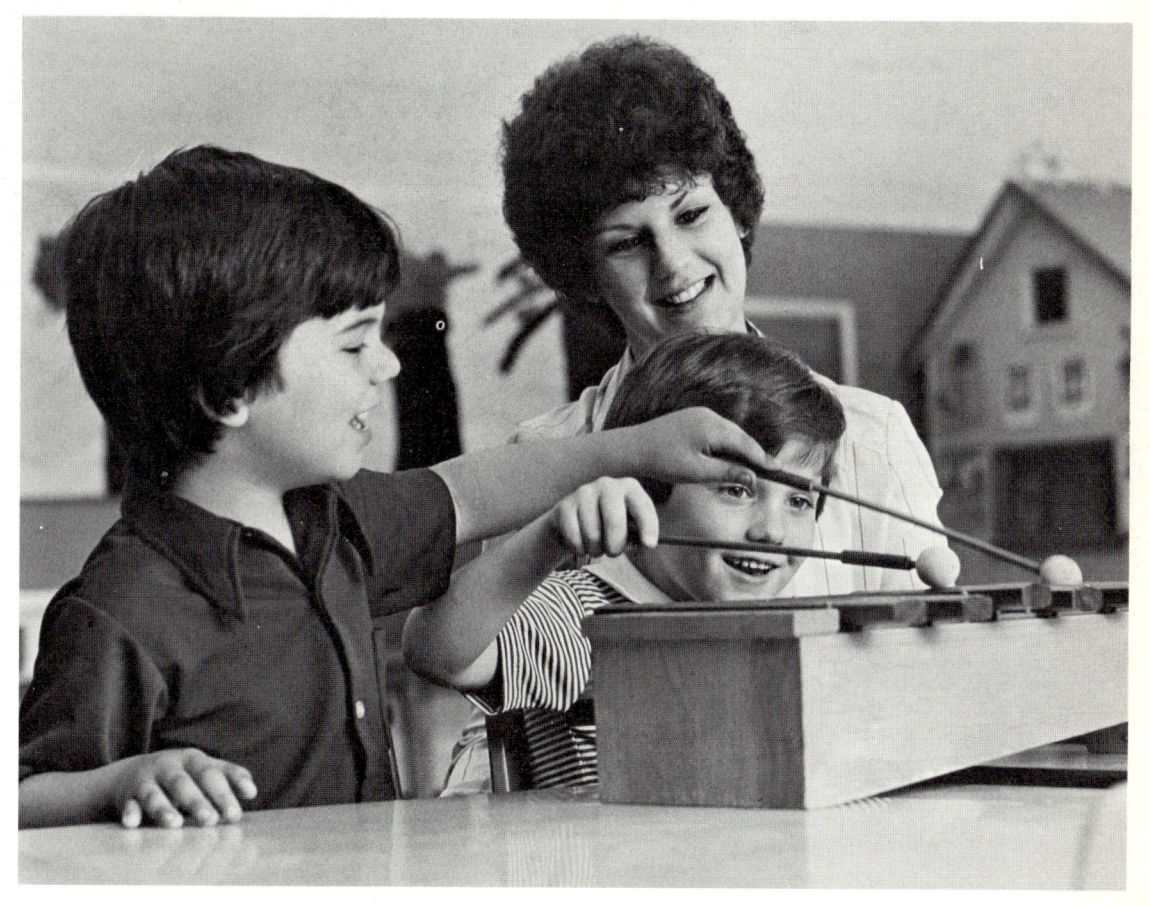

Now Mike has begun to actually play with Tommy, to share the instrument, and to enjoy the interaction with teacher and peer.

widespread and increasing phenomenon, but accurate records are not usually kept. We have argued strongly that delinquency is a composite phenomenon for the most part, made up of many contributing factors; occasionally one overriding factor can be pinpointed, but more typically, an intricate combination of factors produce this situation. Finally, we have suggested that a search for more useful methods and new understanding to help us cope with juvenile delinquency is required.

Throughout the unit, the classroom teacher and other school personnel were viewed as essential to early detection and facilitation of treatment for emotionally handicapped children and youth.

References and resources

Anthony, E., and Benedek, T. eds. *Parenthood—Its Psychology and Psychopathology.* Boston: Little, Brown, 1970.

Azrin, N. H., and Nunn, R. G. "Habit-Reversal: A Method of Eliminating Nervous Habits and Tics." *Behavior Research and Therapy* 11 (1973): 619–28.

Bell, R. "Alternatives for the Disruptive and Delinquent, New Systems or New Teachers." *NASSP Bulletin* (1975): 53–58.

Bowen, M. "Family Therapy and Group Therapy." In *Comprehensive Group Psychotherapy,* edited by H. I. Kaplan and B. J. Sadock, pp. 384–421. Baltimore: Williams and Wilkins, 1971.

Brady, J. P. "Behavior Therapy." In *Comprehensive Textbook of Psychiatry,* vol. 2, edited by A. M. Freedman and H. I. Kaplan, pp. 1824–31. Baltimore: Williams and Wilkins, 1975.

Brenton, M. "School Vandalism." *Today's Education,* vol. 64, no. 2 (1975), pp. 82–85.

Briscoe, C. "Project Vital—Juvenile Offenders Returning to School." *The Clearing House,* March 1974, pp. 411–15.

Buss, A. H. *Psychopathology.* New York: Wiley, 1966.

Calhoun, J. F.; Acocella, J. R.; and Goodstein, L. D. *Abnormal Psychology: Current Perspectives.* 2nd ed. New York: CRM, Random House, 1977.

Chwast, J. "Delinquency and Criminal Behavior as Depressive Equivalents in Adolescents." In *Masked Depression,* edited by S. Lesse, pp. 219–35. New York: Aronson, 1974.

Clarizio, H. F., and McCoy, F. *Behavior Disorders in School-Aged Children.* Scranton, Pa.: Chandler Publishing Co., 1970.

Cooledge, J. C.; Hahn, P. B.; and Peck, A. L. "School Phobia: Neurotic Crisis or Way of Life." *American Journal of Orthopsychiatry* 27 (1957): 296–306.

Everett, R. B., and Schechter, M. D. "A Comparative Study of Prenatal Anxiety in the Unwed Mother." *Child Psychiatry and Human Development,* vol. 2, no. 2 (1972), pp. 84–91.

Finley, W. F., and Wansley, R. A. "Use of Intermittent Reinforcement in a Clinical-Research Program for the Treatment of Enuresis Nocturnal." *Journal of Pediatric Psychology,* vol. 4, no. 1 (1976), pp. 24–27.

Fish, B. "Limitation of New Nomenclature for Children's Disorders." In *The Child: His Psychological and Cultural Development,* vol. 2, edited by A. Freedman and H. I. Kaplan, p. 75. New York: Atheneum, 1972.

Fontana, V. *Somewhere a Child is Crying.* New York: Macmillan, 1973.

Freedman, A. M., and Kaplan, H. I., eds. *The Child: His Psychological and Cultural Development,* vol. 2. New York: Atheneum, 1972.

Hammer, M. "A Teacher's Guide to the Detection of Emotional Disturbance in the Elementary School Child." *Journal of Learning Disabilities* 3 (1970): 517–19.
Haskell, M. R., and Yablonsky, L. *Juvenile Delinquency.* 2nd ed. Chicago: Rand McNally, 1978.
Helfer, R. E., and Kempe, C., eds. *The Battered Child.* Chicago: University of Chicago Press, 1974.
Herskovitz, H. H. "A Psychodynamic View of Sexual Promiscuity." In *Family Dynamics and Female Sexual Delinquency,* edited by O. Pollak and A. S. Friedman, pp. 89–98. Palo Alto, Calif.: Science and Behavior Books, Inc., 1969.
Homme, L., and Tosti, D. *Behavior Technology: Motivation and Contingency Management.* San Rafael, Calif.: Individual Learning Systems, 1971.
Johnson, A. M. "Sanctions for Super Ego Lacunae of Adolescents." In *Searchlights on Delinquency,* edited by K. R. Eissler et al., pp. 225–46. New York: International Universities Press, 1949.
Joint Commission on Mental Health of Children. *Digest of Crisis in Child Mental Health: Challenge for the 1970s,* p. 28, 1969.
Kalogerakis, M. G., "Treatment of Violence Prone Adolescents." *Scientific Proceedings in Summary Form.* American Psychiatric Association, Annual Meeting. Washington, D.C.: 1975.
Kanner, L. *Child Psychiatry.* 3rd ed. Springfield, Ill.: Charles C Thomas, 1957.
Kempe, C. H.; Silverman, F. N.; Steele, B. F.; Droegemueller, W.; and Silver, H. K. "The Battered-Child Syndrome." *Journal of the American Medical Association* 181 (1962): 17.
Kennedy, A. "School Phobia: Rapid Treatment of Fifty Cases." *Journal of Abnormal Psychology* (1965): 285–89.
Kiev, A., ed. "Somatic Manifestations of Depressive Disorders." *Excerpta Medica,* London, 1974.
Kisker, G. V. *The Disorganized Personality.* New York: McGraw-Hill, 1964.
Lesse, S. "Depressive Equivalents and the Multi-variant Masks of Depression." In *Masked Depression,* edited by S. Lesse, pp. 3–23. New York: Aronson, 1974.
Ludwig, A. M. "Psychedelic Drugs and Masked Depression." In *Masked Depression,* edited by S. Lesse, pp. 339–49. New York: Aronson, 1974.
McCord, W., and McCord, J. *Origins of Crime.* New York: Columbia University Press, 1959.
Mishara, B. L.; Baker, A. H.; and Mishara, T. J. "The Frequency of Suicide Attempts: A Retrospective Approach Applied to College Students." *American Journal of Psychiatry* 133 (1976): 841–44.
Morris, M. G., and Gould, R. W. "Role Reversal: A Concept in Dealing with the Neglected/Battered Child Syndrome." In *The Neglected/Battered Child Syndrome.* Child Welfare League of America (1963): 29–49.
Muir, M. "Psychological and Behavioral Characteristics of Abused Children." *Journal of Pediatric Psychology,* vol. 1, no. 2 (1976), pp. 16–19.
Paulsen, M. G. "The Law and Abused Children." In *The Battered Child,* edited by R. E. Helfer and C. H. Kempe, pp. 153–78. Chicago: University of Chicago Press, 1974.
Powell, G. F.; Brasel, J. A.; and Blizzard, R. M. "Emotional Deprivation and Growth Retardation Simulating Idiopathic Hypopituitarism: Clinical Evaluation of the Syndrome." *The New England Journal of Medicine* 276 (1967): 1271–78(a).
Powell, G. F.; Brasel, J. A.; Raiti, S.; and Blizzard, R. M. "Simulating Idiopathic Hypopituitarism: Endocrinologic Evaluation of the Syndrome." *The New England Journal of Medicine* 276 (1967): 1279–83(b).

Quay, H. C.; Gerard, R.; and Levingon, R. C. *Differential Treatment—A Way to Begin.* Washington, D.C.: Bureau of Prisons, U. S. Department of Justice, 1970.

Quay, H. C., and Peterson, T. R. *Manual for the Behavior Problem Checklist.* Champaign, Ill.: University of Illinois, Children's Research Center, 1967.

Quay, H. C., and Werry, J. S., eds. *Psychopathological Disorders of Childhood.* New York: Wiley, 1972.

Rimland, B. *Infantile Autism.* New York: Appleton-Century-Crofts, 1964.

Ritvo, E. R. "Autism: From Adjective to Noun." *Readings in Autism,* pp. 4–6. Guilford, Conn.: Special Learning Corporation, 1978.

Ross, A. O. *Psychological Disorders of Children: A Behavioral Approach to Theory, Research and Therapy.* New York: McGraw-Hill, 1974.

Rulo, J. H. "High School Equivalency Programs: A Method of Rehabilitating Suburban School Drop-Outs." *Juvenile Justice* 25 (1974): 23–30.

Schechter, M. D. "The Recognition and Treatment of Suicide in Children." In *Clues to Suicide,* edited by E. S. Schneidman and N. C. Farberow, pp. 109–14. New York: McGraw-Hill, 1957.

Schechter, M. D., and Sternlof, R. E. "Suicide in Adolescents." *Postgraduate Medicine,* vol. 47, no. 5 (1970): pp. 220–23.

Schechter, M. D.; Toussieng, P.; Sternlof, R. E.; and Pollack, E. "Normal Development in Adolescence." In *Manual of Child Psychopathology,* edited by B. Wolman, part 1, chapter 2. New York: McGraw-Hill, 1972.

Science News. "Vitamin B6 Helps Autistic Children." Vol. 1, no. 19 (1978), pp. 308–09.

Shaw, C., and Lucas, A. R. *The Psychiatric Disorders of Childhood.* 2nd ed. New York: Appleton-Century-Crofts, 1970.

Siegal, A. W. "Toward Comprehensive Etiological Models of Delinquent Behavior in Adolescents: The Contributions of Recent Neuropsychological Studies." Unpublished manuscript, 1976.

Skinner, B. F. *The Behavior of Organisms.* New York: Appleton-Century-Crofts, 1938.

Skinner, B. F. *Science and Human Behavior.* New York: Macmillan, 1953.

Steele, B. F., and Pollock, C. B. "A Psychiatric Study of Parents Who Abuse Infants and Small Children." In *The Battered Child,* edited by R. E. Helfer and C. Kempe, pp. 89–133. Chicago: University of Chicago Press, 1974.

U.S. Office of Education. *Estimated Number of Handicapped Children in the United States, 1971–72.* Washington, D. C.: U.S. Office of Education, 1971.

United Press International. "Girls Delinquency Soars, Study Reports." *Tulsa Daily World,* April 12, 1972, Tulsa, Oklahoma.

Walker, C. E. "Toilet Training, Enuresis and Encopresis." *Psychological Management of Pediatric Problems,* vol. 1, edited by P. Magrab, pp. 129–89. Baltimore, Md.: University Park Press, 1978.

Warson, S. R.; Caldwell, M. R.; Waunier, A.; and Kirk, A. J. "The Dynamics of Encopresis." *American Journal of Orthopsychiatry* 24 (1954): 402–15.

Weinberg, W., and Malmquist, C. "Depression in School Children." *Child Guidance Notes.* Division of Maternal and Child Health, vol. 3, no. 9 (1971), Oklahoma Department of Health.

Williams, G. "Abused and Neglected Children." *Journal of Pediatric Psychology,* vol. 1, no. 2 (1976), pp. 3–5.

Willis, D. J. "Preventive Model for Child Abuse." *Journal of Pediatric Psychology,* vol. 1, no. 2 (1976), p. 98.

Wright, L. "Handling the Encopretic Child." *Professional Psychology,* 4 (1973): 137–44.

Wright, L. "Outcome of a Standardized Program For Treating Psychogenic Encopresis." *Professional Psychology* 6 (1975): 453–56.

Wright, L., and Walker, C. E. "Behavioral Treatment of Encopresis." *Journal of Pediatric Psychology,* vol. 1, no. 1 (1976), pp. 35–37.

American Association of Psychiatric Clinics
 for Children
250 West 57th Street
Room 1032
New York, New York 10019

American Civil Liberties Union
Juvenile Rights Project
22 East 40th Street
New York, New York 10019

American Orthopsychiatric Association
1790 Broadway
New York, New York 10019

American Psychological Association
1200 Seventeenth Street, NW
Washington, D. C. 20036

Child Welfare League of America
44 East 23rd Street
New York, New York 10010

Family Service Association of America
44 East 23rd Street
New York, New York 10010

Mental Health Law Project
1220 Nineteenth Street, NW
Washington, D.C. 20036

National Association for Mental Health
10 Columbus Circle
New York, New York 10019

National Congress of Parents and Teachers
700 Rush Street
Chicago, Illinois 60611

National Society for Autistic Children
621 Central Avenue
Albany, New York 12206

State Mental Health Associations
(in all fifty states)

4
Sensorimotor exceptionality

Most children and youth with a sensorimotor exceptionality (speech, hearing, visual or physical disability) are normal in intelligence, but they can be hampered in their learning process by the sensory deficit if specialized and very early educational opportunities are not available to them. Part Four of the text stresses the need for early intervention and for trained specialists who understand the ramifications of a particular sensory loss. There is a body of documented evidence that demonstrates that children with sensorimotor deficits can progress along a fairly normal developmental continuum if educators, parents, and medical/health personnel intervene at an early stage and provide the necessary specialized services. For multi-handicapped children, often with two or more impairments, early medical diagnosis coupled with educational stimulation and parent consultation are especially crucial to development.

Part Four offers an overview of the causative factors of various sensory or motor impairments, the evaluative procedures used in diagnoses, psychological ramifications and educational strategies. The positive prognosis for children with a sensorimotor disability is stressed, although it is pointed out that a child's prognosis is only as good as the individual educational program, and the training and commitment of the helping professionals and parents to that child.

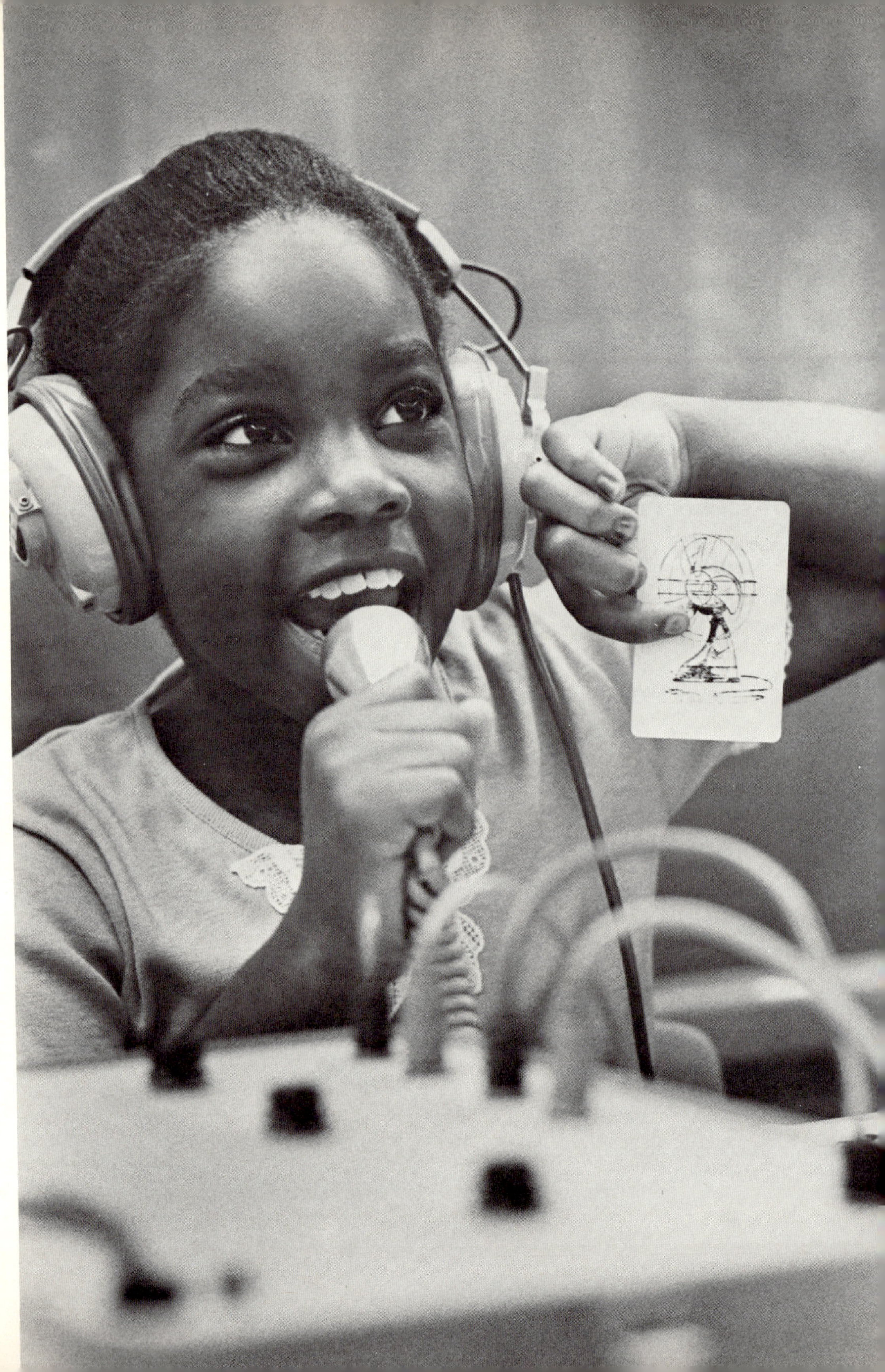

8 Speech and language disabled children and youth
Mary Ann Weiss

What is a communication disorder? • *Language and speech* • *Examples of communication disorders*
Incidence of speech and language disorders
Normal speech development
Types and characteristics of speech disorders • *Articulation disorders* • *Voice disorders* • *Fluency disorders*
Normal language development
Types and characteristics of language disorders • *Causal factors* • *Auditory receptive and expressive language disorders* • *Diagnosing language disorders* • *Remedial techniques*
Speech and language disorders related to other physical disabilities
Summary

Student learning objectives
The student will:
1. identify the major stages of normal speech development in children
2. identify the major stages of normal language development in children
3. become acquainted with specific types of speech and language disorders in children
4. become aware of the difficulties in estimating the incidence and prevalence of speech and language disorders in children

Speech and language disabled children and youth

Student learning objectives

The student will:

5. learn about the characteristics and causes of the following types of communication disorders:
   a. articulation disorders
   b. voice disorders
   c. fluency disorders (stuttering)
   d. auditory receptive-expressive language disorders
6. become familiar with general diagnostic testing and remedial techniques involved in management of speech and language disorders in children
7. learn about the specific classroom interventions that can be helpful to speech and language disabled youngsters
8. learn why a multidisciplinary approach is critical to the development of an individual program for members of this population

Think for a moment of how you rely on verbal communication to share your ideas and feelings with others and to learn new information from them. Most of us take our communication skills for granted because we have never experienced a significant problem in understanding others or in speaking. Some children and youth, however, do not develop adequate communication skills, and the effects of such communication disorders can be devastating to future academic and personal growth if the problems go untreated.

The special educator, psychologist, classroom teacher, or member of some other "helping" profession may be the first to suspect communication difficulties in a particular child. Our purpose here is to provide a basic introduction to speech and language disorders in children and to familiarize the reader with the primary behavioral characteristics associated with these disorders. With such information, a teacher will be better prepared to recognize potential problems and to assure that these children are referred to a speech pathologist for evaluation and necessary training. The teacher's role in early identification cannot be overestimated. In addition, the multidisciplinary nature of the remediation process will become more and more evident as we examine communication disabilities.

What is a communication disorder?

Communication defined

Before attempting to answer this question we must determine what communication itself is. *Communication* may be thought of as an exchange of information among individuals. The message may be sent and received in a variety of ways, ranging from a spoken or written word to a friendly smile or special squeeze of the hand.

Although all forms of animal life presumably have a system of communication, our concern here is *human* communication rather than the sign systems of bees or ants or elephants. In addition, we shall limit our discussion to human *verbal* communication in its oral form and omit consideration of communication through reading and writing or facial expressions and gestures. The spoken word is basic to human communication and it provides the foundation for the written forms of languages.

Language and speech

Oral communication involves speaking and listening, and it involves language as well as speech. Although many people use the two latter terms interchangeably, professionals who deal with communication disorders make important distinctions between them. *Language* may be defined as an arbitrary, conventionalized, and organized system of symbols, with rules for combining these symbols. Its purpose is communicating thoughts, feelings, and ideas among individuals. Every language consists of four primary linguistic systems (Bangs, 1968):

Language defined

1. The *semantic* system deals with the meanings of words and word groups.
2. The *syntactic* system deals with the orderly arrangement of words into phrases or sentences.
3. The *morphologic* system deals with modifications in the base words to indicate such things as tense, number, and possession.
4. The *phonologic* system deals with the sounds, or phonemes, of the language.

Normal language functioning involves both the ability to comprehend the spoken communication of others and the ability to express oneself meaningfully and effectively to others.

Speech, on the other hand, is the motor act, or "process by which oral symbols are perceived and produced" (Bangs, 1968, p. 13). That is to say, speech is the perception and oral expression or production of language. As a motor act, speech involves the coordination of four major processes: (1) respiration, or the act of breathing to provide the airstream used for speaking; (2) phonation, or the production of sound by the larynx and vocal folds; (3) resonance, or the vibratory response of the air-filled cavity above the vocal folds which changes the quality or identity of the sound wave; and (4) articulation, or the use of the lips, tongue, teeth, and hard and soft palates to produce speech sounds such as vowels and consonants (see Figure 8-1). Speech also involves input from various sensory modalities, such as the auditory, visual, tactile, and kinesthetic systems, as we monitor and modify the sounds we produce.

Speech defined

Both speech and language are affected by an individual's anatomical structures, physiological and neuromuscular functioning, cognitive capabilities, and psychosocial maturity and adjustment. Deviations or abnormalities in any of these factors may produce a communication disorder involving speech and/or language.

Examples of communication disorders

Speech and language disorders appear in persons of all ages, from one-year-olds to one-hundred-year olds. They vary in severity from mild to profound, and their effect may be minimal or devastating. They may exist as a single entity or be part of a complex picture of multiple handicaps. They may be short in duration or persist for a lifetime.

The chances are good that you have had contact with someone who has a communication disorder. You may have known Johnny, an eight-year-old who

Figure 8.1
Human vocal organs

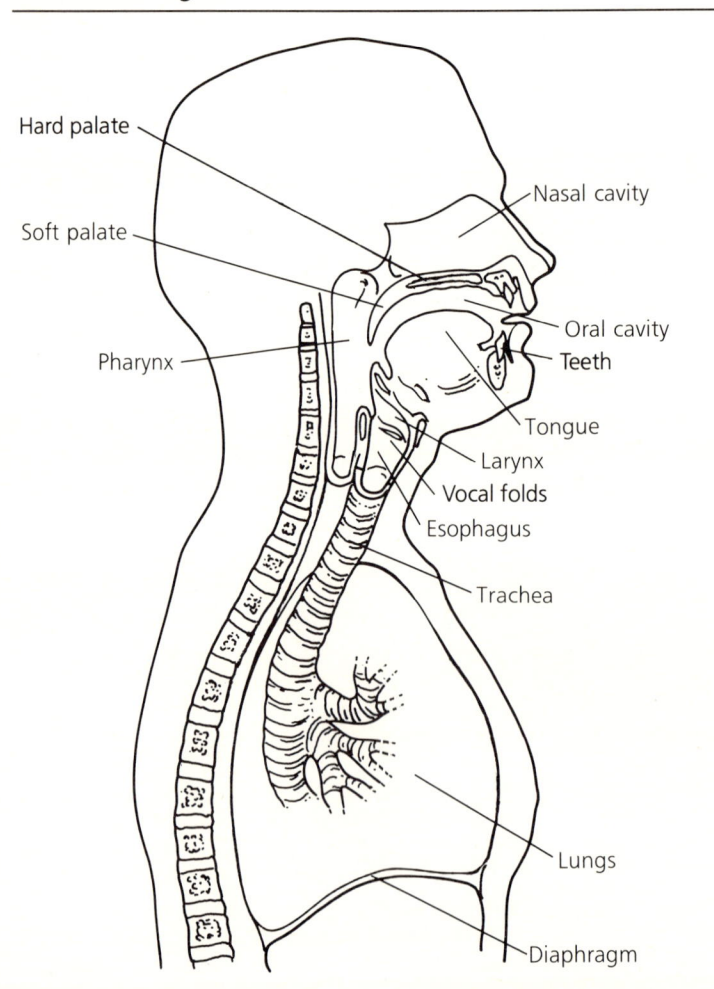

mixes up his sounds and says "wug" for "rug" and "thun" for "sun." Or Susie, a teenager who speaks in a breathy voice that has a very hoarse quality. Or Ted, a college student who struggles with every word he tries to say and accompanies each speaking effort with grimaces and head jerks. Or Michele, a ten-year-old with a cleft palate, whose speech is very nasalized. Or Bill, who is a victim of cerebral palsy and must rely on a communication board which he manipulates with his hands because he has no oral communication. Or Terry, a four-year-old whose vocabulary is limited and who speaks in only two- or three-word telegraphic phrases. You may have known Ms. Smith, an elderly woman whose hearing has begun to deteriorate and whose production of speech sounds has become distorted. Or Mr. Jones, who had his larynx removed because of cancer and who now speaks in a special way called esophageal speech. Or Ms. Green, who suffered a stroke that severely limited her ability to understand others and to speak in full sentences.

All of these persons have communication disorders of various kinds. In the great majority of instances, speech and language disorders can be treated, and the individual's communication skills can usually be improved, if not totally rehabilitated. Speech pathologists are the professionals primarily concerned with the evaluation and treatment of speech and language disorders. Because such disorders do not exist in a vacuum, however, speech pathologists are not the only professionals on the rehabilitation team. The coordinated efforts of a variety of additional specialists, including educators, psychologists, physicians, occupational therapists, and others are involved. Because oral communication is so vital to our functioning as human beings, it is critical that deficits in speech and language be identified early and that appropriate treatment procedures be initiated.

Rehabilitation team

Incidence of speech and language disorders

A classic textbook in speech pathology notes that "speech-handicapped children are not only the largest group of exceptional children within the total population but also the largest group in the area of special education in the nation's elementary and secondary schools" (Johnson et al., 1967, pp. 1–2). According to the 1976 statistics published recently by the American Speech and Hearing Association (ASHA), one out of every twenty persons in the United States suffers from a speech or language disorder. Considering the population of our country today, this translates to nearly ten million people! Articulation disorders, which involve a disturbance in a person's ability to produce speech sounds, constitute the largest single group of speech disorders. The ASHA statistics indicate that approximately three out of five speech and language disorders are related to articulation deficits. ASHA further reports that more than one million Americans stutter, and more than one-half of these are children.

Communication disorders affect one of twenty persons

One-half million American children stutter

As Table 8-1 reveals, estimates of the incidence and prevalence of speech and language disorders vary considerably depending on the particular survey and the age range studied. Based on his extensive review of incidence studies, Milisen (1971) noted that all of the surveys found a greater proportion of males than females in the school-age speech-defective population, especially in the upper grades. All surveys also reported a greater percentage of speech-disordered children in the first three grades of school.

Table 8-1 also indicates that the percentage of children reportedly having defective articulation *decreases markedly* from the first to fourth grades. It is likely that the figures for the lower grades are elevated because children up to the age of seven or eight years are still acquiring their adult articulatory skills. Therefore, many children included in these percentages probably did not present true, clinically significant articulation disorders.

Voice disorders and stuttering occur less frequently than articulation disorders, with a higher incidence in males than females (Hull & Hull, 1973; Johnson et al., 1967; Milisen, 1971; Van Riper, 1971). This sex difference is particularly evident among stutterers where, according to Van Riper, the ratio is approximately four males to one female.

The incidence and prevalence of oral language disorders are extremely difficult

Table 8.1
Estimated incidence and prevalence of speech and language disorders

Disorder	Incidence/prevalence (percent)
1. Speech disorders (all types combined)	
Kindergarten–4th grade children	12–15
5th–12th grade children	4–5
2. Defective articulation	
1st grade children	15–20
Children above 4th grade	2–3
Elementary school children	4–6
1st–12th grade children	2
3. Voice disorders	
Total population	1
School-age children	0.2
1st–12th grade children	3
4. Stuttering	
Total population	1
Preschool children	4
1st–12th grade children	0.8
5. Oral language disabilities	
School-age population	6½

Source: Based on data from Hull & Hull, 1973; Johnson et al., 1967; Marge, 1972; Milisen, 1971; Van Riper, 1971

to determine because of widespread differences in definitions and the lack of well-established norms for language development. In addition, there has been a drastic increase in our knowledge of, and interest in, normal and disordered child language since 1960, and better language measurement techniques have been developed in the past ten or fifteen years. As more children with language disorders have been identified and have begun to dominate the caseloads of speech pathologists, it may appear that the incidence of childhood language disorders has increased significantly. It is more likely, however, that what has changed is our awareness of language disorders and ability to identify them.

An attempt to estimate the magnitude of the language disability problem has been made by pooling data from several studies that investigated the existence of

Introducing Jackie—On the opening page of the unit she is practicing a new sound on the playback machine. Above, she is learning correct word order from picture cues. Jackie "reads" the sequences to produce "where-questions."

language disorders among children with other handicaps, such as mental retardation, deafness, emotional disturbance, cerebral palsy, and cleft palate. In this manner, it has been estimated that 6½ percent of this school-age population presented oral language disabilities, or over 3½ million children, based on 1969 U.S. Census Bureau figures (Marge, 1972). Of course, the incidence of all types of speech and language disorders is known to be much higher among multihandicapped children and youth.

We can see at this point that speech and language disorders are a widespread exceptionality which have a negative impact on a person's ability to realize his or her full potential. Hence, knowledge of and appropriate action regarding communication disorders is an important responsibility shared by all of us.

Normal speech development

We need to understand normal speech development before we can determine if a given child is progressing as he or she should and speaking in a manner acceptable for the age level, or if the child presents a significant speech problem that needs special attention. As with essentially all aspects of human behavior, speech is a developmental phenomenon that is influenced by chronological age as well as physical, intellectual, and psychosocial maturation. Speech development is normally completed by the age of seven or eight years, at which time most children have usually acquired adult speech standards.

Speech development complete by age eight

Table 8-2 outlines the various stages and major milestones of normal speech development. Although the specific ages given for different skills vary slightly by source, we shall attempt to identify general developmental trends.

The initial stage of speech development may be thought of as occurring with the birth cry, when infants begin using the organs of speech. As Table 8-2 indicates, children proceed from that point through various stages as they learn to produce speech sounds and experiment with their voices. Three important stages during the first year of life are (1) the *babbling stage,* characterized by self-initiated pleasurable use of vocalization and a few speech-like sounds; (2) the *lalling stage,* characterized by pleasurable repetition of strings of sounds and syllables; and (3) the *echolalia stage,* characterized by nonmeaningful parroting, or imitation, of sound sequences produced by others. During the period of echolalia, many overanxious parents think their child has begun to talk, but these vocalizations lack meaning.

Development during first year

During the second year, children's speech is characterized by considerable jargon. *Jargon* may be described as nonsense-sound syllable patterns that copy the melody patterns of adult speech. Thus, young children may be heard "scolding," "soothing," or "questioning" their doll and toys, although what they are saying is gibberish.

Use of nonmeaningful jargon

A classic study of children's speech and language skills found that the accuracy of children's speech-sound production "increases with age until essential maturity in

Table 8.2
Stages of normal speech development

Age	Speech characteristics
Birth–3 mos.	Birth cry. Undifferentiated then differentiated crying. Random vocalizations.
4–6 mos.	Babbling stage. Some speech-like sounds, with vowel-like sounds predominating.
6–9 mos.	Lalling stage. Vary intonation patterns (pitch and loudness). Use voice projectively to manipulate others.
9–11 mos.	Echolalia. Greater variety of speech-like sounds.
12 mos.	First true words.
18 mos.	One- and two-word sentences. Frequent jargon. Greater variety of speech sounds.
2 yrs.	Jargon decreases. More real words used. Increased accuracy in speech sound production.
3 yrs.	Intelligible but unstable pronunciation. Many consonants misarticulated. Vowels usually produced correctly. Pitch of voice may be high and uncontrolled. Voice may have nasal quality. Speech often contains repetitions and nonfluencies.
4–5 yrs.	Increased accuracy in production of consonants. May yell and scream as typical speech modes. Frequent and almost compulsive repetitions.
6–8 yrs.	Achieves adult articulation standards. Repetitions and nonfluencies diminish and speech is fluent.

Source: Based on data from Berry, 1969; Dale, 1976; McCarthy, 1954; Menyuk, 1971; Templin, 1957; Winitz, 1969

Table 8.3
Ages at which 75 percent of the subjects correctly produced consonant sounds in words in the Templin study

Age (in years)	Consonants
3	m, n, ng, p, f, h, w
3½	y
4	k, b, d, g, r
4½	s, sh, ch
6	t, th (voiceless), v, l
7	th (voiced), z, zh, j

Source: Templin, 1957, p. 53

articulation is reached by eight years" (Templin, 1957, p. 58), with girls preceding boys by about one year. Table 8-3 indicates the ages at which 75 percent of the subjects produced various consonants correctly in all positions of words. Although the course of development of individual children obviously varies, other studies have identified similar general developmental trends.

Types and characteristics of speech disorders

Articulation disorders

Articulation disorder defined

An articulation disorder is defined as a problem in producing speech sounds in the correct manner. The errors or misarticulations may occur on vowels, single consonants, or consonant clusters (i.e., blends such as *st*, *sk*, *str*, *bl*, and *kr*) and may involve some or all of the sounds in any position of a word. As noted earlier, articulation disorders are by far the most common type of speech disorder, and thus will likely comprise the majority of the speech disorders heard in the classroom or clinic.

Types of misarticulations   There are three major types of articulation errors: (1) *omissions,* (2) *substitutions,* and (3) *distortions.* Some authorities also recognize a fourth category, called *additions.*

Omissions. In this type of error, a sound is left out so that only part of the word is spoken. For example, "-a-y" for *baby,* "fi" for *fish,* or "og" for *dog.* Individual sounds or whole syllables may be omitted. If the omissions involve many sounds and are consistent, the child's speech may be completely unintelligible, even to such familiar listeners as parents. Omission errors tend to occur more commonly in younger children than older children and are most likely to appear on consonants that end words rather than those in the initial and medial positions (Carrell, 1968; Johnson et al., 1967; Templin, 1957).

Substitutions. Substitution errors are present when an inappropriate sound is produced in place of the desired sound. For example, a child may say "fith" for *fish*, "wabbit" for *rabbit* or "toofbrush" for *toothbrush.* When a *th* is substituted for an *s* or *z*, it is often called a *frontal lisp.* Substitution errors are also common in the speech of young children and will reduce the child's intelligibility if they occur frequently.

Frontal lisp

Distortions. Distortion errors exist when a sound is produced in an incorrect manner that still approximates the desired sound. These distorted productions cannot be identified as any other specific phoneme of the language and thus are not classified by most speech clinicians as substitution errors. The target speech sound, for example, may appear mushy or sloppy because the air is coming out the wrong place or the tongue position is incorrect. Distortion errors seem to be more common in older children and adults, and they often involve the *s, z, sh, r,* and *l* sounds or vowels. When a sibilant sound (e.g., *s, z, sh*) is produced with the air escaping over the sides of the tongue, it is often called a *lateral lisp.*

Lateral lisp

Additions. Errors of addition are present when a word is produced with an extra sound or syllable, such as "belue" for *blue* or "runth" for *run*. Errors of addition are the least common type of misarticulation.

During the normal development of speech and articulation skills, children often omit, substitute, or distort speech sounds, with substitution errors being the most common type of developmental misarticulation (Templin, 1957). Table 8-3 should be helpful in an assessment of a specific child's articulation skills. For example, it should not be considered unusual for four-year-old Jimmy to mispronounce his *th* and *r* sounds or five-year-old Sally to say her *t* and *z* sounds incorrectly; but if seven-year-old Betty mispronounces her *p*, *k*, and *s* sounds, she may well have an articulation problem.

Substitution errors most common

The four types of misarticulations described above can occur with any frequency and pattern, and one or any combination of the four can be present in the speech of a particular child. Also, children are often inconsistent in their misarticulations. A child may say a sound correctly some of the time, or in some phonetic contexts, and omit, substitute, or distort the sound at other times.

Patterns of errors

It is important for the speech pathologist to determine whether an error on a speech sound truly represents an articulation error or if it is a language error, because the therapeutic goals and procedures are quite different for the two. For example, if Susie says "scat" for *cat,* the clinician must determine if she is substituting *sk* for *k* or if she is using a verb to label a picture when a noun was called for. Articulation errors and morphological errors may also be confused if one does not evaluate the errors carefully. Omission of the final *s* in "cats" may represent a misarticulation (omission of the phoneme *s*) or it may represent a morphological error (omission of the plural marker /s/).

Dialectical variations   Pronunciation variations that are related to different geographical regions or ethnic groups, such as "pin" for *pen,* "git" for *get,* "dis" for *this,* "aks" for *ask,* "set" for *sit,* "harse" for *horse,* "ca-" for *car,* and so on, should not be considered articulation errors. Children with such characteristic pronunciations should neither be labeled as speech defective nor referred for evaluation and therapy if their speech is not atypical among their peers.

Degree of severity   Articulation disorders range from mild to severe. If they are severe and overall intelligibility is poor, the child may suffer greatly when attempting to express his or her ideas and needs at school, at home, and with friends. The degree to which overall intelligibility is impaired is not the only factor affecting the judgment of severity. The age of the child is certainly important, particularly in light of the developmental nature of articulation pointed out previously. A seven-year-old child who misarticulates many of the early developing sounds has a more severe problem than a child of the same age who misarticulates only the late developing sounds. The persistent misarticulations of an older child are usually more difficult to

Judgment on degree of severity

remediate than the inconsistent errors of a child in the lower grades. Generally, consistent errors are less amenable to treatment. The *number* of misarticulations and sounds in error and the *types* of errors also influence severity, with omission errors considered more infantile than substitutions and distortions. Errors involving sounds which occur frequently in the language, such as *r* and *s*, will be more noticeable and detrimental to intelligibility than errors on such infrequently occurring sounds as *zh* and *j*. If a child can correct the errors when provided with auditory and visual stimulation, it is usually a good prognostic sign that he or she will be able to learn the correct productions. Error sounds that are not "stimulable" (i.e., errors that persist even with extra stimulation or cueing from the clinician) are typically more difficult to train.

Causal factors   It is often difficult, if not impossible, to determine the specific cause or causes of an articulation disorder. Certain organic and physical conditions, such as a hearing loss, oral structural deviations (e.g., dental abnormalities, cleft palate), muscular or neurological involvement of the articulators (e.g., muscular dystrophy, cerebral palsy), and mental retardation, often have an adverse effect on speech, and these disabilities will be considered later in this unit. (Problems associated with auditory disabilities are the subject matter of Unit 9, and conditions associated with mental retardation are discussed in Units 2 and 3.) In the majority of instances, however, children with articulation disorders do not present such obvious organic abnormalities, and their speech disorders appear to be related to some type of faulty learning during the developmental period. Such problems are typically referred to as *functional articulation disorders.*

In an effort to determine the potential causes of functional articulation problems, many different variables have been studied over the years. Reviews of the literature (Johnson et al., 1967; Powers, 1971; Winitz, 1969) suggest that the following factors do *not* relate significantly to articulation skills and do not differentiate between children with articulation disorders and children who speak normally: general motor skills; oral structures (e.g., shape of palate, size of tongue, "tongue-tie"), personality and adjustment, socioeconomic level, and intelligence. (In terms of intelligence, we are referring to children within the normal range of intelligence rather than retarded children who are delayed in all aspects of communication development.)

In regard to the relationship of dental irregularities to articulation, research results have been inconsistent; however, the relationship does not appear to be high, and many persons with significant dental abnormalities have normal articulation skills. Similar inconclusive results have been obtained in several investigations of the relationship of oral sensation to articulation. Oral and facial motor skills directly involved in the production of speech sounds *do* appear to be related to articulation, and children with articulation problems appear to differ from normal speakers in these skills although more research is needed to clarify the relationship.

The effect of abnormal swallowing patterns on speech has been of considerable interest over the past two decades. Various labels, including *tongue thrust* and *reverse swallow,* have been used to identify this swallowing pattern, which is usually characterized by a forward thrust of the tongue against or between the anterior teeth. A number of specialists in the fields of speech pathology and orthodontics consider tongue thrust to be detrimental to normal dental occlusion (alignment of the teeth) and to speech-sound production, and they believe that these children should be taught normal swallowing patterns (Carrell, 1968). Other specialists in these fields disagree and cite research which indicates that children with tongue-thrust swallowing patterns do not have significantly greater articulation errors or dental malocclusions (Joint Committee on Dentistry & Speech Pathology, 1975; Mason & Proffit, 1974). Recently, Mason and Proffit (1974) concluded that there is little research support for the point of view that tongue thrust routinely leads to dental and articulation problems. They indicate that tongue thrust is a normal developmental phenomenon in children up to the age of puberty and that "approximately 80 percent of children who have a tongue thrust and anterior open bite at age eight show improvement without therapy by age twelve" (p. 129). Therefore, they believe that swallowing therapy is not indicated for prepubertal children even if a dental malocclusion is present. If tongue thrust and lisping are both present in a young child, the child should receive regular articulation treatment for the speech problem. For older children in whom the tongue thrust, dental malocclusion, and speech problems persist, coordinated orthodontic, swallowing, and articulation treatment may be beneficial.

Abnormal swallowing patterns

Auditory perceptual skills (discussed in Unit 6) have also been investigated as potential causes of functional articulation disorders. It appears that auditory memory span, involving the immediate recall of items, is usually *not* a significant factor in articulation disorders (Winitz, 1969). But auditory discrimination, on the other hand, does appear to relate significantly to articulation, especially when the task involves discrimination judgments of speech sounds or the child's own articulation errors (Johnson et al., 1967; Winitz, 1969). While research results have varied, it seems safe to conclude at this time that children with functional articulation disorders are likely to have inferior speech-sound discrimination.

Auditory memory and discrimination

Two important environmental factors that may influence articulation are the speech models to which the child is exposed and the amount of stimulation and motivation received for speech development. If the speech of important people in the child's world, such as parents, siblings and peers, contains misarticulations and grammatical errors, the child can be expected to develop similar communication patterns. Poor speech models will typically lead to inadequate speech skills in developing children. Likewise, if the child lacks adequate stimulation and motivation to develop good speech, articulation patterns may remain infantile.

Environmental causes

To sum up, any of the potential causes of functional articulation disorders discussed above *may* have an adverse effect on a particular child's development of articulation. It is important to remember, however, that these factors do not *necessarily* interfere with normal speech development.

Early identification and appropriate referral Our purpose here is to cover some of the major considerations of diagnosis and assessment, with a few examples of current procedures. (In-depth coverage of techniques employed by speech pathologists can be found in the works of Emerick and Hatten [1974] and Johnson et al. [1963])

Finding communicative problems

First, let's consider diagnosis of communication disorders in general. The importance of early identification has already been stressed, and, when possible, a child with a communication disorder should begin receiving treatment *before* reaching school age. If a young child is suspected of having a speech or language problem, the first step should be a thorough evaluation by a speech pathologist.

Teacher referral

Schoolwide survey

Several different techniques are available for identifying speech and language disorders among school-age children. Besides referral of suspected children to a speech and hearing clinic by parents or such specialists as audiologists, physicians, dentists, nurses, and psychologists, two identification procedures are often employed in school systems. One procedure involves observations and referrals by classroom teachers of children who appear to be having communication difficulties. The other involves a speech and language survey of all or some of the grades, conducted early in the school year by the school speech clinician. In both instances, the clinician will briefly screen each child's articulation, voice, fluency, and language skills to determine if potential problems exist and further diagnostic testing is needed.

If such is the case, the clinician will see the child for additional in-depth testing to attempt to determine the specific type and severity of the communication disorder and its cause or causes, and to make appropriate recommendations for the child. These recommendations may include individual and/or group speech and language therapy, consultation with the teacher regarding ways to handle the problem in the classroom, or referrals to other specialists for additional evaluations.

During the diagnostic evaluation, the clinician will want to obtain a case history covering all aspects of the child, to make observations of the child's general and verbal functioning, and to administer formal and/or informal speech and language tests. Related skills such as auditory acuity and perception, visual-motor functioning, oral structures and function, intelligence, and general motor skills will also be evaluated.

Diagnosis an ongoing process

By the end of the evaluation, a tentative diagnosis will usually have been reached, and an appropriate treatment program can be initiated. It is important to remember that diagnosis is, or should be, a continuous and ongoing process which does not terminate at the end of the initial formal evaluation. The child with a communication disorder should be continually reevaluated throughout the treatment program, so that appropriate modifications can be made to meet changing needs.

Diagnosing articulation problems   A number of different tests are commercially available for evaluating articulation. Many clinicians also devise their own informal tests for particular children. Most articulation tests use pictures to evaluate the child's spontaneous production of each vowel and/or consonant in various positions of words. Through such an inventory of a child's speech sounds, the clinician can determine which sounds are produced correctly or incorrectly, and can specify the type of misarticulations made. The clinician will also want to assess the stimula-

Auditory, visual and tactile cues help Jackie to remember to say the sound correctly. Here she watches herself carefully in the mirror as she and the speech clinician say the new word together.

bility of the child's errors (see p. 263) by asking him or her to attempt to produce the error sounds correctly after being given additional auditory, visual, and tactile-kinesthetic cues. By evaluating the child's articulation and intelligibility in conversational speech, consistency of the misarticulations can also be assessed. With this information and the results of the rest of the evaluation, the speech clinician can plan an appropriate treatment program.

Remedial techniques In general, the goal of articulation therapy is to train the child to produce the error sounds correctly. There are probably as many different ways to accomplish this goal as there are speech pathologists in the profession. Regardless of the particular treatment approach, methods, and activities selected, articulation therapy involves training the child to recognize the errors, to produce the sounds correctly, and to use the corrected sounds in all speaking situations. The training program typically consists of individual and/or group therapy sessions with the speech pathologist, although it may be possible for the regular teacher to handle some milder cases in the classroom with the school speech pathologist serving primarily as a consultant. In addition to establishing appropriate articulatory habits, the overall treatment program will also include, when necessary and possible, the elimination or modification of any factors uncovered during the multidisciplinary evaluation that are contributing to the articulation disorder. Examples of such factors would be medical attention for a middle ear infection that is causing a hearing loss detrimental to speech; surgical treatment of a palatal malformation; therapy for improving self-concept or overcoming emotional problems.

Working on target sounds. The speech clinician will usually begin work on only one sound and will introduce a second sound only after the child has begun to use the first in words and phrases. The number of sounds that may be taught simultaneously will depend on the particular child, however. The target sound may be given a name, such as the "Sammy Snake sound" for *s*, the "quiet sound" for *sh*, and the "angry cat sound" for *f*, to help the child identify the sound.

Age-appropriate materials such as toys, pictures, games, stories, mirrors, and tape recorders are employed during the therapy activities to increase the child's motivation, and success at each level is necessary before proceeding to the next stage. Although the above general steps may appear simple, it often requires considerable time and effort for the child to acquire and habituate the new response. The difficulty can be appreciated if one compares it to trying to learn a foreign language that includes non-English sounds, or to trying to speak for five minutes while tapping the table each time an *s* sound is uttered.

Although basic learning principles such as imitation, practice, motivation, and reward can and should be considered regardless of the particular treatment method employed, some speech pathologists have suggested a more formal application of behavior modification and operant conditioning techniques to articulation therapy. In these treatment models, major emphasis is placed on: (1) selecting a target for change (e.g., the *r* sound); (2) establishing the frequency of occurrence prior to treatment; (3) evoking the behavior; (4) providing consequences to increase the frequency of the correct response and/or decrease the incorrect response; and (5) generalizing the correct response to situations outside the therapy sessions. Keeping accurate records of the child's responses is extremely important in planning the successive stages of therapy and in determining when he or she is ready to progress to the next level of difficulty.

The classroom teacher can be very helpful in carrying out the activities suggested by the speech clinician. Examples of classroom activities include: (1) being aware of the particular sounds the child is working on and praising the child when the sounds are produced correctly; (2) reminding the child to use the "new" sound(s) during oral reading lessons and keeping a good speech chart posted near the reading circle; or (3) helping the child find the words in spelling drills that contain the sounds being worked on in therapy and giving extra practice in pronouncing them. General speech improvement activities such as phonic drills, describing how different speech sounds are made, and listening drills to identify sounds at the beginning or end of words may also be helpful. In all instances, care should be taken to assure that the child is not teased or ridiculed by peers.

In the classroom

Voice disorders

Voice disorders occur much less frequently than articulation disorders. But they are still of concern because they may interfere with interpersonal communication, cause embarrassment or adjustment problems, or, most importantly, signal an underlying laryngeal pathology.

What is a voice problem?

The criteria for determining the existence of a voice problem are somewhat difficult to specify because our voices reflect considerable individualism. Vocal characteristics are influenced by one's sex, age, and physical stature, and our voices also vary with different moods and communicative purposes. Although certain voices may be more pleasant and appealing than others, some voices seem to call attention to themselves and elicit judgments of deviancy or abnormality from listeners. These abnormal vocal characteristics are what we label as voice disorders.

The properties of voice *Pitch* refers to the highness or lowness of one's voice in relation to the musical scale. Children and young people may use a habitual pitch level that is too high or too low for their age and physical stature, such as a male high school sophomore who speaks in a high-pitched, squeaky voice, or a female first-grader who sounds as if she's speaking from the bottom of a well. Such pitch disorders not only call attention to themselves but may also be harmful to the vocal mechanism, which is not being used appropriately. Examples of other pitch disorders include pitch breaks (rapid, uncontrolled changes in pitch during speech), the tremulous, or shaky, voice, and the monotone voice.

Intensity refers to the loudness or softness of the voice during ordinary conversational speech. Voices must be loud enough for efficient communication and should contain variations in loudness that are appropriate for the speaker's intended meaning. Voices that are too loud or too soft may reflect deviant speaking habits, or they may reflect underlying physical conditions, such as a hearing loss or neuromuscular involvement of the laryngeal mechanism.

Quality relates to those characteristics of the voice other than pitch or loudness, which give each person's voice its distinctiveness and pleasantness. (While many writers include resonance problems in their discussions of voice quality disorders, we shall consider resonance problems separately below.) Quality and resonance deviations are the most common types of voice disorders. Although the choice of labels and terms varies considerably among speech pathologists, the quality disorders most often recognized are breathiness, harshness, and hoarseness. The *breathy* voice is characterized by weakness and excessive airflow and wastage, and it often sounds like a forced whisper. It may also be accompanied by intermittent but complete lack of voice (aphonia). The *harsh,* or strident, voice has an unpleasant, rough, rasping sound (Johnson et al., 1967, p. 203) and is usually loud in intensity and low in pitch. Vocalization is often sudden and accompanied by strain and hypertension. The *hoarse* voice is typically described as a combination of breathiness and harshness, and it is often a symptom of laryngeal irritation from excessive shouting or a cold, or a symptom of laryngeal pathology. Hoarse voices tend to be low in pitch, and a low-pitched, gravelly sound produced by the vocal folds (glottal fry) is often prevalent.

Resonance refers to sound modification in the oral and nasal cavities above the larynx, and resonance disorders are usually related to the openness of the nasal passages. English contains only three nasal sounds, *m*, *n*, and *ng*, and the nasal cavity is normally separated from the speech mechanism by the action of the soft palate (velum) during the production of all other speech sounds. If the nasal cavity is not closed off, the person's voice will have a nasal quality as if "talking through the nose." Nasality, or hypernasality, is a common characteristic of cleft palate speakers. The opposite condition, denasality, results when the nasal cavity remains closed when it should be open for the nasal consonants. Denasality usually occurs when a person has a "stuffy nose" or "head cold," although it may be chronic if there is a persistent nasal obstruction.

Nasality

Denasality

Causes of voice disorders There are numerous organic and nonorganic causes of voice disorders. Organic conditions involving the larynx that may cause voice disorders include tumors, infections, paralysis of the vocal folds, and congenital abnormalities of the larynx. As noted earlier, persons with a cleft palate condition often have difficulty separating the oral and nasal passages during speech. This causes their voices to sound hypernasal. Enlarged tonsils and adenoids are not uncommon among school-age children, and they may lead to denasality and a muffled voice quality. A significant hearing loss which affects the child's ability to monitor his or her own vocal pitch, loudness, and quality can also cause voice problems. (Temporary vocal deviations, such as pitch breaks, often accompany pubertal voice

Organic causes

changes, especially in males, and these conditions usually do not require voice therapy.)

Voice disorders may also be caused by nonorganic, or functional, factors. Boone (1971) has noted that "most voice disorders are related to the misuse and abuse of the voice" (p. 1). Vocal misuse can take many different forms, including excessive speaking and singing, speaking at an unnatural pitch level, speaking too loudly, excessive yelling and screaming, or speaking with excessive tension. These vocal patterns can result in hyperfunction of the vocal mechanism. If habitual, they may abuse the larynx and lead to such organic pathologies as vocal fold edema (swelling), vocal nodules, vocal polyps, and contact ulcers. A child's voice problem may also be related to poor breathing habits. Psychological disturbances and emotional maladjustment may also be reflected in voice disorders, although voice problems of psychogenic origin appear to be more common in adults than children. *Nonorganic or functional causes*

To sum up, anything that alters or interferes with the normal and efficient functioning of a person's respiratory, phonatory, or resonance mechanisms is a potential cause of voice disorders.

Diagnosing voice disorders   From the above discussion of types of voice problems and their causes, it is clear that a multidisciplinary approach to diagnosis and treatment is critical. A medical examination is an essential early step to determine if an organic pathology is present and to initiate necessary medical and/or surgical treatment. In general, there are four major phases which should be included in the evaluation by the management team: (1) determination of the history of the voice problem; (2) systematic analysis of the voice in regard to pitch, loudness, quality, and resonance; (3) examination of the structure and function of the speech mechanism; and (4) assessment, as needed, of other variables (hearing, general health, intelligence, motor skills, and psychological adjustment). Detailed descriptions of diagnostic and therapy procedures used by speech pathologists in dealing with voice disorders are available in a number of sources (Boone, 1971; Emerick & Hatten, 1974; Johnson et al., 1967). *Multidisciplinary team needed*

In a voice analysis, the speech pathologist evaluates the child's vocal pitch, loudness, quality, and resonance during conversational speech and structured speaking activities. The child's speech mechanism and breathing patterns are also examined during various speech and nonspeech activities. A hearing screening, which is a routine part of speech and language evaluations at most speech and hearing clinics, is also completed. Appropriate referrals are made if the child appears to present other problems, such as motoric, intellectual, or emotional disturbances. *Voice analysis*

Remedial techniques   Regardless of the specific causes of the voice disorder, a period of voice therapy is almost always needed to help the child learn to use the vocal mechanism more appropriately and to eliminate or reduce any vocal abuse that may be evident. The therapy program must be carefully designed for the spe- *Voice therapy* cific child and the particular voice problem; therefore, any of the following methods and procedures may or may not be appropriate in any given case.

The overall goal of voice therapy is to develop effective and efficient vocal habits, and one of the major aspects of therapy is vocal education or reeducation. The child or youth must understand exactly what the voice problem is, what is causing it, and what must be done to improve it. Obviously, the child must be motivated to change the inappropriate voice and be willing to modify some old, established habits or the therapy will be doomed to failure. There is little the clinician can do *to* the child to remediate the voice problem, and the child must work diligently *with* the clinician to identify and habituate the "new voice." Therefore, he or she will need much encouragement and reinforcement from the clinician as well as from parents, teachers, and friends throughout the voice training program.

Eliminating vocal abuse

Although the specifics vary across clinicians and cases, voice therapy usually has four major areas of emphasis. If the voice problem appears to be related to vocal abuse, one important aspect of therapy will be identification and elimination of its sources. Since the clinician cannot rely solely on the verbal reports of young children, it's a good idea to observe the child in a number of different situations to determine how the voice is habitually used. For example, be sure to watch Susie out on the playground, in gym class, and during basketball practice, or Johnny as he cheers at a ballgame or yells at his brother. Reports from parents and teachers are essential in identifying the child's vocal habits. Once identified, the specific types of vocal misuse and their effects on voice should be discussed with the youngster and ways of reducing and eliminating them planned. The child's understanding and cooperation are critical because the clinician cannot be there to tap him or her on the shoulder and point out the bad vocal habits.

Relaxation exercises

Relaxation exercises are often another important part of the treatment program. The child must be trained to vocalize in a relaxed, easy manner, especially if he or she usually speaks in a strained and forced way. Although the results with young children are not always successful, training in general bodily relaxation may be necessary in addition to more specific relaxation of the face, mouth, and throat areas. Such lack of tension in the vocal mechanism will facilitate all other aspects of the therapy program. Activities such as "playing ragdoll," rolling the head round and round, or alternately tensing and relaxing specific parts of the body can be helpful in achieving the desired relaxed state.

Vocal exercises

A third aspect of voice therapy involves vocal exercises and direct training in voice production. Specific exercises are available for improving pitch range, raising or lowering habitual pitch, increasing pitch flexibility, achieving a more appropriate loudness level, and improving overall vocal quality. The particular exercises employed and the goals of each exercise must be developed for the individual child. For example, Todd may need to lower his habitual pitch level three tones, and Carolyn may need to increase her pitch range by half an octave. During the early stage of voice therapy, the clinician will ask the child to experiment with his or her voice in various ways to discover the combination of pitch, loudness, and so on which results in the best vocal quality. Once the "new voice" is identified, the child will need lots of practice in recognizing and using it with various kinds of speech materials. Ear training and improvement of general listening skills are important features of the vocal exercises.

Breathing exercises often comprise the fourth major aspect of voice therapy. The goal of these exercises is typically to train the child or youth to use the breath stream more efficiently, rather than to increase the breath supply. Breathing for speech requires no greater air supply than breathing for life, although speech breathing does require control of the exhaled airstream. Different exercises are available for improving the rate of speaking, phrasing, and control of the breath stream. *Breathing exercises*

When the sources of vocal abuse have been eliminated and the new voice has begun to be stabilized, the difficult job of carry-over must be tackled. Habituation of the new vocal habits and generalization to all speaking situations are the most difficult stages of therapy. Continued success in remediation requires teamwork by the clinician, the child, the classroom teacher, the child's parents, and others in the child's environment.

Fluency disorders

More articles and books have been written about stuttering than any other type of communication disorder. Stuttering has been described, defined, researched, and debated for many years, and authorities do not yet agree on what stuttering is and what causes it. One's definition of stuttering is typically influenced and biased by one's theory of its causes and it is extremely difficult to separate the two aspects.

Recognizing these difficulties and the limitations of any definition, we can describe stuttering as a complex condition characterized by excessive disfluencies, such as repetitions of sounds, syllables, words, and phrases, prolongations, hesitations, and interjections. There is more to stuttering than disfluent speech, however, because disfluencies also occur in the speech of persons who are *not* considered to be stutterers. Therefore, a description of the problem of stuttering should also include the speaker's self-concept and negative reactions to the disfluencies, as well as listeners' acknowledgments of the behavior as stuttering. The secondary, or accessory, nonspeech behaviors such as head jerks, eyeblinks, and avoidance of eye contact, which are often present, should also be a part of our description of stuttering. *Stuttering defined*

The above definition or description is limited, however, because stuttering is extremely variable. It appears to be a developmental phenomenon, which follows different courses in different stutterers. Although stuttering tends to get progressively worse over time, it may plateau at various levels of severity. In addition, stutterers are not equally nonfluent at all times and in all speaking situations, and they may have relatively long periods of normal fluency. For example, many stutterers are normally fluent on the majority of words they speak in conversation, and also when they are singing, speaking, or reading in unison with someone else, talking to their *Variability of stuttering*

pets, or whispering. Some persons who label themselves stutterers are not considered so by others, and the opposite may also be true. Such variability makes stuttering very difficult to define precisely, and it may well be that the definition once proposed by Wendell Johnson is still the best: Stuttering is what the stutterer does when trying not to stutter again (Johnson et al., 1967).

Stuttering usually begins gradually, and the onset typically occurs during early childhood. As noted earlier, it is considerably more prevalent among males than females. There are suggestions in the literature that four out of five children who begin to stutter will recover spontaneously (Van Riper, 1971), although this high recovery rate has been questioned by others.

Theories of stuttering A description of each of the many different theories of stuttering is beyond the scope of this text. It is possible, however, for us to make some generalizations about these theories. Stuttering theories can be categorized into three general groups: (1) physical, or constitutional, differences, (2) psychological, or neurotic, conditions, and (3) learning theories.

Since the time of Aristotle, *physical* or *constitutional factors* have been considered by some as the cause of stuttering. Some of the organic conditions proposed in early theories of stuttering were an abnormal tongue, brain damage, and motor incoordination. In the 1930s, the theory that stutterers lack normal cerebral dominance (that is, a dominant hemisphere in the brain) was very popular (Carrell, 1968; Van Riper, 1971). The possibility of a hereditary factor in stuttering was considered by Wendell Johnson (1959) and others, although environmental and learning factors could also account for the tendency for stuttering to run in families.

Physical or constitutional theories

Two additional physical or constitutional theories deserve mentioning. One is the recent theory that stuttering is a disorder of timing, which results from disturbed auditory feedback and disrupts the motoric sequencing of speech (Van Riper, 1971, 1973). The other is the controversial theory that the core of the stuttering block is related to the functioning of the larynx in stressful situations (Schwartz, 1976). The stutterer's "airway dilation reflex" is triggered, causing the vocal folds to remain open, thus preventing the production of sound. To try to overcome the open vocal folds, the stutterer tenses the folds along with the lips, tongue, jaw, or other body parts, and these reactions become part of the behavior labeled as stuttering. Although many of the early organic theories are considered ludicrous today, the possibility of constitutional differences in stutterers cannot be ruled out entirely.

Psychological theories

Some theorists have considered stuttering to be a *neurotic symptom* related to unconscious needs, hostility, anxiety, or deep-seated emotional problems. Although psychoanalytic approaches to stuttering continue to have their proponents, for example, the theories of Blanton, Froeschels and Barbara (Bloodstein, 1969; Eisenson, 1958; Van Riper, 1971), many speech pathologists agree that if emotional problems are present in stutterers, they are usually the result, rather than the cause, of the stuttering.

Learning theory accounts of stuttering have been stressed recently, although the specifics of the different learning theories vary considerably. One of the early learning theory accounts of stuttering proposed that stuttering develops when parents react negatively to their young child's normal disfluencies (Johnson, 1959; Johnson et al., 1967; Van Riper, 1971). This causes a vicious circle to begin. The child senses the parents' negative reactions and then begins to struggle in an attempt to avoid the disfluencies. This in turn only causes more rather than fewer disfluencies. Thus, stuttering as a definite problem occurs after it is labeled as such by the parents or some other layman. As Van Riper (1971) has stated, much of stuttering behavior *is* learned, although present learning theories do not account completely for the origin and maintenance of stuttering. One thing is certain—the theoretical controversy over its causes will probably continue as long as the condition exists.

Learning theories

Overt and covert stuttering features The observable features of stuttering include the speech disfluencies and associated nonspeech mannerisms which may be present at different times and in varying degrees. The disfluencies most often related to stuttering are *sound* and *syllable repetitions* and *prolongations.* Other disfluencies that may occur are word and phrase repetitions, interjections ("uh," "hmm," "ah"), revisions, and silent gaps or blocks. Hard contacts of the articulators (the lips, tongue, and teeth) and prolonged articulatory postures (positioning the articulators for a sound and holding that position for an extended period) are not uncommon.

Overt disfluency and mannerisms

Nonspeech mannerisms often develop as part of the stuttering behavior. Examples of this secondary, or accessory, behavior include loss of eye contact; tremors of the lips, eyelids, and jaw; head, jaw, and arm jerks; facial grimaces; tongue protrusion; increased body tension; breathing irregularities; and nasal snorts.

The above overt behavior is thought to be related to stutterers' covert, or hidden, feelings about their stuttering. The reactions and attitudes of persons who stutter often include fear of particular sounds, words, and speaking situations, as well as anxiety and frustration regarding their stuttering. Feelings of guilt and hostility may also be reported. These feelings often cause stutterers to avoid or postpone speaking, especially when they anticipate having difficulty.

Covert feelings re stuttering

Stutterers are typically very accurate in predicting when they will stutter, and the disfluency tends to recur in the same situations and on the same words. In general, stuttering behaviors are most likely to occur on the initial sound of a word, the first words of sentences, and longer words (Bloodstein, 1969; Johnson et al., 1967; Van Riper, 1971).

The terms *primary* and *secondary* are used by many clinicians to differentiate between mild and severe stuttering. As noted earlier, stuttering tends to be a developmental phenomenon which gets progressively worse over time if appropriate intervention or therapy is not provided.

Worsens without therapy

Diagnosing stuttering problems   Generally, the speech pathologist must determine if, in fact, a stuttering problem exists, or if the child is manifesting normal disfluencies typical for his or her age. If the child or youth is stuttering, the onset and development of the problem are investigated through an extensive case history.

Since few formal diagnostic tests for stuttering are available, the clinician will typically devise informal procedures for evaluating and describing the specific features of the stuttering behavior. The clinician will need to determine the kinds of disfluencies and secondary mannerisms present, using various kinds of speaking and reading materials and situations. Procedures for measuring the *adaptation* of stuttering (the tendency for stuttering to decrease with repeated reading of the same passage) and the *consistency* of stuttering (the tendency for stuttering to recur on the same words in successive readings of the same passage) are often employed as additional indices of severity (Johnson et al., 1963; Luper & Mulder, 1964). The child's awareness of and reactions to the stuttering should be determined, along with the techniques he or she uses to overcome the disfluencies (postponement, avoidance, starting and releasing devices). The clinician may then try various stuttering therapy techniques briefly during the diagnostic evaluation to determine which ones appear to have the best potential for modifying the stuttering behavior.

This information, plus the results of the general diagnostic procedures described earlier, will be used for estimating the severity or developmental phase of the child's stuttering and for determining an appropriate therapy program. Detailed descriptions of specific diagnostic procedures are available in a number of sources (Emerick & Hatten, 1974; Johnson et al., 1963; Luper & Mulder, 1964).

Remedial techniques   There are as many different approaches to stuttering therapy as there are theories of stuttering. Most of the published therapy programs, however, have been directed toward the advanced adolescent or adult stutterer who has developed significant secondary symptoms and negative feelings about the condition. Hence, as Williams (1971) and Van Riper (1973) have noted, these therapy programs cannot be used indiscriminately with young children in the early developmental stages of stuttering. Here we will explore some of the professionally popular ideas of various authorities.

Many speech pathologists still agree with the idea proposed several decades ago by Wendell Johnson that reducing the stutterer's fear and consequent attempt to avoid stuttering will help eliminate so-called struggle behavior, which comprises a large part of stuttering behavior (Bloodstein, 1969; Johnson et al., 1967). In Johnson's approach, training the child or youth to talk about his stuttering behavior objectively and descriptively rather than evaluatively and emotionally is a significant part of reducing the stutterer's fears. The youth might say, "I closed my eyes and jerked my shoulder as I repeated the *m* sound in the word *my*," rather than "I just couldn't go on because my lips got stuck and my eyes closed. Then my shoulder started a spasm."

In another therapy program for children, Luper and Mulder (1964) recommend goals and procedures based on the child's developmental phase of stuttering. Phase 1, incipient stuttering, calls for completely environmental, or indirect, preventative procedures, involving parent counseling rather than clinical contact with the child. Helping the parents understand normal disfluencies and the development of stuttering, encouraging them to accept and react only positively to their child's speaking efforts, improving parent-child relationships, and altering the environment

Parent counseling

Jackie and Pierre take turns making sentences with words that contain the sounds they've been drilling. With each correct sentence they move closer to the treasure.

to reduce speech pressures and increase the child's enjoyment of speaking are important goals of the parent counseling. For Phase 2, transitional stuttering, Luper and Mulder (1964) recommend a parent-counseling program and direct, face-to-face contact with the child, although they use relatively nondirective play therapy techniques. The emphasis is primarily on providing positive and enjoyable speaking experiences and helping the child learn to overcome or ignore the things that are presently disrupting fluency (e.g., being interrupted, being hurried or pressured to provide information, and so on). Phase 3, confirmed stuttering, calls for a direct therapy approach aimed at improving ways of handling stuttering moments and reducing associated secondary mannerisms. Confirmed stutterers are very aware of their problem and use various maladaptive devices to "get through" their disfluencies. Therapy activities are also directed toward lessening their sensitivity to how stuttering appears to others. The overall goal is easy, or fluent, stuttering. Phase 4 advanced stutterers are usually adolescents. For this group most attention is devoted to encouraging positive attitudes, countering fears and negative emotional reactions, and reducing or eliminating the youth's struggle to avoid stuttering. Various procedures are also used to modify the overt stuttering responses.

Van Riper (1971) sets up a different kind of four-phase therapy program comprising: (1) an *identification phase* in which the stutterer identifies and analyzes her own behavior; (2) a *desensitization phase* to decrease the stutterer's negative reactions to the behavior; (3) a *modification phase* to reduce the struggle and avoidance behavior and achieve "a new fluent, less abnormal way of stuttering"; and (4) a *stabilization phase* to habituate more fluent speech. Various behavior modification and counseling techniques for each of the phases are also important. A therapy program for young stutterers that emphasizes "talking easy" has also been described by Williams (1971, p. 1084).

Learning theory principles and behavior modification techniques have been applied in a number of therapy approaches (Brutten & Shoemaker, 1967; Gray & Egland, 1969; Perkins, 1973). Delayed auditory feedback (DAF), in which the speaker hears her own speech played back with a slight delay as she is speaking is one example of this approach. DAF is used to establish a slowed but fluent pattern of speaking which is then shaped to a normal rate and generalized to nonclinic situations. In the behavior modification techniques, the emphasis is on the stutterer's overt speech and nonspeech behaviors, rather than on her underlying attitudes and feelings. Suggestions that will be helpful to the classroom teacher or other nonspeech pathologist in handling nonfluent children include providing positive speaking experiences and eliminating undue pressure and teasing in the classroom (Egland, 1970).

Normal language development

As we noted in our earlier discussion of speech disorders, an understanding of normal speech development is necessary to determine if there is a problem. The same holds true when we turn our attention to language disorders; we must first become acquainted with normal language development. An outline of the major milestones of normal language development would take us up to approximately school age. By the age of five or six, most children have acquired the basic grammatical rules of their language. Vocabulary skill, however, continues to develop, subject to many variables (IQ, educational opportunities, etc.). Table 8-4 outlines the various stages and milestones.

Basic grammar acquired by age six

Children usually begin to comprehend the meanings of a few words around the age of nine months and begin to say their first true words around eleven or twelve months. For several months thereafter, they express themselves in one-word statements. This period is often called the *holophrastic stage* to indicate that the child is expressing a whole idea or "sentence" in a single word. For example, the child says "Mama" and the meaning appears to be, "Mama, I'm hungry, so feed me." At eighteen months of age, most children begin to produce *two-word syntactic constructions* in which the word order (syntax) is important to meaning.

Early stages

As Table 8-4 indicates, children between the ages of eighteen and twenty-four months express many different meanings and semantic relations, although the length of their utterances is restricted to approximately two words. Typical utterances during this period include: "Donnie hit" (agent + action); "Drink milk" (action + object); "Pretty baby" (modifier + noun); "No bed" (negation + noun); "Mommy here" (noun + locative); and "Daddy hat" (possessive noun + noun).

Table 8.4
Stages of normal language development

Age	Language characteristics
Birth–8 mos.	Prelinguistic period. Develops awareness of world without understanding or producing words symbolically.
9–11 mos.	Transitional period. Begins to comprehend meanings of a few words.
11–12 mos.	Linguistic period. First true words are produced.
12–18 mos.	Holophrastic stage. Increasing vocabulary.
18–24 mos.	Two-word syntactic constructions. Greater variety of meanings and semantic relations. Rapid vocabulary growth. Increased understanding of others.
2–3 yrs.	Three-word constructions and telegraphic sentences. Continued vocabulary growth. Increasing syntactic complexity. Beginning use of morphological markers.
4–5 yrs.	Sentences increase in length and complexity. Fewer grammatical errors. Continued vocabulary growth.
6 yrs.	Long, complex sentences with few grammatical errors. Understands and uses all general rules of adult grammar. Continued vocabulary growth.

Source: Based on data from Berry, 1969; Brown, 1973; Dale, 1976; Lee, 1974; Menyuk, 1971; Templin, 1957

They also begin to give commands: "Give ball," and ask questions using a rising intonation: "Baby shoe?"

Table 8-4 reveals that two- and three-year-old children increase both the length and syntactic complexity of their utterances. The sentences of two-year-olds are often *telegraphic;* that is, they include only the important content words, such as "Daddy go work" and "Sissy give cookie." By three years of age, children's sentences are more grammatically complex and complete, and they begin to use simple inflections. Sentences such as the following are common: "That's daddy's hat," "I jumped on the bed," "Big boys don't cry," "I wanna' go home," "What is that?" It is also not unusual at this age for grammatical errors to occur, such as "Him wanted to go" and "Lisa have a brother too."

Later stages

Four- and five-year-olds have larger vocabularies and their sentences contain fewer grammatical errors. They often have difficulty with irregular forms, however, and it is not uncommon to hear them say things such as "foots," "childs," "runned," "caughted," and "goodest." By six years of age, most children are able to verbalize their ideas quite effectively with long, complex sentences and few grammatical errors.

Sequence and rate

One must remember that these are general developmental trends and individual children may demonstrate considerable variation. Many psycholinguists have emphasized that the *sequence* of language development is quite consistent across children although the *rate* of development varies for individual children.

Types and characteristics of language disorders

Causal factors

Language skills inhibited by cognitive deficit

Physical, psychosocial, and environmental factors all affect language development. Thus, language disorders are closely related to other disabilities and multihandicapping conditions discussed in this text. For instance, in our examination of mental retardation (Units 2 and 3), we saw that speech and language skills will be determined by and consistent with the intellectual functioning level. The greater the cognitive deficit, the greater the delay and inhibiting effect on language development.

Nonstandard dialect is not substandard language

We noted in the discussion of societally neglected children (Unit 5) that environmental factors, such as poor language models in the home and lack of adequate language stimulation, can contribute to a child's language delay. We also saw that patterns of language acquisition among children from low socioeconomic-level families can differ from middle-class language patterns. In the past decade or so, sociolinguists studying inner-city and ethnic minority children have found, however, that many of these children are *not* using a substandard language system filled with grammatical errors and vocabulary deficiencies (Dale, 1976). Rather, their language patterns represent fully developed, rule-governed linguistic systems that are different from standard English but equally effective for communication. The critical point for our consideration here is that we not confuse *nonstandard* dialects with language disorders. A misdiagnosis could lead to an inappropriate treatment program with undesirable consequences for the child. For nonstandard dialect speakers to understand and use standard English, the preferred approach would be to help them become *bidialectal* and to teach them to switch dialects appropriately as the communicative situation requires.

Central nervous system impairment, possibly interfering with language centers of the brain, received attention in Unit 6 in the discussion of medical or neurological approaches to specific learning disabilities. Normal language development is also dependent on normal psychological and emotional adjustment. Some emotionally handicapped children and youth exhibit language disorders, especially in interpersonal communication (see Unit 7). *Neurological and psychological factors*

Additionally, children must *hear* language if they are to develop it normally without special help. Thus, a child with a moderate or severe loss of auditory acuity can be expected to have language problems if the peripheral hearing loss is not identified early and corrected by surgery or amplification. (Children with peripheral hearing loss are discussed in greater detail in Unit 9.) *Hearing acuity disabilities*

Auditory receptive and expressive language disorders

Auditory verbal language disabilities can involve the child's *receptive* skills (comprehension) and/or *expressive* skills (production). In general, a receptive language disorder will be accompanied by expressive deficits, since expression is based on comprehension; but an expressive language disorder will not necessarily be accompanied by receptive deficits. Any or all of the language systems defined in the first part of this unit can be deficient.

Semantic system deficits A language-disordered child may demonstrate deficits in receptive or expressive vocabulary. The child may also demonstrate deficiencies in understanding or use of word relationships such as opposites, synonyms, and categories (food, clothing, colors) or restrictions on word usage (for example, that a bachelor cannot have a wife or that an inanimate object such as a rock cannot eat). Problems such as these represent semantic system deficits, or problems related to meaning. *Problems with meaning*

Syntactic system deficits Deficits in the syntactic system include problems in word order or in understanding and using different types of sentences. Examples of syntactic errors include such things as the use of telegraphic or short, incomplete sentences by a child four years of age or older ("Mommy going store now.") or inappropriate word order in sentences ("Where the boy is running?"). A child may also demonstrate difficulty understanding sentences, such as questions, negatives, and passives, which involve grammatical rules not yet acquired. Of course, the child's developmental age must be considered in determining if the grammatical errors are indeed abnormal for his or her age. *Problems with word order*

Morphological system deficits These deficits include problems in understanding and/or using the various inflectional markers on nouns, verbs, adjectives, and so on. For example, the child may not understand that an *s* at the end of *car* means more than one or that the *d* sound at the end of *jumped* means the action occurred in the past. The child may also fail to use the required markers or use the wrong inflections in sentences, and subject-verb agreement may be poor ("He run home," "The children play at my house," "Me have two dog").

Problems with sounds

Phonological system deficits Deficits in this system appear to be less common than other types of language disorders. They typically involve incomplete development of the sound system, so that the child's repertoire of sounds is limited. Rather than learning all of the forty-three sounds (phonemes) of English, the child may have only two or three vowels and a scattering of consonants. In other instances, the child with a phonological deficit has all the sounds of English but uses them in ways that are inappropriate for the language.

Problems with higher-level thought

Deficits in higher-level language use Children's auditory verbal language disabilities may also be reflected in deficiencies in using language for higher-level thought processing and problem solving. For example, these children may have difficulty describing and categorizing objects or explaining similarities and differences, cause and effect relationships, or temporal sequences. They may do poorly in storytelling activities and demonstrate gaps in information which they are expected to know at their age.

Behavioral concomitants Problems such as those described above may appear in any combination, and they may be mild or severe. If severe, they will make interpersonal communication and academic achievement very difficult for the child. They seldom exist in isolation and are often accompanied by behavior problems, perceptual deficits, and academic learning disabilities.

Diagnosing language disorders

When a child is suspected of having a language disorder, the diagnostic evaluation will include formal and informal tests to evaluate his or her comprehension and use of semantic, syntactic, and morphologic rules, as well as overall use of language for interpersonal communication and problem solving. During the past decade, a wide variety of tests has become available (Berry, 1969; Irwin & Marge, 1972; Wiig & Semel, 1976). Since no single test provides all the pertinent information needed, however, a test battery consisting of several different instruments should be administered to assess all aspects of the child's language functioning.

Analysis of a child's language sample

Informal language testing procedures are also important in determining the child's specific language abilities and disabilities. An analysis of a spontaneous language sample from the child provides some of the most useful information for planning the remediation (Johnson, Darley & Spriestersbach, 1963; Lee, 1974). By identifying and describing the linguistic rules the child is using and comparing these to normative data, one can determine the *content* of the language remediation program—that is, what specific features to emphasize in therapy.

Although new language tests are appearing on the market every year, and each contributes something to the speech pathologist's diagnostic battery, in the final analysis the best testing instrument available is a clinician who has some knowledge of recent research and theory in language, and who can apply that knowledge in evaluating a child's language functioning (Siegel, 1975).

Remedial techniques

In addition to the general suggestions that have appeared in the literature for improving a child's language, a number of specialized programs have been developed. For example, Bangs (1968) has published a curriculum guide that is helpful in planning a preschool language program; Gray and Ryan (1973) have published a programmed approach to teaching grammatical rules used at the Monterey Institute for Speech and Hearing in California; and several language programs based on the Illinois Test of Psycholinguistic Abilities (Kirk et al., 1968) have been developed to improve the language and language-related skills tapped by that test (Bush & Giles, 1969; Kirk & Kirk, 1971). The Interactive Language Development Teaching program of Lee et al. (1975) teaches language-disordered children the vocabulary and grammatical rules they should know through storytelling and group activities. Also, language-training programs primarily devised for mentally retarded children (Miller & Yoder, 1972) or for the societally neglected school population (Dunn & Smith, 1966) contain many useful language stimulation materials and procedures for children who do not present intellectual deficits or environmental deprivation. *(Specialized language programs)*

Chomsky's theory of grammar (1965) and the field of psycholinguistics have had an immense impact on the evaluation and treatment of childhood language disorders. Many of the therapy approaches of the 1970s emphasize the importance of developing the child's underlying knowledge of linguistic rules, which is then used to generate an infinite number of new utterances (Gray & Ryan, 1973; Ingram & Eisenson, 1972; Lee et al., 1975; Leonard, 1973; MacDonald & Blott, 1974; McReynolds, 1974; Miller & Yoder, 1972; Weiss & Duffy, 1974; Wiig & Semel, 1976). These language programs provide a more powerful and flexible tool than programs that teach an arbitrarily limited set of sentences which are learned by rote. *(Recent influence of linguistics)*

Although imitation may be used in some activities in the linguistically oriented therapy programs, other procedures such as *expansion* and *modeling* are also used to teach the child increasingly complex grammatic rules (Leonard, 1973). *Expansion* is a child-initiated technique in which the child's telegraphic utterance is repeated by the adult, who adds missing words and morphological inflections to make the utterance more grammatically complete. For example, the child says, "Boy jump," and the adult responds with "Yes, the boy is jumping." *Modeling* is also a child-initiated *(Expansion and modeling)* technique, but in this procedure the adult comments on what the child has said, thus providing semantic rather than syntactic elaboration. For example, the child says, "Kitty scratch," and the adult responds with "The kitty can hurt you when she's angry."

Auditory perception activities

A language therapy program will also include activities for improving the child's auditory perceptual deficits or use of language in problem-solving tasks, if necessary. For example, the youngster may be asked to blend sequences of three isolated sounds into the appropriate monosyllabic words to improve his or her auditory synthesis or sound blending skills. Or a "going shopping game" may be played, in which each person in the group adds another item to the list which must be remembered to improve short-term auditory sequential memory skills. Problem-solving tasks such as explaining simple cause-and-effect relationships with and without visual cues, matching and verbalizing pictorial opposites, or finding the picture that doesn't belong in a group and explaining the reason can help children learn to use language for thought processing.

Teamwork   Regardless of the particular techniques and methods preferred by the clinician, the language remediation program must be tailored to the individual child's specific abilities and disabilities if it is to be effective. And because the language-disordered child may also present problems in reading or other academic subjects as well as in behavior or perceptual skills, he or she is often involved in several special programs concurrently. In such cases, all of the specialists and the classroom teacher work together to plan an appropriate educational and remediation program for the child. For example, the classroom teacher, speech pathologist, remedial reading teacher, school counselor or psychologist and occupational therapist frequently form the child's educational team. When possible, of course, modifications are made within the child's regular classroom so that improvements can be achieved without placement in special classes or therapy programs. When this is not feasible, however, every effort is made to incorporate the special services into the regular school day so that the child can spend as much time as possible in the regular classroom. The goal of all the programs is to help the child achieve full potential as quickly and as efficiently as possible. Teamwork among the various professionals who may be involved becomes a necessity.

Child may be in several programs concurrently

Games and exercises

Classroom intervention   Activities guided by the teacher or aide in the regular classroom, of course, can be valuable supplements to the child's language therapy program. Games and exercises such as the following examples will often aid the language-disordered child: twenty-questions games requiring descriptions of objects; identifying and defining words with multiple definitions; describing similarities and differences; telling stories with emphasis on appropriate temporal sequencing; describing possible outcomes of different problem situations; building sentences, with each student adding another word and discussing incorrect sentences when they develop; finding the irregular nouns or verbs in oral and written sentences; identifying what is wrong with sentences and making the necessary changes; vocabulary expansion activities through field trips; and so on.

Speech and language disorders related to other physical disabilities

Several specific physical disabilities (see Unit 11) are often accompanied by speech and language problems. Because of the multiplicity of concerns associated with these conditions, a multidisciplinary approach to treatment is crucial.

In this carryover activity, Jackie uses "where-questions" and her new sound to tell her classmates a story. The speech clinician lauds her good job.

Common problems of a child with cleft palate are voice or articulation disorders, such as hypernasality, and difficulty with certain consonant sounds. These are usually related primarily to inadequate closure in the soft palate and pharynx area, and secondarily to bilateral hearing loss. Significant dental abnormalities, such as jumbled and missing or extra teeth, also are involved. Children who have a surgically repaired cleft lip with a normal palate usually do not present special speech or language problems.

Cerebral palsied children often have speech and language problems too. For example, these children may have significant respiratory problems which disturb the energy source for speech. They may be unable to control their breathing or to coordinate it with speech sound production, leading to voice disorders such as loss of voice, inadequate pitch and loudness, or hypernasality. Weakness and lack of coordination of the muscles controlling the articulators often cause an inability to articulate (dysarthria) and the rhythm of speech is often disturbed. The incidence of hearing loss is also high among cerebral palsied children and contributes to their articulation, voice, and language problems. Receptive and expressive language disorders caused by central nervous system impairment are not uncommon. If the cerebral palsy condition is extensive and the motoric involvement severe, the child may be completely nonverbal and an alternate means of communication must be developed.

Summary

This overview of the types and characteristics of speech and language disorders in children stresses early identification of these problems so that appropriate evaluation and remediation procedures can be initiated. As noted throughout the chapter, articulation, voice, fluency, and language disorders will have a significant impact on the child's future if the problems are allowed to grow and worsen. With the cooperation of everyone who has contact with the communicatively disabled child, an individualized remediation program can be developed and carried out. In this manner, the handicap can be minimized or eliminated so that the child will have a maximum opportunity to achieve academic success and healthy interpersonal relationships.

References and resources

American Speech and Hearing Association. *Speech and Language Disorders and the Speech and Language Pathologist.* Washington, D.C.: 1976.

Bangs, T. *Language and Learning Disorders of the Pre-Academic Child.* New York: Appleton-Century-Crofts, 1968.

Berry, M. *Language Disorders of Children: The Bases and Diagnoses.* New York: Appleton-Century-Crofts, 1969.

Bloodstein, O. *A Handbook on Stuttering.* Chicago: National Easter Seal Society for Crippled Children and Adults, 1969.

Boone, D. *The Voice and Voice Therapy.* Englewood Cliffs, N.J.: Prentice-Hall, 1971.
Brown, R. *A First Language: The Early Stages.* Cambridge, Mass.: Harvard University Press, 1973.
Brutten, E., and Shoemaker, D. *The Modification of Stuttering.* Englewood Cliffs, N.J.: Prentice-Hall, 1967.
Bush, W., and Giles, M. *Aids to Psycholinguistic Teaching.* Columbus, Ohio: Merrill, 1969.
Carrell, J. *Disorders of Articulation.* Englewood Cliffs, N.J.: Prentice-Hall, 1968.
Chomsky, N. *Aspects of the Theory of Syntax.* Cambridge, Mass.: MIT Press, 1965.
Dale, P. *Language Development: Structure and Function.* 2nd ed. New York: Holt, Rinehart and Winston, 1976.
Dunn, L., and Smith, J. *Peabody Language Development Kits.* Circle Pines, Minn.: American Guidance Service, 1966.
Egland, G. *Speech and Language Problems: A Guide for the Classroom Teacher.* Englewood Cliffs, N.J.: Prentice-Hall, 1970.
Eisenson, J., ed. *Stuttering: A Symposium.* New York: Harper and Row, 1958.
Emerick, L., and Hatten, J. *Diagnosis and Evaluation in Speech Pathology.* Englewood Cliffs, N.J.: Prentice-Hall, 1974.
Gray, B., and Egland, G., eds. *Stuttering and the Conditioning Therapies.* Monterey, Calif.: Monterey Institute for Speech and Hearing, 1969.
Gray, B., and Ryan, B. *A Language Program for the Non-Language Child.* Champaign, Ill.: Research Press, 1973.
Hull, F., and Hull, M. "Children with Oral Communication Disabilities." In *Exceptional Children in the Schools: Special Education in Transition,* edited by L. Dunn, pp. 297–348, 2d ed. New York: Holt, Rinehart and Winston, 1973.
Ingram, D., and Eisenson, J. "Therapeutic Approaches III: Establishing and Developing Language in Congenitally Aphasic Children." In *Aphasia in Children,* edited by J. Eisenson, pp. 148–88. New York: Harper and Row, 1972.
Irwin, J., and Marge, M., eds. *Principles of Childhood Language Disabilities.* New York: Appleton-Century-Crofts, 1972.
Johnson, D., and Myklebust, H. *Learning Disabilities: Educational Principles and Practices.* New York: Grune and Stratton, 1967.
Johnson, W. *The Onset of Stuttering.* Minneapolis: University of Minnesota Press, 1959.
Johnson, W.; Brown, S.; Curtis, J.; Edney, C.; and Keaster, J. *Speech Handicapped School Children.* 3rd ed. New York: Harper and Row, 1967.
Johnson, W.; Darley, F.; and Spriestersbach, D. *Diagnostic Methods in Speech Pathology.* New York: Harper and Row, 1963.
Joint Committee on Dentistry and Speech Pathology-Audiology. "Position Statement of Tongue Thrust." *Asha* 17 (1975): 331–37.
Kirk, S., and Kirk, W. *Psycholinguistic Learning Disabilities: Diagnosis and Remediation.* Urbana, Ill.: University of Illinois Press, 1971.
Kirk, S.; McCarthy, J.; and Kirk, W. *Illinois Test of Psycholinguistic Abilities.* Rev. ed. Urbana, Ill.: University of Illinois Press, 1968.
Lee, L. *Developmental Sentence Analysis.* Evanston, Ill.: Northwestern University Press, 1974.
Lee, L.; Koenigsknecht, R.; and Mulhern, S. *Interactive Language Development Teaching.* Evanston, Ill.: Northwestern University Press, 1975.
Leonard, L. "Teaching by the Rules." *Journal of Speech and Hearing Disorders* 38 (1973): 174–83.

Luper, H., and Mulder, R. *Stuttering Therapy for Children.* Englewood Cliffs, N.J.: Prentice-Hall, 1964.

McCarthy, D. "Language Development in Children." In *Manual of Child Psychology,* edited by L. Carmichael, pp. 492–630. New York: Wiley, 1954.

MacDonald, J., and Blott, J. "Environmental Language Intervention: The Rationale for a Diagnostic and Training Strategy through Rules, Context, and Generalization." *Journal of Speech and Hearing Disorders* 39 (1974): 244–56.

McReynolds, L., ed. *Developing Systematic Procedures for Training Children's Language.* ASHA Monographs, no. 18, 1974.

Marge, M. "The General Problem of Language Disabilities in Children." In *Principles of Childhood Language Disabilities,* edited by J. Irwin and M. Marge, pp. 75–98. New York: Appleton-Century-Crofts, 1972.

Mason, R., and Proffit, W. "The Tongue Thrust Controversy: Background and Recommendations." *Journal of Speech and Hearing Disorders* 39 (1974): 115–32.

Menyuk, P. *The Acquisition and Development of Language.* Englewood Cliffs, N.J.: Prentice-Hall, 1971.

Milisen, R. "The Incidence of Speech Disorders." In *Handbook of Speech Pathology and Audiology,* edited by L. Travis, pp. 619–33. Englewood Cliffs, N.J.: Prentice-Hall, 1971.

Miller, J., and Yoder, D. "A Syntax Teaching Program." In *Language Intervention with the Retarded,* edited by J. McLean, D. Yoder, and R. Schiefelbusch, pp. 191–211. Baltimore: University Park Press, 1972.

Perkins, W. "Replacement of Stuttering with Normal Speech: 2. Clinical Procedures." *Journal of Speech and Hearing Disorders* 38 (1973): 295–303.

Powers, M. "Clinical and Educational Procedures in Functional Disorders of Articulation." In *Handbook of Speech Pathology and Audiology,* edited by L. Travis, pp. 877–910. Englewood Cliffs, N.J.: Prentice-Hall, 1971.

Schwartz, M. *Stuttering Solved.* Philadelphia: Lippincott, 1976.

Siegel, G. "The Use of Language Tests." *Language, Speech, and Hearing Services in Schools* 6 (1975): 211–17.

Templin, M. *Certain Language Skills in Children.* Minneapolis: University of Minnesota Press, 1957.

Van Riper, C. *The Nature of Stuttering.* Englewood Cliffs, N.J.: Prentice-Hall, 1971.

Van Riper, C. *The Treatment of Stuttering.* Englewood Cliffs, N.J.: Prentice-Hall, 1973.

Weiss, M., and Duffy, M. "Syntactic Slot-Filler: An Alternative to Davis's Sentence Construction Board." *Journal of Speech and Hearing Disorders* 39 (1974): 230–31.

Wiig, E., and Semel, E. *Language Disabilities in Children and Adolescents.* Columbus, Ohio: Merrill, 1976.

Williams, D. "Stuttering Therapy for Children." In *Handbook of Speech Pathology and Audiology,* edited by L. Travis, pp. 1073–93. Englewood Cliffs, N.J.: Prentice-Hall, 1971.

Winitz, H. *Articulatory Acquisition and Behavior.* New York: Appleton-Century-Crofts, 1969.

American Speech and Hearing Association
10801 Rockville Pike
Rockville, Maryland 20852

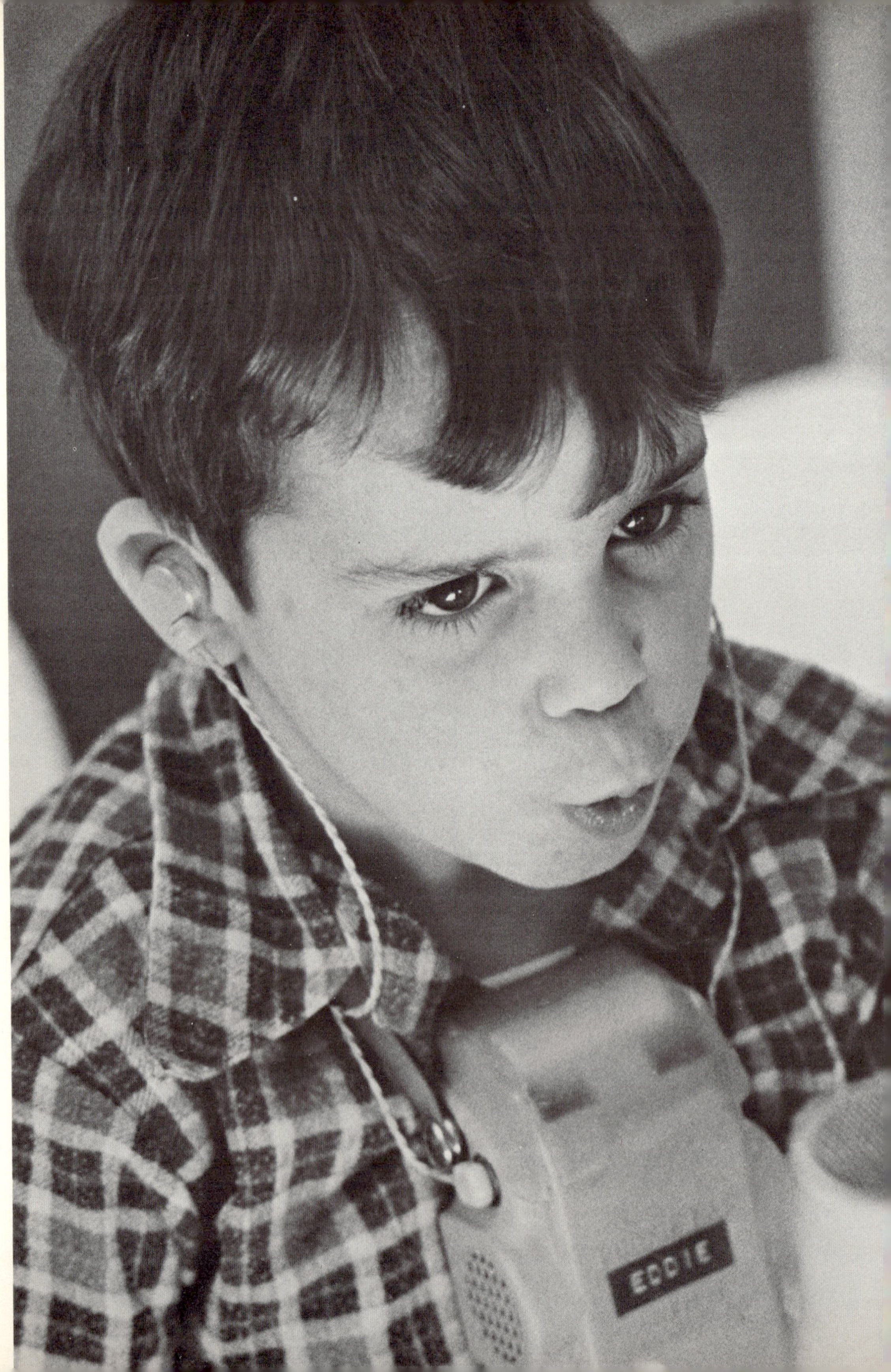
EDDIE

9 Hearing disabled children and youth
Diane J. Willis
Joan H. Faubion

The role of hearing
Effects of hearing loss upon the developing child
Facts and fallacies · Facts · Fallacies
Attitudes toward the "deaf-mute"
Symptoms of possible hearing disabilities · Auditory specialists
Who are the hearing disabled? · Incidence
Causes of hearing disabilities · Genetically linked hearing disabilities · Hearing disabilities of nongenetic origin
The auditory system · The external ear · The middle ear · The inner ear · The cochlea and sensory pathways
Types of hearing loss · Conductive hearing loss · Sensorineural hearing loss · Mixed hearing loss · Central auditory disorder
Assessment of auditory disabilities · Audiometric procedures · Hearing aids
Social and psychological impact of hearing disabilities · Social development · Intelligence · Cognitive development · Personality development
Education of the hearing disabled · Oral communication · Manual communication · Fingerspelling · Total communication · Parental participation in educational programs · General educational achievement · Academic curriculum · Directions in educational programs
General trends and needs in today's society
Summary

Student learning objectives

The student will:
1. be able to distinguish between facts and fallacies about hearing disabilities
2. become acquainted with symptoms accompanying hearing disability
3. learn about the appropriate specialists trained to evaluate hearing
4. learn about the main types of hearing loss, their causes, and means of assessment
5. learn about the general structures that make up the outer, middle, and inner ear
6. be able to discuss the differences among the various audiometric procedures
7. learn about the achievement level of deaf students and the reasons for given achievement levels
8. become acquainted with the effects of hearing loss on social/psychological development
9. recognize the educational, emotional, and vocational needs of the hearing disabled
10. become aware of the various educational approaches used to teach the hearing disabled to communicate and to read, and be able to compare the effectiveness of these approaches

Does thinking occur without language? Is language a necessary ingredient for emotional and social adjustment? Are hearing disabled children cognitively, socially, and emotionally very different from hearing children? How are they taught? What level of work do they perform later in life? Is hearing loss permanent and irreversible? What causes this condition?

These and other questions about the hearing impaired will be discussed in this unit. To appreciate their condition, compare the difficulty in understanding language per se with the difficulty you would have in understanding a foreign language you have never studied. Although you would not comprehend the words, you could at least hear the language. The hearing disabled may hear undistinguishable sounds; or not even that if they are profoundly deaf.

The role of hearing

As you scan this printed page, think a moment about how you learned to read. Better yet, how or where did you learn the words you are reading? How did they get into your vocabulary? The answers to such questions come out of the first four-and-one-half or five years of life.

At birth, your hearing was intact and functioning normally. You did not grow up in a world of silence, for doctors, nurses, and your parents, assuming that everything was fine, began talking to you. As you developed physically and mentally, the verbal barrage typically found within the childhood environment became meaningful. You soon learned to respond to the sound of your mother's voice, to anticipate her presence when she walked across the room. The sound of the table being set for a meal evoked certain responses in you. Usually, the sound of a car door slamming in the driveway indicated that Dad was home from work. The language and sounds surrounding a situation became symbols. Through them you could begin to understand the world around you.

Children learn to interpret sounds in their environment

By the time you were about a year old, you began testing your verbal ability. Important words in the environment were repeated, and the first approximations were praised. When someone said the word "mama," you tried to reproduce it in the same way. You could hear your own vocalizations, and because of auditory memory you continued to shape this approximation of "mama" until it was exactly like the word you heard. At least it was exact enough to evoke a reaction of delight from those who heard you try.

Baby's imitations of sounds

At first, the responses of a hearing disabled infant are like those of an infant with normal hearing; hence, physicians and parents are often unaware of a hearing loss until the child is a few months old. By that time, the social motive for vocalizing has diminished, since the child cannot hear to imitate others. The sound play characteristic of normal infants is soon dropped by the baby who is hearing disabled, and vocalizations become monotonal and brief.

Hearing plays a critical role in *language learning.* Humans learn their language —the appropriate system of verbal symbols—through hearing, interpreting, and imitating it in the form of speech. Later, when children enter school, the verbal symbols are transferred into printed or written symbols and the process of reading begins. But almost without exception, each word that beginning readers meet in print has already been in their speaking vocabulary perhaps for several years.

How language is learned

Effects of hearing loss upon the developing child

If medical diagnosis, home programs, and educational remediation are not initiated early in a child's life, hearing loss can be a great handicap to human growth, development, and learning. A hearing loss is frequently, though not always, permanent and irreversible. It is especially debilitating when it occurs during the most critical and vulnerable period, the readiness years. During these first two or three years of life the child is biologically programmed and ready to learn language (Lennenberg, 1970). When a child is born deaf, the normal channel for language learning is nonfunctional. A deaf child is enveloped in silence, relying upon vision and touch to maintain contact with others. Although the child is exposed to verbal language of

Early detection is important

parents and peers, he or she cannot reproduce it without the earliest and best assistance from qualified personnel; even then the child will not develop vocal expression as intelligible as the average hearing person's speech.

When verbal language or some adequate communication skill does not develop normally along with ability to use it appropriately, human development can be blocked to a varying degree (Levine, 1960). The ability to use and understand language has a direct influence on social and emotional development. Hearing disabled individuals are not necessarily disturbed in these areas, but a hearing loss can alter their social interaction. Deaf children notice family members communicating freely and effortlessly. They see people talking and reacting—perhaps a joke is being told at the dinner table—but they may not totally grasp the magic of the words. "Why," a deaf child might wonder, "did the other family members laugh, as if on cue, while eating?" "Were they laughing at me?"

Why are they laughing?

Emotional and social disruptions in a deaf child with normal intelligence are not the cause of language retardation but are more likely its result. Two case examples will illustrate this point:

Herbie Three-and-a-half-year-old Herbie is a congenitally deaf child enrolled in an oral day-school program, who was referred to the consulting psychologist because of behavior problems. He displayed frequent temper outbursts, rolled and kicked on the floor, and was aggressive with his peers. Herbie had no means of communication other than gestures, so he almost completely sealed himself off from his family, hearing children, and teachers. His low tolerance for frustration was being taxed by the structured classroom setting in the oral school. He wanted to run and play, and he wanted his desires understood. At home, Herbie's parents carried over an oral approach to learning language, but observation revealed that they did not make adequate or clearly understandable use of gestures. Unless his present school and home environment are altered, or unless Herbie is transferred to another program, he will likely continue to manifest behavior problems. Demonstrating his frustration through action, Herbie is letting everyone know that he felt isolated.

Rhonda Congenitally deaf, three-year-old Rhonda was referred for psychological assessment prior to being staffed at a communication disorders conference (an interdisciplinary teaching conference for teachers, medical students, speech pathologists, audiologists, and psychology interns). A psychological assessment was routine for all children staffed at the conference. Rhonda was observed in the waiting room manually communicating to her parents, who in turn responded manually and with speech to Rhonda's communications. She was later observed at play attempting to interact with hearing children. Rhonda was under much less social and emotional pressure because of her communication outlet. She was attending a preschool program with normal hearing children, but she had been taught to communicate manually with at least a few people.

Without effective language (or other communication) skills, progressing from one stage of human development to the next is immensely difficult. Often, the emotional and social problems that develop from this lack are not recognized until the readiness years have long passed. As hearing disabled children approach adolescence, the need to communicate is at an all-time high. They need explanations for the many psychological and biological changes they are experiencing. Without adequate oral or manual language to express feelings, the hearing disabled can only muddle through, using whatever forms of communication they have been able to grasp. This struggle for self-expression will continue throughout life unless they acquire communication skills. The social and psychological impact of hearing loss and the various modes of communication the hearing disabled can learn will be discussed later in this unit.

Adolescents have greatest need to communicate

Facts and fallacies

The hearing population is exposed to far more fallacies than facts about the hearing disabled. No exceptionality has been more misunderstood, perhaps because hearing disorders are not a noticeable handicap (unless, of course, the person is wearing a hearing aid), and perhaps because society's preconceived attitudes are difficult to dispel. Individual contact and interaction between hearing and hearing disabled people can do much to change preconceived ideas.

Misconceptions are hard to dispel

Facts
Let us look at a few facts:

1. A high percentage of the hearing disabled work for the federal government, in the newspaper business, and in wholesale-retail trade or manufacturing. They also work as bakers and in laundering and cleaning, shoe repair, and tailoring businesses. Many hold professional jobs in accounting, law, medicine, or teaching (Schein, 1968).
2. The hearing disabled belong to one or more organizations for the deaf, and their participation in club activities is comparable to that of the hearing population.
3. One large-scale study disclosed that 84 percent of the hearing disabled adults spent their leisure time engaging in hobbies; 91 percent of the sample participated in social and/or cultural activities, with sports (particularly baseball) occupying much of their leisure time (Schein, 1968).
4. The hearing disabled enjoy television, particularly quiz shows.
5. Most of the participants in a large-scale study of hearing disabled adults subscribed to a newspaper, and about one-half of the sample subscribed to more than one (Schein, 1968).

6. In spite of the attempts by legislatures and insurance companies to restrict the hearing disabled from operating motor vehicles, driving records of the hearing disabled are generally better than those of hearing individuals. They have no more accidents than hearing people.
7. The hearing disabled are proud and independent people who do not seek extra privileges other than educational assistance (Schein, 1968).

While this list of facts is not all-inclusive, it does reveal that hearing disabled people have more commonalities than differences with the hearing population.

Fallacies

Deaf people who have regular contact with a variety of hearing people are usually those whose above-average speech and language skills make them relatively easy to understand. They may be leaders in the deaf community who lost their hearing *after* acquiring considerable speech and language. Because they make very favorable impressions, the misconception arises that all deaf people are or can become like these few. This is far from the case.

Another misconception surrounds lipreading, or speechreading. Some people think that it requires little more than extra concentration on the speaker's lips, whereas it really is more of an innate ability, one that bears no significant relationship to intelligence. Many hearing disabled people with above-average IQs are poor lipreaders, and many with less native intelligence are phenomenal at it.

Lipreading ability is not related to intelligence

Contrary to popular belief, a hearing aid does not sharpen or clarify speech; it amplifies sounds, but the user must learn to discriminate and identify them. In the same way, we cannot eliminate static on a radio program by simply turning up the volume. Nor does hearing loss necessarily create keener eyesight. The hearing disabled still must rely on whatever visual acuity they possess with or without correction.

Hearing aids amplify, not clarify, sounds

A fact to be kept in mind is that all deaf people whose deafness is their only handicap have the same innate ability to learn language as do hearing people. If they are exposed to it in a way that is clearly understandable, they will learn it. They will learn what they are exposed to and no more, which of course is true of anyone, hearing or deaf.

Attitudes toward the "deaf-mute"

Society's basic attitude toward the hearing disabled has changed little over the past thousand years. Although they are no longer dismissed as uneducable or mentally retarded, as they were from Aristotle's time through the Middle Ages, deaf people today are in many instances still looked upon as different or peculiar. Employers seem to have the greatest tendency to look askance at the hearing disabled, particularly at the totally deaf. This is evidenced by the fact that the deaf as a whole are grossly *underemployed* (Vernon, 1969). Many work at jobs unrelated to their inter-

The deaf are underemployed

ests and far below their aptitudes and skills. Another reflection of a cultural attitude that borders on discrimination is seen in the shabby legal treatment the deaf receive at the hands of social service agencies, insurance firms, civil law, and the courts (Mays, 1970).

The terms "deaf-mute" and "deaf-and-dumb," both of which carry negative connotations, are incorrect and unenlightened. The totally deaf, as they are technically referred to, are not mute—their vocal mechanisms are intact and function as anyone else's for laughing, crying, screaming, and talking. They are not dumb—many learn to talk with special training. The nonverbal intelligence range of the deaf is similar to that of the hearing population. But society's attitudes, grounded in misinformation, are slow to change. Hearing disability is not an obvious defect like cerebral palsy or a broken leg. Hearing impaired children sometimes are mistakenly

Inaccurate terminology

Introducing Eddie—a youngster with a hearing loss of 100-plus decibels. On the opening page of the unit Eddie is receiving auditory training with sentence cards. Above, we see a chalkboard exercise stressing self-awareness.

thought to be retarded or disturbed because they cannot always respond to verbal questions, and their vocalizations sometimes consist of grunts and other noises.

When parents first discover that their child is deaf, they too may fear that the child will be, or is, retarded or "dumb." At this point the parents need counseling to arm them with facts about hearing loss. They should also be referred to a clinic, agency, or school that can provide their child with auditory training and teach them techniques to stimulate their child's communication skills, cognitive development, and social growth. With early intervention and treatment, the hearing disabled child can have a very positive future in most spheres of adult life.

Symptoms of possible hearing disabilities

Hearing is not always checked in full-term, normal infants, although neonatal screening for hearing disorders has been established in many hospitals throughout the United States. While hearing losses can be detected at birth, a reliable audiogram is difficult or impossible to obtain until the child is four to six years of age. Impaired hearing may be suspected if the following symptoms are observed:

1. The child does not respond to a normal tone of voice or to loud noises.
2. The child is delayed in speech and language development and/or does not imitate sounds. (Delayed speech and language development may also be related to language disorders or retardation.)
3. The child sits close to the television set and turns the volume up high.
4. The child vocalizes as an infant but soon abandons further attempts at verbal communication.
5. The child suffers serious articulation problems, with many sounds missing in his or her speech.

This list is not exhaustive, but the alert adult will want to see that a child who displays any of the preceding symptoms is scheduled for an examination. In conjunction with these symptoms, *or* if hearing screening at school yields a suspect report, a medical and/or audiological referral is imperative.

Auditory specialists

Referral for a hearing examination may be made to either an otorhinolaryngologist or an audiologist. Generally, the child would see a physician first to rule out medical problems within the ear—for example, severe inflammation, structural abnormality to the ear, and wax, to name a few. An otorhinolaryngologist (sometimes referred to as an ENT or ORL specialist) is a medical doctor who specializes in treatment of the ear, nose, and throat, including medication and surgery.

An audiologist is a professional who specializes in identification and measurement of hearing disorders. Additionally, the audiologist can be involved in the management of the nonmedical rehabilitative procedures that are available for the hearing disabled person.

Both a hearing-aid dealer and an audiologist can examine an individual and recommend certain types of hearing aids, but only a hearing-aid dealer sells the aids, routinely checks them for defects, and repairs them. Deaf education teachers and auditory rehabilitation counselors are among the many specialists involved with the hearing disabled.

Hearing aid dealer

Who are the hearing disabled?

The *age of onset* of a hearing disability coupled with its *degree of severity* are important determinants of the child's acquisition of speech and language skills. Generally speaking, a deaf or hard-of-hearing person is one "who requires specialized education because of a hearing impairment" (Committee on Professional Preparation Certification, 1972, p. 1).

For educational purposes the following definition will be used for the deaf and hard-of-hearing. *The deaf are those whose hearing loss precludes the normal acquisition of speech and language. The hearing is so severely diminished that it is not functional for the person in ordinary life.* Usually the loss occurs at birth or before the age of two years. *The hard-of-hearing, or partially hearing, are those whose hearing loss, at birth or later, is not severe enough to prevent the acquisition of some speech and language, but whose educational performance may be adversely affected.* This group may or may not need amplification (hearing aid), and their hearing level is at least functional (Conference of Executives of American Schools for the Deaf, 1938). In this unit we will focus on those children whose *primary* disability appears to be a hearing loss rather than on the multihandicapped or deaf-blind child.

Definitions

Incidence

Approximately 0.5 percent of hearing disabled children (1 in 200 persons) are partially hearing, and 0.08 percent (3 in 4000) are deaf (U.S. Office of Education, 1971). These are only estimates, and many children who have hearing losses in at least one ear are not included in this sample. Additionally, many children have intermittent hearing loss due to infection, which adds up to a high percentage of infants and children who suffer from conductive losses (that is, losses due to problems in the transmission of sound to the cochlea). Approximately 3½ to 4 percent of all children in this group fail screening tests and require medical intervention (McConnell, 1973). Early intervention can avert more serious auditory disabilities. It is essential that we screen the hearing of children at least yearly since intermittent hearing losses due to infections or fluid in the ears can interfere with the child's ability to discriminate sounds, a skill that is vital in learning to read, speak, or articulate.

Intermittent hearing loss

A study of 41,109 hearing disabled students has yielded interesting audiological data and information relative to educational placement (Office of Demographic

Studies, 1973). Almost 10,000 of these students had no audiological data available for their teachers, thus hindering educational planning. Only 10.6 percent of the 41,109 students were enrolled in itinerant programs or were receiving part-time special educational services. Most of the students were in residential schools for the deaf (45.5 percent), day schools for the hearing impaired (7.2 percent), or self-contained classes for the hearing impaired (30.8 percent) (Northcutt, 1973).

Mainstreaming

You will recall that Public Law 94-142, discussed in Unit One, stressed mainstreaming, the integration of exceptional children into regular classes. From the above statistics we can only conclude that the vast majority of hearing disabled students today are receiving their education in residential or self-contained classes. The new laws mandate a different approach, so local schools must provide alternative ways of educating the hearing disabled. Mainstreaming is felt to be a very positive and challenging means of educating this population.

Causes of hearing disabilities

There are genetic and nongenetic causes of hearing disabilities, both of which will be discussed briefly in succeeding pages. Factors that may contribute to hearing problems can be categorized as prenatal, neonatal, and postnatal. Prenatal factors include toxemia of pregnancy, prematurity, antepartum bleeding, maternal infections (rubella, mumps, syphilis), and drugs administered to the mother during pregnancy that are toxic to the hearing mechanism. Neonatal factors include prolonged labor and difficult delivery, craniocerebral trauma (deprivation of oxygen to the brain, bleeding, contusion, skull fracture to the base of the brain), meningitis, encephalitis, head trauma, toxic drugs administered to the infant, cranial tumors, and maternal deprivation (Northern & Downs, 1974).

Prenatal, neonatal and postnatal factors

Genetically linked hearing disabilities

Genetically linked conditions are transmitted from parents to child. Hereditary childhood deafness is described as a profound, irreversible, bilateral sensorineural hearing loss of early onset. Congenitally deaf children include those with hearing losses due to bone malformation in the middle ear, a condition often surgically treatable (Northern & Downs, 1974). A high percentage of congenital deafness is hereditary (Konigsmark, 1972).

Hereditary congenital deafness

A question frequently arises concerning the incidence of inherited hearing loss when two deaf people marry, as they often do. There is evidence that deaf parents have only a slight risk of producing a deaf child (Bergstrom et al., 1971). Since it is unlikely that both parents would be afflicted with the same genetic deafness, the notion that deaf parents usually produce deaf offspring is erroneous. There are many examples of deaf parents producing offspring who are highly gifted in expressive language. One case that quickly comes to mind is Oscar-winning film actress Louise Fletcher, who manually communicated a message to her totally deaf parents at the 1976 Academy Awards presentation.

Offspring of deaf parents

Treacher-Collins Syndrome and Waardenburg's Syndrome are genetic defects with related hearing problems. The former is characterized by small or displaced ears, a large fishlike mouth with dental abnormalities, receding chin, depressed cheekbones, and other facial bone abnormalities. Hearing problems associated with the condition range from conductive deafness to sensorineural loss. Children suffering from Waardenburg's Syndrome frequently have a white forelock of hair, bicolored eyes (each eye a different color), a prominent nose (particularly at the root), and a "cupid's bow" configuration of the lips. Congenital sensorineural deafness, i.e., deafness due to damage to the cochlear hair cells or the auditory nerve (see Figures 9-1 and 9-2 on pp. 303–304) is characteristic of this condition. Mental retardation is not necessarily associated with the genetic disorders, although both conditions may have associated cleft palate conditions (Northern & Downs, 1974).

Genetic defects

Hearing disabilities of nongenetic origin
A few of the more common disorders associated with a hearing loss will be presented here to give you an idea of the scope of the problem. Detailed descriptions of each disorder can be found in audiology textbooks or medical texts under the heading *otorhinolaryngology*.

Drug-related impairment   Few people are aware that certain drugs, notably kanomycin and neomycin, can cause permanent hearing damage in a fetus, an infant, or an adult. Streptomycin and other members of the mycin group may cause permanent injury to the cochlea (Hawkins, 1967; also see Figures 9-1 and 9-2). Individuals differ in their susceptibility to the various drugs, but those who are affected would likely be affected in both ears. Some hearing losses are temporary and improve when medications such as aspirin, quinine, and diuretics are withheld.

Mycin drugs can cause hearing problems

Offspring of mothers who ingest certain drugs harmful to the hearing mechanism during pregnancy can suffer not only hearing loss but other congenital malformations as well. The thalidomide babies of the 1960s were born with cleft palate, impaired hearing, and many other malformations of the cardiovascular (heart and blood vessels) and skeletal systems, and urinary and genital tracts (Northern & Downs, 1974). It is important to note that the resulting malformations in the fetus depend on the time during pregnancy when the prospective mother ingested the drugs or medication. Their effects are most devastating during the first trimester of pregnancy. Knowledge of the effects of drugs (as well as poor nutrition and inadequate medical care) should encourage a woman to be extremely careful about her health. The healthier a pregnant woman is, the less likely her offspring are to suffer from some abnormality. Students interested in reading more on ototoxic deafness in children should consult Hawkins (1967).

Drug effects during first trimester of pregnancy

Viruses   Maternal rubella, the virus most recognizable to the general public, can cause hearing loss as well as other congenital abnormalities. Although the rubella epidemic of the 1960s is now thought to be over, it affected approximately 10,000

Maternal rubella

to 20,000 children in the early and midyears of that decade. Units 2 and 10 offer more detailed discussion of maternal rubella.

Other viruses that have caused congenital deafness are chicken pox, infectious meningitis, inflammation of the membranes sheathing the brain and spinal cord (meningoencephalitis), mumps, measles, and influenza.

Otitis media

Diseases of the middle ear Serous otitis media, better described as fluid in the middle ear, occurs when the eustachian tube becomes blocked, thus creating negative middle-ear pressure. This is a common problem in preschool and early school-age children. Otitis media can be acute or chronic, with or without sudden ear pain. In both conditions a secretion is discharged from the middle ear, and parents may discover fluid on the child's pillow or bed. Perforation or rupture of the tympanic membrane relieves pressure and allows the fluid to flow out of the ear. Chronic otitis media may damage and scar the ear. Otitis media requires medical treatment, sometimes in the form of a myringotomy, which may involve placing tubes in the child's ear to promote drainage. It is best to give preferential classroom seating to children with known otitis media or those with tubes in the ear, since their hearing level is likely to fluctuate. Children with cleft palates have a high incidence of otitis media.

Preferential classroom seating

Other inflammatory diseases of the middle ear include cholesteatoma (a growth of skin accumulating in the middle ear) and conditions caused by respiratory infections. Hearing sensitivity can also be diminished by a buildup of earwax or by foreign objects (crayons, toys, food) in the auditory canal. The child should be referred to a specialist for these complaints to prevent perforation of the tympanic membrane.

Diseases of the inner ear Viral diseases such as meningitis, chicken pox, streptococcus, staphylococcus, mumps, measles, and influenza can cause inner-ear damage resulting in deafness. The viruses are able to infiltrate the inner ear by way of the internal meatus (see Figure 9-1). Again, medical treatment is important any time a child develops a fever or illness of unknown origin. Diseases to the inner ear can result in mild to profound sensorineural hearing loss (Northern & Downs, 1974).

The auditory system

The human auditory system is a uniquely arranged mechanism that enables us to convert environmental signals into meaningful sounds. Structurally, the ear is divided into two major areas: the peripheral auditory mechanism, which is subdivided into the outer, middle, and inner ears; and the central auditory mechanism, which consists of neural pathways in the brain. Figures 9-1 and 9-2 highlight these landmarks.

The external ear

Pinna locates sound

The outer ear includes the pinna and the external auditory canal, which terminates at the eardrum. The pinna aids the listener in locating the sound source and gathers in and focuses sound waves down the external auditory canal to vibrate the eardrum. Because of its length, the external auditory canal protects the eardrum and acts as a resonator.

The middle ear
The middle ear is a small, laterally compressed space filled with air, which is conveyed to it from the back of the nose and throat through the eustachian tube. Three very small bones (malleus, incus, stapes) called the ossicles are suspended by ligaments within the middle ear space. The eardrum has embedded within it a portion of the malleus. The malleus then connects to the incus, which in turn connects to the stapes, thus forming the ossicular chain. Figures 9-1 and 9-2 illustrate this relationship. The stapes inserts into an area called the oval window, which may be thought of as a connecting point between the middle ear and inner ear. Sound waves create ossicular chain vibrations that are conveyed along the eardrum to the inner ear.

The ossicular chain

The inner ear
The inner ear actually serves two functions: it provides for the maintenance of our balance and the capability of hearing. The portion of the inner ear involved with

Figure 9.1
Pathway of sound reception: Outer, middle and inner ear

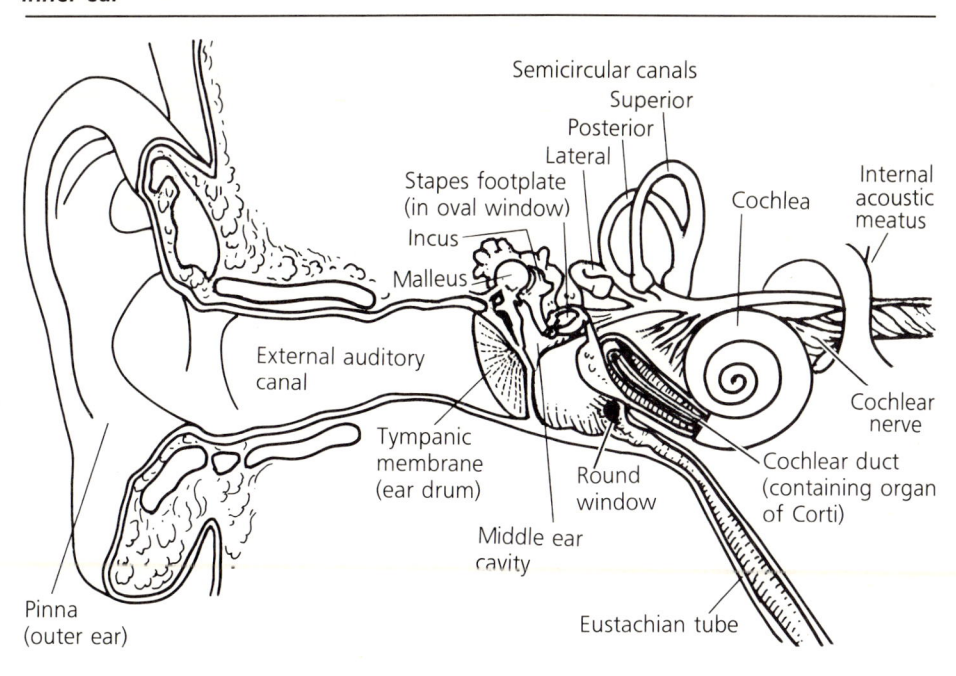

hearing is the cochlea (see Figure 9-1), a small snail-shaped network of fluid-filled ducts. One of these, the cochlea duct, houses a highly specialized receptor called the organ of Corti. This receptor contains many hair cells, which are innervated by fibers of the cochlear branch of the eighth cranial nerve (see *cochlear nerve* in Figure 9-1).

The cochlea and sensory pathways

The vibrations that are transmitted via the eardrum and ossicular chain initiate a displacement of inner-ear fluids. The displaced fluids distort hair cells within the cochlea, which results in the discharge of neural impulses (see Figure 9-2). These im-

Figure 9.2
Simplified drawing of the transmission of vibrations from eardrum through the cochlea

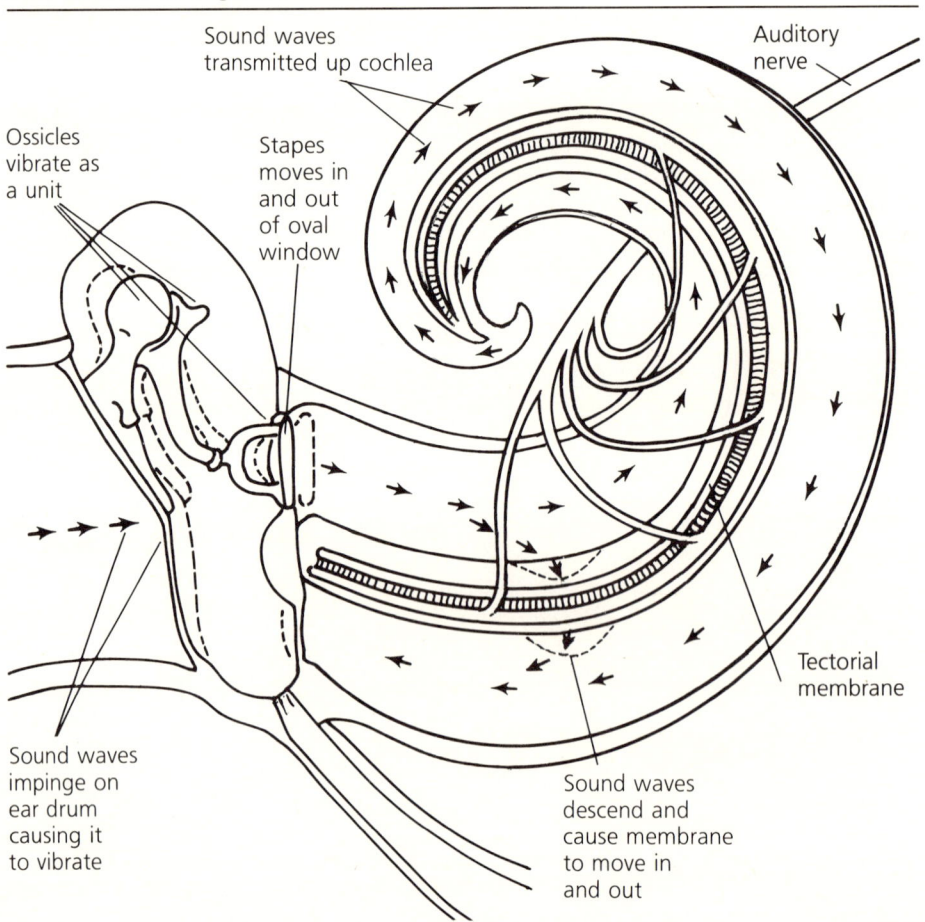

pulses are carried by nerve fibers in the cochlear portion of the eighth cranial nerve to the central auditory pathways in the brain. The impulses then proceed to and through the various levels of the auditory pathways in the brain stem and are ultimately received at the cortex, where we derive meaningful interpretation of sound.

Types of hearing loss

As we have learned, our ability to develop speech and language and to communicate effectively throughout our lives is dependent upon an intact auditory system. Disease or damage in the hearing mechanism can trigger a communicatively handicapping hearing loss and, in some cases, an attendant medical condition requiring treatment. We have also seen that there are numerous causes of impairment to the auditory system, and that the resultant type of hearing loss is related to the portion of the system that is involved. The two major types of hearing loss are graphically analogized below (see Figure 9-3). *Two types of hearing loss*

It is extremely important to be able to (1) hear sounds as loud as they truly are and (2) to hear sounds with complete clarity. The two illustrations in Figure 9-3 depict the difference between (1) conductive and (2) sensorineural hearing loss.

When we look at Illustration A we are able to read the small print that spells *loudness*. If we hold the book at arm's length or further, it is difficult to read the word, but as we bring the book closer, the letters become more distinct. This condition is analogous to a conductive hearing loss. The softer the sound or the further *Example 1: conductive*

Figure 9.3
Visual depiction of two dimensions of hearing loss

A. Inability to hear sounds as loud as they really are

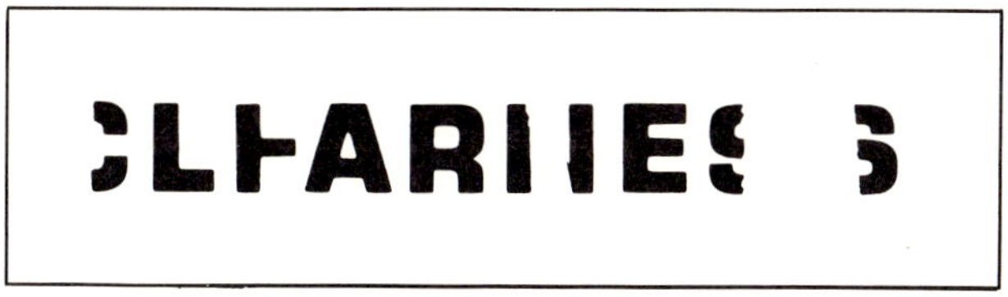

B. Inability to hear sounds with complete clarity

Source: Harford, 1964

away the speaker, the more difficult it is to hear; hearing improves as we approach the sound source. If any part of the outer or middle ear is damaged, we will be unable to hear speech of normal loudness.

We are unable to read the print easily in Illustration B, whether we hold the book far or near. The word *clearness* is difficult to read and we cannot readily decipher it. This is analogous to a sensorineural hearing loss. Clarity of speech and speech sounds is determined by the inner ear and by nerve fibers leading to the brain. If we sustain damage to these fibers or to any portion of the inner ear, speech will sound muffled or fuzzy. In these cases, the person has trouble understanding even loud speech.

Example 2: sensorineural

Conductive hearing loss

Conductive hearing loss is not an uncommon problem among children. It usually results when any dysfunction of the outer or middle ear prevents normal transmission of sound waves to the fluids of the inner ear. In other words, the problem lies in the conduction of eardrum vibrations to the cochlea. Speech is perceived normally once it is loud enough to overcome the hearing loss. Causes for this condition include excessive accumulation of earwax in the external auditory canal, improper eustachian function, middle-ear infection, growths in the middle ear, immobilization of the ossicles (usually the stapes), and perforations of the eardrum. Conductive hearing loss is generally temporary, for most children and adults respond to medical treatment. Once the cause of the conductive impairment is treated, hearing levels often return to normal or near normal. In order to prevent permanent ear damage it is important to obtain medical consultation, preferably from a specialist in the treatment of ear, nose, and throat disease.

A common problem

Sensorineural hearing loss

Sensorineural hearing loss is the result of damage to inner-ear fiber structures of the auditory nerve along the pathway to the brain stem. Sound waves that reach the inner ear are not correctly transformed into normal impulses. Quite frequently speech is not perceived normally even if it is rendered loud enough to overcome the loss of hearing. This type of hearing loss is usually permanent. The varied causes of sensorineural hearing loss include congenital factors such as genetic defects and maternal rubella contracted during pregnancy. Trauma and/or oxygen deprivation at birth also can damage the sensorineural structures. Other causes already discussed are childhood diseases such as mumps or measles, certain drugs, viral and bacterial infections, head injuries, aging, sudden or prolonged exposure to hazardous noise levels, and benign or malignant tumors.

Generally a permanent condition

Mixed hearing loss

This condition occurs when conductive hearing loss and sensorineural hearing loss exist simultaneously. Any of the previously described causes of conductive and sensorineural hearing loss can combine to produce this type of impairment. The conductive portion of a mixed hearing loss usually responds to medical treatment, but the sensorineural condition is generally permanent.

Central auditory disorder

All hearing tests may prove to be normal with this type of impairment but the child may have difficulty comprehending or interpreting speech. This complex disorder is discussed in Unit 6 (Specific Learning Disabilities) and Unit 8 (Speech and Language Disabilities).

Assessment of auditory disabilities

Hearing is routinely checked or screened at school. If the child does not pass the screening test, an appointment with an audiologist may be scheduled. The audiologist uses a variety of tests to determine the status of a person's hearing. The most common is the basic hearing evaluation, which includes pure-tone and speech audiometry.

Frequency and intensity— parameters for describing sound

Audiometric procedures

Pure-tone audiometry   Sound is described by two parameters. The first is the frequency in hertz units (Hz), which indicates the number of complete sound waves or cycles occurring in one second. Frequency determines the pitch of a sound; the higher the frequency the higher the pitch. Pure tones represent one single frequency occurring over time. The second parameter is the intensity of sound expressed in decibel units (db). Intensity determines the loudness of a sound; the greater the intensity, or db level, the louder the sound.

The pure-tone audiometer is an instrument used to make pure-tone measurements. It produces discrete tones of different frequencies at controlled intensity (loudness) levels. Typically, two measurements are made in pure-tone audiometry: (1) air conduction thresholds, in which test tones are presented through an earphone placed over the child's test ear; and (2) bone conduction thresholds, in which test tones are produced by a vibrator placed against the skull, usually directly behind the pinna on the mastoid bone. (The latter procedure is usually carried out in the physician's office.)

Air- and bone-conducted thresholds

Air and bone conduction measures reflect the faintest intensity levels in decibels at which the test tones can be detected. These db levels at each test frequency are called *thresholds*. They are plotted on an audiogram, which is a chart depicting the hearing level at which threshold occurred as a function of test frequency. Figure 9-4 illustrates an audiogram showing normal hearing sensitivity for air- and bone-conducted pure tones.

Speech audiometry   The basic hearing evaluation also includes two speech audiometric measures. The first is the speech reception threshold (SRT), gauged by presenting spondaic words (two syllables of equal stress) separately to each ear through

Speech reception threshold

308
Hearing disabled children and youth

earphones. Threshold is the faintest hearing level in db at which 50 percent of a group of spondaic words can be repeated.

The second measure is the speech discrimination test, which determines a child's or adult's ability to differentiate the individual speech sounds within the English language. Fifty monosyllabic words are presented through the test earphone at a level above the speech reception threshold that is sufficiently loud for all the individual elements of speech to be heard. Each successful identification is scored 2 percent, and a speech discrimination score of 90 percent or above is considered normal. Speech audiometric results, including speech reception thresholds and speech discrimination scores, are also presented on the audiogram in Figure 9-4. The figure also displays the area on the audiogram where the hearing thresholds can be categorized into degree of hearing loss.

Speech discrimination test

Figure 9.4
Audiogram

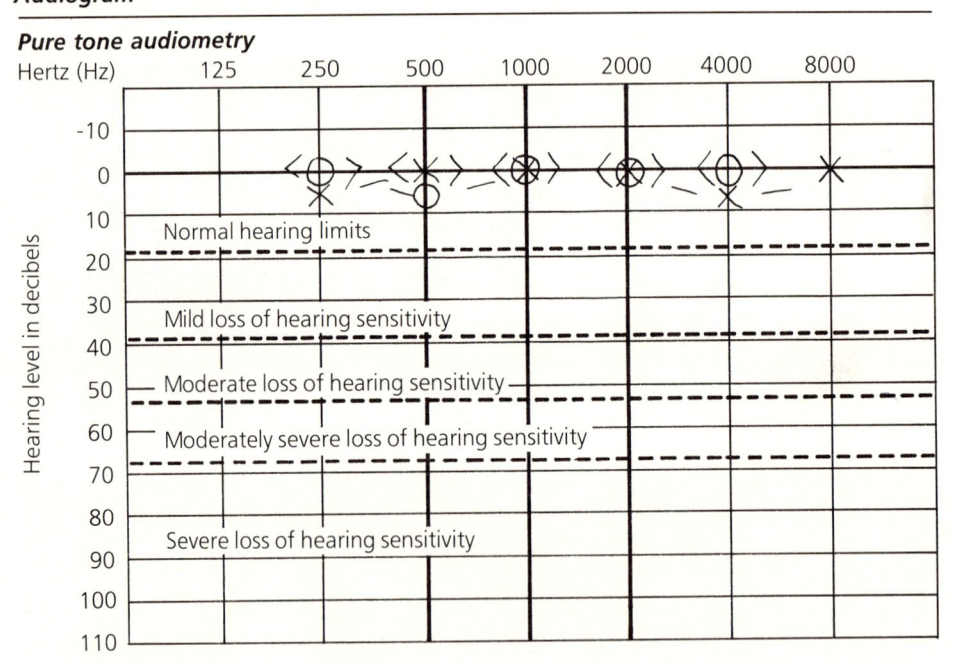

Pure tone audiometry

| Hertz (Hz) | 125 | 250 | 500 | 1000 | 2000 | 4000 | 8000 |

Hearing level in decibels: -10, 0, 10, 20, 30, 40, 50, 60, 70, 80, 90, 100, 110

Normal hearing limits
Mild loss of hearing sensitivity
Moderate loss of hearing sensitivity
Moderately severe loss of hearing sensitivity
Severe loss of hearing sensitivity

Audiogram key	Right ear	Left ear
Air conduction	O	X
Bone conduction	>	<
Speech reception threshold	Right ear 0 dB	Left ear 0 dB
Speech discrimination score	100%	100%

Conditioned play audiometry   The conventional hearing evaluation can be utilized with most adults and children, but behavioral conditioning techniques must be used for younger children down to the age of two-and-one-half years. This modification, termed *conditioned play audiometry,* conditions the child to carry out a given task (for example, block moving) when he or she hears the pure-tone signals, thus generating an audiogram. Picture identification can be used for the speech measures.

Effective techniques with young children

Sound-field audiometry   Sound-field audiometry is one of several measurement techniques that can be used if age or other factors make it impossible to con-

Eddie and Monique are learning to associate words with colors and vice versa, with the aid of body-type hearing aids and in-the-ear receivers. Teachers use a sending set with antenna.

dition a child to respond. Various types of test signals are presented through high fidelity speakers situated in the test room and the db levels at which the child reacts, turns to, or responds to sound are determined.

Impedance audiometry   Impedance audiometry is another frequently used procedure. A battery of tests is administered to measure the relative and static acoustic impedance characteristics of the ear. In this sense the term *acoustic impedance* denotes the ear's ability to accept sound energy. Since pathology can alter the ear's normal impedance to sound, these measures contribute considerable diagnostic information about the status of the middle ear, inner ear, and neural structures. By modifying normal procedure, one can use impedance audiometric data to predict degree of hearing loss, a flexibility that renders the test extremely valuable in the evaluation of the infant and child population.

Evoked response audiometry   Although not a routine clinical test, evoked response audiometry (ERA) is another evaluative procedure that can disclose information about the auditory system. The basis of ERA is that an audible sound event changes the ongoing electroencephalographic (EEG) activity, which can be recorded from the scalp.

Hospital screening in neonatal nurseries   A considerable number of hospitals and clinics have established identification programs designed to detect hearing loss at the neonatal and early postnatal stage. Generally, noisemakers with controlled frequency and intensity output are used to produce the intense sound levels necessary to elicit a response from a baby in the first few months of life. ERA and variants of it are also being utilized for this purpose. The infants who are identified are then thoroughly evaluated and given the necessary treatment, which may include a hearing aid and specialized therapy to enhance the child's speech and language development.

Hearing aids
After a hearing loss has been discovered in a child, it is important to take immediate action so as not to delay language development. The treatment plan usually begins with a hearing aid. The aid is fitted by an audiologist or hearing aid dealer, who performs several tests to determine the most appropriate instrument for each child.

A hearing aid can be thought of as a miniature loudspeaker system composed of three basic electronic parts: a microphone to pick up sound, an amplifier to make the sound louder, and a receiver to deliver the loud sound to the ear. There are four types of hearing aids, varying in size and amount of power delivered. The *body-type* hearing aid is the largest and generally provides the most amplification (see picture story of Eddie). The microphone and the amplifier are housed in a small box worn on the listener's chest, with wires connecting to the receiver worn in the ear. The *eye-*

glass, behind-the-ear, and *all-in-the-ear* models enclose the electronic parts in a single case. They are smaller and more comfortable to wear, but they are not as powerful as the body-type instrument.

When fitting a child with a hearing aid, several factors must be considered. Naturally, the amount of hearing loss is important, but so is the age of a child. Children under three years of age are often fitted with a body-type hearing aid even though their hearing loss may not be great enough to require a very powerful instrument. This is done for practical reasons. Since an ear-level (behind-the-ear, all-in-the-ear) hearing aid is much smaller than a body aid, it is more likely to be misplaced or damaged by an active child. Then, too, a small child's ears are more difficult to fit with an ear-level instrument than with a smaller "button" receiver used with a body aid. Probably the most important consideration, however, is that the controls on an ear-level instrument are very small and difficult for tiny fingers to manipulate. The goal when fitting a hearing aid on a child is to make that child an independent, full-time wearer as soon as possible. If the child is able to adjust the controls easily and to wear the aid in many different surroundings without constant supervision and assistance, this goal is reached more easily. If a child's hearing loss is not severe, an ear-level instrument can be worn at age five or six.

Which type of hearing aid is best?

The single most important factor in determining successful language development in hearing disabled children is probably the age at which they are fitted with a hearing aid. Normal hearing infants must listen and develop the hearing sense for about one year before attempting to produce words. The hearing disabled must go through the same process; no matter how old they are when the aid is first fitted, their "hearing age" is one day. The younger the children are at fitting, the less lost time they will have to make up. The two case studies that follow point up the difference that early fitting makes in a child's speech and language development.

Age when fitted affects language development

Lorna   At the age of ten months Lorna was first diagnosed as hearing disabled. Her hearing loss was judged as severe, meaning she could hear only very loud sounds. She was fitted with a body-type hearing aid at age eleven months and placed in hearing therapy. At eighteen months, her language delay was considered very mild. She had learned several single words. By the time she was two-and-a-half, her speech and language development were considered normal for her age. She attends a normal hearing nursery school. Although Lorna will require speech therapy for several years, she probably will attend regular public school. Of course, she will wear a hearing aid for the rest of her life.

Nicky   At the age of five, Nicky was first diagnosed as hearing disabled. His hearing loss was judged to be severe, so he was fitted with a body-type hearing aid. Nicky had no speech. He communicated through gestures and grunts. Although he was placed in a hearing therapy program where he received much language and speech training, at age six he still could not speak. He was placed in a classroom for hearing disabled children where total communication, or speech plus sign language, is used.

Although the amount of hearing loss and the treatment plan of these two cases were almost identical, the end result, or the degree of handicap each will feel, is very different. Nicky was unable to make up the first five years he lost in speech development.

The aid is only a first step

Fitting a hearing aid on a child is the first step toward developing his or her communication skills, but it is only the first step. The child must be taught to use the aid, to improve his or her hearing, and to develop speech. A multidisciplinary team of qualified therapists and teachers is best equipped to guide the hearing disabled child's overall development.

Social and psychological impact of hearing disabilities

Social development

The hearing disabled child is like the hearing child in the early stages of development. With the exception of the emergence of language by eighteen months to two years of age, the hearing disabled child crawls, walks, smiles, coos, cries, recognizes others, and manifests the many facets of behavior observed in all children. If reared in an accepting and realistic environment, the child need not be handicapped except in the clarity of verbal communication. The child is blissfully ignorant of the grief and agony the parents feel upon discovering that their healthy baby is deaf or hard-of-hearing. The conflicting opinions of experts who examine the infant add to the parents' anxiety and make them hope for a change in the diagnosis. Once a hearing loss is confirmed, the parents must recognize the fact that they have a healthy but hearing disabled child (Furth, 1973). The readjustments in thinking and the accommodations in everyday life that are required of parents in this situation were analyzed in Unit 1.

Parental reactions affect social development

We mention parental reactions to their child's disability at this point because too often parents overprotect their children, which can stifle social and emotional development even in hearing children. Thus, early counseling regarding the effects of hearing loss on the developing child is essential. It is equally important to guide the family to professionals skilled in teaching the hearing disabled, because parents have the most important psychosocial influence on a deaf or hearing disabled child. The educational process to which the youngster is exposed and the extent of his or her communication skills also affect social development (Vernon & Mindel, 1971).

While verbal interaction is of course impeded, hearing disabled children are no less curious or less interested in what is going on around them than are normal children. Hence, hearing loss does not necessarily hinder their social development. They play with toys and games, watch TV, and enjoy playing with other children (although they tend to be followers rather than leaders). Parents can enhance their hearing disabled children's understanding of events by talking and gesturing to them, even though the children are extremely observant and quite often figure things out for themselves.

By the time hearing disabled children begin interacting with hearing children in a school setting, their unfamiliarity with the rules of culturally transmitted games and their difficulty in organizing the rules of these games are apparent. Hence, "their play in primary school takes on a roughhouse character that strikes the observer as decidedly immature. But by and large these children manifest patterns of social interaction, friendship, play, and games that are similar to those of hearing children" (Furth, 1973, p. 44).

Hearing loss need not hinder social development

By adolescence and adulthood the hearing disabled gravitate to one another and, as was pointed out earlier in this unit, their lives are not so different from those of the hearing. Deafness is often mistakenly associated with helplessness and the need for protection; hence, the greatest obstacle facing the hearing disabled child or adolescent is not the hearing disability but the failure of parents, professionals, and the general public to understand and accept the person with this disability (Furth, 1973).

Social attitudes can be an obstacle

Intelligence

Many parents, physicians, and lay persons have the erroneous notion that deafness in and of itself affects the intelligence of the hearing disabled. Almost all of the many studies investigating the intellectual development and functioning of the hearing disabled lead to two conclusions: (1) intelligence of the hearing disabled is normally distributed, as it is within the hearing population (see Figure 2-1 in Unit 2); and (2) the average IQ of the deaf population is comparable to that of the hearing population. Unless a hearing disabled child has other disabilities such as brain damage, there is no causal relationship between deafness and intelligence (White & Stevenson, 1975). However, the child will be slow in reaching his or her full potential without early stimulation and training in communication.

Deafness is not related to intelligence

Psychological evaluation Several factors combine to make it difficult to evaluate the intellect and personality of the hearing disabled child. There are few standardized tests for the hearing disabled population, and those that are used must be relatively free of language. Since language deficiency should not be equated with intelligence, tests measuring performance abilities are preferred over others (Levine, 1960). We cannot be certain whether a low IQ score obtained on a hearing disabled child is due to intellectual deficiency, the unsuitability of the test, additional perceptual problems, or other intervening factors. When evaluating a hearing disabled child it is generally best to observe the child's behavior at school, play, or home and then to administer at least two performance (nonverbal) measures. Bear in mind that assessment is necessary only when specific information is

Psychological evaluation is difficult

needed. A profile of strengths and weaknesses obtained from test data can be helpful only when it aids the child. The IQ *score,* unless we suspect retardation, does not provide much useful information about the individual. Hearing disabled children perform very well on performance sections of various intelligence tests, and it must be reiterated that IQ scores for this group are comparable to those of the general population.

Cognitive development

Thought without language

At the beginning of this unit we asked whether thinking can occur without language. The answer, that language is *not* a necessary ingredient for complex cognitive processes, has been well documented (Furth, 1966; Rosenstein, 1960, 1961). Children who were born deaf or who lost their hearing prior to developing verbal language have been the subjects of many investigations that assessed the relationship between thinking and verbal language. If the hearing disabled are indeed able to figure out complex cognitive tasks that are free of verbal instructions, as Furth (1966) demonstrated in his book *Thinking Without Language,* then educators face a challenge. Those who cling to the misconception that the deaf or hard-of-hearing are limited in cognitive areas must now consider whether the current methods used to teach and reach this group impose the limitations.

Linguistic vs. perceptual skills

Another misconception is that the deaf or hard-of-hearing are delayed in visual-motor-perceptual functioning (Myklebust, 1960). This may be the case if brain damage is involved, but if the disability is solely in the hearing mechanism, then this appears to be false (Willis et al., 1972; 1973). In fact, limited data obtained from school for the hearing disabled suggest that far too much teaching time is spent on visual-motor-perceptual tasks and not enough on linguistic training. All of the participants in this study excelled on perceptual tasks but failed on even simple verbal language tasks (Willis et al., 1973). Naturally, since the children could neither read nor understand verbal language, the verbal items were failed.

Another study compared children segregated in a school for the deaf with those in regular school. The mental/cognitive development of the deaf children in the mainstream school surpassed the level of the children in the segregated school. On Piaget-type tasks no differences existed between hearing and deaf children in the regular school (Raviv et al., 1973). Furth (1966) offers excellent suggestions for teaching symbolic logic to the hearing disabled and is recommended for those interested in teaching this population.

Personality development

The hearing disabled population as a group does not have significantly more psychopathology than does the hearing population. They are not prone to mental illness as a result of their hearing loss. In a comprehensive study of hearing disabled children and youth who do present mental health problems, by far the greatest percentage (27 percent) were diagnosed as behavior disorders. Other problems were diagnosed as transient situational personality disorders, social maladjustments, or other special symptoms (Schlesinger & Meadow, 1972).

For adequate personality development, the hearing disabled need an early means of communication and accepting parents who foster autonomy and independence. Preferably, the children are not isolated or segregated from their normally hearing peers. Those who do have emotional problems serious enough to warrant hospitalization must be treated in sign language since very few of the hearing disabled profit from traditional psychotherapy. Even college-educated individuals must be treated by someone who can use sign language.

Communication is the key to mental health

Education of the hearing disabled

There are numerous approaches used in teaching hearing impaired children. Educators have long, and at times heatedly, debated the relative merits of oral, manual,

Debate about methods

To observe and "listen" is to understand. Planting bulbs brings flowers. Eddie needs the same range of experiences as a hearing child.

and total communication in teaching the hearing disabled. While the controversy has subsided to a degree, it nonetheless continues.

Oral communication

The educational approach referred to as the oral method emphasizes the oral environment, with speech and speechreading as the main avenues of communication (Farwell, 1976). These, of course, are supplemented by reading, writing, and residual hearing developed through hearing aids and auditory training equipment. Many educators of the deaf who espouse oralism would accept the following as an accurate statement of their purpose and objective:

Advantages of oralism

> We believe that each hearing impaired child should be given every opportunity to learn to communicate through speech, speechreading, hearing if possible, reading, and writing; that he [or she] be given every opportunity to develop this ability with the help of home, school, and community so that he [or she] may take his rightful place in the world of today (Miller, 1970, pp. 216–17).

It is interesting to note that in most American schools for the deaf, the child traditionally begins in oral classrooms and later is allowed to use a manual method. Children may begin training in the oral approach as soon as a hearing loss is detected. At first the program may be initiated in the home, but by two years of age the child could be attending school for at least part of the day.

Proponents of oralism cite several advantages of the oral method. Not only can many deaf students learn intelligible speech through this technique, but by lipreading (speechreading) they can establish communication with the rest of society. That is to say, oralism can bring the deaf into the world of the hearing, while sign language restricts communication to those others who have mastered that specialized form of expression.

Disadvantages of oralism

On the other hand, it is extremely difficult for profoundly deaf children to reproduce speech, since they cannot hear others produce it and thus cannot monitor their own vocal attempts to imitate it. Speech reading is at best a guessing game because of the multitudes of words in our English language that look alike when spoken. Approximately 40 to 60 percent of English speech sounds (individual phonemes) are homophonous: that is, their formation on the lips is identical to that of other sounds. Success in speechreading presupposes an adequate language base, knowledge of syntax and grammar, and a wealth of vocabulary. Research has shown that the best speechreaders in one-to-one situations understand from 26 to 36 percent of what is said. Many deaf people understand less than 5 percent (Mindel & Vernon, 1971). All deaf people, or hearing people for that matter, do not have a talent for lipreading, and some find it extremely ineffective and frustrating as a means of reciprocal receptive communication. To realize the difficulty, turn off the sound on your television set and try to guess what is being said.

In recent years an approach using a combination of hand signals and speechreading—called cued speech—has been most effective in enhancing the oral abilities of deaf children. This approach, developed at Gallaudet School for the Deaf, is not strictly speaking an oral method. The end result of cued speech training, however, is improvement in the ability to lip-read as well as improvement in basic reading and communication skills. Cued speech essentially consists of eight hand shapes used in four different positions near the lips. The hand shapes and positions serve to visually differentiate sounds in the English language that are similar in appearance on the lips. As stated above, 40 to 60 percent of English speech sounds have identical formation. Children taught by the cued speech method are achieving success in regular classroom placement. Their academic skills, especially in reading, are improved as is their general scholastic achievement and their ability to participate in class activities and discussions.

The cued speech approach

Manual communication

Technically, manual communication refers to the use of sign language—a system of specific hand symbols that represent specific words, concepts, or ideas. Sign language is a highly visual and unambiguous means of communication. Unlike speechreading, very few signs for different words look alike when executed. Take for instance the words *man* and *pan*. These are identical on the lips, yet the sign symbols are as different as are the mental images we create when seeing the words in print.

Sign language is particularly suited to young children because it is easy to see and does not require fine muscle coordination to execute. Moreover, the signs for the most common objects and action verbs are much like pictures of them. Extremely young deaf children grasp signs easily and use them readily to express themselves. When a hearing loss is so severe that a child cannot understand conversational speech even with a hearing aid, the child will find other ways to communicate efficiently (Mindel & Vernon, 1971). Throughout history, those so afflicted have devised some form of manual communication simply as a matter of expediency.

Particularly suited to young children

Fingerspelling

The Manual Alphabet designates a specific hand configuration for each letter of the English alphabet (see Figure 9-5). Fingerspelling usually supplements manual communication or sign language when there is no sign for a word or if the signer does not happen to know a particular sign. The amount of fingerspelling used in communication is an individual matter.

Fingerspelling used with sign language

Differences in fingerspelling skills are not unlike the differences in handwriting from one person to another. Some handwriting is easy to read, and some is not; with a little getting used to most words can be deciphered. Just as the period of readiness for acquiring certain communicative skills varies according to the developmental stage of the child, so too does the ability to understand and use fingerspelling. However, it has been our experience that deaf children who are exposed to sign language and fingerspelling from birth acquire proficiency with this skill much earlier than hearing children usually learn to read. The reason may be simply that they are exposed to it earlier and more continuously (Quigley, 1969).

Figure 9.5
The manual alphabet

As seen by the receiver

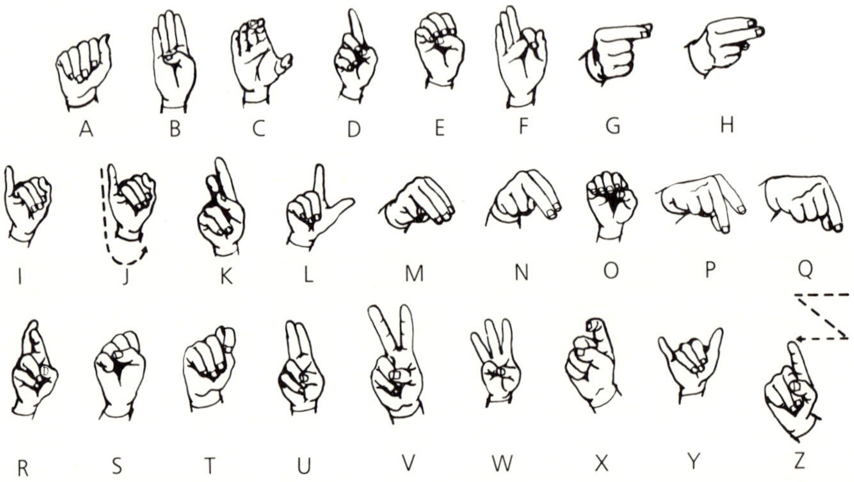

As seen by the sender

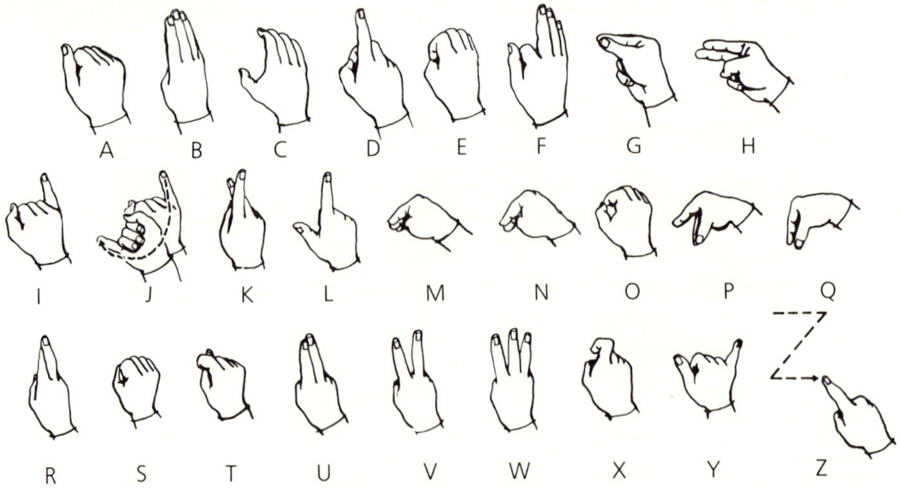

Source: Courtesy of The National Association of the Deaf

Total communication

The term *total communication* was introduced by the Maryland School for the Deaf in 1969. This was an all-out attempt to end the controversy that has existed since public education of the deaf began approximately two hundred years ago. The following excerpts give the definition of and rationale for this approach (Denton, 1970, pp. 1–4, 7–9):

> It has long been recognized that schools for the deaf must find more effective means for developing communication skills and teaching language to very young deaf children. It has also been recognized, and widely accepted as fact, that the level of academic achievement of most deaf students is unacceptably low. Recognition of the existence of these problems is reason enough for a fundamental shift in educational practices in schools for the deaf in America. *[Fundamental shift long overdue]*
>
> By total communication is meant the right of every deaf child to learn to use all forms of communication in order that he [or she] may have the full opportunity to develop language competence at the earliest age possible. This implies the introduction of a reliable receptive expressive symbol system in the preschool years between the ages of one and five. Total communication includes the full spectrum of language modes; child-devised gesture, formal sign language, speech, speechreading, fingerspelling, reading and writing. With total communication every deaf child has the opportunity to develop every remnant of residual hearing by aids and/or high fidelity group amplification systems. *[Definition of total communication]*
>
> Communication between parents and child begins at birth, evolving from primitive gestures to more sophisticated forms. The parent is not asked to become a teacher but is encouraged to communicate to the deaf child through normal day-to-day experiences using a medium which is mutually understood. Thus, communication grows out of positive human interaction.
>
> . . . the early and consistent use of a system of total communication serves as a springboard for intellectual development and subsequent academic achievement. The ultimate key to academic success appears to be reading and comprehension skills. To fully understand the relationship between a total communication system and reading skills, . . . trace the steps backward, beginning with reading comprehension. Reading comprehension is based upon and grows out of rich and vast language experiences. Language experiences are amassed through communication. Finally, communication is based upon and grows out of human interaction. Meaningful human interaction should not arbitrarily be postponed, and the natural sequence in the developmental process of communication should not be violated arbitrarily. *[Interaction → communication → language → reading ability]*

The natural sequence in developing the process of communication can be summed up as follows:

1. Signs are the easiest means of getting the very young congenitally deaf child to communicate in the true sense of the word, that is, to express *his own* ideas. When this happens, we see positive changes in behavior and improvement in interpersonal relationships. The deaf child joins the family as a fully participating member.
2. Signs reinforce speechreading and audition when the adult (teacher, parent, houseparent) signs and talks simultaneously and the child is using amplification adequate for his needs. For the child who cannot benefit from amplification (very few in number), signs reinforce speechreading. Speech for this child must be developed purely on a kinesthetic basis. Language development, however, is not tied to his progress in speech. When speech and signs are practiced simultaneously, acceptable syntactic structure is more likely to occur. This is usually the way a hearing person learns to associate signs with words. The combination of speech and sign provides a syntactical model for the deaf child to imitate, both visually and auditorially. When a deaf adult uses speech with signs, he consciously organizes his signing syntactically. Consequently, deaf persons improve their oral skills and hearing persons improve their manual skills. The result is better communication skill for both.
3. Audition (high gain amplification) reinforces aural-oral skills (speech and speechreading) for many deaf children when equipment is of a quality to facilitate hearing. Success in this area is dependent upon auditory feedback or the degree to which the child can hear his own as well as the speech of others.
4. Fingerspelling reinforces reading and writing. Fingerspelling requires about the same level of maturation and background of language experience as reading and writing. We do not consider it any more practical to start the preschool deaf child with fingerspelling than we do to start the hearing preschool child's language development with reading and writing. Signs provide the "coin of exchange" for transmission of ideas and for generation of syntax at any early age (Denton, 1970).

Oral vs. total approach depends on degree of loss

Total communication is now widely used throughout the United States, and in 1970 the National Association of the Deaf joined in support of the concept. Many other state residential schools and day schools have since incorporated this approach to develop a firm language base during the child's early formative years and to enhance the effectiveness of training programs. Total communication works well with profoundly deaf children and with those who do not have sufficient hearing to benefit from a strictly oral method of teaching; *but for children with sufficient resid-*

ual hearing or only mild to moderate hearing losses, an oral approach is extremely effective.

Periodic reassessment   Since not all children (whether hearing or hearing disabled) learn in the same manner, no one method of teaching is appropriate for all children. Teachers must continually assess the program and the child's progress in it. They should not be locked into one particular approach but should be willing to explore available alternatives in order to provide the best possible educational program (Nix, 1974). Figure 1-6 in Unit 1 clearly points out the need for periodic reassessment of each child to determine whether the educational program needs to be modified.

Avoid being locked into one approach

Morning activities take a lot of concentration. Lunch period is a good time for refueling, then relaxing with a short siesta.

Research findings The studies cited here were conducted on the deaf, not the hard-of-hearing or those children who benefit from amplification (hearing aids). Research indicates that these students appear to assimilate more information when taught by manual and total communication than when taught by the oral technique (White & Stevenson, 1975). English, or the oral approach, is often taught as a second language to young deaf students whose primary means of communication is sign language. Educators speculate that early experience with sign language may facilitate the deaf student's effort to learn English at a later time (Charrow & Fletcher, 1974). Studies suggest that deaf people themselves prefer total communication and that manual communication facilitates the development of other communicative skills (Vernon, 1972). The most convincing study to support teaching the deaf by total or manual communication is reported by Vernon and Koh (1971). Deaf children who had completed an intensive three-year oral preschool education were compared with deaf children who had no preschool education but who were raised in an environment that encouraged early manual communication skills. The latter were superior academically and in language skills to those attending the oral school. In fact, children who were reared in an oral environment but who had not attended preschool nor learned manual communication performed comparably to children who had attended the oral school for three years. In essence, it would appear that total or manual communication is more effective for the deaf, and that it at least gives them a means of communicating that is superior to the oral approach.

Again, bear in mind that these studies are comparing deaf children, not the hard-of-hearing. Obviously, controversy still exists over the relative merits of the various teaching methods discussed above. Educators will utilize the approach that works best with their particular students. It behooves the teacher, therefore, to be thoroughly familiar with all the techniques available to teach the hearing impaired.

Parental participation in educational programs

Educational programs that take place in day schools, special education classrooms, institutions and with itinerant teachers are detailed in Unit 1. Here we will focus on home intervention and parental involvement.

Home programs Some of the earliest programs to develop correspondence courses, model home demonstrations and summer schools for parents of deaf children are from the John Tracy Clinic in Los Angeles, Central Institute for the Deaf in St. Louis, and the Bill Wilkerson Hearing and Speech Center in Nashville. These agencies and others in various parts of the country have instituted helpful developmental programs for parents to use with their very young deaf children. Correspondence courses are available to anyone, and in some instances they are free. Demonstration homes that simulate home surroundings are available to help parents recognize and use the multiplicity of opportunities for language development that exist in their own homes. Summer schools are planned for both parents, when possible, and their hearing disabled children. They receive instruction and practicum supervision and guidance is provided.

A more recent innovation is the Family Learning Vacation sponsored by the Department of Continuing Education, Gallaudet College, Washington, D.C. Currently this program operates two-week summer sessions. As in the aforementioned programs, demonstrations are given to explain how parents can interact with their children in various home activities—by reading to them, for example. The program also offers lectures on various considerations in communication development, ways of expanding language and exposing the child to new and needed vocabulary, and sign language instruction. Guest speakers include deaf adults and instructors from the Kendall Elementary Demonstration School and the Model Secondary School for the Deaf, both located on the Gallaudet College campus. Finally, parents who have reared deaf children are on hand for peer counseling.

A home program that has recently been successful in several individual states, Language Development Programs Through Home Intervention, is an educational service developed in Utah. It has since been adopted successfully by several other states and supported by their appropriate state agencies. The objectives and activities of the model program in Utah are as follows (Clark, 1975):

Objectives

The project identifies hearing impaired infants, birth to five years, provides audiological treatment and services, then provides home visit services to develop an infant-parent program which facilitates language development in the home environment. All services are correlated with existing agencies serving target children.

Expanding children's hearing opportunities

(1) Hospitals administer a high-risk screening questionnaire to detect hearing loss in infants. (2) An infant recheck program to screen hearing at six months of age is used. (3) Audiological testing and fitting of hearing aids follows. (4) A test battery including language, psychological, and social adjustment is available. (5) Parent groups are formulated for peer counseling adjustment. (6) Each home is visited regularly to assist parents in maximizing the linguistic environment in the home. (7) The home visit program is to make the parent an effective manager of the child's language environment. Parents are instructed in the use and maintenance of the hearing aid and how to develop the child's residual hearing to its maximum. The parent then learns to use home-family activities in a way that will be linguistically and auditorally meaningful to the child. Information about child growth and development is given (pp. 1–2).

General educational achievement

Educational achievement appears to be closely correlated with reading comprehension. The ability to read, sometimes stated as the ability to get information from printed material, is a goal for all children. Poor readers, whether they are hearing disabled or not, are also most likely to be low academic achievers.

The overall academic achievement of those affected by hearing loss is shockingly low. Investigations over the last fifty years show that the deaf and hard-of-hearing possess the same intelligence range as the general hearing population. However, further studies reveal gross academic retardation for a great majority of these children as compared to their hearing peers, pointing to relative failure on the part of existing educational systems (Vernon, 1969).

One of the most extensive national surveys of educational achievement included 93 percent of deaf students sixteen years or older in the United States. *Only 5 percent of the students achieved at a tenth-grade level or better, and most of these were hard-of-hearing or adventitiously deaf. Sixty percent were at grade level 5.3 or below and 30 percent were functionally illiterate* (Vernon, 1969). These are appalling statistics, particularly when we take into account that these children and youth are of average or above-average intelligence. Another study citing similar statistics, based on the Metropolitan Achievement Test, included seventy-three school programs and 54 percent of all school-age deaf children between the ages of ten and sixteen. Reading scores revealed that 88 percent of the sixteen-year-olds were below grade 4.9 and that the average reading gain over this six-year span was slightly less than one grade level (Wrightstone et al., 1962).

Deaf children have the innate ability to learn language. The hearing loss need not be an insurmountable barrier. If they are exposed to language in its most visible forms during the earliest years of life, it is postulated that they will learn and use language chronologically at a rate comparable to their hearing peers. Until such opportunities are available to the majority of deaf children, using a combination of teaching methods, it is doubtful, indeed, that their educational achievement will be significantly improved.

Academic curriculum

Quite often, the academic curriculum in schools for the hearing disabled is patterned after school models for hearing children. A difficulty may arise with textbooks, particularly if the school follows a state-adopted list as required for certification of school graduates by many state boards of education. More light is shed on the difficulty when we realize that such books are based on hearing language; therefore, reading them is usually a frustrating experience for the deaf pupil (Levine, 1960). Even though the educational process may be slower than it is in regular schools for hearing children, schools for the deaf offer the full range of academic subjects, vocational training, and sports.

Schools for the hearing disabled naturally place great emphasis on the early development of language skills. Of their many structured systems for teaching language, perhaps the most widely used are the Fitzgerald Key and Wing's Symbols (North Dakota School for the Deaf, 1950; Doctor, 1969; Fitzgerald, 1949). These systems are used primarily with *written language* and were devised to illustrate proper sentence structure. Incorrectly written and spoken language can be restructured.

Another system used to teach early language skills is known as the natural method (Groht, 1958). Based on the theory that hearing disabled children can become as fluent in English as are hearing children and that the capacity to use language appropriately is developed only through opportunities to practice it correctly in meaningful situations, this method attempts to make language learning as natural and normal a process for the hearing disabled as it is for hearing children. They are taught appropriate language to accompany their activities in meaningful situations. Emphasis is placed on the belief that a concept should be learned in the way it will be used, and this fact should prompt the teacher to ensure that there is sufficient motivation present for learning. This approach can be quite positive.

The "natural" method

Visuomotor perceptual training is an area that receives considerable attention in the curriculum of the hearing disabled. This area includes training in motor coordination, figure-ground perception, perceptual constancy, perception of position in space, perception of spatial relationships, and sensorimotor development (Frostig et

Visuomotor perceptual training

Assessing Eddie's hearing level. The pure-tone audiogram obtained in this audiometric test will indicate the decibel level at which Eddie can hear the signal for pegging.

al., 1972; Manolakes et al., 1968). Essentially, such training is designed to raise the students' deficient skills to a level that is necessary for academic success, as usually measured by adjustment and/or progress. The students are also presented with experiences that will stimulate them to explore and discover the world about them.

Directions in educational programs

The hearing disabled as resource people

Recent years have seen more consumer involvement in educational program planning than ever before. Because of national priorities concerning the severely handicapped, many hearing disabled adults are now being consulted by schools in an attempt to improve services through client feedback. The total communication approach is being incorporated more fully into the education of hearing disabled children, particularly in public day and residential schools.

Another popular concern is mainstreaming, discussed at length in Unit 1. Public Law #94-142 mandates that communities provide education locally for hearing disabled children rather than send them to special state or regional schools. When one considers that hearing impairment is the single most prevalent physical disability in America, the need for greater local support is understandable.

Early detection and treatment of hearing loss and language development programs that involve parents are examples of current directions in deaf education. Home intervention programs enable the parent to be an active participant in the child's development rather than a confused, frustrated bystander.

General trends and needs in today's society

A clearinghouse and a platform

Even though society has improved its treatment of hearing disabled people and become more accepting of them, a stigma still remains. People who have had little or no contact with this population often imagine them to be less intelligent or less capable than themselves. Organizations for the deaf and hard-of-hearing have cooperated with professional service groups to form a Council for the Hearing Impaired that gives hearing disabled people a unified voice, a centralized source of information, a clearinghouse for exchange of views, and a platform for establishing action plans on behalf of hearing disabled consumers (Williams, 1971). Councils of organizations now serve the deaf and hard-of-hearing in every state and a national headquarters has been established.

Parent groups give support and advocacy

The need for strong parent organizations becomes apparent each time parents discover that they have a hearing disabled child. Becoming involved with other parents who have reared hearing disabled children can do wonders to dispel the guilt, fear, and frustration that usually accompany the unanticipated (Foreman, 1975). Parent groups provide peer support and solutions that no professional or agency can. The International Organization of Parents of the Deaf, currently located at the headquarters of the National Association of the Deaf in Silver Spring, Maryland, has done much to promote parent organizations at the local level.

Adequate mental health services are also in great demand. Counselors of all kinds abound in our country, but very few are able to communicate with the deaf through sign language or any means other than the most superficial. As a result, not many deaf people receive the professional counseling they need. Many people, simply because they know sign language, are being called upon to help with problems they are unqualified to handle. Clergy who have learned this skill are forced to deal with concerns that are the province of social workers. The obvious solution is for mental health agencies to train staff members to work with hearing impaired clients and to teach them manual communication skills. In some states, rehabilitation counselors, social workers, nurses, law enforcement officers, and others are being given deafness sensitivity training, which consists of information about the problems and needs of the deaf and elementary sign language instruction.

Mental health services are limited

Perhaps the greatest need is for public awareness and education about problems confronting the hearing disabled. This would make it easier for them to gain acceptance at home, in school, on the job, and in the community. Efforts to sensitize the public to the needs of the deaf and to make the deaf aware of services available to them are enjoying more success. Groups like the National Theater of the Deaf, which tours the United States and other countries, and the World Deaf Olympics have done much to correct misconceptions about the limitations of the deaf. Through community service organizations, educational television, and other means the deaf world and hearing world are coming together. It is not unusual to see the evening news broadcast simultaneously in sign language, or captioned, and soon it will be equally common to see the hearing disabled use the telephone, although the device is still too expensive for most. A flashing light in one or more rooms indicates that the telephone is ringing. When it is answered, the parties can communicate by means of a telephone-typewriter system on which messages are typed and read.

National Theater of the Deaf

Summary

This unit has reviewed types of hearing problems, their causes, and the effects of a hearing loss upon the child's social, cognitive, personality, and intellectual development. It has outlined the educational approaches most often adopted with the hearing disabled and has compared their educational achievement level to that of the hearing population.

It is not sympathy the deaf seek, but acceptance for what they are and for what they have the right to become. They merely ask for an opportunity to lead as normal and full a life as possible, with respect to language acquisition, academic achievement, vocational training, placement and security, and social development.

References and resources

Bergstrom, L.; Hemenway, W. G.; and Downs, M. P. "A High Risk Registry to Find Congenital Deafness." *Otolaryngology Clinics of North America* 4 (1971): 369–99.

Charrow, V. R., and Fletcher, J. D. "English as the Second Language of Deaf Children." *Developmental Psychology* 10 (1974): 463–70.

Clark, T. *Project Ski-Hi, A State-wide Program for Identification and Language Facilitation for Hearing Handicapped Children Through Home Management.* Presented at a workshop at the Oklahoma School for the Deaf, Sulphur, Okla., 1975.

Committee on Professional Preparation Certification. *Standards for the Certification of Teachers of the Hearing Impaired.* Council on Education of the Deaf, 1972.

Conference of Executives of American Schools for the Deaf. "Report of the Conference Committee on Nomenclature." *American Annals of the Deaf* 83 (1938): 1–3.

Denton, D. M. "Total Communication." Maryland School for the Deaf, 1970.

Doctor, P. V., ed. *Communication with the Deaf: A Guide for Parents of Deaf Children.* Washington, D.C.: The American Annals of the Deaf, 1969.

Farwell, R. N. "Speech Reading: A Research Review." *The American Annals of the Deaf* 121 (1976): 19–30.

Fitzgerald, E. *Straight Language for the Deaf.* Washington, D.C.: The Volta Bureau, 1949.

Foreman, W. J. "Importance of Early Counseling for Parents of Deaf Children." *Tulsa Speech and Hearing Association Newsletter,* 1975.

Frostig, M.; Horne, D.; and Miller, A. *Pictures and Patterns.* Rev. ed. Chicago: Follett, 1972.

Furth, H. G. *Thinking Without Language.* New York: Free Press, 1966.

Furth, H. G. *Deafness and Learning: A Psychosocial Approach.* Belmont, Calif.: Wadsworth, 1973.

Groht, M. A. *Natural Language for Deaf Children.* Washington, D.C.: Alexander Graham Bell Association for the Deaf, 1958.

Harford, E. R. *How They Hear.* Northbrook, Ill.: Gordon N. Stowe and Associates, 1964.

Hawkins, J. E., Jr. "Antibiotic Insults to Corti's Organ." In *Sensorineural Hearing Processes and Disorders,* edited by A. B. Graham, pp. 411–25. Boston: Little, Brown, 1967.

Konismark, B. W. "Genetic Hearing Loss with No Associated Abnormalities: A Review." *Journal of Speech and Hearing Disorders* 37 (1972): 89–99.

Lennenberg, E. "What Is Meant by Biological Approach to Language." *The American Annals of the Deaf* 115 (1970): 67–72.

Levine, E. S. *The Psychology of Deafness: Techniques of Appraisal for Rehabilitation,* New York: Columbia University Press, 1960.

Manolakes, G.; Weltman, R.; Scian, M. J.; and Waldo, L. *Try: Experiences for Young Children.* New York: Noble and Noble, 1968.

Mays, T. *The Deaf Man and the Law.* Washington, D.C.: Council of Organizations Serving the Deaf, 1970.

McConnell, F. "Children with Hearing Disabilities." In *Exceptional Children in the Schools,* edited by L. C. Dunn, pp. 349–410. 2nd ed. New York: Holt, 1973.

Miller, J. B. "Oralism." *Volta Review* 72 (1970): 211–17.

Mindel, E., and Vernon, M. *They Grow in Silence.* Silver Spring, Md.: National Association of the Deaf, 1971.

Myklebust, H. B. *The Psychology of Deafness.* New York: Grune and Stratton, 1960.

Nix, G. "Total Communication: A Review of the Studies Offered in Its Support." *Volta Review* 77 (1974): 470–94.

North Dakota School for the Deaf. *An Exposition of Wing's Symbols.* Devil's Lake, N.D.: 1950.

Northcutt, W. H., ed. *The Hearing Impaired Child in a Regular Classroom.* Washington, D.C.: Alexander Graham Bell Association for the Deaf, 1973.

Northern, J. L., and Downs, M. P. *Hearing in Children.* Baltimore, Md.: Williams and Wilkins, 1974.

Office of Demographic Studies. *Annual Survey of Hearing Impaired Children and Youth, United States: 1970–71.* Washington, D.C.: Gallaudet College Press, 1973.

Quigley, S. P. *The Influence of Fingerspelling on the Development of Language, Communication and Educational Achievement in Deaf Children.* Washington, D.C.: Rehabilitation Services Administration, Department of Health, Education and Welfare, 1969.

Raviv, S.; Sharan, S.; and Strauss, S. "Intellectual Development of Deaf Children in Different Educational Environments." *Journal of Communication Disorders* 6 (1973): 29–36.

Rosenstein, J. "Cognitive Abilities in Deaf Children." *Journal of Speech and Hearing Research* 3 (1960): 108–19.

Rosenstein, J. "Perception, Cognition, and Language in Deaf Children." *Exceptional Children* 27 (1961): 276–84.

Schein, J. D. *The Deaf Community: Studies in the Social Psychology of Deafness.* Washington, D.C.: Gallaudet College Press, 1968.

Schlesinger, H. S., and Meadow, K. P. *Sound and Sign: Childhood Deafness and Mental Health.* Berkeley, Calif.: University of California Press, 1972.

Stone, A. V. "Oral Education: A Challenge and a Necessity." *Volta Review* 70 (1968): 287–92.

U.S. Office of Education. *Estimated Number of Handicapped Children in the United States, 1971–72.* Washington, D.C.: USOE, 1971.

Vernon, M. "Sociological and Psychological Factors Associated with Hearing Loss." *Journal of Speech and Hearing Research* 12 (1969): 541–63.

Vernon, M. "Mind over Mouth: A Rationale for Total Communication." *Volta Review* 74 (1972): 529–40.

Vernon, M., and Koh, S. D. "Effects of Oral Preschool Compared to Early Manual Communication on Education and Communication in Deaf Children." *American Annals of the Deaf* 116 (1971): 569–74.

Vernon, M., and Mindel, E. "Psychological and Psychiatric Aspects of Profound Hearing Loss." In *Audiological Assessment,* edited by D. E. Rose, pp. 87–132. Englewood Cliffs, N.J.: Prentice-Hall, 1971.

White, A. H., and Stevenson, V. M. "The Effects of Total Communication, Manual Communication, Oral Communication and Reading on the Learning of Factual Information in Residential School Deaf Children." *The American Annals of the Deaf* 120 (1975): 48–57.

Williams, B. R. "The Deaf Community Matures." Paper presented at the Guest Lecture Series, North Carolina School for the Deaf. Morgantown, N.C., 1971.

Willis, D. J.; Wright, L.; and Wolfe, J. "WISC and Nebraska Performance of Deaf and Hearing Children." *Perceptual and Motor Skills* 34 (1972): 783–88.

Willis, D. J.; Walcott, S.; and Jones, J. "Cognitive and Perceptual Development of Deaf Children as Measured by the Grassi Basic Cognitive Evaluation Test." Unpublished manuscript, 1973.

Wrightstone, J. W.; Aronow, M. S.; and Moskowitz, S. "Developing Reading Test Norms for the Deaf Child." *The American Annals of the Deaf* 108 (1962): 311–16.

Alexander Graham Bell Association
  for the Deaf
3417 Volta Place, NW
Washington, D.C. 20007

Center on Deafness
600 Waukegan Road
Glenview, Illinois 60025

Developmental Learning Materials
7440 Natchez Avenue
Niles, Illinois 61148

Dormac, Inc.
P.O. Box 1622
Lake Oswego, Oregon 97034

Educational Activities, Inc.
Freeport, New York 11520

Educational Distribution Center
Captioned Films for the Deaf
5034 Wisconsin Avenue, NW
Washington, D.C. 20016

Follett Publishing Company
1010 W. Washington Boulevard
Chicago, Illinois 60607

Gallaudet College Book Store
Florida Avenue and 7th St., NE
Washington, D.C. 20002

General Educational Materials
P.O. Box 842
Independence, Missouri 64052

Gordon W. Stowe and Associates
P.O. Box 233-A
Northbrook, Illinois 60062

International Association of Parents
 of the Deaf
814 Thayer Avenue
Silver Spring, Maryland 20910

John Tracy Clinic
806 West Adams Blvd.
Los Angeles, California 90007

National Association of the Deaf
814 Thayer Avenue
Silver Spring, Maryland 20910

Noble and Noble, Publishers, Inc.
750 Third Avenue
New York, New York 10017

Phonics Corporation
814 Thayer Avenue
Silver Spring, Maryland 20910

Photo School Films, Inc.
3770 Tracy Street
Los Angeles, California 90027

Volta Speech Association for the Deaf
1537 35th Street, NW
Washington, D.C. 20036

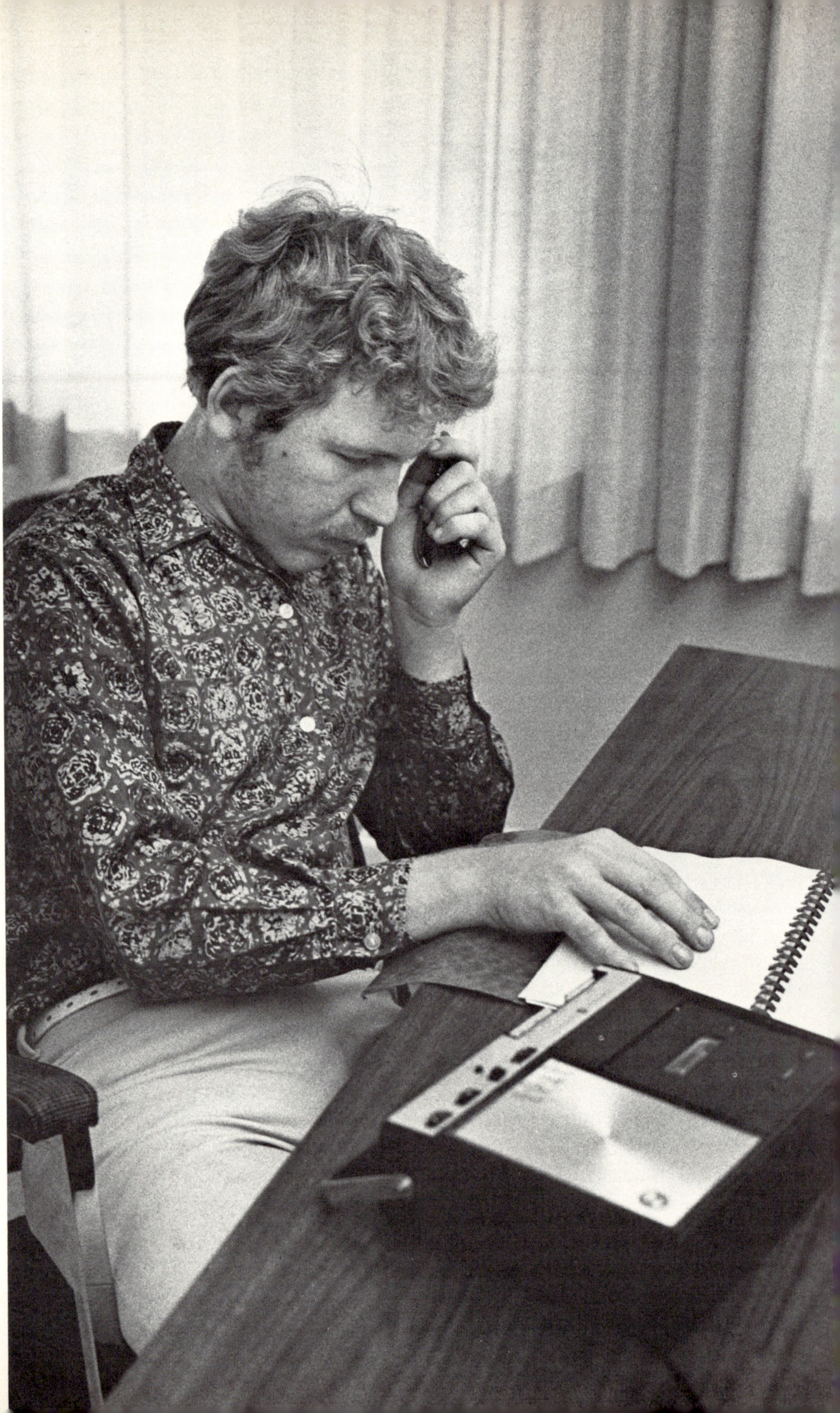

10 Visually disabled children and youth

Diane J. Willis
Cathy Groves
Wanda Fuhrmann

Facts and fallacies about visually disabled children and youth
Who are the visually disabled? · Prevalence and incidence · Causal factors · Symptoms of possible visual disorders · Eye specialists
Anatomy and function of the eye · Protective structures · Refractive structures · Muscular structures · Receptive structures
How visual disabilities are assessed · Snellen chart · Barrage visual efficiency scale
Personal-social development of visually disabled children · Mother-child interaction · Stimulation techniques
Motor milestones · Sitting · Crawling
Language development
Cognitive development
Psychological overview of the visually disabled · Self-concept · Body image · Concept formation · Mannerisms · Adjustment problems · Psychological testing · Fostering social and emotional growth in the school environment
Academic curriculum and training programs · Mobility training and orientation · Decisions about primary mode of learning · Braille · Reading print · The Optacon for reading
Combined visual and hearing disorders · Causes · Diagnosis and evaluation · Prevention
Trends in educational programs
Summary

333

Student learning objectives

The student will:
1. distinguish between fact and fiction about the blind and partially sighted
2. recognize the range of abilities and limitations of the visually disabled
3. learn the major causes of visual problems
4. learn the major anatomical structures of the eye and will recognize major visual problems associated with each
5. learn the symptoms that suggest possible visual problems
6. learn about visual assessment techniques and how to assess the visually disabled child's primary mode of learning
7. be aware of the impact that blindness can have on the personal-social, motor, and language development of the child and of the importance of early stimulation
8. become familiar with the psychological development of the visually disabled, including influences on self-concept and ways of enhancing self-esteem
9. recognize blindisms, and learn ways to eliminate adverse mannerisms
10. become acquainted with relevant mobility and educational aids used to enhance the learning of the visually disabled
11. become aware of the ways a teacher can facilitate social and emotional growth and reduce adjustment problems at school
12. become familiar with major resources where special materials and equipment can be obtained for teaching the visually disabled to read

In the film "Butterflies are Free" a young blind man, Don Baker, is attempting to live independently in the adult world. He meets, courts, and almost loses his girl, Jill. We are caught up in the struggles Don faces. He is portrayed as a healthy, sensitive young man, a characterization that contradicts prevailing attitudes toward the visually disabled. While interaction with this group has done much to change public opinion, there are still those who consider visually disabled people to be extremely limited in what they can attain. Fortunately, the last ten years have witnessed many educational, vocational, and personal-social-cognitive attainments for this population.

Facts and fallacies about visually disabled children

Stereotypes about the blind

Observers have noted similarities as well as differences in the behavior of sighted and visually disabled children. Severely visually disabled children do not necessarily move out spontaneously like their sighted counterparts; they must be taught to play. Once adequately stimulated and taught, the visually disabled enjoy play activities, but in a slightly different manner.

Visually disabled children can vary in their motor and verbal behavior. Although somewhat restricted, their later vocational choices are not nearly as limited as we would believe. In fact, society's attitude rather than their physical disability often circumscribes the job and training activities of the blind or visually impaired. As we noted, some sighted people persist in the false notion that the blind and visually impaired are helpless, unproductive, and maladjusted and hence to be pitied, feared, or avoided. Others think that they are superior in their ability to use senses other than sight, or that they live in a world of darkness, gifted with magical or supernatural powers. Such attitudes are devastating, as well as untrue. The visually disabled, even the blind, enjoy riding bicycles, roller skating, snow skiing, dancing, and any number of activities that sighted youngsters perform. In this unit we will find that societal and particularly parental attitudes toward a visually disabled child influence not only the child's self-image and self-confidence, but his or her academic and vocational attainment as well. *Parental attitudes are crucial*

All children develop in a sequential manner, although their timetables can vary; that is to say, visually disabled children may develop more slowly than others. This is due in part to the fact that a very large percentage are multihandicapped and require a team approach to their medical, social, and educational problems.

This unit will concern itself mainly with the visually disabled (a term that refers to both blind and partially sighted people) who do not present other compounding handicaps, but it also contains a section on the deaf-blind child. In addition to providing general information about the visually disabled, the unit will emphasize early identification and intervention strategies, which are so crucial to this population. If the child is to be adequately prepared for life, appropriate resources must be available to aid the parents as they learn to adapt to their child's needs. *Early intervention strategies*

Who are the visually disabled?

Before discussing precise definitions in this area of exceptionality, it is important that we become familiar with state and federal legislation that directly affects the visually disabled and other exceptional children. For example, recent laws offer tax relief to parents who are paying for special services needed by their exceptional children. This has been a tremendous help to many families, and professional people working with the visually disabled child should be knowledgeable enough about the laws to inform parents of these special benefits.

The definitions for the visually disabled were first adopted in 1935 from the Social Security Act passed by Congress. The guidelines were subsequently passed by most states. The visually disabled must satisfy state and federal definitions in order to be eligible for income tax exemptions, for special teaching materials from the American Printing House for the Blind, and for state service programs. The Social Security definitions of *blind* and *partially sighted* are as follows: *Congressional guidelines*

Blindness is generally defined in the United States as visual acuity for distant vision of 20/200 or less in the better eye, with best correction; or visual acuity of more than 20/200 if the widest diameter of field of vision subtends an angle no greater than 20 degrees or, in some states, 30 degrees.

The partially seeing are defined as persons with a visual acuity greater than 20/200 but not greater than 20/70 in the better eye after correction (National Society for the Prevention of Blindness, 1966, p. 10).

What do these definitions mean? In general, a measure of 20/200 visual acuity means that a blind person can see at a distance up to twenty feet after visual correction what a person with normal vision can see at two hundred feet. Blind people, then, are not *necessarily* totally blind (without light perception), although a few people are totally blind. The partially sighted are generally capable of seeing at twenty feet what we can see at seventy feet.

Functional definition

For more practical purposes we prefer to adopt the functional definitions proposed by Harley (1973). The blind, for educational purposes, are children whose visual impairment is severe enough that they read primarily through the medium of braille. Partially seeing children are those who can generally read large or regular print under optimum conditions.

Prevalence and incidence

Prevalence refers to the number of blind or partially sighted people in our population in a given year. Because the state registers of the blind are not completely reliable, prevalence data (number of blind or partially sighted in our population in a given year) cannot be presumed accurate.

The incidence rates of the number of children with visual defects severe enough to warrant special educational services, are estimated to be 0.14 percent (fourteen per ten thousand) partially seeing and 0.01 percent (one per ten thousand) blind (U.S. Office of Education, 1971). As of 1971 and 1972 there were approximately 30,630 children in the U.S. enrolled in special education classes for the blind and visually impaired (USOE, 1971). In the same report, the American Printing House for the Blind projects higher estimates based on the number of legal and educationally blind school age children registered with them. They cite an incidence figure of 0.04 percent.

Least widespread exceptionality

With the number of school-age children decreasing and the number of elderly increasing, it is not surprising that most visual disabilities in the U.S. occur in people sixty-five years of age or older (National Society for the Prevention of Blindness, 1966). Only about 10 percent of the total population of legally visually disabled people are school-age children, and about one-third to one-half of that 10 percent have some other handicap in addition to their visual problem.

What these statistics tell us is that visual impairment is the least widespread exceptionality requiring special education, and that there are more partially sighted children than blind. A great many children wear glasses and need professional eye care, but their visual problems are not serious enough to warrant special education.

Causal factors

Prenatal influences, including hereditary and congenital problems, are the leading cause (64.4 percent) of visual disability in children and youth. Prenatally determined visual disabilities cannot be prevented until this causal relationship is better understood. Infectious diseases such as syphilis are the second leading cause (23.2 percent) of visual disabilities in children under five years of age. *Congenital and hereditary problems*

Sixteen percent of visual disabilities in children and youth are of undetermined origin and occur postnatally. Such a high incidence arising from unknown origins suggests that there is a need for medical investigation in this area. General diseases, such as diabetes and vascular disorders, and conditions such as glaucoma, myopia, and senile cataract, whose origins are unknown to science, can lead to visual disabilities in people of all ages (National Society for the Prevention of Blindness, 1966). *Diseases*

In the 1940s and 1950s retrolental fibroplasia (caused by excessive oxygen affecting the retina) was responsible for a high incidence of visual impairment in children. Premature infants were most vulnerable to this condition because of the excessive amount of oxygen they received while in an incubator. The cause for retrolental fibroplasia was discovered in 1952 and thereafter oxygen content was more carefully monitored, thus drastically reducing the number of children blinded by this type of poisoning. *Retrolental fibroplasia*

Our educational systems are still feeling the impact of the rubella epidemic in the 1960s that accounted for about one-half of all legal blindness with other multi-handicapping conditions. (The rubella epidemic is discussed later in this unit in the section on deaf-blind children and youth.)

Visual disabilities due to infections and poisonings have been greatly reduced in the 1970s because of advanced medical knowledge and more sophisticated monitoring equipment used to regulate oxygen for premature infants. Visual disabilities due to undetermined causes, prenatal influences, conditions not yet understood by science, and diabetes will continue to contribute to visual problems in children and youth, as will eye injuries caused by accidents. The National Society for the Prevention of Blindness has published information pertaining to prevention, incidence, and screening techniques useful in early identification of visual impairment.

Symptoms of possible visual disorders

Vision is not routinely checked in full-term, normal infants and children. Until a child is at least three years of age it is difficult or impossible to get a completely accurate assessment of either visual or hearing acuity. Parents, teachers, and other professionals working with children may suspect impaired vision in youngsters who *Early assessment of visual acuity is difficult*

1. frequently fall or bump into objects

2. hold objects unusually close or unusually far from their eyes (This includes children who hold reading material too close to their eyes.)
3. exhibit abnormal eye movements, such as rapid eye movements
4. are slow or poor readers (It is sensible to rule out the most obvious explanations for poor reading before looking further to see if the child's problem is attributable to other factors such as mental retardation or a learning disability.)
5. suffer frequent eye irritations, swollen eyelids, or watery eyes
6. rub their eyes, shake their head, frown, or squint as they look at near or far objects
7. complain of fuzzy vision or are unable to read or see something at a distance (Children who become restless and tired from visual strain may be mistakenly called hyperactive.)
8. tilt their head to one side while reading or close one eye or seem to be unable to see part of the visual field that is not directly in front of them
9. hold tightly to railings when walking down stairs and seem fearful of running freely (Bray, 1969; National Society for the Prevention of Blindness, 1969; Winebrenner, 1952)

This list does not exhaust the possible symptoms. The alert adult will sense when visual disabilities may be present and will schedule the child for a good examination.

Eye specialists

A visual examination may be conducted by either an ophthalmologist or an optometrist. An ophthalmologist (sometimes referred to as an oculist) is a medical doctor who specializes in treatment of the eye, including medication, surgery, and prescription of glasses (English & English, 1966). An optometrist is not a physician, but the field of optometry overlaps with ophthalmology in that the optometrist is trained to measure the eye and check its visual functions. The optometrist may prescribe glasses, visual training, or corrective exercises but may not perform surgery or use medication. An optician, as distinguished from an optometrist or ophthalmologist, is one who makes lenses for prescribed glasses.

Anatomy and function of the eye

The eye is an extremely complex sense organ that develops as a protrusion of a part of the third ventricle in the brain. Its amazing evolution is not totally understood by those who study its structure. The eye is shaped like a globe and operates something like a camera, that is, an image is focused by a lens and the amount of light entering the eye is adjustable, but the similarities end here.

The functioning of the visual system can be better understood if we first examine the structure of the eye (see Figure 10-1). The four parts of the visual system are: (1) protective, (2) refractive, (3) muscular, and (4) receptive (Harley, 1973).

Protective structures

The *protective structures* include the outer portions of the eye—the bony socket in which the eye is housed, the eyelashes, eyebrows, eyelids, and tears—which prevent or ward off trauma to the eyeball itself. Trachoma, or pink eye, a chronic contagious conjunctivitis, is a visual defect commonly found in this portion of the eye. Poor hygiene is thought to be a predisposing factor to this viral infection, whose early symptoms include pain and visual disturbances, drooping of the eyelid, and a foreign body sensation in the eye (Ophthalmologic Staff of Toronto Hospital, 1967).

Pink eye

Refractive structures

The *refractive structures* of the visual system include the cornea, aqueous humor, lens, and vitreous fluid. The parts are designed to focus light on the retina; that is, the lens changes shape to focus objects on the retina and the cornea seems to refract light (Figure 10-2). The more common refractive visual problems occurring in childhood are hyperopia (farsightedness), myopia (nearsightedness), cataract, astigmatism, and glaucoma. Figure 10-2 illustrates near- and farsightedness. If either the

**Figure 10.1
Structures of the human eye**

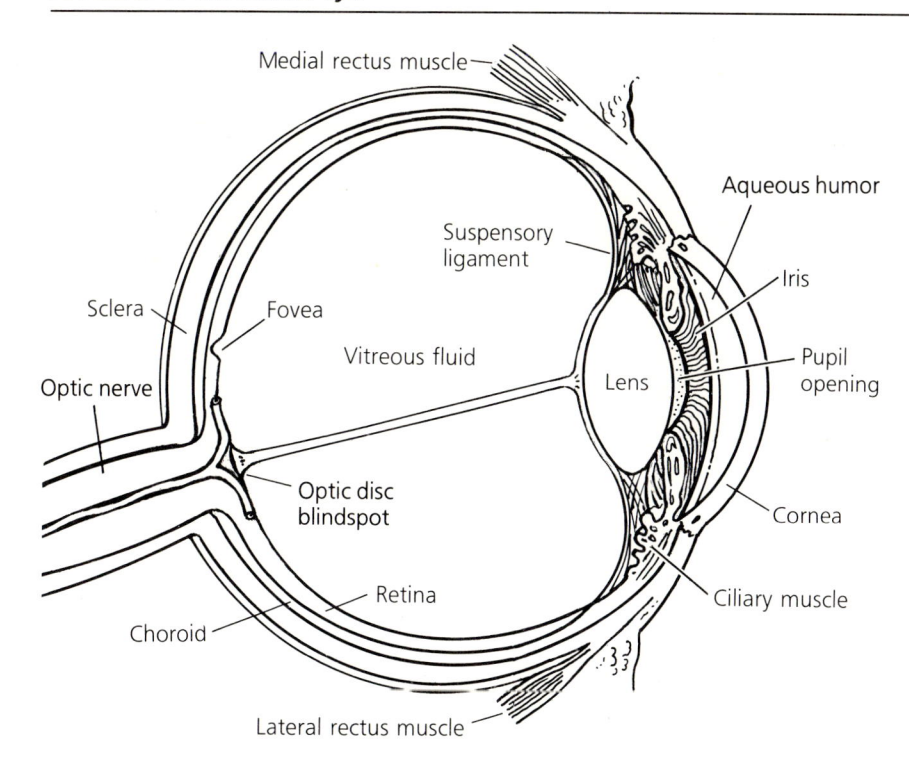

cornea or the lens of the eye is irregular, astigmatism develops. These three conditions sometimes require correction with glasses, since eye exercises alone do not necessarily produce any change or improvement. Glaucoma is a deficiency in aqueous flow that causes increased intra-ocular pressure. A diagnostic sign of glaucoma can be invaluable in preventing blindness, but diagnosis and treatment are not always successful. Glaucoma may be congenital (present at birth), or it may occur later. The same is true of cataracts, a cloudiness of the crystalline lens. Generally, children with cataracts should avoid bright light. Surgical treatment is usually recommended (Ophthalmologic Staff of Toronto Hospital, 1967).

Muscular structures

The *muscular structures* are six muscles connected to the eyeball. We use these muscles to turn our eyes up, down, left, or right. Children with muscular defects can have strabismus (crossed eyes), nystagmus (rapid, involuntary eye movements), or amblyopia (dimness of vision resulting from improper muscle balance). Strabismus may be corrected by surgery, nystagmus by the use of contact lenses in therapy, and amblyopia by wearing glasses and intermittently occluding the normal eye to strengthen the weak eye (Ophthalmologic Staff of Toronto Hospital, 1967).

Receptive structures

The *receptive structures* of the visual system include the retina, optic nerves, and occipital area of the brain (where vision takes place). Optic atrophy, retinitis pigmentosa, and retrolental fibroplasia are examples of visual impairment to the receptive structures. When the nerve fibers connecting the retina to the brain degenerate, the result is optic atrophy. Children suffering from this condition often have a restricted field of vision and may see smaller print better than large print on a chalkboard. The same is true of children who have retinitis pigmentosa. The latter is a hereditary degenerative process that affects the retina (Ophthalmologic Staff of Toronto Hospital, 1967). As was mentioned, retrolental fibroplasia is caused by giving too much oxygen to premature infants.

In addition to the above-mentioned disabilities, diseases, tumors or multihandicapping conditions that affect the central nervous system can also cause visual problems and disorders.

How visual disabilities are assessed

The Snellen Chart

The Snellen Chart is recommended as a yearly screening test for school-age children, but it must be supplemented by close observation of the child's visual behavior. It is used widely by physicians, nurses, and teachers because of the ease and quickness with which vision can be assessed. As shown in Figure 10-3, the Snellen Chart consists of rows of letters or objects (for the nonliterate) of different sizes. These repre-

Figure 10.2
*Accommodation of the lens
and examples of farsightedness and nearsightedness*

**The lens changes shape
to focus objects on the retina.**

Lens accommodation
for far objects

Lens accommodation
for near objects

The accommodation of the lens.
The lens flattens to focus images of objects far away, and it thickens to focus images of nearby objects. Note that much of the refraction, or bending, of the light is done by the cornea. This does not change. The changes due to the lens are added to this constant refraction caused by the cornea.

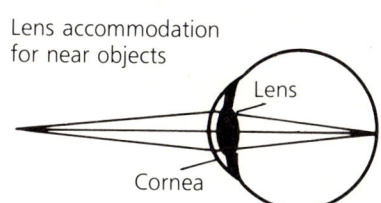

**When the eyeball is too short, a person
is farsighted: when it is too long,
a person is nearsighted.**

Normal eye — In focus on retina

Farsighted eye — Out of focus on retina, Focus here

Nearsighted eye — Focus here, Out of focus on retina

Farsightedness and nearsightedness.
In the normal person (top) the image is focused on the retina. The farsighted person (middle) has an eyeball that is too short and focuses images on a plane behind the retina. The nearsighted person (bottom) has an eyeball that is too long and focuses images on a plane in front of the retina. (Modified from Ruch, 1958.)

Source: Morgan & King, 1966, p. 287

sent what the person with normal vision sees at various distances. For example, if one has to stand twenty feet from the chart to see what the average person can see at one hundred feet, this would be 20/100 vision, which is not very good. If, however, one is standing twenty feet from the chart and can see the letters that the average person sees at ten feet, he or she has 20/10 vision, which is very good.

Snellen Chart has limitations

While the Snellen Chart is most widely used, it does have limitations—it mainly measures central distance vision. Far-sightedness or strabismus (squinting of eyes due to muscular incoordination, where the eyes may not be able to accommodate equally to an object), for instance, would not necessarily be detected unless supplemental vision tests such as the Massachusetts Vision Test were also administered. In general, if one carefully observes and records the child's visual behavior during the screening test, and if there is a history of presenting symptoms as outlined earlier, it is possible to obtain a fairly accurate assessment of the child's vision. Nothing, however, can supplement a thorough ophthalmological assessment, and when vision appears to be impaired according to results obtained on the Snellen Chart, an in-depth assessment should be recommended.

Barraga visual efficiency scale

Utilizing remaining vision

Often, children who do have perception of light, objects or motion are mistakenly assumed to be "too blind" to use vision as the primary means of learning (Barraga, 1970). Barraga (1964) developed a scale for assessing the visual efficiency of children with low vision. The purpose of this scale is to assess functional vision with the idea of teaching low-vision children to "look" or "see."

The scale is helpful to teachers or other specialists working with the visually disabled. It requires children to study an object or geometric design and find one like it or different from it (see Figure 10-4). One correct choice must be made out of four figures presented. The figures, objects, or words are of varying sizes and complexity to assess the child's ability to match them with the original stimulus figures. Visual learning can be maximized if low-vision children learn to use their remaining vision (Barraga, 1964).

The general objectives of the Barraga Scale are:

1. to determine the visual functioning level of each child who shows any visual potential (light perception, motion-object perception).
2. to develop individual prescriptive plans for the stimulation and development of all visual potential.
3. to develop an interest in and to foster a positive attitude toward "learning to see" activities.
4. to encourage greater control of eye muscles to facilitate fixation, tracking, and focus.
5. to offer encouragement, motivation, reinforcement, and support to the child in all visual activities.
6. to involve the child in preparing and assimilating a booklet relating to his or her daily accomplishments and overall achievement in visual performance.

Figure 10.3
The Snellen Chart

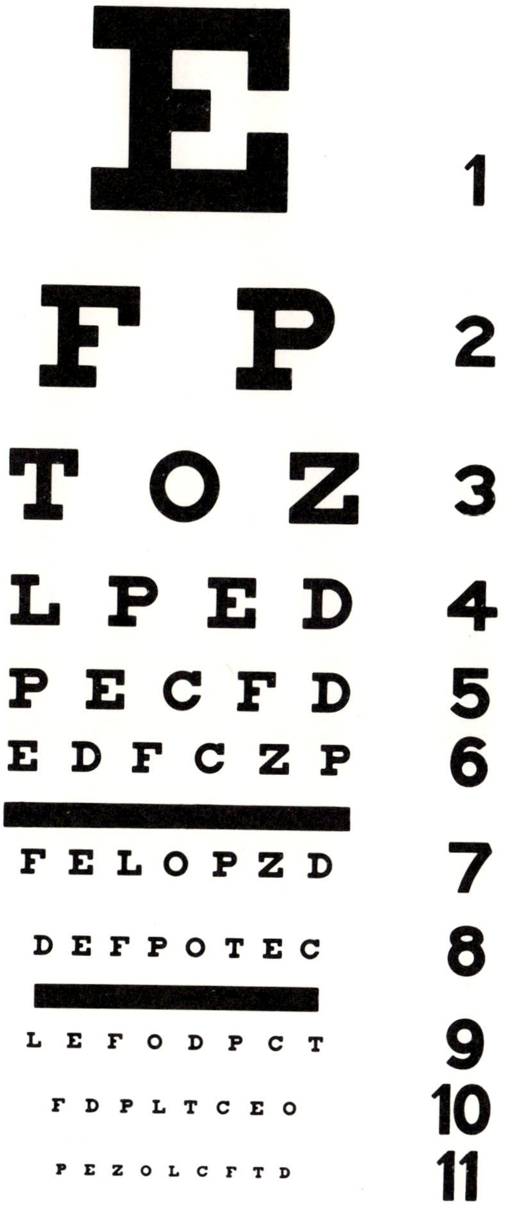

E   1

F P   2

T O Z   3

L P E D   4

P E C F D   5

E D F C Z P   6

F E L O P Z D   7

D E F P O T E C   8

L E F O D P C T   9

F D P L T C E O   10

P E Z O L C F T D   11

Source: Courtesy of the National Society for the Prevention of Blindness

344
Visually disabled
children and youth

7. to reassess visual functioning and efficiency after a period of training in visual development (1970, pp. 7–14).

Personal-social development of visually disabled children

Mother-child interaction

The visually disabled infant cannot participate fully in the stimulation that is typical of early interaction activities such as feeding, rocking, fondling, cuddling, bouncing, and body molding. Not only are these types of activities mutually enjoyed by mother

Figure 10.4
Sample test page from the Barraga Visual Efficiency Scale

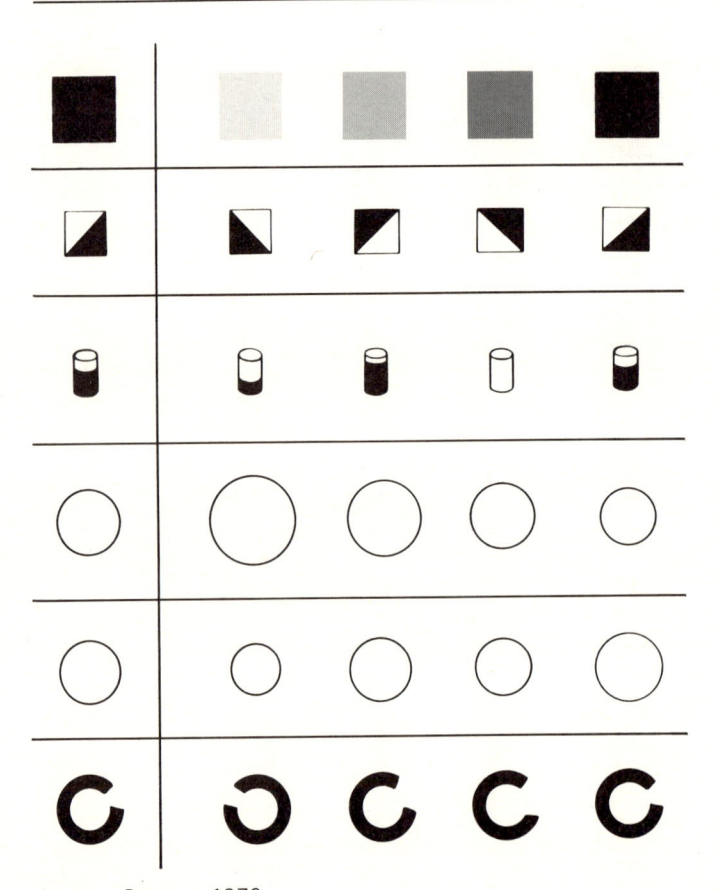

Source: Barraga, 1970

and child, they provide the kind of enriched stimulation and patterns of exchange that lay the foundation for the child's organization and understanding of the more complex stimulation presented by the larger environment. There is a "catch-22" with visually disabled children. Their *cueing modes* (varying means of signaling others to elicit certain responses) may develop in unconventional ways. One must be flexible enough to read these atypical cues. This is no easy task for a family. A case example of a visually disabled infant illustrates this process:

Visually disabled infants give atypical cues

> **Jimmy**   He was a difficult child to hold. Any type of typical snuggling that his mother tried to initiate was met with rebuff, and upon occasion, rage. Despite the understandable rejection and hurt his mother felt about Jimmy's response to her overtures, she dared to be different. She allowed Jimmy to remain on his pallet when taking his bottle. She stayed with him during the whole process, at first only singing to him. Then gradually she began to make body contact with him while he was feeding by sitting quite close to him. Several days later, Jimmy rested his head on her lap, while the rest of his body remained on his pallet. In this way his body movement was not restrained. Jimmy began to nuzzle his face close to his mother's abdomen intermittently during the feeding process.
>
> About a month after she had begun this process an occasion arose that prevented her from participating in the feeding ritual. Jimmy refused to eat. Eating had become more than nourishment time. It had become a mutually shared exchange between Jimmy and his mother, and she discovered she was indeed important to him. Jimmy was not rejecting *her* when he rejected *her style of holding*. She had taken the risk of coming to know Jimmy's unique system and she had responded within the confines he had imposed.
>
> As a consequence of meeting Jimmy where he was, his mother received in reciprocal fashion the type of "feeding" she needed from her child. This mutuality and reciprocity is critical to the evolution of the mother-child relationship. Without the child cueing the mother, the mother cannot be expected to continue to nurture, stimulate, and interact with the child.

The dilemma for the family of the visually disabled child is to decipher the cues and the modes of pressuring used by the infant to notify the family of who he or she is. Sometimes these clues are very difficult to read. In the case example cited above, how easy it would have been for Jimmy's mother to conclude from his signaling that "Jimmy just doesn't like me," rather than "Jimmy needs to be held in a different way."

Picture the infant who tightly grasps a mother's thumb and in a fleeting moment of wakefulness fixes on her face with ever-widening eyes. This type of response encourages the mother to interact with the infant and allows them to gaze at each other in mutual admiration. Now picture the opposite situation, in which the mother does not receive this response because the infant cannot focus on her face.

Absence of attachment behavior bonds

Attachment behavior may be totally lacking in the visually disabled child or may become evident only at later intervals. The insult caused by the lack of visual functioning deals a blow to the mother-child relationship. It can significantly alter the nature of the attachment process that binds the mother to the child and the child to the family, particularly if the child is totally, congenitally blind or has only dim light perception.

Stimulation techniques

Parents often are unsure about how they can contribute to their child's growth and development. There are a number of exercises for the visually disabled that can be carried out at home. Since the visually disabled, like the deaf, require early diagnosis and stimulation to achieve optimally, educators can help by providing parents with specific exercises.

The following letter sent by teachers Jane Giles and Barbara Ketchum at the Child Study Center of Oklahoma Children's Memorial Hospital to parents of blind and multihandicapped children illustrates one technique used to teach parents ways of stimulating their visually disabled child. It serves a second purpose too—teaching parents how their child might react and why.

Stimulation group review

> We thought it might help you to review some of the activities that we've done in the stimulation group and offer some suggestions for carry-over at home. All of the activities in the group are basically designed to bring your child more fully into contact . . . with other people (adults, children, and you!) and with the environment. A simple activity like the greeting, therefore, helps the child to be [self-] aware as separate and unique in the group. At the same time the child is expected to respond to adults and other children with at least some eye contact, and to listen to the sounds from the environment. When activities like this are repeated over and over again, they set up what we call an *anticipation response*. . . .
>
> Children without learning problems say "hi" or roll over or play music or sing songs hundreds of times in a week's period. Your children need this too, but we must bring it to them—over and over again. What can get boring to us is new to them for a long, long time. So, here is a review of activities we've done here, and how you can carry them over at home. Get other family members and relatives—even neighbors!—to help you out. You can only tolerate so much repetition!

Stroking or touching your child

> The atmosphere and the nonverbal communication that you provide for your child during stroking is every bit as important as the actual movements of stroking you do. Be sure to begin in a quiet, softly lit room and allow your body to transmit a feeling of tranquillity. Be aware that your own body tension and the rhythm of your movements will be communicated to your child. The goal of stroking is that you communicate relaxation

and "togetherness" between you and your child. Stroking ought to be an enjoyable experience for both you and your child—so enjoy yourself! Stroking experiences at home may be different from here at school, but both are valuable. In the group, your child can see others experiencing the process and at home [he or] she experiences the quiet, nonverbal intimacy of stroking with you or other family members.

Because of the very repetitive nature of dressing, it provides many

Introducing Jim, blinded as a teenager. Jim is continuing his education with tape-recorded and braille lessons. Above, his partially sighted teacher is instructing him in sewing as part of his daily living class.

learning opportunities if you *actively* involve your child. Through coactive involvement your child learns that [he or] she can have a part in what's happening in the world around. . . . Sit so your child is between your legs and in contact with your body. As often as possible during dressing, hold your child's hands in yours. . . . Remember to give verbal description of each body part and associated article of clothing at the moment you are *performing the task*.

Tactual sensations

You provide a wide variety of tactual sensations so your child's sense of touch can become sensitive to the world around. The greater the variety and the repetition of textures presented, the more your child will be able to learn to feel the differences. By encouraging exploration and giving verbal descriptions you help your child be aware of the many textures encountered every day—dry, crunchy cereal and wet soggy cereal, Daddy's scratchy whiskers, smooth bars on the crib, silky pajamas and fuzzy houseshoes, bumpy carpet, and rough tree bark. Remember that the experience of touching new textures may be frightening to a child who has limited contact with the environment. Although your child may show strong aversion (screaming and hollering) to the initial experience, it is through repetition that [he or] she loses her fear of contact with the environment.

Another excellent intervention program for the visually disabled infant and child is discussed by Fraiberg (1976, 1977) and demonstrated in other selected publications (Child Study Center, 1973, 1974; Napier et al., 1974).

Motor milestones

Blindness can interrupt motor development

Our mastery of gross motor milestones such as rolling from stomach to back, sitting, pivoting, crawling, standing, and walking is guided by vision. These motor milestones are often initiated by the sight of an enticing toy to be reached or touched. For the visually disabled child these motor milestones may neither take place in the normal sequential time frame nor result in the same quality of acquisition that one sees in the normal child (Burlingham, 1961). Case examples might be helpful in illustrating how achievement of the motor milestones sequence may be interrupted by blindness.

Caren She is four-and-one-half months old, and has been blind since birth. She is what is referred to as a "supine baby," meaning that she insists upon lying on her back. When Caren was placed on her stomach, the prone position, she began to show distress. She wiggled, fussed, and banged her head on the mattress, before finally surrendering to the confines of this imposed body position. She modified it to simulate the fetal position and placed her fisted hands under her eyes.

Daniel At the same age as Caren, Daniel, a sighted child, was placed in the prone position and immediately lifted his head into a vertical position.

He did this while supporting all the weight of his head, neck, and chest with his hands and arms. With an easily executed movement of his head from left to right, Daniel scanned the visual environment. If by chance Daniel sighted a toy, he could shift his weight and reach toward the toy as he pivoted on his stomach to shorten the distance between the desired object and his hand. Additionally, Daniel had in his repertoire a motor maneuver by which he could change his position from prone to supine. In this way, he could get a different visual perspective of his surroundings.

As will be remembered, in the prone position Caren did *not* elevate her head and extend the upper part of her body to survey all that was surrounding her. As a consequence, she is missing out on the exercise necessary to strengthen the neck muscles. She will need to be able to hold her head and neck upright in order to sit by herself without support. As early as four months we see the effects of visual loss on Caren's motor development. It is not that she is incapable of achieving this head-up, arm-support position; rather, it has no purpose for her. There is no reason for Caren to engage in this movement because she can see nothing in her environment. *Caren is missing out*

When Caren was in a supine position, she stretched her arms and legs in rapidly alternating circular motions. But Caren, like most blind infants, does not use her hands to bring objects to her mouth or to the midline of her body. The sighted child would, around this time, bring the interesting object to the "center of self," the mouth. In the midline position the object is available for mouthing, for a centered manipulation, and for visual exploration.

It is in this middle position also, that the eyes can capture the mutually engaged hands simultaneously as they act one upon the other. Prior to this time, the tactual and visual sensory modalities were separate, independent, and unintegrated ways of exploring objects. Now, as demonstrated through visual regard and study of the hands, these two modes of sensory motor exploration become coordinated. The child's manual ways of exploring begin at this time to come under the direction of the visual information the child is receiving. Because of Caren's blindness the visual environment could not induce her to remove her hands from her eyes into active exploration of spatially removed people and objects. This position provided a secure and known base of operation for her. Consequently, rather than pulling her hands from her eyes for object manipulation, it would be wise to consider bringing the object to Caren's known base—her hands as they rest against her eyes. In this manner she can be encouraged to reach out toward a heard, touched, smelled, and/or tasted object. *Coordination of sensory modalities in sighted child*

Inducing Caren to use her hands

When Caren was on her back she did not mimic Daniel's absorbed hand play; instead she kept her arms close to her sides, with the arms bent at the elbows and her hands positioned next to her shoulders. In this manner, she could use her shoulder as a *tactual* support against which she could finger objects. Caren had devised a clever body "playpen." Objects could not roll away from her body contact with them.

Sighted children at this stage forget an object once it rolls out of sight. The same is true of Caren with her sensorial understanding of objects. If the object moves from contact with her body, it no longer exists. Figures 10-5 and 10-6 demonstrate simple but highly effective materials used with infants such as Caren. The frame and sitting box provide a tactual support in which the visually disabled child can be offered a variety of stimulation experiences.

Let us review briefly the possible implications of loss of vision on the acquisition of the following motoric skills.

Figure 10.5
Stimulation frame

The frame provides many early stimulation experiences. The 32" × 18" × 15" lightweight frame is easy to make.

The multipurpose frame allows for one's creativity to expand when adapting it for a specific child's needs. The child may be placed in supine, prone, and side positions. Objects may be arranged to facilitate such movements as mid-line activity, head raising, forward motion, rotation, and many others.

Since there is no floor in the frame, many different materials may be used. Materials used might range from fuzzy rugs or towels to grass and other natural surfaces. The sides of the frame offer another opportunity for exposure to various stimuli. Different materials are easily attached or sewn to the sides. These, again, can range from silk or burlap to paper sacks or aluminum. Objects of your choosing may also be hung from the sides.

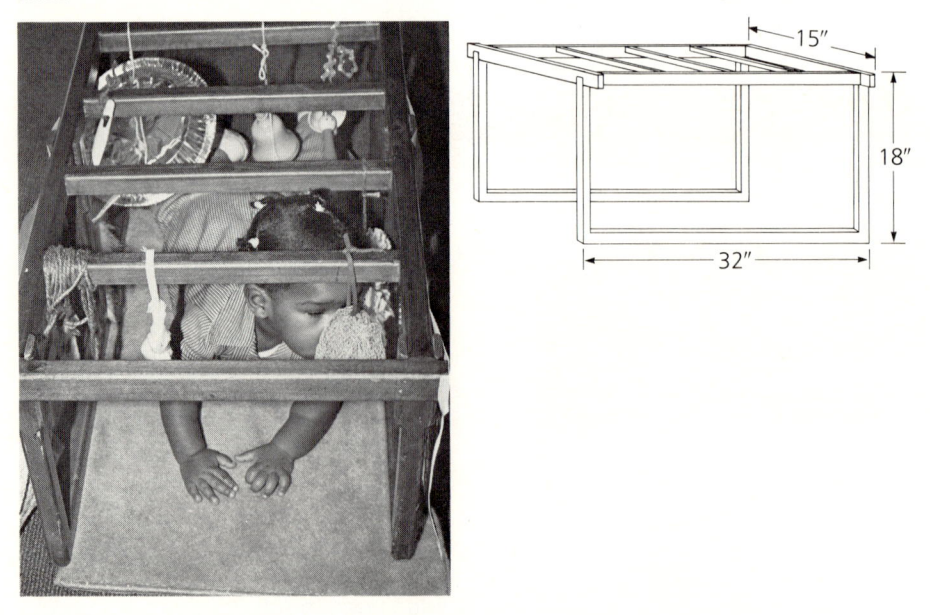

Source: Courtesy of Gertrude Forde, Child Study Center, Oklahoma City

Sitting

One can safely say that unless special exercises are initiated, the ability to sit will be delayed in a visually disabled child. Remember Caren's flexed arms next to the sides of her body? In order to sit without propping, a child needs protective responses. Try gently pushing a six-month-old sighted child on the shoulder. The child will protect himself from a fall by extending his arm or arms toward the surface on which he sits. Caren selected the supine position as her favorite orientation because her body was more manageable and the world more knowable in this position. When we put

Figure 10.6
Sitting box

The sitting box provides support and security to the child who is not sitting independently. Boxes should be sized according to the individual child, the amount of support he needs and the purpose it will serve. One should observe the child's development closely and alter box sizes when the child is ready for less support and/or more exploration.

A second box can easily function as a table when positioned in front of the child. Various objects can be attached securely to the table or tied using different lengths and textures of materials, depending on the purpose. Objects can be positioned on the table or hung from the larger box in mid-line, on the sides or to the front. You may also wish to line the box with different textures.

As the child becomes more active the box can be turned open-side up and used as a playpen. The bigger box will facilitate more adventurous play and provide room for later standing and cruising.

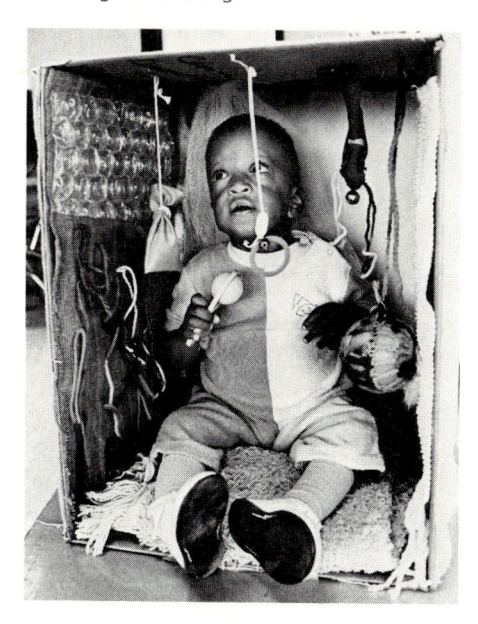

Source: See Figure 10-5

Caren in the seated position, she lost her body reference; her back was no longer in contact with a surface. Placing her in a sitting box would encourage more active exploration, since she could establish body reference with greater ease (Figure 10-6).

Crawling

Ambulation and mobilization

There is a great deal of difference between becoming ambulatory and becoming mobile. Ambulation is the achievement of the motor skill. Mobilization is the purposeful use of that skill to get things done. It is goal-directed ambulation.

Many visually disabled children skip the crawling or creeping stage and progress right to the walking stage. Most propel themselves by scooting on their backs or rolling over and over. To creep or crawl in the typical fashion— as Daniel did—Caren would have had to tolerate the prone position. This was not for her, so she developed unique mobilization skills. She began to pivot on her back, much as Daniel had done on his stomach. She then began to scoot on her back, with her feet thrusting her forward toward her destination. When she reached it, her delight was evident. Caren was mobile, but not classically ambulatory.

Language development

Multisensory approaches to teaching

What about the benefit gained by the visually disabled child from his sense of hearing? It is thought that we have overrated and overtaxed this sensory channel in our education of the visually disabled. For auditory input, or sound, to acquire meaning and content the visually disabled child must be exposed simultaneously to the touch, taste, weight, and possible functions of the object (Burlingham, 1961; Fraiberg et al., 1966). For example, one would not tell a blind child to catch a ball without first allowing the child to manipulate for himself the real, three-dimensional ball. While the child was engaged with the object, the language label would be applied.

"Showing" the ball

We would also "show" the child the possible functions of the ball, always keeping the object close to or against the child's body surface. Balls can be squeezed, bounced, tasted, felt, rolled, or suspended from a string. They can be tossed up, down, or to the side. Appropriate language would accompany these motor experiences with the ball. After all this preparation, we would ask the child to anticipate when we say "let's play ball" or "roll the ball." We might want to play with rhymes about balls after providing some solid content about them.

Passive listening

Young visually disabled children often indulge in passive listening because the sound stimulus is not paired with other stimulus elements, such as touch or motor movements. The echolalic and content-vacant vocal expression of the young visually disabled child may be a direct result of this lack of object-directed vocalization. In this case the sound of a word has not been linked to concrete sensorimotor experiences with the object.

In the example above, the child might have focused primarily on the interesting sounds, rhythms, and intonations in the phrase "roll the ball" and become preoccupied with repetition of this phrase. We might have mistakenly assumed that the child's ability to articulate the phrase implied an understanding of it as well. If we were to ask this child who is repeating it to actually find the ball that is in his or her lap, it is more than likely he or she would be unable to do so beyond chance probabilities. This child has not yet associated the appealing sounds of words with the actual events or objects that they represent. There is only a memory of a sequence of sounds, which are really no more than sequenced nonsense syllables.

Vocalization does not always mean understanding

When Caren's family spoke to her, they always touched her body first. They often placed Caren's hands on their lips to allow her to explore their mouth movements and discover the causes and effects of sound and its source. Sound and the music of language must become *coordinated with the multitude of other sensory information* about the objects in question.

Cognitive development

Construction of an object concept—an internal (mental) representation of the object when it is not present—is a prerequisite for a child's cognitive growth and development. An object concept is based on a thorough sensorimotor experience with a variety of objects (Piaget, 1952). All of the impressions we have gained from our various senses about an object become organized into a whole image of the object.

How object concepts are formed

For example, when Caren was placed in the box shown in Figure 10-6 (a corrugated cardboard box textured with linoleum or other fabric), she began to learn that objects leaving her hands and her grasp continued to exist in space. Without the boundaries provided by the box, Caren might have been discouraged from reaching out into unknown and vast space in search of an object. The box provided a confined space in which her retrieval efforts had a greater chance of success. When objects slipped out of her grasp, Caren could hear them drop against the bottom or feel them touch a part of her body. She would then activate her hands and feet in a random search for them.

Not all visually disabled infants and children would be expected to respond exactly like Caren; yet all infants, sighted and visually disabled, progress through a series of normal developmental stages. We have placed great emphasis on early development of the child, because without early stimulation programs the sensorially disabled child will lag behind peers in overall social, emotional, motor, and cognitive development. With early intervention, the visually disabled child can progress close to or at the level of the sighted child.

Early stimulation is critical

Psychological overview of the visually disabled

Social environment has a strong influence upon the personal and social adjustment of the visually disabled. Negative or oversolicitous attitudes toward this population can make them feel inferior. Some investigators have even linked the emotional problems of the blind to the negative attitudes that sighted people exhibit toward them (Cutsforth, 1951). While this is an extreme view, there is no doubt that people who are significant to the visually disabled exert a tremendous influence on their personal-social development. Visual disability may well be the most difficult exceptionality for sighted people to accept. In fact, severely visually disabled people were found to be least well accepted when rated with twelve other types of exceptionality on a social distance scale. Partially seeing people were more readily accepted (Jones et al., 1966). Fortunately, the more experience and interaction that sighted people have with the visually disabled, the more positive their reactions and attitudes become. The visually disabled are thus encouraged in their struggle to cope with their handicap (Wright, 1974).

The visually disabled are least well-accepted

Self-concept

Formation of an adequate self-concept, a person's view of self and the feelings one might have about oneself, is thus dependent on feelings and attitudes of significant others. Peers, teachers, neighbors, and especially parents all shape a person's view of self. Lukoff et al. (1972) found that when the blind associate with the sighted, they are most influenced by the standards of the sighted, not by those of their blind counterparts. But when the blind associate with other blind people, they are quite responsive to the standards of their counterparts. When in Rome, they do as the Romans do: significant people in their lives will have a greater impact on the way they feel about themselves.

How self-concept is formed

Early medical, educational and social intervention, including parental counseling, can promote self-esteem in visually disabled children. (Unit 1 suggests a number of intervention techniques to foster positive mental health in exceptional children; for example, channeling parents' reactions to their child's exceptionality in helpful directions.) For the most part, visually disabled persons have tremendous obstacles to overcome in learning to trust the environment and in feeling self-confident. As with any group, some surmount these obstacles and some do not. Scores in one large-scale study disclosed that visually disabled adolescents viewed themselves much more negatively than did the normative group. Their self-concept measures were extremely low on physical, moral-ethical, and identity items (Meighan, 1971). The visually disabled often feel that their condition prevents others from recognizing their positive attributes and that the visual disability penetrates all relationships in which they would like to engage (Lukoff et al., 1972).

Low self-esteem among visually disabled adolescents

If the visually disabled person's personal-social adjustment and self-concept is as contingent upon attitudes of parents, teachers, and peers as we have suggested, it is imperative to educate the general public about this exceptionality. Educators can do much to change parental perceptions and attitudes toward the visually disabled once a child is enrolled in an educational stimulation program. Teachers in public schools relieve the fear and anxiety of their visually disabled students by integrating them in a structured manner into the class. Teacher-pupil ratio must be kept

Keep teacher-pupil ratio low

low so that visually disabled students can be given the individual attention and support they need. A case example reinforces this observation.

> **Tony** The special services director at a local school district requested a consult on a severely visually disabled child formerly enrolled in the Child Study Center's program for the developmentally disabled. The child had begun talking to himself aloud in class, seemed to be inattentive, was not getting his work completed, and appeared fearful. Observation in the regular classroom demonstrated that Tony became disoriented when trying to localize the children's voices. Soon he would tire of trying to "find" the children talking. It was at this point that he would lose interest and begin entertaining himself. Similarly, he was observed to become anxious and inattentive when the teacher or the other students talked to him. Observation revealed that students would suddenly pounce on him in play, hit his shoulder, and talk while walking away. In looking at his classroom assignments it was found that math or matching problems were crowded on a single page so that very close visual work was required. The following recommendations were made to the classroom teacher:
>
> (1) Touch Tony gently when talking to him and help him to orient where you are in relation to him.
> (2) Do not suddenly walk up to him and tap or hit him on the back when he least expects it.
> (3) Help him to orient to other children during show and tell.
> (4) Place fewer math or other problems on each page and increase their size for him.
>
> When these recommendations were followed, Tony's difficulties diminished. Informally, Tony confided to the psychologist that he talked to himself because he got bored. When the psychologist explained that sometimes Tony's talking to himself aloud made others look at him and think he was different, the youngster agreed. On subsequent visits, Tony informed the psychologist that he no longer felt a need to talk out loud.

Body image

Body image is a concept that lays the foundation for further development in all children; yet attention is not drawn to it until something happens to interfere with its formation. The process of body image formation can be explained this way:

How body image is formed

> As a normal child matures, he at first unconsciously, and subsequently in an academic way, learns about his body, his body's shape, his movement capabilities, the relationship of his body and its parts to events near and distant space and the names of specific body movements and body parts (Cratty & Sams, 1968, p. 11).

This awareness of one's body in space seems a simple matter until one understands the role that vision plays in it. Personal-social development, with which we dealt in the preceding section, is closely related to the visually disabled person's body image.

At the moment of birth, an infant begins to discover the ways he or she can move. Much of the infant's movement is reinforced by seeing body parts or interesting objects in the environment. For the child who cannot see well, auditory and tactual clues can be motivators for movement if they are presented along with input from others. For example, bringing the arms of the visually disabled child together and stroking them gives tactual feedback to the child. A noise-making mobile over the crib encourages the child's arms and feet to move in a new way, upward, whereas items to the side of the child encourage rotation of the trunk. Fraiberg and Freedman (1964) explain also how gross kinesthetic stimulation can heighten an infant's awareness of his or her own body. Placed in different positions, the infant develops a "feel" for the movement and will want to repeat it. Sometimes it is easier to bring a prepared environment to a visually disabled child than it is to allow the child to experience his or her own body moving about the environment. How much easier it is to pick up something under the table than to have a child go through the process of discovering how to get under the table and then out again. Yet the child must do so in order to understand the causes and effects of his or her own movements within the environment. In this manner one begins to have some awareness of one's own body. Since body image and intellectual development may be significantly related, body-image training programs in schools or clinics are invaluable to the visually disabled (Walker, 1973).

Kinesthetic stimulation heightens body awareness

Concept formation

There is considerable debate regarding the effect of visual impairment on the child's ability to conceptualize. It has been suggested that like the deaf child, the congenitally blind child, or one whose loss of vision occurs quite early in life (before the age of five), may be restricted in the area of concept formation. The lack of sensory input due to deafness or blindness forces the child to rely upon other senses to gain information. The blind child's motor limitations may discourage exploration and subsequent learning from the environment.

Visually disabled children have demonstrated a lack of fantasy and imagination in play, suggesting a deficiency in abstraction, or at least more concreteness than their sighted counterparts. These children usually must be *taught* before play becomes of any significance to them. Whether this is the result of environmental deprivation or sensory impairment alone, their play patterns are different. If the visually disabled have inadequate patterns of play, can it be assumed that their intellectual development will be more constricted and concrete? There seems to be some evidence to warrant this conclusion at least tentatively (Singer & St. Reiner, 1966; Tait, 1972). However, it also seems reasonable to suppose that toys designed for sighted children may be of little interest to the blind (Rogow, 1975). We need to investigate

Play activities and intellectual development

this possibility thoroughly before charging the blind with deficient play patterns that are related to poor intellectual or conceptual development.

Recent studies suggest that congenitally blind children, who must use other sense data such as the shape, size, weight, texture, and temperature of objects, are equal to their sighted peers on tactual perception and object recognition (Gottesman, 1971). Also, blind and sighted children appear to acquire the concept of conservation (i.e., a tall narrow glass may hold the same amount of water as a cup, even though the glass looks bigger) at comparable ages, particularly when sighted chil-

Lunch hour is a good time to socialize with other students. Aspirations and mutual interests can be shared.

dren are blindfolded (Cramer, 1973). From this study Cramer concluded that blind children are not deficient in their thinking processes; they merely arrive at conclusions in a different manner than do sighted children.

Through early diagnosis, concept formation in the visually disabled can proceed at a rate that is normative to that group. The child must then be provided with a highly stimulating environment using a multisensory approach to teaching. Infant stimulation programs are effective, but they should be conducted by highly skilled teachers who are familiar with the development of visually disabled children. Teaching must be practical, using the intact senses that are at the child's disposal. A number of aids that can be used in teaching basic concepts to the visually disabled are suggested by the American Printing House for the Blind (Barraga et al., 1973). Only through early identification, a highly stimulating environment maximizing the other senses, and skilled teachers can the visually disabled child hope to overcome difficulties in concept formation.

Mannerisms

The visually disabled often display certain mannerisms, called *blindisms,* which are associated with self-stimulating behaviors like eye-rubbing or rocking. The following case studies illustrate blindisms:

Christopher This totally blind six-year-old constantly moved his head from side to side. When he was walking, he also rotated his shoulders and trunk and occasionally stiffened his entire body and walked on his tiptoes. He moved his hands in a finger-clicking motion when they were not in contact with something else in the environment. His behavior had reached a point at which it interfered with his academic progress, social skills, mobility, and even self-help tasks. Much of his behavior was not unlike that seen in autistic children.

Marilyn Twenty-five-year-old totally blind Marilyn snapped her fingers, fidgeted quite often, blinked her eyelids almost constantly, talked so fast as to not be understood, and generally had many extraneous movements. She was able to go through regular daily routines with no difficulty, but socially and psychologically she ran into problems because her behavior caused people to avoid her company.

The behavior described above may appear to be perseverative and meaningless to observers, but visually disabled children can supply personal input through such motor actions when they feel a void within their sensory channels. Sometimes visually disabled children may not explore their environment even through touch. They do not move their bodies through space and thus do not get kinesthetic feedback about their body in space. Not having a model of what everyone else does, they turn inward for stimulation.

Lowenfeld (1971, 1973) suggests that anxiety and frustrations are the cause of these mannerisms, and that additional impairments can increase and prolong blindisms. Studies do indeed show that sensory deprivation can heighten tension, confusion about reality, and fear of the unknown. Knight (1970) attributes blindisms to the visually disabled child's attempts to "cope with tensions created by situations of frustration, fear, excitement, stimulation deficit, physical activity deprivation, insecurity, etc." (p. 301). The increased danger to which a visually disabled child is exposed contributes to the tension.

Sensory deprivation heightens tension

Dealing with blindisms The attitude of the visually disabled person towards blindisms depends largely on his or her social environment and the demands made therein. Visually disabled peers in a residential setting probably would not place the same demands on fellow students that sighted classmates would. On the other hand, a teacher, mobility instructor, or house parent might place more demands on the child to cease unnecessary mannerisms than would a teacher in a class that included sighted peers. A teacher with just one or two visually disabled children may not want to point them out continuously. Classmates, however, usually let the visually disabled child know when he or she is not acting like "part of the crowd." The child will have to change these mannerisms to be accepted by peers.

Attitudes toward blindisms

As we all know, younger people can adapt to new situations more easily than older people can. Rather than change, the blind adult may decide not to pursue friendships with sighted individuals who cannot accept his or her mannerisms.

If intervention begins in early infancy, mannerisms can be modified so that the child behaves more like sighted children. Parents, teachers, and other professionals can do much to help visually disabled children develop a more normal way of acting and living. The child can be spared much grief and pain if this is done at a young age, so that he or she may be teased and excluded less often. Visual disability itself can set the child apart, and allowing its attendant mannerisms to persist can only increase the social gap.

Blindisms can isolate a child from peers

Adjustment problems

Several factors determine the degree to which satisfactory adjustment is attained. Feelings of inferiority, lack of self-confidence, and poor self-esteem often plague the visually disabled child and adolescent—especially one who has not had optimal early intervention in the form of parent education, infant stimulation, and close work with educators at school. Depression, anxiety, and grief are common reactions to the loss of sight in later childhood. The person who is visually disabled since birth is not faced so overwhelmingly with the realization of the vast experiences that are being missed. Oddly enough, studies have demonstrated that the partially sighted are less well adjusted than the blind or severely visually disabled. In one large-scale study, in which adjustment measures for the visually disabled were comparable to those of the sighted, the study concluded that in the minds of the public and professionals visual disability must not presuppose maladjustment (Cowen et al., 1961, p. 127). Intervention strategies that can help with a child's adjustment problems include:

1. promoting family involvement while teaching family members to adapt their home life to acceptance of the child
2. teaching peer groups at school to accept the child, coupled with attempts to alter any negative attitudes that sighted peers have toward the visually disabled
3. involving the child in school-related activities (This must be done in a very warm, supportive, and accepting manner, not from an overprotective stance that encourages dependence.)
4. encouraging early independence and autonomy by treating the child as normally as possible within the confines of the disability
5. recognizing the natural tendency for a visually disabled child or teenager to feel anxious and fearful in new situations (Additional support can be offered at these times.)

It is heartening to note the increasing number of programs that the 1970s have brought into operation. The visually disabled are now offered appropriate psychological and educational aid early in life. Teaching and training programs designed in recent years allow visually disabled children and youth to participate in almost any sighted activity: dancing, playing ball, running, skating, skiing, and bowling.

Psychological testing

Evaluating the intellect and personality of the visually disabled is a challenging task for any psychologist. It should be understood that psychological testing can be extremely helpful if one examines *all* of the data and does not concentrate on a single IQ score. It is beneficial to obtain a profile of the child's strengths and weaknesses and to assess them *when the information can answer specific referral questions,* not simply to obtain a numerical score that tells us very little. The visually disabled perform very well on verbal sections of tests and, in general, their intellectual range is roughly comparable to that of the general population.

Fostering social and emotional growth in the school environment

The visually disabled child entering school for the first time is placed in the position of getting acquainted with many new people at once. A teacher or parent has to be sensitive to situations in which the visually disabled need help in establishing healthy, friendly relationships. Visually disabled children may want to prove their strength to friends, but they cannot if the others want to play games like baseball.

When visually disabled children are left out of activities, they do not have the opportunity to prove themselves, and their peers may assume they can do very little. The teacher can arrange other games, such as tug-of-war, that require everyone's participation. As visually disabled children show what they can do, their peers look on them with more respect and may even invite them to participate in other games. The children gain confidence in themselves as members of the group and eventually feel free to invite their classmates to join them in some of their favorite games.

Fostering good mental health

A visually disabled child cannot learn by visual imitation. Again, teachers, parents, and even other children may need to step in to help the child be a part of the peer group. Every generation, for example, has some preferred style of clothing. If the visually disabled child is wearing striped knit pants while other children are wearing blue jeans, then the child has another visible eccentricity to set him or her apart from the others.

As was mentioned earlier, the mannerisms of the visually disabled also can set them apart unless someone takes the time to demonstrate behavior that will communicate to their peers. For example, a blind person may express intense listening by holding his or her head downward. To others, this posture communicates just the opposite intent. Thinking that the posture indicates lack of interest, they may cease the conversation. We can teach the blind that their relationships with others can be improved by holding up their heads and facing the speaker when engaged in conversation. As they become more aware of what others are doing to express certain moods or thoughts, the visually disabled will want to imitate and communicate with others in a similar manner. It is important to remember that the teacher is not asking the visually disabled child to change what he or she is thinking, but to communicate so that others will understand the child's interest in them; in this way, the sighted child might be more willing to accept the visually disabled child.

Demonstrating communicative behavior

Fostering independence The blind adolescent wants to be self-sufficient but is often dependent on others for mobility and transportation. It is not feasible for the adolescent to hop into a car and drive across town to see a friend; he or she must wait on someone else's convenience. This is especially hard on the adolescent because it limits him or her in meeting peer expectations. A self-confident blind person could probably come up with creative yet realistic ways to fulfill that role, but this attitude requires experience and an opportunity to be around someone who is confident.

Problems of the blind adolescent

In our society, the mother bears more day-to-day responsibility for rearing the children. Although the blind boy may want to model his father he may not have much contact with him, especially when we remember that the visual mode is absent. At school, his friends may not ask him to join them in activities because of his lack of self-confidence; yet he cannot gain self-confidence until he is involved in situations that are typical for his age group. If the adolescent is to progress in his emotional growth, a sensitive person can and must intervene at this point.

Break the cycle

A very useful book for teachers is one that suggests ways to help the visually disabled in areas of personal management—applying makeup, shaving, cooking, sewing, and so forth (American Foundation for the Blind, 1974).

Academic curriculum and training programs

Mobility training and orientation

Mobility is an important aspect of a visually disabled person's life because it gives some degree of independence, freedom, and confidence. Mobility training, basically is learning to negotiate environments one would normally encounter in daily living (Cratty, 1971). Mobility can be encouraged in the home environment long before teachers begin formal training in class. The home is, after all, the center of focus for many years to come.

Young children may go many places with their parents and still be deprived of the experiences that will strengthen their later mobility skills. For example, if doors are always opened for a child, she does not have the experience of opening a door for herself. Or perhaps a child is always picked up and placed in a car rather than being allowed to get in independently and orient herself properly in the seat. Again, parents can help visually disabled children by exposing them to these experiences and, at the same time, describing the environment through language.

Expose children to environmental landmarks

The more environmental situations children are exposed to, the more easily they can interpret the structures they encounter. Some structures move and others are stationary; the wall does not move but the door might, so they can anticipate this. Significant landmarks, such as the curb of a street or the steps of a building, are also clues that the child can anticipate. Visually disabled children can use these landmarks to gauge where they are and where they need to go next. They can then apply this information to new situations. Understanding spatial relationships is the key to good mobility, and the children must learn this early. Larson (1975) has outlined methods for teaching orientation and mobility to the visually disabled.

Safety techniques

Teachers in public schools begin formal mobility training with visually disabled children soon after the children are enrolled in class. The students learn general mobility techniques that can be used in the school environment and surrounding neighborhood. These children want to be able to walk down to the local store or over to a friend's house to play. Many have already been doing just that, anxious for independence but unaware of the hazards involved. Mobility training enables them to use techniques that give them a greater degree of safety (Cratty, 1971).

Mobility aids and habilitation programs

Sonic guide aids mobility

Mobility can be enhanced by the use of a cane, guide dog (for older blind people), sonar sensor cane, or electronic echo-sounding device. The latter is a battery-powered transducer system that is worn on polyester headgear (Clark & Agust, 1975). The system transmits an ultrasonic pulse approximately six feet in front of the person and covers about an 80-degree cone area (see Figure 10-7). Signals vary in pitch and intensity depending on the size, distance, and hardness or softness of objects in the path. It is suitable for use with children six months of age and older. Other electronic devices also have been devised to aid mobility in the visually disabled (Farmer, 1975).

Habilitation or rehabilitation programs develop the skills necessary for independence within one's own home in later life. Young visually disabled people learn cooking, dressing, housekeeping, grooming, and related skills. Additional emphasis is placed on special job skills if the individual is to terminate education at the high-school level. Those planning to continue their education can concentrate on subjects that will prepare them for college.

Developing job skills

Decisions about the primary mode of learning

Prior to learning to read (by braille or large print) the visually disabled child must have certain basic readiness skills. The ability to discriminate sizes, shapes, and textures is an important perceptual (readiness) skill. Basic concepts like the *top* or *bottom* of a page are important ingredients in learning to read and follow instructions.

Reading readiness skills

Figure 10.7
Sonicguide: A mobility aid and environmental sensor for the blind

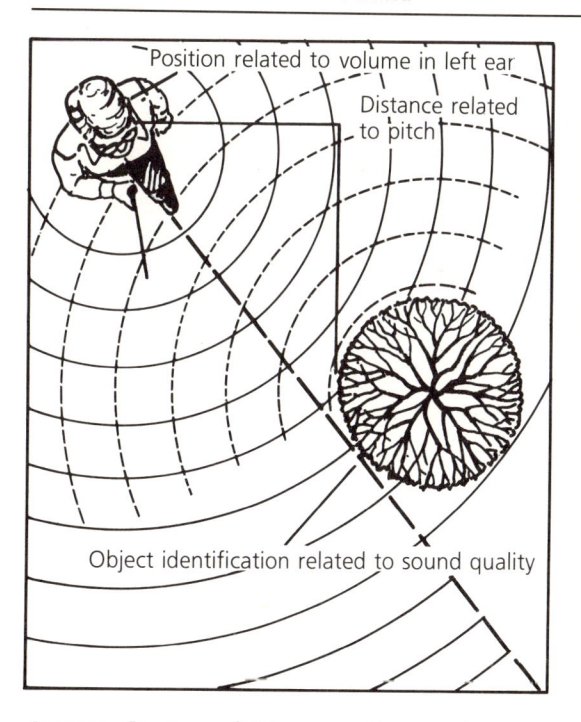

Source: Courtesy of Telesensory Systems, Inc. Palo Alto, California

364 Visually disabled children and youth

Left and *right*, *big* and *little*, *short* and *long*, *up* and *down*—all are concepts a child should be able to demonstrate.

Either commercial products or easily prepared homemade materials can be used to teach the concepts that will prepare a child for reading. Figure 10-8 illustrates one such useful teaching tool. The child's hand can be moved from left to right over the textured line and, as the teacher reads, the child learns about the versatility of a line. Homemade books that encourage tactual discrimination are also a good teaching tool. Pieces of yarn, cloth, or popcorn glued to the page are tactually interesting to the child and encourage exploration. .

Beth Two-and-a-half-year-old Beth, a low-vision child, was diagnosed by a physician as blind. When she first entered an educational program she visually attended to lights and could tell when a large object was immediately in front of her. Beth was required to use this vision in a structured setting. In a dark room she had to find the spot in the floor where a flashlight beam was shining. This was an easy task for her, but it was a good place to start because it gave her a sense of success and taught her to follow verbal instructions. The activities changed to finding objects on the table in front of her. Gradually, Beth became more confident in her abilities. She

Figure 10.8
Learning basic readiness concepts

The lines are grilled or textured by gluing sand to the sheet or pressing a crayon in a firm manner so that it leaves a slightly textured surface. Then the child feels the line and learns the various concepts.

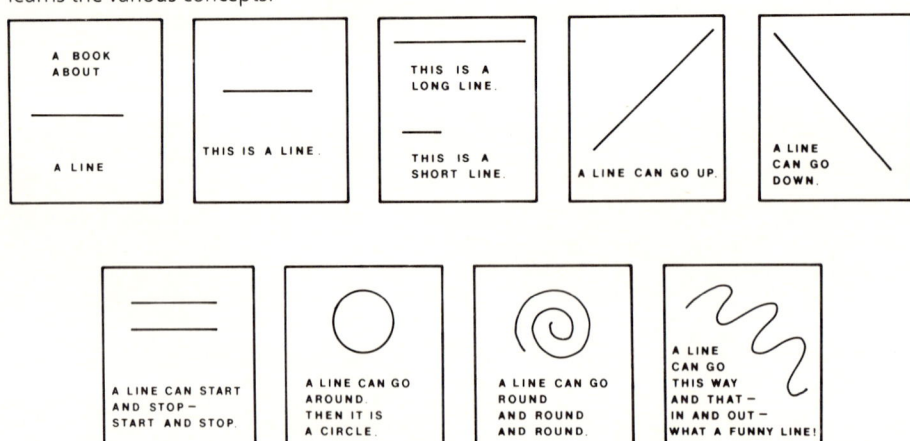

Source: Courtesy of Gertrude Forde, Child Study Center, Oklahoma City.

enjoyed the challenge of visually finding an object and then matching it to one that was the same. The materials were three-dimensional. Beth matched colors and shapes in outline and even sequenced pictures according to size. She was also introduced to chalkboard drawing at this time. She traced lines, then copied a line or circle, and identified various shapes drawn on the board. Language was tied in closely so that she could verbalize what she saw to others.

By the age of four, Beth was beginning to identify so many shapes at such small sizes that she was ready to start on letters and sight words written in large print. Without structured intervention, she might have entered school at the age of six not having actualized her visual abilities. By learning how to "see," she acquired visual skills that she can continue to improve.

After helping parents to pinpoint the visually disabled child's strengths and weaknesses, the educator can teach them activities that will stimulate their child's vision. Observation of the child's responses is the key to both short- and long-term planning.

Beth's initial visual responses suggested several structured activities that would help to evaluate her vision, and further observations led to more emphasis on visual training. Her parents and teachers were pleased with Beth's ability to carry over this training into unstructured settings. Realizing that we do not learn via one sensory channel alone, they did not ignore tactual stimulation, which was Beth's primary mode of learning at the age of two-and-a-half years. She could perceive that an object was in front of her but could not identify it until she had touched it. She learned by pairing tactual information and language. Visual training did not deny her this form of learning; rather, it added another form of sensory input. *Visual stimulation can supplement other sensory input*

A decision must be made at some time concerning the use of braille or large print. Visually impaired children who still use vision as their primary means of sensory input are good candidates for reading print. In fact, if braille were provided as the principal reading material to these youngsters, many would read it visually rather than tactually. On the other hand, those who need a great deal of visual amplification in order to distinguish even one letter may find it more efficient to read by braille. To decide what mode of learning a child should use on the basis of a visual acuity score alone is too cursory. The child's visual functioning (gauged by observation and evaluation) and personal preference also should be considered. *Braille or large print?*

Braille

Charles Barbier, a French army officer during the early 1800s, designed a tactual system for sending messages that could be read at night with no light. This night writing system was based on phonetics. It was later introduced at the Institution for the Blind in Paris. Louis Braille, a student there, adapted it to touch reading. Braille's system, comprising an alphabet and contractions, was officially accepted in the *Origins of braille system* school in 1854. It has been changed and modified through the years because of controversy surrounding the formation of the cell (see below) and the use of contractions. But regardless of controversies and modifications, the importance of braille as an aid to communication for the blind cannot be overestimated.

In braille the cell consists of two vertical rows with three raised dots in each row, which allows for 63 possible combinations (see Figure 10-9). These combinations can be used to present any literary, musical, numerical or scientific material that can be presented in print. Since each braille cell requires a quarter-inch of line space, many space-saving features have been added to Braille's original code in the form of

Figure 10.9
Alphabetic index for braille reading

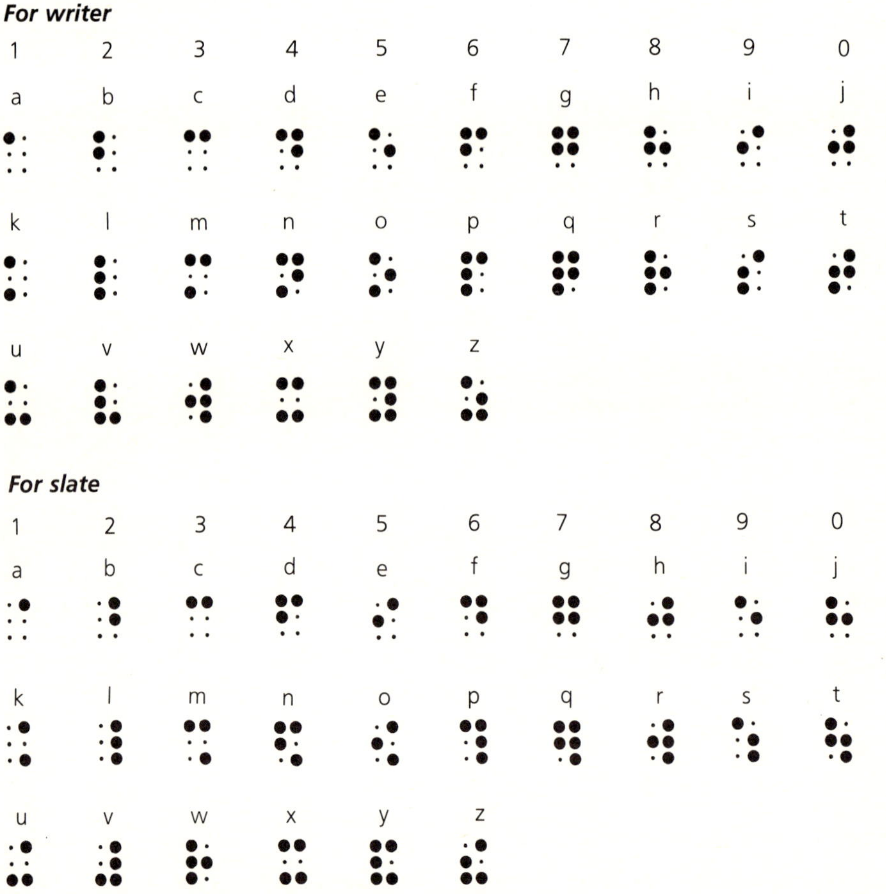

For writer

1	2	3	4	5	6	7	8	9	0
a	b	c	d	e	f	g	h	i	j

k	l	m	n	o	p	q	r	s	t

u	v	w	x	y	z

For slate

1	2	3	4	5	6	7	8	9	0
a	b	c	d	e	f	g	h	i	j

k	l	m	n	o	p	q	r	s	t

u	v	w	x	y	z

Source: Dorf & Scharry, 1973, p. xvii

signs, abbreviations and contractions. To illustrate, the word *knowledge,* if spelled letter for letter in braille, would require two-and-a-half inches of line space. To save space, *knowledge* is always represented in braille by the letter *k*—dots 1 and 3 standing alone (Figure 10-9), requiring only one-half inch and saving two inches of

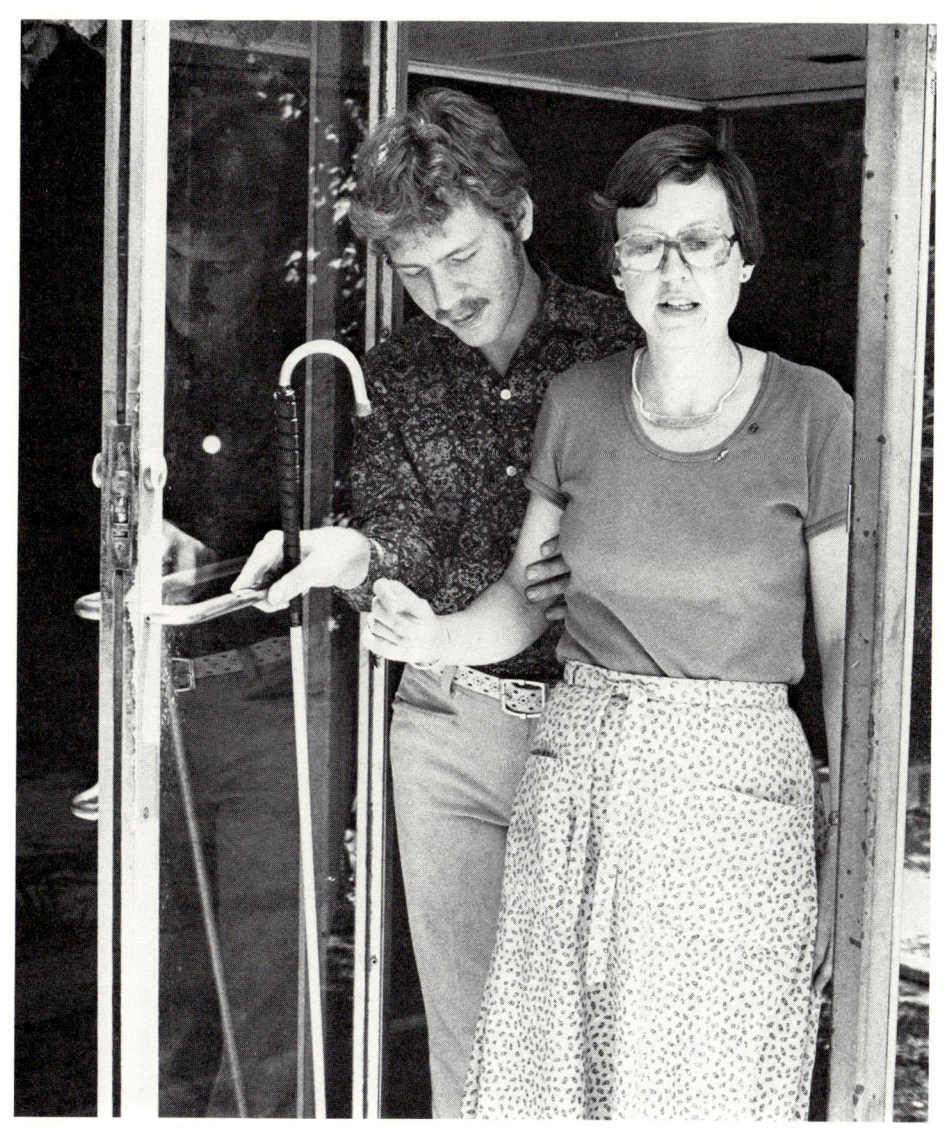

Jim's world can be as wide as he wants to make it. Mobility training, shown here, will help him maintain his independence.

space (Ashcroft, 1963, p. 447). Numerical and musical notation systems in braille make it possible for blind children and youth to read musical scores for instrument and voice.

Reading print

Low-vision students learning to read print follow most of the methods of their sighted peers but need special materials to accomplish the same tasks. Because they are often unaware of how effectively they can use their vision, they might not attempt the same visual tasks as their sighted peers. Through training, however, low-vision students can learn to maximize their visual functioning. (Effective lesson plans have been outlined by Barraga [1964].)

Figure 10.10
Optiscope Illuminated Enlarger System in use

The optiscope enlarger makes large type of any printed material by magnifying the images four times and projecting the images on a 9 × 14 inch polarized screen in color or black and white.

Source: Courtesy of Stimulation Aids, Ltd., Lynbrook, New York 11563

Classroom teachers can order enlarger systems so that low-vision pupils can work from the same texts as their peers. The Optiscope Illuminated Enlarger System magnifies regular print images or words to four times their original size and displays them on a large screen in color or black and white (see Figure 10-10).

Enlarger systems

Braille or large print materials for the visually disabled are used in the classroom. Textbooks containing maps or drawings must be prepared with a tactual medium, enlarged by an Optiscope, or in some way adaped to the needs of the student. The American Printing House for the Blind provides books, materials, and other services for the blind in both residential and local schools. In addition to its research projects, the agency produces a variety of special materials to meet the needs of the visually disabled—from maps for high school students to toys for infants. The Division for the Blind and Physically Handicapped of the Library of Congress provides free reading material for the blind. Regional libraries serving the blind receive their materials from the Library of Congress and then make them available to the local community.

Till now, teachers and helping professionals have not utilized the many services available to the visually disabled population to their fullest, but with passage of Public Law 94-142 (discussed in Unit 1) inquiries to regional and state resources for the visually impaired have increased substantially. Materials like "talking books" (recorded books that can be played like a record or cassette) are now in greater demand. But unless we continue to inform parents, teachers, and the visually disabled themselves of the many services available to them, these resources will not be tapped.

Underuse of services and resources

The Optacon for reading

The Optacon, an amazing electronic device introduced in 1971, has brought in a new era for the severely visually disabled by opening the door for them to all types of reading material. The Optacon converts the visual images of letters into tactile forms that can be felt and read. Anything the blind child or adolescent knows how to read, can be read by this device after approximately forty to fifty hours of instruction coupled with considerable practice. Most well-equipped classrooms for the visually disabled will have at least one Optacon (see Figure 10-11). Those who are skilled in its use have more opportunities for advancement and enjoy more freedom and privacy. They can now pay bills by check, look up numbers in a telephone directory, vote by truly secret ballot, and complete many other tasks that once required the aid of a guide or friend.

Liberating effects of the Optacon

Combined visual and hearing disorders

The child with a combined vision and hearing problem presents a special need for a multidisciplinary team approach to evaluation and program planning. When designing an educational program, one should consider not only sensory impairments, but

Special need for multidisciplinary team

Sharing information

also associated medical and psychological problems, some of which may require specific intervention. The family situation has to be assessed regularly, for home life influences the child's response to an educational program. If the child is to respond fully, the teacher must be aware of inhibiting medical and family factors that might necessitate altering some part of the child's program, either permanently or temporarily. These problems can be brought to the teacher's attention through interdisciplinary sharing of information.

Causes

German measles

Maternal infections during the first three months of pregnancy, such as measles (rubeolla) or German measles (rubella), have been a major cause of visual and hearing deficits in children. While nationwide inoculations have now practically nullified rubella, the epidemic of 1964 and 1965 left thousands of children with multihandicapping conditions. Their educational needs could not be ignored; hence, programs were planned specifically for deaf and blind children. Their care—medical, social, and educational—became a prototype for care of children who are deaf and blind from other causes and for those who suffer multihandicapping conditions of any sort. As the vanguard, however, these deaf-blind children were exposed to the trial-

**Figure 10.11
Optacon apparatus in use**

Source: Courtesy of Telesensory Systems, Inc. Palo Alto, California

and-error efforts of professionals who tried various ways of designing optimum programs for them.

Vision and hearing problems, accompanied by other handicapping conditions, may also be caused by chromosome abnormalities such as Turner's Syndrome. Under certain circumstances, combined hearing and vision defects can arise from central nervous system infections, prematurity, hypoxia, toxins, and trauma—including battering.

Diagnosis and evaluation

Because so many conditions are accompanied by vision and hearing impairment, each child must be diagnosed and evaluated individually. This group does, however, share general health-care needs. All deaf-blind children need a determination of developmental level, and all should be checked by eye and ear specialists. The Bureau of Education for the Handicapped has sponsored an excellent manual to help in assessing the deaf-blind multihandicapped child (Midwest Regional Center for the Deaf-Blind, 1978). The specific etiology also determines what other disciplines or specialties will be needed for evaluation. For example, since the possibility of a cardiac problem must be considered in the child with congenital rubella, a cardiologist should participate in the evaluation (see Unit 1, team approach). Low-vision clinical or itinerant services are springing up in large cities. They provide many optical aids for the partially sighted, plus a team of professionals to evaluate, diagnose and counsel this population (Jose et al., 1975).

Clinical services

In short, evaluation and care of a child who is deaf-blind consists of (1) health-care needs common to all children, (2) special evaluation in common as a group, and (3) evaluation specific to the causal factors. An intensive and well-rounded approach will ensure that information necessary for optimum program planning is not overlooked.

Prevention

Prevention is the best treatment for diseases that can cause deafness and blindness. Prevention of rubella is straightforward—immunization of school-age children. Public awareness is important and a sustained, organized immunization program is necessary. That these conditions cannot be taken for granted is brought to our attention periodically by public health officials who warn that the number of susceptible individuals is reaching unacceptably high levels.

Immunization and public awareness

Trends in educational programs

Early childhood education, such as has been described in this unit, is a current educational trend for the visually disabled and multihandicapped. Whereas an exceptional child traditionally started school in kindergarten or first grade, home and educational settings are now being combined to provide very early stimulation for

Early childhood education is the trend

Areas for further research

high-risk children. The multisensory stimulation of exceptional or high-risk infants facilitates their integration into school and promotes mental health. The idea to be kept in mind is that education, if it *is* education, benefits those around the child as well as the child itself.

Other trends in education of the visually disabled have been noted, but not yet fully explored (Ashcroft, 1963). "There seems to be 'a new era in education' but 'a paradox in research'" (Ashcroft & Harley, 1967). More research is still needed to evaluate the visually impaired child's ability to utilize residual vision and optical aids and to progress in concept formation. Further research is also required to develop adequate assessment tools to diagnose educational strengths and weaknesses. The effects of early infant stimulation on later development is another important area to study. Finally, the teacher education programs and ongoing programs for the visually disabled need further evaluation of their effectiveness. The development of leadership personnel to work with the visually disabled is worthy of further examination, also (Ashcroft et al., 1971).

Summary

The foregoing discussion of the visually disabled (blind and partially sighted) child or youth has shown that this handicap need not be debilitating. With early diagnosis and stimulation, and with parent education, the child can progress much like a sighted child. Although their tools for learning and their vocational choices may vary, visually disabled children and adolescents have more commonalities than differences with sighted people. Society's attitudes toward the sensorially disabled can do much to stifle or encourage their productivity, independence, and self-confidence. In recognizing this we can do much to raise public consciousness to a more enlightened level.

References and resources

American Foundation for the Blind. *A Step-by-Step Guide to Personal Management for Blind Persons.* New York: American Foundation for the Blind, 1974.

Ashcroft, S. C. "Blind and Partially Seeing Children." In *Exceptional Children in the Schools,* edited by L. Dunn, pp. 413–61. New York: Holt, Rinehart and Winston, 1963.

Ashcroft, S. C., and Harley, R. K. *The Visually Handicapped: Vision and Its Disorders.* U.S. Department of Health, Education, and Welfare, National Institute of Neurological Diseases and Blindness. Monograph no. 4. Bethesda, Md.: 1967.

Ashcroft, S. C.; Harley, R. K.; and Hart, V. "Development of Leadership Personnel in Visually Handicapped." *Education for the Visually Handicapped* 3 (1971): 109–10.

Barraga, N. C. *Increased Visual Behavior in Low Vision Children.* New York: American Foundation for the Blind, 1964.

Barraga, N. C., *Teacher's Guide for Development of Visual Learning Abilities and Utilization of Low Vision.* New York: American Printing House for the Blind, 1970.

Barraga, N. C.; Doriward, B.; and Ford, P. *Aids for Teaching Basic Concepts of Sensory Development.* Louisville, Ky.: American Printing House for the Blind, 1973.
Bray, P. F. *Neurology in Pediatrics.* Chicago: Year Book Medical Publishers, 1969.
Burlingham, D. "Some Notes on the Development of the Blind." *Psychoanalytic Study of the Child* (1961): 121–45.
Burlingham, D. "Hearing and Its Role in the Development of the Blind." *Psychoanalytic Study of the Child* (1964): 95–112.
Child Study Center. *Services to deaf-blind children.* No. 1. Oklahoma City: 1973.
Child Study Center. *Services to deaf-blind children.* No. 1. Oklahoma City: 1974.
Clark, M., and Agust, S. "Sonar for the Blind," *Newsweek,* July 29, 1975, p. 69.
Cowen, E. L.; Underberg, R. P.; Verrillo, R. T.; and Benham, F. G. *Adjustment to Visual Disability in Adolescence.* New York: American Foundation for the Blind, 1961.
Cramer, R. F. "Conservation by the Congenitally Blind." *British Journal of Psychology* 64 (1973): 241–50.
Cratty, B. J. *Movement and Spatial Awareness in Blind Children and Youth.* Springfield, Ill.: Charles C Thomas, 1971.
Cratty, B. J., and Sams, T. A. *The Body-Image of Blind Children.* New York: American Foundation for the Blind, 1968.
Cutsforth, T. D. *The Blind in School and Society.* New York: American Foundation for the Blind, 1951.
Dorf, M. B., and Scharry, E. R. *Instruction Manual for Braille Transcribing.* Louisville, Ky.: American Printing House for the Blind, 1973.
English, H. B., and English, A. C. *A Comprehensive Dictionary of Psychological and Psychoanalytic Terms.* New York: David McKay, 1966.
Farmer, L. W. "Travel in Adverse Weather Using Electronic Mobility Guidance Devices." *New Outlook for the Blind* 69 (1975): 433–39.
Ficociello, C. *Manual for Visual Assessment Kit.* Dallas, Tex.: South Central Regional Center for Services to Deaf-Blind Children, 1974.
Fraiberg, S. "Intervention in Infancy." In *Infant Psychiatry,* edited by E. N. Rexford, L. W. Sander and T. Shapiro, pp. 264–84. New Haven: Yale University Press, 1976.
Fraiberg, S. *Insights from the Blind.* New York: Basic Books, 1977.
Fraiberg, S., and Freedman, D. A. "Studies in the Ego Development of the Congenitally Blind Child." *Psychoanalytic Study of the Child* 19 (1964): 113–69.
Fraiberg, S.; Seigal, B. L.; and Gibson, R. "The Role of Sound in the Search Behavior of the Blind Infant." *The Psychoanalytic Study of the Child* 21 (1966): 227–57.
Gottesman, M. "A Comparative Study of Piaget's Developmental Schema of Sighted Children with That of a Group of Blind Children." *Child Development* 42 (1971): 573–80.
Gruber, K. F., and Leslie, M. *Cumulative Record of Visual Functioning of Children and Youth with Severe Visual Impairment.* Portland, Ore.: Portland State University, 1967.
Harley, R. K. "Children with Visual Disabilities." In *Exceptional Children in the Schools,* edited by L. Dunn, pp. 411–67. 2nd ed. New York: Holt, Rinehart and Winston, 1973.
Jones, R. L.; Gottfried, N. W.; and Owens, A. "The Social Distance of the Exceptional Child: A Study at the High School Level." *Exceptional Children* 32 (1966): 551–56.
Jose, R. T.; Cummings, J.; and McAdams, L. "The Model Low Vision Clinical Service: An Interdisciplinary Vision Rehabilitation Program." *New Outlook for the Blind* 69 (1975): 249–54.

Knight, J. J. "Mannerisms in the Congenitally Blind Child." *New Outlook for the Blind* 65 (1970): 297–301.
Larson, R. W. "Teaching Orientation to Blind Children." *Education of the Visually Handicapped* 7 (1975): 26–31.
Lowenfeld, B. *Our Blind Children: Growing and Learning with Them.* Springfield, Ill.: Charles C Thomas, 1971.
Lowenfeld, B., ed. *The Visually Handicapped Child in School.* New York: John Day Co., 1973.
Lukoff, I. F.; Cohen, O.; et al. *Attitudes Toward Blind Persons.* New York: American Foundation for the Blind, 1972.
Meighan, T. *An Investigation of the Self-Concept of Blind and Visually Handicapped Adolescents.* New York: American Foundation for the Blind, 1971.
Midwest Regional Center for Services to Deaf-Blind Children. *A Manual for the Assessment of a "Deaf-Blind" Multiple Handicapped Child.* Lansing, Mich.: 1978.
Morgan, C. T., and King, R. A. *Introduction to Psychology,* 3rd ed. New York: McGraw-Hill, 1966.
Napier, G. D.; Kappan, D. L.; Tuttle, D. W.; and Schrotberger, W. L. *Handbook for Teachers of the Visually Handicapped.* Louisville, Ky.: American Printing House for the Blind, 1974.
National Society for the Prevention of Blindness. *Estimated Statistics on Blindness and Vision Problems.* New York: National Society for the Prevention of Blindness, 1966.
National Society for the Prevention of Blindness. *Visual Screening in Schools.* Publication #257. New York: National Society for Prevention of Blindness, 1969.
Ophthalmologic Staff of the Hospital for Sick People, Toronto. *The Eye in Childhood.* Chicago: Year Book Medical Publishers, 1967.
Piaget, J. *Origins of Intelligence in Children.* New York: International University Press, 1952.
Rogow, S. "Perceptual Organization in Blind Children." *New Outlook for the Blind* 69 (1975): 226–33.
Singer, J. L., and St. Reiner, B. F. "Imaginative Content in the Dreams and Fantasy Play of Blind and Sighted Children." *Perceptual and Motor Skills* 22 (1966): 475–81.
Tait, P. "Play and the Intellectual Development of Blind Children." *New Outlook for the Blind* 66 (1972): 361–69.
U.S. Office of Education. *Estimated Number of Handicapped Children in the United States, 1971–1972.* Washington, D.C.: USOE, 1971.
Walker, D. L. "Body Image and Blindness: A Review of Related Theory and Research." *American Foundation for the Blind Research Bulletin,* no. 25, 1973, pp. 211–31.
Winebrenner, D. K. "Finding the Visually Inadequate Child." *Visual Digest* 16 (1952): 21–34.
Wright, B. "An Analysis of Attitudes: Dynamics and Effects." *New Outlook for the Blind* 68 (1974): 108–18.

American Association of Workers
  for the Blind
1511 K Street, NW
Suite 637
Washington, D.C. 20005

American Foundation for the Blind
14 West Sixteenth Street
New York, New York 10011

American Printing House for the Blind
1639 Frankfort Avenue
Louisville, Kentucky 40206

Association for Education of the
  Visually Disabled
711 Fourteenth Street, NW
Washington, D.C. 20005

Library of Congress Division for the Blind
10 First Street, SE
Washington, D.C. 20540

National Association of Sheltered
 Workshops and Homebound Programs
1522 K Street, NW
Washington, D.C. 20005

National Society for Low Vision People
2346 Clermont
Denver, Colorado 80207

US Office of Vocational Education
400 Maryland Avenue, SW
Washington, D.C. 20202

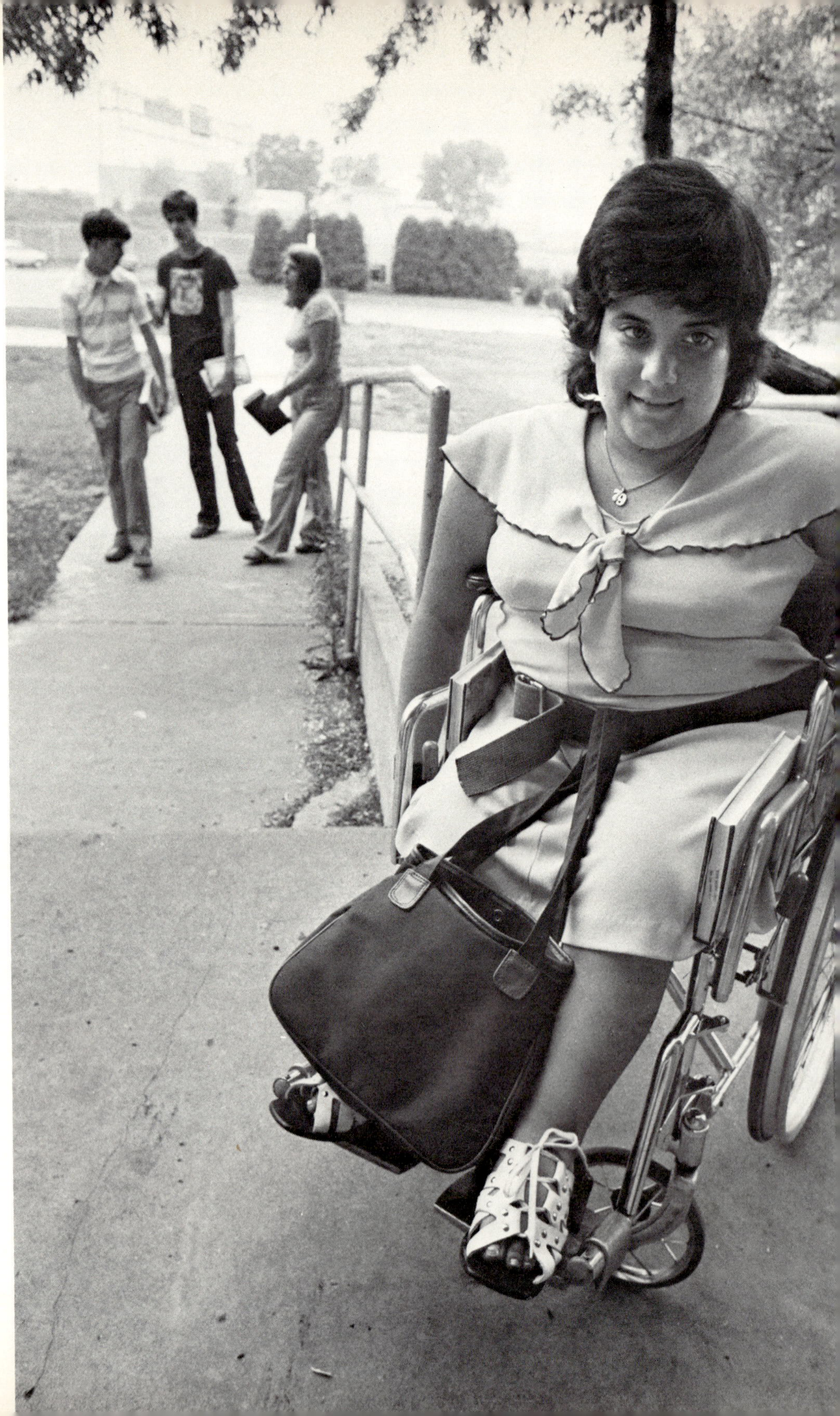

11 Children and youth with physical and health disabilities
Harry J. Parker

Introduction
Disorders of the nervous system—cerebral dysfunction • Cerebral palsy • Epileptic seizures
Disorders of the musculoskeletal system • Juvenile rheumatoid arthritis • Muscular dystrophy
Disorder of the cardiovascular system • Rheumatic fever
Disorder of the endocrine system • Diabetes
Disorders of the respiratory system • Allergies and bronchial asthma
Life-threatening disorders • Leukemia • Cystic fibrosis
Other disorders and their educational implications
Multihandicapped children
Summary

Student learning objectives
The student will:
1. become acquainted with some of the physical and health disabilities in children that school personnel may face in the classroom
2. become acquainted with definitions, causative factors, incidence, treatment strategies, secondary behavioral characteristics, and educational and career planning for youngsters with physical and health disabilities
3. be able to group certain disabilities according to a disorder system
4. be able to identify some of the key elements associated with causation

Children and youth with physical and health disabilities

Student learning objectives

The student will:
5. gain a knowledge of the comparative incidence of various health disorders
6. gain a knowledge of some of the treatment and therapeutic techniques used with various health disorders and of the meaning of some of the descriptive terms used in the symptomology of these disorders
7. become aware of various behavior that may emerge from the child, family, home, and peers as a result of physical/health disabilities, and learn how teachers can help to offset psychological problems
8. recognize the necessity for realistic educational and career planning in relation to certain disabilities
9. learn about the relationship between teachers' attitudes toward physical/health disabilities and student school adjustment and achievement

Overview

In this unit we deal with consequences of physical and health disabilities, which range from mild to very severe. Certain of these disabilities may demand an inordinate amount of time and attention from parents, and the expenses incurred for needed medical services can add further family strain. In addition, parents of exceptional children and youth often face a difficult task in coping with feelings about how their child is different from other children. Extra efforts on the part of educational personnel to understand and work with such children and their families are imperative. In some cases the child, the family members, and the school personnel must accept the fact that certain conditions are permanent or may even culminate in death.

Regular and special classroom teachers are vital to the provision of needed supportive services for the physically or health disabled child and his or her family. Teacher interest and concern is supported by federal legislation, which specifies the rights of each individual to equal educational provisions and equal access to later employment opportunities. Most importantly, school people and government are trying to eliminate unwarranted stereotypes about certain physical and/or health disabilities, such as epilepsy and cerebral palsy.

Aspects studied

We will be looking at the following aspects of the various disabilities: (1) definition and causes; (2) incidence and prevalence; (3) treatment and therapeutic techniques; (4) secondary characteristics or behavioral implications as they may affect the child, family, school, and peer situations; and (5) educational and career planning. Agencies, institutions, and programs serving various disabilities are listed as resources in the references at the end of the unit. Federal legislation designed for a specific disease or health disorder is also listed there.

Introduction

Children and youth with physical and health disabilities present a unique challenge to teachers and health-related professionals. The teacher must see that ongoing education and support are provided to such children and youth, who will frequently be absent from school and may be hospitalized for varying periods of time. Everyone (parent, health professional, and teacher) must recognize and appreciate how difficult it is for a child to have a chronic illness that requires so much medical attention. Open communication and close cooperation among the various professionals and the family become critical for the educational, emotional, and actual physical health of the child.

Children and youth with health disabilities are so defined when the medical problem limits the alertness, vitality, or strength of the individual to such an extent that his or her educational performance is adversely affected. Depending on the severity of the condition, the child's social and emotional status is also affected.

Definition of health disability

The disabilities of this young population can be caused by: (1) diseases, such as polio or tuberculosis; (2) congenital anomalies, such as clubfoot, cleft lip/palate, or the absence of some limb or part of the body; (3) prenatal and postnatal complications (known or unknown), such as those represented in cerebral palsy and epilepsy; and (4) other systemic health disorders, such as rheumatoid arthritis and diabetes.

Origins

Many health-related problems will come to the attention of the teacher in the classroom setting. In this unit our discussion will focus on those physical and health disabilities that have greatest relevance for teachers and other educational personnel.

Disorders of the nervous system—cerebral dysfunction

Cerebral palsy (CP)

Paralysis or neuromotor disabilities resulting from organic damage to motor control centers of the brain is termed cerebral palsy. Cerebral refers to the brain, and *palsy* refers to a weakness, lack of control, or paralysis of any voluntary muscle due to a disorder in the nervous system. The United Cerebral Palsy Associations call the disability of cerebral palsy "a group of medical conditions—not a disease" (1976, p. 1).

Cerebral palsy defined

Clinical symptoms vary, depending on the part(s) of the brain affected. They include the following (Cobb, 1973; Department of HEW, 1975):

1. *Spasticity.* In the spastic type of CP the muscles are still and resistive in all four limbs with variation in contraction-flexion of upper versus lower limbs, but with only one side of the body involved. Spastic paralysis represents from 50 to 65 percent of all cases seen.
2. *Athetosis.* The athetoid type of CP appears more disabling than the spastic. Athetosis is evidenced by a constant twisting, writhing motion; drooling; fa-

cial contortions; imbalance of the head, neck, and shoulders; and involuntary muscle contractions resulting in marked uncoordination.
3. *Ataxia.* The ataxic type of CP is reflected in uncoordinated movement, inability to balance, and difficulty with magnitude or direction of equilibrium or orientation in space.
4. *Rigidity.* This is a most severe type and is characterized by continuous tension when limbs are extended. There is no flexibility, hence there is difficulty in walking or mobility of any type.
5. *Tremor.* Various types of tremors (coarse or fine, rapid or slow) may appear but are usually limited to certain muscle groups and appear rhythmic and totally involuntary.
6. *Atonic, or flaccid.* This CP condition refers to a flabby, lifeless function so that no coordination is possible.

Many cases of CP can involve a combination of the six types noted, with severity ranging from a relatively mild limitation to complete absence of directed motion. Strictly speaking, only damage in the early developmental years to the central nervous system related to motor coordination is CP.

Causes

Causation of CP is related to: (1) prenatal complications (blood-type incompatibility, rubella and other viral diseases in the mother or toxic substances in the mother's blood); (2) perinatal complications (difficult childbirth, prolonged labor); (3) postnatal complications in the early years of life (encephalitis or meningitis).

Multihandicaps of CP children

Other disabilities can accompany motor-control difficulties in CP children, and these conditions will have a direct bearing on the child's education. Intellectual limitations may be present, and these are usually in direct relation to the degree of physical impairment. Hearing losses are usually not significant, but visual problems are common, with studies suggesting over one-half of the CPs are affected in the visual modality. Speech defects remain the most common of all accompanying disabilities. As we can see from the above, CP children are often multihandicapped; they require the services of a team of professionals.

Incidence and prevalence Friedman and MacQueen (1971) found 1.7 children per 1000 with CP and in need of special education. Perhaps 3 in 1000 might be a good estimate; though with a more enlightened public, better medical care, and state and federal programs, the earlier diagnosis of conditions may make for a lowering of this estimate. Kurland et al. (1973) indicate an incidence of one per thousand and a prevalence of 0.6 per thousand total population.

Treatment and therapeutic techniques Physical therapy or training of body areas to take over needed muscle functions represents one means of helping CP children and youth to achieve more controlled mobility and psychomotor behavior. Training in muscle relaxation to promote movement and produce some measure of control over involuntary movement is a long-term process. Occupational therapy can aid in activities of daily living and occupational mobility.

Bracing, support, and even surgery on muscles and tendons have been employed to produce better motion. Medication programs have been used to modify hyperactivity, control emotions, and relax muscle groups. Improvement of treatment must be an ongoing team effort, consistently striving to serve the child's best interests. For school personnel, the CP child represents one of the most challenging of all exceptional children to educate for independent living. They may have multihandicaps, be unable to communicate and/or walk, and yet be free of any intellectual exceptionality. *Treatment requires ongoing team effort*

Secondary behaviorial characteristics   Since many of the neuromuscular problems previously described are easily seen, they may overshadow consideration of other difficulties. Perceptual problems, including tactile and muscular impairment, difficulty in identifying concepts, problems with spatial orientation, writing irregularities, and reading difficulties may also be evidenced.

Behavioral aspects associated with cerebral palsy can include accident proneness, mood fluctuation, perseveration, short attention span, and hyperactivity. Peer rejection because of speech inadequacy may result in withdrawal, shyness, immature behavior, or an attempt by the CP child to avoid communication. It is most important that the teachers and the family do not set overly high expectations and unrealistic goals for the CP child, particularly concerning speech and writing skills. *Academic and emotional considerations*

Educational and career planning   In planning educational goals for the CP child, the multidisciplinary approach is emphasized. Scherzer et al. (1972) found that analysis of the factors of (1) medical involvement, (2) level of intelligence, (3) social development, and (4) family stability is 80 percent accurate in predicting educational placement and development—especially in regular schools. CPs may require placement in a special CP center, where the total team approach and expertise of diverse professionals can be applied consistently. In some cases special classes for CPs in the public school system represent a more economical and manageable educational venture. Accommodations can be made for mainstreaming a CP child in regular classes if adequate physical facilities are present. *Placement and mainstreaming*

The inclusion of a physical education program in public schools is being urged, including organized competitive sports collateral to any other medical effort, in order to create independence and physical freedom (Huberman, 1976). On follow-up, it was shown that with appropriate services, approximately 60 percent of a CP group were living independently and/or employed (O'Reilly, 1975).

Because of the multiple physical problems that are presented, it is crucial that the family be counseled early in the life of the CP child; the earlier that educators can begin a stimulation program, the better the progress. There is presently a dearth of day-care centers and preschool facilities with trained personnel who can ade- *Early intervention is crucial* quately provide the socialization and cognitive stimulation that the CP child needs so desperately. A wider range of social programs and sheltered workshops for continued development and occupational involvement are needed, too. CP centers are few and far between, so a considerable amount of travel time and transportation arrangements are required.

Epileptic seizures

The approximately four million persons with epilepsy (children, youth and adults) are faced with enormous problems throughout life. They are forced to combat extensive stigma still associated with this type of disorder of the nervous system. The Epilepsy Foundation of America (EFA), notes references to epilepsy are contained in the earliest of writings, including the Bible; yet the extent of misinformation and the lack of information concerning the true nature of this disability is still overwhelming (EFA, 1974).

Misinformation about epilepsy is widespread

In today's society, epileptics still may be the victims of others' misunderstandings, as evidenced in the following examples:

> A college student suddenly acts confused and disoriented, is approached and searched by a suspicious policeman, and a vital anticonvulsant drug is taken away from him on the way to the police station. An airline passenger becomes convulsive, turns blue, and the pilot immediately requests an emergency landing for medical help. A nightclub entertainer falls unconscious on the street and is subsequently arrested and charged with public drunkenness. All three people had experienced epileptic seizures and were penalized because their symptoms were not recognized. But these drastic actions are not unusual, for epilepsy is still one of the least known, most misunderstood of all medical disorders (EFA, 1971a, pp. 2–3).

What is epilepsy? The term *epilepsy* is derived from the Greek word meaning *seizure*. The Epilepsy Foundation of America defines the term as *a series of disorders of the nervous system, centered in the brain.* While it may be more exact to refer to such disorders as "epilepsies," since there is a wide variation in types, severity, frequency, and treatability, we will use the term *epileptic seizure* throughout. *Epileptic seizures are the result of intermittent imbalance in the electrical activity present in the brain cells.* This instability can be manifested in muscular spasms, loss of consciousness for periods ranging from a few seconds to several minutes, seizures or convulsions, or behavior viewed as odd or bizarre, resulting from temporary loss of awareness.

Definition

While various types of seizures can result from disease or injury to the brain cells, no specific causes can be thoroughly identified. However, certain events can be traced to conditions before, during, or after birth. These include such factors as head trauma, chemical imbalance, nutritional deficiency, fevers, tumors, and infec-

Causes are unknown and may be variable

tious diseases. We know only that the brain cells discharge electrical energy abnormally.

Diagnosis of epileptic seizures   Diagnosis of seizures includes the usual pattern of obtaining pertinent past history that may relate to the child's or youth's present difficulties. The examining physician will want to know when seizuring symptoms or activities began, the descriptive behavior during the seizure, and the circumstances that may have precipitated or contributed to seizure activity. As much information as the family, teacher, or child can provide about early developmental history, previous illnesses, and present patterns of behavior contributes to adequate diagnosis and future therapeutic methods.

Developmental history important to diagnosis

Introducing Wendy—Although she has a spina bifida condition (defective closure around the spinal cord), Wendy attends a regular school and participates in classroom and extracurricular activities.

An essential part of diagnosis is a neurological examination to further determine the type of seizure difficulty present and the possible source of neurological disturbance. Use of electroencephalography (EEG) to record the brain's electrical activity is primary to diagnosis and to suggested anticonvulsant therapy. While a normal EEG does not rule out a seizure disorder, the EEG does aid in detecting possible structural abnormalities that may need to be assessed further by skull X-ray, computerized axial tomography (CAT) scan of the brain, and other neurological tests.

Types of seizure activity The most commonly recognized kinds of seizure behavior fall into the following categories: (1) petit mal, (2) grand mal, and (3) psychomotor. A more clinically or medically oriented classification scheme uses four groups of seizures (partial, generalized, unilateral, and unclassified). Classroom teachers need to be acquainted, however, with the more common grouping of seizures so they may recognize them if they occur in the school environment. (See Figure 11-1 for distribution of seizure types among children.)

Petit mal

Petit mal seizures occur most often in children between the ages of four and ten years (EFA, 1973a). Staring or daydreaming may be the initial manifestations but classroom learning may suffer as periods of memory lapses are experienced. Other symptoms can include rapid eye blinking and small jerking or twitching movements of the head or arm. This type of seizure may occur as frequently as one hundred times per day, although duration is generally less than a minute (EFA, 1974, p. 8). If the classroom teacher lacks knowledge of the nature of petit mal, such symptoms may go unrecognized. Following petit mal seizure, the child or youth is able to resume activities as if no interference was encountered. This type of seizure some-

Figure 11.1
Distribution of seizure types in children age 11

Petit mal only		3%
Minor only		20%
Grand mal and other (includes petit mal)		9%
Grand mal and minor (includes psychomotor)		17%
Grand mal only		51%

Source: Rutter, Graham & Yule, 1970

times disappears spontaneously at puberty, but it can continue to adulthood. Early identification followed by proper treatment can reduce future complications.

Grand mal takes the form of blackouts and convulsive, violent shaking of the body. It may last from one to twenty minutes, but usually less than five minutes. Other symptoms are irregular breathing, drooling, and blue pallor of the face and lips. Some children and youth identify a warning signal (often referred to as *aura*) which alerts them to the onset of a seizure. Such signals may include a feeling of numbness or tingling in the body or the sensation of experiencing a particular or peculiar smell or sound. If the grand mal seizure is of brief duration, the child or youth may be able to resume activity but may be confused for a brief period of time. The child will often be drowsy after an episode and may need to sleep.

Grand mal

The tonic-clonic type of grand mal seizure is the most common and is described as follows:

> In this case, the patient, if standing, becomes rigid (*tonic* phase) and falls in the direction he [or she] is leaning. This phase soon changes to generalized *jerking* movements (*clonic* phase). In other cases, however, the patient may remain rigid for the duration of the seizure (tonic type) or go into generalized convulsions (clonic type) without passing through the tonic phase (EFA, 1973a, p. 6).

A responsible, knowledgeable person should monitor the child or youth experiencing a grand mal seizure during his or her loss of consciousness and subsequent reactions. The child or youth should be allowed to awaken voluntarily. Instructions for first aid are spelled out below (EFA, 1973a, p. 9):

1. *Keep calm* when a major seizure occurs. You cannot stop a seizure once it has started. Do not restrain the patient or try to revive him.
2. *Clear the area* around him or hard, sharp or hot objects which could injure him. Place a pillow or rolled-up coat under his head.
3. *Do not force anything between the teeth.* If his mouth is open, you might place a soft object like a handkerchief between his side teeth.
4. *Turn the patient's head to the side,* and make sure his breathing is not obstructed. Loosen necktie and tight clothing but do not interfere with his movements.
5. *Do not be concerned* if he seems to stop breathing. *Do be concerned* if the patient seems to pass from one seizure into another without gaining consciousness. This is rare but requires a doctor's help.
6. Carefully observe the patient's actions during the seizure for a full medical report later. When the seizure is over let the patient rest if he wishes.

Psychomotor seizures occur more often in older children and adults. Symptoms generally include a sudden, rapid onset of confused or dazed behavior (e.g., dizziness) in which the individual ceases any current activity. Psychomotor seizures

Psychomotor seizure

vary in form but can include purposeless movements (called *automatism*). Repetitious and poorly coordinated movements such as lip-smacking or chewing, rubbing of legs or hands, or picking at clothing may be evidenced. Incoherency of speech may be shown as well as inappropriate emotional behavior, such as sudden onset of fear, temper tantrums, or anger (EFA, 1973a; 1974).

During a psychomotor seizure, no restraint should be used unless necessary for the personal safety of the seizuring person. Suggestions "made in a pleasant and friendly manner" (EFA, 1974) are usually sufficient to control psychomotor seizures while the seizure is going on (about fifteen to twenty minutes).

Victim may be totally unaware of seizure

If the psychomotor seizure is of brief duration, normal activity is usually resumed and the child or youth may be totally unaware of his or her seizure behavior. This can be upsetting to the child, particularly if unusual behavior was exhibited in the presence of classmates. When the seizure subsides, the child may think that others are laughing at him or her and may not understand what occurred. If the seizure is lengthy, confusion can be present for a period of time.

Other types of seizures include infantile myoclonic (very brief, characterized by involuntary muscle contractions on both sides of the body) seizures, with jerking, crying, and loss of interest in surroundings; focal motor (Jacksonian) seizure, which relates to motor or body movements; and autonomic seizure, in which repeated symptoms of headache, nausea, and fever may affect school learning, behavior, and emotional control. The latter may be misdiagnosed, and the child or youth thought to be malingering to avoid going to school.

Incidence and prevalence   From a wide array of studies the Professional Advisory Board of the Epilepsy Foundation of America has concluded that at least 2 percent of the present population of the United States, or approximately 4 million people, suffer from some form of epileptic seizure disorders (EFA, 1970). If one assumes that a prevalence figure of 2 percent remains constant, the population growth alone will result in 70,000 new cases per year (Kurland et al., 1973; Kurtzke et al., 1973).

Incidence rates may be increasing

However, there are some indications that incidence rates may be increasing slightly. Although preventive medicine is making some inroads via prenatal and postnatal care and in treatment of infections, the number of head injuries (especially in the young) due to automobile accidents is increasing. Hence we can cite 80,000 people as newly afflicted and one million diagnosed as having recurrent convulsive disorders. Prevalence figures may be underestimated because both the parents of children with seizures and the youth and adults with seizures themselves are reluctant to disclose the presence of the disorder. School nurses, for example, indicate that frequently school officials detect the condition only after a student experiences seizures within the school setting. Furthermore, older youths and adults may sometimes feel *forced* to conceal the presence of seizures. The following portion of a letter to the editor of the Epilepsy Foundation Association Newsletter reveals one of the reasons.

Reluctance to disclose the presence of the disorder

Thanks, EFA

> Ten years ago, when I was a teenager, I suffered a blow to the head. A few days later I experienced my first epileptic seizure. I was placed on anticonvulsant medication by my neurologist and I resumed a normal active life through high school and one year of college.
>
> When I entered the job market, I discovered that employers were afraid of people with epilepsy. The only job I could find was in a sheltered workshop.
>
> In 1969, on the advice of my physician, I went underground. No longer would I admit on job application forms that I had epilepsy. Within a few weeks I secured a good job at a decent wage with a local airline.
>
> For six years I worked without incident. Last month I had a seizure on the job and was terminated for falsifying my employment application (EFA, 1975, p. 2).

The writer of the letter goes on to express his appreciation for support from his San Francisco chapter on epilepsy. A series of public presentations were launched via television and other media explaining in factual terms the nature of the disability and discussing employment problems. Aided by these and other private efforts, he was able to resume his employment.

While job discrimination is still practiced, the public is becoming more enlightened and less prejudiced toward epileptics, who are no less capable in terms of job performance than a person who is free of seizures.

Dispelling the myths about epilepsy

Treatment and therapeutic techniques   Although there is no absolute cure for seizures, control can be achieved by proper intervention procedures. Since a seizure disorder is a medical problem, it can often be controlled through the use of medication. Medical management of seizures with anticonvulsants represents the primary method of control. It is estimated that approximately "50 percent of people can achieve complete control and 30 percent more [can achieve] partial control through careful use of different medicines" (EFA, 1973b, p. 6). Children with seizures may eventually become seizure-free, have a normal EEG, and be taken off medication. Since each anticonvulsant drug acts uniquely upon the particular kind of seizure, careful medical diagnosis must precede selection and administration of anticonvulsant medication. Some medications require periodic checks of the level of dosage by measuring the blood level. Occasionally some children and youth become overdosed and act extremely lethargic. Other treatment for seizures may include biofeedback conditioning, and in very rare cases, surgical intervention.

Medication is primary method of control

Secondary behavioral characteristics   We have discussed the need for medical treatment of the physical aspects of seizures. The psychosocial and emotional aspects must also be examined. School personnel can be vital in helping to minimize adjustment difficulties among children and youth with seizures. Our society places a good deal of emphasis on conformity and individuals with seizures are subject to these pressures to attempt to conform, "but the social stigma attached to epilepsy (in addition to the basic nonconformity of a seizure) often [constrains] conforming or norm-accepted behavior" (Arangio, 1975, p. 8).

Independence is another value that is highly prized by most people in our culture. Seizure-disordered children or youth can easily feel dependent on medications and people around them who can help during a seizure. Anxiety about this dependency and insecurity about uncertain seizure control may extend to seizure-free periods of time. Feelings of self-doubt concerning abilities may become "so frustrating and painful that the person will withdraw totally from social relationships and regress into greater dependence than is actually warranted" (Arangio, 1975, p. 8).

Secondary psychosocial problems

Of course, no psychological or behavioral aberrations *necessarily* occur as a consequence of seizures. But if a child or youth does develop secondary emotional or psychosocial problems, it is likely due to one or more of the following (Livingston, 1972):

1. *attitudes of the parents and significant others* who may try to hide the fact of seizures, be embarrassed, overprotective, or fearful of being around the child or youth during seizures
2. *social stigma and outdated laws still associated with seizures,* including the false notion that people with seizures are either crazy or mentally retarded, sterilization laws, insurance and auto drivers' license exclusions, and similar restrictions and prohibitions based on ignorance and misinformation
3. *overdosage or adverse drug reactions* that lead to emotional side-effects and unusual behavior. Once the drug is changed or discontinued, the child returns to a normal state
4. *anxiety over anticipation of having a seizure,* which may include fear of dying or fear of being hurt

Two case examples will illustrate problems relating to points 3 and 4.

Ellie   A bright teenager whose seizures began recurring as she entered puberty, Ellie was placed on a new anticonvulsant medication. Soon afterward her teacher became concerned about Ellie's erratic behavior. She had crying spells, reacted aggressively against any classmate who seemed to upset her, and, in general, was not her previous self. The teacher consulted Ellie's mother, and she, in turn consulted the pediatric neurologist, who immediately changed the anticonvulsant medication he had prescribed. Within twenty-four to forty-eight hours Ellie resumed her previous acceptable behavior.

If Ellie had been referred for psychiatric evaluation and her medical problem had not been shared with the neurologist, her erratic behavior might have gone on for months. She herself might even have begun to believe that she was indeed mentally disturbed.

Jerry   A six-year-old boy diagnosed as having seizures was receiving special tutoring because of his visual-motor perceptual problem. He asked his special teacher to write the following: "Hello, I'm Jerry. I have seizures. Don't be afraid." Jerry went on to explain that in the past his seizures sometimes had occurred where people reacted fearfully, and he was concerned about his classmates' reactions if he were to have a seizure now that he was at school.

Educational planning   Even though current opinion reflects the view that exceptional children should be placed in the least restrictive environment possible (see Unit 1), sources of placement for children and youth with seizures must be consigned on an individual basis. The degree of physical disability must be appraised and a decision must be based on how the specific child's needs can best be met. Many children with seizures are diagnosed as learning disabled. But, depending on the severity of the seizure and whether it is well controlled by medication, these children may not require special education.

Arguments for special educational treatment include the availability of: (1) specially trained teachers, (2) special teaching resources, (3) social adjustment emphasis, and (4) sports and recreation under defined conditions. While studying two hundred children with epilepsy, Harlin (1965) found 30 percent were being provided with some form of special education. Arguments against special education include: (1) segregation of the child or youth from peers and the outside world, (2) probable restrictions on freedom of movement and activity, (3) the limited number of children and youth with seizures in the same school environment, precluding special class provision, and (4) problems of adaptation to the real world upon school completion.

Pros and cons of special treatment

With respect to educational problems, school achievement of a child with seizures is found to be related to teacher attitudes about the disorder. Teachers' knowledge about the role of seizures in shaping the behavior of this student population is regarded as a critical factor in adjustment.

Teacher's knowledge of seizure behavior is a critical factor

Studies suggest that many children with seizures have psychological problems that may interfere with school achievement and subsequent career endeavors. Harlin (1965) identifies these problems as resulting from: (1) impending feelings of doom that precede a seizure, (2) post-seizure awakening to agitated, anxious adults, (3) daily intake of pills, (4) oversolicitousness by family, (5) strong reactions from other children toward the seizures, (6) the need for frequent physician or hospital visits, and (7) interruption of school, family, and social programs because of medical problems.

Specific career planning   The majority of individuals subject to epileptic seizures are completely capable of providing for themselves when given the opportu-

Eliminating job discrimination

nity. They have the ability to perform many types of jobs in a variety of settings. Hence, one of the most important goals of persons and organizations concerned with this exceptionality is to acquaint future employers with these facts. Public education concerning this aspect of epilepsy has made some progress, but a great deal still needs to be accomplished to eliminate job discrimination. Well-informed teachers can be a vital link in helping these youth to make appropriate career choices according to their physical, personal, educational, and social capabilities.

Disorders of the musculoskeletal system

Juvenile rheumatoid arthritis (JRA)

This is a serious, painful, and oftimes crippling inflammatory disorder that can affect the whole body. It primarily attacks the joints, but can affect the lungs, skin, muscles, heart, and even the eyes. It is a chronic illness that may subside but may also then flare up again. While JRA can begin at any age, it most often strikes a child between eighteen months and four years of age. The cause of JRA is unclear; it has been found, however, that many children develop a respiratory infection before its onset. Since JRA mimics other serious childhood diseases, the diagnosing physician will want the child to undergo numerous tests. Because of the painful and tender feeling in the child's joints, he or she may be limited in activity. The illness is not necessarily life-threatening, but the child does feel pain and stiffness in body joints.

JRA mimics other diseases

About one-half of the children will have complete abatement of symptoms and no crippling evidence; one-fourth will have abatement and some crippling evidence; but the rest will continue to have sustained active symptoms, such as difficulty in joint movement and related pain. The span of JRA is about three years, with a range of one to ten years. Prognosis for recovery is excellent; however, school absence for varying lengths of time will occur, and school activities, particularly on the playground, may have to be modified for the JRA child.

Causal theories

Two causal theories for JRA have been proposed: (1) that it is caused by a virus and (2) that the body's defense system has been disrupted, producing antibodies that attack its own joints and tissues. Emotional stress is acknowledged as a possible factor in the aggravation of the disease (Arthritis Foundation, 1974).

Prevalence Estimates by the Arthritis Foundation (1974) suggest that 250,000 children are affected. About three times as many girls as boys have JRA.

Treatment and therapeutic techniques Educators play a significant role in the team effort involved in working with a JRA child. Treatment includes a good pattern of rest, supervised exercise, massage, special physical therapy, careful monitoring of infections, counseling to deal with emotional stress, and a well-balanced diet. No single drug has been found that will cure JRA. The steroid cortisone is helpful but must be carefully supervised due to its potentially harmful side effects.

Exercises for developing and strengthening all the child's muscles are essential and should be carried out scrupulously in formative years. Physical therapy support in exercise is recommended. Hydrotherapy (warm water massage), heat therapy, surgery, and prosthetic devices (braces, splints, crutches) are other means of aiding a child to cope with the condition and to be as independent as possible. In the moderate to severe cases of JRA the educators, parents, and health professionals must communicate with each other so that the teacher will know what activities must be limited for the child and whether or not homebound instruction will be necessary.

Teacher needs to know limits on child's activities

Secondary behavioral characteristics   Because of the possible disfiguring aspects of JRA, children with this illness may tend to avoid contact with others and have a poor self-image. Feeling inferior or less worthy than peers can become evident. It is not unusual for JRA children to be overly sensitive to criticism, to be extremely dependent upon others, and to exhibit general frustration over the physical

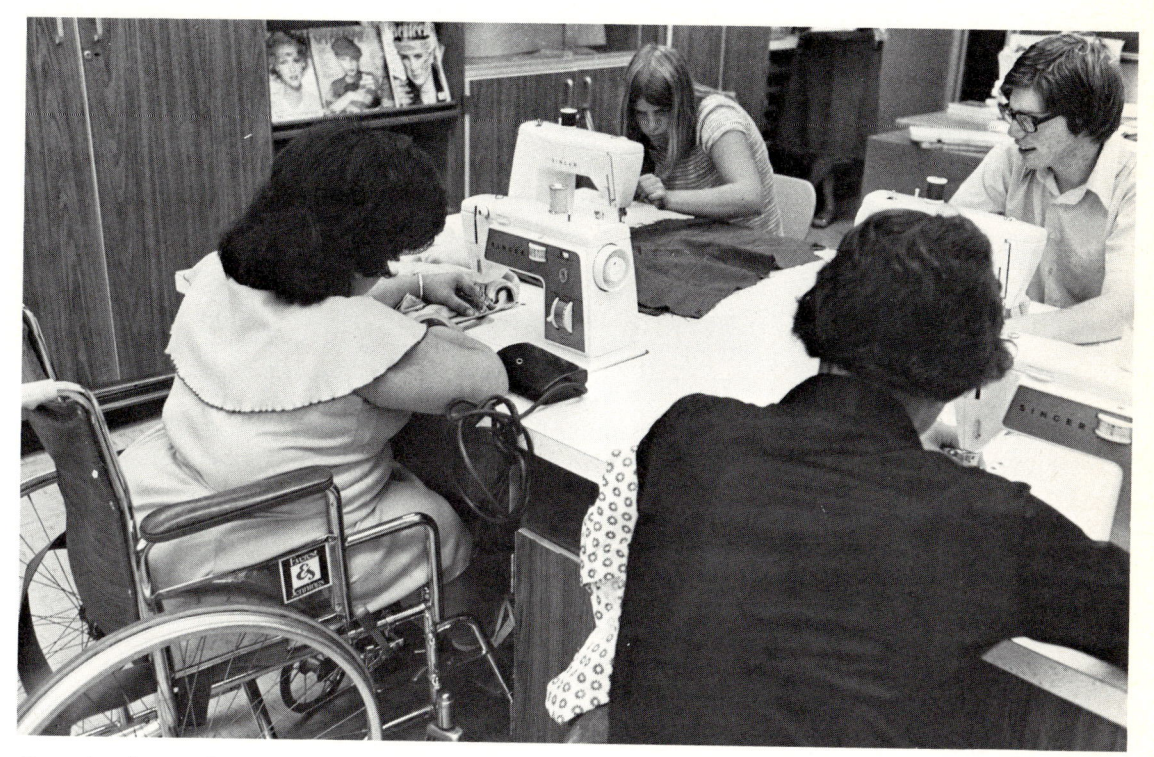

Despite her wheelchair, which necessitates the use of ramps instead of stairs, Wendy is able to pursue her school interests in the same way as the other, nonexceptional students shown here in a home economics class.

limitations imposed by their disorder. We often observe, too, that these children have difficulty expressing anger in appropriate ways (Cleveland & Brewer, 1970).

Parents must avoid overprotection of the child since this can contribute to his or her long-term difficulty (Brewer, 1970). Failure to get support from school or age-mates can cause feelings of estrangement and isolation, particularly if home support is based upon the child's dependency and being different. A case example will illustrate some of the problems encountered by the child with JRA and the resulting effects this disease can have on his or her family and school life.

Kelly   A physical examination of Kelly shows a very thin, twelve-year-old who looks chronically ill. She complains about joint pains and has difficulty with joint movement.

Compound problems of the child pose significant family crises. There are six children in the family; the mother cannot work because she takes full-time care of Kelly. The father has all he can do to make ends meet. Kelly is reacting with apathy, extreme dependency, crying spells, excessive fears, and inordinate demands upon other members of the family. Her father avoids contact, and work is a convenient excuse to remain out of the serious family upheaval.

Kelly has found school unappealing, although she makes friends easily. The time she must spend in hospitals and her difficulty in moving around have disrupted her potential interest in school. Kelly's mother feels school is desirable, but the youngster's physical difficulties make getting her to school a problem. With ambulation restricted, Kelly's mother seems to have found it convenient to keep her at home. When Kelly does go to school, her swollen joints are conspicuous to others, and are painful to her. In Kelly's case, actual restrictions on certain school activities, such as participation in physical education classes, seem necessary.

Education and career planning   Under the mainstreaming concept, public school teachers will be directly involved with JRA children; only in severe cases do home teaching, hospital-based classes, and special arrangements need to be considered. With the varied treatments available and the degree of symptom reduction, nearly all children can be kept in the classroom. Special schools have been recommended only under definite medical criteria. The freedom, self-help, and responsibility the child needs can best be provided in a regular school program (Arthritis Foundation, 1974).

Studies have found school programs to be critical factors in the fullest development of youth with this disorder. McAnarney et al. (1974) found that juveniles with JRA had rated poorer in school adjustment and progress than a control group of normals. However, Morse (1972) studied aspiration and achievement in one hundred patients who have been diagnosed as JRAs when younger. He found they had uniformly high levels of aspiration and evidenced greater educational achievement than the normal group. A follow-up of JRAs into adulthood found one-third had prolonged absences from school, but special arrangements resulted in makeup and continuation. Failure of schools, agencies, and state services to help provide achievement opportunities were determined to be detriments. Communication among all groups was strongly urged to aid JRA youngsters maintain aspiration levels and achievement according to individual capacity (Cleveland & Brewer, 1970). Thus the teacher has a key role in providing the opportunity for the JRA child to achieve at optimum levels.

Teacher's key role

Muscular dystrophy (MD)

This disease manifests itself in the destruction or deterioration of the voluntary muscles in the arms and legs; muscle fiber and tissue are replaced by fatty tissue and the loss of muscle fiber weakens and wastes the limbs.

The nature of MD is not fully known. Research findings lead the Muscular Dystrophy Association (1976) to conclude that there is no single disease called MD, but a wide variety of muscle-destroying dystrophies. These may vary by hereditary pattern, age at onset, initial muscles attacked, and rate of progression.

Three types are apparently related to age. One is the childhood Duchenne type, where onset can begin at age one to four, with a greater onset occurring around three years of age. A second type of MD related to age is the juvenile Limb-Girdle type, generally appearing in the teens or early twenties. The muscle degeneration appears in the shoulder girdle and affects the arms, or appears in the pelvic girdle and affects the legs. Girls are affected with this second type nearly as often as boys. Third, is the Facio-Scapulo-Humeral type, occurring in the early twenties in both sexes. Deterioration begins in the muscles of the face, moves to the shoulder girdle or blades, and then to the upper arm.

Types of MD

Prevalence For all of the muscle-destroying dystrophies except the juvenile Limb-Girdle type, males are five to six times more often the bearers than females. Estimated prevalence in the U.S. population is around 250,000, two-thirds of whom are children between the ages of three and thirteen (Muscular Dystrophy Association, 1976). Children affected at an early age have a low probability of living to adulthood.

Males are affected far more than females

Treatment and therapeutic techniques No treatment has been found to deal with the pathology of MD and its progressive deterioration. Generally the earlier the symptoms appear, the more rapid the deterioration. Death usually results from respiratory failure. Physical therapy has been of value in delaying the muscle contractures, and antibiotics tend to prolong the child or youth's life and retard respiratory infection.

Secondary behavioral characteristics Even if a child's intellectual abilities are not affected by the disease, motoric loss may still prevent social entry and development of interaction with others. As the child tries to cope with progressive muscular

Retreat into self must be counteracted

deterioration, we may see withdrawal, loss of interest in people and environment, passivity, and retreat into self (Ziter & Allsop, 1975, 1976). Television watching—rather than schoolwork—frequently tends to be a central activity. For those who are not ambulatory, social play and/or hobbies may not occupy a significant amount of time. Physical care represents the pre-eminent challenge to parents and to school personnel. Eating, dressing, and toilet functions and physical lifting, carrying, or stabilizing in walking are the demanding elements.

One of the greatest needs of MD children is the development of a feeling of self-assurance. This can often be accomplished by teaching MD children to perform necessary physical tasks, such as feeding and dressing themselves and making things with their hands. By showing visible pleasure at the student's accomplishments, parents, teachers, and peers can reinforce self-confidence. Attitudes of the parents and siblings with regard to the possible early mortality of the child with MD also need to be dealt with. The teacher can be a crucial and important person in offering supportive understanding to the child and his or her family.

Educational and career planning   The primary goal for school-age MD children is that they remain in school if at all possible. When homebound classes become necessary due to the degree of muscle weakness, opportunities still should be provided for these youngsters to make career plans and to participate in all possible activities of an intellectual-educational-vocational nature (Mearig, 1973). For school personnel, the physical loss aspects of a child with MD comprise the most demanding elements. It is often all too easy to adopt a commiserative attitude toward the child because of possible early death. Most teachers will recognize, however, that this is counterproductive, and will attempt to set up realistic expectations for the child, along with providing supportive emotional components.

Cardiovascular system disorder

Rheumatic fever (RF)
In this disorder of the cardiovascular system, the joints become inflamed and there is accompanying high fever. Several other parts of the body may be attacked at the same time.

Streptococcal infections are usually regarded as the cause, particularly after the age of four (American Heart Association, 1970). Ages five to fifteen are the susceptible years for RF (American Heart Association, 1976). As adolescence approaches, strep infection is more often found in the throat and upper respiratory passages. This infection causes a thickening in the valves of the heart muscle, thereby impeding the flow of blood to the heart chambers.

Susceptibility to upper respiratory infections is common with children who have RF. Since one does not become immune to RF, each incidence of the disease increases the child's susceptibility to upper respiratory infections.

Incidence and prevalence   As early adolescence is approached, incidence rates increase to an estimated 1 to 6 per 1000 (American Heart Association, 1976a). The highest incidence in the U.S. occurs in urban poverty areas, especially those populated by minority groups (Brownell & Bailen, 1973). In the last decades, however, a general decreasing trend has been noted, with a death rate of 1.3 per 100,000 (American Heart Association, 1976a).

    Climate appears to be an important factor in the incidence of RF. Cooler, rainier regions of the U.S. and/or colder, rainier seasons of the year favor higher prevalence of RF cases. Substandard home conditions, such as high-density living circumstances, poor diet, and poor health habits (often associated with socioeconomic conditions discussed in Unit 5), can enhance the incidence of RF.

Cold, wet climate is a factor

Treatment and therapeutic techniques   There appears to be no agreement on the prescribed therapy for RF, although bed rest is used differentially and antibiotics are employed to retard further susceptibility (American Heart Association, 1971). Since there is no "miracle drug" to cure RF, prevention is critical. Integration of an RF child into a normal school situation requires both medical management and the efforts of school personnel and the family to help the child achieve educational objectives.

No miracle drug

Secondary behavioral characteristics   If a long-term confinement and convalescence period is indicated, the child may have difficulty appreciating the reason for restricted activity. It is important to help the child realize that school and parents are not trying to overcontrol or punish him or her for being sick.

Educational and career planning   For some decades, studies have indicated that elementary-school RF children were generally below their peers in achievement, although there is a wide range of variability. Irregular attendance is offered as a reason for these limitations. Homebound and/or hospital instruction should be utilized as necessary to prevent the child from falling too far behind in achieving to his or her potential. The medical problem itself should not produce specific learning problems and classroom instruction can progress as with other children.

Irregular school attendance

Disorder of the endocrine system

Diabetes

Diabetes mellitus is a chronic condition of high levels of sugar in the blood and urine. While technically a genetic disorder rather than an endocrine disorder, it does involve metabolism of carbohydrates. Normally, the pancreas gland produces a hormone called insulin, which is used to facilitate combustion of glucose (sugar), the source of energy in the tissues.

Definition and causes

    In the diabetic, the pancreas may manufacture little or no insulin. Thus sugar is not used and collects or is concentrated in the blood (hyperglycemia). Then this sugar collects in the urine. The kidneys try to eliminate the glucose, pulling water from the body and causing dehydration and thirst. Because the body cannot use carbohydrates without insulin for energy, it consumes fats stored in the body instead. Conversion of this fat into energy produces acid in the urine as a by-product. If continued, serious loss of weight, acidosis, vascular disease, or coma result. Heredity, infection, overeating, endocrine dysfunction, and psychological aspects are causative factors.

Incidence and prevalence   Diabetes is a major health problem, affecting at least 10 million people, or 5 percent of the population. Incidence rates rose by more than 50 percent in the U.S. between 1965 and 1974, meaning a 6 percent increase per year. The child born today has a better than one-in-five chance to develop diabetes. In 1974, 38,000 people died as a direct result of the disorder, but there is strong evidence that as many as 300,000 deaths could be attributed to diabetes and its complications. It ranks third as a cause of death, behind heart disease and cancer, and is the second leading cause of new cases of blindness (National Commission on Diabetes, 1975).

Approximately half of all children with diabetes will die of kidney disease within an average of twenty-five years after the diagnosis of diabetes. The National Commission on Diabetes (1975) estimated 86,000 of juvenile-onset diabetics face the prospect of blindness and death from kidney failure prior to age forty. While the mortality rate for diabetic children has been declining, the symptoms in the juvenile diabetic remain severe—in fact more severe than the symptoms found in adults. Greater variability and day-to-day control problems are also noted for juvenile diabetics. As the child gets older, the conditions stabilize themselves.

It is uncommon to see diabetes in a newborn; the juvenile period usually starts between ages eight and twelve. One child in 2,500 under age fifteen is estimated to have diabetic symptoms, which are unmistakable and rapid in development.

Insulin reaction on the child's physiology often is disturbing and uncomfortable, being characterized by faintness, pallor, and excessive perspiration. The more visible behavior resulting from hypoglycemic effects (low concentration of sugar in the blood) includes irritability, temper tantrums, drowsiness, and lack of concentration.

Treatment and therapeutic techniques   Insulin injection, preferably self-administered, is the most essential control for the rest of the person's life. Oral medication, accompanying or in place of insulin, is also used. Diet control, too, will continue to be an integral part of the life-style to which the person must adjust. Family, peers, and teachers have a responsible role in reinforcing the crucial importance of this treatment.

Teachers need to be alert to emotional and physiological changes in the child and must be aware of the need for urine testing. These aspects must also be communicated effectively to the diabetic child in order to ensure health maintenance.

Secondary behavioral characteristics Due to the limitations placed on diet, activities, and social relations, the diabetic child perceives himself or herself as different (Collier, 1969). The resulting emotional stress can produce undesirable behavior (especially social behavior) and can affect metabolic processes (Newman, 1967). The child may adjust either by becoming extremely anxious and fearful or by becoming rigid, compulsive, and preoccupied with the diabetic condition. Because of the emotional impact of the disease on the child, dealing with feelings is an important part of the treatment regimen. Optimum time with medical personnel to help reduce anxiety is a crucial factor.

Important to deal with feelings

Food matters in particular may become a source of child-family conflict. Issues such as failing to maintain a prescribed diet are often used by the child as a weapon against parents and helping professionals. By far the most highly charged emotional area for the diabetic child, however, is the administration of insulin injections (Davis, 1965). Children often view the administration of insulin as a punishment and something to be avoided if at all possible.

Insulin injection may be viewed as punishment

The family has been cited as reacting readily in two obvious ways: overprotection or resentment-rejection of the child (Collier & Etzwiler, 1971; Etzwiler & Robb, 1972). Both reactions are debilitating to the child and can significantly impair normal personality development. Depending on the child's makeup he or she may, on the one hand, become rebellious, self-destructive, and hostile or, on the other hand, become submissive, passive, and highly dependent.

Etzwiler and Robb (1972) see parent education in adolescent diabetes management as a necessity. Earlier delegation of self-care and responsibility to the adolescent was viewed by parents in one study as part of the growing-up process of the youngster with diabetes (Garner, 1974). Teenagers have indicated that they can be partially responsible for self-care as early as the age of twelve, and fully responsible by fifteen. The impact of a diabetic child on the integrity of the family has been found to be significant and not unlike the impact of other disabilities.

Earlier self-care responsibility

Teachers too play an important role in facilitating the adjustment of the child or adolescent with diabetes. The child needs to be accepted and treated as any other child, with concerned interest and support in his or her educational and emotional development. The teacher can understand the possible sullenness or anxiety that may appear in the child, and can react in a supportive and caring manner.

Educational and career planning In general, the needs of the diabetic child have been met within the regular classroom. The only special requirement is that the teacher be aware of the medical regimen required and that he or she reinforce the child in maintaining firm control of diet and regularity of medication (Friedland, 1976). Collier (1969) found that both teachers and counselors had inadequate

Teacher must work closely with family and physician

knowledge of diabetes and that special preparation was warranted. In order to accomplish educational goals, school personnel must work closely with the family of the diabetic child.

Given the normal life span expectancy of the diabetic who undergoes sound medical management, any educational or vocational goal is possible and not precluded by the disease. Only in very severe cases, where special classes or homebound study is necessary, should educational or vocational plans be modified.

Disorders of the respiratory system

Allergies and bronchial asthma (BA)

Allergens and antibodies

Allergies represent the presence of extreme sensitivity to certain foreign substances (allergens). Specifically, when various allergens enter the body, the protective mechanism in some cells (called antibodies) are released to resist the presence of such substances. Sometimes, however, antibodies react in ways *opposite* to that expected and produce allergic symptoms such as hay fever and asthma-like conditions.

Allergic reactions can involve a variety of body organs: the nose and eyes in sinus problems or hay fever; the lungs, as in asthma; or the skin, as in hives, insect stings, and food and drug reactions.

Definition and causes of asthma

Asthma is defined as *an intermittent, variable, reversible form of airway obstruction,* where the bronchial tubes or air passages of the lungs go into spasm due to hypersensitivity to various stimuli (food, dust, fumes, bacteria, very cold air, or overexertion). Asthmatic symptoms include labored breathing, wheezing, coughing, chest tightness, excessive mucus, and tissue swelling. Asthma is more common among children and, without treatment, can persist to debilitating levels. The following case example illustrates the known association of asthma and stress:

Anxiety aggravates the condition

Dennis Eight-year-old Dennis had bronchial asthma attacks that required periodic hospitalization. His attacks were greatly aggravated by the fear that he could die during an attack because the bus ride to his school took him so far from the hospital and his home.

Dennis's teacher was aware of his medical problem and with the physician's help was able to transfer Dennis to a school three blocks from his home, eliminating the need for a long bus ride. His new teacher was informed of Dennis's medical problem, and offered him additional calming support. The teacher made it clear to Dennis that he would be well cared for should he have an attack. By lessening Dennis's environmental stress and giving him assurance that responsible adults could and would care for him, Dennis's hospitalizations sharply declined.

Incidence and prevalence Approximately 4 percent of school children have asthma (Schwartz, 1972); in fact, it is the leading cause of chronic disease in children under seventeen years of age and the most common pediatric disorder requiring hospitalization in the U.S. (HEW, 1971). In addition, asthma-allergy conditions account for the largest categorical cause of school absenteeism. Gordis (1973) noted that incidence of asthma-allergy is higher in non-Caucasian and lower socio-economic level samples. He suggested that quality of care is a contributor to differences. He also found over one-half of those who develop asthma in youth do so before age five.

More school absences than other categories

The student lounge provides a great opportunity for encouraging social interaction and group acceptance. She need not feel isolated from the mainstream of her fellow classmates.

Treatment and therapeutic techniques   Although there is no known cure for asthma and allergies, treatment and management can reduce the symptoms to less debilitating levels. While drugs represent a preponderant method of control, physician management is essential. Bronchodilator drugs, aerosol mists, and breathing therapy are the approaches used when episodes are mild to moderate. Injection of epinephrine (a hormone secreted in the adrenal gland that stimulates the heart, increases muscular strength, and relaxes bronchial muscles) and ingestion of steroids represent the drug regimen for moderate to severe attacks, but their side effects must be carefully managed. Severe asthma symptoms require hospitalization for treatment.

Controlling the symptoms

A number of therapeutic measures are suggested for the child with asthma or allergies including: (1) elimination of direct contact with known or suspected allergens (pollens, molds, fabrics, animal hair, and bird feathers); (2) modification of home climate control (air conditioning, purification filters, humidity regulation, etc.); (3) consideration of a change of locale if this would be beneficial; (4) exclusion of known allergens from the diet; (5) resolution of psychological problems through psychotherapy; (6) regulation of physical education activities in school (programs that emphasize general physical fitness, especially breathing, are unquestionably beneficial) and (7) continuing medical management to monitor changes in regimen and ensure that an accurate record is maintained (Ghory, 1975).

Secondary behavioral characteristics   Both school personnel and family members should be aware that psychological variables influence the frequency and severity of asthmatic episodes. Anxiety, insecurity, and dependency may be prominent in the asthmatic child. A continuing level of anxiety may be produced by the child's inability to understand how an attack is precipitated. In some cases panic, fear, or irritability may frequently occur (Purcell & Weiss, 1970; Purcell et al., 1972). Crying behavior can become silent and awkward because the asthmatic child soon learns that crying, like laughing and coughing, can trigger an attack of asthma.

Encouraging self-confidence

In the family milieu, restrictions may produce reactive behavior. Children sometimes feel they are being punished and become depressed. The asthmatic child, as any child, needs to gain self-confidence and a greater feeling of freedom to act. A group of asthmatic boys who participated in a program stressing physical activities with peers showed improvement of physical fitness, a decrease in school days lost, and a consistent improvement in sociability, self-assertion, and group activity. In addition, an increase in intelligence test scores from pre- to post-assessment was noted (Purcell & Weiss, 1970; Purcell et al., 1972).

Educational and career planning   Premedication has been proposed as a way of dealing effectively with chronically asthmatic students in physical education and music classes, as well as in regular classes (Bharani & Hyde, 1976). Whatever allergens affect the child, this source of reaction can be readily controlled. It must be monitored in the educational environment through communication between physician, educational personnel, and the family. Except for falling behind in course work due to illness, the asthmatic child should be able to adjust to regular classroom curricula. In cases of severe chronic asthma, the other available options include hospital-based educational programs (sometimes in different parts of the country for optimum climate control), homebound programs, and special classes.

Life-threatening disorders

School personnel may see many other physical and health disabilities among children in their classrooms. Some of these disabilities are life threatening, such as leukemia and cystic fibrosis (CF).

Leukemia

While commonly thought of as a blood disease, *leukemia* is actually a disease of the tissues that produce white cells in the bone marrow, lymph nodes, and spleen. It is a generalized disorder, since the tissues are those protecting the body against bacteria, viruses, and other foreign substances. Overproduction of white cells disrupts production of red cells and prevents blood clotting (Leukemia Society of America, 1975). *Definition*

    Acute leukemia, which occurs in children, represents more than half of the cases of leukemia seen. It is the most common fatal illness in children between ages two and fifteen in the United States, and is exceeded in child fatality rates only by accidents (Leukemia Society of America, no date). Ninety percent of the children with acute leukemia achieve some remission of symptoms and 50 percent of these children survive for at least five years. No accurate figures are available on the number of children and adults with this disease; however, the Leukemia Society of America (1975) projected that 45,000 would be stricken in 1976. *Incidence*

    Leukemia in children and youth is diagnosed by blood tests and a sample of blood from the bone marrow. In fact, periodic bone marrow tests may be required, and these are both painful and frightening for the child.

    Although there is no known cure, radiation therapy and a few of the newer drugs have shown a capacity to lengthen life a few years and offer promise of greater efficacy in the future. Refinement of transfusion techniques is also being pursued. *Diagnosis and treatment*

Secondary behavioral characteristics   Children and youth with leukemia present personality reactions much like other chronically ill children. Tremendous anxiety and fear are experienced by child and parents because of the strong possibility that the child may die. Both parents and child, depending upon the age of the child, will proceed through a grief reaction like that discussed in Unit 1. Most parents feel terrible guilt even though there is no way they could have caused the disease. The *Grief reactions* children experience two particular fears: the fear of separation from their parents and the fear of being hurt.

Dominic Nine-year-old Dominic was readmitted to the hospital because of a worsening in his leukemia condition. He was so agitated that the physicians requested a psychology consult. In talking with the child, the psychologist found that Dom wanted desperately to go home to be with his parents. To him, being hospitalized meant that he would die. Since both parents worked and could not be with him, he was even more frightened. When this was discussed with the parents, one of them took time off from the job and stayed with Dom until his discharge from the hospital. This greatly reduced the boy's agitation.

Fear of separation

Children taking medication for leukemia may become bald and feel very self-conscious about it. Teachers can prepare classmates ahead of time to expect this, making it easier for the child with leukemia to return to school. Often these children and youth feel isolated and alone even at school; it is as if no one can understand what they might be feeling. Teachers and classmates cannot fully appreciate the feeling that death may be near, but the teacher can be an invaluable support to the child by including him or her fully in class activities.

Usually no special classes are necessary, although tutorial assistance may be needed if the child has missed a lot of school time. The teacher must also consider the effect on classmates if the child dies. Despondency, fear, or anger may be presented by some of the classmates for a period of weeks without anyone really understanding why the youngsters' behavior has changed. The teacher must be aware of this possible reaction and be prepared for it. Support and understanding helps the class members and even allowing special, private time to talk about the death may be necessary.

Classmates' reactions to death

Cystic fibrosis (CF)

This is a genetic disorder that affects the lungs and digestive system of the child. The exocrine glands do not function properly, causing a thick mucus to be secreted in the lungs. Respiratory limitation and predisposition to infection ensue. The excessive mucus prevents digestion and the flow of enzymes from the pancreas, and the sweat glands produce a salty excretion. Obvious symptoms such as coughing, wheezing, and loss of weight often cause the disorder to be mistaken for asthma, bronchitis, or allergy; there is one test, however, that clearly distinguishes the disorder from all others: the sweat chloride test.

The National Cystic Fibrosis Research Foundation (1975) estimates that 1 in 15,000 newborns have this condition, and about 10 million carry the gene. Fifty percent of CF patients can be expected to live beyond eighteen years of age (NCF Research Foundation, 1975). Cystic fibrosis is a serious illness and can be life threatening.

CF can result in death

Treatment and therapeutic techniques Antibiotics, aerosol mist dispensers, and drugs to aid the digestive process are ways to deal with the disease if initiated at the early stages. A child can participate in regular classes and physical activity under the guidance of a physician. Physical activity and the psychological problems related to the disorder require that school personnel work as a team with such a child.

These children may require frequent hospitalization; hence, they will miss considerable amounts of school time. Individualizing instruction may be necessary, but care must be taken not to isolate the child any more than he or she already is by the nature of the medical problem.

Other disorders and their educational implications

Other disorders, either life threatening or crippling, with which school personnel may come in contact are club foot, scoliosis (spine curvature), spina bifida and, less

Playing Frisbee is a favorite form of recreation. Here Wendy demonstrates her ability during a free period in the school day.

frequently, polio, tuberculosis, and hemophilia. The most expedient way of educating oneself about these and any other disorders is to have a good general pediatric disorders text available in the school's professional library to use as a reference. Teachers are urged to educate themselves about the various disorders in children they will encounter within the regular or special class setting. In this way they can better understand the child, his or her possible limitations, and any equipment that the child's condition might require. Because of the multitude of disabilities that can be encountered, the educator would do well to request that in addition to the pediatrics-disorder reference text, the library order several texts related to general pediatric health problems and specialized methods or techniques for teaching these children.

Teachers need a good reference library

Generally, children with chronic illnesses develop their own set of personality variables. These variables, however, are influenced by amount of parental support, acceptance by school personnel, reaction of close relatives and others, and extent to which such children understand their own condition. Children have an amazing ability to adapt and cope with painful medical tests, medicine that may make them feel very ill, or even the knowledge that they may die. In the experience of the present author, the most important members of the team working with children with physical and health problems are physicians, parents, and teachers. The teacher can do more to offset psychological problems and provide therapeutic help than almost any individual psychotherapy program. Of course, the teacher's attitude and manner in relating to children is all-important. The concerned, supportive, and caring teacher —who takes into account children's feelings, fears, and anxieties—is equally as important to the child's psychological adjustment as the psychologist or the physician on the team.

Children adapt and cope amazingly well

Teachers can do wonders

Multihandicapped children

The multihandicapped child presents a special challenge to all professionals. We noted that children who are cerebral palsied are often multihandicapped (Adams, 1968). In the case of these children or others with multiple handicaps, a multidisciplinary team approach is necessary for adequate diagnosis and integration of all the findings in order to suggest appropriate remedial efforts. Medical and educational assessment and reassessment may be important, and the earlier a diagnosis is made and remediation begun, the better chance the child has for optimal development. Careful and constant education and counseling of the parents is crucial, since many tasks will have carry-over value at home and the parents must carry out home stimulation programs.

Multihandicapped need multiplicity of services

Educating the children with a multiplicity of health problems may be no different from educating any child. Or it may vary enormously and need to be supplemented by a number of specialists, such as a speech pathologist, physical therapist, or educator of the deaf.

Summary

We have examined various physical and health disabilities through a criteria framework of definition and causative factors; incidence, treatment and therapeutic techniques; behavioral implications for the child, youth, family, school and peers; and education and career planning aspects. All disabilities discussed reveal varying implications for educational personnel. Some pose a challenge in terms of physical management; others are less complicated in terms of classroom instructional activities and needed adaptation, but all require a completely supportive posture on the part of the teacher.

Placement in the regular classroom is, of course, strongly advocated whenever possible. The need for psychosocial and regular peer group experiences is intrinsic to the child or youth's total development for participation in society. Educational personnel play an integral part in furthering such development through greater knowledge and subsequent total acceptance of children and youth with various physical and health disabilities.

References and resources

Adams, M. E. "Problems in the Management of Mentally Retarded Children with Cerebral Palsy." *Cerebral Palsy Journal* 29 (1968): 3–7.

American Heart Association. *Prevention of Rheumatic Fever.* New York: American Heart Association, 1970.

American Heart Association. *You, Your Child, and Rheumatic Fever.* New York: American Heart Association, 1971.

American Heart Association. *Heart Facts, 1975.* New York: American Heart Association, 1976.

American Heart Association. *1976 Heart Facts Reference Sheet.* New York: American Heart Association, 1976.

Arangio, A. A. "Behind the Stigma." *National Spokesman,* March 1975, p. 8.

Arthritis Foundation. *Arthritis, the Basic Facts.* New York: Arthritis Foundation, 1974.

Bharani, S. N., and Hyde, J. S. "Chronic Asthma and the School." *Journal of School Health* 46 (1976): 24–30.

Brewer, E. J. *Juvenile Rheumatoid Arthritis.* Philadelphia: W. B. Saunders, 1970.

Brownell, K. D., and Bailen, R. F. "Acute Rheumatic Fever in Children." *Journal of the American Medical Association* 224 (1973): 1593–97.

Cleveland, S. E., and Brewer, E. J. "Psychological Aspects of Juvenile Rheumatoid Arthritis." In *Juvenile Rheumatoid Arthritis,* edited by E. J. Brewer, pp. 116–31. Philadelphia: W. B. Saunders, 1970.

Cobb, R. B. *Medical and Psychological Aspects of Disability.* Springfield, Ill.: Charles C Thomas, 1973.

Collier, B. N. "The Adolescent with Diabetes and the Public Schools: A Misunderstanding." *Personnel and Guidance Journal* 47 (1969): 753–57.

Collier, B. N., and Etzwiler, D. D. "Comparative Study of Diabetic Knowledge Among Juvenile Diabetics and their Parents." *Diabetes* 20 (1971): 51–57.

Crawford, D. P. "PEP-SIE Project Reveals School Practices, Attitudes, Information Needs." *National Spokesman,* July 1976, p. 8.

Davis, D. M. "Attitudes of Boys and Girls Toward Diabetes." *Diabetes* 14 (1965): 106–09.

Department of Health, Education and Welfare. "Chronic Conditions and Limitations of Activity and Mobility in the U.S." *Vital and Health Statistics, 1971.* Series 10, no. 61. Washington, D.C.: U.S. Government Printing Office, 1971.

Department of Health, Education and Welfare. *Cerebral Palsy: Hope Through Research.* DHEW Publication no. 75-159. Washington, D.C.: U.S. Government Printing Office, 1975.

Epilepsy Foundation of America. *Basic Statistics on the Epilepsies.* Philadelphia: F. A. Davis Co., 1970.

Epilepsy Foundation of America. *Recognition and First Aid for Those with Epilepsy.* Washington, D.C.: 1973a.

Epilepsy Foundation of America. *Answers to the Most Frequent Questions People Ask about Epilepsy.* Washington, D.C.: 1973b.

Epilepsy Foundation of America. *Facts and Figures on the Epilepsies.* Washington, D.C.: 1974.

Epilepsy Foundation of America. "Letter to the Editor." *National Spokesman,* Sept. 1975, p. 2.

Etzwiler, D. D., and Robb, J. R. "Evaluation of Programmed Education among Juvenile Diabetics and Families." *Diabetes* 21 (1972): 967–71.

Friedland, G. "Learning Behavior of a Pre-adolescent with Diabetes." *American Journal of Nursing* 76 (1976): 39–61.

Friedman, R. J., and MacQueen, J. C. "Psycho-Educational Considerations of Physically Handicapped Conditions in Children." *Exceptional Children* 37 (1971): 538–39.

Garner, A. M., and Thompson, C. W. "Facts in the Management of Juvenile Diabetes." *Pediatric Psychology* 2 (1974): 6–7.

Ghory, J. H. "Exercise and Asthma: Overview and Clinical Impact." *Pediatrics* (supplement) 56 (1975): 844–46.

Gordis, L. *Epidemiology of Chronic Lung Diseases in Children.* Baltimore: Johns Hopkins University Press, 1973.

Harlin, V. "Experiences with Epileptic Children in a Public School Program." *Journal of School Health* 35 (1965): 20–24.

Huberman, G. "Organized Sports Activities with Cerebral Palsied Adolescents." *Rehabilitation Literature* 37 (1976): 103–06.

Kurland, L. T. "Incidence and Prevalence of Convulsive Disorders in a Small, Urban Community." *Epilepsia* 1 (1959): 143–61.

Kurland, L. T.; Kurtzke, J. F.; and Goldberg, I. D. *Epidemiology of Neurologic and Sense Organ Disorders.* Cambridge, Mass.: Harvard University Press, 1973.

Kurtzke, J. F.; Kurland, L. T.; Goldberg, I. D.; Choi, N. W.; and Reeder, F. A. "Convulsive Disorders." In *Epidemiology of Neurologic and Sense Organ Disorders,* edited by L. T. Kurland, J. F. Kurtzke, and I. D. Goldberg, pp. 15–40. Cambridge, Mass.: Harvard University Press, 1973.

Leukemia Society of America. *Annual Report, 1975.* New York: Leukemia Society of America, 1975.

Leukemia Society of America. *Leukemia: The Nature of the Disease.* New York: Leukemia Society of America, no date.

Livingston, S. *Comprehensive Management of Epilepsy in Infancy, Childhood, and Adolescence.* Springfield, Ill.: Charles C Thomas, 1972.

McAnarney, E. R.; Pless, I. B.; Satterwhite, B.; and Friedman, S. B. "Psychological Problems of Children with Chronic Juvenile Arthritis." *Pediatrics* 53 (1974): 523–28.

Mearig, J. S. "Some Dynamics of Personality Development in Boys Suffering from Muscular Dystrophy." *Rehabilitation Literature* 34 (1973): 226.

Morse, J. "Aspiration and Achievement: A Study of One Hundred Patients with Juvenile Rheumatoid Arthritis." *Rehabilitation Literature* 33 (1972): 299–303.

Muscular Dystrophy Association. *1976 Fact Sheet.* New York: Muscular Dystrophy Association, 1976.

National Commission on Diabetes. "Diabetes Forecast." *Diabetes* (Supplement no. 1, special edition) 28 (1975): 1–60.

National Cystic Fibrosis Research Foundation. *Your Child and Cystic Fibrosis.* Atlanta: National Cystic Fibrosis Research Center, 1975.

Newman, R. G. *Psychological Consultations in Schools.* New York: Basic Books, 1967.

O'Reilly, D. R. "Care of the Cerebral Palsied: Outcome of the Past and Needs of the Future." *Developmental Medicine and Child Neurology* 17 (1975): 141–49.

Purcell, K., and Weiss, J. H. "Asthma." In *Symptoms of Psychopathology,* edited by C. D. Costello, pp. 597–624. New York: Wiley, 1970.

Purcell, K.; Weiss, J. H.; and Hahn, W. W. "Certain Psychosomatic Disorders." In *Manual of Child Psychopathology,* edited by B. B. Wolman, ch. 4, pp. 706–40. New York: McGraw-Hill, 1972.

Rutter, M.; Graham, P.; and Yule, W. *A Neuropsychiatric Study in Childhood. Clinics in Developmental Medicine,* no. 35/36. Philadelphia: Lippincott, 1970.

Scherzer, A. L.; Ilson, J. B.; Mike, V.; and Landoli, M. "Educational and Social Development among Intensively Treated Young Patients Having Cerebral Palsy." *Archives of Physical Medicine and Rehabilitation* 54 (1972): 478–84.

Schwartz, D. D. "Chronic Asthma in Children." *Journal of American Medical Association* 222 (1972): 485.

United Cerebral Palsy Associations. *What is Cerebral Palsy?* New York: United Cerebral Palsy Associations, 1976.

Willis, D. J., and Thomas, E. D. "Seizure Disorders." In *Psychological Management of Pediatric Problems,* vol. 2, edited by P. Magrab, pp. 49–88. Baltimore: University Park Press, 1978.

Ziter, F. A., and Allsop, K. G. "Comprehensive Treatment of Childhood Muscular Dystrophy." *Rocky Mountain Medical Journal* 72 (1975): 329.

Ziter, F. A., and Allsop, K. G. "The Diagnoses and Management of Childhood Muscular Dystrophy." *Clinical Pediatrics* 15 (1976): 540–48.

Allergy Foundation of America
801 Second Avenue
New York, New York 10017

American Academy of Neurology
4015 West 65th Street, Suite 302-A
Minneapolis, Minnesota 55438

American Cancer Society
219 East 42nd Street
New York, New York 10017

American Diabetes Association
1 West 48th Street
New York, New York 10020

Children and youth with physical and health disabilities

American Epilepsy Society
Montreal Neurological Hospital
McGill University
3801 University Street
Montreal, Canada H3A2B

American Heart Association
7320 Greenville Avenue
Dallas, Texas 75231

American Lung Association
1740 Broadway
New York, New York 10019

American Medical Association
Education Research Foundation
535 North Dearborn Street
Chicago, Illinois 60610

American Occupational Therapy Association
6000 Executive Boulevard
Rockville, Maryland 20852

American Orthotic and Prosthetic Association
1440 N Street, NW
Washington, D.C. 20005

American Physical Therapy Association
1156 15th Street, NW
Washington, D.C. 20005

American Speech and Hearing Association
9030 Old Georgetown Road
Washington, D.C. 20014

Arthritis Foundation
7212 Avenue of the Americas
New York, New York 10036

Epilepsy Foundation of America
1828 L Street, NW
Suite 406
Washington, D.C. 20036

Leukemia Society of America
211 East 43rd Street
New York, New York 10017

Muscular Dystrophy Associations of America
810 Seventh Avenue
New York, New York 10019

National Cystic Fibrosis Research Foundation
3379 Peachtree Road, NE
Atlanta, Georgia 30326

National Easter Seal Society for Crippled Children and Adults
2023 West Ogden Avenue
Chicago, Illinois 60612

National Foundation/March of Dimes
1275 Mamaroneck Avenue
White Plains, New York 10605

National Hemophilia Foundation
25 West 39th Street
New York, New York 10018

National Institutes of Health
Bethesda, Maryland 20014
    National Cancer Institute
    National Heart and Lung Institute
    National Institute for Arthritis, Metabolism, and Digestive Diseases
    National Institute of Allergy and Infectious Diseases
    National Institute of Child Health and Human Development
    National Institute of Neurological and Communicative Disorders and Stroke

National Kidney Foundation
116 East 27th Street
New York, New York 10016

National Multiple Sclerosis Society
257 Park Avenue South
New York, New York 10010

National Rehabilitation Association
1522 K Street, NW
Washington, D.C. 20005

Rehabilitation Services Administration
330 C Street, SW
Washington, D.C. 20201

Spina Bifida Association of America
P.O. Box 5568
Madison, Wisconsin 53705

United Cerebral Palsy Associations
66 East 34th Street
New York, New York 10016

U.S. Office of Education
Bureau of Education for the Handicapped
400 Maryland Avenue, SW
Washington, D.C. 20202

Applicable federal legislation

Developmental Disabilities Services Act (PL91-517), 1971

National Cancer Act (PL92-218), 1971

National Heart, Blood Vessel, Lung and Blood Act (PL92-423), 1972

National Commission on Multiple Sclerosis Act (PL92-563), 1972

Rehabilitation Act (PL93-112), 1973

National Diabetes Mellitus Research and Education Act (PL93-354), 1974

National Arthritis Act (PL93-640), 1975

Education for All Handicapped Children Act (PL94-142), 1975

National Commission for the Control of Epilepsy and its Consequences (PL94-63), 1975

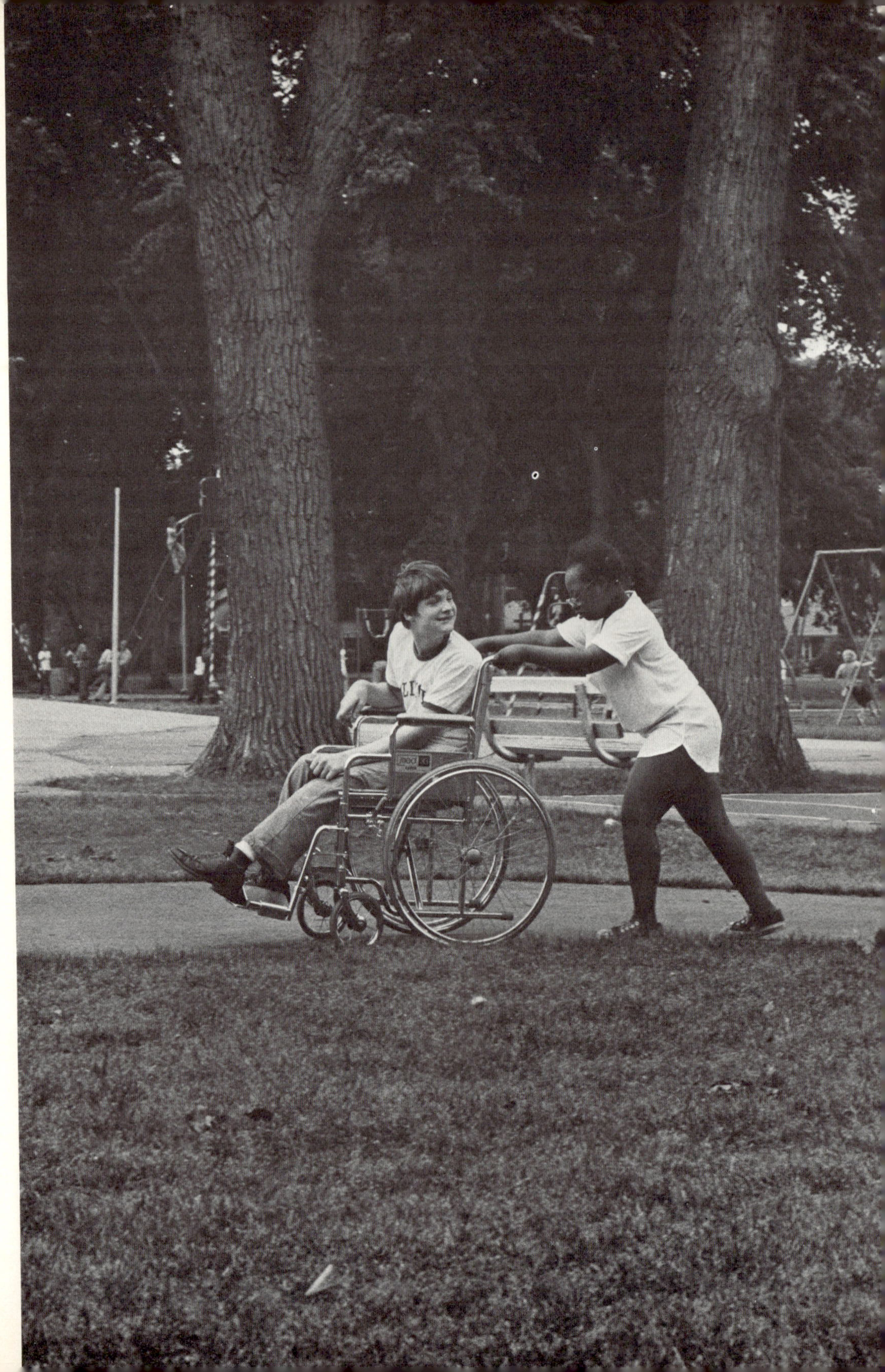

Summing up

We will not attempt to summarize all the information you have received in this text concerning the complex subject of exceptionality. We will, however, pinpoint some of the most salient facts presented for your study and consider their implications for the future.

Throughout history we have seen varying degrees of progress made in better educational approaches to exceptional children and youth. Affording handicapped individuals their full human rights, however, is a very recent development. With the enactment in 1975 of Public Law 94-142, The Education for All Handicapped Children Act, however, massive change has been mandated. This newest federal legislation serves our present society as a means of guaranteeing a free and appropriate public education for *all* handicapped children. To make sure these goals do not remain elusive, the major provisions deal with due process rights of all parties concerned (e.g., children and their families, classroom teachers and other professional personnel, local and state education agencies) and with ensuring needed special services for the handicapped in the "least restrictive environment" possible.

In the same legislative context, early identification and procedures for comprehensive assessment are important tools for verifying handicaps and determining eligibility for special services. The multidisciplinary team approach is necessary, too, to fulfill the above provisions. So is the placement committee with its specific responsibilities in planning, implementing, and reviewing special services as set forth through the written individual education programs (IEPs).

In the population designated as having intellectual deficits we are seeing greater inclusion of those previously unserved because of the severity of their disabilities, and major revisions in identification procedures. An intelligence quotient score alone will no longer be the sole criterion for designating a child as mentally retarded. Similarly, the definition of another intellectually exceptional population—the gifted—includes criteria other than an IQ score (e.g., creativity and special talent).

The focus of concern for those exceptional children and youth whose educational progress is impeded by many societal circumstances is twofold: better understanding and social programs of prevention and alleviation of the societally neglected. Concerning the newest group included within the handicapped population, those with specific learning disabilities, identification and remediation procedures are still evolving. Further knowledge and consensus is needed among all professionals in this area of exceptionality.

Another major effort among educators in present-day society is enrolling the aid and support of families, psychologists, social workers, and/or agencies involved with or representing children and youth who have been evaluated as having emotional difficulties and/or adjudged delinquent. Only through the sharing of knowledge and joint cooperation of the multidisciplinary approach can greater successful participation ensue in the regular classroom.

For youngsters with hearing, visual, and/or physical and health disabilities, each particular disability (or combination thereof in the case of the multihandicapped) presents a specific challenge to educators. They have a responsibility as part of the placement team to determine the extent of special services needed and the variety or types of special equipment required (e.g., hearing amplification aids, visual amplification and/or braille materials, structural modifications for the physically handicapped). Fortunately, appropriate remediation techniques and necessary materials for speech and language therapy is more often a part of present resource room services provided through a speech and language pathologist working in cooperation with the regular classroom teacher.

Future outlook

It becomes increasingly clear that parents, educators, and other helping professionals must make a major investment in time, effort and funds to activate their total commitment to the goals discussed at the beginning of this summation.

Any item of legislation—as enacted for a good and exemplary purpose—is only effective when implemented by many individual efforts to carry out in good faith the original intent. Frequently, governmental calls for basic changes to be made in any profession will encounter resistance. Some individuals (no matter how well-documented the need for change is) will actively voice their opposition. Others may continue operating in their previous roles while giving lip service to the new requirements.

Responsibility for compliance rests first with state education agencies (SEAs) as they set the state standards. Second, responsibility rests with school superintendents and principals in the local education agency (LEA) setting. The commitment of such local administrative personnel to compliance with legislative changes will set the tone for teacher attitudes and teachers' willingness to prepare themselves and regular students in their school for the successful inclusion of handicapped children and youth within the mainstream of education.

School administrators will also need to involve themselves and their respective teaching staffs in in-service and other training opportunities to gain increased knowledge of how best to serve the handicapped or exceptional child or youth. Participation must be encouraged and arrangements made for attendance by teachers at state or national conventions representing various areas of exceptionality and/or state or federal agency-sponsored workshops and seminars. Educators need to encourage and challenge each other to stay abreast of the latest research, legislation, and educational strategies pertaining to exceptional children and youth.

While teachers must personally and professionally seek to increase their understanding of the field, there is also a need for greater availability and dissemination of research findings related to the goal of free and appropriate education for all. Three aspects, in particular, would benefit from increased funding in research: (1) further clarification of the *individual* needs of exceptional children, (2) greater emphasis on studies that tell us how best to maximize the capabilities of exceptional children for their own as well as society's benefit; and (3) expansion of studies of preventive methods that will reduce the number of disabilities in the child population.

The Bureau of Education for the Handicapped has begun to compile studies relating to the goals of P. L. 94-142. The implications and consequences of (1) the multidisciplinary team approach, (2) early diagnosis and interventional strategies employed, and (3) least restrictive educational placement for handicapped students are beginning to emerge. Accountability procedures necessarily will be a part of considerations for strengthening the effectiveness of the Education for All Handicapped Children's Act.

The current "taxpayers' revolt" notwithstanding, adequate funding must be assured for materials, supplies, and facilities necessary to successfully implement the prescribed individual educational plans (including, for instance, modifying any present architectural barriers preventing the handicapped from attending local schools). Class-size reduction and complete elimination of overcrowded classrooms—long-standing goals of dedicated educators—must come to pass. The individualization of instruction now mandated to meet specific educational needs of any child is another approach that has always been utilized by conscientious professionals.

Greater use of child advocates and greater cooperation among federal, state, and local education agencies in order to meet federal guidelines can complement the efforts of those who have recognized all along the importance of a diagnostic-prescriptive approach and have striven for years to meet individual children's needs.

Some universities and colleges are already offering special training for students entering or already involved in the helping professions. These individuals will become members of multidisciplinary teams, whose objectives will be to identify exceptional children and youth and devise appropriate educational strategies for them; hence, various programs for them are being revamped and/or expanded.

Academic instruction and practical learning experiences that will lead to greater teacher competency are becoming a more and more important part of the curriculum. Many state education agencies now require at least one course involving understanding of the handicapped or exceptional child prior to teacher certification. Further learning experiences that will give the teacher greater skill in understanding and handling a wide range of student behavior are not only becoming a part of teacher education, but of other disciplines related to understanding human behavior.

Thus, society—individually and collectively—at the end of the 1970s has its course clearly outlined. The impetus for progress in the '80s and subsequent years will come through further knowledge and continued dedication.

Contributors' biographies

B. Marian Swanson, Ph.D., is currently professor of psychology in the College of Behavioral Sciences at Northeastern Oklahoma State University. As a licensed psychologist—specializing in school psychology—she also serves as a consultant to schools and guidance centers. She received her doctorate in counseling psychology from the University of Oklahoma, and her former professional experience includes regular classroom teaching; special education classroom teaching; school administration; directing special education services; and coordinating a state regional guidance center. She has also contributed to the American Psychological Association's visiting psychologist program, under the sponsorship of the National Institute of Mental Health. Dr. Swanson is listed in *Who's Who of American Women; The Compendium, International Biography of Persons of Eminence in Exceptional Education;* and *The National Register of Health Service Providers in Psychology*. She has published in numerous professional and educational journals and literature, and has written a children's book used in regular and remedial reading instructional programs. She also serves as a member of the editorial staff for the *Journal of Clinical Child Psychology*.

Diane J. Willis, Ph.D., is associate director and chief of pediatric psychology services, at the Child Study Center of Oklahoma Children's Memorial Hospital (OCMH), affiliated with the University of Oklahoma Health Sciences Center. She is also an associate professor in the Department of Pediatrics and clinical associate professor in the Department of Psychiatry and Behavioral Sciences. Dr. Willis is a clinical psychologist who has worked with exceptional children and their families for more than ten years. She has served as a consultant to a school for the deaf for five years. Now she serves as a consultant to the deaf-blind preschool program at the Child Study Center and to a Montessori school serving children age three to twelve. Dr. Willis is past president of the Society of Pediatric Psychology, editor of the *Journal of Clinical Child Psychology,* and a consulting editor of *Professional Psychology* and *Journal of Pediatric Psychology*. For her work in the area of learning disabilities, Dr. Willis was given a Distinguished Contribution Award by the Oklahoma Association for Children with Learning Disabilities. She has published numerous articles on seizures, hearing disabilities, child abuse, parental grief, and Public Law 94-142.

Henry R. Angelino, Ph.D., is professor of psychology at The Ohio State University, where he has been on the faculty since 1969. He received his doctorate from The University of Nebraska at Lincoln and from 1950 to 1969 he taught in the College of Education at the University of Oklahoma, where he held appointment as professor of education. He has had a twenty-year concern with gifted children, including a number of summer institutes on the gifted at the University of Oklahoma. Currently he teaches both an undergraduate and a graduate seminar on the gifted. He is a fellow of the American Psychological Association and has published more than forty professional articles and contributions to larger works, including publications on the gifted.

Joan H. Faubion, Ph.D., is an assistant professor in the Department of Educational Psychology and Child Development at Oklahoma City University and supervisor of the graduate program in Montessori training. For three-and-one-half years she produced a weekly television series on the exceptional. Dr. Faubion taught junior and senior high school before obtaining her doctorate in educational psychology at the University of Oklahoma. She has been a member of the Governor's Committee on the Deaf and Hearing Impaired, the Governor's Committee on Children and Youth and the Governor's Committee on the Handicapped. The television program SIGN-POST, produced by Dr. Faubion, has been recognized by civic leaders as outstanding in its service to people with disabilities.

Wanda Fuhrmann graduated with honors from the University of Texas where her area of concentration in elementary education was with the visually impaired and the deaf. At the Child Study Center in Oklahoma City, which she joined in 1972, Ms. Fuhrmann worked for a number of years with deaf-blind preschool children. During her tenure as teacher of the deaf-blind and blind children, the Child Study Center served as a model program for regional deaf/blind centers. Prior to joining the staff of the Child Study Center, Ms. Fuhrmann taught first-grade blind children and special education classes for preschool-aged children.

Cathy Groves, Ph.D., is currently a psychology interne in the Department of Psychiatry at Kaiser Permanente Medical Center in San Francisco. She has taught at San Francisco State University in the Department of Special Education, and also serves as a consultant and conducts training workshops for professionals and paraprofessionals involved in work with multihandicapped children and their families. Ms. Groves has worked with multihandicapped infants and children for nine years in the capacities of teacher, supervisor, consultant, and family counselor. Her academic background includes the study of speech pathology, early child development, Montessori training, education of neurologically impaired children, and psychology. She obtained her doctorate in psychology at the California School of Professional Psychology in Berkeley. Her dissertation dealt with the effects of handicapping conditions on the attachment process between adult caretakers and the handicapped child, on the effects of the handicapping condition on family members, and on the consequent elaboration of family relationships.

John S. Howland, M.D., is director of Prevention and Education at the Southern Arizona Mental Health Center in Tucson. He was trained in adolescent psychiatry at Massachusetts General Hospital and served as unit chief for youth services at the Richard Hutchings Psychiatric Center in Syracuse, New York.

Harry J. Parker, Ph.D., is professor of physical medicine and rehabilitation, psychology, and rehabilitation science, all in the University of Texas Health Sciences Center at Dallas. He has also been associate dean of the School of Allied Health Sciences, in addition to his current appointments. Dr. Parker, who obtained his doctorate from Northwestern University, was professor of education, preventive medicine and public health, and human ecology at the University of Oklahoma prior to his current academic affiliation. He is a fellow in the American Psychological Association, and has held office in the Dallas Psychological Association, the Southwestern Psychological Association, and the Texas Psychological Association. Dr. Parker is the author of more than thirty-five publications, monographs, research reports, and contributions to larger works. He has received grants from federal, state, and private agencies to support research and has served as consultant to various governmental entities and health organizations. He also maintains a consulting private practice as a licensed psychologist.

Marshall D. Schechter, M.D., is presently the director of the Division of Child and Adolescent Psychiatry, University of Pennsylvania School of Medicine. He previously held faculty positions at the University of Oklahoma, and Upstate Medical Center, Syracuse, New York. Dr. Schechter received his M.D. from the University of Cincinnati, and his postgraduate studies in psychiatry were pursued at Barnes Hospital in St. Louis. He trained in adult and child psychoanalysis at the Veterans Administration Center in Los Angeles and the Los Angeles Psychoanalytic Institute. Dr. Schechter is certified in adult and child psychiatry, and in adult and child psychoanalysis. He has been an examiner for the boards in general psychiatry and child psychiatry and is a fellow of the American Psychiatric Association. Dr. Schechter has published numerous articles dealing with emotionally handicapped children on such topics of interest as adoption, early infantile autism, and suicide among children and youth.

William J. Ward, Ed.D., is professor of special education at Northeastern Oklahoma State University. After obtaining a doctorate from the University of Tulsa in special education, he taught in a number of private and public school programs involving the full range of mental retardation among all ages. He founded and directs a summer program for exceptional children. Dr. Ward has served as state president of the Council for Exceptional Children, state president of the Teacher Education Division of CEC, and state president of the Mental Retardation Division of the CEC in Oklahoma. He is a member of the Board of Governors for the Oklahoma Council for Exceptional Children, has served on the state task force on mental health, and has been active in the local, state, and national Special Olympics program.

Mary Ann Weiss, Ph.D., is director of the Division of Communication Disorders at North Texas State University in Denton, Texas. She supervises student clinicians in diagnostic and therapeutic practicum experiences and directs research in language disorders of children. After obtaining her doctorate in speech pathology from the University of Oklahoma, she held faculty appointments and directed language diagnostic services at Colorado State University, the University of Oklahoma Health Sciences Center, and Bradley University. Dr. Weiss serves as the chair of the Clinical Certification Board of the American Speech and Hearing Association and has held office in several state affiliates. She has been selected as an Outstanding Young Woman of America, an Outstanding Teacher in Exceptional Education, and is listed in *Who's Who of American Women*. She has presented many workshops and seminars in language disorders of children, and has published a number of scientific and professional articles.

Credits

Photo credits
Unit 1   Photography by Michael Goss with the kind permission of Park School, Evanston, Illinois
Unit 2   Photography by Pat Lasko
Unit 3   Photography by Gary Mason with the kind permission of Lakemary Center, Paola, Kansas
Unit 4   Photography by Michael Philip Manheim with the kind permission of the Walnut Hill School for College Preparation and the Performing Arts, Natick, Massachusetts
Unit 5   Photography by Richard Younker
Unit 6   Photography by Martha Leonard with the kind permission of the Dyslexia Institute and the Board of Education of the City of Chicago
Unit 7   Photography by Michael Goss with the kind permission of Cook County Illinois School District #73½
Unit 8   Photography by Martha Leonard with the kind permission of Siegel Institute, Michael Reese Clinic, Chicago, Illinois
Unit 9   Photography by Michael Philip Manheim with the kind permission of Clarke School for the Deaf, Northampton, Massachusetts
Unit 10   Photography by Steve Saunders with the kind permission of the State of Illinois Department of Children and Family Services
Unit 11   Photography by Michael Goss with the kind permission of Cook County Illinois School District #219
Summing Up   Photography by Michael Goss with the kind permission of Park School, Evanston, Illinois

The following copyrighted figures and tables are reprinted with permission:
Table 1-3   From *Exceptional Children in the Schools,* 2nd ed., edited by Lloyd M. Dunn, pp.18–19. Copyright 1963, 1973 by Holt, Rinehart and Winston, Inc. Reprinted by permission of Holt, Rinehart and Winston.
Figures 1-1 and 1-2   Adapted from figures 1 and 2 on pp. 18, 20 in "Exceptional Children: Clinical Evaluation and Coordination of Services; An Ecological Model" by E. E. Thomas and M. Marshall, *Exceptional Children* 44 (1977): 16–22 by permission of the Council for Exceptional Children. Copyright 1977 by the Council for Exceptional Children, 1920 Association Drive, Reston, Virginia 22091.

Table 3-1 From "The Profoundly Retarded: A New Challenge for Public Education" by R. E. Luckey and M. R. Addison, *Education and Training of the Mentally Retarded* 9 (1974): 123–30. Reprinted with permission.

Figure 5-1 Data for figure is based on Hierarchy of Needs in "A Theory of Human Motivation" in *Motivation and Personality,* 2nd ed. by Abraham H. Maslow. Copyright 1970 by Abraham H. Maslow.

Figure 6-1 From *Effective Teaching: A Guide to Diagnostic-Prescriptive Task Analysis* by Robert E. Valett. Copyright 1970 by Fearon-Pitman Publishers, Inc., 6 Davis Drive, Belmont, California 94002. Reprinted by permission.

Figure 9-3 From *How They Hear* by Carol Harford, 1964. Reprinted by permission of Gordon N. Stowe and Associates, P.O. Box #233, Northbrook, Illinois 60062.

Figure 10-2 Modified from *Psychology and Life,* 5th ed. by Floyd L. Ruch, p. 242. Copyright 1958 by Scott, Foresman and Company. Reprinted by permission.

Figure 10-4 From *Teacher's Guide for Development of Visual Learning Abilities and Utilization of Low Vision* by Natalie C. Barraga. Copyright 1970 by American Printing House for the Blind, 1839 Frankfort Avenue, Louisville, Kentucky 40206. Reprinted with permission.

Figure 10-9 From *Instruction Manual for Braille Transcribing* by Maxine Dorf and Earl Scharry. Copyright 1971 by American Printing House for the Blind, 1839 Frankfort Avenue, Louisville, Kentucky 40206. Reprinted with permission.

Name index

Abeson, A., 8, 25, 43
Adams, M. E., 404, 405
Addison, M. R., 91, 96
Agust, S., 362, 373
Aiello, B., 31, 41
Allsop, K. G., 394, 407
Ammons, C. H., 104, 125
Ammons, R. B., 104, 125
Anastasi, A., 50, 70
Angelino, H. R., 119, 125
Anthony, E., 218, 246
Arangio, A. A., 388, 405
Arasteh, A. R., 112, 125
Arasteh, J. D., 112, 125
Aronow, M. S., 324, 329
Ashcroft, S. C., 368, 372
Atkinson, R. C., 137, 159
Azrin, N. H., 215, 246

Bailen, R. F., 395, 405
Baker, B. M., 156, 158
Baker, Don, 334
Ballard, J., 30, 31, 41
Bangs, T., 255, 283, 286
Bannatyne, A., 176, 194
Barbara, D., 274
Barbier, Charles, 365
Barraga, N. C., 342, 344, 368, 372, 373
Bayley, N., 54, 70
Bell, R., 242, 246
Bender, L., 68, 70, 168, 194

Benedek, I., 218, 246
Benham, F. G., 360, 373
Bennett, E. M., 168, 194
Bernstein, B., 149, 158
Bergstrom, L., 300, 327
Berman, A., 190, 194
Berry, M., 261, 286
Bharani, S. N., 400, 405
Biller, H. B., 146, 158
Binet, Albert, 50
Birch, J. W., 110, 127, 171, 197
Bishop, W., 122, 125
Blackham, G. J., 192, 194
Blanton, S., 274
Blom, G. E., 181, 195
Bloodstein, O., 274, 275, 276, 286
Blott, J., 283, 288
Boder, E., 178, 181, 182, 195
Bookbinder, S., 31, 41
Boone, D., 271, 287
Borden, J. P., 153, 158
Bowen, M., 240, 246
Bradley, R. C., 133, 158
Brady, J. P., 241, 246
Braille, Louis, 365
Brandwein, P. F., 123, 125
Bray, P. F., 338, 373
Brenton, M., 10, 32, 41, 242, 246
Brewer, E. J., 392, 393, 405
Brickman, W. W., 134, 158
Bridges, S. A., 118, 125
Briggs, D., 143, 147, 158
Briscoe, C., 242, 246

423

Brolin, D. E., 79, 96
Bronfenbrenner, U., 152, 155, 158
Brown, B. S., 34, 41
Brown, R., 279, 287
Brownell, K. D., 395, 405
Brutten, E., 278, 287
Bryson, C. Q., 67, 70
Burks, B. S., 106, 125
Burlingham, D., 348, 352, 373
Burt, C., 104, 113, 125
Bush, W. J., 187, 195, 283, 287
Buss, A. H., 205, 246

Cain, L. F., 54, 70
Caldwell, B. M., 18, 20, 41
Caldwell, Erskine, 14
Calhoun, J. F., 33, 41, 215, 246
Carlyle, Thomas, 158
Carpenter, R. L., 176, 181, 195
Carrell, J., 262, 287
Carter, H., 59, 60, 61, 62, 63, 64, 65, 66, 67, 70
Carter, T. O., 147, 158
Chaffin, J. P., 86, 96
Charrow, V. R., 322, 327
Chomsky, N., 283, 287
Chwast, J., 238, 246
Clarizio, H. F., 211, 218, 219, 246
Clark, M., 362, 373
Clark, T., 323, 328
Clements, S. D., 171, 195
Cleveland, S. E., 392, 393, 405
Cobb, R. B., 379, 405
Cohen, O., 354, 374
Colfax, J., 142, 146, 147, 158
Collier, B. N., 397, 405
Conway, L., 154, 158
Cooledge, J. C., 221, 246
Corbett, G. R., 48, 71
Cordasco, F., 151, 158
Cowen, E. L., 360, 373
Cowles, M., 150, 158
Cox, C. M., 101, 125
Cramer, R. F., 358, 373
Cratty, B. J., 355, 362, 373

Crow, L. D., 134, 135, 159
Cummings, J., 371, 373
Cutsforth, T. D., 354, 373

Dale, P., 261, 279, 280, 287
Daniels, J. C., 118, 125
Davis, D. M., 397, 406
Davis, S. P., 4, 41
Dawson, H. S., 143, 144, 159
Dayton, D. H., 138, 139, 159
De La Cruz, F. F., 92, 96
Demos, G. D., 121, 126
Denton, D. M., 319, 320, 328
Deutsch, C., 148, 149, 150, 152, 159
Deutsch, M., 149, 159
Doctor, P. V., 324, 328
Dodds, J. B., 54, 70
Doll, E. A., 54, 70
Dorf, M. B., 366, 373
Doriward, B., 358, 373
Downs, John Langdon, 64
Downs, M. P., 300, 301, 302, 327, 329
Drotar, D., 34, 36, 41
Duffy, M., 283, 288
Dunn, L. M., 4, 5, 7, 30, 41, 283, 287

Egland, G., 278, 287
Ehlers, W. H., 93, 96
Einstein, Albert, 4
Eisenson, J., 274, 283, 287
Emanuel, J., 153, 159
Emerick, L., 266, 271, 287
English, A. C., 338, 373
English, H. B., 338, 373
Etzwiler, D. D., 397, 405
Everett, R. B., 208, 246
Eyman, R. K., 68, 96

Faas, L. A., 168, 195
Fairchild, T. N., 191, 192, 195
Fantini, D., 144, 148, 159
Farmer, L. W., 363, 373
Farwell, R. N., 316, 328

Feingold, B. F., 192, 195
Feingold, M., 59, 60, 61, 62, 63, 64, 66, 67, 70, 77, 78, 96
Finley, W. F., 213, 246
Fish, B., 211, 246
Fishbein, M., 59, 60, 68, 70
Fitzgerald, E., 324, 328
Fletcher, J. D., 322, 327
Fletcher, Louise, 300
Foerster, L. M., 152, 159
Fontana, V., 226, 246
Ford, P., 358, 373
Foreman, W. J., 326, 328
Forgus, R. H., 172, 174, 195
Foster, R., 55, 71
Fraenkel, W. A., 79, 96
Fraiberg, S., 348, 352, 356, 373
Frankenburg, W., 54, 70
Freedman, A. M., 215, 218, 224, 228, 246
Freedman, D. A., 356, 373
Friedland, G., 397, 406
Friedman, R. J., 380, 406
Frierson, E. C., 105, 126, 178, 181, 195
Froeschels, E., 274
Frostig, M., 173, 175, 192, 326, 328
Fulton, R., 146, 159
Furth, H. G., 312, 313, 314, 328

Gaddis, W. H., 168, 173, 195
Gallagher, J. J., 8, 27, 41, 124, 126
Galton, F., 101, 126
Garner, A. M., 397, 406
Gearheart, R., 49, 64, 70
Gellis, S. S., 59, 60, 61, 62, 63, 64, 66, 67, 70, 77, 78, 96
Gesell, A., 54, 70
Getman, G. N., 171, 195
Getzels, J. W., 112, 126
Ghory, J. H., 400, 406
Gibley, G., 85, 96
Gibson, R., 352, 373
Giles, Jane, 346
Giles, M., 283, 287
Ginsberg, L. H., 8, 41

Golann, E., 112, 126
Gold, M. J., 120, 122, 126
Goldberg, M., 118, 126
Goodman, Y. M., 135, 159
Gordis, L., 399, 406
Gottesman, M., 357, 373
Gottfried, N. W., 354, 373
Gottlieb, D., 133, 148, 159
Gottlieb, M. I., 38, 39, 43
Gould, N., 144, 159
Gould, R. W., 227, 247
Gowan, J. C., 121, 126
Grant, W. V., 7, 42, 105, 126
Gray, B., 278, 283, 287
Groht, M. A., 325, 328
Grossman, J., 52, 59, 60, 62, 65, 67, 68, 70, 75, 78, 96
Grost, A., 124, 126
Guilford, J. P., 112, 113, 126

Hammer, M., 232, 247
Hammill, D. D., 168, 176, 187, 195, 196
Harford, E. R., 305, 328
Harley, R. K., 336, 338, 372, 373
Harlin, V., 389, 406
Harlow, H., 18, 41
Harlow, M. H., 18, 41
Hart, V., 372
Haskell, M. R., 143, 146, 159, 234, 247
Hatten, J., 267, 271, 287
Havard, J., 192, 195
Havemann, E., 176, 195
Hawkins, J. E., Jr., 301, 328
Heber, R., 58, 70
Helfer, R. E., 226, 247
Hemenway, W. G., 300, 327
Herskovitz, H. H., 237, 247
Hess, E. H., 18, 41
Hildreth, G. H., 116, 126
Hilgard, E. R., 137, 159
Hingtgen, J. W., 67, 70
Hirsch, S. J., 119, 120, 126
Hobbs, N., 8, 41

425

Name index

Homme, L., 231, 247
Horne, D., 326, 328
Huberman, G., 381, 406
Hull, F., 258, 287
Hull, M., 258, 287
Husen, T., 109, 126
Hutt, L., 85, 96
Hyde, J. S., 400, 405

Ingram, D., 283, 287
Irwin, J., 282, 287

Jensen, D. W., 106, 125
Jervis, G. A., 48, 70
Johnson, A. M., 239, 247
Johnson, D., 176, 178, 181, 195, 281, 287
Johnson, G. O., 30, 41, 62, 70
Johnson, J. L., 30, 41
Johnson, O. C., 139, 160
Johnson, President Lyndon B., 7
Johnson, W., 266, 274, 275, 276, 282, 287
Jones, J., 314, 329
Jones, N. W., 181, 195
Jones, P. R., 30, 41
Jones, R. L., 85, 96, 354, 373
Jose, R. T., 371, 373
Justin, N., 151, 159

Kagan, J., 176, 195
Kalogerakis, M. G., 241, 247
Kanner, L., 214, 222, 247
Kaplan, D. L., 348, 374
Kauffman, J. M., 186, 197
Keller, Helen, 4
Kempe, C. H., 226, 247
Keniston, K., 119, 120, 126
Kennedy, A., 220, 247
Kennedy, President John F., 4
Kennedy, Rosemary, 4
Kennedy, W. A., 85, 97
Keogh, B. K., 188, 196

Kephart, N. C., 172, 178, 188, 196
Ketchum, Barbara, 346
Khatena, J., 116, 126
Kiev, A., 208, 215, 247
King, R. A., 341, 374
Kirk, S. A., 62, 70, 85, 96, 165, 166, 175, 176, 196, 283, 287
Kirk, W. D., 114, 126, 175, 176, 283, 287
Kisker, G., 207, 247
Klausmeier, H. J., 116, 126
Knight, J. J., 359, 374
Knight, R. A., 191, 196
Koh, S. D., 322, 329
Kollar, D. E., 149, 159
Koppitz, E. M., 168, 196
Kolstoe, O. P., 48, 49, 70, 88, 96
Konigsmark, B. W., 300, 328
Koocher, G., 8, 41
Krisher, C. H., 92, 96
Kubler-Ross, E., 34, 41
Kugel, R. B., 92, 96
Kurland, L. T., 380, 386, 406
Kurtzke, J. F., 386, 406

Lambert, N., 49, 54, 56, 71
Larson, R. W., 362, 374
Lee, L., 279, 282, 283, 287
Lehtinen, L., 170, 197
Leland, H., 55, 71
Lennenberg, E., 293, 328
Leonard, L., 283, 287
Lerner, J. W., 165, 171, 196
Lesse, S., 238, 247
Levine, D. U., 142, 159
Levine, E. S., 294, 313, 328
Lewis, J. F., 54, 71
Lewis, O., 135, 159
Lind, C. C., 105, 126
Litton, W., 49, 64, 70
Lively-Weiss, M. A., 149, 159
Livingston, S., 388, 406
Lombroso, C., 101, 126
Lowenfeld, B., 359, 374
Lucas, N. R., 214, 215, 248

Luckey, R. E., 91, 96
Ludwig, A. M., 238, 247
Lukoff, I. F., 354, 374
Luper, H., 276, 277, 278, 288

McAdams, L., 371, 373
McAnarney, E. R., 392, 407
McCarthy, D., 261, 288
McClurg, W. H., 183, 196
McConnell, F., 299, 328
McCord, J., 239, 247
McCord, W., 239, 247
MacDonald, J., 283, 288
Mackie, R. P., 7, 42
Mackinnon, D., 104, 113, 126
McQueen, J. C., 380, 407
McReynolds, L., 283, 288
McWilliams, B. J., 39, 42
Madsen, C. L., 34, 42
Malmquist, C., 219, 249
Manolakes, G., 326, 328
Marge, M., 258, 260, 282, 287
Marland, S. P., 102, 104, 114, 126
Marsh, R. W., 113, 126
Marshall, M. J., 15, 16, 42
Martens, E. H., 7, 42
Martin, E. W., 7, 11, 32, 42
Martinson, R. A., 102, 104, 126
Martinus, J. W., 176, 192, 196
Maslow, A. H., 119, 126, 136, 143, 145, 148, 159
Mason, R., 265, 288
Mays, T., 297, 328
Meadow, K. P., 315, 329
Mearig, J. S., 294, 328
Meighan, T., 354, 374
Melcher, J. W., 4, 42
Menyuk, P., 261, 279, 328
Mercer, J. R., 25, 42, 54, 71
Milgram, N. A., 106, 127
Milgram, R. M., 106, 127
Milisen, R., 258, 288
Miller, A., 326, 328
Miller, J., 283, 288
Miller, J. B., 316, 328

Mindel, E., 312, 316, 317, 328, 329
Ming, R. W., 119, 120, 127
Minskoff, E. H., 176, 177, 196
Mishara, B. L., 229, 247
Moltz, H., 18, 42
Monckeberg, F., 140, 159
Morgan, C. T., 341, 374
Morris, M. G., 227, 247
Morse, J., 392, 406
Moskowitz, S., 324, 329
Muir, M., 228, 247
Mulder, R., 276, 277, 278, 288
Mullins, J., 184, 196
Murdock, C. W., 8, 42
Mussen, P. H., 23, 42
Myers, P. L., 168, 196
Myklebust, H. B., 176, 178, 181, 281, 287, 314, 328

Napier, G. D., 348, 374
Nelson, A. P., 191, 197
Newland, T. E., 124, 127
Newman, R. G., 397, 407
Nihira, K., 55, 71
Nix, G., 321, 328
Noland, R. L., 35, 42
Northcutt, W. H., 300, 328
Northern, J. L., 300, 301, 302, 328
Nunn, R. G., 215, 246

Oden, M. H., 101, 105, 106, 107, 108, 127
Oettinger, L., 191, 196
O'Reilly, D. R., 381, 407
Organ, J. J., 138, 139, 141, 159, 160
Ortiz, Rafael, 155—156
Owens, A., 354, 373

Page, J. G., 191, 196
Parker, F., 134, 143, 144, 160
Parker, H., 190, 197
Patterson, E. G., 59, 71
Paulsen, M. G., 226, 247

Name index

Pegnato, C. W., 110, 127
Penrose, L. S., 58, 72
Perkins, W., 278, 288
Peterson, C., 31, 42
Peterson, J., 31, 42
Peterson, T. R., 232, 233, 248
Piaget, J., 353, 374
Plato, 101
Pollock, C. B., 227, 248
Porteus, S. D., 48, 71
Powell, G. F., 209, 247
Powers, M., 264, 288
Pressey, S. L., 104, 127
Proffit, W., 265, 288
Purcell, K., 400, 406

Quay, H. C., 208, 232, 233, 241, 248
Quigley, S. P., 318, 329

Ramsey, C. E., 133, 148, 159
Raviv, S., 314, 329
Reiber, M., 144, 160
Rendon, R., 68, 71
Renzulli, J. S., 110, 127
Rice, J., 115, 127
Riesen, A. H., 23, 42
Riggs, R., 134, 160
Rimland, B., 222, 224, 248
Ripple, R. E., 116, 126
Ritvo, E. R., 222, 248
Robb, J. R., 397, 406
Robinson, H. B., 68, 71
Robinson, N. M., 68, 71
Rogow, S., 356, 374
Rolands, P., 124, 127
Roosevelt, President Franklin D., 4
Rosenstein, J., 314, 329
Ross, A. O., 208, 211, 215, 231, 248
Rotter, J. B., 148, 160
Ruch, F. L., 341, 374
Rulo, J. H., 242, 248
Rutter, M., 384, 407
Ryan, B., 283, 287
Ryback, D., 191, 196

Sagan, E., 153, 159
St. Reiner, B. F., 356, 374
Sams, T. A., 355, 373
Sanchez-Hidalgo, E., 146, 160
Sarason, S. B., 48, 64, 71
Sawrey, J. M., 27, 42
Schaefer, A. E., 139, 160
Scharry, E. R., 366, 373
Schechter, M. D., 208, 229, 248
Schein, J. D., 295, 296, 329
Scherzer, A. L., 381, 407
Schlesinger, H. S., 315, 329
Schmidt, R. P., 68, 71
Schrotberger, W. L., 348, 374
Schwartz, D. D., 398, 407
Schwartz, M. P., 274, 288
Scian, M. J., 326, 328
Scott, J. P., 18, 42
Scott, W. S., 147, 160
Scriven, G., 31, 42
Scriven, M., 27, 42
Seashore, H. G., 51, 71
Séguin, Edouard, 49
Semel, E., 282, 283, 288
Sharan, S., 314, 329
Shaw, C., 214, 215, 248
Shellhaas, M., 55, 71
Shipe, D., 92, 97
Shotwell, A. M., 92, 97
Siegal, A. W., 190, 194, 234, 248
Siegal, B. L., 352, 373
Siegel, G., 283, 288
Silberman, A., 192, 194
Simon, K. A., 7, 42
Simon, Theodore, 50
Simpson, D. D., 191, 197
Singer, J. L., 356, 374
Skinner, B. F., 33, 42, 231, 241, 248
Slingerland, B. H., 168, 197
Smead, V. S., 187, 197
Smith, D. W., 64, 71
Smith, H. W., 85, 97
Squanto, 186
Staats, A., 191, 196
Stanley, J. C., 114, 127
Steele, B. F., 227, 248

Stephen, E., 68, 71
Sternlof, R. E., 229, 248
Stevens, G. D., 171, 197
Stevenson, V. M., 313, 322, 329
Stewart, W. A., 33, 42
Stockton, Carol, 156
Stone, A. V., 329
Strauss, A., 170, 197
Strauss, S., 314, 329
Stubblefield, J. H., 176, 197
Sullivan, Anne, 4
Swanson, B. M., 190, 197

Tait, P., 356, 375
Telford, C. W., 27, 42
Templin, M., 261, 262, 263, 279, 288
Terman, L. M., 50, 57, 71, 101, 105, 106, 108, 116, 127
Thomas, E. D., 4, 15, 16, 42, 43, 171, 178, 197
Thompson, C. W., 397, 407
Todd, M., 38, 39, 43
Torrance, E. P., 111, 112, 127
Trent, J. W., 120, 127
Tuttle, D. W., 348, 374

Underberg, R. P., 360, 373

Valett, R. E., 167, 197
Van Gogh, Vincent, 4
Van Riper, C., 258, 274, 288
Vernon, M., 296, 312, 316, 317, 322, 324, 329
Verrillo, R. T., 360, 373
Vogel, S. A., 181, 197
Vogeli, B. R., 122, 127

Wadsworth, H. G., 93, 97
Wadsworth, J. B., 93, 97

Wakefield, R. A., 30, 43
Walcott, S., 314, 329
Waldo, L., 326, 328
Walker, C. E., 213, 214, 248
Walker, D. L., 356, 374
Walker, S., 188, 197
Wallace, G., 186, 197
Wallach, M. A., 112, 127
Wansley, R. A., 213, 246
Warson, S. R., 213, 214, 249
Wechsler, D., 52, 57, 71
Weinberg, W., 219, 249
Weinstein, G., 144, 148, 159
Weintraub, F. J., 8, 25, 43
Weiss, J. H., 400, 406
Weiss, M., 283, 288
Weltman, R., 326, 328
Wender, P., 170, 178, 197
White, A. H., 313, 322, 329
Wiig, E., 282, 283, 288
Wilder, B. J., 68, 71
Williams, B. R., 326, 329
Williams, D., 276, 278, 288
Williams, G., 226, 248
Willis, D. J., 4, 43, 171, 197, 227, 249, 314, 329
Wilson, H., 144, 146, 160
Winebrenner, D. K., 338, 375
Winitz, H., 261, 265, 288
Wolfe, J., 314, 329
Wright, B., 354, 375
Wright, L., 214, 249, 314, 329
Wrightstone, J. W., 324, 329

Yablonsky, L., 143, 146, 159, 234, 247
Yamamoto, K., 111, 127
Yoder, D., 283, 288
Young, C. E., 176, 197

Zetter, J., 30, 31, 43
Ziter, F. A., 394, 407

Subject index

Ability grouping, 115, 118, 119
Abnormal eye movements, 338
Academic curriculum
    for hearing disabled, 324–26
    for visually handicapped, 362
Academically gifted exceptional children. *See* Gifted children
Acceleration, 115, 116
Acoustic impedance, 310
ACTION, 160
Adaptive behavior, 48, 54, 55, 56
    assessment in retardation, 48, 54–56
    defined, 54
    in mildly retarded, 84–89
    in moderately retarded, 76–83
    in profoundly retarded, 90, 91
    tests used to measure, 54–56
        AAMD Scale, 54, 55, 56
        Bayley Scale, 54
        Cain-Levine, 54
        Denver Developmental, 54
        Gessell, 54
        System of Multicultural Assessment, 54
Adaptive management, 190–92
Adjustment to visual handicaps, 359
Advocacy representation, 8, 10, 25, 27, 37, 94, 226, 327
Aggressive and destructive behavior, 217
Alexander Graham Bell Association for the Deaf, 329
Allergies, 398

Amblyopia, 340
Ambulation, 352
American Academy of Pediatrics, 43
American Association for Gifted Children, 127
American Association for Education of the Severely and Profoundly Handicapped, 97
American Association of Psychiatric Clinics for Children, 249
American Association on Mental Deficiency, 48, 50, 52, 54–56, 59–68, 97
American Civil Liberties Union, 249
    Juvenile Rights Project, 160
American Epilepsy Society, 408
American Foundation for the Blind, 362, 372
American Foundation on Learning Disabilities, 198
American Heart Association, 294, 295, 327, 408
American Lung Association, 408
American Orthopsychiatric Association, 249
American Medical Association, 43, 408
American Occupational Therapy Association, 43, 408
American Orthotic and Prosthetic Association, 408
American Physical Therapy Association, 408
American Psychological Association, 24, 41, 249

Subject index

American Speech and Hearing Association, 257, 288, 408
Anorexia nervosa, 215
Aqueous humor, 339
Arithmetic problems, 184
Arthritis Foundation, 390, 392, 408
Articulation, 255, 261, 262
Articulation disorders
 causal factors, 264–66
 cerebral palsy, 286
 cleft palate, 266
 defined, 262
 diagnostic testing, 266–68
 incidence, 257–60
 remediation, 268–69
 severity of, 263–64
 types, 262–63
Assessment. See Evaluation
Association for Children with Learning Disabilities, 198
Association for the Help of Retarded Children, 97
Asthma. See Bronchial asthma
Astigmatism, 339–40
Audiogram, 298, 307–09
Audiologist, 298, 307, 310
Auditory perception, 176
 articulation disorders, 265
 closure, 177
 discrimination, 176–77
 expressive language disorders, 281
 memory, 177
 reception, 177
Auditory system, 302–05
Autism, 222

Babbling, 260
Barraga Scale, 343
Behavior, approaches to understanding, 31–34
 behavioristic, 33, 34, 75, 191, 213, 215, 220, 231, 241
 biophysical, 31, 33
 medical, 31, 207–08, 221–23

Behavior, approaches to understanding (cont'd)
 psychodynamic or psychodevelopmental, 33
 psychosocial, 33
Behavior modification, 75
Behavioral variations, classification of, 210–12
Bill Wilkerson Hearing and Speech Center, 322
Binet-Simon Scale, 50. See also Stanford-Binet
Blindisms, 358–59
Blindness, 336, 348–49
Body image, 355
Braille, 336, 363, 365–68
Bronchial asthma, 398–401
Bureau of Education for the Handicapped, 7, 409, 413

Cardiovascular system disorder, 394–95
Cataract, 339–40
Center on Deafness, 329
Central auditory disorder, 307
Central Institute for the Deaf, 322
Central nervous system, 168–71
Cerebral palsy, 68, 257, 260, 264, 286, 379–81
Child abuse, 226–28
Child advocates, 413. See also Advocacy
Child Study Association of America, 43
Child Study Center, 348, 373
Child Welfare League of America, 249
Chromosome abnormalities, 64, 65
 Down's Syndrome, 64, 65
 Klinefelter's Syndrome, 66
 Turner's Syndrome, 66
Cleft palate, 257, 260, 264, 270, 286
Closer Look, 198
Club foot, 403
Cochlea, 304–05
Cognition, 179
Committee for Economic Development, 153, 156, 158, 160

Committee on Professional Preparation Certification, 299, 328
Communication, 254–57, 266. *See also* Speech disorders; Language disorders
Community attitudes toward retardation, 93
Community responsibilities toward the gifted, 121
Community Services Administration, 160
Compensatory education, 152–56
  alternative schools, 153
  community colleges, 153
  early diagnosis, 154
  follow-through programs, 153
  for the gifted and talented, 153, 154, 155
  Head Start, 153
  health and nutrition provisions, 154
  innovative strategies, 154–56
  language provisions, 154
  migrant education, 156
  Upward-Bound Projects, 153
Compensatory services, 152, 154
Conditioned play audiometry, 309
Conductive hearing loss, 305, 306
Conference of Executives of American Schools for the Deaf, 299, 328
Confidentiality
  access rights, 10, 26
  amendment of records, 26
  definition of, 10
  hearing opportunities and procedures, 26
  notice of rights, 10, 26, 27
Congenital deafness, 300–01
Cornea, 339, 341
Cortex, 305
Council for Exceptional Children, 43
Council on Education of the Deaf, 299
Counseling, 121
  of parents, 59, 93
Creativity, 110–13
Cretinism, 61

Cued speech, 317
Cystic fibrosis, 402–03

Day school provisions
  emergence of, 5–7
  placement alternatives to, 29–31
Deaf-blind child, 335, 369
"Deaf mute," 296, 297
Deafness. *See* Hearing disabilities
Decibel units, 307
Delayed auditory feedback, 278
Delinquency, 146, 412
Developmental Disabilities Act, 27
Developmental learning materials, 330
Diabetes, 395–98
Diagnosis. *See* Evaluation
Dialects, nonstandard, 263
Directory of Educational Facilities for the Learning Disabled, 198
Distractibility, 189
Diseases of the ear and auditory mechanism, 302
Dormac, Inc., 330
Down's Syndrome, 64, 65
Drug abuse, 228
Drug-related hearing impairment, 301
Due process, 10, 11, 26, 27, 411
Dysgraphia, 183
Dyslexia, 180
Dysorthography, 183

Ear, anatomy and function of, 302–05
Echolalia, 260
Education for All Handicapped Children Act. *See* Public Law 94-142
Education of the Handicapped Amendment, 10
Education of the Handicapped (Title VI, ESEA), 7
Educational Activities, Inc., 330
Educational categories, 52–53
Educational classification, 52–53
Educational Distribution Center, 330

Educational Policies Commission, 85, 96
Educational provisions
  administrative procedures, 115
  for emotionally handicapped, 231–32, 241–44
  for gifted and talented, 102, 114–22
  for hearing disabled, 315–26
  for mentally retarded, 74–92
  for physical and health disabled, 381, 389, 392, 394, 395, 397, 403–05
  program planning and operation, 114–15
  for societally neglected, 152–56
  for specific learning disabled, 167, 171–92
  for speech and language disabled, 268, 271, 276, 283–84
  for visually disabled, 346–68
Educational readiness, 20–23
Educational strategies, 186–87
  combination approach, 188
  process or modality training, 175, 187
  task analysis, 187–88
Electronic echo-sounding device, 362
Elementary and Secondary Education Act (Title I, ESEA), 6
Emotional lability, 189
Emotional and social adjustment, 106, 206, 281, 412
Encopresis, 312
Endocrine system disorders, 395–98
Enrichment for the gifted, 115, 117, 118
Enuresis, 212
Environmental influences, 67
Epilepsy Foundation of America, 382, 384–87, 406, 408
Epileptic seizures, 382–90
Equal educational opportunity, 6, 7, 8, 10
Eustachian tube, 303
Evaluation (assessment and diagnosis)
  of creativity, 110–13

Evaluation (assessment and diagnosis) (cont'd)
  early, need for, 18, 20–23
  of educational readiness, 20–23
  of emotionally handicapped, 233
  of gifted, 108–14
  group tests, 109
  of hearing disabled, 298, 307–10, 313–14
  individual tests (IQ), 109
  of mentally retarded, 48, 50–56
  of physical and health disabled, 376–414
  rating scales, 110
  of societally neglected, 132, 156
  of specific learning disabled, 165–86
  of speech and language disabled, 266–68, 271, 276, 282
  teacher assessment, 110, 114
  of visually disabled, 337–38, 340, 342–44, 360, 371
Evoked response audiometry, 310
Exceptional learner education. See Special education
Exceptionality, 3–11
  among societally neglected, 132–35
External auditory canal, 302–03
External ear, 302
Eye, anatomy and function of, 338–41
Eye specialists, 338

Facts and fallacies
  about hearing disabilities, 295
  about visual handicaps, 334
Family. See Parents and family
Family Service Association of America, 43, 249
Farsightedness, 339, 341, 343
Federal legislation. See specific Public Laws
Fingerspelling, 318
First priority children, 10
Fitzgerald Key, 324
Fluency disorders, 258, 273–75
Follett Publishing Company, 330
Foundation for Child Development, 43

Free and appropriate education, 10, 11, 74, 411

Galactosemia, 61
Gallaudet College 323
  Book Store, 330
Gang affiliations, 146
General Educational Materials, 330
Genetically linked hearing defects, 300
Gestational disorders, 67
Ghetto children, 135
Giftedness, 98–127
  defined, 102–04
  ethnic and socioeconomic variables, 108, 133
  male-female variance, 107–08
Gordon W. Stowe and Associates, 330
Grand mal, 385
Glaucoma, 339–40

Habilitation, 363
Hard of hearing, 299, 314, 322, 324
Head Start, 153
Health disabilities, 379
Hearing-aid dealer, 299
Hearing aids, 310–12
Hearing disabilities, 7, 11, 290–331
  causal factors, 300–02
  defined, 299
  education, 315–26
  psychological evaluation of, 313
  types of, 305–07
  and visual handicaps, 369–71
Hemophilia, 404
Hierarchy of needs, 136–37
Historical perspectives
  attitudes toward exceptionality, 4–5
  church-sponsored asylums, 5
  on the gifted, 101, 102
  legislation, 6–10
  on mental retardation, 48, 49
  President's Panel on Mental Retardation, 49
  on public day schools, 5, 6
  on residential schools, 5

Holophrastic stage, 279
Homebound services, 30
Hospital services, 30
Housing and societal neglect, 141–42
Hydrocephaly, 64
Hyperkinesis, 188
Hyperopia, 339

IEP. See Individualized education program
Illinois Test of Psycholinguistic Abilities, 283
Impedance audiometry, 310
Incidence. See Prevalence
Individualized education program
  content, 14–17
  definition of, 11
  development, 14–20, 74
  parent participation in, 15–20, 22
  review, 11, 17, 22
  synopsis, 19
Infant and child mortality, 138
Infections and intoxications, 59, 60
Inner city poor, 134, 135
Inner ear, 303, 304
Institute for the Study of Mental Retardation and Related Disabilities, 97
Institutionalization. See Residential schools
Integration. See Least restrictive environment
Intelligence quotient, 50–53, 75, 84, 103, 104, 109, 110, 412
Intelligence testing, 50–53
  controversy over, 24, 25, 53
  group, 109, 110
  individual, 109, 110
  normal curve, 51
  standard deviation, 50, 51
  Stanford-Binet, 50, 51
  Wechsler Scale, 51
International Association for the Scientific Study of Mental Deficiency, 97

International Association of Parents of
 the Deaf, 330
Intervention strategies and techniques,
 36–40, 152–56, 242–44
IQ. *See* Intelligence quotient

Jargon, 260
John Tracy Clinic, 323, 330
Joint Committee on Dentistry and
 Speech Pathology-Audiology,
 265, 287
Joint Committee on Mental Health of
 Children, 8, 41
Joseph P. Kennedy Foundation, 94
Juvenile delinquency, 170, 232–44
Juvenile rheumatoid arthritis, 390–93

Kinesthetic stimulation, 356
Klinefelter's Syndrome, 66

Labeling, 27
Lalling, 260
Language
 bilingualism, 151
 defined, 255
 development, 278–79, 352
 dialectical differences, 151, 152
 disabilities and disorders, 184–86,
  257–60, 280–86
 elaborated, 149, 150, 151
 expressive, 149–51
 holophrastic, 279
 learning, 293, 294, 314
 linguistic systems, 255
 receptive vocabulary, 144, 150, 151
 restricted, 149, 150, 151
 telegraphic, 280
Learning problems
 fatigue or restlessness, 142
 irregular attendance, 134
 language experiences, 149, 151
 mental development, 139–41
 motivation, 148

Learning problems (*cont'd*)
 reading difficulties, 132, 152
Least restrictive environment, 10, 11,
 28–31, 74, 411
Legislation. *See* specific laws
Lens, 339–40
Lesch-Nyhan's disease, 61
Leukemia, 401, 402
Leukemia Society of America, 401, 406,
 408
Life-threatening disorders, 401–03
Local education agencies, 26

Mainstreaming, 30–31, 90, 300, 326.
 Also see Least restrictive environment
Malleus, 303
Malnutrition, 137, 138, 140
Manic depression, 225
Mannerisms, 358. *Also see* Blindisms
Manual communication, 315,
 317–19, 327
Mastoid bone, 307
Measles, German. *See* Rubella
Mental age, 50
Mental development, 140–42
Mental health, 205
Mental Health Law Project, 249
Mental retardation, 46–97, 411–12
 adaptive behavior deficit, 48, 54
 causal factors, 59, 60–68
 defined, 48
 educational categories, 52–53
 IQ (AAMD classification), 52
 and language disability, 260
Metabolic disorders, 61–62
Microcephaly, 62
Middle ear, 303
Midwest Regional Center for Services to
 Deaf-Blind Children, 371, 374
Migrants, 134, 156
Mild retardation, 52, 84–91
Minority groups, 24, 25, 104, 133–36,
 138, 140, 141, 147, 151
Mixed hearing loss, 306

Mobility training, 352, 362
Moderate retardation, 52, 53, 77–83, 91
Mongolism. *See* Down's Syndrome
Morphologic system, 255, 282, 279–80
Motivation, 119, 148–49
Motor development, 348–52
Multidisciplinary approach, 11–22, 254, 257, 271, 285, 378–79, 381, 411, 414
Multihandicapped, 3, 68, 335, 340, 369–71, 404
Muscular dystrophy, 393–94
Muscular Dystrophy Association, 393, 406, 408
Musculoskeletal system disorders, 390–94
Myopia, 339

National Advisory Committee on the Handicapped, 7
National Advisory Council on the Education of Disadvantaged Children, 160
National Association for Mental Health, 249
National Association for Retarded Citizens, 97
National Association of Sheltered Workshops and Homebound Programs, 97
National Association of Social Workers, 43
National Association of State Directors of Special Education, 14, 42
National Center for Law and the Handicapped, 43
National Center on Educational Media and Materials for the Handicapped, 43
National Commission on Diabetes, 396, 406
National Committee for Multihandicapped Children, 43

National Congress of Parents and Teachers, 249
National Council of Organizations for Children and Youth, 198
National Cystic Fibrosis Research Foundation, 402, 406, 408
National Easter Seal Society for Crippled Children and Adults, 408
National Education Association, 43, 154, 159, 160
National Foundation/March of Dimes, 408
National Hemophilic Foundation, 408
National Information Center for the Handicapped, 43
National Institute of Child Health and Human Development, 61, 71
National Institutes of Health, 408
National Kidney Foundation, 408
National Learning Disabilities Assistance Project, 198
National Multiple Sclerosis Society, 408
National Rehabilitation Association, 408
National Society for Autistic Children, 249
National Society for the Prevention of Blindness, 336–38, 374
Native language requirements, 25
Nearsightedness, 339, 341
Needs, hierarchy of, 136–37
Needs, human, 136–47
Neonatal screening, 298
Nervous system disorders, 379–80. *Also see* Cerebral palsy; Epilepsy
Neurofibromatosis, 62
Neuroses, 219–20
Noble and Noble, Publishers, 330
Nondiscrimination, 25
Nonverbal communication, 246
Normal curve, 50–52
Normalization, 49
Normal language, 255
North Dakota School for the Deaf, 324, 328
Nutritional disorders, 62
Nystagmus, 340

Oculist, 338
Office of Child Development, 160
Office of Demographic Studies, 299, 300, 329
Oklahoma Association for Children with Learning Disabilities, 198
Operant conditioning. *See* Behavior; behavioristic approach
Ophthalmologic Staff of Toronto Hospital, 339, 340, 374
Ophthalmologist, 338
Optacon, 369
Optic atrophy, 340
Optic nerves, 340
Optician, 338
Optiscope, 369
Optometrist, 338
Oral communication, 316
Organic approach to SLD
    hard neurological signs, 169–70
    soft neurological signs, 170–71
    Strauss syndrome, 170–71
    minimal brain dysfunction, 171
Organ of Corti, 304
Orton Society, Inc., 198
Ossicles, 303
Otitis media, 302
Otorhinolaryngology, 298, 301
Ototoxic deafness, 301
Oval window, 303

Parents and the family
    communication, 150
    counseling of, 36, 37, 40, 59, 93
    delinquency patterns, 238–43
    emotional problems among, 208
    of gifted children, 124
    of hearing disabled, 322
    involvement, 8, 13, 16–20, 22, 26, 36–40, 74, 104, 113, 120–21, 124
    in poverty, 143–49
    reaction to disability, 34–40, 92
    therapy, 230
    of visually disabled, 344–48

Parental love, 136–43
Partially seeing, 336
Part-time special placement, 30
Pennsylvania Association for Retarded Children, 8
Perception
    auditory aspects, 176
    defined, 172
    visual aspects, 173
Perceptual deficits, 282
Perceptual-motor theory, 171–80
Peripheral auditory mechanism, 302
Perseveration, 189
Petit mal, 384
Phenylketonuria, 61
Phonics Corporation, 330
Phonologic system, 255
Photo School Films, Inc., 330
Physical growth, 105–06, 138–42
Pica, 214
Pinna, 302
Placement alternatives, 29–31
Placement committee, 411
Placement provisions, 28–31
    review, 11, 17, 22
Placement team, 11–22
Polio, 404
Postnatal brain disease, 62
Poverty
    and family unit, 143–46
    and malnutrition, 137–41
    and self-esteem, 146–49
Prenatal influences, 62–67
President's Committee on Mental Retardation, 97
President's Panel on Mental Retardation, 58, 71, 84, 96
Prevalence of exceptionality, 2, 56–58, 104–05, 135–36, 165–67, 207, 236–37, 257–60, 299–300, 336–37, 380, 382, 386, 390, 393, 395, 396, 398, 401, 402
Priorities, 10
Profound retardation, 52, 75, 76, 90, 91
Project URBAN, 160

Psychological testing, 360
Psychomotor seizures, 385
Psychoses, 222–25
Public Law 89-750, 7
Public Law 93-380, 10
Public Law 94-103, 27
Public Law 94-142, 3, 10–11, 26, 411
Pure-tone audiometry, 307

Reading comprehension, 323
Reading difficulties, 180–83
   among low vision children, 368
Rehabilitation Services Administration, 408
Residential placement, 5, 28
Reinforcement therapy. See Behavior; behavioristic approach
Remediation, 175, 180–92, 213, 215, 216, 220, 221, 230, 231, 241
Resonance, 255, 270
Resource services, 30
Respiration, 255
Respiratory system disorders, 398–401
Retina, 339–40
Retinitis pigmentosa, 340
Retrolental fibroplasia, 337, 340
Rheumatic fever, 394, 395
Rights of children and parents, 7, 8, 10, 11, 25, 26, 27
Rubella, 59, 300, 301, 331, 337, 370–71
Rural poor, 134

Safety, 142, 143, 146
Schizophrenia, 224
Science News, 223, 248
Scoliosis, 403
Second priority children, 10
Self concept, 354
Self-contained placement, 30
Self-esteem, 146–48, 155, 165, 170–71, 354, 359
Semantic system, 255

Semantic system (*cont'd*)
   deficits, 281
   development of, 278–80
Sensorineural hearing loss, 306
Serous otitis media, 302
Severe retardation, 52, 53, 75, 76, 90
Sitting box, 351–52
Snellen Chart, 340–43
Social and emotional growth
   of the gifted, 107
   of hearing impaired, 312–14
   of visually disabled, 360–62
Sound field audiometry, 309
Spasticity, 379
Special Learning Corporation, 198
Specific learning disabilities, 163–98, 412
   behavioral aspects of, 187–90
Special Olympics, 94
Special services. See Special education
Speech, 255, 260–62
Speech and language disorders, 257–58, 262–64, 267–68, 286, 412
Speech discrimination test, 308
Speech reception threshold, 307
Speechreading, 296, 316–17, 319–20
Spelling and writing problems, 183–85
Spina bifida, 403
Spina Bifida Association of America, 408, 409
Spondaic words, 307–08
Standard deviation, 50–53
Stanford-Binet, 50, 51, 57, 76, 84, 101, 110
Stapes, 303
Sterilization, 92
Strabismus, 340, 342
Stroking, 346–47
Stuttering, 274–78
Suicide, 229
Syntactic system, 255
Syphilis, 300, 337
   as cause of retardation, 59

Tay-Sachs disease, 61
Teenagers for the Retarded, 94
Testing. *See* Intelligence testing
Thalidomide, 301
Tics, 214
Total communication, 319–21
Trachoma, 339
Transient situational disorders, 216–17
Treacher-Collins Syndrome, 301
Tuberculosis, 404
Tuberous sclerosis, 62
Turner's Syndrome, 66, 371
Tympanic membrane, 302

Underachievers, 119–20
United Cerebral Palsy Association, 379, 407, 409
United Press International, 141, 160, 237, 248
U.S. Department of Health, Education, and Welfare, 86, 97, 165, 197, 379, 399, 407
U.S. Office of Education, 3, 5–7, 11, 25, 32, 43, 165, 166, 192, 193, 197, 207, 248, 299, 329, 336, 375

VISTA program, 160
Visual acuity, 336
Visual disability, 412
   causal factors, 337
   defined, 335
   and hearing impairment, 369–71
   psychological overview of, 353
   symptoms, 337
Visual limitation, 361
Visual perception, 173–76
Visuomotor perceptual training, 325
Vitreous fluid, 339
Voice disorders
   causes, 270–73
   definition and types, 269–70
   diagnostic testing, 271
   with hearing loss, 270
   incidence of, 258–59
   with other disabilities, 286
   remedial techniques, 271–73
Voice properties, 269–70
Volta Speech Association for the Deaf, 330

Waardenburg's Syndrome, 301
Wechsler Scale, 51, 52, 57, 76, 84, 110
Wing's Symbols, 324
World Health Organization, 58, 71

Printed in USA

DISCHARGED 1981
DISCHARGED
MAY 9 1984
DISCHARGED
DISCHARGED
DISCHARGED
DISCHARGED
DISCHARGED
MAR 2 2 1990
DISCHARGED 1981
DISCHARGED
DISCHARGED

MAR 2 2 1999

DEC 7 1981
DISCHARGED
DISCHARGED
DISCHARGED
OCT 17 1983
DISCHARGED
DISCHARGED